The "Other" in Second Temple Judaism

John J. Collins

The "Other" in Second Temple Judaism

Essays in Honor of
JOHN J. COLLINS

Edited by

Daniel C. Harlow,
Karina Martin Hogan,
Matthew Goff &
Joel S. Kaminsky

WILLIAM B. EERDMANS PUBLISHING COMPANY
GRAND RAPIDS, MICHIGAN

Wm. B. Eerdmans Publishing Co.
4035 Park East Court SE, Grand Rapids, Michigan 49546
www.eerdmans.com

© 2011 William B. Eerdmans Publishing Co.
All rights reserved

Hardcover edition 2011
Paperback edition 2022

ISBN 978-0-8028-8294-3

Library of Congress Cataloging-in-Publication Data

The "other" in Second Temple Judaism : essays in honor of John J. Collins /
  edited by Daniel C. Harlow, Karina Martin Hogan,
  Matthew Goff, and Joel S. Kaminsky.
    p.   cm.
  Based on a conference held Apr. 4-5, 2008, at Amherst College.
  Includes bibliographical references and index.
  ISBN 978-0-8028-8294-3 (pbk.: alk. paper)
1. Gentiles — Congresses. 2. Judaism — History —
Post-exilic period, 586 B.C.-210 A.D. — Congresses. 3. Other (Philosophy) —
Congresses. 4. Bible. O.T. Apocrypha — Criticism, interpretation, etc. —
Congresses. 5. Apocalyptic literature — History and criticism — Congresses.
6. Dead Sea scrolls — Congresses. 7. Apocryphal books (Old Testament) —
History and criticism — Congresses. 8. Hellenism — Congresses.
I. Collins, John Joseph, 1946- II. Harlow, Daniel C.

BM720.N6O84   2010
296.3'909014 — dc22

2010040493

Contents

Contributors	ix
John J. Collins: Cursus Vitae	xii
Doctoral Dissertations Directed by John J. Collins	xiv
A Select Bibliography of the Publications of John J. Collins, 1973-2010	xvi
Abbreviations and Symbols	xxxiii

INTRODUCTION

"Showing the Wisdom of What He Has Learned":
The Scholarly Contributions of John J. Collins   3
   Daniel C. Harlow

PART ONE: THE HEBREW BIBLE AND ITS RECEPTION

Israel's Election and the Other in Biblical, Second Temple,
and Rabbinic Thought   17
   Joel S. Kaminsky

Contents

God's Other: The Intractable Problem of the Gentile King
in Judean and Early Jewish Literature   31
    Carol A. Newsom

The Original Sin of the Canaanites   49
    Katell Berthelot

Defining and Controlling Others Within: Hair, Identity,
and the Nazirite Vow in a Second Temple Context   67
    Susan Niditch

Otherworldly Music and the Other Sex   86
    Susan Ackerman

How Good Was Ruth's Hebrew? Ethnic and Linguistic
Otherness in the Book of Ruth   101
    Timothy H. Lim

The Other in Haggai and Zechariah 1–8   116
    Antonios Finitsis

When the King Is the Other: Nebuchadnezzar's Hibernian Cousin   132
    Naomi S. Jacobs

PART TWO: WISDOM

Elusive Wisdom and the Other Nations in Baruch   145
    Karina Martin Hogan

The Lady Vanishes: Wisdom in Ben Sira and Daniel   160
    Shannon Burkes Pinette

"The Foolish Nation That Dwells in Shechem":
Ben Sira on Shechem and the Other Peoples in Palestine   173
    Matthew Goff

Poverty and Otherness in Second Temple Instructions 189
    Samuel L. Adams

Transcending Death: The Reasoning of the "Others"
and Afterlife Hopes in Wisdom 1–6 204
    Daniel J. Harrington, S.J.

PART THREE: APOCALYPTICISM

The Apocalyptic Other 221
    Lorenzo DiTommaso

Apocalypticism as the Rejected Other: Wisdom and
Apocalypticism in Early Judaism and Early Christianity 247
    Sean Freyne

The We and the Other in the Worldview of *1 Enoch*,
the Dead Sea Scrolls, and Other Early Jewish Texts 262
    George W. E. Nickelsburg

Monsters and the Crippled Cosmos:
Construction of the Other in *Fourth Ezra* 279
    Rebecca Raphael

Idolatry and Alterity: Israel and the Nations
in the *Apocalypse of Abraham* 302
    Daniel C. Harlow

PART FOUR: THE DEAD SEA SCROLLS

Religious Epistemology and the History of the
Dead Sea Scrolls Community 333
    Shane Berg

Contents

The Wicked Priest Revisited — 350
  James C. VanderKam

Poetry of the Heavenly Other: Angelic Praise
in the *Songs of the Sabbath Sacrifice* — 368
  Eric D. Reymond

"At the Crossroads": Anti-Samaritan Polemic
in a Qumran Text about Joseph — 381
  Esther Chazon with Yonatan Miller

PART FIVE: JEWS AMONG GREEKS AND ROMANS

Romans, Jews, and Christians on the Names of the Jews — 391
  Martin Goodman

Jews and Greeks as Philosophers: A Challenge to Otherness — 402
  Erich S. Gruen

The Persecution of Judeans by Antiochus IV:
The Significance of "Ancestral Laws" — 423
  Robert Doran

Constructing Jewish Identity in Ptolemaic Egypt:
The Case of Artapanus — 434
  Patricia D. Ahearne-Kroll

Dispelling an Illusion of Otherness?
Judicial Practice in the Heracleopolis Papyri — 457
  Robert A. Kugler

Index of Authors — 471
Index of Scripture and Other Ancient Texts — 480

Contributors

Susan Ackerman, Preston H. Kelsey Professor of Religion, Dartmouth College, Hanover, New Hampshire

Samuel L. Adams, Assistant Professor of Old Testament, Union Theological Seminary & Presbyterian School of Christian Education, Richmond, Virginia

Patricia D. Ahearne-Kroll, Assistant Professor of Religion, Ohio Wesleyan University, Delaware, Ohio

Shane Berg, Assistant Professor of New Testament, Princeton Theological Seminary, Princeton, New Jersey

Katell Berthelot, Chargée de recherché, Centre de recherche français de Jérusalem, Israel

Shannon Burkes Pinette, San Antonio, Texas

Esther Chazon, Senior Lecturer in Hebrew Literature, Mandel Institute of Jewish Studies, Hebrew University of Jerusalem, Israel

Lorenzo DiTommaso, Associate Professor of Religion, Concordia University, Montréal, Quebec

Robert Doran, Samuel Williston Professor of Greek and Hebrew, Amherst College, Amherst, Massachusetts

Contributors

Antonios Finitsis, Assistant Professor of Hebrew Bible, Lutheran Pacific University, Tacoma, Washington

Sean Freyne, Emeritus Professor of Theology, School of Religions and Theology, Trinity College, Dublin, Ireland

Matthew Goff, Associate Professor of Religion, Florida State University, Tallahassee, Florida

Martin Goodman, Professor of Jewish Studies, The Oriental Institute, University of Oxford, England

Erich S. Gruen, Gladys Rehard Wood Professor of History and Classics Emeritus, University of California, Berkeley

Daniel C. Harlow, Professor of Biblical and Early Jewish Studies, Calvin College, Grand Rapids, Michigan

Daniel J. Harrington, S.J., Professor of New Testament, Boston College School of Theology and Ministry, Boston, Massachusetts

Naomi S. Jacobs, Postdoctoral Fellow in Hebrew Bible, Washington University, St. Louis, Missouri

Joel S. Kaminsky, Professor of Religion, Smith College, Northampton, Massachusetts

Robert A. Kugler, Paul S. Wright Professor of Christian Studies, Lewis & Clark College, Portland, Oregon

Timothy H. Lim, Professor of Hebrew Bible and Second Temple Judaism, University of Edinburgh School of Divinity, New College, Edinburgh, Scotland

Karina Martin Hogan, Assistant Professor of Theology, Fordham University, New York, New York

Yonatan Miller, Graduate Student in Jewish Studies, Harvard University, Cambridge, Massachusetts

Carol A. Newsom, Charles Howard Candler Professor of Old Testament, Candler School of Theology, Emory University, Atlanta, Georgia

George W. E. Nickelsburg, Emeritus Professor of Religious Studies, University of Iowa, Iowa City, Iowa

Contributors

Susan Niditch, Samuel Green Professor of Religion, Amherst College, Amherst, Massachusetts

Rebecca Raphael, Assistant Professor of Philosophy, Texas State University, San Marcos, Texas

Eric D. Reymond, Lecturer in Biblical Hebrew, Yale Divinity School, New Haven, Connecticut

James C. VanderKam, John A. O'Brien Professor of Hebrew Scriptures, University of Notre Dame, Notre Dame, Indiana

John J. Collins: Cursus Vitae

1946	Born in Newport, County Tipperary, Ireland
1967	B.A., Semitics and Classics, University College Dublin
1969	M.A., Semitics and Classics, University College Dublin
1972	Ph.D., Near Eastern Languages and Literatures, Harvard University
1973-76	Assistant Professor of Scripture, St. Mary of the Lake Seminary, Mundelein, Illinois
1976-78	Associate Professor of Scripture, St. Mary of the Lake Seminary
1978-82	Associate Professor of Religious Studies, DePaul University
1979	Election to Studiorum Novi Testamenti Societas
1980-85	Chair, Pseudepigrapha Group, Society of Biblical Literature
1982-85	Professor of Religious Studies, DePaul University
1985-91	Professor of Theology, University of Notre Dame
1987-88	National Endowment for the Humanities Fellowship
1989-94	Editor in Chief, *Journal of Biblical Literature*
	Member of Executive Committee, Society of Biblical Literature
1991-2000	Professor of Hebrew Bible, University of Chicago Divinity School, with Appointments in the Committees on the Mediterranean World and Jewish Studies

John J. Collins: Cursus Vitae

1994-2008	Editor in Chief, Supplements to the Journal for the Study of Judaism
1995-96	President, Chicago Society for Biblical Research
1996	President, Catholic Biblical Association
2000-	Holmes Professor of Old Testament Criticism and Interpretation, Yale University Divinity School and Department of Religious Studies
2000-01	Henry Luce Fellowship
	Vice President, Society of Biblical Literature
2002	President, Society of Biblical Literature
2003-08	Editor in Chief, *Dead Sea Discoveries*
2004	The Roland Murphy Memorial Lecture, Catholic University of America
	The Gunning Lectures, University of Edinburgh
2006	The Speaker's Lectures, Oxford University
	The Mowinckel Lecture, University of Oslo
2007	The Brodie Lecture, Stockholm School of Theology
2008-	General Editor, Anchor Bible
2008	President, Northeastern Regional Society of Biblical Literature
	The Other in Second Temple Judaism: A Conference in Honor of John J. Collins, Amherst College, Amherst, Massachusetts
	The Inaugural Wold Lecture, Union College, Schenectady, New York
2009	The Ray Frank Robbins Memorial Lecture, Samford University
	The Ernst Lohmeier Lecture, Greifswald University
	Doctor of Literature, *honoris causa*, University College Dublin

Doctoral Dissertations Directed by John J. Collins

Joel S. Kaminsky, "Punishment Displacement in the Hebrew Bible," University of Chicago Divinity School, 1993

Daniel C. Harlow, "The Greek Apocalypse of Baruch (3 Baruch) in Hellenistic Judaism and Early Christianity," codirected with James VanderKam, University of Notre Dame, 1994

Shannon Burkes, "Death and Qoheleth and Egyptian Biographies of the Late Period," University of Chicago Divinity School, 1997

Rebecca Raphael, "Divine Word, Divine Song: Inspiration and Authority in Hesiod and First Isaiah," codirected with Michael Murrin, University of Chicago Divinity School, 1997

Michael C. Douglas, "Power and Praise in the Hodayot: A Literary-Critical Study of 1QH 9:1–18:14," University of Chicago Divinity School, 1998

Dereck M. Daschke, "Loss, Fantasy, and Recovery in Ancient Judaism: Ezekiel, 4 Ezra, and the Baruch Apocalypses as Texts of Mourning," codirected with Peter Homans, University of Chicago Divinity School, 2000

Brenda J. Shaver, "The Prophet Elijah in the Literature of the Second Temple Period: The Growth of a Tradition," University of Chicago Divinity School, 2001

Matthew J. Goff, "The Worldly and Heavenly Wisdom of 4QInstruction," University of Chicago Divinity School, 2002

Karina Martin Hogan, "Theologies in Conflict in 4 Ezra: Wisdom Debate and Apocalyptic Solution," University of Chicago Divinity School, 2002

Patricia Ahearne-Kroll, "Joseph and Aseneth and Jewish Identity in Greco-Roman Egypt," codirected with David Schloen, University of Chicago Divinity School, 2005

Doctoral Dissertations Directed by John J. Collins

Samuel L. Adams, "Wisdom in Transition: Act and Consequence in Second Temple Instructions," Yale Divinity School, 2006

Antonios Finitsis, "Visions and Eschatology: A Socio-Historical Analysis of Zechariah 1–8," codirected with David Schloen, University of Chicago Divinity School, 2007

Claudia D. Bergman, "Childbirth as a Metaphor for Crisis: Evidence from the Near East, the Hebrew Bible, and 1QH XI, 1-18," codirected with Tikva Frymer-Kensky, University of Chicago Divinity School, 2007

Shane Berg, "Religious Epistemologies in the Dead Sea Scrolls: The Heritage and Transformation of the Wisdom Tradition," Yale Divinity School, 2008

Ryan Stokes, "Rebellious Angels and Malicious Spirits: Explanations of Evil in the Enochic and Related Literature," Yale Divinity School, 2010

Kyong-Jin Lee, "The Authority and Authorization of the Torah in the Persian Period," Yale Divinity School, 2010

A Select Bibliography of the Publications of John J. Collins, 1973-2010

John Collins has published more than two hundred book reviews; but since he never kept a list, they do not appear here. Also excluded here are the more than three dozen articles he has written for popular, church-related readerships.

1973
"The Date and Provenance of the Testament of Moses." Pages 15-32 in *Studies on the Testament of Moses*. Edited by George W. Nickelsburg, Jr. SBLSCS 4. Cambridge: Society of Biblical Literature, 1973.

"Some Remaining Traditio-Historical Problems in the Testament of Moses." Pages 38-43 in ibid.

1974
The Sibylline Oracles of Egyptian Judaism. SBLDS 13. Missoula, Mont.: Scholars Press, 1974.

"Apocalyptic Eschatology as the Transcendence of Death." *CBQ* 36 (1974): 21-43.

"The Son of Man and the Saints of the Most High in the Book of Daniel." *JBL* 93 (1974): 50-66.

"History and Tradition in Amos." *ITQ* 41 (1974): 120-33.

"The Provenance and Date of the Third Sibyl." *Bulletin of the Institute of Jewish Studies* 2 (1974): 1-18.

"Structure and Meaning in the Testament of Job." Pages 35-52 in vol. 1 of *SBL Seminar Papers, 1974*. Edited by George W. MacRae. SBLSP 7. Missoula, Mont.: Society of Biblical Literature, 1974.

"The Symbolism of Transcendence in Jewish Apocalyptic." *BR* 19 (1974): 5-22.

"The Place of the Fourth Sibyl in the Development of the Jewish Sibyllina." *JJS* 25 (1974): 365-80.

1975

"The Mythology of Holy War in Daniel and the Qumran War Scroll." *VT* 25 (1975): 596-612.

"The Court-Tales of Daniel and the Development of Apocalyptic." *JBL* 94 (1975): 218-34.

"Jewish Apocalyptic against Its Hellenistic Near Eastern Environment." *BASOR* 220 (1975): 27-36.

1976

"The Jewish Response to Hellenism." *Int* 30 (1976): 311-14.

1977

The Apocalyptic Vision of the Book of Daniel. HSM 16. Missoula, Mont.: Scholars Press, 1977.

"The Biblical Precedent for Natural Theology." *JAAR* 15/1 (1977) Supplement B: 35-67.

"Pseudonymity, Historical Reviews and the Genre of the Apocalypse of John." *CBQ* 39 (1977): 329-43.

"Cosmos and Salvation: Jewish Wisdom and Apocalyptic in the Hellenistic Age." *HR* 17 (1977): 121-42.

"The Meaning of Sacrifice: A Contrast of Methods." *BR* 22 (1977): 19-34.

"Apocalypse: Towards the Morphology of a Genre." Pages 359-70 in *SBL Seminar Papers, 1977*. Edited by P. J. Achtemeier. SBLSP 11. Missoula, Mont: Scholars Press, 1977.

1978

"Methodological Issues in the Study of 1 Enoch." Pages 315-22 in vol. 1 of *SBL Seminar Papers, 1978*. Edited by P. J. Achtemeier. SBLSP 13. Missoula, Mont.: Scholars Press, 1978.

"The Root of Immortality: Death in the Context of Jewish Wisdom." *HTR* 71 (1978): 177-92.

1979

Apocalypse: The Morphology of a Genre. Edited by John J. Collins. Semeia 14. Missoula, Mont.: Scholars Press, 1979.

"Introduction: Towards the Morphology of a Genre." Pages 1-20 in ibid.

"The Jewish Apocalypses." Pages 21-60 in ibid.

"The Persian Apocalypses." Pages 207-18 in ibid.

"The 'Historical' Character of the Old Testament in Recent Biblical Theology." *CBQ* 41 (1979): 185-204.

"Dualism and Eschatology in 1QM: A Reply to P. R. Davies." *VT* 29 (1979): 212-16.

Select Bibliography

"The Son of Man Who Has Righteousness." Pages 1-14 in vol. 2 of *SBL Seminar Papers, 1979*. Edited by P. J. Achtemeier. SBLSP 17. Missoula, Mont.: Scholars Press, 1979.

1980

Ideal Figures in Ancient Judaism. SBLSCS 12. Edited with George W. Nickelsburg. Chico, Calif.: Scholars Press, 1980.

"The Heavenly Representative: The Son of Man in the Similitudes of Enoch." Pages 111-33 in ibid.

Proverbs and Ecclesiastes. Knox Preaching Guides. Atlanta: John Knox Press, 1980.

"Proverbial Wisdom and the Yahwist Vision." Pages 1-17 in *Gnomic Wisdom*. Edited by J. D. Crossan. Semeia 17. Missoula, Mont.: Scholars Press, 1980.

"The Epic of Theodotus and Hellenism of the Hasmoneans." *HTR* 73 (1980): 96-104.

1981

Apocalyptic Symbols and Social Reality. Edited by John J. Collins. Biblical Research 26. Chicago: Chicago Society of Biblical Research, 1981.

Daniel, 1 and 2 Maccabees. Old Testament Message 16. Wilmington, Del.: Glazier, 1981.

"Patterns of Eschatology at Qumran." Pages 351-76 in *Traditions in Transformation: Turning Points in Biblical Faith*. Edited by B. Halpern and J. D. Levenson. Winona Lake, Ind.: Eisenbrauns, 1981.

"Apocalyptic Genre and Mythic Allusion in Daniel." *JSOT* 21 (1981): 83-100.

1982

"Process Hermeneutic: Promise and Problems." Pages 107-116 in *Old Testament Interpretation from a Process Perspective*. Edited by William A. Beardslee and David J. Lull. Semeia 24. Missoula, Mont.: Scholars Press, 1982.

"The Apocalyptic Technique: Setting and Function in the Book of Watchers." *CBQ* 44 (1982): 91-111.

1983

Between Athens and Jerusalem: Jewish Identity in the Hellenistic Diaspora. New York: Crossroad, 1983. Revised edition: Grand Rapids: Eerdmans, 1999.

"The Apocalyptic Context of Christian Origins." *Michigan Quarterly Review* (Spring 1983): 250-64.

"Apocalyptic Eschatology as the Transcendence of Death." Pages 61-84 in *Visionaries and Their Apocalypses*. Edited by Paul D. Hanson. Issues in Religion and Theology 2. Philadelphia: Fortress, 1983.

"The Sibylline Oracles." Pages 317-472 in *The Old Testament Pseudepigrapha*, vol. 1. Edited by James H. Charlesworth. Garden City, N.Y.: Doubleday, 1983.

"The Genre Apocalypse in Hellenistic Judaism." Pages 531-48 in *Apocalypticism in the Mediterranean World and the Near East*. Edited by D. Hellholm. Tübingen: Mohr-Siebeck, 1983.

1984

The Apocalyptic Imagination: An Introduction to the Jewish Matrix of Christianity. New York: Crossroad, 1984. Revised edition: Grand Rapids: Eerdmans, 1998.

Daniel, with an Introduction to Apocalyptic Literature. FOTL 20. Grand Rapids: Eerdmans, 1984.

"Testaments." Pages 325-56 in *Jewish Writings of the Second Temple Period.* CRINT 2, 2. Edited by Michael E. Stone. Assen: Van Gorcum; Philadelphia: Fortress, 1984.

"The Sibylline Oracles." Pages 357-82 in ibid.

"The Intertestamental Literature." *List* 19 (1984): 41-52.

1985

"Artapanus." Pages 889-903 in *The Old Testament Pseudepigrapha,* vol. 2. Edited by James H. Charlesworth. Garden City, N.Y.: Doubleday, 1985.

"Daniel and His Social World." *Int* 39 (1985): 131-43.

"A Symbol of Otherness: Circumcision and Salvation in the First Century." Pages 163-86 in *"To See Ourselves as Others See Us": Christians, Jews, "Others" in Late Antiquity.* Edited by Jacob Neusner and Ernest S. Frerichs. Chico, Calif.: Scholars Press, 1985.

"The Testament (Assumption) of Moses." Pages 145-58 in *Outside the Old Testament.* Edited by M. de Jonge. Cambridge Commentaries on Writings of the Jewish and Christian World 200 BC to AD 200, vol. 4. Cambridge, UK: Cambridge University Press, 1985.

1986

The Biblical Heritage. Edited with John Dominic Crossan. Wilmington: Glazier, 1986.

"Old Testament Theology." Pages 11-33 in ibid.

Isaiah. Collegeville Bible Commentary. Collegeville: Liturgical Press, 1986. Italian translation: *Isaia.* Brescia: Queriniana, 1995.

"The Testamentary Literature in Recent Scholarship." Pages 268-86 in *Early Judaism and Its Modern Interpreters.* Edited by R. A. Kraft and G. W. E. Nickelsburg. Atlanta: Scholars Press, 1986.

"Apocalyptic Literature." Pages 345-70 in ibid.

1987

"The Development of the Sibylline Tradition." Pages 421-59 in *Aufstieg und Niedergang der Römischen Welt* 20.1. Edited by W. Haase and H. Temporini. Berlin: de Gruyter, 1987.

"Apocalypse: An Overview." Pages 334-36 in *Encyclopedia of Religion,* vol. 1. Edited by M. Eliade. New York: Macmillan and Free Press, 1987.

"The Place of Apocalypticism in the Religion of Israel." Pages 539-58 in *Ancient Israelite Religion: Essays in Honor of F. M. Cross.* Edited by P. D. Miller, P. D. Hanson and S. D. McBride. Philadelphia: Fortress, 1987.

"The Kingdom of God in the Apocrypha and Pseudepigrapha." Pages 81-95 in *The*

Kingdom of God in Twentieth-Century Interpretation. Edited by W. Willis. Peabody, Mass.: Hendrickson, 1987.

"Daniel and His Social World." Pages 249-60 in *Interpreting the Prophets*. Edited by J. L. Mays and P. J. Achtemeier. Philadelphia: Fortress, 1987.

"The Apocalyptic Context of Christian Origins." Pages 257-71 in *Backgrounds for the Bible*. Edited by M. P. O'Connor and D. N. Freedman. Winona Lake, Ind.: Eisenbrauns, 1987.

"Prophecy and Fulfillment in the Qumran Scrolls." *JETS* 30 (1987): 267-78.

"The Biblical Vision of the Common Good." Pages 50-69 in *The Common Good and U.S. Capitalism*. Edited by O. F. Williams and J. W. Houck. Lanham, Md.: University Press of America, 1987.

1988

"Messianism in the Maccabean Period." Pages 97-109 in *Judaisms and Their Messiahs*. Edited by J. Neusner, W. Green and E. Frerichs. Cambridge: Cambridge University Press, 1988.

"Introduction to the Apocrypha." Pages 758-68 in *The Harper Bible Commentary*. Edited by James L. Mays. San Francisco: Harper & Row, 1988.

"3 Maccabees." Pages 916-21 in ibid.

"Isaiah." Pages 411-52 in *The Collegeville Bible Commentary*. Edited by Dianne Bergant and Robert J. Karris. Collegeville: The Liturgical Press, 1989.

1989

"Old Testament Eschatology and Apocalypticism." Pages 298-304 in *The New Jerome Biblical Commentary*. Edited by R. Murphy, R. Brown, and J. Fitzmyer. Englewood Cliffs: Prentice-Hall, 1989.

"Biblical Theology and the History of Israelite Religion." Pages 16-32 in *Back to the Sources: Biblical and Near Eastern Studies in Honour of Dermot Ryan*. Edited by Kevin J. Cathcart and John F. Healey. Dublin: Glendale, 1989.

"The Origin of the Qumran Community: A Review of the Evidence." Pages 159-78 in *To Touch the Text: Biblical and Related Studies in Honour of Joseph A. Fitzmyer, S.J.* Edited by Paul J. Kobelski and Maurya P. Horgan. New York: Crossroad, 1989.

"The Wisdom of Solomon." Pages 51-63 in *The Books of the Bible*. Edited by Bernhard W. Anderson. New York: Scribners, 1989.

"Judaism as Praeparatio Evangelica in the Work of Martin Hengel." *RelsRev* 15 (1989): 226-28.

1990

Hebrew Bible or Old Testament. Edited with Roger Brooks. Notre Dame: University of Notre Dame Press, 1990.

"Introduction." Coauthored with Roger Brooks. Pages 1-8 in ibid.

Of Scribes and Scrolls: Studies on the Hebrew Bible, Intertestamental Judaism and Chris-

tian Origins. Edited with Harold W. Attridge and Thomas H. Tobin. Lanham, Md.: University Press of America, 1990.

"The Meaning of 'The End' in the Book of Daniel." Pages 91-98 in ibid.

The Catholic Study Bible. Edited with D. Senior, C. Stuhlmueller, and M. A. Getty. New York: Oxford University Press, 1990.

"Inspiration or Illusion: Biblical Theology and the Book of Daniel." *Ex Auditu* 6 (1990): 29-38.

"Was the Dead Sea Sect an Apocalyptic Movement?" Pages 25-51 in *Archaeology and History in the Dead Sea Scrolls*. Edited by Lawrence H. Schiffman. Sheffield: JSOT, 1990.

"The Sage in the Apocalyptic and Pseudepigraphic Literature." Pages 343-54 in *The Sage in Israel and the Ancient Near East*. Edited by John G. Gammie and Leo Perdue. Winona Lake, Ind.: Eisenbrauns, 1990.

"Is a Critical Biblical Theology Possible?" Pages 1-17 in *The Hebrew Bible and Its Interpreters*. Edited by William H. Propp et al. Winona Lake, Ind.: Eisenbrauns, 1990.

"Nebuchadnezzar and the Kingdom of God: Deferred Eschatology in the Jewish Diaspora." Pages 257-62 in *Loyalitätskonflikte in der Religionsgeschichte: Festschrift für Carsten Colpe*. Edited by Christoph Elsas and Hans G. Kippenberg. Würzburg: Königshausen & Neumann, 1990.

1991

Mysteries and Revelations: Apocalyptic Studies since the Uppsala Colloquium. Edited with J. H. Charlesworth. JSPSup 9. Sheffield: JSOT, 1991.

"Genre, Ideology and Social Movements in Jewish Apocalypticism." Pages 11-32 in ibid.

1992

Creation in the Biblical Traditions. Edited with R. J. Clifford. CBQMS 24. Washington, D.C.: The Catholic Biblical Association of America, 1992.

"The Son of Man in Ancient Judaism." *NTS* 38 (1992): 448-66.

"'The King Has Become a Jew': The Perspective on the Gentile World in Bel and the Snake." Pages 335-46 in *Diaspora Jews and Judaism: Essays in Honor of, and in Dialogue with, A. Thomas Kraabel*. Edited by J. Andrew Overman and R. S. MacLennan. South Florida Studies in the History of Judaism 41. Atlanta: Scholars Press, 1992.

"Apocalypses and Apocalypticism: Early Jewish Apocalypticism." Pages 282-88 in vol. 1 of *The Anchor Bible Dictionary*. 6 vols. Edited by David Noel Freedman. New York: Doubleday, 1992.

"Daniel, Book of." Pages 29-37 in vol. 2 of ibid.

"Dead Sea Scrolls." Pages 85-101 in vol. 2 of ibid.

"Essenes." Pages 619-26 in vol. 2 of ibid.

"Nabonidus, Prayer of." Pages 976-77 in vol. 4 of ibid.

"Sibylline Oracles." Pages 2-6 in vol. 6 of ibid.

Select Bibliography

1993

Daniel: A Commentary on the Book of Daniel. Hermeneia. Minneapolis: Fortress, 1993.

"The Impact of Dogmatism on Rational Discourse: Comments on the Paper of Michael Dummett." Pages 23-30 in *Hermes and Athena: Biblical Exegesis and Philosophical Theology.* Edited by Eleonore Stump and Thomas P. Flint. Notre Dame: University of Notre Dame Press, 1993.

"The Son of God Text from Qumran." Pages 65-82 in *From Jesus to John: Essays on Jesus and Christology in Honour of Marinus de Jonge.* Edited by M. de Boer. Sheffield: JSOT, 1993.

"A Pre-Christian 'Son of God' Among the Dead Sea Scrolls." *BRev* (June 1993): 34-38, 57.

"Stirring Up the Great Sea: The Religio-Historical Background of Daniel 7." Pages 121-36 in *The Book of Daniel in the Light of New Findings.* Edited by A. S. van der Woude. Leuven: Leuven University Press, 1993.

"Historical Criticism and the State of Biblical Theology." *Christian Century* (July 28–August 4, 1993): 743-47.

"Wisdom, Apocalypticism, and Generic Compatibility." Pages 165-85 in *In Search of Wisdom: Essays in Memory of John Gammie.* Edited by L. Perdue, B. B. Scott, and W. J. Wiseman. Louisville: Westminster, 1993.

"The Suffering Servant at Qumran?" *BRev* (Dec. 1993): 25-27, 63.

"The Works of the Messiah." *DSD,* sample issue (1993): 1-15. Reprinted in *DSD* 1 (1994): 98-112.

1994

Methods of Investigation of the Dead Sea Scrolls and the Khirbet Qumran Site: Present Realities and Future Prospects. Edited with M. O. Wise, N. Golb, and D. Pardee. Annals of the New York Academy of Sciences 22. New York: The New York Academy of Sciences, 1994.

"Messiahs in Context: Method in the Study of Messianism in the Dead Sea Scrolls." Pages 213-30 in ibid.

"The Sibyl and the Potter: Political Propaganda in Ptolemaic Egypt." Pages 57-69 in *Religious Propaganda and Missionary Competition in the New Testament World.* Edited by Lukas Bormann, Kelly Del Tredici and Angela Standhartinger. Leiden: Brill, 1994.

"Introduction to Early Jewish Religion." Pages 284-291 in *Genesis to Leviticus,* vol. 1 of *The New Interpreter's Bible.* Edited by Walter Brueggemann et al. Nashville: Abingdon, 1994.

"Teacher and Messiah? The One Who Will Teach Righteousness at the End of Days." Pages 193-210 in *The Community of the Renewed Covenant.* Edited by Eugene Ulrich and James VanderKam. Notre Dame, Ind.: University of Notre Dame Press, 1994.

"A Thrice-Told Hymn." Coauthored with D. Dimant. *JQR* 85 (1994): 151-55.

1995

The Scepter and the Star: The Messiahs of the Dead Sea Scrolls and Other Ancient Literature. ABRL. New York: Doubleday, 1995. Second edition: Grand Rapids: Eerdmans, 2010.

Death, Ecstasy and Otherworldly Journeys. Edited with Michael Fishbane. Albany: SUNY Press, 1995.

"A Throne in the Heavens: Apotheosis in Pre-Christian Judaism." Pages 41-58 in ibid.

"Asking for the Meaning of a Fragmentary Qumran Text: The Referential Background of 4QAaron A." Pages 579-90 in *Texts and Contexts: Biblical Texts in Their Textual and Situational Contexts: Essays in Honor of Lars Hartman.* Edited by Tord Fornberg and David Hellholm. Oslo: Scandinavian University Press, 1995.

"The Origin of Evil in Apocalyptic Literature and the Dead Sea Scrolls." Pages 25-38 in *Congress Volume, Paris 1992.* Edited by J. A. Emerton. Leiden: Brill, 1995.

"'He Shall Not Judge by What His Eyes See': Messianic Authority in the Dead Sea Scrolls." *DSD* 2 (1995): 145-64.

"Daniel." Pages 413-16 in *Dictionary of Deities and Demons.* Edited by K. van der Toorn et al. Leiden: Brill, 1995.

"Gabriel." Pages 640-42 in ibid.

"Liers in Wait." Page 967 in ibid.

"Prince." Pages 1249-52 in ibid.

"Saints of the Most High." Pages 1359-64 in ibid.

"Watcher." Pages 1681-85 in ibid.

"Before the Canon: Scriptures in Second Temple Judaism." Pages 225-41 in *Old Testament Interpretation, Past, Present and Future: Essays in Honor of Gene M. Tucker.* Edited by J. L. Mays, D. L. Petersen, and K. H. Richards. Nashville: Abingdon, 1995.

"The Exodus and Biblical Theology." *BTB* 25 (1995): 152-60.

1996

Qumran Cave 4. XVII. Parabiblical Texts, Part 3. Edited with G. Brooke et al. DJD XXII. Oxford: Clarendon, 1996.

"Pseudo-Daniel." Coauthored with P. Flint. Pages 95-164 in ibid.

"Prayer of Nabonidus." Pages 83-93 in ibid.

"Introduction: The Bible and Christian Theology." *JR* 76 (1996): 167-71.

"Wisdom, Apocalypticism and the Dead Sea Scrolls." Pages 19-32 in *"Jedes Ding hat seine Zeit. . . ." Studien zu israelitischen und altorientalischen Weisheit: Diethelm Michel zum 65 Geburtstag.* Edited by A. A. Diesel et al. Berlin: de Gruyter, 1996.

"Jesus and the Messiahs of Israel." Pages 287-302 in *Geschichte — Tradition — Reflexion: Festschrift für Martin Hengel.* Edited by H. Lichtenberger. Tübingen: Mohr-Siebeck, 1996.

"Pseudo-Daniel Revisited." *RevQ* 17 (1996): 111-35.

Select Bibliography

1997

Families in Ancient Israel. Coauthored with L. G. Perdue, J. Blenkinsopp, and C. Meyers. Louisville: Westminster, 1997.

"Marriage, Divorce and Family in Second Temple Judaism." Pages 104-62 in ibid.

Apocalypticism in the Dead Sea Scrolls. London: Routledge, 1997. Italian translation: Milan: Massimo, 1999.

Seers, Sibyls and Sages in Hellenistic-Roman Judaism. Leiden: Brill, 1997. Paperback edition: Boston: Brill Academic, 2001.

Jewish Wisdom in the Hellenistic Age. Old Testament Library. Louisville: Westminster, 1997.

"L'influence perse sur le judaisme." *Le Monde de la Bible* 106 (1997): 76-77.

"Varieties of Judaism in the Hellenistic and Roman Periods." *JR* (1997): 605-11.

"The Expectation of the End in the Dead Sea Scrolls." Pages 74-90 in *Eschatology, Messianism and the Dead Sea Scrolls.* Edited by C. A. Evans and P. W. Flint. Grand Rapids: Eerdmans, 1997.

"A Herald of Good Tidings: Isaiah 61:1-3 and Its Actualization in the Dead Sea Scrolls." Pages 225-40 in *The Quest for Context and Meaning: Studies in Biblical Intertextuality in Honor of James A. Sanders.* Edited by C. A. Evans and S. Talmon. Leiden: Brill, 1997.

"The Background of the Son of God Text." *BBR* 7 (1997): 51-62.

"Jewish Monotheism and Christian Theology." Pages 81-105 in *Aspects of Monotheism.* Edited by H. Shanks and J. Meinhardt. Washington, D.C.: Biblical Archaeology Society, 1997.

"McKenzie, John L." Page 891 in *The Encyclopedia of American Catholic History.* Edited by M. Glazier and T. J. Shelley. Collegeville: The Liturgical Press, 1997.

"Vawter, Bruce." Pages 1430-31 in ibid.

"Wisdom Reconsidered in Light of the Scrolls." *DSD* 4 (1997): 265-81.

"The Dead Sea Scrolls and Christian Origins." The Henry Barton Robison Lecture in Religion. Culver-Stockton College, Canton, Missouri. October 30, 1997. 25 pages.

1998

The Encyclopedia of Apocalypticism. Edited with Bernard McGinn and Stephen J. Stein. 3 vols. New York: Continuum, 1998. Winner of Choice Outstanding Book Award, 1999.

"From Prophecy to Apocalypticism: The Expectation of the End." Pages 129-61 in vol. 1 of ibid.

"Ideas of Messianism in the Dead Sea Scrolls." Pages 20-41 in *The Dead Sea Scrolls and the Christian Faith.* Edited by J. H. Charlesworth and W. P. Weaver. Harrisburg, Pa.: Trinity Press International, 1998.

"Jerusalem and the Temple in Jewish Apocalyptic Literature of the Second Temple Period." International Rennert Guest Lecture Series 1. Bar Ilan University, 1998. 31 pages.

"Natural Theology and Biblical Tradition: The Case of Hellenistic Judaism." *CBQ* 60 (1998): 1-15. Presidential address to the Catholic Biblical Association, 1997.

"Apocalyptiek: Het genre, de ideologie en de bewegung." Pages 19-38 in *Visioenen aangaande het einde*. Edited by J. W. van Henten and O. Mellin. Zoetermeer: Meinema, 1998.

"New Light on the Book of Daniel from the Dead Sea Scrolls." Pages 180-96 in *Perspectives in the Study of the Old Testament and Early Judaism: A Symposium in Honour of A. S. van der Woude*. Edited by F. García Martínez and E. Noort. Leiden: Brill, 1998.

"The Jewish Transformation of Sibylline Oracles." Pages 369-87 in *Sibille e Linguaggi Oracolari. Atti del Convegno Macerata-Norcia — Settembre 1994*. Edited by Ileana Chirassi Colombo and Tullio Seppilli. Rome: Istituti Editoriali e Poligrafici Internazionali, for the University of Macerata, 1998.

1999

"In the Likeness of the Holy Ones: The Creation of Humankind in a Wisdom Text from Qumran." Pages 609-18 in *The Provo International Conference on the Dead Sea Scrolls*. Edited by D. W. Parry and E. Ulrich. Leiden: Brill, 1999.

"Pseudepigraphy and Group Formation in Second Temple Judaism." Pages 43-58 in *Pseudepigraphic Perspectives: The Apocrypha and Pseudepigrapha in Light of the Dead Sea Scrolls*. Edited by E. G. Chazon and M. Stone. Leiden: Brill, 1999.

"The Christian Appropriation of the Apocalyptic Genre." Pages 513-26 in *The 1900th Anniversary of St. John's Apocalypse: Proceedings of the International and Interdisciplinary Symposium, September 17-26, 1995*. Edited by Elias V. Oikonomou et al. Athens: Monastery of St. John, 1999.

"Faith without Works: Biblical Ethics and the Sacrifice of Isaac." Pages 115-31 in *Recht und Ethos im Alten Testament: Gestalt und Wirkung: Festschrift für Horst Seebass zum 65. Geburtstag*. Edited by S. Beyerle, G. Mayer, and H. Strauss. Neukirchen-Vluyn: Neukirchener Verlag, 1999.

"Apocalypticism and Literary Genre in the Dead Sea Scrolls." Pages 403-30 in *The Dead Sea Scrolls after Fifty Years: A Comprehensive Assessment*. Edited by P. W. Flint and J. C. VanderKam. Leiden: Brill, 1999.

"Jesus, Messianism and the Dead Sea Scrolls." Pages 100-119 in *Qumran-Messianism: Studies on the Messianic Expectations in the Dead Sea Scrolls*. Edited by J. H. Charlesworth, H. Lichtenberger, and G. S. Oegema. Tübingen: Mohr-Siebeck, 1999.

"The Tales from the Persian Court (4Q550^{a-e})." Coauthored with Deborah A. Green. Pages 39-50 in *Antikes Judentum und Frühes Christentum: Festschrift für Hartmut Stegemann zum 65. Geburtstag*. Edited by B. Kollmann, W. Reinbold, and A. Steudel. Berlin: de Gruyter, 1999.

"The Sense of an Ending in Pre-Christian Judaism." Pages 25-43 in *Fearful Hope: Ap-*

Select Bibliography

proaching the New Millennium. Edited by C. Kleinhenz and F. Lamont. Madison: University of Wisconsin Press, 1999.

"The Hellenization of Jerusalem in the Pre-Maccabean Era." International Rennert Guest Lecture Series 6. Bar Ilan University, 1999. 20 pages.

"Scrolls Scholarship as Intellectual History." Pages 101-6 in *The Dead Sea Scrolls at Fifty*. Edited by R. A. Kugler and E. M. Schuller. Atlanta: Society of Biblical Literature, 1999.

Preface to reprint of *Hellenistic Civilization and the Jews*, by V. Tcherikover. Peabody, Mass.: Hendrickson, 1999.

2000

Religion in the Dead Sea Scrolls. Edited with Robert Kugler. Grand Rapids: Eerdmans, 2000.

"Powers in Heaven: God, Gods, and Angels in the Dead Sea Scrolls." Pages 9-28 in ibid.

"The Afterlife in Apocalyptic Literature." Pages 119-39 in *Judaism in Late Antiquity, Part 4: Death, Life-After-Death, Resurrection and The World-to-Come in the Judaisms of Antiquity*. Edited by A. J. Avery Peck and J. Neusner. Handbuch der Orientalistik. Leiden: Brill, 2000.

"Apocrypha and Pseudepigrapha." Pages 35-39 in *Encyclopedia of the Dead Sea Scrolls*. Edited by L. H. Schiffman and J. C. VanderKam. New York: Oxford University Press, 2000.

"Daniel, Book of: Pseudo-Daniel." Pages 176-78 in ibid.

"Eschatology." Pages 256-61 in ibid.

"Family Life." Pages 287-90 in ibid.

"Strugnell, John." Pages 895-96 in ibid.

"Teacher and Servant." *RHPR* 80 (2000): 37-50.

"Qumran, Apocalypticism and the New Testament." Pages 133-38 in *The Dead Sea Scrolls Fifty Years after Their Discovery: Proceedings of the Jerusalem Congress, July 20-25, 1997*. Edited by L. H. Schiffman, E. Tov, and J. C. VanderKam. Jerusalem: Israel Exploration Society, in cooperation with the Shrine of the Book, 2000.

"Models of Utopia in the Biblical Tradition." Pages 51-67 in *A Wise and Discerning Mind: Essays in Honor of Burke O. Long*. Edited by S. M. Olyan and R. C. Culley. BJS 325. Providence, R.I.: Brown University, 2000.

"Apocalyptic Literature." Pages 40-45 in *Dictionary of New Testament Background: A Compendium of Contemporary Biblical Scholarship*. Edited by C. A. Evans and S. E. Porter. Downers Grove, Ill.: Intervarsity Press, 2000.

"Enoch, Books of." Pages 313-18 in ibid.

"Eschatologies of Late Antiquity." Pages 330-37 in ibid.

"Sibylline Oracles." Pages 1107-12 in ibid.

"Reinventing Exodus: Exegesis and Legend in Hellenistic Egypt." Pages 52-62 in *For a Later Generation: The Transformation of Tradition in Israel, Early Judaism and*

Early Christianity. Edited by R. A. Argall, B. A. Bow, and R. A. Werline. Harrisburg, Pa.: Trinity Press International, 2000.
Eerdmans Dictionary of the Bible. Grand Rapids: Eerdmans, 2000. Consulting editor. Editor-in-chief: David Noel Freedman; associate editor: Allen C. Myers; managing editor: Astrid B. Beck.

2001

Hellenism in the Land of Israel. Edited with Gregory Sterling. Notre Dame, Ind.: University of Notre Dame Press, 2001.
"Cult and Culture: The Limits of Hellenization in Judea." Pages 38-61 in ibid.
The Book of Daniel: Composition and Reception. Edited with Peter W. Flint. 2 vols. Leiden: Brill, 2001.
"Current Issues in the Study of Daniel." Pages 1-15 in ibid.
"The Construction of Israel in the Sectarian Rule-Books." Pages 25-42 in *Judaism in Late Antiquity, 5.1, The Judaism of Qumran: A Systematic Reading of the Dead Sea Scrolls*. Edited by A. J. Avery-Peck, J. Neusner and B. Chilton. Leiden: Brill, 2001.
"Spells Pleasing to God: The Binding of Isaac in Philo the Epic Poet." Pages 3-13 in *Antiquity and Humanity: Essays on Ancient Religion and Philosophy Presented to H. D. Betz*. Edited by A. Yarbro Collins and M. M. Mitchell. Tübingen: Mohr-Siebeck, 2001.
"The Wisdom of Jesus Son of Sirach." Pages 667-98 in *The Oxford Bible Commentary*. Edited by J. Barton and J. Muddiman. Oxford: Oxford University Press, 2001.
"The Development of the Exodus Tradition." Pages 144-55 in *Religious Identity and the Invention of Tradition*. Edited by J. W. van Henten and A. Houtepan. Assen: van Gorcum, 2001.
"Apocalyptic Literature." Pages 432-37 in *The Blackwell Companion to the Hebrew Bible*. Edited by L. G. Perdue. Oxford: Blackwell, 2001.
"Culture and Society in Hellenistic Judaism." Pages 17-36 in *Honeycomb of the Word: Interpreting the Primary Testament with André Lacocque*. Edited by W. D. Edgerton. Chicago: Exploration Press, 2001.

2002

The History of Apocalypticism. Edited with B. McGinn and S. Stein. New York: Continuum, 2003. Condensation of *The Encyclopedia of Apocalypticism*.
"Death and Afterlife." Pages 357-77 in vol. 2 of *The Biblical World*. Edited by John Barton. New York: Routledge, 2002.
"Apocalyptic Eschatology in Philosophical Dress in the Wisdom of Solomon." Pages 93-107 in *Shem in the Tents of Japhet: Essays on the Encounter of Judaism and Hellenism*. Edited by J. L. Kugel. Leiden: Brill, 2002.
"Ethos and Identity in Jewish Apocalyptic Literature." Pages 51-65 in *Ethos und Identität: Einheit und Vielfalt des Judentums im hellenistisch-römischer Zeit*. Edited by Matthias Konradt and Ulrike Steinert. Munich: Schöningh, 2002.

Select Bibliography

"The Literature of the Second Temple Period." Pages 53-78 in *The Oxford Handbook of Jewish Studies*. Edited by M. Goodman. Oxford: Oxford University Press, 2002.
"Theology and Identity in the Early Enoch Literature." *Hen* 24 (2002): 57-62.

2003
"Forms of Community in the Dead Sea Scrolls." Pages 97-111 in *Emanuel: Studies in Hebrew Bible, Septuagint and Dead Sea Scrolls in Honor of Emanuel Tov*. Edited by S. M. Paul, R. A. Kraft, L. H. Schiffman, and W. W. Fields. Leiden: Brill, 2003.
"Temporality and Politics in Jewish Apocalyptic Literature." Pages 26-43 in *Apocalyptic in History and Tradition*. Edited by C. Rowland and J. Barton. JSPSup 43. Sheffield: Sheffield Academic Press, 2003.
"The Zeal of Phinehas: The Bible and the Legitimation of Violence." *JBL* 122 (2003): 3-21. Reprinted on pages 11-33 in *The Destructive Power of Religion: Violence in Judaism, Christianity, and Islam*. Edited by J. Harold Ellens. Westport, Conn.: Praeger, 2004. Presidential Address to the Society of Biblical Literature, 2002.
"The Book of Truth: Daniel as Reliable Witness to Past and Future in the United States of America." Coauthored with Adela Yarbro Collins. In *Europa, Tausendjähriges Reich und Neue Welt: Zwei Jahrtausende Geschichte und Utopie in der Rezeption des Danielbuches*. Edited by M. Delgado, K. Koch, and E. Marsch. Freiburg: Universitätsverlag; Stuttgart: Kohlhammer, 2003.
"An Enochic Testament? Comments on George Nickelsburg's Hermeneia Commentary." Pages 373-78 in *George W. E. Nickelsburg in Perspective: An Ongoing Dialogue of Learning*. Edited by J. Neusner and A. Avery-Peck. Leiden: Brill, 2003.
"Weisheit/Weisheitsliteratur III. Judentum." *Theologische Realenzyklopädie* 35 (2003): 497-508.
"Journeys to the World Beyond in Ancient Judaism." Pages 20-36 in *Apocalyptic and Eschatological Heritage: The Middle East and Celtic Realms*. Edited by Martin McNamara. Dublin: Four Courts, 2003.
"Life after Death in Pseudo-Phocylides." Pages 75-86 in *Jerusalem, Alexandria, Rome: Studies in Ancient Cultural Interaction in Honour of A. Hillhorst*. Edited by F. García Martínez and G. P. Luttikhuizen. Leiden: Brill, 2003.
"The Jewish World and the Coming of Rome." Pages 353-62 in *Symbiosis, Symbolism, and the Power of the Past: Canaan, Ancient Israel and Their Neighbors from the Late Bronze Age through Roman Palestine: Proceedings of the Centennial Symposium, W. F. Albright Institute of Archaeological Research and American Schools of Oriental Research, Jerusalem, May 29-31, 2000*. Edited by W. G. Dever and S. Gitin. Winona Lake, Ind.: Eisenbrauns, 2003.
"The Eschatology of Zechariah." Pages 74-84 in *Knowing the End from the Beginning: The Prophetic, the Apocalyptic, and Their Relationship*. Edited by L. L. Grabbe and R. D. Haak. New York: T&T Clark International, 2003.
"Prophecy, Apocalypse and Eschatology: Reflections on the Proposals of Lester Grabbe." Pages 44-52 in ibid.

"The Mysteries of God." Pages 287-306 in *Wisdom and Apocalyptic*. Edited by F. García Martínez. Leuven: Peeters, 2003.

2004

The Hebrew Bible: An Introduction. Minneapolis: Fortress, 2004.

Does the Bible Justify Violence? Facets. Minneapolis: Fortress, 2004.

Sapiential Perspectives: Wisdom Literature in Light of the Dead Sea Scrolls. Edited with Gregory E. Sterling and Ruth A. Clements. STDJ 51. Leiden: Brill, 2004.

"The Eschatologizing of Wisdom in the Dead Sea Scrolls." Pages 49-66 in ibid.

Apocalypse and Violence. Edited with Abbas Amanat. New Haven: Yale Center for International and Area Studies, 2004.

Religions of the Ancient World: A Guide. Cambridge, Mass.: Belknap/Harvard University Press, 2004. Editorial board member with responsibility for ancient Israel and Judaism. General Editor: Sarah Iles Johnston.

"Cosmology: Time and History." Pages 59-70 in ibid. Reprinted on pages 59-70 in *Ancient Religions*. Edited by Sarah Iles Johnston. Cambridge, Mass.: Harvard University Press, 2007.

"Israel." Pages 181-88 in ibid. Reprinted on pages 181-88 in *Ancient Religions*.

"Death, the Afterlife, and Other Last Things: Israel." Pages 480-83 in ibid.

"Before the Fall: The Earliest Interpretations of Adam and Eve." Pages 293-308 in *The Idea of Biblical Interpretation: Essays in Honor of James L. Kugel*. Edited by H. Najman and J. H. Newman. Leiden: Brill, 2004.

"La Reinterpretazione delle Tradizioni Apocalittiche nell Sapienza di Salomone." Pages 157-71 in *Il Libro della Sapienza: Tradizione, Redazione, Teologia*. Edited by Giuseppe Bella and Angelo Passaro. Roma: Città Nuova, 2004. Reprinted as "The Reinterpretation of Apocalyptic Traditions in the Wisdom of Solomon." Pages 143-57 in *The Book of Wisdom in Modern Research*. Edited by Giuseppe Bella and Angelo Passaro. Deuterocanonical and Cognate Literature Yearbook 2005. Berlin: de Gruyter, 2005.

"The Politics of Biblical Interpretation." Pages 195-211 in *Biblical and Near Eastern Essays in Honour of Kevin J. Cathcart*. Edited by Carmel McCarthy and John F. Healey. London and New York: T&T Clark International, 2004.

"Amazing Grace: The Transformation of the Thanksgiving Hymn at Qumran." Pages 75-85 in *Psalms in Community: Jewish and Christian Textual, Liturgical, and Artistic Traditions*. Edited by Harold Attridge and Margot E. Fassler. Symposium Series 25. Atlanta: Society of Biblical Literature, 2004.

"The Third Sibyl Revisited." Pages 3-19 in *Things Revealed: Studies in Early Jewish and Christian Literature in Honor of Michael E. Stone*. Edited by E. G. Chazon, D. Satran, and R. A. Clements. JSJSup 89. Leiden: Brill, 2004.

"Marriage in the Old Testament." Pages 12-20 in *Marriage in the Catholic Tradition: Scripture, Tradition, and Experience*. Edited by Todd A. Salzman, Thomas M. Kelly, and John J. O'Keefe. New York: Crossroad, 2004.

Select Bibliography

2005

Jewish Cult and Hellenistic Culture. JSJSup 100. Leiden: Brill, 2005.
Encounters with Biblical Theology. Minneapolis: Fortress, 2005.
The Bible after Babel: Historical Criticism in a Postmodern Age. Grand Rapids: Eerdmans, 2005.
"Anti-Semitism in Antiquity? The Case of Alexandria." Pages 9-29 in *Ancient Judaism in Its Hellenistic Context.* Edited by Carol Bakhos. JSJSup 95. Leiden: Brill, 2005. Reprinted in *Archiv für Religionsgeschichte* 7 (2005): 86-101.
"Joseph and Aseneth: Jewish or Christian?" *JSP* 14 (2005): 97-112.
"Foreword: Mowinckel's *He That Cometh* in Retrospect." Pages xv-xxxii in reprint of *He That Cometh,* by Sigmund Mowinckel. Grand Rapids: Eerdmans, 2005.
"Interpretations of the Creation of Humanity in the Dead Sea Scrolls." Pages 29-43 in *Biblical Interpretation at Qumran.* Edited by M. Henze. Grand Rapids: Eerdmans, 2005.
"The Judaism of the Book of Tobit." In *The Book of Tobit: Text, Tradition, Theology.* Edited by Géza Xeravits and József Zsengellér. JSJSup 98. Leiden: Brill, 2005.
"Response: The Apocalyptic Worldview of Daniel." Pages 59-66 in *Enoch and Qumran Origins.* Edited by Gabriele Boccaccini. Grand Rapids: Eerdmans, 2005.
"Enoch, the Dead Sea Scrolls, and the Essenes: Groups and Movements in Judaism in the Early Second Century B.C.E." Pages 345-530 in ibid.
"Hellenistic Judaism in Recent Scholarship." Pages 969-80 in *The Encyclopaedia of Judaism,* Vol. 2 (F-K). Edited by Jacob Neusner, Alan J. Avery-Peck and William Scott Green. Leiden: Brill, 2005.

2006

Christian Beginnings and the Dead Sea Scrolls. Edited with Craig A. Evans. Grand Rapids: Baker, 2006.
"A Messiah before Jesus?" Pages 15-35 in ibid.
"An Essene Messiah? Comments on Israel Knohl, *The Messiah Before Jesus.*" Pages 37-44 in ibid.
"Apocalyptic Theology and the Dead Sea Scrolls: A Response to Jonathan Wilson." Pages 129-33 in ibid.
The Catholic Study Bible. Revised edition. Edited with D. Senior. New York: Oxford, 2006.
"The Time of the Teacher: An Old Debate Renewed." Pages 212-29 in *Studies in the Hebrew Bible, Qumran, and the Septuagint Presented to Eugene Ulrich.* Edited by Peter W. Flint, Emanuel Tov, and James C. VanderKam. VTSup 101. Leiden: Brill, 2006.
Foreword to *Qumran: The Site of the Dead Sea Scrolls: Archaeological Interpretations and Debates.* Edited by Katharina Galor, Jean-Baptiste Humbert, and Jürgen Zangenberg. STDJ 57. Leiden: Brill, 2006.
"The Yahad and the Qumran Community." Pages 81-96 in *Biblical Traditions in Trans-*

mission: Essays in Honour of Michael A. Knibb. Edited by Charlotte Hempel and Judith Lieu. JSJSup 111. Leiden: Brill, 2006.

"The Essenes and the Afterlife." Pages 35-53 in *From 4QMMT to Resurrection: Mélanges qumraniens en homage à Émile Puech*. Edited by Florentino García Martínez, Annette Steudel and Eibert Tigchelaar. STDJ 61. Leiden: Brill, 2006.

"Some Issues in the Study of Apocalyptic Literature." *Hen* 27 (2006): 21-26.

"What Was Distinctive about Messianic Expectation at Qumran?" Pages 71-92 in *The Bible and the Dead Sea Scrolls: The Princeton Symposium on the Dead Sea Scrolls*. Edited by J. H. Charlesworth. Waco, Tex.: Baylor University Press, 2006.

"Messianism and Exegetical Tradition: The Evidence of the Pentateuch." Pages 129-49 in *The Septuagint and Messianism*. Edited by M. A. Knibb. BETL 195. Leuven: Peeters, 2006.

2007

A Short Introduction to the Hebrew Bible. Minneapolis: Fortress, 2007.

The Early Enoch Literature. Edited with Gabriele Boccaccini. JSJSup 121. Leiden: Brill, 2007.

"'Enochic Judaism' and the Sect of the Dead Sea Scrolls." Pages 283-99 in ibid.

"Conceptions of Afterlife in the Dead Sea Scrolls." Pages 103-25 in *Lebendige Hoffnung-ewiger Tod? Jenseitsvorstellungen im Hellenismus, Judentum und Christentum*. Edited by Michael Labahn and Manfred Lang. Arbeiten zur Bibel und ihrer Geschichte 24. Leipzig: Evangelische Verlagsanstalt, 2007.

"Mowinckel's *He That Cometh* Revisited." *ST* 61 (2007): 3-20.

"Sectarian Consciousness in the Dead Sea Scrolls." Pages 177-92 in *Heavenly Tablets: Interpretation, Identity and Tradition in Ancient Judaism*. Edited by Lynn LiDonnici and Andrea Lieber. JSJSup 119. Leiden: Brill, 2007.

"Pre-Christian Jewish Messianism: An Overview." Pages 1-20 in *The Messiah in Early Judaism and Christianity*. Edited by Magnus Zetterholm. Minneapolis: Fortress, 2007.

"Enoch and the Son of Man: A Response to Sabino Chialà and Helge Kvanvig." Pages 216-27 in *Enoch and the Messiah Son of Man: Revisiting the Book of Parables*. Edited by Gabriele Boccaccini. Grand Rapids: Eerdmans, 2007.

"Apocalyptic Eschatology in the Ancient World." Pages 40-55 in *The Oxford Handbook of Eschatology*. Edited by Jerry L. Walls. Oxford: Oxford University Press, 2007.

"The Nature and Aims of the Sect Known from the Dead Sea Scrolls." Pages 31-52 in *Flores Florentino: Dead Sea Scrolls and Other Judaic Studies in Honour of Florentino García Martínez*. Edited by Eibert Tigchelaar. STDJ 122. Leiden: Brill, 2007.

"How Distinctive Was Enochic Judaism?" *Meghillot* 5-6 (2007): 1-18.

Introduction to "Philo and the Dead Sea Scrolls." *SPhilo* 19 (2007): 81-83.

"The Life Angelic, according to the Dead Sea Scrolls." Pages 126-28 in *Complexity: Inter-*

disciplinary Communications. Edited by Willy Østreng. Oslo: Centre for Advanced Study at the Norwegian Academy of Science and Letters, 2006/2007.

2008

King and Messiah as Son of God. Coauthored with Adela Yarbro Collins. Grand Rapids: Eerdmans, 2008.

"Isaiah 8:23–9:6 and Its Greek Translation." Pages 205-21 in *Scripture in Transition: Essays on Septuagint, Hebrew Bible, and Dead Sea Scrolls in Honour of Raija Sollamo*. Edited by Anssi Voitila and Jutta Jokiranta. JSJSup 126. Leiden: Brill, 2008.

"The Sons of God and the Daughters of Men." Pages 259-74 in *Sacred Marriages: The Divine-Human Sexual Metaphor from Sumer to Early Christianity*. Edited by Martti Nissinen and Risto Uro. Winona Lake, Ind.: Eisenbrauns, 2008.

2009

Beyond the Qumran Community: The Sectarian Movement of the Dead Sea Scrolls. Grand Rapids: Eerdmans, 2009.

"The Idea of Election in 4 Ezra." *JSQ* 16 (2009): 83-96.

"The Angelic Life." Pages 291-310 in *Metamorphoses: Resurrection, Body and Transformative Practices in Early Christianity*. Edited by Turid Karlsen Seim and Jorunn Økland. Ekstasis 1. Berlin: de Gruyter, 2009.

"The Interpretation of Psalm 2." Pages 49-66 in *Echoes from the Caves: Qumran and the New Testament*. Edited by Florentino García Martínez. STDJ 85. Leiden: Brill, 2009.

"The Beginning of the End of the World." Pages 137-55 in *Thus Says the Lord: Essays on the Former and Latter Prophets in Honor of Robert R. Wilson*. Edited by John Ahn and Stephen Cook. New York: Continuum, 2009.

"Josephus on the Essenes: The Sources of His Information." Pages 51-72 in *A Wandering Galilean: Essays in Honor of Seán Freyne*. Edited by Zuleika Rodgers, with Margaret Daly Denton and Anne Fitzpatrick McKinley. JSJSup 132. Leiden: Brill, 2009.

"Beyond the Qumran Community: Social Organization in the Dead Sea Scrolls." *DSD* 16 (2009): 351-69.

"Apocalypses, Apocryphal." Pages 315-16 in volume 2 of *The Encyclopedia of the Bible and Its Reception*. Edited by H. J. Klauck, B. McGinn et al. Berlin: de Gruyter, 2009.

2010

The Eerdmans Dictionary of Early Judaism. Edited with Daniel C. Harlow. Grand Rapids: Eerdmans, 2010.

The Oxford Handbook of the Dead Sea Scrolls. Edited with Timothy Lim. Oxford: Oxford University Press, 2010.

"Prophecy and History in the Pesharim." Pages 209-26 in *Authoritative Scriptures in Ancient Judaism*. Edited by Mladen Popović. Leiden: Brill, 2010.

Abbreviations and Symbols

Abbreviations for the names of writings in the Bible, Apocrypha, Pseudepigrapha, and Dead Sea Scrolls may be found in Patrick Alexander et al., eds., *The SBL Handbook of Style* (Peabody, Mass.: Hendrickson, 1999).

Abbreviations

AB	Anchor Bible
ABD	*Anchor Bible Dictionary.* 6 vols. Edited by D. N. Freedman. New York, 1992
ABRL	Anchor Bible Reference Library
Aet.	Philo of Alexandria, *De Aeternitate Mundi*
Ag. Ap.	Josephus, *Against Apion*
AGJU	Arbeiten zur Geschichte des antiken Judentums und des Urchristentums
Anab.	Xenophon, *Anabasis*
AnBib	Analecta biblica
ANEP	*The Ancient Near East in Pictures Relating to the Old Testament.* Edited by J. B. Pritchard. Princeton, 1954
ANET	*Ancient Near Eastern Texts Relating to the Old Testament,* 3d ed. Edited by James B. Pritchard. Princeton, 1969
ANRW	*Aufstieg und Niedergang der römischen Welt*
Ant.	Josephus, *Antiquities of the Jews*
AOT	*The Apocryphal Old Testament.* Edited by H. F. D. Sparks. Oxford, 1984
Artap.	Artapanus

xxxiii

Abbreviations and Symbols

ASTI	Annual of the Swedish Theological Institute
AUSS	Andrews University Seminary Studies
b.	Babylonian Talmud tractate
BA	Biblical Archaeologist
BAC	Biblioteca de autores cristianos
BASOR	Bulletin of the American Schools of Oriental Research
BBR	Bulletin for Biblical Research
BCH	Bulletin de correspondance hellénique
BDB	F. Brown, S. R. Driver, and C. A. Briggs. *A Hebrew and English Lexicon of the Old Testament.* Oxford, 1907
BEHE	Bibliothèque de l'Ecole des hautes études
BETL	Bibliotheca ephemeridum theologicarum lovaniensium
BGU	Aegyptische Urkunden aus den Königlichen Staatlichen Museen zu Berlin, Griechische Urkunden. 15 vols. Berlin, 1895-1983
BHT	Beiträge zur historischen Theologie
Bib	Biblica
BJRL	Bulletin of the John Rylands Library
BJS	Brown Judaic Studies
BR	Biblical Research
BRev	Bible Review
BTB	Biblical Theology Bulletin
BZ	Biblische Zeitschrift
BZAW	Beihefte zur Zeitschrift für die alttestamentliche Wissenschaft
CBC	Cambridge Bible Commentary
CBQ	Catholic Biblical Quarterly
CBQMS	Catholic Biblical Quarterly Monograph Series
CBR	Currents in Biblical Research
chap(s).	chapter(s)
CIG	*Corpus inscriptionum graecarum.* Edited by A. Boeckh, 4 vols. Berlin, 1828-1877
CIS	Corpus inscriptionum semiticarum
Cl. Ant.	Classical Antiquity
col(s).	column(s)
CP	Classical Philosophy
CPJ	*Corpus Papyrorum Judaicarum.* 3 vols. Edited by V. Tcherikover and A. Fuks. Cambridge, Mass., 1957-64
CRINT	Compendia rerum iudaicarum ad Novum Testamentum
CSCO	*Corpus scriptorum christianorum orientalium.* Edited by I. B. Chabot et al. Paris, 1903-
CTM	Concordia Theological Monthly
DCH	*Dictionary of Classical Hebrew.* Edited by D. J. A. Clines. Sheffield, 1993-

De Div.	Cicero, *De divinatione*
De Nat. Deor.	Cicero, *De natura deorum*
DJD	Discoveries in the Judaean Desert
DSD	*Dead Sea Discoveries*
DSS	Dead Sea Scrolls
DSSSE	*Dead Sea Scrolls Study Edition*. Edited by F. García Martínez and E. Tigchelaar. Leiden, 1999
EvT	*Evangelische Theologie*
FOTL	Forms of Old Testament Literature
GCS	Die griechische christliche Schriftsteller der ersten [drei] Jahrhunderte
Gen. Rab.	Genesis Rabbah
Giṭ.	*Giṭṭin*
GKC	*Gesenius' Hebrew Grammar*. Edited by E. Kautzsch. Translated by A. E. Cowley. 2nd ed. Oxford, 1910
HDR	Harvard Dissertations in Religion
Hen	*Henoch*
Her.	Philo of Alexandria, *Quis Rerum Divinarum Heres Sit*
HR	*History of Religions*
HSM	Harvard Semitic Monographs
HSS	Harvard Semitic Studies
HTR	*Harvard Theological Review*
HTS	Harvard Theological Studies
HUCA	*Hebrew Union College Annual*
IEJ	*Israel Exploration Journal*
INR	*Israel Numismatic Research*
Int	*Interpretation*
IRT	Issues in Religion and Theology
ITQ	*Irish Theological Quarterly*
JAAR	*Journal of the American Academy of Religion*
JAOS	*Journal of the American Oriental Society*
JB	Jerusalem Bible
JBL	*Journal of Biblical Literature*
JEA	*Journal of Egyptian Archaeology*
JETS	*Journal of the Evangelical Theological Society*
JHS	*Journal of Hellenic Studies*
JJS	*Journal of Jewish Studies*
JNES	*Journal of Near Eastern Studies*
JQR	*Jewish Quarterly Review*
JR	*Journal of Religion*
JRS	*Journal of Roman Studies*
JSJ	*Journal for the Study of Judaism*

Abbreviations and Symbols

JSJSup	Journal for the Study of Judaism Supplements
JSOT	*Journal for the Study of the Old Testament*
JSOTSup	Journal for the Study of the Old Testament: Supplement Series
JSP	*Journal for the Study of the Pseudepigrapha*
JSPSup	Journal for the Study of the Pseudepigrapha: Supplement Series
JSQ	*Jewish Studies Quarterly*
JTS	*Journal of Theological Studies*
J.W.	Josephus, *Jewish War*
KJV	King James Version
LCL	Loeb Classical Library
Leg. Alleg.	Philo of Alexandria, *Legum Allegoriarum*
LSJ	H. G. Liddell, R. Scott, and H. S. Jones, *A Greek-English Lexicon*. 9th ed. with revised supplement. Oxford, 1996
LXX	Septuagint
m.	Mishnah
MGWJ	*Monatschrift für Geschichte und Wissenschaft des Judentums*
MT	Masoretic Text
NAB	New American Bible
NEB	New English Bible
NETS	New English Translation of the Septuagint
NIB	*The New Interpreter's Bible*
NJPS	Tanakh: The Holy Scriptures: The New JPS Translation according to the Traditional Hebrew Text
NovTSup	Novum Testamentum Supplements
NRSV	New Revised Standard Version
NTS	*New Testament Studies*
OGIS	*Orientis Graeci Inscriptiones Selectae*. Ed. W. Dittenberger
OLA	Orientalia lovaniensia analecta
OTL	Old Testament Library
OTP	*Old Testament Pseudepigrapha*. Edited by J. H. Charlesworth. 2 vols. New York, 1983-1985
P.Alex.Giss.	*Papyri variae Alexandrinae et Gissense*. Edited by J. Schwartz. Brussels, 1969
P.Amh. II	*The Amherst Papyri*. Vol. 2. *Classical Fragments and Documents of the Ptolemaic, Roman and Byzantine Periods*. Edited by B. P. Grenfell and A. S. Hunt. London, 1901
P.Berl.Dem.	*Demotische Papyri aus den Staatlichen Museen zu Berlin*. Vols. 1 and 3. *Papyri von der Insel Elephantine*. Edited by K.-Th. Zauzich. Berlin, 1978, 1992.
P.Bingen	*Papyri in Honorem Johannis Bingen Octogenarii*. Edited by H. Melaerts. Leuven, 2000

Abbreviations and Symbols

P.Bub.	*Die verkohlten Papyri aus Bubastos.* Vol. 1. Edited by J. Frösén and D. Hagedorn. Opladen, 1989
P.Cair.Masp.	*Papyrus grecs d'époque byzantine, Catalogue général des antiquités égyptiennes du Musée du Caire.* Vol. 3. Edited by J. Maspero. Cairo, 1916
P.Dryton	*The Bilingual Family Archive of Dryton, His Wife Apollonia and Their Daughter Senmouthis.* Edited by K. Vandorpe. Brussels, 2002
P.Eleph.	*Aegyptische Urkunden aus den Königlichen Museen in Berlin: Griechische Urkunden,* Sonderheft. *Elephantine-Papyri.* Edited by O. Rubensohn. Berlin 1907.
P.Fay.	*Fayum Towns and Their Papyri.* Edited by B. P. Grenfell, A. S. Hunt and D. G. Hogarth. London, 1900
P.Gen.	*Les Papyrus de Genève.* Edited by J. Nicole. Geneva, 1896-1906
P.Giss.	*Papyri variae Alexandrinae et Gissenses*
P.Harr.	*The Rendel Harris Papyri of Woodbrooke College, Birmingham.* Vol. 1. Edited by J. E. Powell. Cambridge, 1936. Nos. 1-165. Vol. 2. Edited by R. A. Coles et al. Cambridge, 1985. Nos. 166-240
P.Hausw.	*The Hauswaldt Papyri.* Edited by J. Manning. Sommerhausen, 1997
P.Heid.	*Papyri der Heidelberger Papyrussammlung*
P.Hever	*Aramaic, Hebrew and Greek Documentary Texts from Nahal Hever and Other Sites, with an Appendix Containing Alleged Qumran Texts (The Seiyâl Collection II).* Edited by H. M. Cotton and A. Yardeni. Oxford, 1997
P.Köln	*Das Papyrus-Projekt Köln*
P.Lond. VII	*Greek Papyri in the British Museum.* Vol. 7. *The Zenon Archive.* Edited by T. C. Skeat. London, 1974
P.Mich.	*Michigan Papyri I, Zenon Papyri.* Edited by C. C. Edgar. Ann Arbor, 1931
P.Moscow	*Koptskie teksty Gosudarstvennogo muzeia izobrazitel'nykh iskusstv imeni A. S. Pushkina.* Edited by P. V. Ernshtedt (Jernstedt). Leningrad, 1959
P.Oxy. XXXVIII	*The Oxyrhynchus Papyri.* Vol. 38. Edited by G. M. Browne et al. London, 1971
P.Petaus	*The Flinders Petrie Papyri.* Edited by J. P. Mahaffy. Dublin, 1891-1905
P.Phrur.Diosk.	*Das Archiv des Phrurarchen Dioskurides (154-145 v. Chr.?).* Edited by James M. S. Cowey et al. Paderborn, 2003
P.Polit.Iud.	*Urkunden des Politeuma der Juden von Herakleopolis (144/3–133/2 v. Chr.* Edited by K. Maresch and J. M. S. Cowey. Wiesbaden, 2001

Abbreviations and Symbols

PSI	*Papiri greci e latini.* (Pubblicazioni della Società Italiana per la ricerca dei papiri greci e latini in Egitto)
P.Strasb. I	*Griechische Papyrus der Kaiserlichen Universitäts- und Landesbibliothek zu Strassburg.* Vol 1. Edited by F. Preisigke. Leipzig, 1912
P.Tebt.	*The Tebtunis Papyri.* Vol 1. Edited by B. P. Grenfell, A. S. Hunt, and J. G. Smyly. London, 1902
P.Thmouis	*Le Papyrus Thmouis 1, colonnes 68-160.* Edited by S. Kambitsis. Paris, 1985
P.Vindob.	*Papyri der Österreichischen Nationalbibliothek,* Wien
PVTG	Pseudepigrapha Veteris Testamenti Graece
P.Yadin	*The Documents from the Bar Kochba Period in the Cave of Letters.* Vol. 1. *Greek Papyri.* Edited by N. Lewis. Jerusalem, 1989
Praep. Evang.	Eusebius of Caesarea, *Praeparatio Evangelica*
Qad	*Qadmoniot*
QC	*Qumran Chronicle*
RB	*Revue biblique*
RBL	*Review of Biblical Literature*
REB	*Revised English Bible*
REJ	*Revue des études juives*
RelSRev	*Religious Studies Review*
RevQ	*Revue de Qumran*
RHPR	*Revue d'histoire et de philosophie religieuses*
RHR	*Revue de l'histoire des religions*
SAOC	Studies in Ancient Oriental Civilizations
SB	*Sammelbuch griechischer Urkunden aus Aegypten*
SBLDS	Society of Biblical Literature Dissertation Series
SBLEJL	Society of Biblical Literature Early Judaism and Its Literature
SBLMS	Society of Biblical Literature Monograph Series
SBLSCS	Society of Biblical Literature Septuagint and Cognate Studies
SBLSP	Society of Biblical Literature Seminar Papers
SBLStBL	Society of Biblical Literature Studies in Biblical Literature
SBLSymS	Society of Biblical Literature Symposium Series
SBLTT	Society of Biblical Literature Texts and Translations
SBLWAW	Society of Biblical Literature Writings from the Ancient World
SBT	Studies in Biblical Theology
SCI	*Scripta Classica Israelica*
SemeiaSt	Semeia Studies
SJ	*Studia judaica*
SJLA	Studies in Judaism in Late Antiquity
SJSJ	Supplement to the Journal for the Study of Judaism
ST	*Studia theologica*
STDJ	Studies on the Texts of the Desert of Judah

Abbreviations and Symbols

Strom.	Clement of Alexandria, *Stromata*
SUNT	Studien zur Umwelt des Neuen Testaments
SVTP	Studia in Veteris Testamenti pseudepigraphica
TAD	*Textbook of Aramaic Documents from Ancient Egypt*. Edited by B. Porten and A. Yardeni. Jerusalem, 1986-1999
TSAJ	Texte und Studien zum antiken Judentum
UF	*Ugarit-Forschungen*
UPZ	*Urkunden der Ptolemäerzeit (ältere Funde)*. Vol 1. *Papyri aus Unterägypten*. Berlin/Leipzig, 1927
v(v)	verse(s)
VT	*Vetus Testamentum*
VTSup	Supplements to *Vetus Testamentum*
WBC	Word Biblical Commentary
W.Chr.	L. Mitteis and U. Wilcken, *Grundzüge und Chrestomathie der Papyruskunde*. I Bd.: *Historischer Teil*. II Hälfte: *Chrestomathie*. Leipzig/Berlin, 1912
WMANT	Wissenschaftliche Monographien zum Alten und Neue Testament
WUNT	Wissenschaftliche Untersuchungen zum Neuen Testament
ZÄS	*Zeitschrift für ägyptische Sprache und Altertumskunde*
ZAW	*Zeitschrift für die alttestamentliche Wissenschaft*
ZTK	*Zeitschrift für Theologie und Kirche*

Symbols

[ ]	a break in the text (lacuna); the text is supplied by the editor
< >	a mistaken omission by the scribe
{ }	superfluous letter or letters
[[ ]]	letter or letters deleted by the scribe
\ /	insertion above the line
vac.	vacat (indicates that the papyrus is blank at that point)
. . .	uncertain reading

INTRODUCTION

"Showing the Wisdom of What He Has Learned": The Scholarly Contributions of John J. Collins

Daniel C. Harlow

At its commencement exercises in June 2009, University College Dublin honored six outstanding individuals, among them Brian Friel, Ireland's greatest living playwright. The other honorees included John J. Collins, whom the awarding body recognized as "the leading expert in the scholarly field of Near Eastern apocalyptic writings" and "a true world-leader." The citation that accompanied the bestowal on Collins of an honorary Doctor of Literature gives a fitting summary of his preeminent place in the world of biblical scholarship:

> Among the main contributions that John Collins has made as a biblical scholar and historian of religion has been to encourage us to see the biblical text as the product of a particular time and place, rooted in the history, archaeology and literature of the Ancient Near East. In his work in the relationship between biblical interpretation and theology, he advocates an approach of dialogue and cross-fertilisation between the two distinct disciplines. His overall approach has been characterized as combining a lucid and detailed exposition of primary texts — where fluency in five ancient and at least as many current languages is merely an entry ticket — with responsible interaction with the best of current scholarship.

The twenty-seven essays collected in this volume form a tribute to a great scholar and a great human being, offered in gratitude by colleagues and former students on the occasion of his sixty-fifth birthday. Earlier drafts of ten of the papers included herein were read at a conference held in John's honor at Amherst College on April 4-5, 2008. Joel Kaminsky of Smith College masterminded that conference with the collaboration of Susan Niditch and Robert Doran of the Amherst Religious Studies Department. Their department's administrative assistant, Diane Dix, provided invaluable logistical support, and Amherst's Willis D. Wood Fund generously supplied financial sponsorship. The organizers of the conference and editors of this volume have chosen "the Other" as their theme not only because it has become a prominent topic in study of Jewish identity, but because it affords a useful, unifying entrée into the manifold areas of inquiry to which John Collins has devoted a lifetime of scholarship.[1] Over the past few decades, the issue of identity has become a major focus of attention in scholarly discourse on a wide range of social, cultural, political, and religious phenomena. Several different theoretical approaches to this topic converge on the recognition that human beings forge their own sense of self only by constructing a sense of the Other. This general fact of human existence receives striking confirmation when one examines sources for the experience of Jews living in Palestine and in the Diaspora during the Greco-Roman age, arguably one of the most tumultuous and consequential periods in Jewish history. The essays in this volume approach its broad theme from a variety of angles and employ a variety of methodologies. They are arranged under five headings that reflect the main areas to which John Collins has contributed over the course of more than thirty-five years of distinguished teaching and scholarship.

---

1. For other forays into this area of inquiry, see, for example, Jacob Neusner and Ernest S. Frerichs, eds., *"To See Ourselves as Others See Us": Christians, Jews, "Others" in Late Antiquity* (Chico, Calif.: Scholars Press, 1985); that volume includes one of the best essays John Collins ever wrote: "A Symbol of Otherness: Circumcision and Salvation in the First Century" (163-86); it is reprinted in his *Seers, Sibyls, and Sages in Hellenistic-Roman Judaism* (Leiden: Brill, 1997), 211-35; Laurence J. Silberstein and Robert L. Cohn, eds., *The Other in Jewish Thought: Constructions of Jewish Culture and Identity* (New York and London: New York University Press, 1994); Frank Anthony Spina, *The Faith of the Outsider: Exclusion and Inclusion in the Biblical Story* (Grand Rapids: Eerdmans, 2005); Florentino García Martínez and Mladen Popović, eds., *Defining Identities: We, You, and the Other in the Dead Sea Scrolls: Proceedings of the Fifth Meeting of the IOQS in Groningen* (STDJ 70; Leiden: Brill, 2008); and Lawrence M. Wills, *Not God's People: Insiders and Outsiders in the Biblical World* (Lanham, Md.: Rowman & Littlefield, 2008).

"Showing the Wisdom of What He Has Learned"

I. The Hebrew Bible and Its Reception

John Collins did not begin his scholarly career focused on the Hebrew Bible, but he was quickly recognized as an expert in it. His interest in the Jewish Scriptures and their theology deepened when he started teaching biblical literature to undergraduates and seminarians. In the 1970s and early 80s, while he was mainly occupied with research on apocalypticism, he was invited to write several church-oriented commentaries on books in the Old Testament (Proverbs and Ecclesiates for the Knox Preaching Guides; Daniel and 1 and 2 Maccabees for the Old Testament Message series; Isaiah for the Collegeville Bible Commentary; Amos for the Catholic Study Bible). Then throughout the 1980s and 1990s, when he was busy preparing his Hermeneia commentary on Daniel and engaged in major projects related to apocalypticism and the Dead Sea Scrolls, he collaborated in coauthoring and editing books devoted to various themes in the Old Testament (*The Biblical Heritage*, 1986; *Hebrew Bible or Old Testament*, 1990; *Creation in the Biblical Traditions*, 1992; *Families in Ancient Israel*, 1997). Three decades of teaching courses in Old Testament were then distilled in his magisterial and widely used *Introduction to the Hebrew Bible* (2004).

To the field of biblical theology proper, Collins has contributed numerous seminal essays, fifteen of which came together in *Encounters with Biblical Theology* (2005). In the same year, he published *The Bible after Babel: Historical Criticism in a Postmodern Age*. Originally delivered as the Gunning Lectures at the University of Edinburgh School of Divinity, the successive chapters in this book offer a penetrating assessment of the impact that various postmodern approaches — postcolonial, deconstructionist, and feminist criticisms among them — have had on study of the Hebrew Bible over the last three decades, with special attention to Scripture's concern for the Other. "The main gain of postmodern criticism," Collins has written, "is that it has expanded the horizons of biblical studies, by going out to the highways and byways to bring new 'voices from the margins' to the conversation." Yet these new approaches bring with them the potential for "the disintegrating of the conversation in a cacophony of voices." He has urged that if biblical scholars want to engage the wider public, they must be forthright in facing troubling theological and moral aspects of the biblical text. "Biblical theology and biblical ethics will have to be more skeptical and self-critical in the wake of postmodernism, but they remain viable enterprises for people who are willing to enter a conversation in good faith and to pursue consensus, but not assume it." Between the time he authored his now-classic essay "The

Biblical Precedent for Natural Theology" (1977) and published *The Bible after Babel*, Collins's thinking underwent a marked development. Reflecting on this in recent conversation, he said,

> When I started out, one could assume a reliable historical core to the biblical record. That has collapsed. More importantly, I have come to realize that the "moral core" is questionable too. For a time, I would have subscribed to a kind of natural theology, but I realize now that this is more problematic. I would still defend it as a starting point, as opposed to a Barthian stress on revelation. But I think we have to take the postmodern critique of universals seriously. There does not seem to be any one truth on which everyone can agree.

To honor John's work in the Hebrew Bible, the first part of the volume assembles eight essays. Joel Kaminsky opens it with an overview of the differing and at times conflicting ways in which various ancient Jewish writers portrayed outsiders. He shows that the Hebrew Bible conceptualizes the "elect," that is, God's chosen people Israel, over against two broad categories of Other: the anti-elect and the non-elect, while a number of late biblical and Second Temple texts entertain the possibility that certain non-Israelites could attach themselves to the people of Israel or its God and obtain something like the status of a convert. The rabbis developed a formal procedure of conversion but did not, like early Christian groups, presume that only the elect could be saved or made righteous in God's eyes. In her essay "God's Other: The Intractable Problem of the Gentile King in Judean and Early Jewish Literature" — the keynote address at the Amherst conference held in John's honor — Carol Newsom adapts aspects of Emanuel Levinas's account of the Other and Miroslav Volf's typology of exclusion to map the various attempts by the Jewish people in antiquity to reckon with rule by foreign empires. Although different political circumstances called for different symbolic strategies of coping in various texts — elimination, domination, or assimilation — common to many of them is a preoccupation with the foreign king's thoughts, beliefs, and (mis)perceptions. In the next entry, Katell Berthelot examines early Jewish interpretations of Noah's curse of Canaan in Genesis 9. She explains how they deal with the oddity of Noah cursing his grandson instead of his son, and how they appeal to the curse to justify the later conquest of Israel's ancestral Other, the Canaanites. Susan Niditch utilizes recent theoretical insights from several disciplines to illumine the social significance of the Nazirite vow in Numbers 6. With that vow's emphasis on hair, the body, and identity, both males and females could voluntarily assume a temporary but regulated sacral status. Yet the vow also tended paradoxically to reinforce a male, hereditary status quo. In the following essay, Susan Ackerman traces the progressive marginalization of women from cultic music-making in exilic and postexilic Israel. Their new status as outsiders stands in stark contrast to their participation in preexilic times in victory songs after war, singing and dancing at festivals, and life-cycle rituals. Timothy Lim reveals how ethnic Otherness is subtly expressed in a linguistic mode in the book of Ruth. The biblical author renders the spoken Hebrew of the Moabite protagonist of the book good but uneven. Antonios Finitsis draws on social identity theory to explain why the two early postexilic prophets Haggai and Zechariah define their "in-group" differently, despite their common goal of community identity-formation. In the final essay in Part 1, Naomi Jacobs offers a careful analysis of the *Buile Shuibhne*, a fascinating Middle Irish text that is part of the reception history of the story of Nebuchadnezzar's madness in Daniel 4.

II. Wisdom

John Collins has made several important contributions to the study of early Jewish wisdom literature. His research in this quarter began in the 1970s and came to fruition in his monograph *Jewish Wisdom in the Hellenistic Age* (1997), now a standard resource for researchers investigating texts such as Ben Sira and the Wisdom of Solomon. Thanks in no small part to John's insights, scholars now generally acknowledge the generic and ideological compatibility of wisdom and apocalypticism, worldviews that are not antithetical but that merged and interacted in a variety of ways in the Second Temple period. The results of his and others' investigations have had an impact on New Testament studies, especially the ongoing debates surrounding the historical Jesus and the composition history of the Synoptic sayings source Q. The publication in 1999 of a Qumran wisdom text known as 4QInstruction has forced scholars to revise their assessments of the early Jewish wisdom tradition, and Collins has been a leading figure in this effort.

The five essays gathered in the second part of the volume begin with a paper by Karina Martin Hogan, who looks at the wisdom poem in the book of Baruch, arguing that the poem's ethnocentrism is mitigated by the more nuanced view of other nations reflected in the rest of the work. Shannon Burkes Pinette's contribution demonstrates that whereas Lady Wisdom is a public and forthright figure in Proverbs, wisdom is associated with the Torah in Ben Sira, and in Daniel becomes something mysterious and otherworldly. In his essay "The Foolish Nation That Dwells in Shechem," Matthew Goff focuses on Sirach 50:25-26, verses that he maintains are original to the text and that make sense in light of both their placement in the book and Judean views of the Samaritans in the early second century B.C.E. In the next essay, Samuel L. Adams documents the diversity of perspectives on wealth and poverty in a variety of sapiential texts from the Second Temple period, as they negotiated complex financial dynamics, apocalyptic ideas, and the assumptions of an established wisdom tradition. He demonstrates that while 4QInstruction continues to affirm wealth as a sign of favor from God, other wisdom texts, such as the *Epistle of Enoch*, do not. Daniel J. Harrington rounds out the section with an essay on Wisdom 1–6. He clarifies how these chapters combine Greek notions of immortality with Jewish apocalyptic eschatology to express a hope for transcending death, a theme developed in a number of New Testament texts.

III. Apocalypticism

Harrington's essay forms a nice bridge to the third part of the volume, since his point of departure is Collins's essay of 1974, "Apocalyptic Eschatology as the Transcendence of Death." In that landmark study, John identified the feature of apocalyptic eschatology which distinguishes it from the eschatology of the Hebrew prophets as hope in a personal afterlife. Drawing attention to this and other features of apocalyptic literature — such as the periodization of history, *ex eventu* prophecy, otherworldly journeys, cosmology, and judgment of the dead — Collins established that apocalypticism was quintessentially an ideology of the Hellenistic age and not simply a development of late Israelite religion. In *Apocalypse: The Morphology of a Genre*, a theme issue of the journal *Semeia* (vol. 14; 1979), he collaborated with Harold Attridge, Adela Yarbro Collins, and others to produce the first systematic study of apocalypse as a literary genre. His groundbreaking work in this field began earlier, with a number of important articles published in the mid 1970s and his monograph *The Apocalyptic Vision of the Book of Daniel* (1977). His book *The Apocalyptic Imagination* (1984; rev. ed. 1998) remains the best introduction to early Jewish apocalyptic literature, and his Hermeneia *Daniel* (1993) is the leading critical commentary on this pivotal biblical book. John has also written a very learned but accessible monograph on *Apocalypticism in the Dead Sea Scrolls* (1997) and edited the first volume of the *Encyclopedia of Apocalypticism* (1998). His scholarly articles on apocalyptic subjects are too numerous to describe, but perhaps his greatest contribution has been to make available to a wide readership a sympathetic yet critical understanding of apocalypticism and its cultural influences.

Part three of this Festschrift opens with a provocative essay by Lorenzo DiTommaso that scrutinizes the epistemological basis of apocalyptic Otherness. He presents a scathing indictment of apocalypticism as an "adolescent" and "escapist" worldview that is inherently "dehumanizing" and "poisonous." A thoughtful counterpoint to DiTommaso's thesis comes in the following paper by Sean Freyne. Though well aware of the disturbing aspects of apocalyptic rhetoric, Freyne avers that rejecting apocalypticism altogether requires adopting a literalist approach to its symbolism and ignoring its positive aims. His essay attempts to retrieve apocalypticism from its status as the rejected Other of modern scholarship by showing how interwoven apocalyptic and sapiential features are in works such as 1 Corinthians, the Gospel of Mark, and 4QInstruction. The next entry, by George Nickelsburg, surveys passages in *1 Enoch*, the Dead Sea Scrolls, and the *Psalms of Solomon* to illustrate how often the We in early Jewish literature are not defined in their own right but only in reference to the Other. Rebecca Raphael's "Monsters and the Crippled Cosmos" analyzes the cosmology and anthropology of *4 Ezra* from the perspective of disability studies, explaining that images of anomolous bodies constitute a major means by which the text constructs the Other. The section concludes with Daniel Harlow's essay on the *Apocalypse of Abraham*, which gives a close reading of the entire text, detailing how not only its haggadic section but also its heavenly ascent epitomizes evil as idolatry and pictures worship of the one God as the defining practice which sets Israel apart from the other nations of the world.

IV. The Dead Sea Scrolls

John Collins first came to Dead Sea Scrolls research as an offshoot of his work on early Jewish apocalypticism. After publishing various articles on the eschatology and origins of the Qumran community between 1979 and 1989, he was commissioned to write the two substantial articles on the Essenes and the Dead Sea Scrolls for the *Anchor Bible Dictionary* (1992), entries that nearly two decades later still serve remarkably well as authoritative introductions to these topics. Then, when the international team editing the

Scrolls was expanded in the early 1990s to expedite the long-delayed publication of the numerous fragmentary texts from Qumran Cave 4, he was called on to prepare the *editio princeps* of the *Pseudo-Daniel* writings and the *Prayer of Nabonidus* for the Discoveries in the Judaean Desert series (DJD XXII, 1996). In the field of Qumran studies, John is perhaps best known for his work on messianism and the nature of the sectarian movement described in the Scrolls. His book *The Scepter and the Star* (1995; rev. ed. 2010) remains the essential study of the messianic texts found at Qumran and in other ancient Jewish literature. And his recently published *Beyond the Qumran Community* (2009) reaffirms his place at the forefront of the ongoing reexamination of the variety of forms of sectarian community reflected in the Scrolls.

The fourth part of this volume opens with an essay by Shane Berg which suggests that it was the advent of the Teacher of Righteousness that led the Qumran sectarians to view inspired exegesis of biblical texts as a vehicle for divine revelation and to develop a separatist self-consciousness and communal organization. In the following entry, James VanderKam embarks anew on a quest that commenced almost as soon as the first Dead Sea Scrolls were discovered — the identification of the Qumran community's arch-Other, the Wicked Priest. After collecting descriptions of the Wicked Priest in the *Pesher Habakkuk* and *Pesher Psalms*^{a}, comparing the language of those texts with scriptural and other texts to determine whether it is traditional, and then removing stereotypical or generic elements from the remainder, he arrives at the most likely candidate. Eric D. Reymond turns to the *Songs of the Sabbath Sacrifice* and analyzes the paradoxical language of a blessing at the end of the sixth Sabbath song, which may qualify as the only direct quotation of angelic speech in the entire work. The section closes with a short piece by Esther Chazon (with Yonatan Miller) that approaches 4Q371-373 (4QNarrative and Poetic Composition^{a-c}) as a case study in early Jewish biblical exegesis. She discusses how the Qumran text subtly adapts the phrase אם הדרך ("at the fork of the road," a *hapax legomenon* in the Hebrew Bible) from Ezek. 21:26 in order to bolster its anti-Samaritan polemic.

V. Jews among Greeks and Romans

The final portion of this Festschrift contains essays that touch on various aspects of the scholarly discipline that may fairly be labeled John Collins's intellectual first love — Hellenistic Judaism. John studied Classics in high school and took his B.A. and M.A. in Semitics and Classics from Trinity College Dublin. His Hebrew teacher at Trinity, Dermot Ryan (who later became the archbishop of Dublin) encouraged him to pursue graduate study in Hellenistic Judaism. One of Ryan's scholarly contacts, Harry Orlinsky, recommended that John apply to Harvard to study with John Strugnell. An extremely gifted scholar, Strugnell had made his reputation back in the 1950s as the youngest member of the small team of scholars editing the Dead Sea Scrolls. In the 1960s and 70s he had become distinguished for his knowledge of early Jewish texts and for a time was practically the only professor at a major university training students in the literature of Second Temple Judaism. Due in no small measure to the influence of Strugnell on the research agendas of his students, the 1970s saw a renaissance in study of the early Jewish pseudepigrapha. John combined his interests in apocalypticism and Hellenistic Judaism by writing his dissertation on the Jewish *Sibylline Oracles* under Strugnell's direction, and in 1974 had it published in the Society of Biblical Literature's recently inaugurated dissertation series. His deep engagement with the Sibylline tradition in that work and in subsequent articles brought about the most significant advance in appreciating this important body of material since the foundational work of Johannes Geffcken in 1902. And in volume 1 of *The Old Testament Pseudepigrapha* (1983), he presented the first English translation of the entire Sibylline corpus in almost a century.

In the late 1970s, John participated in a research project at McMaster University on Jewish and Christian self-definition headed by E. P. Sanders. This led to his writing *Between Athens and Jerusalem: Jewish Identity in the Hellenistic Age* (1984; rev. ed. 2000). In that remarkable book, Collins studied the numerous so-called minor authors of the Jewish Diaspora in the Greco-Roman era, giving attention both to national and political identity, and identity as expressed through ethics and piety. He combined careful historical and sociological study of the experience of Diaspora Jews with insightful interpretations of some three dozen texts. In response to E. P. Sanders's proposal that "covenantal nomism" was the dominant construction of Jewish identity in antiquity, Collins showed how Diaspora Jews could appropriate their tradition in a variety of other ways by appealing alternately to higher revelation, philosophical wisdom, and mystical piety, for example. His study underscored the remarkable extent to which Jews adapted themselves to foreign rule and Hellenistic culture by, *inter alia*, sharing a common ethic with their Gentile neighbors while still finding creative ways to maintain their distinctive cultural and religious identity.

Daniel C. Harlow

In 1999 John invited Martin Hengel to attend a conference he was convening on the Jewish encounter with Hellenism. The occasion afforded Hengel the opportunity to revisit the theses of his classic *Judaism and Hellenism,* and brought other scholars together to examine various aspects of the incursion of Greek culture into Judea, Galilee, and Egypt. The colloquium was cosponsored by the University of Chicago and the University of Notre Dame, and its proceedings appeared in print as *Hellenism in the Land of Israel* (2001). Then in 2005 John assembled a dozen of his own articles on Hellenistic Judaism in *Jewish Cult and Hellenistic Culture.* His contributions to the study of Hellenistic Judaism continue unabated, as a glance at the select bibliography printed in this volume will show.

In the first essay of the fifth and final section of this book, Martin Goodman inventories the variety of names for the Jewish people used in Jewish, Roman, and Christian sources between 200 B.C.E. and 300 C.E. After proferring explanations for certain shifts in the nomenclature applied to Jews, he documents how Christians not only came to adopt the general denigration of Jews typical in the Roman world but exploited it to distance their own communities from Jewish ones. Erich Gruen's paper explores the reciprocal ways in which Greeks perceived Jews as philosophers and Jews considered Greek philosophers as indebted to Jewish lore. His investigation illustrates how confidently Jews embraced and enriched aspects of Hellenistic intellectual culture, in a way that problematizes the notion that Jews regarded the Greeks as the Other. Robert Doran's contribution addresses the rhetoric within and the reality behind the account in 2 Maccabees of Antiochus IV Epiphanes' persecution of Judeans in the second century B.C.E., an anomalous act whose motivations have long puzzled historians. Doran makes the brilliant proposal that Antiochus imposed Greek cultic rites and abolished circumcision, Sabbath observance, and kosher dietary regulations in Jerusalem not because he wanted to abolish the Jewish religion as such, but because he was intent on not allowing the city to live by its ancestral laws *(patrioi nomoi)* as his father had done to Apollonia at Rhyndacos. Antiochus could not foresee the consequences of his act because he did not know that the Judeans regarded their distinctive customs and observances as laws instituted by the one God. In the next essay, Patricia Ahearne-Kroll directs her attention to Ptolemaic Egypt, meticulously defending the view that the author Artapanus was Jewish, notwithstanding his claim that Moses originated certain Egyptian cultic practices. Robert Kugler brings both the section and the volume to a close in an essay that looks at the Jewish experience in Ptolemaic Egypt from the perspective of two recently published legal papyri from Heracleopolis. His analysis highlights cases in which Jews relied on the hybrid Greco-Egyptian common law of the Ptolemaic kingdom but also resorted to the juridical norms of their Judean ancestry in order to attain their litigative goals. On his reading, though Jews living in Egypt held much in common with their non-Jewish neighbors, they were also aware of having a distinct identity.

VI. Colleague, Mentor, Friend

The title of this introduction draws on Ben Sira's descripton of the ideal sage (Sir. 39:8). Co-opting it as a description of the prolific career of John Collins seems more than fitting. It would be difficult to exaggerate the breathtaking range and depth of John's contributions to the study of ancient Judaism. The author of twenty monographs and more than 240 academic articles, as well as the editor of seventeen books — and counting! — he has advanced scholarship in five cognate disciplines, any one of which might occupy a person's entire career. Yet any adequate assessment of his accomplishments must also include mention of how he has provided leadership within the wider academy and nurtured the labors of others in the field, especially that most vulnerable group of Others — graduate students.

From 1974 to the present, John has served on the editorial boards of more than a dozen scholarly organs, including the *Harvard Theological Review*, the *Catholic Biblical Quarterly*, the *Journal for the Study of the Pseudepigrapha*, the *Journal of Jewish Studies*, the *New Interpreter's Bible*, the *Encyclopedia of the Dead Sea Scrolls*, and the *Encyclopedia of Religions in the Ancient World*. In the first half of the 1980s, he chaired the Pseudepigrapha Group in the Society of Biblical Literature, and from 1989 to 1994 served as editor-in-chief of the *Journal of Biblical Literature* and member of the SBL's executive committee. John's three decades of outstanding leadership in the Catholic Biblical Association and in the SBL were acknowledged by his being elected president of both those learned societies in 1996 and 2002, respectively.

The reach of John's mentoring influence has been truly international in scope. During the five years that he edited the journal *Dead Sea Discoveries* (2003-2008) and the fourteen years he served as editor-in-chief of the Supplements to the *Journal for the Study of Judaism* (1994-2008), John shaped the work of scores of scholars from all around the world. Indeed, his years at the helm of JSJSup have led many budding young scholars to regard him as a de facto codirector of their doctoral dissertations.

Daniel C. Harlow

John's fellow professors at the five institutions where he has taught witness unanimously to how delightful a colleague he has been, and his students at Notre Dame, Chicago, and Yale can attest to what a steady, reassuring presence he has been in their lives. He has taken an interest in *their* interests and in them as individuals, and offered them his unstinting support and encouragement. And it goes without saying that a letter or phone call from him has frequently helped secure a job for a freshly minted Ph.D. and helped advance junior scholars along the path toward tenure. Perhaps the best measure of his greatness is how unprepossessing he is; here indeed is a man who wears his immense learning lightly and has not a pretentious bone in his body. Only one of many marks of his generous nature is how often he has invited former students and younger colleagues to collaborate with him in various projects. A devoted husband and father, a man possessed of great warmth, wit, and charm, John Collins is regarded by all who know him as a beloved colleague, mentor, and friend. As he turns a youthful sixty-five, we can be sure that he has many productive years — nay, decades — ahead of him.

PART ONE

THE HEBREW BIBLE AND ITS RECEPTION

Israel's Election and the Other in Biblical, Second Temple, and Rabbinic Thought

Joel S. Kaminsky

It is a sociological axiom that identity formation is inherently bound up with defining who one is not, that is, the category of the Other. In terms of Jewish self-definition and Judaism's construal of the Other, there have been a host of important recent monographs including ones by Shaye Cohen, Christine Hayes, and Robert Goldenberg.[1] This necessarily brief tour through some extremely complex terrain will inevitably involve making a few generalizations. I refer readers to my latest book, *Yet, I Loved Jacob: Reclaiming the Biblical Concept of Election,* for fuller argumentation of a number of these points.[2]

The first thing that must be said is that most biblical and rabbinic texts are addressed to their own communities and thus unsurprisingly they are

---

1. Shaye J. D. Cohen, *The Beginnings of Jewishness: Boundaries, Varieties, Uncertainties* (Berkeley: University of California Press, 1999); Robert Goldenberg, *The Nations That Know Thee Not: Ancient Jewish Attitudes towards Other Religions* (New York: New York University Press, 1998); Christine Hayes, *Gentile Impurities and Jewish Identities: Intermarriage and Conversion from the Bible to the Talmud* (New York: Oxford, 2002).

2. Joel S. Kaminsky, *Yet, I Loved Jacob: Reclaiming the Biblical Concept of Election* (Nashville: Abingdon, 2007).

I offer this essay as a small token of appreciation to my mentor John J. Collins. He has taught me much about the Hebrew Bible and ancient Judaism, and even more about mentoring students in a generous fashion that allows them to learn from the wisdom of previous scholars while helping them find their own voice (even when that voice challenges one's own teachers).

overwhelmingly focused on issues internal to each community. Contemporary scholars interested in biblical and rabbinic views of non-Israelites must often deduce how a given text or theological school understood Israel's relationship to or perception of various foreign individuals, groups, or nations from texts that generally do not lavish tremendous attention directly upon such issues. Thus most scholarly constructions of Israel's understanding of the Other are attempts to systematize ideas that are often implied rather than explicit.

With that caution in mind, one of the central contentions of my recent work on Israel's election theology is that Israel appears to conceive of herself over against two broad categories of the Other. Large swaths of the Hebrew Bible conceptualize the "elect," that is God's chosen people Israel, over against the anti-elect and the non-elect. The "anti-elect" are those few groups who are deemed to be enemies of God and whom Israel is commanded to annihilate, such as the Canaanites and the Amalekites. Even here it seems clear that biology and ethnicity do *not* rule the day inasmuch as one finds exceptions like Rahab, a character who manages to save herself and her extended family from annihilation by helping the Israelite spies (Joshua 2). Alternatively, you have the example of Achan, an Israelite who is treated like a Canaanite when he and his entire family are wiped out for violating the war ban by taking booty (Joshua 7).[3] Texts that deal with the anti-elect do pose serious difficulties to anyone seeking to use the Bible as a moral compass. However, most texts that affirm Israel's elect status view the vast majority of foreign individuals and nations as members of the "non-elect" rather than the "anti-elect." These non-elect peoples were always considered full participants in the divine economy, and, in a very real sense, Israel was to work out her destiny in relation to them, even if in separation from them.

With some exceptions and qualifications to be noted below, ancient Israel's bipartite way of conceiving non-Israelites continues to be upheld within a broad array of late biblical, Second Temple, and early rabbinic texts. In contrast, major streams of classical Christianity tended to conceive the Other as a single entity, producing the belief that Christians belonged to the saved while those who failed to put their faith in Christ would be lost to God

---

3. For a nice discussion of how these two inverse characters demonstrate that the categorization of anti-elect is not driven primarily by ethnic concerns, see Frank Anthony Spina, *The Faith of the Outsider: Exclusion and Inclusion in the Biblical Story* (Grand Rapids: Eerdmans, 2005), 52-71.

(e.g., John 14:6; Acts 4:12). Of course, Christian thinkers derived this more dualistic approach to the divine economy from certain eschatological currents that first appear in postexilic biblical texts, but these currents became more magnified within early Christianity than they did within rabbinic Judaism. I would contend that frequently authors who condemn Jewish chosenness tend to read classical Christianity's more dualistic notions of the saved and the damned into biblical and rabbinic texts that operate with a different and more complex view of the Other, one rooted in a distinct understanding of the meaning of election.

I. Late Biblical and Second Temple Texts

Let us now turn to a few select late biblical and Second Temple texts and the issues raised by them. One exceptional phenomenon in the late biblical period deserving comment is the growing possibility that certain non-Israelites could attach themselves to the people of Israel or its God and obtain something like the status of a convert. Here Moshe Greenberg suggests it may be useful to draw a distinction between those who "join themselves to the Jews" (cf. Esth. 9:27; Isa. 14:1; Dan. 11:34), a socioethnic group who attach themselves to a community, and those who "joined themselves to the Lord" (Isa. 56:6), foreigners who have experienced a "conversion to the God of Israel."[4] The late biblical movement toward greater openness to non-Israelites who wished to participate in the Second Temple community is found within more inclusive as well as within more exclusivistic postexilic texts. Not only does Isaiah 56 speak of certain foreigners attaching themselves to Israel's God, but also, it appears, so do the authors of Ezekiel 40–48 and Ezra and Nehemiah, as demonstrated by Ezek. 47:22-23, Ezra 6:21, and Neh. 10:29. In fact, the closest thing to an actual conversion ceremony within the Hebrew Bible might be found in Exod. 12:48-49, often viewed as a late P passage, which permits an alien who is willing to be circumcised along with the males in his family to participate in the Passover ritual.

An additional point worth making is that even in texts like Exod. 12:48-49 or Isaiah 56, those foreigners who attach themselves to the people

---

4. Moshe Greenberg, "A House of Prayer for All Peoples," in *Jerusalem: A House of Prayer for All Peoples in Three Monotheistic Religions*, ed. Alviero Niccacci (Studium Biblicum Franciscanum Analecta 52; Jerusalem: Franciscan Printing Press, 2001), 31-37, here at 32-33.

of Israel or her God do not necessarily become part of Israel. Rather, as Isa. 56:7 notes, God welcomes worship by those foreigners who join themselves to the Lord because his house is now a house of prayer for all peoples. In a similar manner, Lev. 24:22 speaks of having one law for natives and resident aliens, implying that group boundaries remained intact. Truth be told, Lev. 25:44-46, a law allowing one to keep Gentiles or resident aliens as slaves in perpetuity, makes clear that there is not one law for both groups. Thus, even very welcoming texts maintained Israel's distinction from non-Israelites, a fact supported by the book of Ruth. While the dating of Ruth is contested, many scholars believe it may have been produced to counter more exclusivist definitions of Judean identity put forward in late books like Ezra and Nehemiah. Interestingly enough, Ruth is still called "the Moabitess" in chapter 4 (vv. 5 and 10), long after she has pledged herself to Israel and her God back in 1:16, in what some scholars suggest may be an ancient conversion formula.

Slightly different from these texts are passages such as Isaiah 66 or Zech. 14:16-21, which imagine all of humanity worshipping Israel's God. But even these passages seem to maintain the idea that Israel is distinct from these other nations though they all worship Israel's God. Thus Isa. 66:22 appears to proclaim that Israel will always have descendants and that her name will forever be preserved, even while verse 23 speaks of all flesh regularly worshiping the Lord.

I suspect that something similar is going on in Tobit 14:6. The NRSV translates: "Then the nations in the whole world will all be converted and worship God in truth." But the continuation of this text, which pictures the reunited people of Israel persisting as a separate enclave safely in the land of Abraham, speaks against rendering the verb *epistrephō* as "convert." A more accurate translation might be "to turn toward," in this case speaking of the Gentiles' turning toward God by abandoning their idolatry and acknowledging that Israel's God is the only true God. This action does not transform these Gentiles into Israelites, or suddenly dissolve Israel's unique status.

Although texts such as Isaiah 66 and Zechariah 14 show a new and somewhat radical openness to foreigners and thus exhibit what could be labeled as a new form of tolerance, that tolerance is based on the assumption that these foreigners submit to Israel's God or face a grisly doom (Isa. 66:24 and Zech. 14:12, 18-19). These apocalyptically tinged texts begin to move away from the idea that a non-Israelite could be righteous while practicing his or her own religion. Thus they are less tolerant of non-Israelite religious practice than the earlier theology espoused by Deuteronomy, which appears to permit non-Israelites to worship other deities (Deut. 4:19; 29:25; 32:8-9 as worded in 4QDeut^j and LXX). Contrary to popular belief today, a growing universalism is not always accompanied by greater acceptance of the Other.

One should note yet another late biblical propensity, that is the growing demonization of Edom and the Edomites, a movement that stands in stark contrast to the much more nuanced view of Esau and his descendants found in Genesis and in certain texts from Deuteronomy. Deuteronomy 2 and 23 warn Israel to respect the territorial integrity of Edom and not to abhor the Edomite people, while Genesis 27 and 33 present Esau as a complex and sympathetic character. Yet, in a number of late prophetic texts the Edomites become the axis of evil in the symbolic universe of Israel and her God. One thinks particularly of the rather graphic and gory passages found in Isaiah 34, Ezekiel 35, the book of Obadiah, and the beginning of Malachi. I have no intention of trying to solve the perplexing question of why this imagery arose, although I do think Bert Dicou has advanced a plausible set of arguments.[5] While these negative portrayals may have been set off by certain Edomite actions, they appear to function metaphorically. Perhaps Edom comes to represent the *goyim*, the non-Israelite nations in general, as Dicou argues. Or perhaps these texts seek to reassure the returning Judeans that the Babylonian exile did not signal God's rejection of Israel and the election of Edom in Israel's place, as recently argued by Elie Assis.[6] In any case, the Hebrew Bible is not systematic in its descriptions of the final disposition of the nations. Thus, one finds texts like Isaiah 19 proclaiming that after a period of judgment against Israel's arch-adversaries Assyria and Egypt, these nations will themselves worship Israel's God and even become divinely favored peoples alongside Israel.

A final trend worth exploring is the theological move to exclude certain native Israelites from Israel on behavioral grounds. Note the following passage from Isa. 65:13-15.

> Therefore thus says the Lord GOD:
> My servants shall eat, but you shall be hungry;
> My servants shall drink, but you shall be thirsty;

---

5. Bert Dicou, *Edom, Israel's Brother and Antagonist: The Role of Edom in Biblical Prophecy and Story* (JSOTSup 169; Sheffield: Sheffield Academic Press, 1994).

6. Elie Assis, "Why Edom? On the Hostility Towards Jacob's Brother in Prophetic Sources," *VT* 56.1 (2006): 1-20.

> My servants shall rejoice, but you shall be put to shame;
> My servants shall sing for gladness of heart, but you shall
>   cry out for pain of heart, and shall wail for anguish of spirit.
> You shall leave your name to my chosen ones to use as a curse,
>   and the Lord GOD will put you to death;
> But to his servants he will give a different name.

Passages like this one, in combination with those strongly dualistic images found in the anti-Edomite prophetic polemic, stand at the beginning of a long process that eventuated, in the New Testament and Dead Sea Scrolls, in a revisioning of the three categories of the elect, non-elect, and the anti-elect into the saved and those lost to God. Certain sectarian texts from Qumran, especially the *War Scroll*, the *Damascus Document*, and the *Rule of the Community*, exhibit the same tendency to exclude many ethnic Jews from the people of Israel that occurs in Isaiah 65. As Larry Schiffman observes, "For the sectarians, the renewed covenant was the indication of their particular relation with God — what made them the true Israel and disqualified the rest of the Jewish people. In this respect, some affinity does exist between the Qumran 'new covenant' and that of the early Christians."[7]

While it is impossible to do justice to the full variety of late biblical images of the Other within the confines of a single essay, this survey highlights some of the major ways that later biblical passages represent the Other. So far we have seen that there are many texts that view the outsider in neutral or positive ways, some even moving to include select aliens within Israel's cultic life, and others going so far as to imagine a time when all the nations would worship Israel's God alongside Israel. However, juxtaposed against these positive images, there are alternative texts that conjure up negative portrayals of the Other and envision the total destruction of at least certain non-Israelite nations. While one might be tempted to systematize these variant images by arguing that the final disposition of various Gentiles depends on how they interact with Israel and her God, I suspect that such readings obscure the complexity behind these tensions.

There are at least two more probable explanations for these variant eschatological views of the Gentile nations. Sometimes, it seems best to acknowledge that distinct images stem from different streams of biblical tra-

---

7. Lawrence Schiffman, "The Concept of Covenant in the Qumran Scrolls and Rabbinic Literature," in *The Idea of Biblical Interpretation: Essays in Honor of James L. Kugel*, ed. Hindy Najman and Judith Newman (Leiden: Brill, 2004), 276.

dition that contain divergent assessments of the Other. Not only do various biblical books present unique images, but sometimes later editors may add insertions that qualify an earlier theology. Thus, toward the end of Isaiah 66 many scholars see verse 20 as an attempt by a later tradent to ameliorate the implications of this very inclusive text. Of course, another possible explanation is that such tensions may have been more tolerable to those who produced these mythic and poetic texts. I have often wondered whether we sometimes misread these passages by reifying each image and explaining any tensions as the result of internal societal divisions. While this type of socio-historical analysis has great explanatory power, sometimes what appear to us as textual tensions or outright contradictions may stem from the juxtaposition of poetic images describing Israel's restoration. While variant images may stand in uneasy relationship to each other when one attempts to put them into a systematic rational schema, we need to recognize that within the mytho-poetic universe occupied by the biblical writers they may not have seemed nearly as discordant as they do to most contemporary readers.

II. Rabbinic Texts

Turning our attention to rabbinic Judaism, we discover that the situation here is equally complex. While there are elements of continuity with biblical understandings of the Other, there are some differences and some new developments as well. One very important change in the rabbinic era was the development of a conversion procedure that normalized the path for joining the chosen people. It is important to note that while the rabbis made the community's boundary more porous, they did not presume, as Christianity did, that only the elect could be saved or could be righteous in God's eyes. In fact, many rabbinic texts explicitly discourage Gentile conversion, recognizing that Gentiles who observe the (seven) Noahide commandments can attain the rewards of the righteous without converting. Note the following exchange from *Tosefta Sanhedrin* 13:2. Initially, Rabbi Eliezer argues that none of the Gentiles have a portion in the world to come on the basis of Psalm 9:18 (Eng. 9:17), which states, "the wicked will return to Sheol, all the nations *(goyim)* who forget God." However, Rabbi Joshua has the best of this argument when he responds by noting that inasmuch as the verse says "all the *goyim* who forget God" it "indicates that there are also righteous people among the nations of the world, who do have a place in the world to come (i.e., those Gentiles who do not forget God.)"[8] Rabbi Eliezer's statement mirrors the more dualistic view found in early Christian texts. However, Rabbi Joshua's position, which imagines many non-Israelites occupying a positive place in the divine economy, became dominant within rabbinic and later Judaism.

It may well be that this belief in the existence of the righteous non-elect, a belief the rabbis carried over from the Hebrew Bible's theology, best explains the lack of full-blown missionary activity within late antique and early rabbinic Judaism.[9] Of course one should not oversimplify matters. Rabbinic Judaism's preservation of major tribal/familial aspects of ancient Israelite identity may too have played a role in rabbinic reserve concerning missionizing. A brief word should be said here about Marc Hirshman's recent arguments that texts associated with the school of Rabbi Ishmael were much more open to proselytizing, although these traditions eventually fell out of favor. While the texts that Hirshman discusses deserve much greater attention than they have received previously, Hirshman overstates his case when he argues that this school of ancient Jewish thought had a missionary orientation.[10] The texts he discusses are proof that the ancient rabbis saw Torah as universally available to all, not that they believed Jews should actively seek to convert all Gentiles to Judaism.

A particularly interesting innovation is the rabbinic maneuver to soften or at times almost dissolve the concept of the anti-elect. Thus the *Sifre* creatively rereads Deut. 20:16-18 to prove that if the Canaanites repent, they

---

8. The implication of the verse is that only those of the nations who forget God will end up in Sheol. Translation taken from *The Tosefta, Neziqin,* trans. Jacob Neusner (New York: Ktav, 1981), 238. See the similar statement attributed to Rabbi Joshua in *Midrash Proverbs* 19:1: "Anyone who lives blamelessly before his Creator in this world will be saved from the torment of Gehenna in the coming future." *The Midrash on Proverbs: Translated from the Hebrew with an Introduction and Annotations,* by Burton Visotzky (Yale Judaica Series; New Haven: Yale University Press, 1992), 87. For a deeper introduction to this subject see the following works: Benjamin Helfgott, *The Doctrine of Election in Tannaitic Literature* (New York: King's Crown Press, 1954); David Novak, *The Image of the Non-Jew in Judaism: An Historical and Constructive Study of the Noahide Laws* (Toronto Studies in Theology 14; New York: Edwin Mellen, 1983); and Gary Porton, *Goyim: Gentiles and Israelites in Mishnah-Tosefta* (BJS 155; Atlanta; Scholars, 1988).

9. For in spite of the claims by some scholars that rabbinic Judaism was such a missionary faith, Martin Goodman has made a very strong argument that the evidence suggests otherwise. Martin Goodman, *Mission and Conversion: Proselytizing in the Religious History of the Roman Empire* (Oxford: Clarendon Press, 1994).

10. Marc Hirshman, "Rabbinic Universalism in the Second and Third Centuries," *HTR* 93.2 (April 2000): 101-15.

Israel's Election and the Other

are not to be slain.[11] A similar but more elaborate tradition is found in *b. Soṭa* 35b, which informs us that the Canaanite nations were not only given an opportunity to repent but received a clear warning to do so in that they could read the stones that Joshua erected in the Jordan. Both these texts imply that the Canaanites were not annihilated for being Canaanites, but for failing to act in a particular manner. A similar midrashic reflex softens the anti-Amalek polemic, another arch-foe included among the anti-elect. Thus *b. Sanhedrin* 96b reports that the descendants of Haman, a character linked to the king of the Amalekites in Esth. 3:1, studied Torah in the academies of Bnei Braq.

Now in fairness, there are many rabbinic texts that remain skeptical about the possibility of the Gentile nations acting righteously. Often the Gentiles as a whole are pictured as doomed for destruction and incapable of keeping even the few Noahide commandments, let alone the Torah's 613. One sees this quite clearly in an elaboration of the midrashic motif of God offering the Torah to various nations who each in turn refuse to accept it.[12] This unusual passage found near the beginning of tractate *'Avodah Zara* in the *Babylonian Talmud* (2b-3a) reads as follows:

> The nations will then contend: "Lord of the Universe, did you give us the Torah, and we declined to accept it?" But how can they argue thus, seeing that it is written, *The Lord came from Sinai and rose from Seir unto them, He shined forth from Mount Paran* (Deut. 33:2)? And it is also written, *God comes from Teman* (Hab. 3:3). What did He seek in Seir, and what did He seek in Mount Paran? R. Johanan says: This teaches us that the Holy One, blessed be He, offered the Torah to every nation and every tongue, but none accepted it, until He came to Israel who received it. . . . This, then, will be their contention: "Lord of the Universe, did you suspend the mountain over us like a vault as you did to Israel and did we still decline to accept it?" . . . Thereupon the Holy One, blessed be He, will say to them: "Let us then consider the happenings of old," as it is said, *Let them announce to us former things* (Isa. 43:9), "there are seven commandments which you did accept, did you observe them?" How do

---

11. *Sifre on Deuteronomy* (Louis Finkelstein, ed.; New York: JTS, 1993), 238. The standard English translation is *Sifre: A Tannaitic Commentary on the Book of Deuteronomy,* trans. Reuven Hammer (Yale Judaica Series 24; New Haven: Yale, 1986), §202, p. 218.

12. For a more standard version of this midrashic motif, see *The Mekilta de Rabbi Ishmael,* trans. J. Z. Lauterbach (Philadelphia: Jewish Publication Society, 1976 [1933]), 2.234-35.

we know that they did not observe them? — For R. Joseph learned: *He stands and shakes the earth, He sees and makes the nations tremble* (Hab. 3:6): what did He see? He saw that the nations did not observe even the seven precepts which the sons of Noah had taken upon themselves, and seeing that they did not observe them, He stood up and released them from them [punning on the two differing roots of נטר in Hab. "to cause to tremble," in the rabbinic mind, "to free from responsibilities"]. . . . The nations will then plead. "Offer us the Torah anew and we shall obey it." But the Holy One, blessed be He, will say to them, "You foolish ones among peoples, he who took trouble [to prepare] on the eve of the Sabbath can eat on the Sabbath, but he who has not troubled on the eve of the Sabbath, what shall he eat on the Sabbath? Nevertheless, I have an easy command which is called Sukkah; go and carry it out." . . . Straightaway will every one of them betake himself and go and make a booth on the top of his roof; but the Holy One, blessed be He, will cause the sun to blaze forth over them as at the Summer Solstice and every one of them will trample down his booth and go away, as it is said, *Let us break their bands asunder, and cast away their cords from us* (Psalm 2:3).[13]

Often when this midrashic theme is evoked the implication is that the Torah was intended for every nation, an idea somewhat in tension with the notion of the seven commandments of Noah, which suggests a Torah reserved for Israel alone.[14] Here both notions are asserted at once. The nations complain that although they refused to accept the Torah, God never threatened them as he did Israel when (according to midrashic tradition) he held Mt. Sinai over the Israelites' heads; thus he cannot convict them of wrongdoing. Here God goes on to assert with scriptural proof that the nations were not even capable of keeping the seven Noahide commandments let alone the whole Torah. After first having God state in language reminiscent of the parable of the wise and foolish virgins (Matt. 25:1-13) that it is too late for the nations to save themselves, this midrash narrates a last-chance offer God gives the Gentiles. He commands them to observe a single non-Noahide mitzvah,

---

13. The Soncino translation is taken from Davka Software, *Soncino Classics* (2007). I have modernized some of the archaic English usage in the biblical quotations.

14. Recently, Marc Hirshman, *Torah for the Entire World* (Tel Aviv: Hakkibbutz Hameuchad, 1999) [in Hebrew], has cogently argued that there was an alternative rabbinic position on Gentile salvation that did not survive the talmudic period, according to which Gentiles can keep the Torah (or at least parts of it) without converting to Judaism, rather than observing only the seven Noahide commandments.

building and dwelling in a sukkah. However, they utterly fail at even this simple task and so are consigned to destruction. Similar treatments of the Gentile nations' inability to act righteously that imply their ultimate destruction could be multiplied many times over, as even a quick perusal through Sacha Stern's book *Jewish Identity in Early Rabbinic Writings* demonstrates.[15]

A different type of negative rabbinic portrayal of the Gentile nations can be found in the rabbinic propensity to describe certain non-elect characters that have close connections to the people of Israel in much harsher terms than the biblical text does. Thus in the Bible characters like Ishmael and Esau, while not chosen children, do share in the blessings of God. But note the following midrash from the *Sifre* on Deuteronomy:

> *For the portion of the Lord is His people* (Deut. 32:9): A parable: A king had a field which he leased to tenants. When the tenants began to steal from it, he took it away from them and leased it to their children. When the children began to act worse than their fathers, he took it away from them and gave it to (the original tenants') grandchildren. When these too became worse than their predecessors, a son was born to him. He said to the grandchildren, "Leave my property. You may not remain therein. Give me back my portion, so that I may repossess it." Thus also, when our father Abraham came into the world, unworthy (descendants) issued from him, Ishmael and all of Keturah's children. When Isaac came into the world, unworthy (descendants) issued from him, Esau and all the princes of Edom, and they became worse than their predecessors. When Jacob came into the world, he did not produce unworthy (descendants), rather all his children were worthy, as it said, *And Jacob was a perfect man dwelling in tents* (Gen. 25:27). When did God repossess His portion? Beginning with Jacob as it said, *For the portion of the Lord is His people, Jacob the lot of His inheritance* (Deut. 32:9), and *For the Lord chose Jacob for Himself* (Ps. 135:4).[16]

This rabbinic text contains an argument with close affinities to Paul's negative descriptions of Hagar and Ishmael in Galatians 4 as well as to the parable of the wicked tenants in Matthew 21. Here Ishmael, Keturah's children, and Esau are no longer portrayed with the complexity found within

---

15. Sacha Stern, *Jewish Identity in Early Rabbinic Writings* (Leiden: Brill, 1994).
16. *Sifre*, Piska 312, page 318 (trans. Reuven Hammer).

Genesis, where Ishmael is explicitly blessed by God in Gen. 17:20 and Esau is the wronged party who in the end appears more willing to let bygones be bygones than does Jacob. Rather these rival siblings are now pictured as totally reprobate characters who stand beyond God's blessing.[17] In turn Jacob and his children, characters who are far from perfect in Genesis, are here described in a totally positive fashion. This set of interpretive moves is widespread within the rabbinic corpus, perhaps most clearly seen in the further rabbinic extension of the late prophetic anti-Edomite polemic in which the rabbis completely demonize Esau, who in the rabbinic mind is a symbol of the oppressive Roman Empire.

This brief survey reveals that in some ways the rabbis maintained the biblical heritage they received, as can be seen in their assertion that Gentiles could be in right relationship to God without converting if they observe the Noahide commandments. However, in other ways the rabbis took both harsher and more lenient positions towards the Other. On the lenient side, they normalized the process of conversion, at times moving to neutralize the idea of the anti-elect, and in some texts they go so far as to imagine the nations eventually acknowledging the correctness of the Torah and perhaps observing it.[18] However, while they erected a theoretical framework that is potentially quite inclusive of Gentiles, often their depiction of the utter depravity of the nations of the world led them to conclude that the Gentiles are beyond redemption. This negative assessment of the Gentile nations is further reinforced by the tendency to rewrite, in rather negative terms, biblical texts that are more open to the Other. So it seems that even while the rabbis, likely on biblical precedent, recognized that the non-elect Gentiles could in theory be righteous, their experience often led them to assimilate the Gentile nations to the anti-elect, dooming them. It may be that the rabbis were more open to the possibility of select Gentile individuals acting in a righteous fashion than whole nations (one finds similar thinking in *4 Ezra* 3:34-36). If so, the rabbis may be guilty of stereotyping, condemning whole groups while making exceptions for individuals who leave a positive impression on the sterotyper.

---

17. On the rich midrashic tradition surrounding Ishmael in particular, see Carol Bakhos, *Ishmael on the Border: Rabbinic Portrayals of the First Arab* (Albany: SUNY Press, 2006).

18. Thus Goldenberg, *The Nations*, 91, correctly notes that "much (though not all) rabbinic thinking expected eventual recognition by the whole world of the sole power of the God of Israel. . . . Sometimes this recognition of the God of Israel entailed adoption of his followers' way of life, that is, conversion to Judaism." See *b. Berakot* 57b.

In fairness, these harsh assessments of Gentiles are at least partially attributable to the experience of Jews living under Roman authority and witnessing Roman excesses that the rabbis wrongly generalized to all Gentiles. However, it is likely that condemnations of the Gentiles also served an internal theological purpose. The rabbis often wrestled with the issue of theodicy, and these constructs would explain that the success of the Gentiles is only temporary. Soon enough, God will restore Israel and punish the wicked Gentile nations who cannot observe even the most basic standards of decency.

III. Contemporary Concerns

Before concluding, it seems appropriate to link our tour through these biblical and rabbinic perceptions of the Other to the contemporary interest in communal identity formation and the attempt to foster greater tolerance among different religious or political communities. It is evident that there are many under-utilized resources within classical Jewish texts for contemporary Jews seeking to construct a more tolerant theological stance towards non-Jews. This task must begin with an honest appraisal of the full range of relevant texts, both those with which we are sympathetic and those that we find disturbing. Now that a number of scholars have begun to collect and analyze the relevant data, one can imagine employing a constructive approach that would seek a sophisticated way to utilize more tolerant texts as a critique against the less palatable ones, perhaps emphasizing certain more generous elements of biblical thinking over problematic rabbinic views, and vice versa.

But even such constructive theological critiques must acknowledge that all biblical and rabbinic construals of the Other, both positive and negative, grow out of an affirmation of Israel's special divine election. Of course this deeply particularistic affirmation of Israel's identity need not spell intolerance, let alone doom, of all outsiders. Interestingly enough, there is substantial evidence within both the Hebrew Bible and the rabbinic corpus to suggest that a number of the most universalistic statements found in these texts are penned by sources who highlight Israel's special election. It seems quite reasonable to argue that the heightening of Israel's sense of her divine election found in texts like Second and Third Isaiah may well have given rise to the growing universalism expressed in these same texts. It is worth noting that arguably the single most universalist statement in the whole biblical tradition, that all humans were created in the image of God, comes from P, an author who is far from shy about asserting Israel's special status. A close rabbinic analogue to this biblical tendency can be found in *Pirqe 'Abot* 3:14. In this text, Rabbi Akiva first proclaims God loves human beings in general, using Gen. 9:6b as a prooftext. He immediately goes on to assert God's special love of Israel in particular by citing Deut. 14:1.

While today many assume that a growing universalism must imply a waning of particularism, the biblical and rabbinic evidence suggests that it was only through a deepening understanding of her unique identity that Israel came to glimpse the universalistic aspects inherent in her special election. This very insight might in fact provide a critique of a certain intellectual schizophrenia that is widespread today. Why is it that in personal psychology we tend to accept the notion that through deepening one's own unique self a person matures and comes to interact with others in an ever more sympathetic fashion, but in social psychology we too easily assent to the opposite belief, that only by weakening our unique national and ethnic identities can we ever hope to understand and respect the Other?

In my recent book, I argue that the Hebrew Bible's election theology is much more complex and nuanced than many of its cultured despisers recognize, but that it remains an inherently particularistic and exclusivistic idea. I also point out that election is an idea that Judaism (and for that matter Christianity as well) cannot easily discard inasmuch as the Hebrew Bible's central theological affirmations concerning God and his personal character are tightly interlinked with the claim that Israel is God's chosen people. This interlinking is already fully in place in the preexilic edition of Deuteronomy and is amplified greatly in rabbinic and later Jewish thinking. Thus, contemporary Jews who wish to maintain their core theological assumptions — and much the same could be said of Christians affirming the New Testament's elective language — will face certain insurmountable theological hurdles in the quest to belong to a religion that offends or excludes no one.

God's Other: The Intractable Problem of the Gentile King in Judean and Early Jewish Literature

Carol A. Newsom

Throughout the Hebrew Bible where the God of Israel is represented as having an opponent, this opponent is more often framed, not as another god, but as a human king.[1] To be sure, the rivalry between YHWH and Baal is explicit in the Elijah-Elisha cycle and in the book of Hosea, but this is the exception that proves the rule. There the conflict is much more an internal debate about the Israelite deity to whom honor should be paid, for Baal was certainly, for many centuries, a deity associated with Israelite and Judean worship.[2] One can find a few references to Babylonian gods as humiliated deities in Second Isaiah (Isa. 46:1) and in Jeremiah (Jer. 50:2-3; 51:44), but for the most part the gods of other nations are simply ignored. Not so their kings. From beginning to end in Israelite and early Jewish literature, from Pharaoh of Egypt to Pompey of Rome,[3] a succession of kings appears as the opponent of the God of Israel.

The opposition between YHWH and the foreign king is in one sense an asymmetrical relationship. They belong to different orders of being. But their opposition stands in, of course, for a more complex set of relationships

---

1. The exception, of course, is the mythic opponent of God in creation accounts, typically the Sea, Rahab, or Leviathan (cf. Pss. 74:12-14; 89:10-11; Isa. 27:1; 51:9-10). See John Day, *God's Conflict with the Dragon and the Sea: Echoes of a Canaanite Myth in the Old Testament* (Cambridge: Cambridge University Press, 1985).

2. Mark Smith, *The Early History of God: Yahweh and Other Deities in Ancient Israel* (San Francisco: Harper & Row, 1990), 12-14, 41-60.

3. Pharaoh: Exodus 5–15; Pompey: *Psalms of Solomon* 17.

that include both identity and opposition. YHWH and the Judean king are different in that YHWH is a deity and the Judean king is not. But they are linked in a relationship of identity in that they are both kings. More than that, in Judean royal ideology, it is YHWH who as divine king (1) authorizes the earthly king's rule ("I have found my servant David; with my holy oil I have anointed him; my hand shall always remain with him," Ps. 89:20-21), (2) associates him with YHWH's own rule ("sit at my right hand," Ps. 110:1), and (3) even adopts the earthly king as son ("you are my son; today I have begotten you," Ps. 2:7). Thus they mirror one another's identity as king. Although each ancient Near Eastern culture had somewhat different ways of articulating this relationship, all of them in one way or another understood the earthly king to manifest the divine royal authority and to receive his own royal identity from that of the deity.[4] Thus both vertical relationships mirror the other: YHWH and his king, the foreign god and his king.

YHWH ↕ Davidic king   Foreign god ↕ Foreign king

The opposition between these two sets of forces is, of course, the relationship of military and political aggression that so characterized the ancient Near East. It manifested itself on the ground in the presence of the foreign armies led by their king. But since the Judean royal ideology spoke of YHWH as the effective power of the Judean king's military success ("I will crush his foes before him and strike down those who hate him," Ps. 89:23), it becomes a quite natural "shorthand" for the entire set of oppositions to be summed up in terms of YHWH versus the foreign king. This is to trace the opposition in terms of the diagonal line (see p. 33). This configuration has the advantage of being able to attribute even reverses of the foreign king not inflicted by the Judean king as nevertheless due to the Judean god.[5] But the

---

4. See, e.g., R. J. Leprohon, "Royal Ideology and State Administration in Pharonic Egypt," in *Civilizations of the Ancient Near East*, 4 vols., ed. J. Sasson et al. (Peabody, Mass.: Hendrickson Publishers, 1995), 1.273-87, esp. 274-75; J. N. Postgate, "Royal Ideology and State Administration in Sumer and Akkad," in *Civilizations of the Ancient Near East*, 1.395-411. P. Jones, "Divine and Non-Divine Kingship," in *A Companion to the Ancient Near East*, ed. Daniel Snell (Malden: Blackwell, 2005), 330-42.

5. E.g., the death of Sennacherib in 2 Kings 19:37/Isa. 37:38 and 2 Chron. 32:20-21. The

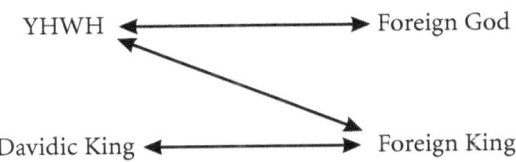

other sets of oppositions (the upper and lower parallel lines of the square: human king versus human king; deity versus deity) also find their symbolic embodiments. The outcome of king versus king opposition was enacted in rituals of surrender, abasement, humiliation, and punishment (Judg. 1:5-7; 2 Kings 25:5-7; 2 Chron. 33:11; cf. Esarhaddon's holding the Tyrian and Egyptian rulers on a leash, *ANEP* 447).[6] The outcome of deity versus deity opposition was enacted in the capture of divine images or symbols and their placement in the temples of the victorious deity. In both of these cases we have several accounts of the Judeans on the losing side (e.g., the deportations and executions of various Judean monarchs in 597 and 586, and the capture of the ark, described in 1 Samuel, and of the temple vessels, described in 2 Kings 24:13; 25:13-17, in 2 Chron. 36:7, 18, and in Dan. 1:2).[7] Thus the "diagonal" configuration of YHWH versus the foreign king is only one of several ways in which this set of oppositions was articulated, but it is the one that figures most prominently in the literary texts of the Hebrew Bible.

Before turning to particular texts, there are two terms from my title that require clarification. The first is the term Other. It has a number of different, often overlapping uses in contemporary critical discourse. It is easiest

---

Assyrians made use of the same motif. As Cynthia Chapman observes in *The Gendered Language of Warfare in the Israelite-Assyrian Encounter* (HSM 62; Winona Lake, Ind.: Eisenbrauns, 2004), 148, "when an Assyrian king failed to catch and kill a fleeing king, the annals often noted his death by some natural catastrophe that was understood as the revenge of the Assyrian king's gods."

6. The Assyrian inscriptions regularly refer to rituals of submission performed by defeated kings (bowing in submission, kissing the feet of the Assyrian king), to being carried away in fetters, and occasionally to more gory symbolic acts, such as decapitation of the king (see Esarhaddon's report of the defeat of Abdimilkutte of Sidon, *ANET* 291). Defeated kings might even be required to wipe the Assyrian king's sandals with their beards as a symbol of "compromised masculinity," as noted by Chapman, *Gendered Language of Warfare*, 39.

7. The deportation of divine statues, or "godnapping," was a regular practice of Mesopotamian kings. See Steven W. Holloway, *Assur Is King! Assur Is King! Religion in the Exercise of Power in the Neo-Assyrian Empire* (Leiden: Brill, 2002), 145-45; Zainab Bahrani, *Rituals of War: The Body and Violence in Mesopotamia* (New York: Zone Books, 2008), 159-75.

to say what I do not mean. I do not find particularly useful for this investigation the various Lacanian usages. Thus in using the term Other I do not mean the "specular" other of Lacan's hypothetical mirror stage of human development, the other that embodies the elusive image of wholeness that persons both desire and fear. Nor do I mean the Lacanian "symbolic" other, the alien Other of language and the symbolic order that structures our subjectivity.

Better, but still not quite adequate for my purposes, is the common anthropological use of the Other to refer to that person or group of people symbolically constructed as foreign or alien so as to serve as a definitional boundary for the self or for one's own group. In poststructuralist discussions of identity formation, the other is the devalued half of a binary opposition.[8] What is helpful about these perspectives is that they recognize that identity is always dialogical — the other is necessary for the self to exist. As warrior kings, YHWH and his Judean counterpart must have opponents — that is definitionally necessary to warrior kings. Such is the logic of Psalm 2, which opens with the conspiracy of "the kings of the earth" against "the one enthroned in heaven." Their presence and provocation are what permits the assertion of identity of the divine king and his Davidic representative through derisive laughter and annihilating fury. But in contrast to the way this definitional other functions in forming identity, the individual foreign king does not neatly fit the description of "the devalued half of a binary opposition." Occasionally, to be sure, one finds language that inscribes the foreign king as the dragon of chaos as opposed to the creator deity, as in Ezek. 32:2-8, a passage that vividly depicts Pharaoh king of Egypt as "a dragon in the seas," destroyed by YHWH in language evocative of the cosmogonic battle. But in most of the cases where the opposition between YHWH and the foreign king is described, this type of "othering" is not the rhetorical strategy employed.

Consequently, some additional analysis of the Other is needed to explain the dynamics. I think what is lacking can be supplied by aspects of Emanual Levinas's account of the Other. There is much of Levinas's thinking that is not germane. But one aspect of his discussion seems to be quite significant for this inquiry. In *Totality and Infinity* Levinas describes the Other

---

8. This approach is associated in particular with the analysis of Jacques Derrida (e.g., in *Positions* [Chicago: University of Chicago Press, 1981]) and is an important element in Judith Butler's theoretical description of identity as performative (*Gender Trouble* [London: Routledge, 1993]).

not in terms of that which is opposite to me but rather as that which is separate from me, that which is radically exterior to me, that which is utterly transcendent, exceeding me. The encounter with the Other makes me aware that the world is not simply my possession or an extension of me, but that I share the world.[9] And it is the matter of sharing the world that I think illumines the remaining aspect of the problem. The ideological claims concerning sovereignty that are made on behalf of any divine king are more or less incompatible with sharing the world with another sovereign who makes ultimate claims. Consequently, such an Other presents problems. In fact, intractable problems, which brings me to the second important term of my title — "intractable."

In his book *Exclusion and Embrace*, Miroslav Volf examines the dynamics of the encounter between self and other and catalogues the ways in which the logic of exclusion deals with the problem of the other.[10] These strategies of exclusion are four: elimination, domination, assimilation, and abandonment.[11] For my purposes the equivalent of abandonment is "simply ignoring the problem." And that is what most of the divine royal ideologies do. They ignore the parallel claims of other nations concerning their deities and the kings who represent them on earth. When no active military/political conflict exists, this is the most effective strategy. When active conflict exists, however, then the rival and incompatible claims have to be ideologically resolved in some fashion. And the nature of the conflict will dictate which of the strategies — elimination, domination, assimilation — is most effective in defusing the discomfort and cognitive dissonance represented by this theo-political Other.

I am, of course, primarily considering ideological strategies as they are represented in the Hebrew Bible and related texts. So it is necessary to consider the interface between reality and ideology. Particularly helpful for this issue is the trajectory of rhetorical and ideological analysis that runs from Kenneth Burke through Fredric Jameson. Kenneth Burke's dictum that

---

9. Emmanuel Levinas, *Totality and Infinity: An Essay on Exteriority*, trans. A. Lingis (Pittsburgh: Duquesne University Press, 1981), 198-203.

10. Miroslav Volf, *Exclusion and Embrace* (Nashville: Abington Press, 1996). I think one can take it for granted that in antiquity there would be no resolution of the problem by an ethical "embrace" of the claims to sovereignty by the deities of other nations. Obviously, I am adapting Volf's analysis for a sort of ideological problem that is different from the concrete ethical issues he is concerned with, but I find the logical analysis of exclusion very helpful.

11. Volf, *Exclusion and Embrace*, 75.

"words are strategies for encompassing situations" and his characterization of utterances as "symbolic acts" are perspectives that should always be borne in mind when reading texts of any nature, but particularly those engaged in negotiating power relations.[12] Even more useful, however, is Jameson's analysis of the relation of history to text. "History," he says, "is *not* a text, not a narrative, master or otherwise, but . . . it is inaccessible to us except in textual form."[13] That is to say, one has to render historical reality in some symbolic or narrative fashion if one is to grasp it and engage it at all. What the literary text does is to draw the historical reality into itself where it is malleable, and by narrativizing it, to make it possible to invent "imaginary or formal 'solutions' to unresolvable social contradictions."[14] This is the symbolic act that relieves the tension of the contradiction, the tension of the intractable problem of sharing the world with rival claims. But the problem, as Jameson concludes, can be seen in "Kenneth Burke's play of emphases, in which a symbolic act is on the one hand affirmed as a genuine *act*, albeit on the symbolic level, while on the other it is registered as an act which is 'merely' symbolic, its resolutions imaginary ones that leave the real untouched, suitably dramatiz[ing] the ambiguous status of art and culture."[15]

With these preliminary theoretical considerations in mind, I want to examine the ways in which — depending on the particular political circumstances — the varying symbolic strategies of elimination, domination, and assimilation are worked out in various texts to attempt to resolve the anxiety producing contradiction represented by the foreign king. One feature of these strategies which is particularly striking is the extent to which the foreign king's psyche — his thoughts, beliefs, perceptions, and misperceptions — become the preoccupation of the biblical and early Jewish texts. This concern with what is going on in the foreign king's head is not evenly distributed, however, but becomes both more prominent and differently inflected as the strategy moves into the part of the spectrum represented by domination and assimilation.

---

12. These and related ideas permeate Burke's extensive works. Particularly recommended are *A Grammar of Motives* (Berkeley: University of California Press, 1969); *A Rhetoric of Motives* (Berkeley: University of California Press, 1969); and *Language as Symbolic Action: Essays on Life, Literature, and Method* (Berkeley: University of California Press, 1966).

13. Fredric Jameson, *The Political Unconscious* (Ithaca, N.Y.: Cornell University Press, 1981), 35.

14. Jameson, *Political Unconscious*, 79.

15. Ibid., 81.

I. Elimination

The simplest way to deal with the disturbing claims implicit in the foreign king is to kill him — physically, if possible; but certainly, within the text. Three examples that serve as temporal bookends illustrate this strategy: on the one hand, the Song of the Sea in Exodus 15, a very early Hebrew composition; and on the other hand the death of Antiochus IV Epiphanes, as it is described in Daniel 7 and 11, and the death of Pompey, as it is described in the *Psalms of Solomon*. The Song of the Sea frames this mythic-legendary confrontation in terms of the conflict between two warriors, the triumphant warrior YHWH and the defeated and destroyed warrior Pharaoh, whose chariots, army, and officers are all drowned in the sea. Pharaoh's perception of the situation is of no interest whatsoever. He is given no thoughts or words. Similarly, in the apocalypses in Daniel, Antiochus IV is said to have spoken "big words" in Dan. 7:8b, 20b, and 25a; and in 8:25b and 11:36 there are references to his considering himself great, but there is neither an exploration of the content of his boasts nor any interest in a "recognition scene" in which he perceives that he was mistaken. Similar is the treatment of the death of Ptolemy in the *Psalms of Solomon*. The psalmist prays "Do not delay, O God, to repay them [i.e., the Gentiles] on their heads, to declare dishonorable the arrogance of the dragon. And I did not wait long until God showed me his insolence pierced on the mountains of Egypt" (2:25),[16] a description then filled out with the details of Pompey's death. Pompey is cited as having spoken one arrogant statement, "I shall be lord of land and sea" (2:29), but he, too, apparently dies in ignorance of the true state of affairs, namely, "that it is God who is great . . . king over the heavens" (2:29-30).

II. Elimination Plus Domination

Even when the foreign king dies, there may be an interest in giving him a more developed psychological experience of the meaning of his death. In these situations, I would say that the text is interested not simply in elimination of the rival but in psychological domination as well as elimination. In the prose traditions of the Exodus, the domination and manipulation of Pharaoh's psyche is a central trope. Most famously, Pharaoh is not even his own agent, but has his heart repeatedly "hardened" by God, so as to prolong the drama of the contest between God and Pharaoh (Exod. 4:21; 9:12; 10:1, 20,

---

16. Trans. R. B. Wright in *OTP* 2:653.

27; 11:10; 14:4, 8). Nevertheless, it is not enough merely to manipulate him. The theme of knowledge is made explicit. In Moses and Aaron's first encounter with Pharaoh, he says, "Who is YHWH, that I should listen to him and let Israel go? I do not know YHWH, and I will not let Israel go" (Exod. 5:2). And the drowning at the Reed Sea is twice described in terms of this purpose. In Exod. 14:4, "I will gain glory for myself by means of Pharaoh and all his army; and the Egyptians shall know that I am YHWH"; and similarly in vv. 17-18. Thus the text is concerned not just that Pharaoh die but that he die in the knowledge that another monarch has dominated him.

A similar combination of elimination and domination occurs in the way in which 1 Maccabees, but even more, 2 Maccabees, deals with the death of Antiochus IV. In 1 Maccabees 6, Antiochus, already frustrated by a failed attempt to plunder a temple, hears news of the defeat of his army by Judah. He takes to bed, "sick from disappointment" and finally dying. On his deathbed he "recall[s] the wrong [he] did in Jerusalem," plundering the Temple vessels and killing the inhabitants, and sees that as the reason that he is now "dying in bitter grief in a strange land" (1 Macc. 6:12, 13). But this is not an explicitly theological moment of recognition. That is supplied by 2 Maccabees, however. There in 2 Maccabees 9 Antiochus responds to a similar set of frustrations by an outburst of rage and intent to destroy Jerusalem utterly. "But the all-seeing Lord, the God of Israel, struck him with an incurable and invisible blow" (v. 5). The events are described in full melodramatic mode. As Antiochus succumbs to his disgusting disease, his arrogance diminishes, and he declares, "It is right to submit to God and not to think his mortal being equal to God" (v. 12). Moreover, he promises to free Jerusalem, to make its inhabitants equal to citizens of Athens, to make lavish offerings to the Temple, and even to "become a Jew and to visit every inhabited place, proclaiming the power of God" (v. 17). Here the text moves not only to domination but seems to toy with the notion of assimilation by conversion. But that is just a feint. What the reader is treated to is purely the pleasure of the domination, humiliation, and ultimate rejection and elimination of the vile Antiochus, who gives up hope of recovery because, the narrator informs us, "the judgment of God had justly come upon him" (v. 18).

III. Domination and the Strategy of False Consciousness

Where the foreign king actually dies, one can successfully make use of the strategy of elimination, with or without domination. But what if the king inconveniently does not die? In the monarchical period, the strategy is to compose texts that make the case for domination. The best examples of this strategy are the poems concerning the "King of Assyria" in Isa. 10:5-19 and 37:21-29.[17] Obviously, in light of the extraordinary conquests and threats against Jerusalem, the competing ideology of Assyrian sovereignty must be confronted. One cannot ignore or share space with *this*. The available ideological strategy is to assert domination through contesting claims of agency, as well as to make threats. Here, however, no "recognition scene" is described, perhaps because the relationship between YHWH and Sennacherib does not have a completed plot and a definitive outcome. But the king's psyche is quite clearly the focal issue of these texts. His thoughts and words are extensively represented in both poems. In Isaiah 37, Sennacherib is presented as bragging about ascending mountains, felling the forests of Lebanon, digging wells, and drying up the streams of Egypt.[18] In chap. 10, the claims are more explicitly military, concerning what the king has done to peoples, their kings, their lands, and their wealth. What is threatening about these claims is that they are true. The king of Assyria and his predecessors have in fact done what he boasts about.[19] What kind of strategy for encompassing this situation can the prophet offer?

Rather than excluding and ignoring the Assyrian royal rhetoric, it is brought into the text itself, and the facts that are asserted are implicitly acknowledged. The prophet's strategy is to shift the plane of the argument to raise the question of agency. In chap. 37 what the king claims regarding his cutting of forests and digging wells would not seem to be a direct challenge to YHWH, but the repetition of the emphatic pronoun 'ani in vv. 24 and 25 suggests that it is the very claim of personal agency that is offensive. The mocking "have you not heard" that begins YHWH's counterclaim (v. 26) casts doubt on the king's own understanding of the nature of his actions. YHWH goes on to claim that it was he, not the king, who in fact determined

---

17. Scholarly opinion is divided as to the date and identity of the king in Isa. 10:5-14 and the relationship between these verses and vv. 15-19. For present purposes, the identification of the king is not crucial, though I am inclined to associate this passage with Sennacherib and to consider the sections as parts of one rhetorical whole; cf. Joseph Blenkinsopp, *Isaiah 1–39* (New York: Doubleday, 2000), 256. The words attributed to the king in Isaiah 10 telescope the achievements of more than one Assyrian king.

18. Cf. *ANET* 276, 291.

19. The cities listed had all been conquered by Assyrian monarchs: Calno (738 B.C.E.), Carchemish (717), Hamath (738 and 720), Arpad (740 and 720), Samaria (722), Damascus (732).

all of these deeds and planned them "from days of old," including Sennacherib's military victories. Thus psychological domination comes from disclosing the king's consciousness to be false consciousness, as well as by relocating effective agency. YHWH does not threaten Sennacherib with elimination here, but concludes rather with a final image of physical domination that makes use of the binary opposition between human and animal. Sennacherib is represented as an unruly animal who can be controlled and led about by placing "my hook in your nose and my bit in your mouth," a humiliating punishment that was often inflicted on defeated kings and nobles after a military defeat (see *ANEP* 447).

In Isaiah 10 many of the same strategies are employed. Here, the king's own words, in which he brags about what he has done to other peoples and cities and what he will therefore do to Jerusalem, are surrounded by a series of images that use the trope of tools and the relation between tool and tool user. The king is variously a rod and a club (v. 5), an ax, a saw, a rod and a staff (v. 15). The imagery efficiently organizes the relationship of agency, inscribing the king as a mere instrument, an inanimate object. The notion that such an object might have its own intentionality or engage in aggression against the one who wields it is the point of the parody — and provides the force of the poem's claim that despite the Assyrian king's victories over other cities, he will not in fact be able to do the same to Jerusalem, because the intentionality that wields the king's power is not his own. After the initial description of the king as the rod of God's own anger (v. 5), the king's words are introduced with the line, "But this is not what he intends, nor does he have this in mind" (v. 7). Yet it turns out, he is wrong. From the perspective of the audience for Isaiah's words, the king is disclosed as psychologically dominated by having his fundamental misperception of the situation disclosed.

Having contained the Assyrian king's boasting through these tropes, the poem also concludes with a threat of physical domination, the claim that YHWH of hosts "will send a wasting sickness among his stout men" (v. 16). This is perhaps a taking of credit for an outbreak of plague that put an end to Sennacherib's siege of Jerusalem.[20] Despite the fact that Judah ended up as a vassal state dominated by Assyria, events permitted enough ideological space to make claims that the relationship of domination ran in the other direction.

---

20. Josephus preserves a tradition from Berossus that Sennacherib's army suffered an outbreak of plague (*Ant.* 10.21-23). Whether this is to be associated with Herodotus's account of mice attacking the bows and quivers of Sennacherib's army, as Josephus surmises, is suggestive but uncertain.

IV. Assimilation — and a Hope for Elimination

The situation changed decisively with the Babylonian hegemony in the ancient Near East, and the agonized struggle to interpret events and plan strategies within the resources of the available ideologies of power is reflected above all in the book of Jeremiah. This book strains under the tension of its various interpretive strategies. In the poetic oracles in chaps. 50–51, which a brief narrative describes as the contents of a scroll thrown into the Euphrates as a sign act of Babylon's destruction (51:59-64), the imagery is of pure elimination, indeed annihilation. Although most of the imagery is directed against the city itself, Nebuchadnezzar figures repeatedly. He is "the arrogant one" who will fall "with no one to raise him up" (50:31-32). He is the object of the lament of the people of Zion, who accuse him of devouring them, provoking God to promise vengeance (51:34-39). Although there is a brief reference to Babylon as an instrument, "the golden cup in the Lord's hand" (51:7), for the most part these poems speak in the pure idiom of the elimination of Babylon and its king as God's Other.

Utterly different is the interpretation of the prose portions of Jeremiah. These texts describe an ideological conflict between two Judean parties, one urging surrender to Nebuchadnezzar and one urging resistance and rebellion (see especially, Jeremiah 25; 27–29; 37–38). The party urging resistance had, of course, the traditions of "Zion theology" upon which to draw, with its ideological commitment to the inviolability of Zion (Jer. 7:4). The party urging submission had to employ their ideological resources in a new way. Here one has to be careful to track what was apparently a tradition that developed over time.[21] It is difficult, if not impossible, to uncover the terms of the argument as they unfolded in the final years of Zedekiah's reign. The differences between the Septuagint and the MT, however, allow one to discern some of the layers of this novel interpretation in the developing text of the book of Jeremiah.

Concerning the characterization of Nebuchadnezzar, the Septuagint text corresponding to MT 27:5-6 appears to be the least developed. Here YHWH speaks: "Because I have made the earth through my great strength and by my lofty effort, I will give it to whoever seems good in my eyes. I have

---

21. Indeed, the prose traditions themselves may reflect an internal conflict between those Jeremiah traditionists who remained in Judah and those in the Babylonian diaspora. Such, at least, is the argument advanced by Carolyn Sharp, *Prophecy and Ideology in Jeremiah: Struggles for Authority in the Deutero-Jeremianic Prose* (London: T&T Clark, 2003). See in particular her summary on pp. 157-59.

given the earth to Nabouchodonosor, King of Babylon, to serve him, and the wild animals of the field to work for him." What is said here goes far beyond mere instrumental use of a king for a specific purpose. Nebuchadnezzar is not identified here as the rod of God's anger. Nor is there any hint here, as is expressed elsewhere in the book of Jeremiah, of the Judeans' own sin as reason for Nebuchadnezzar's power over them. This statement reflects a truly novel configuration — the assimilation of the foreign king into the one whom YHWH chooses as his royal representative on earth. This new role does not mean a displacement of the Davidic monarch, however, since Nebuchadnezzar's fiefdom is broader than Judah. In the Septuagint it is "the earth," in the MT "all these lands." For the first time, YHWH establishes an imperium.

Where does such an idea come from? It appears to be difficult to ground it in native Judean ideologies, at least not entirely. The old tradition in Deuteronomy 32 that the Most High apportioned the nations according to the number of the gods is not really parallel, though it does provide some analogy for Judah's god making decisions about the governance of the nations. But neither is Jeremiah's claim likely to be simply an appropriation of what Nebuchadnezzar was saying about himself. Neo-Babylonian kings did not use the titulature of king of the world.[22] More likely, the book of Jeremiah is appropriating and adapting imperial ideological constructs, but probably Assyrian ones known in Judah from the long period of Assyrian hegemony. To illustrate, one might consider the beginning of Sennacherib's annals:

> Sennacherib, the great king, the mighty king, king of the universe, king of Assyria, king of the four quarters (of the earth); the wise ruler, favorite of the great gods, guardian of the right. . . . The god Assur, the great mountain, an unrivaled kingship has entrusted to me, and above all those who dwell in palaces, has made powerful my weapons; from the upper sea of the setting sun to the lower sea of the rising sun all humankind he has brought in submission at my feet. (col. 1.1-4, 10-15)[23]

---

22. David Vanderhooft, "Babylonian Strategies of Imperial Control in the West: Royal Practice and Rhetoric," in *Judah and the Judeans in the Neo-Babylonian Period*, ed. Oded Lipschits and Joseph Blenkinsopp (Winona Lake, Ind.: Eisenbrauns, 2003), 249. The exception is Nabonidus, who modeled his titulature after that of the neo-Assyrian kings. See Paul-Alain Beaulieu, *The Reign of Nabonidus, King of Babylon, 556-539 B.C.* (New Haven and London: Yale University Press, 1989), 143, 214.

23. D. D. Luckenbill, *The Annals of Sennacherib* (Chicago: University of Chicago

Thus in a radical move, Jeremiah both assimilates Mesopotamian imperial ideology and assimilates the foreign king, who is now positioned not as an opponent but as a chosen king, creating a three-tiered hierarchy of sovereignty: YHWH, Nebuchadnezzar, Zedekiah.[24]

A comparison of the LXX and the MT illustrates the development and naturalization of this new conception, as the MT adds to the king's name the epithet "my servant," which it also inserts into Jer. 25:9. This phrase echoes the frequent royal designation "David my servant" and so emphasizes the parallel between YHWH's choice of Nebuchadnezzar and his choice of David.[25] This is not merely an instrumental but a personal relationship. At the same time the MT attempts to bridge the distance between this breathtaking new assimilation of the foreign king and the tradition of elimination by incorporating a time limit for his rule: "All the nations will serve him and his son and his grandson, until the time of his own land comes. Then many nations and great kings shall make him their slave" (27:7). Nevertheless, a vitally important new possibility is added to the repertoire of ways in which the threatening otherness of the foreign king can be dealt with.

V. Assimilation Only

With the exile and the gradual realization that the Davidic dynasty might not be restored, the strategy of assimilation, innovated in extraordinary circumstances by Jeremiah, was developed to good advantage in negotiating the new state of affairs introduced by the conquest of Cyrus the Persian. The ways in which Cyrus was assimilated to the Davidic dynastic role have been often recounted,[26] so a brief summary will suffice, focusing on the Cyrus oracle in Isa. 44:24–45:13. It is important to remember, however, the religious

---

Press, 1924), 23. I am not claiming that the authors of Jeremiah had direct access to Assyrian inscriptions but rather that the gist of Assyrian imperial rhetoric would have been familiar to Judeans who were involved in political matters.

24. Cf. Ezek. 17:11-21, where YHWH is represented as the guarantor of the vassal treaty sworn by Zedekiah to Nebuchadnezzar (cf. 2 Chron. 36:13), a not uncommon practice in antiquity. Perhaps the recent fact of the swearing of the oath of fealty in the name of YHWH facilitated the ideological innovations in the Jeremianic tradition.

25. "David my servant": 2 Sam. 3:18; 7:5, 8; 1 Kings 11:13, 32, 34, 36, 38; 14:8; 2 Kings 19:34; Isa. 37:35; Jer. 33:21, 22, 26; Ezek. 34:23, 24; 37:24, 25; Ps. 89:3, 20; 1 Chron. 17:4, 7.

26. See, e.g., Roddy L. Braun, "Cyrus in Second and Third Isaiah, Chronicles, Ezra and Nehemiah," in *The Chronicler as Theologian*, ed. M. P. Graham, S. L. McKenzie, and G. N. Knoppers (London: T&T Clark International [Continuum], 2003), 146-64.

propaganda free-for-all that was Babylon in the years leading up to and just after the conquest by Cyrus. First, there had been the furor over Nabonidus, who claimed authorization for his kingship through the moon god Sin, although for most of his kingship publicly adhering to the official Babylonian theology that acknowledged Marduk as the dynastic god.[27] Second, there was the decision by Cyrus, presumably in cooperation with the priests of Marduk, to present himself as having been chosen by Marduk for rulership ("[Marduk] pronounced the name of Cyrus, king of Anshan, declared him to be the ruler of all the world," *ANET* 316). Morton Smith may (or may not) have been too imaginative in envisioning Persian agents infiltrating Babylon and persuading various segments of the population to participate in a joint propaganda campaign to prepare the way for Cyrus,[28] but it is important to situate Second Isaiah's own positioning of Cyrus in the context of the lively discursive struggle to account for Cyrus's stunning success. Moreover, for the first time the foreign king was *not* someone threatening violence against Judah or the Judeans. Thus assimilation becomes the most useful way of encompassing the new imperial ruler.[29]

As in Jeremiah, Second Isaiah begins the assimilation of Cyrus by identifying YHWH as the creator, and as the agent who has determined everything that will happen. Here, however, the assimilation of Cyrus to the Davidic tradition is much stronger. Cyrus is "my shepherd" and "YHWH's anointed." YHWH not only grasps his right hand but also gives him a throne name. Above all, he charges Cyrus to rebuild Jerusalem and refound the Temple, tasks previously carried out by the Davidic kings.

One significant difference between Jeremiah and Second Isaiah is that in Jeremiah's assimilation of Nebuchadnezzar, no attention at all was given to Nebuchadnezzar's consciousness. In Jeremiah's view, does Nebuchadnezzar *know* he has been given the rulership of the world? The issue never comes up. For Jeremiah's limited purposes, it did not matter. The persistence of the exile, however, and the succession of Persia to imperial rule, made the issue of the foreign king's psyche once more a matter of concern. One can see Second Isaiah negotiating this issue in the Cyrus oracle. The theme of

---

27. Beaulieu, *Reign of Nabonidus*, 49-50, 137-38, 203.
28. Morton Smith, "II Isaiah and the Persians," *JAOS* 83 (1963): 415-21.
29. See the similar analysis of Lisbeth Fried, "Cyrus the Messiah? The Historical Background to Isaiah 45:1," *HTR* 95 (2002): 373-93. In particular, "I suggest instead that the Deutero-Isaianic writer wrote as a contemporary of Cyrus, and that he wrote to legitimize him as the Davidic monarch, heir to the Davidic throne. The line of the Achaemenid kings would now take the place of the Davidides" (p. 374).

what Cyrus knows or does not know occurs intensely in vv. 4-6a. "For the sake of my servant Jacob, and Israel my chosen, I call you by your name, I give you a title, though you do not know me. I am the LORD, and there is no other; besides me there is no god. I arm you, though you do not know me, so that they may know, from the rising of the sun and from the west, that there is no one besides me." Here it is made explicit that Cyrus is *not* aware of the true state of affairs, though the ultimate purpose of this election of Cyrus is universal knowledge of the nature and power of YHWH. (The "so that you may know" phrase in v. 3b is probably a secondary addition.) Why would Cyrus be said not to know? Perhaps because of his public declaration that his kingship comes from Marduk. Thus the claim of false consciousness again has a role to play, although in this case a more subtle one.

VI. Colluding in Assimilation?

What was missing in Second Isaiah, Cyrus's awareness of the source of his imperial power, is, of course, made explicit in the decree of Cyrus that concludes the book of 2 Chronicles and begins the book of Ezra: "Thus says King Cyrus of Persia: YHWH, the God of heaven, has given me all the kingdoms of the earth, and he has charged me to build him a house at Jerusalem, which is in Judah" (2 Chron. 36:23a; Ezra 1:2). A long and inconclusive debate has raged as to whether this decree is or is not authentic, though the balance of opinion currently favors the skeptics.[30] I doubt the issue will ever be resolved. I would like to lay out two alternative possibilities, however, either of which I think makes sense in the context of the power relations of empire. First, the Persians did represent themselves in Babylon as kings authorized by the Babylonian gods and in Egypt as the successors of the Pharaohs, authorized by the Egyptian gods.[31] What is not known is whether or not they extended this practice to the minor peoples of the empire. One could imagine good reasons for doing so. The subject peoples would receive the dignity and ideological power of being able to affirm that their Persian overlord

---

30. See Lester Grabbe, "The 'Persian Documents' in the Book of Ezra: Are They Authentic?" in *Judah and the Judeans in the Persian Period*, ed. Oded Lipschitz and Manfred Oeming (Winona Lake, Ind.: Eisenbrauns, 2006), 541-44. For arguments in favor of authenticity, see E. J. Bickerman, "The Edict of Cyrus in Ezra 1," in idem, *Studies in Jewish and Christian History*, vol. 1 (Leiden: Brill, 2007), 71-107. For a nuanced analysis see H. G. M. Williamson, *Ezra, Nehemiah* (WBC 16; Waco, Tex.: Word Books, 1985), 6-15.

31. Fried, "Cyrus the Messiah?" 383-86.

reigns at the command of their own god. The advantage to the Persians is that people who have acknowledged that Persian rule is what their own god desires are less likely to join in revolts. If such a practice were in fact the case, then the Persian overlords would themselves be colluding in assimilation to local religious ideologies throughout the empire as a strategy of rule. But there is no hard evidence that this was the case, outside of the contested biblical passages in Ezra and 2 Chronicles.

The other option is that the Judeans themselves, aware of the Persian practices with respect to the gods of Mesopotamia and Egypt, constructed by analogy a Persian acknowledgment that Persian rule was authorized by the God of Israel. It is not difficult to appreciate the ideological double bind of a persistent life under imperial control *without* native kingship. In the ancient Near East kingship is divinely authorized. There may be bad kings, but kingship itself mediates the divine rule on earth. Nativist revolts (as opposed to revolts by satraps) were usually associated with a claimant to the native throne (the likely expectations of restoration of the Davidic monarchy associated with Zerubbabel [Zech. 3:8-10; 4:6-7]; the revolts of Nidintu-Bel and Arakhu, each of whom took the name of Nebuchadnezzar and claimed to be the son of Nabonidus[32]). If revolt in the name of one's own kingship was not possible, then there were strong ideological pressures to envision the imperial ruler as divinely authorized by one's own god. Otherwise the world simply did not make sense.

VII. Assimilation with Domination — and Back to Elimination

What appears in Chronicles and Ezra in brief form (the conscious and explicit confession by the king that he has received rule from YHWH) becomes the obsession of the narrative cycle in Daniel 1–6.[33] Much more than in previous texts, the consciousness of the king becomes the field of struggle itself. Here the genre of court stories (which regularly patronize or even satirize kings) is turned to a new purpose. In Daniel, the king rather than the courtier becomes the protagonist. This is especially true of what I would call "the Nebuchadnezzar cycle" in MT Daniel 1–4. Although originally probably sep-

---

32. Beaulieu, *Reign of Nabonidus*, 232. See also Pierre Briant, *From Cyrus to Alexander: A History of the Persian Empire*, trans. P. T. Daniels (Winona Lake, Ind.: Eisenbrauns, 2002), 115, 120.

33. One might note also the story of Alexander the Great and the Jewish high priest, preserved by Josephus, *Ant.* 11.329-39.

arate stories, with chap. 1 composed as an introduction to Daniel 1–6, in the MT tradition especially, the material in chaps. 1–4 have been carefully linked to form something almost like a *Bildungsroman* for Nebuchadnezzar, showing the slow and painful development of his consciousness of the source of his sovereignty.[34] As has often been noted, the theme of divine sovereignty is carried throughout the narratives by the various doxologies uttered by the kings, mostly at the end of the chapters, doxologies that have a crescendo pattern.[35] At the end of chap. 2, Nebuchadnezzar praises the God of Daniel as "God of gods and Lord of kings and a revealer of mysteries," though the juxtaposition of chap. 3, where Nebuchadnezzar builds the statue of gold and demands worship of it, suggests that he has not in fact grasped the full meaning of the revelatory dream. At the end of chap. 3 he answers his own earlier rhetorical question concerning what god could save the three young men from his hand by blessing "the God of Shadrach, Meshach, and Abednego who sent his angel and delivered his servants who . . . disobeyed the king's command" (3:28). But then he makes a decree offering to protect this deity from insult and blasphemy by means of his own royal power, suggesting again that he has still not quite grasped the principle involved. Chapter 4 tells the story of Nebuchadnezzar's redemptive humiliation for his arrogant presumption. Cast in the form of a public letter to all the peoples of the earth, the letter is framed by doxologies in which he explicitly affirms the Most High God's sovereignty and his confession that "he is able to bring low those who walk in pride" (4:37). The story makes clear that Nebuchadnezzar receives back his own kingship only after he has uttered his confession concerning divine sovereignty. The domination of Nebuchandezzar by YHWH in this story is what makes the outcome ideologically satisfying. The final two stories stand as counterpoints: Nebuchadnezzar's son Belshazzar serves as the negative counterpart to Nebuchadnezzar's redeemed consciousness (a point underscored in the MT) and is summarily eliminated. In the final narrative concerning Darius the Mede, the concluding doxology is not simply a personal confession by the king but "a decree that in all my royal dominion people should tremble and fear before the God of Daniel" (6:26). Not only are the foreign kings happily dominated by the sovereign God of Israel but all the peoples of the empire will be as well.

---

34. Evidence exists in the Old Greek of Daniel that chaps. 4–6 (or 3–6) may have circulated separately as the core of the narrative cycle. See Collins, *Daniel* (Minneapolis: Fortress, 1993), 4-7. Later editorial activity in the MT tradition, however, links the Nebuchadnezzar stories tightly together.

35. Sibley Towner, "The Poetic Passages of Daniel 1–6," *CBQ* 31 (1969): 317-26.

Fredric Jameson would recognize in this narrative cycle a clear example of the use of narrative to invent formal and imaginary solutions to unresolvable social contradictions. By positing the kings' acknowledgment of YHWH's sovereignty, and indeed the recognition of it as the source of their own sovereignty, the text can create a tightly framed narrative world in which YHWH's sovereignty is indeed a present reality, exercised through the foreign kings. If there were ways in which the imperial rulers did in fact "collude" in the wording of their proclamations, then the cycle of stories would not be wild fantasies so much as they would be narrative ways of opening up the ideological space made possible by such royal rhetoric. In any event, such was the tradition embedded in Chronicles and Ezra, which the author of Daniel presumably knew. The Daniel stories appear to be a highly stable way to discharge cognitive dissonance by asserting YHWH's sovereignty within the context of foreign imperial rule. The problem with symbolic acts, however, as Jameson warned, is that such an imaginative resolution is "symbolic only." The contradiction cannot be put to rest once and for all. And the tension surfaces in the Daniel cycle in the content of the revelatory dream to Nebuchadnezzar in chap. 2. A debate exists as to whether the eschatological elements of the dream are secondary, for the resolution proposed by the dream is quite different from that devised by the narrative cycle.[36] The resolution in the dream is, once again, the strategy of elimination. "Then the iron, the clay, the bronze, the silver, and the gold, were all broken in pieces and became like the chaff of the summer threshing floors; and the wind carried them away, so that not a trace of them could be found. But the stone that struck the statue became a great mountain and filled the whole earth" (2:35).

In the end, elimination is the only ideologically stable option. Although various strategies for dealing with the foreign king as YHWH's other may answer particular situations, the ideology of divine sovereignty is incompatible with other rival claims. Even the re-establishment of a kingdom under the Hasmoneans does not fully resolve the cognitive dissonance, and the eschatological projection of the elimination of rival claims to sovereignty, both on earth and in heaven, becomes the project of apocalyptic literature.

---

36. The case has been most forcefully argued by Reinhard Kratz, *Translatio Imperii: Untersuchungen zu den aramäischen Danielerzählungen und ihrem theologiegeschichtlichen Umfeld* (WMANT 36; Neukirchen-Vluyn: Neukirchener Verlag, 1991), 33-35, 55-62. But see the review by John Collins, *JBL* 111 (1992): 702-4, who questions the somewhat circular argumentation.

The Original Sin of the Canaanites

Katell Berthelot

The Canaanites belong to the ancient peoples described in the Bible as idolatrous. However, they hold a special status among the peoples surrounding the children of Israel, because they live in the land that God promised to give, and eventually gave, to the people of Israel.[1] According to Deuteronomy 20, whereas idolatry can be tolerated in countries that are not part of the land of Israel, in the latter it has to be rooted out. According to the Deuteronomic worldview, this entails the annihilation of the seven nations of Canaan (the commandment of *ḥerem*).[2] Other biblical texts demand that the Canaanites be expelled from the land but not necessarily killed. Their cultic places and objects, though, have to be utterly destroyed.[3]

Now, according to the biblical narrative, in contrast with the Egyptians and the Amalekites, who inflicted great suffering upon Israel, the Canaanites who lived in the land at the time of the conquest had not done any harm to the Hebrews. Therefore, their expulsion or destruction is especially shocking.[4]

---

1. The special challenge that the Canaanites present to Israel, as the nearest Other, has been aptly analyzed by Robert L. Cohn in "Before Israel: The Canaanites as Other in Biblical Tradition," in *The Other in Jewish Thought and History: Constructions of Jewish Culture and Identity*, ed. L. J. Silberstein and R. L. Cohn (New York: New York University Press, 1994), 74-90. But he does not deal with nonbiblical texts.

2. See Deut. 7:2; 20:17.

3. See, for instance, Exod. 23:23-33; Num. 33:51-53.

4. In Joshua, a book that is heavily influenced by the Deuteronomic perspective, the Canaanites are to be banned; see Josh. 6:21, 8:26, 10:28, etc.

49

What is the reason for their punishment, in what way(s) did they become guilty? The main answer in the biblical texts consists in underlining Canaanite idolatry and emphasizing that it implies all kinds of moral and religious "abominations" (תועבות). The expulsion or destruction of the inhabitants of Canaan is thus justified by their sinful behavior (it is a just, divinely ordained punishment) and by Yahweh's desire to keep Israel, his chosen people, from imitating them.

Whereas most biblical texts focus on the abominations or idolatrous practices of Canaanites who lived at the time of the conquest or later on (since many of them ultimately remained in the land), the book of Genesis contains a story that implicitly connects the fate of the Canaanites with that of their ancestor, Canaan himself, the son of Ham and grandson of Noah. However, the story of the curse of Canaan in Gen. 9:21-27 is altogether strange. Canaan is cursed by Noah even though it was Ham, not Canaan, who did something wrong to his father.[5] The idea that sons are punished on account of the sins committed by their fathers is found in other biblical texts as well, but is ultimately difficult to defend from an ethical point of view. The difficulty is acknowledged in the Hebrew Bible itself, for instance in Ezek. 18:14-20, which states that every person will have to account for his own deeds. Moreover, if the intention of the writer of Genesis 9 was to establish a connection between the fate of the ancestor and that of his descendants — that is, to explain the dispossession and destruction of the Canaanites by appeal to the original curse of Canaan — he apparently failed to make his point clear. Indeed, the texts in the Torah and in the book of Joshua that pertain to the fate of the Canaanites do not even mention slavery.[6]

Moreover, there is no link between the curse pronounced in Genesis 9 and the following story in Genesis 10, the so-called Table of Nations, which enumerates the peoples which descended from Japheth, Ham and Shem, and describes the territories in which their descendants settled. In Genesis 10, Canaan and his descendants settle in a country that is subsequently called by

---

5. On the nature of Ham's deed according to traditional Jewish interpretations, see *Genesis Rabbah* 36.7; b. *Sanhedrin* 70a; L. Ginzberg, *The Legends of the Jews* (Philadelphia: The Jewish Publication Society of America, 1909), 168-69; D. M. Goldenberg, *The Curse of Ham: Race and Slavery in Early Judaism, Christianity and Islam* (Princeton: Princeton University Press, 2003), 157-67; idem, "What Did Ham Do to Noah?" in *"The Words of a Wise Man's Mouth Are Gracious" (Qoh 10,12): Festschrift für Günter Stemberger on the Occasion of His 65th Birthday*, ed. M. Perani (Berlin: de Gruyter, 2005), 257-65.

6. Except in the case of the Gibeonites (Joshua 9), but only because they successfully deceived the children of Israel.

the same name (implying, apparently at least, that their settlement is legitimate). No allusion whatsoever is made to a political or economic dependency of Canaan upon his brothers or cousins. In the following chapters, again, one can find no hint of the lower status of the Canaanites. One explanation, of course, could be that the result of the curse — slavery — was supposed to take place only when the children of Israel had entered the land to settle in it as a people after receiving the Torah at Sinai. But then, why does no text from Exodus to Deuteronomy call for reducing the Canaanites to slavery? On the contrary, these texts specify that they are forbidden to stay in the country, and must be either expelled or killed. Thus, we are left with inner contradictions between the different biblical texts.[7]

The lack of connection between the story of the curse in Genesis 9 and the distribution of the lands among the children and grandchildren of Noah in Genesis 10, is reflected in modern research as well. Biblical commentaries obviously follow the order of the chapters in Genesis,[8] but they rarely connect their analysis of chapter ten with that of chapter nine. Moreover, articles and books that focus on the curse of Canaan (or Ham)[9] hardly attend to the division of the territories among the children of Noah, and vice-versa.[10]

What about ancient Jewish exegesis? In this article, I wish to analyze several ancient Jewish interpretations of the curse of Canaan, in order to

---

7. As correctly noticed by C. Westermann (*Genesis 1–11: A Continental Commentary*, trans. J. J. Scullion [Minneapolis: Fortress Press, 1994], 493), who writes concerning Gen. 9:26: "No promise was ever made to Israel that Canaan would be its slave. The promise was that it would drive out or destroy the Canaanites but not that it would exercise dominion over them."

8. See, for instance, E. A. Speiser, *Genesis: Introduction, Translation and Notes* (AB; New York: Doubleday, 1964), 60-73; Westermann, *Genesis 1–11*, 481-530; G. J. Wenham, *Genesis 1–15* (WBC 1; Waco: Word Books, 1987), 197-232; J. A. Soggin, *Genesi 1–11* (Genova: Marietti, 1991), 154-70.

9. See Goldenberg, *The Curse of Ham*; idem, "The Curse of Ham: A Case of Rabbinic Racism?" in *Struggles in the Promised Land: Toward a History of Black-Jewish Relations in the United States*, ed. J. Salzman and C. West (New York: Oxford University Press, 1997), 21-51.

10. See for instance E. Isaac, "Genesis, Judaism, and the 'Sons of Ham,'" *Slavery and Abolition: A Journal of Comparative Studies* 1/1 (1980): 3-17; S. Bakchine Dumont, "Le mythe chamitique dans les sources rabbiniques du Proche-Orient, du début de l'ère chrétienne au XIIIe siècle," *Rassegna Mensile di Israel* 55/1 (1989): 43-71; D. H. Aaron, "Early Rabbinic Exegesis on Noah's Son Ham and the So-Called 'Hamitic Myth,'" *JAAR* 63/4 (1995): 721-59. The articles and books that discuss the existence of a connection between the curse and the Jewish perception of black people generally refer to the geographical localization of the sons of Ham (since, according to Genesis 10, most of Ham's descendants settled in Africa), but only in passing.

clarify two points: (1) the implications of this story for the perception of the Canaanites by ancient Jewish commentators; (2) the possible connections between the story of the curse, the Table of the Nations, and the subsequent fate of the Canaanites during the conquest of the land by the children of Israel. I am pleased to offer this essay in honor of John Collins, a great scholar and friend, in gratitude.

I. Ancient Jewish Interpretations of the Story of the Curse

All the texts referred to in this section have been referred to or analyzed in previous studies,[11] so I shall content myself with a brief overview of the relevant passages.

4Q252

The fragmentary Qumran text entitled *Commentary on Genesis A* (4Q252) seems to have consisted of a brief and selective commentary of chaps. 6 to 49 of Genesis. One preserved section of text (col. II, frgs. 1 and 3) refers to the episode of the curse of Canaan.[12] But this passage is very brief, even shorter than the biblical text itself. Between two blanks, one reads (lines 5-8): "*And Noah awoke from his wine and knew what* ₆*his youngest son had done to him. And he said, 'Cursed be Canaan! A slave of slaves will he be to his brothers'* (Gen. 9:24-25). *But he did not* ₇*curse Ham, but his son, because God blessed the sons of Noah* (Gen. 9:1) *and in the tents of Shem may He dwell* (Gen. 9:27ab); ₈*a land He gave to Abraham his friend* (2 Chron. 20:7)."[13] From line 8 onwards the text moves on to the story of Abraham.

As the italics show, the author adds little to the biblical verses he quotes. But even in such an extremely brief summary of the episode of the

---

[11]. For mere references, see for example Goldenberg, *The Curse of Ham*, 157-58. See also the footnotes in Louis Feldman's translation of and commentary on Josephus, *Jewish Antiquities 1–4* (Leiden: Brill, 2000), 50-51. For analyses of a particular text, see references in the footnotes below.

[12]. For the sake of completeness, one should add that 4Q254 frag. 1 also refers to the curse of Canaan. But the context is lost and it is impossible to know how Genesis 9:21-27 was interpreted in this text.

[13]. Translation by G. J. Brooke, *Qumran Cave 4. XVII: Parabiblical Texts, Part 3* (DJD 22; Oxford: Clarendon Press, 1996), 199.

curse, he succeeds in tackling the main exegetical problem, namely, why Canaan was cursed instead of Ham. According to 4Q252, Noah could not curse any of his sons because they had previously been blessed by God, as indicated in Gen. 9:1. The curse then had to fall on the succeeding generation, and it fell on Canaan. The only point that remains unclear in the text is why the author quotes Gen. 9:27ab as well. George J. Brooke correctly understands the third masculine singular (ישכנון) as referring to God, and not to Japheth.[14] But the blessing or the promise that God will dwell in the tents of Shem hardly explains why Noah did not curse Ham. It makes more sense to connect the words *"and in the tents of Shem may He dwell"* with the following sentence in line 8, "a land He gave to[15] Abraham his friend." This is all the more so since these words are then followed by a *vacat*, indicating that they are still part of the passage dealing with the curse of Canaan.[16] The next "paragraph" starts with Abraham's departure from Ur, before God promises to give the land to Abraham and his descendants (Gen. 12:7; 13:15-17; 15:7, 18-21, etc.); thus, it is not the continuation of the phrase "a land He gave to Abraham his friend."

---

14. See also *Jub.* 7:12.

15. The italics have to be modified, because 2 Chron. 20:7 is very different altogether:

הֲלֹא אַתָּה אֱלֹהֵינוּ הוֹרַשְׁתָּ אֶת־יֹשְׁבֵי הָאָרֶץ הַזֹּאת מִלִּפְנֵי עַמְּךָ יִשְׂרָאֵל וַתִּתְּנָהּ לְזֶרַע אַבְרָהָם אֹהַבְךָ לְעוֹלָם.

What we find in 4Q252 looks like a free use of verses such as Gen. 28:4 or 35:12 (God gives the land to Abraham) and 2 Chron. 20:7 (Abraham is the beloved of God, and the land is given to his descendants). As a consequence, J. L. Trafton does not put these words in italics (or bold) at all in *The Dead Sea Scrolls: Hebrew, Aramaic, and Greek Texts with English Translations*, Volume 6B: *Pesharim, Other Commentaries, and Related Documents*, ed. J. H. Charlesworth et al. (Tübingen: Mohr-Siebeck, 2002), 213.

16. G. J. Brooke rightly connects the two sentences, but I do not understand why the author should have used a source here; moreover, the comparison drawn with CD 2:15–3:2 is both illuminating and slightly misleading, since in CD the issue is not to whom the land belongs, nor where God dwells ("The Thematic Content of 4Q252," *JQR* 85/1-2 [1994]: 33-59, see 41-44; see also idem, "The Genre of 4Q252: From Poetry to Pesher," *DSD* 1 [1994]: 160-79, esp. 167-68). M. Bernstein makes the link clearer by speaking of a lemma and a commentary ("4Q242: From Re-Written Bible to Biblical Commentary," *JJS* 45/1 [1994]: 1-27, esp. 11; idem, "4Q252: Method and Context, Genre and Sources," *JQR* 85/1-2 [1994]: 61-79, esp. 66-68 and 78, where he aptly writes: "The quotation should still be explained as an asyndetic relative clause ('the land which he gave . . .') which defines אהלי שם. The function of the 'poetic' citation is also 'exegetical' "). The connection is missed by A. Caquot, in his translation published in "Suppléments qumrâniens à la Genèse," *RHPR* 80/3 (2000): 339-58 (see 354). But it is noticed by K. Trehuedic in *La Bibliothèque de Qumrân*, Volume 1: *Torah — Genèse*, ed. K. Berthelot, T. Legrand, and A. Paul (Paris: Cerf, 2008), 305.

The link between the end of line 7 and the beginning of line 8 shows that, although the Table of Nations is not referred to in 4Q252, the words *"and in the tents of Shem may He dwell"* nevertheless have territorial implications. The conclusion seems to be that "the tents of Shem," where God will dwell, include or correspond to the land that will later be given to Abraham.[17] If this way of reading the text is correct, it means that the land of Canaan was supposed to be in the lot of Shem, not in that of Ham, an idea also found in the *Genesis Apocryphon* and *Jubilees*.[18] However, in 4Q252 no explicit allusion is made to the future fate of the Canaanites. Moreover, according to the biblical narrative, the gift of the land to Abraham does not prevent him from living rather peacefully alongside the Canaanites. In any case, in what remains of the *Commentary on Genesis A*, there is no explicit link between the curse of Canaan, the partition of territories for the descendants of Noah, and the future fate of the Canaanites. However, the link between Gen. 9:27ab and the gift of the land to Abraham is striking.

Philo

The main passages pertaining to the curse of Canaan in Philo's works are *Quaestiones in Genesim* 2.65, 70, 77[19] and *De sobrietate* 30-69. In the *Quaestiones*, Philo first tries to answer the question: "Why does (Scripture) in mentioning the sons of the righteous men, Shem, Ham and Japheth, tell of the genealogy of the middle one only, saying 'Ham was the father of Canaan,' and after this add, 'these (were) the three sons of Noah' (Gen. 9:18-19)?" He answers,

> ... it may be that (Scripture) foretells to those who are able to see from afar what is distant with the sharp-sighted eyes of the mind that He will take away the land of the Canaanites after many generations and give it to the chosen and god-beloved race. And so (Scripture) wishes to show that Canaan, the ruler and inhabitant of that country, practised peculiar

---

17. As noticed by Brooke, "The Thematic Content of 4Q252," 44; and Bernstein, "4Q242: From Re-Written Bible," 11-12; idem, "4Q252: Method and Context," 78. However, they do not elaborate on the implications of this conclusion, as far as the author's understanding of the distribution of territories among Noah's children is concerned.

18. On *Jubilees*, see part II below. On the *Genesis Apocryphon*, see notes 28 and 40.

19. Although §§75-76 deal with the interpretation of Gen. 9:26-27, they do not tackle the issue of the curse.

evils of his own, as well as those of his father, so that from both sides his ignobility and low-born alienness are shown. (trans. R. Marcus, LCL)

For Philo, the apparently odd reference to Canaan in the middle of a passage about the three sons of Noah is to be explained as a kind of anticipation, indicating the connection between the story of the curse and the unhappy fate of the Canaanites who lived at the time of the conquest. On the other hand, for Philo Canaan was similar to his father, so that the two are in fact one. However, Canaan performed vicious deeds of his own, not only those of his father. In 2.70, concerning Gen. 9:22, which again presents Ham as the father of Canaan, Philo repeats that, on a literal level, the biblical text "convicts both the son through the father and the father through the son, for in common and as one they have committed an act of folly, wickedness and impiety and other evils." Finally, in 2.77, when the question is asked: "Why, when Ham sins, does (Scripture) present his son Canaan as the servant of Shem and Japheth?" Philo again answers that the father and the son were equally perverse. Moreover, the father (Ham) "was to be greatly saddened by the cursing of his son, knowing that it was not so much for his own sake as for his father's that he was punished, for the punishment (fell) on the prime mover and teacher of evil thoughts, words and deeds." The argument is slightly different here and puts less emphasis on the identity of the father and the son, but, as we shall see, the underlying reasoning is that Ham represents thought and Canaan action. However, all the explanations mentioned so far pertain for Philo to the literal level of the text.

In spite of the readings mentioned above, Philo was aware that the biblical text hardly referred to any evil deeds committed by Canaan himself. In *De Sobrietate* 31, Philo correctly observes that "the person cursed is not the apparent sinner, Noah's son, but that son's son, Noah's grandson, though up to this point no clear wrongdoing great or small on his part has been indicated by Moses."[20] The explanation offered by Philo to solve this exegetical problem involves an allegorical interpretation. Ham symbolizes evil in a state of quietness, whereas Canaan represents evil in movement or action.[21] Only evil acts can be punished, not thoughts, and therefore Canaan is cursed, not his father (see also *Sobrietate* 48). However, "virtuously does he curse his son Ham in cursing Canaan, since when Ham has been moved to

---

20. Trans. F. H. Colson and G. H. Whitaker, LCL.
21. *Sobr.* 44: ὁ μὲν υἱὸς τοῦ Νῶε Χὰμ ἠρεμούσης κακίας ἐστὶν ὄνομα, ὁ δὲ υἱωνὸς ἤδη καὶ κινουμένης.

sin, he himself becomes Canaan, for it is a single subject, wickedness, which is presented in two different aspects, rest and motion." Philo's allegorical interpretation here is therefore very congruent with one of the literal readings presented in the *Quaestiones*. Finally, it should be noted that, when Philo comes back to the interpretation of Gen. 9:25-27 (*Sobrietate* 51-68), he hardly explains the meaning of the curse but focuses instead on Shem and Japheth. Only the last paragraph pertains to Canaan, interpreted as the "fool" (ἄφρων):

> It is with good reason that Moses writes down the fool as the slave of them who lay claim to virtue, either that promoted to serve under a higher control he may lead a better life, or that, if he cling to his iniquity, his masters may chastise him at their pleasure with the absolute authority which they wield as rulers.

In short, Philo is aware that the biblical text mentions no evil deed performed by Canaan himself, but explains the unnecessary precision in the statement "Ham (was) the father of Canaan" in Gen. 9:18 and 22 as an indication that Ham and Canaan were identical and equal in wickedness. The curse of Canaan was therefore justified. Moreover, the reference to Canaan in Gen. 9:18 is also an allusion to the future fate of the Canaanites at the time of the conquest, so that an explicit connection is made between the episode of the curse and the biblical texts pertaining to the conquest. But the Table of the Nations is not referred to in this context.

Wisdom of Solomon

The author of the Wisdom of Solomon only randomly refers to the curse of Canaan. As I have shown elsewhere,[22] his condemnation of the Canaanites is influenced by the argumentation of Deuteronomy, a book that presents the Canaanites as so abominable and inhuman that they even sacrifice their children to their idols (Deut. 12:31). The author of the Wisdom of Solomon depicts the Canaanites as worshippers of Dionysos, which explains why he accuses them of cannibalism, a crime unheard of in the biblical texts de-

---

22. K. Berthelot, "'Ils jettent au feu leurs fils et leurs filles pour leurs dieux': une justification humaniste du massacre des Cananéens dans les textes juifs anciens?" *Revue Biblique* 112/2 (2005): 161-91 (see 174-82).

scribing the abominations of the Canaanites. His main point is that they were dispossessed and eradicated because of their monstrous behavior, so that their fate demonstrates God's justice rather than undermines it.

After having affirmed that the children of Israel destroyed the Canaanites by the will of God (12:6), the author adds, apparently with Exod. 23:28-30 or Deut. 7:20-22 in mind:

> Yet these too you spared as being men, and sent wasps as the advance guard of your army to exterminate them gradually. 9It was not through inability to subject the godless to the righteous in pitched battle, or with cruel beasts or a relentless word to wipe them out at once, 10but judging them gradually you gave them space for repentance, not unaware that their seed was evil, and their viciousness innate, and that their mode of thought would in no way vary to the end of time (κρίνων δὲ κατὰ βραχὺ ἐδίδους τόπον μετανοίας οὐκ ἀγνοῶν ὅτι πονηρὰ ἡ γένεσις αὐτῶν καὶ ἔμφυτος ἡ κακία αὐτῶν καὶ ὅτι οὐ μὴ ἀλλαγῇ ὁ λογισμὸς αὐτῶν εἰς τὸν αἰῶνα), 11for their race was accursed from the very first (σπέρμα γὰρ ἦν κατηραμένον ἀπ' ἀρχῆς).[23]

This seems to contradict the book's leitmotif that sinners are capable of repentance *(metanoia)* and therefore responsible for their own fate if they refuse to follow the path that leads to eternal life after death. In chapter 12, the original curse pronounced by Noah upon Canaan and his descendants seems to be understood as the very factor which made them unable to repent and turn to God.[24] As always when a deterministic way of thinking is adopted, the question thus arises: "If the Canaanites were cursed and made unable to repent, then how can they be considered morally responsible?" The author does not really answer this embarrassing question. In any case, in the Wisdom of Solomon the main factor explaining and justifying the destruction of the Canaanite populations lies in their wicked behavior, much more than in the curse of their ancestor, even if the latter may have contributed to the former. Perhaps it is because the Wisdom of Solomon does not

---

23. Translation by D. Winston, *The Wisdom of Solomon: A New Translation and Commentary* (AB 43; Garden City: Doubleday, 1984), 237. Concerning the "evil seed," he writes (p. 241): "A similar notion is found in *4 Ezra* 4:30: 'For a grain of evil seed was sown in the heart of Adam from the beginning.' In our text, however, it is applied only to the Canaanites."

24. That Wisdom 12:11 refers to Genesis 9 can be taken for granted. See among others Winston, ibid., 241.

focus on Gen. 9:21-27 that the author does not explain why Canaan was cursed and not Ham. In any case, there is no connection whatsoever with the Table of Nations.

Josephus

In Josephus' *Jewish Antiquities*, both Genesis 9 and Genesis 10 are paraphrased to some extent. First, it must be underlined that in *Ant.* 1.120-147, the division of the different countries among the descendants of Noah does not seem problematic at all. In §120, Josephus writes, "From that time on they were scattered owing to their diverse languages and they established colonies everywhere, and each group occupied the land that they came upon and *to which God led them* (καὶ γῆν ἕκαστοι κατελάμβανον τὴν ἐντυχοῦσαν καὶ εἰς ἣν αὐτοὺς ἦγεν ὁ θεός), so that every continent, both the interior and the coast, was filled with them. . . ."[25] According to this sentence, there was nothing wrong with the distribution of the lands among them, and it was even led by God. In §134, similarly, one reads: "Chananaios, who was the fourth son of Chamas, after founding the land now called Judea, named it Chananaia after himself. . . ." Elsewhere (in §121-122, for instance), Josephus mentions that those who founded countries called them by their own names, but that the names were changed afterwards in some cases (mainly due to Greek influence!). So there is nothing anomalous about Canaan naming the land after himself. The fact that it was called Judea later on does not imply that it should not have been settled originally by the Canaanites. It is merely a neutral remark.

In §§138-142, when Josephus lists the sons born to Chananaios, he addresses the issue of the fate of the seven Canaanite nations that were eradicated by the children of Israel. In the context of this passage, he only mentions the destruction of their cities; but the destruction of the people is implied, since they are said to have disappeared:

> 139Of the seven others — Euaois, Chettaios, Iebousaios, Amorraios, Gergesaios, Seinaios, Samaraios — we have nothing in the sacred books except their names. For the Hebrews destroyed their cities, which came to misfortune for the following reason. 140After the Flood, when the

---

25. All translations from the *Antiquities* are taken from L. H. Feldman, *Jewish Antiquities 1–4* (LCL).

earth had been re-established to its former nature, Nochos applied himself to labor and planted vines upon it. When, the fruit having become ripe in due season, he harvested it and the wine was ready for use, he offered a sacrifice and feasted. 141Having gotten drunk, he fell asleep, and being naked he lay indecently. The youngest of his sons, having observed him, showed him mockingly to his brothers, but they covered their father. 142And Nochos, realizing this, invoked a blessing for his other sons, but he did not curse Chamas because of his kinship to him, but rather his descendants. And whereas the others escaped the curse, God pursued the children of Chananaios. And with regard to these matters we shall speak in what follows.[26]

Josephus provides here a new reason for Noah's not cursing Ham: not the divine blessing mentioned in Gen. 9:1 but the close family ties between Noah and his son. However, he does not provide any explanation for why Ham's descendants were cursed, but only Canaan's. Moreover, considering, as Josephus does, that the consequence of the curse was the eradication of the Canaanites living at the time of the conquest, he should have explained why only seven peoples among Canaan's descendants were stricken, whereas the others, mentioned in §138, remained safe. The discrepancy between the consequence of the curse in Gen. 9:25-27 (slavery) and the fate of the Canaanites according to other biblical books is not accounted for either. Although Josephus explicitly connects Genesis 9 with the biblical texts that tell about the fate of the Canaanites at the time of the conquest, he does not provide a satisfactory solution to the numerous problems this connection raises.

Genesis Rabbah

There are many rabbinic texts that comment on Gen. 9:21-27 or refer to it in passing, but they are rather late. Here I shall analyze only the oldest rabbinic commentary on Genesis, namely *Genesis Rabbah*. First, I wish to draw attention to one passage that is generally left aside, since it appears in a comment on the story of Joseph. In connection with Gen. 37:27, "Come, and let us sell him to the Ishmaelites," the midrash adds: "Let us follow the ancient paths, said he (Judah). *When Canaan sinned,* was he not cursed to be a slave? So he [Joseph] too, 'Come and let us sell him (to the Ishmaelites).' And his breth-

26. Ibid., 50-51.

ren hearkened unto him" (84.17).²⁷ This text makes clear that the midrash took for granted that Canaan had sinned. He was not cursed only because his father had sinned, but he had sinned himself. Here Philo and *Genesis Rabbah* agree with one another. Of course, it could also be that the author unconsciously confused Ham and Canaan, as happens in commentaries even today.²⁸

The next relevant passage is *Gen. Rab.* 36.2, which, in connection with Gen. 9:18 ("Ham was the father of Canaan"), calls Canaan somewhat abruptly "the father of degradation" (אבוי דפחתה). Maybe the midrash associates the name Canaan (כנען) and the root כנע, which in the *hiphil* means "humble," "subdue," or "oppress." In any case, Gen. 9:24 says that Noah woke up from his wine and "knew what his youngest son *had done* to him" (וַיֵּדַע אֵת אֲשֶׁר עָשָׂה לוֹ בְּנוֹ הַקָּטָן); the word "degradation" (פחתה) here refers to what Ham "did" to his father.²⁹ In this case the midrash may again be compared to what Philo writes about Ham being the idea and Canaan the implementation of the idea, since *Genesis Rabbah* equates Canaan with the deed itself or its result.

In *Gen. Rab.* 36.7, concerning Gen. 9:25 ("Cursed be Canaan . . ."), the midrash asks the fundamental question: "Ham sinned and Canaan is cursed?" According to R. Judah, the reason was, as in 4Q252, that God had already blessed the sons of Noah so that Ham could not be cursed. But R. Nehemiah suggests that "(it was) Canaan (who) saw (Noah's nakedness) and informed them; therefore the curse is attached to the one who did wrong." Here, as in the passage mentioned above in connection with Joseph (84.17), Canaan himself is considered the sinner and is therefore rightly punished. In the same passage, other explanations are provided which try to clarify what Ham "did" to Noah and to establish a connection with Ham's youngest son. According to these explanations, Ham was guilty, but since, for instance, he prevented his father from having a young son who would

---

27. Ed. Theodor-Albeck, 1022. Translation by H. Freedman, *Midrash Rabbah* (London: Soncino, 1961), 2:783.

28. See for instance E. Eshel, "The *Imago Mundi* of the *Genesis Apocryphon*," in *Heavenly Tablets: Interpretation, Identity and Tradition in Ancient Judaism*, ed. L. LiDonnici and A. Lieber (Leiden: Brill, 2007), 129, who writes: "This serves as another explanation for why Canaan was cursed, in addition to his having seen Noah inebriated and naked." Actually it is Ham who saw Noah, not Canaan.

29. Castration is probably implied (note that the word פחתין means "testicles"; see M. Jastrow, *A Dictionary of the Targumim, the Talmud Babli and Yerushalmi, and the Midrashic Literature* [New York: Pardes, 1950], 1154); on this interpretation, see below.

have served him,[30] it was Ham's youngest son who was cursed and doomed to serve his brothers. What the ancient commentator tries to do is to apply the principle "measure for measure," even if somewhat clumsily. In any case, according to these explanations, Canaan suffered the consequences of his father's sin without necessarily being guilty himself.

So far, no connection is established between the curse of Canaan and the future fate of the Canaanites, nor with the Table of Nations. But another passage throws some interesting light on this issue. While commenting upon Gen. 25:6 (which states that Abraham's inheritance was given to Isaac alone), the midrash tells the following story: once, Alexander the Great was asked by the children of Ishmael, the Canaanites, and the Egyptians to perform the task of a judge between them and the children of Israel. The Canaanites came to him and said:

> We base our suit against them on their (own) Torah. It is everywhere written, "The land of Canaan"; so let them return our land. Said he (Gebiah ben Kosem) to him (Alexander): Your majesty! Cannot a man do as he pleases with his slave? Yes, he replied. Then surely it is written, "A slave of slaves he shall be unto his brethren" (Gen. 9:25). (Hence) they are now our slaves.[31] Thereupon they fled and were dismissed in shame (61.7).[32]

According to this text, the fact that the Canaanites were expelled from their country is a consequence of the curse of Canaan, but the text has a distinct legal flavor that takes the nature of the curse into consideration. It is because the Canaanites are enslaved to the children of Israel that the latter can use the property of the former as they wish and are considered the true owners of the land, legally speaking. However, this story does not deny that the land originally belonged to the Canaanites. The whole point is that the properties of slaves belong to their master, who can do as he pleases with them.[33]

---

30. The idea that Ham castrated his father, which is only implicit here, appears explicitly in *b. Sanhedrin* 70a.

31. Some manuscripts, including Vaticanus 30, add the words (with slight variants): "Behold, the land is ours and they are slaves to your majesty."

32. Ed. Theodor-Albeck, 667; trans. H. Freedman, *Midrash Rabbah*, 2:546 (very slightly modified). See also *b. Sanhedrin* 91a. Some manuscripts, including Vaticanus 30, read instead, "they disappeared from there."

33. Note that here the debate takes place on a wholly legal level, not at all on a moral or religious one (in opposition to the *Wisdom of Solomon*, for instance).

Interestingly enough, elsewhere in *Genesis Rabbah* a different perspective rises to the surface. According to *Gen. Rab.* 44.7 and 56.10, Shem is identified with Melchizedek and thus reigns in (Jeru)salem, in the land of Canaan, implying that the land originally belonged to Shem and to his descendants. Moreover, *Gen. Rab.* 26.3 states that the sanctuary was built on Shem's territory, implying once again that the land of Canaan (or at least Judea) was originally in the lot of Shem. Thus, the midrash does not present a coherent and unified picture of who the original owners of the land were. But one has to take into account the fact that in 61.7 the context is polemical. Gebiah ben Kosem mainly replies to the Canaanites by turning their own argument and reference to the Torah against themselves.[34] Thus, even this passage does not necessarily mean that the author or redactor of the midrash considered the land the original property of the Canaanites.

So far, although some texts do indeed link the fate of the Canaanites at the time of the conquest with the curse of Canaan in Gen. 9:25-27 (so Wisdom of Solomon, but only indirectly or secondarily; Philo; Josephus; *Gen. Rab.* 61.7), no connection is established with Genesis 10, except that Josephus does mention the future fate of the Canaanites in the context of his paraphrase of Genesis 10, apparently because he felt compelled to explain why these nations did not exist any more. There is, however, one other significant exception, to which we shall now turn.

II. The Story of the Curse and the Table of Nations in *Jubilees* 7–10

Strangely enough, most studies of the interpretive history of the story of the curse of Canaan fail to deal with *Jubilees* 7–10. The reason is probably that *Jubilees*' retelling of Gen. 9:21-27 in *Jub.* 7:7-12 is very close to the biblical text, whereas the author so freely adds to the biblical account of 10:15-20 that the motif of the curse undergoes great transformations, thus making the connection with Gen. 9:21-27 less obvious.

As rightly noticed by James VanderKam, whereas the biblical account does not connect explicitly the episodes of Gen. 9:21-27 and Genesis 10, *Jubilees* 7 already contains elements that lead to the addition in *Jub.* 10:28-34.[35]

---

34. The full complexity of the picture in *Genesis Rabbah* cannot be presented here. I hope to come back to this issue in a separate article.

35. See J. VanderKam, "Putting Them in Their Place: Geography as an Evaluative

After having told the story of the curse, with a few modifications that mainly clarify the fact that it was Canaan who was cursed, and that he was supposed to serve Shem alone, not Shem and Japheth, the author of *Jubilees* adds that Ham was so displeased by the curse of his father upon his younger son that he separated from his father and his brothers and settled somewhere else with his sons, building a city and naming it after his wife (*Jub.* 7:13-14). Then Japheth imitates Ham, but Shem stays with Noah. As a consequence, a kind of geographical division already occurs, as *Jub.* 7:17 makes clear: "Now these three cities were near Mt. Lubar: Sedeqatelebab [Shem] in front of the mountain on its east side; Neelatamauk [Ham] toward its south side; and Adataneses [Japheth] toward the west."[36]

Then, in *Jubilees* 8–9, the Table of Nations is rewritten with interesting modifications, which have been analyzed elsewhere.[37] What concerns us here is the allotment to Canaan of a country in the western part of Africa,

---

Tool," in *Pursuing the Text: Studies in Honor of Ben Zion Wacholder*, ed. J. C. Reeves and J. Kampen (Sheffield: Sheffield Academic Press, 1994), 46-69 (reprinted in VanderKam, *From Revelation to Canon: Studies in the Hebrew Bible and Second Temple Literature* [Leiden: Brill, 2000], 476-99), in which he writes concerning the biblical text: "The boundaries of the Canaanites are given in a straightforward and generous manner; there seems to be no aftereffect from the curse in 9.25" (p. 53 [483]); and: "The curse which Canaan there receives [in Genesis 9] appears to be of no consequence in Genesis 10, but in *Jubilees*, though it is surprisingly phrased no more vociferously than in Genesis, it manifestly sets the stage for what is to follow" (p. 55 [485]).

36. All English translations are by J. VanderKam, *The Book of Jubilees* (CSCO 511; Louvain: Peeters, 1989), here 45.

37. See G. Hölscher, *Drei Erdkarten: Ein Beitrag zur Erdkenntnis des hebräischen Altertums* (Sitzungsberichte der Heidelberger Akademie der Wissenschaften, Philosophisch-historische Klasse, 1944/48, no. 3; Heidelberg: Carl Winter, Universitätsverlag, 1949), 57-73; P. S. Alexander, "Notes on the 'Imago Mundi' of the Book of Jubilees," *JJS* 33 (1982): 197-213; F. Schmidt, "Naissance d'une géographie juive," in *Moïse Géographe: Recherches sur les représentations juives et chrétiennes de l'espace*, ed. A. Desreumaux and F. Schmidt (Paris: J. Vrin, 1988), 13-30 (a slightly different version has been published in English under the title "Jewish Representations of the Inhabited Earth," in *Greece and Rome in Eretz Israel: Collected Essays*, ed. A. Kasher, U. Rappaport, and G. Fuks [Jerusalem: Yad Izhak Ben-Zvi and The Israel Exploration Society, 1990], 119-34); J. VanderKam, "Putting Them in Their Place"; J. M. Scott, "The Division of the Earth in *Jubilees* 8:11–9:15 and Early Christian Chronography," in *Studies in the Book of Jubilees*, ed. M. Albani, J. Frey, and A. Lange (Tübingen: Mohr-Siebeck, 1997), 295-323; J. M. Scott, *Geography in Early Judaism and Christianity: The Book of Jubilees* (Cambridge: Cambridge University Press, 2002), 23-43; J. T. A. G. M. Van Ruiten, *Primaeval History Interpreted: The Rewriting of Genesis 1–11 in the Book of Jubilees* (Leiden: Brill, 2000), 307-63; E. Eshel, "The *Imago Mundi* of the *Genesis Apocryphon*"; C. Werman, "*Jubilees* in the Hellenistic Context," in *Heavenly Tablets*, 133-58 (esp. 136-41).

which runs contrary to the plain, literal meaning of the biblical narrative (*Jub.* 9:1). Moreover, at the end of chapter 9, the author of *Jubilees* specifies that Noah made his sons "swear by oath to curse each and every one who wanted to occupy the share which did not emerge by his lot. All of them said: 'So be it'! So be it for them and their children until eternity during their generations until the day of judgment . . ." (9:14-15).[38]

The stage having been skillfully set in chapters 7-9, the final *coup de théâtre* comes in chapter 10, when the reader is told that Canaan chose to settle in a country that belonged to the descendants of Shem:

> When Canaan saw that the land of Lebanon as far as the stream of Egypt was very beautiful, he did not go to his hereditary land to the west of the sea. He settled in the land of Lebanon, on the east and west, from the border of Lebanon and on the seacoast. His father Ham and his brothers Cush and Mizraim said to him: "You have settled in a land which was not yours and did not emerge for us by lot. Do not act this way, for if you do act this way both you and your children will fall in the land and be cursed with rebellion, because you have settled in rebellion and in rebellion your children will fall and be uprooted forever. Do not settle in Shem's residence because it emerged by their lot for Shem and his sons. You are cursed and will be cursed more than all of Noah's children through the curse by which we obligated ourselves with an oath before the holy judge and before our father Noah." But he did not listen to them. He settled in the land of Lebanon — from Hamath to the entrance of Egypt — he and his sons until the present. For this reason the land was named the land of Canaan. (*Jub.* 10:29-34)[39]

The text underlines that the transgression of the oath sworn by all the descendants of Noah brought upon Canaan and his descendants an everlasting curse, but it does not explain what the connection between this curse and the one mentioned in chapter 7 was. It is possible that the very fact of transgression, alone among all the descendants of Noah, is already a consequence of the first curse. That reasoning would be similar to the one found in the Wisdom of Solomon (a connection between the original curse and the Canaanites' depravity).

In any case, what this passage from *Jubilees* makes clear is twofold: first,

---

38. VanderKam, *The Book of Jubilees*, 58.
39. Ibid., 63-64.

the land of Israel was never meant to be called Canaan and to be occupied by Canaanites; second, the Canaanites purposely sinned by seizing a country that was not theirs and knew what penalty would ensue.[40] Of course, one could argue that the sin was committed by the ancestors of the Canaanites who, according to the biblical narrative,[41] suffered the loss of their country or their lives, and that the ethical problem of being punished for the sins of one's ancestors remains. However, the answer could be, as in the Wisdom of Solomon, that God granted the Canaanites time to repent, or, as in some midrashim, that God took into consideration some meritorious acts performed by the Canaanites (in particular, in connection with Abraham) and therefore granted them more time in the land.[42] Finally, one could argue that since the promise of the land was for Israel as a people, its fulfillment and the punishment of the Canaanites could occur only after Sinai.

Although the rewriting of Genesis 9–10 in *Jubilees* 7–10 does not solve all the problems raised by the biblical texts pertaining to the curse of Canaan and the fate of the Canaanites at the time of the conquest, it certainly represents the most audacious reworking of the biblical story thus far.[43] More-

---

40. In the *Genesis Apocryphon* (cols. XVI-XVII), one finds a version of the division of the earth between the sons of Noah that both resembles the one in *Jubilees* and differs from it (see in particular the recent article by E. Eshel, "The *Imago Mundi* of the *Genesis Apocryphon*"). According to the *Apocryphon*, the land of Canaan belongs to Shem, as in *Jubilees*. It is possible that the author of *Jubilees* used the *Genesis Apocryphon* as one of his sources. However, the story of the oath and the transgression of Canaan is not part of the *Genesis Apocryphon*, at least according to what is preserved of the text. True, col. XIV tells about a vision of Noah, in which two branches representing Ham and Japheth are said to encroach on the branch that represents Shem, and this has been interpreted as referring to the episode mentioned in *Jub.* 10:28-36. But if we did not know *Jubilees*, we would probably interpret the vision quite differently. Moreover, even if one agrees with this interpretation, there are still no traces left of the story of the oath and the curse, and no evidence that the author of the *Genesis Apocryphon* connected the episode of the division of the earth with Gen. 9:21-27.

41. The biblical narrative in the book of Joshua is actually more complex than just the story of the dispossession and the destruction of the natives. According to the biblical text itself, several groups do indeed remain alive and continue to live in the land alongside the children of Israel. But this is another issue that cannot be dealt with in depth here.

42. See, for instance, *Sifra* אחרי מות parasha 9 (on Lev. 18:3), which quotes Gen. 23:6 (ed. Weiss פה ג).

43. *Jubilees* is sometimes compared to *Sib. Or.* 3:110-128. But the latter is inspired by Hesiod, and its connection with Genesis is looser. Thus, the brothers start to fight with one another after their father's death, but they fight for political supremacy, not for a particular territory. Actually, the territorial or geographical dimension is nearly lost in the *Sibylline Or-*

over, it definitely eliminates the ambiguities of the biblical text concerning the identity of the legitimate owner of the land. Along the way, the picture of the Canaanites has been darkened a little bit more, and their original sin made worse. *Jubilees* very likely reflects tensions between the Judeans and other ethnic groups living in "Canaan" during the second century B.C.E. and debates over the legitimacy of Judean rule over the land.[44]

III. Conclusion

We have seen that in order to solve the difficulty of a son being cursed for the sin of his father, several early Jewish commentators on Genesis 9 argue that Canaan himself had sinned (*Jubilees*, Philo, and two passages in *Genesis Rabbah*). Moreover, several texts also connect the curse of Canaan in Genesis 9 with the fate of the Canaanites at the time of the conquest (*Jubilees*; Wisdom of Solomon, even if only indirectly or secondarily; Philo; Josephus; *Gen. Rab.* 61.7). Among these interpretations, *Jubilees* provides the most consistent explanation of this connection, by adding a second curse (which may be considered a consequence of the first one, although it is not explicitly stated) that envisions a transgression committed by Canaan himself, together with his sons. Moreover, because *Jubilees* establishes a further connection with Genesis 10 and because the nature of Canaan's transgression consists in settling in a land that did not originally belong to him, the Canaanites living at the time of the conquest are presented as committing the same sin as their ancestors, by their very presence in the land. The book of *Jubilees* thus provides a more coherent justification for the expulsion or the destruction of the Canaanites than do other Jewish texts from the Hellenistic and Roman periods that link the conquest and the fate of the Canaanites to the curse in Genesis 9.

---

acles, and there is no curse, probably due to the influence of the Greek model the author had in mind, which lacked these elements.

44. As already argued by Y. Lewy, "Ein Rechtsstreit um Boden Palästinas im Altertum," *MGWJ* 77 (1933): 84-99, 172-80. See also R. H. Charles, *The Book of Jubilees or the Little Genesis* (London: A. & C. Black, 1902), 68; and, more cautiously, VanderKam, "Putting Them in Their Place," 67 [497] and 69 [499].

Defining and Controlling Others Within: Hair, Identity, and the Nazirite Vow in a Second Temple Context

Susan Niditch

My paper in honor of our friend and colleague John Collins approaches the topic of the Other in the Second Temple period as it emerges in Numbers 6, the description of the Nazirite vow. This important Persian-period ritual text that prescribes the growing and cutting of hair is examined within a framework of ideas related to identity, the body, and religion. The Otherness explored deals with priestly status, holiness, and gender — an internal Otherness within the Jewish community rather than ways of defining those outside it.

Over the last decade, there has been an explosion of scholarly interest in the relationship between culture and the body. Particularly influential have been Foucault's and Bourdieu's studies of the complex ways in which culture is "inscribed" on the body.[1] Scholars of religion, including Howard

---

1. Michel Foucault, *The History of Sexuality*, Volume I: *An Introduction*, trans. Robert Hurley (New York: Vintage Press, 1980); Pierre Bourdieu, *Distinction: A Social Critique of the Judgement of Taste*, trans. R. Nice (Cambridge: Harvard University Press, 1984); see also Susan Bordo, *Unbearable Weight: Feminism, Western Culture and the Body* (Berkeley: University of California Press, 1993); Caroline Bynum, *Holy Feast and Holy Fast: The Religious Significance of Food to Medieval Women* (Berkeley: University of California Press, 1987); Elizabeth Grosz, *Volatile Bodies: Toward A Corporeal Feminism* (Bloomington: Indiana University, 1994); Moira Gatens, *Imaginary Bodies: Ethics, Power, and Corporeality* (New York: Routledge, 1996).

A fuller treatment of portions of this essay is available in Susan Niditch, *"My Brother Esau Is a Hairy Man": Hair and Identity in Ancient Israel* (Oxford/New York: Oxford University Press, 2008).

Eilberg-Schwartz, Wendy Doniger, Jon Berquist, and others, have produced a wide range of studies focusing on the body within various traditions.[2] A subset of these studies on the body focuses on hair and identity from a variety of perspectives, including anthropology, sociology, psychology, women's studies, history of art, and history of religion. In our own area are works by Irene Winter,[3] Cynthia Chapman,[4] Megan Cifarelli,[5] Saul Olyan,[6] Greg Mobley,[7] and myself[8] which deal with hair, self-perception, and self-projection in ancient Near Eastern cultures.

The Second Temple period has also seen in recent years a flowering of research and writing. Some, such as Jacob Wright, have grappled anew with complex redactional issues in important sources such as Nehemiah.[9] Others, such as Oded Lipschits,[10] have returned to basics asking what we can know about the boundaries, demographics, ethnography, and economy of ancient Yehud and environs in the light of archaeology, biblical and extrabiblical texts. Lipschits's and Oeming's edited work provides an array of thoughtful

---

2. Howard Eilberg-Schwartz, ed., *People of the Body: Jews and Judaism from an Embodied Perspective* (Albany: SUNY Press, 1992); Howard Eilberg-Schwartz and Wendy Doniger, eds., *Off with Her Head: The Denial of Women's Identity in Myth, Religion, and Culture* (Berkeley: University of California Press, 1995); Jon L. Berquist, *Controlling Corporeality: The Body and the Household in Ancient Israel* (New Brunswick, N.J.: Rutgers University Press, 2002); Sarah Coakley, ed., *Religion and the Body* (Cambridge: Cambridge University Press, 1997); Jane Marie Law, ed., *Religious Reflections on the Human Body* (Bloomington: Indiana University Press, 1995); Linda B. Arthur, ed., *Religion, Dress and the Body* (Oxford: Berg, 1999).

3. Irene J. Winter, "Royal Rhetoric and the Development of Historical Narrative in Neo-Assyrian Reliefs," *Visual Communication* 7/2 (1981): 2-38; "Art *in* Empire: The Royal Image and the Visual Dimensions of Assyrian Ideology," in *Assyria 1995*, Proceedings of the 10th Anniversary Symposium of the Neo-Assyrian Text Corpus Project, Helsinki, Sept. 7-11, 1995, ed. S. Parpola and R. M. Whiting (Winona Lake, Ind.: Eisenbrauns), 359-81.

4. Cynthia R. Chapman, *The Gendered Language of Warfare in the Israelite-Assyrian Encounter* (HSM 62; Winona Lake, Ind.: Eisenbrauns, 2004).

5. Megan Cifarelli, "Gesture and Alterity in the Art of Ashurnasirpal II of Assyria," *The Art Bulletin* 80 (1998): 210-28.

6. Saul Olyan, "What Do Shaving Rites Accomplish and What Do They Signal in Biblical Ritual Contexts?" *JBL* 117 (1998): 611-22.

7. Gregory Mobley, "The Wild Man in the Bible and the Ancient Near East," *JBL* 116 (1997): 217-33.

8. Niditch, *"My Brother Esau Is a Hairy Man."*

9. Jacob Wright, *Rebuilding Identity: The Nehemiah-Memoir and Its Earliest Readers* (Berlin: de Gruyter, 2004).

10. Oded Lipschits, *The Fall and Rise of Jerusalem: Judah under Babylonian Rule* (Winona Lake, Ind.: Eisenbrauns, 2005).

articles that explore worldviews in Persian-period Yehud from a host of interdisciplinary perspectives with interests in ethnicity, geography, economic and geopolitical issues.[11] Another set of readings edited by James Watts deals with questions related to the formation of the Pentateuch in a Persian setting.[12] Did Persian control extend to influence upon the collection, preservation, and form of the Pentateuch itself? Work continues as well concerning the identity of and tensions between various priestly groups, their self-perception and self-presentation in the Hebrew Bible and their actual political, sociohistorical identities. Lester L. Grabbe has attempted to summarize, synthesize, and choose among various positions on these issues in history of religion, biblical composition, and political history.[13] Jon L. Berquist has explored with insight Persian-period Jewish literature in the light of post-colonial studies.[14] One new piece by Leong Seow which will contribute to the present essay deals with the economy of the Persian period and its impact on Jews,[15] an area also explored by Gary Knoppers in connection with an analysis of Samarian-Judean relations.[16]

The analysis of Numbers 6 begins with comments on models and theoretical approaches that help to make sense of the ways in which the body serves to distinguish the self from the Other. The first model is provided by medical anthropologists Nancy Scheper-Hughes and Margaret Lock and applied to the study of hair by Barbara Miller.[17] Scheper-Hughes and Lock sug-

---

11. Oded Lipschits and Manfred Oeming, eds., *Judah and Judeans in the Persian Period* (Winona Lake, Ind.: Eisenbrauns, 2006).

12. James Watts, ed., *Persia and Torah: The Theory of Imperial Authorization of the Pentateuch* (Atlanta: Society of Biblical Literature, 2001).

13. Lester L. Grabbe, *Ezra-Nehemiah* (London/New York: Routledge 1998); idem, *Judaic Religion in the Second Temple Period* (London/New York: Routledge, 2000); idem, *A History of the Jews and Judaism in the Second Temple Period*, vol. 1, *Yehud: A History of the Persian Province of Judah* (London: T&T Clark, 2004).

14. Jon L. Berquist, *Judaism in Persia's Shadow: A Social Historical Approach* (Minneapolis: Fortress, 1995); idem, "Psalms, Post-Colonialism, and the Construction of the Self," in *Approaching Yehud: New Approaches to the Study of the Persian Period*, ed. Jon L. Berquist (Leiden: Brill, 2007), 195-202. See also Jean-Pierre Ruiz, "An Exile's Baggage: Toward a Postcolonial Reading of Ezekiel," in *Approaching Yehud*, 117-35.

15. Leong Seow, "The Social World of Ecclesiastes," in *Scribes, Sages, and Seers: The Sage in the Eastern Mediterranean World*, ed. Leo Perdue (Göttingen: Vandenhoeck & Ruprecht, 2008), 189-217.

16. Gary N. Knoppers, "Revisiting the Samarian Question in the Persian Period," in *Judah and the Judeans in the Persian Period*, ed. Oded Lipschits and Manfred Oeming (Winona Lake, Ind.: Eisenbrauns, 2006), 265-89.

17. Nancy Scheper-Hughes and Margaret Lock, "The Mindful Body: A Prolegomenon

gest exploring the meanings of "body" in terms of three interrelated categories. First is the "individual body," the "phenomenological sense of the lived experience of the body-self."[18] One might ask how a person's hair makes him or her feel, what hair means to people in their personal lives, how hair represents them or serves as an extension of self, a critical source of their own embodiment. In his study of long-haired holy women in Sri Lanka, Gananath Obeyesekere emphasizes the complex ways in which such personal issues intertwine with the public and the cultural. The holy woman's hair helps to define her within and over against others in her social world.[19] Thus a second category offered by Scheper-Hughes and Lock is "the social body."

Influenced by the work of anthropologist Mary Douglas, Scheper-Hughes and Lock explore the ways in which body serves as a natural symbol.[20] Like Bordo and Bourdieu, Douglas asks how the social and cultural is inscribed on the body. Similarly, Raymond Firth argues that hair allows humans to use "their own physical raw material in terms of the social norms to provide indices to their personality and make statements about their conception of their role, their social position and changes in these."[21] James Watson, for example, asks what the destitute young men in colonial Hong Kong of the 1960s were saying about their personal condition and social status by wearing long, unkempt hair. He asks about the "social management of hair" and explores how this modern phenomenon may relate to a lengthy Chinese tradition concerning the demeanor of ghosts, bandits, and rebels.[22] Hair thus can make oneself into the Other.

The third category offered by Scheper-Hughes and Lock is really a subset of the social body, "the body politic." "The body politic" interweaves with "the individual body" as well. This level of meaning, grounded in the work of Michel Foucault, deals with "the regulation, surveillance, and control of

---

to Future Work in Medical Anthropology," *Medical Anthropology Quarterly* 1 (1987): 6-41; Barbara D. Miller, "Afterword: Hair Power," in *Hair: Its Power and Meaning in Asian Cultures,* ed. Alf Hiltebeitel and Barbara D. Miller (Albany: SUNY Press, 1998), 281-86.

18. Scheper-Hughes and Lock, "The Mindful Body," 7.

19. Gananath Obeyesekere, *Medusa's Hair: An Essay on Personal Symbols and Religious Experience* (Chicago: University of Chicago Press, 1981), 7, 37, 40.

20. Mary Douglas, *Purity and Danger: An Analysis of Concepts of Pollution and Taboo* (New York: Praeger, 1966).

21. "Hair as Private Asset and Public Symbol," in *Symbols: Public and Private* (Ithaca, N.Y.: Cornell University Press, 1973), 298.

22. James L. Watson, "Living Ghosts: Long-Haired Destitutes in Colonial Hong Kong," in *Hair,* 179.

bodies."²³ Hair thus expresses and shapes specific messages about power or subversion of that power. As Mageo notes, an issue to consider is whether the hairstyle is worn voluntarily or not.²⁴ Influenced by the suggestion of C. R. Hallpike that "cutting hair equals social control,"²⁵ Weikun Cheng shows how enforced wearing of the queue in Qing China "reflected the Manchus' drive to submit Hans to the minority's political and cultural hegemonies and its symbolic standardization of the people's political ideology."²⁶ What sort of statement would have been made by the voluntary female Nazir who took it upon herself to follow the instructions outlined in Numbers 6 not to cut her hair for a specified period of time?

Another important model is provided by Victor Turner, who seeks to understand how the outsider might discover the meanings of symbols within cultures. Turner refers to three levels of examination, the "exegetical," the "operational," and the "positional."²⁷ At the exegetical level, one attempts to ascertain what people within the culture think about the symbol. Scholars such as Obeyesekere are able to interview living people about the relationship between their hair and their feelings of inclusion and Otherness. Lacking live informants, we have access to the traditional texts of the Hebrew Bible, which mention hair in a variety of ritual and narrative contexts, to an array of archaeological remains that provide evidence of material culture, and to the images of ancient Near Eastern art. All such sources must be handled with care, however. Issues of authorship, provenance, dating, and relevance come to the fore, as do knotty questions concerning the relationship of ancient Israelites and their varied cultures to the multi-voiced, many-layered, often ideologically oriented texts of the Hebrew Bible. The same caution applies to Turner's "operational level."

Turner suggests that we explore the operation of the symbol in specific contexts. What do ancient Israelites appear to do with hair in ritual settings such as those related to the assumption and completion of the Nazirite vow? Where, moreover, does the ritual description of Numbers 6 fit in the larger

23. *The History of Sexuality,* vol. 1, 7.

24. J. Mageo, "Hairdos and Don'ts: Hair Symbolism and Sexual History in Samoa," *Man* 29 (1994): 424.

25. C. R. Hallpike, "Social Hair," *Man* 4 (1969): 262.

26. Weikun Cheng, "Politics of the Queue: Agitation and Resistance in the Beginning and End of Qing China," in *Hair,* 128.

27. "Themes in the Symbolism of Ndembu Hunting Ritual," in *Myth and Cosmos: Readings in Mythology and Symbolism,* ed. John Middleton (Garden City, N.Y.: Natural History Press, 1967), 249-69.

context of symbolic content preserved in the Hebrew Bible and reflected in nonbiblical evidence from the wider ancient Near East? This brings us to Turner's "positional level."

As Olivelle puts the question, what is the symbolic grammar within which such practices are located?[28] Do these various symbols combine to make comments on age, gender, sacredness, and ethnicity, drawing lines between child and adult, male and female, holy and mundane, insider and outsider, us and them?

In addition to frameworks offered by Scheper-Hughes and Lock and Turner, is a third model, offered by Gananath Obeyesekere. In his study of the relationship between the private and the public in symbolic usage, Obeyesekere is particularly interested in the origins, development, and variations upon key defining symbols such as hair. For Obeyesekere, there is a feedback loop between deep-seated symbols of the unconscious, cultural context, personal experience, and the human being's creative capacity for inventiveness.[29] In approaching Numbers 6 we too need to think about universals and specific cultural contexts and to consider the intentions of individual composers who describe ritual actions involving hair.

Numbers 6 describes a vow undertaken by an individual to become a Nazirite for a specified period of time. My study is framed by a larger work in which I take the position that the Nazirism of Samson and Samuel reveals an important symbolic association between hair and manliness, warrior status, charisma, and divine selection.[30] A close reading of Numbers 6, with help from methodological perspectives described earlier, reveals a quite different version of Nazirism. Some of the heroic and charismatic symbolic resonances of the Nazir's long hair may still reside in the culture behind the phenomenon described in Numbers 6, motivating a person to assume a Nazirite vow, but the vow itself has been shaped by a particular priestly worldview that is highly concerned with issues of purity even while democratizing holy status itself. The constitution and significance of Otherness thus differ in the two cases of Nazirism. While the book of Numbers contains more ancient materials, its current form and the contours of much of its content are probably determined by postexilic priestly writers of the Persian period, who shaped the work in a time without Judean kings and during

---

28. Patrick Olivelle, "Hair and Society: Social Significance of Hair in South Asian Traditions," in *Hair*, 12.

29. *Medusa's Hair*, 9, 40.

30. "*My Brother Esau Is a Hairy Man*," 63-80.

subjugation by a foreign empire. They regarded the hereditary priesthood as the critical, stabilizing, and central remaining institution of leadership and guardian of the faith. They preserved ancient customs and ritual traditions while, in more utopian fashion, they reflected a vision of how the world should work. The worldview of such priests emerges in much of Numbers, and tracing the hair motif in context reinforces the suggestion of Martin Noth that "the Nazirite Law of Numbers is far removed from (the) old, original type of Naziriteship" exemplified by Samson and Samuel.[31] Long, uncut hair thus takes on particular connotations, while the vow involving hair reveals a different and later orientation than the one reflected in portrayals of biblical heroes. Victor Turner's exegetical, operational, and positional levels of analysis are especially helpful in understanding the particular worldview behind Numbers 6.

What does the "native informant," the biblical narrator, reveal about Nazirite status? What information is emphasized? In Numbers 6, it is significant that the would-be Nazirite may be a man or a woman. The vow to live as a Nazirite is assumed voluntarily. The verb describing the action of undertaking the vow is rooted in *pl'*, a term with miraculous or extraordinary nuances. NRSV translates "make a special vow" (cf. NRSV Lev. 27:2 "make an explicit vow"). BDB suggests "do a difficult thing" or "make a hard vow." The person thus takes upon himself or herself an extraordinary, unusual responsibility through the means of a vow to God and under God. A Nazirite vow undertaken by an adult is, moreover, a temporary condition, and one sets the time limits oneself.

The vow as described involves not cutting the hair and abstinence from wine and all grape products. The list of wine products is especially detailed, including grapes, raisins, seeds, and skin (the last two terms are difficult to translate). The Nazirite vow in Numbers 6 does not mention abstinence from unclean food. What is mentioned and emphasized is the avoidance of dead bodies, an important source of uncleanness. Two rites of passage are described. One involves actions undertaken when the person under a Nazirite vow encounters a dead body; the other involves ritual passage at the time of the completion of the vow.

At the operational level, we ask what the Nazir does. He or she grows hair, presumably so that it shows. Is the implication that the ordinary person who has not undertaken such a vow trims his or her hair regularly? The

---

31. Martin Noth, *Numbers: A Commentary*, trans. James D. Martin (OTL; London: SCM, 1968), 54. See also Morris Jastrow, Jr., "The 'Nazir' Legislation," *JBL* 44 (1914): 266-85.

question is especially pertinent for women, a matter to be discussed in its social, aesthetic, and literary contexts below. The operational question, difficult to answer, is how long is long? Would the avoidance of all grape products and the avoidance of funerary rituals, even those involving a father, mother, sister, or brother, be even more of a marker of a different or unusual status assumed by the person than the long hair?

At the level of what is done, we also explore more deeply the two ritual passages. In one, the vow is cut short because of contact with the dead. The hair of the Nazirite is cut off, as it is now contaminated (6:9). Purification and burnt offerings make atonement for this unexpected interruption of the holiness. A guilt or reparation offering is provided, and the person begins his or her vow days all over again.

At the normal completion of the promised time, he or she goes to the holy space, the tent of meeting, imagined here in a pre-temple setting. A burnt offering of an unblemished young male lamb, a purification offering of an unblemished young ewe-lamb, and a well-being offering of an unblemished ram, grain offerings, and drink offerings are presented. Then the head is shaved, and the hair of the Nazirite's head is placed on the fire under the offering of well-being. A portion of the food offering is placed in the palm of the Nazir, to be transferred finally to the priest. It is as if the holiness reverts to the institutionalized holy person. The full meaning of the symbolic complex that shapes Numbers 6 emerges in a positional or contextual analysis.

The positional analysis is based upon comparisons with images of Samson and Samuel, upon an important oracle of the prophet Amos, and upon the wider search for parallels and contrasts in language and content between Numbers 6 and other relevant passages. Also important is what can be reconstructed from biblical and extrabiblical evidence concerning the social context of Nazirism as imagined in Numbers 6.

Formulaic language concerning the razor not going upon the head (Num. 6:5) is shared with tales of Samson (Judg. 13:5; 16:17) and Samuel (1 Sam. 1:11). Perhaps most remarkable and surprising about Numbers 6, however, is that women as well as men can bear this "consecrated status" through their own choice. No divine charisma descends nor is a special quality implicit in being the child of a barren mother. This places Numbers 6 in strong contrast to tales of Samson and Samuel and to Amos's juxtaposition of the Nazir with the prophet, called by God. There is no hint of warrior status or political leadership. The term *pr'* is employed here as in Judg. 5:2 and Deut. 32:42, but rather than being linked to the male warrior's prowess, the long hair is linked to a temporary immersion into the sacred (Num. 6:12, 13). To be sure, holy warriors upon whom the divine spirit descends are also immersed in holiness, but in the case of a Samson or a Samuel this descent is not a matter of an optional ritual status assumed by the would-be holy person himself or herself. Its sudden, god-sent explosiveness is a kind of warrior's frenzy; in Number 6, matters are much more controlled. The Nazirite vow has the effect of domesticating, democratizing, or generalizing the possibility of Nazirite status. One need be able only to take the vow and thereby become a temporary Other in terms of holy or sacred status.

The vow is an interesting phenomenon in Israelite and later rabbinic culture. A person makes an oath to the deity to do something, often promising to make a sacrifice involving some sort of self-denial or to provide a gift, giving of himself or herself in a way that goes beyond the usual requirements of liturgical law or custom. This vow allows one to prove devotion to the deity and perhaps is linked to expectations of reciprocity as in the many biblical war vows (Judg. 11:29-40; 1 Sam. 14:24-46; Num. 21:1-3). Broken vows are serious matters that can lead to being cursed rather than blessed. Numbers 30 alludes to and provides a framework for more domesticated varieties of vowing, but these vows are to be taken just as seriously as those involving war, life, and death.

A man or a woman may take a vow to Yahweh upon themselves, although the latter may be subject to the approval of father or husband, depending upon her age and status. Only the widow or divorcee, who is no longer under the control of a man, may take upon herself vows as does an adult male. The lengthy pericope concerning women's vows in Numbers 30 says almost nothing about the content of such vows and seems more concerned to clarify and circumscribe the woman's vow-taking capacity and her father's or husband's veto power (30:3-15) than to describe the process of vowing or typical vows themselves. Nevertheless, it is made clear that such pledges are binding (30:2), cannot be broken, and, as in the case of Jephthah's daughter, "according to all that comes forth from his mouth, he shall do" (30:2). It may be that husband or father is imagined to be able to veto a decision of a woman to become a Nazirite or that the vow might be expected to be undertaken by a widow or divorcee rather than a woman tied to a man. Numbers 6 does not clarify.

The Nazirite vow, like other vows, however, is pictured to be undertaken with full seriousness, a kind of vow worn on the body, and one which must be properly completed. Awareness of the deep significance and often sacrificial nature of vows allows for an understanding of the way the hair is offered up and the way in which the interrupted vow must be resumed and properly completed. One might also suggest that the hair is invested with holiness. Like a whole burnt offering to the Lord, a special variety of sacrifice which is totally consumed by the flame, rising up to God in the smoke (see Lev. 1:9), the hair needs to be transported to him in full by the fire. Holy hair cannot remain on earth once the period of sacred status has passed, nor can it remain attached to the now ordinary, wine-drinking person. The hair is divinely invested through the process of voicing the vow. The power of the word to transform is of special note. It is "opening the mouth" that makes the vow real and visceral. It is concrete in a world in which blessings and curses genuinely have the power to bring about that which they speak. By the same token, the hair is invested with the vow-taker's very person, and is a way in which the Nazir offers himself or herself to the deity. The offered item is a substitute for the most valuable sacrifice of all, one's own person. The Nazirite vow in Numbers is thus deeply integrated into a particular priestly worldview involving the power of words, vowing, and literal offering of sacrifice. The notion of sacrifice may, indeed, always be implicit in the symbol of sacrally assumed long hair (see 1 Sam. 1:11 and Judg. 5:2). In Numbers 6, we see how priests place this sacralizing custom within the contours of their own orientation to life.

The particular priestly orientation of hair customs in Numbers 6 also emerges in the emphasis on staying away from corpses during the long-haired vow. Priests in ancient Israel developed quite sophisticated notions of and rules pertaining to cleanness and uncleanness, purity and impurity, related ultimately to ritual roles in which the mediator between God and human had to be pure, approaching the purist of pure, which is the deity himself. One major source of contamination is death, the ultimate chaos, that which cannot be controlled. If death is a source of chaos, the most one can hope for is to contain that source, to demarcate one's immersion in it and one's cleansing and separation from it. While Numbers 19 portrays death as a source of chaos that exudes uncleanness from which all people need to be cleansed should they come in contact with it (see also Num. 31:19), the priestly text of Lev. 21:1-6 makes a special case for the avoidance of the dead on the part of the hereditary Aaronide priests, except for closest relatives. An alteration of his hairstyle (Lev. 21:5) would signal the defilement of death and the impermanence of life, that which is chaotic and mundane.

For the high priest, avoidance of the dead is even stricter, as seen in a comparison between Lev. 21:1-3 pertaining to priests versus 21:10, pertaining to "the priest who is called above his fellows," i.e., the high priest. He may not attend closely even to the bodies of his deceased mother or father. The same proscription applies to the Nazir. While under the vow, he or she may not defile himself or herself with death even should mother, father, sister, or brother die (Num. 6:6-7), for "the set-apart status of God is upon the head." That holiness must not be in touch with the uncleanness of death; pure wholeness must not touch chaos. Should the Nazir unavoidably come into contact with the dead, he or she must end the vow, shave the holy hair, emerge from sacred status, and recommence the vow period after the process of cleansing. The proscription against contact with the dead, which closely links priestly concerns with the version of the Nazirite status found in Numbers, is all the more serious and extreme in a culture in which kinship bonds are so central to identity and self-definition and in which death, as in so many cultures, is regarded as a core passage in the life of all human beings, one which family members attend and ease.

In a discussion of an Israelite "hierarchy of burial," Saul Olyan points to the positive and critical identity-defining connections between kinship and interment customs. The actual physical presence of those near and dear to the departed during ritual actions related to a kinsman's death is an important symbolic declaration of the visceral connection between the living and the dead and of the continuation of family and lineage.[32] Similarly, Joshua Berman explores the important connections between burial customs and "identity politics" in the biblical telling of the death of Jacob.[33] Thus lack of participation in ceremonies pertaining to the dead, even for a circumscribed period of time, is a significant way in which the Nazir is removed from a normal social role and one of several ways in which the Nazir of Numbers 6 is shaped by priestly preoccupations. No mention of avoidance of the dead is found in connection with Samson, and the proscription seems to belong to a later priestly layer in the development of the Nazirite vow. One sees how Nazirite status paradoxically is both democratized to include any man or woman even while being made stricter in accordance with certain priestly concepts of clean and unclean.

The version of the wine prohibition which is part of the vow also reveals a particular late-biblical, priestly orientation. Notice that the priest, who must be in his most holy and "clean" condition in order to enter the sa-

---

32. Saul Olyan, "Some Neglected Aspects of Israelite Interment Ideology," *JBL* 124 (2005): 601-16.

33. Joshua Berman, "Identity Politics in the Burial of Jacob (Genesis 50:1-14)," *CBQ* 68 (2006): 11-31.

cred locus where God's spirit rests, the tent of meeting," is also not to "drink wine or strong drink" (Lev. 10:8). The prohibition against drinking before engaging in his activities mediating between God and Israel has to do with the need for presence of mind and sobriety in undertaking sacrificial duties, but also, within the symbol system as described by the writer of Leviticus 10, is framed by the need to "distinguish between the holy and the common, and between the unclean and the clean." The Nazir, during his vow, is thus in a perpetual state of priestly style cleanness and holiness, as if he were about to enter the sacred locus. The directive of the divine messenger to Samson's mother is that she not drink "wine or strong drink" (13:7) as the child takes form within her. Judges 13:14 expands the prohibition to include anything that comes from the vine. In Numbers 6, however, a set of specific food products associated with the forbidden wine is listed, so that "wine" comes to include an extended list much as in the style of Rabbinic reasoning.[34]

Equally interesting in a positional analysis is the lack of reference to unclean food in Numbers 6, a prohibition clearly found in Judges 13. Keeping kosher for the author of Numbers is a critical pan-Israelite means of self-definition, so basic that it need not be mentioned; it is assumed by the late priestly writer as customary for all Israelites.

The early material seems to allow Nazirite status to overlap with other sorts of sacred status. Samuel is a Nazir and a priest. Amos juxtaposes the Nazir with the prophet, and Samson, the Nazir, is also a superheroic warrior called a judge. Priestly roles are not mentioned in connection with the latter two instances of Nazirism. In Numbers 6, the divide between hereditary priesthood and voluntary Nazir is clear, but the Levitical priests have control of many aspects of the process, especially due to the sacrifices which mark the interruption of the sacred status in case of contact with death and the conclusion of the specified period of time allotted for completion of the vow. Both in terms of the emphasis on purity and in terms of the management of key ritual aspects of the vow, never mentioned, for example, in connection with Samson, the status of Nazirism, while available to any man or woman, is controlled by the hereditary priesthood in Numbers 6 (see, e.g., vv. 11, 16, and 20).

Scheper-Hughes and Lock's category of the "body politic" is relevant, for the priests, in a sense, take control of the Nazirite vow and of the symbolism of the hair, which is finally sent heavenward in a thoroughly priestly ritual. One might say that the writers of Numbers would like to view Nazirite

---

34. See Jastrow, "The 'Nazir' Legislation," 266, 269.

status as safely hijacked by the institutional, priestly establishment.[35] The very availability of the vow to women makes it less of a threat. No charismatic, divinely-selected leadership is assumed; rather, a person can take on a vow to display his or her piety and to experience temporarily that holiness that rightly belongs to priests as their hereditary purview, and the priests continue to serve as mediators between divine and human realms in the Nazirite process. This is in strong contrast to the direct relationship between God and Samson or God and Samuel or the kind of direct tie between God and man imagined by Amos for those chosen to be Nazirites.

Charismatic Nazirites did not necessarily disappear after the classical period of Amos, and some may have considered themselves chosen from birth in settings of the sixth and fifth centuries B.C.E. No late biblical Nazirites are described with certainty in the chronology of the preserved literature of the Hebrew Bible, although Zech. 13:4 perhaps suggests some nuances of the holy associations of hairiness. For the most part, however, charismatic Nazirites seem to be located in earlier times by preserved traditions in the Hebrew Bible. It may well be that priestly leaders of the postexilic period sought to control the rise of charismatic holy men or to diminish their unique position by making a status of holiness available to everyone, a status surrounded by ritual actions controlled by the priests themselves. The priestly description of Nazirism in Numbers 6 may reflect, in fact, an implicit power struggle between various sources of political and religious power in Persian-period Judah. The hereditary priests, like Ezra, hold power not only because of their particular Levitical genealogy, but also because of the support of Persia, conqueror of Israel. Others may regard themselves as holding power from God himself. The contrast is between the central-establishment hereditary holy men and peripheral, perhaps anti-establishment charismatics. Nazirites could have been as much of a political threat to a Judean establishment as Samson was a military threat to the Philistines. One thinks here of the Christian holy men of late-antique Byzantium, who were a counterpoint of power to the bishops of the institutional church and the imperial bureaucracy.[36] Such figures are often thorns in the side of the establishment, and it is interesting that priestly elites here attempt to domesticate and contain the Nazirite role.

Who might be likely to take on this vow? What would the person get out of it? The questions posed by Obeyesekere concerning the emotional

---

35. Cf. Berquist, *Judaism in Persia's Shadow*, 155-56.

36. See Peter Brown, "The Rise and Function of the Holy Man in Late Antiquity," *Journal of Roman Studies* 61 (1971): 95.

and personal content of the symbolism of hair are important, as is Scheper-Hughes and Lock's attention to the "individual body." Cultural and social context, of course, remain critical as well for a full understanding. The person who takes on the Nazirite vow needs to be able to provide some expensive offerings along the way, a young male lamb if the vow goes awry because of contact with the dead, and several offerings at the conclusion of the vow. No allowance is made, as in other sacrifices, for less expensive substitutes (cf. Lev. 12:8). One must assume, therefore, that the Nazirite is imagined to be a person of some means for whom the loss of these animals would be possible. Such a person might be one of the landed gentry or *'am hā'āreṣ*, "people of the land," perhaps one of the elders imagined to help in adjudicating local disputes at the gates of the city, the local power centers. In the postexilic and Persian periods, such a seeker of status might be one of the newly wealthy Southerners, or Judeans, whose fortunes actually improved in the power vacuum created by the Babylonian conquest and the initial return after the exile. Only a relatively small number of elite Judeans were exiled, and an even smaller number returned. The various passages and situations of political and economic instability may well have led to the acquisition of new wealth in land on the part of those who stayed behind or who returned early after Cyrus's decree. These members of Judean society formed relationships with the hereditary priesthood (see Neh. 13:7, 28) and/or with the emissaries of the Persian central government, some of whom like the leader, Ezra, were themselves priests. Alternatively, the custom of noncharismatic Nazirism may have developed in the Northern Kingdom of Israel, which scholars now believe to have been quite well off economically during the periods of Babylonian and Persian control and quite similar in cultural and religious self-definition to their southern brothers.[37]

Leong Seow's analysis of the social world of the book of Ecclesiastes contributes further to our capacity to speculate about the identity of those who might desire to take on the Nazirite vow in the postexilic period. Employing a variety of biblical and extrabiblical sources, Seow provides relevant detail about income, commercial enterprises, and other aspects of the economy of the Persian period. He points to "a new middle class,"[38] a lively cash economy,[39] the vitality of trade and other commercial activity,[40] and "the

---

37. See Gary N. Knoppers, "Revisiting the Samaritan Question," 271-72, 279-80.
38. Leong Seow, "The Social World of Ecclesiastes," 4.
39. Ibid., 8.
40. Ibid., 11.

democratization of commerce" that led to newly rich members of society[41] and also to the insecurities that come with volatile, vibrant economies. Today's newly rich could become tomorrow's impoverished debtor. Seow paints a socioeconomic portrait of haves and have-nots, the former often being favorites of the Persian-supported aristocracy who received grants from the king which they, in turn, could share with their allies. The newly rich, the insecurely rich, might well have the means and the desire to partake in the expression of religious devotion offered by the Nazirite vow. Nazirite status would allow such a person to exude and experience holiness, while shoring up his or her sense of self-worth in the face of economic insecurity.

Women of means are also alluded to in biblical literature, for example in the description of the "woman of valor" of Proverbs 31. Drawing upon epigraphic, archaeological, and comparative material of the Persian period, Christine Yoder suggests that such a woman is pictured to engage in commerce, to have a successful cottage craft business, to run a complex household, to exercise considerable economic independence, and to hold high status in her family.[42] Similarly, N. Avigad points to the existence of cylinder seals inscribed with women's names in the pre- and postexilic periods (205-206).[43] Since such seals were used to imprint stamps of ownership on material possessions or documents, they would indicate that such named women exercised independent economic and political power and that they had status in the public realm. Such women might also have had the resources and desire to undertake a Nazirite vow and thereby assume the status related to it. Male or female, the person would be seeking to project an aura of holiness. Participation in the vow would probably add to his or her status, for voluntary Nazirites suggest, by their demeanor and behavior, not only that they have the means to take on such a vow but also that they long for a sacred, closer-to-God experience.

To be sure, such vow-takers may not merely be "projecting" sacredness to increase status in a community, but might well desire to be closer to the divine. Here we think of Obeyesekere's attention to the emotional dimension of religious symbolism. Not to drink wine with one's fellows, not to attend to the dead in one's community or one's family, and slowly watching

---

41. Ibid., 21.

42. Christine Roy Yoder, "The Woman of Substance (אשת־חיל): A Socioeconomic Reading of Proverbs 31:10-31," *JBL* 122 (2003): 427-47.

43. N. Avigad, "The Contribution of Hebrew Seals to an Understanding of Israelite Religion and Society," in *Ancient Israelite Religion*, ed. Patrick D. Miller, Paul D. Hanson, and S. Dean McBride (Philadelphia: Fortress Press, 1987), 205-6.

one's hair lengthen would be reminders of and perhaps sources of a spiritual and psychological pilgrimage. Physical factors are involved as well. As Pnina Galpaz-Feller has suggested in explaining preferences among ancient Egyptian men to shave the head, the longer the hair, the more the lice, and the more the need for care and grooming.[44] Long hair thus could well constantly remind the Nazirite himself or herself of his or her status and become a source of contemplation or preoccupation, much as in the case of Obeyesekere's long-haired female informants in Sri Lanka.

Interest in varieties of individual religious expression and preoccupation, in fact, comes more and more to feature in ancient Israelite religion from the period just before the exile and afterward. In the works of the prophets Jeremiah, Ezekiel, and Second Isaiah one begins to see the emergence of a kind of confessional literature that includes autobiographic detail. The prophet Jeremiah, for example, personally addresses the deity about the experience of being a prophet (Jer. 15:16-18).

The literary forms in which the prophets speak are conventionalized as in any traditional literature. Jeremiah 15, like many other biblical passages that contain individual prayers, emotional content, and allusions to personal experience, is rooted in the form of the lament, but the personal stamp of the material is unmistakable (see also Jer. 20:7-18). The sixth-century B.C.E. Ezekiel and the seventh- and sixth-century B.C.E. Jeremiah, moreover, offer critiques of the notion that the children are punished for the sins of the parents (Ezek. 18:2-4; Jer. 31:29-30). Sin is seen in more individual terms, whereby each person is punished for his own misdeeds. Job, a work that grapples with the issue of God's justice and one human being's undeserved suffering, is intensely engaged with the plight of the religious individual, seen apart from community guilt or a divine covenant with an entire people. Finally, the Persian-period memoir of Nehemiah, which includes large portions of the biblical book by his name, is overtly autobiographic. In his memoir, the governor of Judah, who is supported by the Persian government, describes his successes and failures in implementing his program. Within this context, a noncharismatic form of Nazirism might flower. The individual makes a choice to lead a particular kind of religiously conscious existence that sets him or her socially apart from the conviviality of drinking wine or the communal experience of mourning for friends and relatives, and he or she wears the sign of that status in his or her hairstyle.

---

44. Pnina Galpaz-Feller, "Hair in the Hebrew Bible and in Ancient Egyptian Culture: Cultural and Private Connotations," *Biblische Notizen* 125 (2004): 76.

Economic issues again are at play, for noncharismatic Nazirites in ancient Israel might be assumed also to have the leisure and wherewithal to contemplate and act upon this desire to be holy. Nazirism does not seem to be a community-supported status like the priesthood or the prophetic guild, which, as Robert R. Wilson has suggested, no doubt had its support groups, those who preserved what were regarded as valuable prophetic utterances.[45] One also thinks, for example, of the way in which the woman of Shunem supports the holy man Elisha (2 Kings 4:8-37). The vow to live as a Nazir for a certain length of time, taken upon himself or herself by the Nazir, is a self-selected condition by those in an economic and social position to do so. It is also entirely possible that the Nazirism of heroes such as Samson, with its associations of leadership, charisma, and victory in war, would be desirable traits to project for would-be community leaders. Even though we are suggesting that Numbers 6 is a later version of Nazirism than those presented by the authors of tales of Samson and Samuel and by the oracle of Amos, the traditions about the early long-haired heroes are part of the cultural tradition, available to the priestly authors of Numbers and actual members of the community whom they may picture to take on such a vow. Samson's Nazirism, however, is of a wild, explosive variety, whereas the holiness in Numbers seems very controlled and circumscribed by priestly safeguards. How does the Nazirite vow described in Numbers 6 relate to images of hair, in particular, especially in comparison with images of Samson, for the hair would seem to be a critical part of what is projected?

Samson is a life-long Nazir so that, like a Sikh, his hair would be plentiful indeed, and he is pictured to wear it in plaits. There may have been various accepted hairstyles for the manly charismatic Nazir. Unless the Nazir of Numbers 6 took on the vow for a number of years, the length of the hair really would not have been noticeable, unless Israelite men wore their hair cropped enough that even several months' growth would be apparent. Pictorial evidence of premonarchic periods and for the ninth century B.C.E. suggests that men's hair was at least shoulder-length.[46] The Lachish reliefs of the eighth century B.C.E. portray the hair of some of the men who fight for Judah as covered by hats, wraps, or helmets; the length of their hair is not clearly ascertainable.[47] Others, who wear no head covering, have cropped

---

45. Robert R. Wilson, *Prophecy and Society in Ancient Israel* (Philadelphia: Fortress, 1980), 45, 76-83.
46. See Niditch, "My Brother Esau Is a Hairy Man," 34-50.
47. Ibid., 53-59.

hair in tight curls, but there are questions about the Judean versus Nubian or Egyptian identity of the men with visible, short hair.[48] If such portrayals are accurate representations of Judeans, then the uncut hair of the voluntary Nazir would more quickly become an apparent sign of a change in status. The shaving of the head, marking that the person had been under a Nazirite vow (or in mourning), would have been the more dramatic and sudden indication of transition. Abstaining from the social activity of drinking wine and not attending to funerary rites of friends or relatives may well have been the more effective and obvious daily statements of a man's temporary set-aside status, with its priestly and sacral connotations, than the slow growing of hair. The same might be said for women.

We have no evidence that women wore their hair short. To the contrary, the Song of Songs describes the beautiful long hair of a young woman, while the woman accused of adultery has her hair let down, so that presumably it is long enough to put up. Pictorial evidence from the eighth century B.C.E. portrays Judean women of Lachish wearing long cloth headdresses that completely cover the hair.[49] Thus it is possible that in public neither the growing nor the shaving of hair would have been visible. The woman's abstaining from wine and her lack of attendance to funerary rites might be better indicators. There is some evidence, in fact, that women were especially involved in rites of mourning.[50] The hair may have taken a backseat to other symbolic manifestations of Nazirism in the view of the priestly writers of Numbers 6.

In dealing with positional analysis, which has led to priestly interests and motifs in Numbers 6, and in considering in context the perspective of the person who takes on the vow, a special comment on women is necessary. Numbers 6 opens up Nazirism to both genders, thereby radically altering the symbolic web linking Nazirism, hairiness, and maleness. Such a view both democratizes and domesticates holy status even while perhaps reducing its charisma and potency. It is important also to mention that the Levitical priesthood, both in Numbers and Leviticus, does not include women in the ranks of priests. A woman of priestly family can partake of food resulting from special priestly offerings and, to that extent, she can partake of the holiness, but she herself is no priest. In fact, an interesting passage in Numbers

---

48. Ibid., 55, 56, 59.
49. Ibid., 51-53.
50. See Philip J. King and Lawrence E. Stager, *Life in Biblical Israel* (Louisville: Westminster John Knox, 2001), 373, and Jer. 9:17-18.

12 viscerally puts Miriam of the priestly tribe of Levi, sister of Moses and Aaron, in her place in contrast to some genealogical references in which she is listed as having special leadership status (Micah 6:4; 1 Chron. 5:29 [6:3 in English]). She is called a prophet in Exod. 15:20-21. Numbers 12 has been understood to suggest that there may have been priestly clans at some point in the history of Israel, claiming descent from Miriam the Levite or a history of women priests now edited out of the surviving literature of the Bible. Could it be that the priestly authors of Numbers allow women the safe, compensatory holiness of Nazirite status? Paradoxically, this form of Nazirism allows priestly leaders to give women of means an opportunity for some kind of sacred status, but it is temporary and no threat to the male, Levitical priesthood. Voluntary Nazirism makes it clear further that male Nazirites are no competition for the male hereditary priests because even women may assume the holiness! Priestly writers of similar orientation may well be responsible for the first creation account of the Bible, in which both male and female are created in the image of God, and no hierarchy is emphasized between men and women. Such a text is oddly inclusive of women and potentially exclusive at the same time, for the status has to do with primordial times and is no threat to actual social reality. The image makes women feel a part of divine creation without promising them power.

Otherness within the Levitical priestly understanding of the Jewish community can be variously expressed and understood. The priests picture themselves as consummate insiders whose special leadership status relates to a hierarchy of holiness and sacral Otherness. Their androcentric worldview combines with an emphasis on purities to make women the Other gender. The description of the Nazirite vow in Numbers 6 with its emphasis on hair, the body, and identity provides a fascinating study in the manifestation, shaping, and controlling of Otherness within the Second Temple Jewish community. Individuals of either gender may voluntarily assume a sacral status that temporarily attaches to them some of the holiness held by priests, but the status is temporary and regulated; it contrasts with the utter Otherness into which a charismatic figure such as Samson is born. Paradoxically, the Nazirite vow tends to reinforce a male, hereditary status quo with its hierarchical and permanent features. The priests' reliable, inherited, unchanging Otherness assures them the social capital of insiders. Numbers 6 reveals the power to which its composers aspire while providing a sociostructural map reinforced by symbols of and relationships to the body.

Otherworldly Music and the Other Sex

Susan Ackerman

In her book *Fragmented Women: Feminist (Sub)versions of Biblical Narrative* (1993), J. Cheryl Exum includes a chapter whose title, "The (M)other's Place," and especially the parentheses within it, tries to capture the ambivalent position that the matriarchs Sarah, Rebekah, Rachel, and Leah occupy in the book of Genesis. On the one hand, as Exum sees it, these matriarchs are central to the movement forward of the Genesis narrative, since the generational progression on which Genesis relies cannot be accomplished without each patriarch's begetting a son or sons with his "right" or proper wife. What makes a wife "right," moreover, is her *insider* status: she is not of the Canaanites or, like the Egyptian Hagar, some other foreign people. Rather, she is of the patriarchs' ethnos and, indeed, of their own family: Sarah is Abraham's half-sister; Rebekah and Isaac are patrilateral parallel cousins; Rachel and Leah are Jacob's matrilateral cross-cousins. On the other hand, however, the matriarchs stand as outsiders: Rebekah, Leah, and Rachel, for example, are residents of far-away lands that they must leave to dwell with their husbands in Canaan. There, "they are 'other'"; quite literally, that is, the "other" sex. Still, as Exum writes, "they are 'other' who," because of their insider status, "are also 'same.'"[1]

In this paper, which joins with all the essays in this volume to honor John Collins's extensive and extraordinarily learned contributions to the

---

1. J. Cheryl Exum, *Fragmented Women: Feminist (Sub)versions of Biblical Narrative* (Valley Forge, Pa.: Trinity Press International, 1993), 110.

scholarship of the Second Temple period, my focus cannot be these Genesis narratives that, like the majority still of biblical scholars, I would date primarily to the preexilic era. Indeed, my focus will not be narrative at all, but a question of history. Like Exum, though, I am interested in women; more specifically, I am interested in the roles that at least some ancient Israelite women seem to have played as musicians within their communities. To be even more specific: I am interested in the responsibilities these women seem to have assumed as *ritual* musicians during certain cultic and related occasions. It will be my contention that an examination of these responsibilities shows that female ritual musicians were positioned within the world of ancient Israelite religion as Exum's "Others" who are also "Same," especially beginning in the sixth and fifth centuries B.C.E., during Israel's exilic and early Second Temple periods. In order to demonstrate this historical development, my remarks below proceed diachronically, from an examination of women's roles as ritual musicians in preexilic Israel to a description of certain changes I identify as emerging in the exilic and postexilic eras.

I. Women's Roles as Ritual Musicians in Preexilic Israel

Within preexilic tradition, we can identify, in my opinion, at least three major arenas in which women assumed responsibilities as ritual musicians. The first was originally studied by Eunice Poethig in her 1985 Union Theological Seminary dissertation:[2] it is women's responsibility for singing victory songs after an Israelite triumph in holy war. The most famous examples are the two victory "songs" that are commonly called by the names of the women who performed them: the so-called "Song of Miriam" in Exod. 15:1-18, 20-21, which celebrates the Israelite victory over the forces of Pharaoh at the time of the exodus from Egypt, and the similarly named "Song of Deborah" in Judg. 5:1-31, which celebrates the victory of the Israelite militia over the Canaanite army of Sisera during the early days of Israel's emergence in the promised land.

Some analytical nuance is required, however, to appreciate fully women's role — and, more important, women's seemingly *exclusive* role — as singers of these and other victory songs. While Judg. 5:1, for example, identifies both a man and a woman, Deborah and Barak, as singing the Judg.

---

2. Eunice B. Poethig, "The Victory Song Tradition of the Women of Israel" (Ph.D. dissertation; Union Theological Seminary, 1985).

5:1-31 victory hymn, close scrutiny suggests that in some older version of the text, the woman Deborah was identified as the sole performer, as her name comes first in the verse and the verb *šwr*, "to sing," is rendered in the third-person *feminine* singular *(wattāšar)*. Somewhat similarly, although Exod. 15:1 identifies Moses, and not Miriam, as the singer of the Exod. 15:1-18 victory song that praises Yahweh for the Egyptians' defeat, Frank Moore Cross and David Noel Freedman suggested already in their 1955 article "The Song of Miriam" that this attribution may not have been original.[3] This argument is based on the fact that the second half of Exod. 15:21 repeats almost verbatim the second half of 15:1. Yet in the first half of 15:21, the singer of these lines — and presumably, therefore, the singer of the larger hymn of which these lines are the incipit — is identified not as Moses, but as his sister, Miriam.[4] Cross and Freedman further argue that this attribution to Miriam is the older ascription, for it is easy to see how, over time, tradition would have changed from assigning the song to Miriam and attributed it to her more famous brother. It is difficult to imagine, conversely, that a song originally ascribed to Moses would have later been accredited to a more minor character.[5]

Carol Meyers has in addition located evidence for the tradition of women's victory songs in Ps. 68:12-13 (in most of the Bible's English versions, 68:11-12), in which female heralds *(hamĕbaśśĕrôt)* are commissioned to sing out the news of Yahweh's victory in holy war by proclaiming "The kings of the armies, they flee, they flee!"[6] Meyers similarly notes that in vv. 25-26 of

---

3. Frank Moore Cross and David Noel Freedman, "The Song of Miriam," *JNES* 14 (1955): 237-50.

4. It has been argued that Miriam's song does not *begin* with the couplet found in 15:21, but that 15:21 is Miriam's song in its entirety. This view, however, has been well refuted by Cross and Freedman, who write of Exod. 15:1-18 and 20-21, "The opening verse [Exod. 15:1] also served as the title of the song in antiquity. . . . Hence, v. 21 is not a different or shorter or the original version of the song, but simply the title of the poem taken from a different cycle of traditions" ("The Song of Miriam," 237; see also Frank Moore Cross, *Canaanite Myth and Hebrew Epic: Essays in the History of the Religion of Israel* [Cambridge, Mass.: Harvard University Press, 1973], 123-24). Cf. Rita J. Burns, *Has the Lord Indeed Spoken Only Through Moses? A Study of the Biblical Portrait of Miriam* (SBLDS 84; Atlanta: Scholars Press, 1987), 13-16, who quotes these lines from Cross and Freedman only to register her disagreement with them.

5. Cross and Freedman, "Song of Miriam," 237. See also Phyllis Trible, "Bringing Miriam out of the Shadows," *BRev* 5/1 (February 1989): 34, n. 5.

6. Carol Meyers, "Mother to Muse: An Archaeomusicological Study of Women's Performance in Israel," in *Recycling Biblical Figures: Papers Read at a Noster Colloquium in Amsterdam, 12-13 May 1997*, ed. Athalya Brenner and Jan Willem van Henten (Studies in Theology and Religion 1; Leiden: Deo Publishing, 1999), 72, n. 61; see also eadem, "Those Who

this same psalm (in most of the Bible's English versions, vv. 24-25), young women playing hand drums *('ălāmôt tôpēpôt)*, which Meyers defines as "a hoop-shaped drum with a diameter much greater than the width of its frame,"[7] are among those musicians who participate in a procession into Yahweh's *qōdeš*, or sanctuary — most probably (although not definitively) to be identified as God's Temple in Jerusalem (the temple is mentioned specifically in v. 30 [English v. 29] of the following stanza) — in order to celebrate the deity's victory as the divine warrior who has vanquished Israel's foes.[8] Similarly in Exod. 15:20, Miriam's "song" is preceded by a description of how Miriam and all the women of Israel celebrated Yahweh's victory over the Egyptians by playing hand drums *(tuppîm)*, which suggests that the playing of such drums — and also dancing *(měḥōlōt)*, which is mentioned as well in Exod. 15:20 — were features commonly associated with women's victory-song performances.

Thus the daughter of Jephthah, in Judg. 11:34, greets her father beating hand-drums and dancing *(bětuppîm ûbimḥōlôt)* after he returns home victorious from battle against the Ammonites, and in 1 Sam. 18:6-7, the women of the towns of Israel serenade Saul as he marches back from doing battle against the Philistines, again playing hand-drums *(tuppîm)*, dancing *(měḥōlōt)*, and singing hymns of victory. Meyers has further suggested that the several Iron II terracotta figurines that depict women holding hand-drums may be related to the tradition of women's victory-song performance.[9] To be sure, we cannot say definitively, even if Meyers is right, that these terracottas should be associated with a tradition of women's victory-song performance that is *religious* in nature, as fits our interest here, and Rita J. Burns has in addition argued that scholars need to differentiate within the biblical material between women's victory songs that are "cultic" (e.g., Miriam's "Song of the Sea") and the "secular" (e.g., the post-battle music-making of Jephthah's daughter and the women who serenade Saul).[10] But in

---

Bear Tidings: Heralds (Ps. 68:11; Isa. 40:9)," in *Women in Scripture: A Dictionary of Named and Unnamed Women in the Hebrew Bible, the Apocryphal/Deuterocanonical Books, and the New Testament*, ed. Carol Meyers, with Toni Craven and Ross S. Kramer (Boston: Houghton Mifflin, 2000), 299.

7. Meyers, "Mother to Muse," 57.

8. Carol Meyers, "Women with Hand-Drums, Dancing: Exod. 15:20; 1 Sam. 18:6-7; 2 Sam. 1:20; Ps. 68:25; Jer. 31:4, 13," in *Women in Scripture*, 190.

9. Carol Meyers, "Of Drums and Damsels: Women's Performance in Ancient Israel," *BA* 54 (1991): 16-27; eadem, "Mother to Muse," 66-73.

10. Burns, *Has the Lord Indeed Spoken Only Through Moses?* 17-18.

Susan Ackerman

fact, each of our biblical examples concerns a battlefield victory that Yahweh has at a minimum sanctioned, if not participated in, meaning that, as far as our evidence suggests, *all* women's music-making in celebration of a triumph in war should be categorized as cultic in nature.

The second arena I will discuss as a site of Israelite women's ritual musicianship during the preexilic period draws on some of my own previous efforts to describe the special role women may have played as dancers and more generally as music-makers during the fall harvest festival of the ingathering, or Succoth. In my original presentation of this hypothesis, I took as my starting point Judg. 21:15-25 and its descriptions of the young women who come out to dance in the dances *(lāḥûl bamměḥōlôt)* during the "yearly festival of Yahweh held at Shiloh."[11] While this text, unfortunately, does not explicitly state that the "yearly festival" in question was, as I have just suggested, the ingathering, or Succoth festival, commentators almost unanimously agree that the text's indication that the young women's dancing took place in the vicinity of Shiloh's *vineyards* indicates that their dancing was done on the occasion of Succoth, at which the annual grape harvest and the pressing of the new wine were preeminently celebrated (Deut. 16:13; Judg. 9:27).

Another text whose "yearly festival" I would take to be the festival of the ingathering, or Succoth, is 1 Sam. 1:1–2:10, the story of Hannah and her family's annual pilgrimages to Shiloh. Indeed, although this is obscured in Christian Bibles, which interpose the book of Ruth, I would argue that in the older Deuteronomistic History, the story of Hannah in 1 Sam. 1:1–2:10 intentionally parallels Judg. 21:15-25, which it immediately follows. Not only, for example, are both set during celebrations that take place in Shiloh, but both describe the annual nature of the Shiloh festival by using the exact same phrase, *miyyāmîm yāmîmâ*, "year by year" (Judg. 21:19; 1 Sam. 1:3; 2:19), a locution, notably, that is otherwise very rare, found only at two other points in the entire Hebrew Bible (Exod. 13:10 and Judg. 11:40). Judges 21:15-25 and 1 Sam. 1:1–2:10 both stress that their respective festivals are pilgrimage feasts. In 1 Sam. 1:3 (see also 1 Sam. 2:19), Hannah and her husband Elqanah are said to come *up* to Shiloh annually, which is typical language used of a pilgrimage,[12] and Judg. 21:19 explicitly describes its celebration as a *ḥag*, which, al-

---

11. Susan Ackerman, *Warrior, Dancer, Seductress, Queen: Women in Judges and Biblical Israel* (ABRL 17; New York: Doubleday, 1998), 253–87.

12. See, for example, Exod. 34:24, where it is commanded in the Covenant Code that the Israelites shall "go up" to appear before Yahweh three times a year.

though often just translated as "festival" or the like,[13] is actually, of course, a technical term meaning "pilgrimage festival" or "pilgrimage feast."[14] As I have already proposed, moreover, I would take the particular pilgrimage festival being celebrated in both texts to be Succoth. In fact, understanding the Shiloh festival of 1 Sam. 1:1–2:10 as the festival of Succoth — which we are elsewhere told involved copious amounts of eating and drinking (Judg. 9:27) — helps explain an otherwise enigmatic detail in the text: why the priest Eli, as he watches Hannah pray silently (and for the ancient Near East atypically), with only her lips moving, presumes that she is drunk. Yet surely there are other, equally plausible explanations for Hannah's silent prayer: why does Eli, for example, not presume that Hannah is mute? If we understand, though, that the setting of the Hannah story is the Succoth festival, then it makes sense for Eli to leap to the assumption that Hannah, as a celebrant at the feast of the new wine, would be intoxicated.[15]

Understanding the setting of the Hannah story to be the fall festival of the ingathering, or Succoth, also explains a second enigmatic detail in the story: the presence of the so-called "Song of Hannah" in 1 Sam. 2:1-10. Although this hymn of praise and thanksgiving is attributed to Hannah in verse 1, almost all commentators agree it was only secondarily attached to her story. This is in particular indicated by the significant variations that are found among the ancient versions in the verses that surround 1 Sam. 2:1-10, all of which stem from the fact that the original narrative of Samuel's dedication was disturbed at a later point in its transmission when some editor added the "Song of Hannah."[16] It is also indicated by passages such as verse

---

13. As it is, for example, in the NRSV, the JB, the NAB, the KJV, and the NJPS, all of which translate "feast." Cf. the REB, "pilgrimage."

14. See further C. F. Burney, *The Book of Judges, with Introduction and Notes*, 2d ed. (London: Rivington's, 1920), 492; J. Alberto Soggin, *Judges: A Commentary* (OTL; Philadelphia: Westminster, 1981), 299.

15. I am grateful to Julie A. Duncan, my colleague at Garrett-Evangelical Theological Seminary, for this observation.

16. For example, while the verse that immediately precedes the "Song" in 1 Sam. 1:28 reads in the received Hebrew text, "So he [presumably Eli, or perhaps Elqanah] worshipped Yahweh there," the Samuel manuscript from the Dead Sea records, "And she [Hannah] left him [Samuel] there, and she worshipped Yahweh there." As for the Greek tradition, one of its versions has nothing at all at this point but does read in 2:11, "And she [Hannah] left him [Samuel] there before Yahweh." The other major Greek version follows the received Hebrew tradition in 1:28 by reading, "So he [presumably Eli] worshipped Yahweh there," but then, in 2:11, it sides with its Greek counterpart by reading, "And they [Hannah and Elqanah] left him there before Yahweh." It then adds, "And they worshiped Yahweh there." For further dis-

10 of the "Song," which presumes the existence of the monarchy, an institution that is otherwise not a part of the Samuel narrative until Samuel's secret anointing of Saul in 1 Sam. 10:1 and the public proclamation of Saul's kingship that follows in 10:17-27.[17]

So why the addition? According to many, although the hymn itself is anachronistic, the insertion of some song of jubilation for Hannah to sing is nevertheless appropriate, given that her silent prayer — in which she had asked that her barrenness be reversed so that she might bear a son — has been granted. The mention in 2:5 of the barren woman who, through God's gift, bears seven children, as well as the entire poem's sense that Yahweh can bring about great reversals in the natural order, especially indicates to commentators that the ancient curators of the Samuel text acted in a reasonable — albeit inaccurate — fashion in putting this song into Hannah's mouth.[18] But this explanation does not satisfy me completely, for there are, including Hannah, six women in the Hebrew Bible who find that their barrenness has been miraculously and unexpectedly reversed by a God who has given them the gift of a child. Arguably, moreover, the reversal of at least some of these women's barrenness is more miraculous than was the reversal of Hannah's: Sarah, after all, is said to be ninety years of age (Gen. 17:17) and to have ceased to menstruate (Gen. 18:11) before she finally becomes pregnant; Rebekah also, according to Gen. 25:20 and 26, is barren for a prolonged period — twenty years — before eventually giving birth; and Rachel, too, must have been infertile for many years before bearing, given that her sister Leah is able to deliver six sons and a daughter in the interim. But despite the fact that these women receive a gift of fertility from God that must be regarded — after such long delays — as wholly unexpected, and despite the command in Isa. 54:1 to the barren one to "sing" *(rānnî 'ăqārâ)*, the Bible's redactors place a song of thanksgiving *only* on the lips of Hannah.

---

cussion, see P. Kyle McCarter, *1 Samuel: A New Translation with Introduction and Commentary* (AB 8; Garden City, N.Y.: Doubleday, 1980), 57-58, and John T. Willis, "The Song of Hannah and Psalm 113," *CBQ* 35 (1973): 139-40, nn. 8-9.

17. Scholars also suggest that (1) the military metaphor found in verse 4a is difficult to imagine as coming from Hannah's mouth; (2) that verse 5's reference to the *seven* children of the barren woman cannot refer to Hannah, who, according to 1 Sam. 2:21, had only six offspring; and (3) that the overall tone of the poem is nationalistic rather than the sort of personal hymn of thanksgiving Hannah might be expected to sing. See further Ralph W. Klein, "The Song of Hannah," *CTM* 41 (1970): 676-77, n. 4.

18. Klein ("Song of Hannah," 677, n. 4) also adds that verses 1 and 3 express well the difficulties Hannah had suffered at the hands of Peninnah, Elqanah's other wife.

Why just her? I believe that the ritual context of 1 Sam. 1:1–2:10 that I have proposed provides the crucial clue. The biblical tradition, I suggest, assigns Hannah alone among the Bible's barren women a song of thanksgiving to sing because Hannah's story of barrenness, alone among the Bible's six barren women stories, is set during the celebration of the fall ingathering festival. Hannah alone sings, that is, because as a woman participating in the Succoth feast, the tradition expects her to play a special role in the making of ritual music. Hannah's song is thus *not,* according to this thesis, a specific response to her experience of barrenness reversed, but rather an example of the kind of ritual musicianship typically undertaken by women as they participated in the Succoth festival.

Other texts that I would suggest attest to this special role for women as musicians in conjunction with the celebration of Succoth are found in the prophetic books. In Jer. 31:10-14, for example, Jeremiah expresses his hope that Israel will return from its exile in Babylon to experience once more God's goodness and munificence in Jerusalem. At that time, Jeremiah says (v. 12), the people will "sing out on the height of Zion" over the flocks and the herds, and also over the grain *(dāgān),* and over the new wine *(tîrōš),* and over the freshly-pressed oil *(yiṣhār).* Generally, commentators see in this verse a fairly generic description of rejoicing over the bounty God will give to a rejuvenated Israel in a restored Jerusalem with a rebuilt Temple. But the references in this verse to the grain *(dāgān),* the new wine *(tîrōš),* and the freshly-pressed oil *(yiṣhār),* and especially the references to the new wine and freshly pressed oil, make clear that Jeremiah's referent is far more specific; it is the rejoicing that takes place at the pilgrimage festival of Succoth on the occasion of the harvesting and pressing of the freshly ripened grapes and olives. Recognizing this temporal setting gives the next verse of Jeremiah's oracle (v. 13) a whole new significance:

Then the young women[19] will rejoice in the dance *(běmāḥōl),*
The young men and the old will be merry.[20]

The young women, that is, will rejoice in the same sort of dance of the vineyard festival described in Judg. 21:15-25.

---

19. Literally, the MT reads "young woman" (singular), *bětûlâ,* but almost all commentators translate in the plural for the sake of the parallelism with the second half of the verse. See further my discussion below.

20. Reading here *yaḥdû* with the LXX for MT *yaḥdāw.*

The third arena we can describe as a site of women's ritual musicianship in preexilic Israel is the music-making undertaken by women in conjunction with various life-cycle rituals. Best attested is women's role as singers of lamentation in conjunction with Israelite funerary rites. A well-known passage in Jer. 31:15, for example, speaks of how, at the time of the Babylonian invasions of the late seventh and early sixth centuries B.C.E., the voice of the long-dead Rachel is heard weeping and performing a mourning song over her devastated descendants (*nĕhî*, from the verb *nāhâ*, "to wail" or "to lament"). Second Samuel 1:24 similarly describes how David, as a part of the dirge he sings after the deaths of Saul and Saul's son Jonathan, expects the daughters of Israel to weep over their dead king — or we can more specifically imagine, based on Jer. 31:15, that David expects these women to sing songs of lamentation. To be sure, the fact that David voices this expectation as part of his own song of lament, or *qînâ*, makes clear that men, as well as women, could assume roles as lament singers in ancient Israel. Still, for women, or at least for some women, the task of singing ritual laments during funerary rites or at analogous times of mourning seems to have been their *professional* — as opposed to a personal — obligation. This is suggested in Jer. 9:16-20 (in most of the Bible's English versions, 9:17-21), where in verse 16, Yahweh, as part of the lament over the forthcoming devastation of Jerusalem, commands that *the* mourning women should be summoned (*qir'û lamĕqônĕnôt*). The use of the definite article suggests a group of women specializing in lamentation, and this is also indicated in the passage's next line, in which these women are identified as being "skilled" or "learned" (*ḥăkāmôt*) in their craft — meaning, perhaps, specially trained. In verse 19, moreover, these female mourners are commanded to teach their daughters a dirge *(nehî)*, possibly suggesting that the profession of the lament singer was handed down by women from one generation to the next.

II. Women's Roles as Ritual Musicians in Exilic and Early Postexilic Israel

Women may also have assumed responsibility within ancient Israel for making music at other life-cycle rituals: at weddings, for example. Yet even though I omit a discussion of the relevant evidence here, for reasons of space, I still think it fair to say that our survey so far has generated a surprisingly rich list of examples of women's ritual musicianship. It is striking, however, from the point of view of my inquiry, that almost all of our texts attesting to women's music-making within Yahwistic tradition come from sources I would date to the preexilic or early exilic period. When we turn, conversely, to look for evidence of women's roles as cultic musicians in sources that come from the late exilic or postexilic period, it is much more difficult to find. We do find one postexilic text that attests to women as lament singers during funerary rituals, 2 Chron. 35:25, although even this text seems to stress women's role as mourners less than do its preexilic counterparts by describing how both "the singing men and the singing women" chanted laments mourning the death of King Josiah; contrast Jer. 9:16 (in most of the Bible's English versions, 9:17), in which only "the mourning *women*" (emphasis mine) are summoned to come to sing a dirge over the destruction of Jerusalem. Meyers speculates that the addition of men to the retinue of mourners in Chronicles is due to the fact that "the mourning for Josiah, one of the few kings considered a righteous ruler, called for an extraordinary outpouring of mourning, which would have involved professional singers of both genders."[21] My own sense, though, is that during the later exilic and postexilic periods, many of the responsibilities for making ritual music that our evidence shows could be assumed by women in the preexilic and early exilic eras became primarily and eventually perhaps even exclusively assigned to men.

More specifically, according, at least, to the books of Chronicles, the responsibility for music-making in the Yahwistic cult came to lie solely with the male members of certain clans of the tribe of Levi. The kindred books of Ezra and Nehemiah also seem to describe the cult's singers as men from various Levite clans, although these texts are not unambiguous (cf., e.g., Ezra 2:41 and 2:70). Ezekiel apparently believes as well that the cult's singers should be male Levites (Ezek. 40:44-46), although he, differently from Chronicles and the admittedly ambiguous books of Ezra and Nehemiah, envisions these Levitical musicians as tracing their ancestry back both to the Solomonic-era priest Zadok and to other ancestors within the Levitical line. Chronicles, conversely, along with multiple texts in Ezra and Nehemiah, suggests that the cult's musicians are drawn solely from the Levites' non-Zadokite lineages. Particularly noteworthy according to the Chronicles-Ezra-Nehemiah tradition is the line of Asaph (see, e.g., 1 Chron. 16:7; 2 Chron. 35:15; Ezra 2:41; Neh. 11:22), and, consequently, a significant corpus of hymns within the Psalter (Psalms 50, 73–83) becomes attributed to him.

---

21. Carol Meyers, "Singing Women (and Men) Who Lament: 2 Chr 35:25," in *Women in Scripture*, 284.

Still, like Ezekiel, Chronicles suggests that the tradition of levitical musicianship was established already in the tenth century B.C.E., during, according to the Chronicles account, the time of King David (1 Chron. 15:16-22, 24). In scholarly circles, however, a very different view of the preexilic history of the Levites prevails, although determining this history has proven to be in many respects a daunting task. In a recent article, for example, Ernest Nicholson has provocatively challenged the "*communis opinio* among modern commentators" that follows, at least in broad outlines, a hypothesis already put forward by Julius Wellhausen in the late nineteenth century.[22] Still, both the *"communis opinio"* of modern commentators and Nicholson agree that a key text for understanding Levitical history is 2 Kings 23:8-9. They also agree, regarding this text, that the "priests of the towns of Judah" mentioned in 23:8 are members of a non-Zadokite line or lines of Levites who, before the reform efforts of Josiah, served in shrines in the Judean countryside, while the priests of the tribe of Levi who traced their descent back to Zadok (and ultimately to Aaron) had, since the time of Solomon, served in the Temple in Jerusalem.[23] They further agree that when Josiah's reforms began, the non-Zadokite "priests of the towns of Judah" were displaced from these towns and that they — or at least some of them — ultimately ended up in Jerusalem, either immediately in the view of the *communis opinio*, or somewhat later, according to the reconstruction offered by Nicholson.[24] At any rate, the evidence of Ezek. 44:6-16 indicates that by 573 B.C.E. at the latest (Ezek. 40:1), the Jerusalem priesthood was envisioned as consisting both of Zadokite and non-Zadokite Levites.

Ezekiel further envisions these two groups as clearly delineated, with the non-Zadokite Levites responsible for only secondary Temple rituals. They may not approach Yahweh's altar or come near to anything that has been consecrated to Yahweh: that privilege is reserved for "the descendants of Zadok" alone (Ezek. 44:13, 15-16). Instead, they serve as gatekeepers, they slaughter sacrificial animals, and they stand before the people to serve them (Ezek. 44:11). Moreover, they serve as singers, although in Ezekiel, as I have already noted, both non-Zadokite Levites and the Zadokites assume this

---

22. Ernest Nicholson, "Josiah and the Priests of the High Places (II Reg 23, 8a.9)," *ZAW* 119 (2007): 499-513; the phrase *"communis opinio* among modern commentators" is taken from this article, p. 499.

23. See, e.g., Rainer Albertz, *A History of Israelite Religion in the Old Testament Period, II: From the Exile to the Maccabees* (OTL; Louisville, Ky.: Westminster John Knox, 1992), 430-31; Cross, *Canaanite Myth and Hebrew Epic*, 195-215, 237-38.

24. Nicholson, "Josiah and the Priests of the High Places," 503-7, 512.

function (Ezek. 40:44-46). Still, from Ezekiel's preliminary attempts at status differentiation, it is but a short jump to the hierarchy that is established in Chronicles, somewhat in certain P materials in the Pentateuch (e.g., Numbers 3–4), and in Ezra and Nehemiah, whereby Zadokite priests take responsibility for the central rituals of Yahwistic faith while the non-Zadokite Levites serve as the Temple's gatekeepers, musicians, and Temple servants.

Yet if Josiah's act in bringing the Levites of the Judahite countryside into Jerusalem establishes a trajectory that culminates by the fifth and fourth centuries in the conviction that it is the men of certain Levitical lineages who *alone* are responsible for musical performance in the Yahwistic cult, then what of the earlier traditions that assigned to women important roles as music-makers within Yahwistic ritual? Our answer must be that women's ability to participate in the cult as musicians was greatly diminished by the time of the late exilic and postexilic periods. In some cases, as I have already suggested, this may mean that the rituals of music-making associated with mourning that were previously the responsibility primarily of women were reconceptualized so as to include both men and women (2 Chron. 35:25). In other cases, I might suggest, the older traditions that described women as the actual makers of music in conjunction with Yahweh's victories in holy war came to be rendered in far more metaphorical language.

Such a transformation may be found in the late exilic text of Isa. 40:9-10,[25] where the city of Jerusalem, also called Zion and personified as female, seems commissioned to serve as the herald *(mĕbaśśeret)* who proclaims that, as the Babylonian captivity is coming to an end, Yahweh is prepared to march forth as the divine warrior to deliver the Israelites from the enemies that have oppressed them.[26] This task of singing out in celebration of Yahweh's march as the divine warrior recalls the role assumed by women such as Miriam, Deborah, and Jephthah's daughter in making music after Yahweh's victories in holy war, and it is particularly reminiscent of Ps. 68:12, where a divine command to speak out precedes the proclamation by female heralds *(mĕbaśśĕrôt)* of Yahweh's victory in holy war. Yet Isa. 40:9 reconceptualizes the specific way in which the responsibility for making music after a triumph in holy war is envisioned, so that rather than assign this task to actual women, as in the preexilic period, it is only a

---

25. This text brought to my attention by Meyers, "Mother to Muse," 72; see also eadem, "Those Who Bear Tidings: Heralds," 299.

26. It is also possible to translate this text as commissioning an anonymous female herald to call forth good tidings to Jerusalem/Zion.

metaphorically-rendered female, the city Jerusalem/Zion, who is said to sing out tidings of victory.

Other texts in the exilic-era Isaianic corpus (i.e., Isaiah 34–35, 40–55) seem similarly to retain the notion that singing and dancing in celebration of Yahweh's victories in holy war are to be associated with females, yet resist ascribing this music-making to actual women. In Isa. 35:1-2, for example, it is the desert, grammatically gendered as female (*'ărābâ*), that sings songs rejoicing in Yahweh's victorious march against the nations who participated in Judah's destruction in 586 B.C.E. Later on in this same poem, in verse 10, the traditional conception that music-making upon the occasion of a Yahwistic victory in holy war was the responsibility of women is undermined in a somewhat different way, by describing how it is all "the ransomed of Yahweh," presumably, that is, both men and women, who will come to Jerusalem singing in celebration of Yahweh's triumphs. This same undermining is illustrated even more dramatically when 35:10 is repeated, almost verbatim, in Isa. 51:11. Here, the verse is part of a short poem, Isa. 51:9-11, that explicitly appropriates images of the exodus out of Egypt and uses them to describe the journey the Israelites will make out of Babylon. Yet despite the fact that this new exodus is described, as was the exodus of old, as a triumph of Yahweh, the divine warrior, over Israel's enemies, the music that is appropriately made in this victory's aftermath is, as in 35:10, made by "the ransomed of Yahweh," that is, both men and women, instead of by the all-female chorus of musicians who were led by Miriam in the celebration of the actual exodus from Egypt.

There are other texts in the exilic-era Isaianic corpus that divorce women altogether from their traditional role as musicians who celebrate Yahweh's victories in holy war. In Isa. 42:10-12, for example, it is an assembly of natural phenomena and the nations, all grammatically gendered as male, that is commanded to sing a hymn praising Yahweh, the divine warrior, for God's mighty deeds that have defeated Israel's enemies (42:13) and transformed the natural world for the Israelites' benefit (42:15-16). Similarly in 44:23, male imperative forms are used to command the heavens, the depths of the earth, and the mountains to sing in exultation. Note finally 52:7, where, as in 40:9, a herald is to proclaim that Yahweh has acted to bring salvation to the exiled Israelites. But whereas in 40:9 the tradition associating women's music-making with the celebrating of Yahweh's victories in holy war is retained at least to the degree that it is a female herald, the personified Jerusalem, who sings out the news of Yahweh's triumph, here, in 52:7, the herald is male, and the sentinels who sing for joy in 52:8 are male as well.

All these texts lead us to ask of the author of the exilic-era Isaianic materials: what is left, in this corpus's understanding, for the actual women of ancient Israel who would make the ritual music that celebrates Yahweh's triumphs in battle, in the same way that we previously asked of the Priestly tradition and the Chronicles-Ezra-Nehemiah corpus: what is left, according to their vision, for the women of ancient Israel who would render service as musicians generally within Yahwistic worship? Our evidence may well suggest that, within the structures of the Israelite cult that emerge during the exile and early postexilic period, women as ritual music-makers are pushed more and more to the outside. Or, to return to the language of Exum, although women in the exilic and postexilic periods remain the "same" as men in terms of their identities as Israelites and as Yahwists, they become, in terms of their role as cultic musicians, more and more the Other.

One final example of this phenomenon is found in Jer. 30:23–31:4, amid a series of oracles (Jer. 30:1–31:40) that almost all commentators date, at least in the form in which they have come down to us, to the early exilic period[27] — that is, from precisely the period during which, under the terms of my hypothesis, the transition had begun that moved at least some ritual music-making functions from the female arena to the male. Appropriately, therefore, at least as I would see it, this transitional passage still contains two examples — both of which I have previously cited — of women taking responsibility for ritual music-making: women serving as singers of ritual laments (the dirge Rachel sings over her devastated children in Jer. 31:15) and women making music in conjunction with the annual celebration of the vineyard festival (the young women who dance in Jer. 31:13 at the time of the pressing of the newly-harvested grapes and olives). Yet even here, the responsibilities women assumed as ritual musicians in the preexilic period have become somewhat eroded: the dirge-singing Rachel of Jer. 31:15, for example, is, according to the Bible's chronology, at least a thousand years dead and so represents only a specter of a woman past, not an actual woman of Jeremiah's day. And while I have followed all the standard translations in my earlier renderings of Jer. 31:13 and so have read the verse as a reference to young *women* who rejoice in dance, the fact of the matter is that both the subject *(bĕtûlâ)* and the verb *(tiśmaḥ)* are in the singular.[28]

---

27. Although an older source, we can take as representative the comments of John Bright, *Jeremiah: A New Translation with Introduction and Commentary* (AB 21; Garden City, N.Y.: Doubleday, 1965), 284-87.

28. See above, n. 19.

Jeremiah 31:13 is not, moreover, the only point within the series of oracles in Jer. 30:1–31:40 at which the noun *bĕtûlâ* is found. It occurs in Jer. 31:4, in the concluding verse of an oracle (30:23–31:4) in which Jeremiah speaks of how Yahweh, although now requiring that God's people endure suffering, will eventually come like a storm against the Israelites' enemies and destroy them. Following this triumph of Yahweh, the divine warrior, comes the same sort of victory celebration that, as we have already noted, is described in older traditions: the celebration where women, accompanying themselves on hand drums, dance and sing hymns praising Yahweh's saving acts. Yet like Isaiah, Jeremiah changes these earlier traditions of women's music-making after a victory in holy war not insignificantly by suggesting in 31:4 that the celebratory music is no longer made by actual women, but by the *bĕtûlat yiśrā'ēl*, that is, the nation Israel personified as a woman. Perhaps the *bĕtûlâ* of Jer. 31:13 should be similarly interpreted? Note in this regard that the phrase *bĕtûlat yiśrā'ēl* occurs again within the Jer. 30:1–31:40 complex in 31:21, suggesting that at least as the redactor of this complex saw it, the *bĕtûlâ* in Jer. 31:13 who is bracketed between these two evocations of the *bĕtûlat yiśrā'ēl* is not to be envisioned as a real woman.

And so even within this text that at first glance seemed so richly imbued with the various sounds of women's ritual music-making that we have identified — women's victory-song performances in celebration of Yahweh's triumphs in holy war; women's dancing and singing at the time of the Succoth festival; and women's musicianship on the occasion of certain lifecycle rituals — we are ultimately left with only a dirge sung by a thousand-year-old ghost. Would it thus be untoward for us to imagine that this lament not only bewails the fate of Rachel's children as they face the onslaught of the Babylonian army, but also bemoans the fate of Rachel's fellow women performers as they face the silencing of their preexilic musical traditions?

How Good Was Ruth's Hebrew?
Ethnic and Linguistic Otherness in the Book of Ruth

Timothy H. Lim

The theme of Otherness is evident throughout the book of Ruth as it tells a tale of the displacement of the family of Elimelech from Judah to Moab and back again. The story focuses on the migration of two women, Naomi and Ruth, as they adapt to life in a foreign land. In this paper, I will examine one feature of this theme of estrangement by discussing the quality of Ruth's Hebrew. I will suggest that while Ruth's Hebrew is very good, it is uneven. The author of the book intentionally made her stumble over her words in one instance as he reminds the reader that she was "Ruth the Moabitess."

The question that I have posed for myself in the title is more interesting than one might at first suppose. The common view is that Moabite is not that different from Hebrew and consequently Ruth had little difficulty acquiring the language of her husband and in-laws. Edward Ullendorff, in a 1962 article, for instance, asserts that "Hebrews and Moabites could communicate without undue difficulty."[1] He does not specify what linguistic adjust-

---

1. "The Knowledge of Languages in the Old Testament," BJRL 44 (1961-62): 455-65 (esp. 463).

It is a great pleasure to honor my good friend John Collins, whose knowledge of the Hebrew Bible and ancient Judaism is complemented by a humane and hearty character. Earlier versions of this paper were delivered at research seminars in Edinburgh and Sheffield. Many thanks to colleagues in both places, especially Hans Barstad and Cheryl Exum, for their comments that have made this paper better. Thanks also to Raija Sollamo, University of Helsinki, for her comments on a draft of the paper.

ments had to be made for mutual comprehension, but whatever they were they must have been fairly minor. Ullendorff states: "This impression is borne out very fully by the book of Ruth, for neither of the two Moabite women, Ruth and Orpah, seems to have found it hard to understand their Judaean relatives."[2]

The intelligibility of Moabite for ancient Hebrew speakers is the consensus view as evidenced in the recent review of the *status quaestionis* by the late Simon Parker.[3] After a survey of the evidence for Ammonite, Edomite, and Moabite languages, he states that the Moabite language as reflected especially in the Mesha inscription is "strikingly similar in language and even style to classical Hebrew prose."[4] Parker's review takes account of all the existing evidence of Moabite language: the Mesha inscription, the unprovenanced *marzeah* papyrus, the Tell Siran inscription, the Amman citadel inscription and the Tell El-Mazar ostraca. The evidence is not plentiful and no full description of the language could be made. Nonetheless, Parker points out that Moabite shares with Hebrew the use of the relative pronoun *'šr*, the object marker *'t*, and the apocopation of the third weak verb in the *wayyqtl* form. Like Ammonite, it used the article *h-* but with less frequency than Hebrew. Moabite shares with Northern (Israelite) Hebrew and Phoenician the monophthongized dipthongs *aw* and *ay*, and with Old Aramaic and Phoenician the feminine ending on the word *št*, "year." Distinctive to Moabite is the preservation of older features of Canaanite language, namely the use of the final *n* on the absolute plural of masculine nouns and adjectives, the final *t* as the marker of feminine singular absolute nouns, and an infixed *t* stem of the simple conjugation. Parker does not explicitly relate his survey of Moabite to the book of Ruth, but anyone who has read the Moabite evidence with an eye on the review is likely to draw the same conclusion that he and Ullendorff drew.

If I may take the opinion of the two men as representative of the scholarly consensus, then I believe that there is room for refinement of the discussion. I do not mean by this the kind of caveat expressed in connection with the study of inscriptional language as opposed to classical Hebrew

2. "Knowledge of Languages," 463.

3. "Ammonite, Edomite, and Moabite," in *Beyond Babel: A Handbook for Biblical Hebrew and Related Languages*, ed. J. Kaltner and S. L. McKenzie (Atlanta: Society of Biblical Literature, 2002), 43-60. See earlier Kent P. Jackson, "The Language of the Mesha Inscription," in *Studies in the Mesha Inscription and Moab*, ed. A. Dearman (Atlanta: Scholars Press, 1989), chapter 4.

4. "Ammonite, Edomite, and Moabite," 51.

prose of the Bible, however legitimate that may be. This sort of scholarly caution has been made frequently and needs no repetition here. Rather, I believe that we should take full account of the fictional context of the book of Ruth. We do not have Ruth's *ipsissima verba*, to borrow a phrase from New Testament scholarship on Jesus' *logia*, but her and Orpah's words as conceived by the literary author who we assume was Israelite. The evidence for the Moabite language is too paltry to permit one to say whether real, ancient Moabite speakers could easily understand and communicate with their Judean counterparts. Rather, I want to rephrase the question to reflect the literary interests of my study: "How good did the author make Ruth's Hebrew?"

From the outset it would be useful to rehearse some of the basics. The book of Ruth consists of four chapters and 85 verses. Of these, 59 verses (or 69 percent) contain speeches. Ruth speaks by herself ten different times in three chapters (1, 2, and 4), although on two occasions (2:21 and 3:17) she is simply reporting Boaz's speech. She also speaks together with Orpah one other time in 1:9-10. Ruth, then, speaks a total of eleven times in the book.[5] When one studies her speeches, it is evident that she speaks in idiomatic classical Hebrew. Her eloquence reaches its zenith in the expression of the finely balanced and noble sentiments of filial piety in 1:16-17.

I. Young Men or Women

There is, nevertheless, one instance where Ruth's otherwise good Hebrew appears to have faltered, and this is when she is reporting to Naomi what Boaz had said to her earlier.[6] The context is that Ruth had just returned from a day of gleaning in the field and was discussing with Naomi her encounter with Boaz. The masoretic scribes point out that 2:21 is precisely the middle of the book, which in the RSV translation reads as follows:

> And Ruth the Moabitess said, "Besides, he (i.e., Boaz) said to me: 'You shall keep close by my servants, till they have finished all my harvest.'"

---

5. See my discussion of the speeches in "The Book of Ruth and Its Literary Voice," in *Reflection and Refraction: Studies in Biblical Historiography in Honour of A. Graeme Auld*, ed. R. Rezetko, T. H. Lim, and B. Aucker (Leiden: Brill, 2007), 261-82.

6. The other time when Ruth reports his speech (3:17), the original words of Boaz are not preserved.

The translation "by my servants" renders the Hebrew עִם־הַנְּעָרִים, which literally refers to Boaz's male servants. What Boaz actually says in 2:8 is "do not glean in another field or leave this one, but keep close to my maidens (עִם־נַעֲרֹתַי)." When Naomi repeated Boaz's advice, she reverts to the female servants: "it is well, my daughter, that you go out with his maidens (עִם־נַעֲרוֹתָיו), lest in another field you be molested" (v. 22). The reference to female servants is continued by the narrator in v. 23 and repeated in Naomi's speech in 3:2.

Paul Joüon explained away the discrepancy as a scribal error arising out of the accidental, graphical confusion of נערות with נערים. The reading עִם־הַנְּעָרִים in v. 21 is correct, but נערותיו in v. 22 is a mistake. This error arose out of the previous confusion of נערתי for נערי in v. 8. The mistake was then propagated in vv. 22, 23 and 3:2.[7] Joüon maintained that had there been female servants, then Boaz would have asked Ruth to sit beside them rather than by the male servants (2:14). He emended all the instances of the female servants to read "serviteurs." There are problems with Joüon's explanation. It is difficult to see how the scribal error of omitting ת arose in the first place, in v. 8. It also leaves unexplained why the scribe would have presumably made the same mistake in 2:22 when he had just got it right in the immediately preceding verse.

Yair Zakovitch similarly reconciled the different readings by an appeal to scribal error.[8] He suggested that the correct reading was נערות, but that in 2:21 the copyist inadvertently changed it to נערים because he had wrongly assumed that the subject of כלו ("they completed") must only refer to the masculine-plural reapers. Although Zakovitch does not mention it, there is a textual variant of χορασίων ("young maidens") that supports his reading.[9] The main LXX witnesses, however, read παιδαρίων. If the verb caused the supposed scribal error, why did a similar mistake not also occur in verse 23, where the same root is used to refer to the same completion (כלות) of the harvest? Also, Zakovitch would have to assume that when the copyist com-

---

7. *Ruth: Commentaire Philologique et Exégétique* (Rome: Biblical Institute Press, 1986), 52-53, 64-65.

8. *Das Buch Rut: Ein jüdischer Kommentar* (Stuttgart: Verlag Katholisches Bibelwerk, 1999), 65, 129-30.

9. Udo Quast, *Ruth* (Göttingen: Vandenhoeck & Ruprecht, 2006), 177. Wilhelm Rudolph, *Das Buch Ruth. Das Hohe Lied: Die Klagelieder* (Gütersloh: Gütersloh Verlagshaus Gerd Mohn, 1962), 51, also referred to the textual support from the versions, but argued that the MT reading is the *lectio difficilior* and that הנערים (as in Job 1:19) covers workers of both genders.

mitted his scribal error he already had his eye on the following phrase, thus anticipating an understanding of the verb "they have completed" to be an exclusive reference to male harvesters.

Another explanation followed by several commentators is to consider the masculine נערים as generic. Edward Campbell, for instance, suggested that the masculine plural refers to "harvesters" and "young people" who would have included both sexes.[10] Whenever the female-plural form is used, it is a means of reminding the reader of the need to protect the "elected" female from harm or from the wrong marriage. This line of exegesis does not explain why Ruth should use נערים in 2:21 and Naomi נערות in 2:22 when both have in view the same female participation in the harvest with all its potential dangers.[11]

Kirsten Nielsen offers a literal exegesis of 2:21 by suggesting that Ruth, misquoting Boaz, has now chosen to cling to the farm hands, prompting her mother-in-law to admonish her to stay away from the men and to cling to the young women. For Nielsen, Naomi's subsequent advice echoes Boaz's speech in 2:8, although the two had not met.[12] There is support for Nielsen's reading in *Midrash Ruth Rabbah* 5:11 ("in truth she was a Moabitess"), but this Jewish text imputes Ruth's impure thoughts to her Moabite origins,[13] an ethnic propensity that is nowhere found in the biblical text. In Ruth, Moab and Moabites do not play the role of enemies of Israel, as they appear to in other biblical texts, notably Deut. 23:4. Additionally, this reading would portray Ruth in a particularly salacious light as someone who schemed by intentionally misquoting Boaz's advice so that she could stay with the men. In this improbable understanding, Ruth would be seen as someone who chased after any eligible men, even male servants.

A fifth explanation, by Danna Fewell and David Gunn, suggested that Ruth teasingly misreported Boaz's words in order to prompt her mother-in-

---

10. *Ruth: A New Translation with Introduction, Notes and Commentary* (AB 7; Garden City, N.Y.: Doubleday, 1975), 97, 107. He is followed by, among others, Frederic Bush, *Ruth, Esther* (Waco: Word Books, 1996), 120-21, and Robert L. Hubbard, *The Book of Ruth* (Grand Rapids: Eerdmans, 1988), 156-57.

11. Jack M. Sasson, *Ruth: A New Translation with a Philological Commentary and a Formalist-Folklorist Interpretation* (Sheffield: JSOT Press, 1989), 62, glosses over the whole issue by stating that it is Boaz's concession to allow her to gather grain behind the young men that is most important to Ruth's new status.

12. *Ruth: A Commentary* (Louisville: Westminster John Knox, 1997), 64.

13. Zakovitch, *Das Buch Rut*, 130, comments: "Der Midrasch hat den Wechsel von נערים zu נערות für eine despektierliche Bemerkung über Rut benutzt. . . ."

law to express concern for her well-being.[14] Ruth was apparently demanding reciprocal love from Naomi and hinting at the possibility of future separation by cleaving to unknown young men. Moreover, Naomi's advice notably omits the verb "to cleave" (דבק) with its sexual and marital connotations (cf. Gen. 2:24). Fewell and Gunn's reading is based upon their view that the two women were estranged from before the time that they entered Bethlehem. This reading against the grain of the text attributes more to "the young men" than the text allows: in this reading "the young men" constitute both the source of danger and potential, future separation of the two women when only the former reason was explicitly mentioned in Naomi's response of 2:22. Moreover, it is unlikely that דבק has the sexual connotation of Gen. 2:24 as it does in Ruth 1:14; here, Ruth is simply repeating the verb that Boaz used which, in the context of 2:8, has as its referent the young women. It is improbable that Boaz also has in mind sexual connotations when he admonishes Ruth to "keep close to my maidens." The issue in 2:21, as opposed to the one raised later in 3:10 (note the use of a different word, בחורים and not נערים, for young men), is about safety and not marriage.

II. Vestiges of Ruth's Foreign Origins

There is no compelling reason to emend the text as it stands in the MT and LXX. Support for the MT reading is found in *Targum Ruth*, which maintains the distinction by using two different Aramaic words to translate נערים and נערות:

> Ruth the Moabite said, "He even told me, 'Continue with my lads (ריביא דילי), until they conclude all the harvest.'" And Naomi answered her daughter-in-law Ruth, "It is good, my daughter, that you go out with his maidservants (עולימותי), and not be accosted in some other field" (2:21-22).[15]

The usual word for young males in targumic Aramaic is רבי; although, in some cases, including Ruth 1:12, 2:5, 6, and 4:12, it refers to a young fe-

---

14. This is followed by Tod Linafelt and Timothy K. Beal, *Ruth and Esther* (Collegeville: Liturgical Press, 1999), 43-44.

15. Translation by Etan Levine, *The Aramaic Version of Ruth* (Rome: Biblical Institute Press, 1973), 30. Levine notes, "whereas the text has Boaz instructing her to cleave to his maidservants (II, 8), here the word 'lads' is used" (p. 84).

male.¹⁶ In Ruth 3:10 and 4:16, the word refers to males. However עולימותי (2:22, 23 and 3:2) has the feminine plural suffixed ending and clearly indicates that the reference is to Boaz's female servants. It is true that עולים means "young boy or man," but עולימה invariably means "young girl or woman." The meturgeman translates Boaz's earlier command in 2:8 with עולימותי ("my girls").

Midrash Ruth Rabbah, too, supports the MT, but attributes to Ruth a licentiousness that it traces to her Moabite origins. A dictum reported in the name of R. Hanin b. Levi states that she remained a Moabitess because she misreported Boaz's words as a command to abide "by my young men" rather than "by my young women." Apparently she wanted to consort with young males.¹⁷ There is no basis for this reading in Ruth, as previously mentioned, and the midrash otherwise portrays Ruth as an obedient and modest woman. What is important here is that the darshan pays close attention to the different genders of the young workers in exegeting the words נערים and נערות. The interpretation is based upon the gender distinction between male and female youths.

The "author" of the biblical book, whoever he was,¹⁸ intended Ruth to slip up in her use of נערים, which she either misunderstood or misremembered from Boaz's advice. It is a common mistake of bilinguals who otherwise speak fluently in the acquired language. Naomi corrects her by supplying the correct word נערות in the following verse; she does so "in midstream" when she confirms that it is good advice that Ruth should cleave to the young women. Both the narrator and Naomi again use the correct word in the immediately following 2:23 and 3:2. It is only Ruth who uses the wrong word.

Of course, Boaz himself is not a paragon of clarity. What he says in 2:9 is rather confusing. RSV (italics added) translates it as follows:

---

16. The searches in the Complete Aramaic Lexicon Project database of the Hebrew Union College (Ohio) resulted in the following hits for רבי, meaning "boy" and "girl" respectively: in *Onkelos, Jonathan* and the *Writings* (82x and 7x); *Neofiti* and *Esther Sheni* (5x and 30x); *Pseudo-Jonathan* (13x and none); Cairo Genizah (2x and 1x); and Aramaic Targum (Fragments) (4x and none).

17. See the discussion of Tryggve Kronholm, "The Portrayal of Characters in Midrash Ruth Rabbah: Observations on the Formation of the Jewish Hermeneutical Legend Known as 'Biblical Haggadah,'" *ASTI* 12 (1983): 13-54 (esp. 35).

18. See my "Book of Ruth and Its Literary Voice" for the complexities involved in speaking about an author, voice, and narrative perspective.

Let your eyes be upon the field which they are reaping (יקצרון), and *go after them* (אחריהן). Have I not charged the young men (אֶת־הנערים) not to molest you? And when you are thirsty, go to the vessels and drink what the young men (הנערים) have drawn.

The phrase "go after them" translates the Hebrew אחריהן, which has a third-feminine-plural pronominal suffix attached to the preposition and must refer to the female and not the male servants. Since the Moabite language uses a final *nun* on the masculine nouns and adjectives, Ruth may wrongly take the final *nun* of אחריהן as a reference to males and not females.[19]

What Boaz says to Ruth in this verse is "Let your eyes be upon the field which they (i.e., the male servants) are reaping, and follow after them (i.e., the female servants)." In the harvest, apparently the male servants were to lead by cutting down the crop of grain and barley and were to be followed by female bundlers who collected and tied up the sheaves ready for transport to the threshing floor. Ruth is asked to follow after the female bundlers and not the male harvesters when she gathers the grains that have fallen on the ground. It is easy to see how she misunderstands Boaz, because the man's speech is not exactly perspicuous. In 2:9, he switches from a masculine plural (with *paragogic nun*) יקצרון to a feminine reference אחריהן, which is then followed immediately by another reference to a masculine plural, הנערים. Ruth's own understanding of the harvest is less exacting: "Pray, let me glean and gather among the sheaves after the reapers (אחרי הקוצרים)" (2:7). She does not differentiate between reapers and bundlers, males and females. Boaz's speech with its quick succession of switches between grammatically masculine and feminine genders — especially when one also considers the speed at which words flow in any active dialogue (real or imagined) — would have left the poor foreigner terribly confused. The author, drawing on his knowledge of Moabite language, which, like Aramaic, represented the masculine plural by the final *nun*, exploited this linguistic difference to underscore the foreignness of Ruth.

Ruth's infelicitous use of נערים in her speech represents a phenomenon often found among bilinguals, namely, the use of an inappropriate word or term in the target language, as for instance when a native French or Italian may write in English to "my estimated colleague" when he means "es-

---

19. Note, for example, the phrases in the Mesha stele שלשן שת ("thirty years"; l. 2) and ימן רבן ("many days"; l. 5). The preposition "after" occurs only once in this text and without the suffix, "after my father" (אחר אבי; l. 3).

teemed." Both words derive from the Latin root *aestimare*, but the former means an approximation of the colleague's value, while the latter is an expression of that same value in the form of respect and admiration. Ruth misunderstands Boaz's advice in a spectacular way. The effect of her confusion is that Boaz has apparently advised her to cleave to the young men who were wont to molest her (cf. 2:9)! This unevenness in her facility in the Hebrew language, I suggest, is characteristic of people who have learned, but not quite mastered the target language. I do not postulate that the author needed to know linguistics or any modern conception of how language works in stylizing Ruth's speech to underscore the theme of foreignness; creativity is often intuitive and innate more than studied and methodical. He would have instinctively known through observation and life-experience that even among the speech of those who have learned Hebrew well there remain vestiges of their foreign origins.

III. The Speeches as Literary Creations

The literary artistry of the book of Ruth is well known. Campbell opines in the introduction to his commentary, which pays particular attention to literary features: "One more obvious conclusion, to which I have pointed regularly: I stand in awe of this author. He was a genius."[20] Of course "genius" is an overused term, and whether or not one agrees with this description, one cannot but be impressed by the stylized composition of the book, a work that uses narrative structure (balance, parallelism, chiasm), rhetorical tropes (assonance), appeals (pathos), thematic synonymy, and juxtaposition.

What I would like to discuss are the literary features of the speeches that the author has created for his characters. In his article "Art et leçon de l'histoire de Ruth," Paul Humbert noted in passing a literary feature that distinguished the speeches of the characters in the story. He stated that "[t]he narrator takes care to make Boaz speak as the aged, for he makes him use some archaizing verbal forms and the solemnity that he also places in Naomi's mouth no other interlocutor employs in the story of Ruth."[21] What Humbert was referring to by "archaizing verbal forms" is the addition of *nun-paragogicum* or the lengthening of certain prefixed conjugations by the

---

20. *Ruth*, 10.
21. The article was republished in *Opuscules d'un hébraïsant* (Neuchâtel: Université de Neuchâtel, 1958), 83-110 (esp. 92).

addition of a final *nun;* there are 304 cases of the additional *nun* in the Hebrew Bible, especially in the older books, as compared with 6,600 instances without this ending.[22] Most scholars understand this linguistic phenomenon in morphological terms; it indicates the use of older or archaic forms. Jean Hoftijzer, however, has argued that the added *nun,* in some cases, has a "functional opposition" or contrastivity. Thus, when Boaz cautions Ruth to "keep close (תדבקין) to my maidens," he means that she should stay here and not go to other fields.[23]

The use of the *nun-paragogic* occurs six times in the book of Ruth, three times in the speech of Boaz (תדבקין 2:8; יקצרון and ישאבון 2:9) and twice in the mouth of Naomi (תעשׂין 3:4 and תדעין 3:18). Ruth, too, uses it when she is reporting what Boaz said to her (תדבקין 2:21). Apart from this one instance of *nun-paragogic,* Ruth does not use this linguistic feature in her own speech. Humbert understood it as archaic in a literary sense. He did not intend by this to date Ruth on the basis of historical Hebrew grammar. Rather, "verbales archaïsantes" are the forms of speech that mark the aged.

Following Humbert's lead, I have recently suggested that a further feature of the speech of "les gens âges" may be detected. Commentators have long noticed a peculiar feature of the Hebrew of Ruth, namely that pronominal suffixes that appear to be masculine plurals are applied to females. There are seven such cases of apparent gender confusion:[24]

NAOMI SPEAKING: עמכם (1:8), עשׂיתם (1:8), לכם (1:9, 11), מכם (1:13)
NARRATIVE: שׁתיהם (1:19)
PEOPLE OF THE GATE AND ELDERS SPEAKING: שׁתיהם (4:11).

There have been several explanations given for this apparent linguistic anomaly,[25] but the one suggested by Frank Anderson has received the widest

---

22. Jean Hoftijzer, *The Function and Use of the Imperfect Forms with Nun Paragogicum in Classical Hebrew* (Assen: Van Gorcum, 1985), 2.

23. Ibid., 18-19.

24. In 1975 Campbell, *Ruth,* 40, 66, reported that 4QRuth[a] read *qolam* for MT *qolan* (Ruth 1:9) and suggested that this may well be another instance of the old feminine dual.

25. Jaakov Levi, *Die Inkongruenz im biblischen Hebräisch* (Wiesbaden: Otto Harrassowitz, 1987), for instance, surveyed them as part of the widespread phenomenon of grammatical incongruence in Biblical Hebrew. He noted that the incongruence of masculine plural pronominal suffix with feminine plural substantives, a phenomenon found in all sorts of nouns in early and late texts, could be caused by metonymy or attraction. The distinction between ם- and ן- for the feminine suffix is not strictly maintained and both forms

support. Anderson argued that the final *mem* endings are vestiges of an old "Ugaritic dual" and that all seven cases have as their antecedent two women.

The Ugaritic-dual explanation is attractive. However, Frederic Bush's argument that *hemmah* in 1:22 is a further case of the Ugaritic dual built on the third masculine plural (as *hûma* in Ugaritic and Arabic) is questionable on the grounds that this would be the only occurrence of such an independent dual form in Biblical Hebrew.[26] David Freedman has otherwise explained *hemmah* as an emphatic particle from the Ugaritic *hm/hmt*, meaning "behold," with numerous examples from the Psalms and a few from Isaiah.[27]

I have suggested that this linguistic feature, rather than being useful for a linguistic dating of Ruth, constitutes another literary technique that the author used to distinguish the speech of the aged.[28] All but one of the six occurrences appears in the mouth of the aged, Naomi and the elders. The only exception is Ruth 1:19, where the feature occurs in a narrative verse. But 1:19 appears to be a scribal error of assimilation to 4:11. Here, I want to expand on the reasons why I think that this was so by comparing the two verses. Ruth 1:19 reads as follows in the RSV:

> So the two of them (שתיהם) went on until they came (עד־באנה) to Bethlehem (בית לחם). And when they came (כבאנה) to Bethlehem (בית לחם), the whole town was stirred because of them (עליהן); and the women said: "Is this Naomi?"

Ruth 4:11 reads as follows:

> Then all the people who were at the gate, and the elders, said, "We are witnesses. May the Lord make the woman, who is coming into your

---

often occur in the same sentence. He suggested that this linguistic phenomenon may have been influenced by spoken speech. For the eight instances (he included המה of Ruth 1:22 on p. 163), he gave no explanation but simply listed them (pp. 178-79). Levi has underscored how common is the grammatical incongruence, but the passages should not simply be listed and catalogued but studied and explained.

26. Frederic Bush, *Ruth, Esther* (Dallas: Word Books, 1996), 94-95.

27. This suggestion was reported and adopted by Campbell, *Ruth*, 78 (cf. M. Dahood, *Psalms I, 1–50* [New York: Doubleday, 1965], 56). Bush, *Ruth, Esther*, 94, argued that this particle is problematic in Ugaritic and that the syntax required the pronoun to avoid a *vav* consecutive. As for the Hebrew syntax, I do not see how the pronoun but not the emphatic article would avoid a *vav* consecutive. For the Ugaritic particle, see also Josef Tropper, *Ugaritische Grammatik* (Münster: Ugarit-Verlag, 2000), 793-94.

28. "Book of Ruth and Its Literary Voice," 275.

> house (הבאה אל־ביתך), like Rachel and Leah, who together (שתיהם) built up the house of Israel (את־בית ישראל). May you prosper in Ephrathah and be renowned in Bethlehem (בבית לחם)...."

There are several reasons for thinking that שתיהם of 1:19 in Codex L was a scribal error of assimilation: (a) Many other manuscripts read שתיהן at 1:19; (b) שתיהם is used in two different, yet comparable, contexts. Only לכם (1:9, 11) is used twice within the same context; (c) the scribal error was probably caused by the assimilation of 1:19 to 4:11. The link between the two pairs is implied in 4:11. It was explicitly said that Ruth came "to your (i.e., Boaz's) house" like Rachel and Leah, who "the two of them" (שתיהם) built up the house of Israel. Ruth is compared to Rachel and Leah; and Naomi is implied (see end of 4:9). There is lexical affinity in the use of the verb "to come" (בא) and the denominative "house" (בית), and the literary setting is the same (Bethlehem, Ephratha); (d) In 1:19, the two women are referred to (עליהן) with the regular, feminine-plural pronominal suffix, suggesting that שתיהם is a secondary reflex based on what the copyist knew in 4:11.

If 1:19 is a scribal error of assimilation, as I have suggested, then the remaining six instances of the "Ugaritic dual" occur in speeches, five by Naomi and one by the people of the gate and the elders. Of course, there is no instance of Boaz using this linguistic feature; Boaz is not in the scene when Orpah is still with Ruth in chapter 1; Naomi and Boaz do not meet; and in chapter 4 Boaz is the object, not the speaker, of the blessing.

Let us return to 2:8 and 2:21 and combine the feature of archaism with the incorrect word choice in the case of the reported speech. In effect, Boaz and Ruth might have sounded like this in English (with apologies to the Authorized translation):

> BOAZ: "Go not to glean in another field, neither go thence, but abide here fast by my maidens."
> RUTH: "He said to me: 'Abide here fast by my young men until they have completed all my harvest.'"

What I am suggesting is that the author depicted Ruth as someone for whom Hebrew was a second language. As is common among bilinguals who have learned, but not yet mastered, another language, she is both precise and imprecise in her reporting of a speech by someone else. She is overly correct, given that her own speech does not include such features, in replicating

Boaz's archaisms in her reporting (תדבקין "abide here fast"), but she fails to detect the important distinction between נערים and נערות.

IV. Epithets

One final literary feature that should be mentioned is the author's penchant to add epithets and other short descriptors for the various characters in his story. These include: Naomi the mother-in-law in 2:18, 19, 23; 3:1, 6, 16, 17 (also 1:14; 2:11); Boaz, "kinsman of her husband," 2:1; "a relative to us, one of our redeemers," 2:20; "our kinsman"; "redeemer (once removed)," 3:12; "the man," 3:16, 18; and "redeemer," 4:14. The author has a proclivity to make explicit the relationship of the characters: Elimelech, "husband of Naomi," 1:3; "the dead," 1:8; "her husband," 1:5; Naomi, "his wife," 1:1, 2; "our brother," 4:3; Machlon and Chilion, "his two sons," 1:1, 2; "her two sons," 1:3; "her two boys," 1:5; "with the dead," 1:8; Machlon, "your husband," 2:11; "the dead," 4:5 (2x); Ruth, "wife of Machlon," 4:10; "her daughter-in-law," 1:22; 2:22; "my (Naomi's) daughter," 2:22; 3:1; "your (Boaz's) female slave," 2:13; "your (Boaz's) handmaid," 3:9; "my (Boaz's) daughter," 3:10, 11; "a woman of (moral) substance," 3:11; "my (Naomi's) daughter," 3:16, 18; "wife of the dead," 4:5 (cf. "to whom does this young woman belong?" 2:5); "your daughter-in-law," 4:15; Ruth's parents, "your father" and "your mother," 2:11; Orpah and Ruth, "Moabite wives," 1:4; "her daughters-in-law," 1:6; "her two daughters-in-law," 1:7, 8; "my daughters," 1:11; Orpah, "your sister-in-law," 1:15 (2x); entire family, "with the dead" and "with the living," 2:20; unnamed redeemer, "Mr. So-and-So," 4:1, 3, 8; elders, "ten men of the elders of the city," 4:2, 9, "in the gate," 4:11; Obed, "the boy," 4:16; women of Bethlehem, "they said," 1:19; "the women of the neighborhood," 4:17; young man-in-charge of the harvesters, 2:5, 6; male harvesters, 2:4, 7; "young men," 2:9, 15; female servants, "young women," 2:8, 22.

Notable is the way that the author uses "Ruth the Moabitess" five times in three chapters (1:22; 2:2, 21; 4:5, 10; "stranger" 2:10). Why does the author keep telling his reader that Ruth was "the Moabitess"? It seems to me that the author is using the epithet intentionally to underscore the foreign origins of Ruth. She, together with Orpah, is introduced as מאביות in the opening lines of the story (1:4). After Orpah leaves, Ruth is described as "the Moabitess" when she and Naomi first arrives in Bethlehem (1:22 and 2:2) and also when her fate is being discussed by Boaz and the unknown kinsman in a legal context (4:5, 10). There are good reasons for using the epithet in these passages: the former is the introduction of a Moabitess to the Bethlehemite community, and the other is the need to specify which woman would come along with the redemption.

Only 2:21 seems superfluous, as there is no particular reason why she should be called המואביה; the LXX omits the epithet and adds "to her mother-in-law," which seems to be an assimilation to 3:1 (ἡ πενθερὰ αὐτῆς). Sasson explains that המואביה in 2:21 is the writer's stress on Ruth's connection with her native land despite her newly forged links with Boaz and his family.[29] But this is gratuitous. Moab has receded from view, ever since the narrator, through Boaz's words in 2:11, says that it is known about Ruth that she has left her father, mother, and the land of her birth to join a people whom she has come to know only recently. What I would suggest is that this is another instance of how the author emphasized the foreign origins of Ruth. Precisely at the place where her speech falters, the reader is reminded that it is "Ruth the Moabitess" who had earlier described herself in 2:10 as a foreigner (נכריה).

V. Conclusion

The response to the question that I have been answering in this paper is that the author makes Ruth's Hebrew very good, though uneven. She is made to express one of the most memorable lines of filial piety in the Hebrew Bible. Yet, counterbalancing this speech, her understanding lapses in reporting what Boaz has said. The grammatical solecism of 2:21 underscores her foreignness, which is, of course, one of the main themes of the book. It seems that the author intended to emphasize her alien status, her Otherness, by reminding the reader that she was "Ruth the Moabitess" and to underscore this by making her speak with some infelicities of the Hebrew language.

It is true that this is the only instance of a faltering Hebrew, but one has to remember that the book of Ruth is a short story or novella with 85 verses, and only 59 of these contain dialogue. Moreover, Ruth speaks by herself only ten times and in three chapters, and in two of those speeches she is simply reporting Boaz's speech (2:21 and 3:17).[30] She also speaks together with Orpah once in 1:9-10, and the repetition of her speech mentioned in 1:14 is not included. In 3:17, Ruth apparently reports Boaz's speech a second

---

29. Sasson, *Ruth*, 61.
30. See the table of speeches in my "Book of Ruth and Its Literary Voice," 271-72.

time, but שׁ שׁ עׂרים is part of the narrative of what Boaz did (3:15) and not said. Presumably, he did say something about giving the six measures of barley, but we do not have his words. Nor do we have his initial utterance about not going back empty (handed) to Naomi; we only have Ruth's report of his speech in 3:17.

In other words, while 2:21 is the only instance of a faltering Hebrew, it has to be recognized that the author does not make Ruth speak very much at all (1:16-17; 2:2, 7, 10, 13, 19; 3:5 and 9). Each of these speeches is stylized and highly significant for the story. We do not have any of Ruth's casual speech and we cannot reconstruct what she would have sounded like in Hebrew. Both her character and speech are literary creations, and my contention is that the author has exploited what he knew about non-native speakers of Hebrew to underscore the foreignness of Ruth "the Moabitess." How good did the author make Ruth's Hebrew? In short, very good, but not perfect.

The Other in Haggai and Zechariah 1–8

Antonios Finitsis

The definition of the Other in the Hebrew Bible has been based on mutable criteria. The first few books are quite traditional in defining as Other the people outside the religio-ethnic boundary of the people of Israel. In the book of Exodus this identity is taken by the oppressing enemy: the Egyptians. In the Deuteronomistic History it is assumed by the often rehashed list of the peoples of the land. In the book of Kings we witness an interesting inversion when the status of Other is ascribed to a part that was formerly recognized as Self; that is, as personified by the religiously rogue kingdom of the North: Israel. This marks the beginning of a counterintuitive development according to which the traditional ethnic and religious boundaries recede in importance when trying to define the Other. Hence, the Assyrians become the rod of YHWH's anger, Nebuchadnezzar of Babylon is YHWH's servant, and Cyrus of Persia is YHWH's anointed. This trend continues in the postexilic era, when the Other is sometimes a part of the former Self.

It is commonly agreed upon that the construction of Jewish identity began in the postexilic period. The destruction of the kingdoms, the exile, and the return increased exponentially the pressure for definition of Self and Other. In the late postexilic period, not only did the gulf between Jew and Gentile grow to unprecedented proportions but also the separation between "Israel and Israel," so to speak, took root. That does not seem to be the case in the early postexilic period, however. The evidence we have for this period comes from two prophets: Haggai and Proto-Zechariah. Neither of them paints such a polarized picture as the one found in the books of Ezra and

The Other in Haggai and Zechariah 1–8

Nehemiah.[1] In this paper I will attempt to present a more nuanced way to understand why these two prophets adopt a more conciliatory approach. I will argue that their stance stems from the prophets' desire to build a new cohesive group identity for the people in Yehud.

I. The Social Dynamics in Yehud

Evidence from the exilic and early postexilic period suggests that there were a number of disagreements between various groups in Yehud and that the economic conditions were dire. These tensions could lead to further fragmentation of the community and destroy any hope for the formation of a common identity. A major disagreement had to do with the land. As Albertz notes, evidence in Jeremiah suggests that the landless and refugees were installed on the properties of large landowners (39:10; 40:10), which had either been abandoned or confiscated (Lam. 5:2), and according to Ezekiel (11:15), the people who had occupied the land refused to give it back.[2] Japhet argues

---

1. Bedford notes that Haggai and Zechariah, unlike Ezra and Nehemiah, do not distinguish between repatriates and non-repatriates, nor do they exclude the Samaritans from the rebuilding of the Temple. For the two prophets, "temple rebuilding was not undertaken to establish a distinct community of repatriates within Judah." Peter Ross Bedford, *Temple Restoration in Early Achaemenid Judah* (JSJSup 65; Leiden: Brill, 2001), 264. Kessler concludes that "Zech. 1–8 presents a highly inclusivistic, nonpolemical, nonexclusionary perspective. There is no conflict between political and religious authorities, and no heterodox and ethically suspect worshippers of Yahweh from whom to keep separate." John Kessler, "Diaspora and Homeland in the Early Achaemenid Period: Community, Geography and Demography in Zechariah 1–8," in *Approaching Yehud: New Approaches to the Study of the Persian Period*, ed. Jon L. Berquist (SemeiaSt 50; Atlanta: Society of Biblical Literature, 2007), 165.

2. Albertz adds that Ezek. 11:15 and 33:24 imply that those who were left behind not only agreed with the redistribution of property but also found a way to justify it theologically. "For them the exile was Yahweh's judgment on the exploitation of the upper class and often even a de facto liberation from debt." Rainer Albertz, *A History of Israelite Religion in the Old Testament Period*, 2 vols. (OTL; Louisville: Westminster John Knox, 1994), 2:372. Zimmerli adds that Ezek. 11:15 is an "objective claim to legal right" but it is also a theological statement. This argument holds that "the land was the sacramental assurance of the favor of Yahweh," and those who "lost the land had visibly lost the sign of his favor and were far from Yahweh's salvation." Walther Zimmerli, *Ezekiel 1: A Commentary on the Book of the Prophet Ezekiel, Chapters 1–24*, trans. Ronald E. Clements (Hermeneia; Philadelphia: Fortress, 1979), 261. Paul D. Hanson concludes that the polemical confrontation depicted in Ezekiel led to an inevitable acrimonious confrontation when the return took place; see his *The Dawn of Apocalyptic*, rev. ed. (Philadelphia: Fortress, 1979), 240-42.

that Ezek. 11:15-21 and 33:23-29 as well as Jeremiah 24 preserve arguments that seek to exclude either the returnees or those who remained from making a claim to the land.[3] One would expect that these arguments would have become even more heated once the exiles began returning to Jerusalem, which is the time when Haggai and Proto-Zechariah were active.

With his fourth vision, Zechariah alludes to yet another debate in early postexilic Yehud. The goal of the vision seems to be the absolution of Joshua, the high priest, of all guilt and his reinstatement to ritual purity. This implies that in the opinion of the prophet, and possibly of the people, Joshua was deemed unfit for his office and criticized.[4] In Zech. 3:7, Joshua is explicitly told that his position of power will be retained only as long as he is faithful to YHWH. The conditionality of Joshua's rule possibly betrays the prophet's attempt to mediate fairly an argument between the people and the high priest. Although we do not know the extent or the nature of the argument, it seems that Zechariah helped them reach a compromise by absolving the high priest, on the one hand, and reassuring the people that this absolution was both conditional and unique, on the other.

Both Haggai and Zechariah declare that the economic conditions in Yehud are poor. The poverty of the people and the land are integral to Haggai's oracle in the first chapter of his book, and I will examine them more closely below. Zechariah (in 7:14) relates that the land "was desolate, so that no one went to and fro, and a pleasant land was made desolate."[5] In 8:10,

---

3. Japhet believes that both prophets defend the interests of the Babylonian exiles. Sara Japhet, "People and Land in the Restoration Period," in eadem, *From the Rivers of Babylon to the Highlands of Judah: Collected Essays on the Restoration Period* (Winona Lake, Ind.: Eisenbrauns, 2006), 96-116 (100-103).

4. Von Rad suggests that it is better to perceive Joshua here as representing the guilt of the community in the eyes of YHWH rather than to think that he is accused of a personal transgression. Gerhard von Rad, *Old Testament Theology,* 2 vols., trans. D. M. G. Stalker (New York: Harper & Row, 1962-65), 2:287. Meyers and Meyers offer that his uncleanness is related to his having lived part of his life in exile away from the earthly locus of holiness and purity; i.e., Jerusalem and the Temple. Carol L. Meyers and Eric M. Meyers, *Haggai, Zechariah 1–8* (AB 25b; Garden City, N.Y.: Doubleday, 1987), 188-89, 218. I think that it is more likely, however, that he is tried for his personal guilt since the guilt of the community is removed later, in 3:9. Furthermore, I agree with Ben Zvi's observation on prophetic utopias, that "the very portrayal of an imaginary ideal world carries a critique and ideological rejection of present conditions." Ehud Ben Zvi, "Utopias, Multiple Utopias, and Why Utopias at All? The Social Roles of Utopian Visions in Prophetic Books within their Historical Context," in *Utopia and Dystopia in Prophetic Literature,* ed. Ehud Ben Zvi (Göttingen: Vanderhoeck & Ruprecht, 2006), 59.

5. Unless otherwise noted, all translations are from the New Revised Standard Ver-

he adds that "there were no wages for people or for animals, nor was there any safety from the foe for those who went out or came in." These dire social circumstances, he continues, "set them all against one another." The tight fiscal situation would have aggravated existing arguments and increased friction in their community. The challenge for Haggai and Zechariah would be to inspire unity among their audience despite the divisive arguments, lest internal discord should prohibit any effort at restoration.

II. The Other in Haggai

Haggai's primary objective is to get the Temple rebuilt. In order to succeed in this campaign he has to elicit and secure support from the target audience. His understanding of who constitutes this audience becomes clear from the way he addresses them. In the opening of the first oracle, Haggai describes them with the vague designation "these people," which is probably used to convey the estrangement between YHWH and the population.[6] This estrangement had a very concrete manifestation and an adverse side effect. First, the people had a callous disregard for the fact that YHWH's house lay in ruins and, as a result, YHWH was disciplining them with adverse climatological, agricultural, and livestock conditions. Haggai points out these facts and stirs up a reaction from his audience, which is now identified as Zerubbabel son of Shealtiel, governor of Judah, Joshua son of Jehozadak, the high priest, and "all the remnant of the people."[7] Since the term "remnant" can be used in several different ways, it is important to discern in which way this prophet seems to understand it. For Haggai it does not denote a righteous or a purified remnant as it does in other postexilic texts.[8] That they

---

sion. Kessler notes that the themes of destruction, exile, and abandonment figure prominently in the root *(šmm)* that Zechariah uses in this verse. John Kessler, "Diaspora and Homeland," 160-61.

6. Hag. 1:2. Kessler posits that this term is frequently one of reproach (e.g., Hag. 2:14; Zech. 8:11; Isa. 6:9-10; 8:6, 12; Jer. 4:11). He observes that it is used extensively in Isaiah, the Deuteronomic tradition, and in Jeremiah. John Kessler, *The Book of Haggai: Prophecy and Society in Early Persian Yehud* (VTSup 91; Atlanta: Society of Biblical Literature, 2002), 123.

7. Hag. 1:12, 1:14, 2:2. Meyers and Meyers note that all three occurrences of this term are in the editorial framework of Haggai. Meyers and Meyers, *Haggai, Zechariah 1–8*, 34.

8. Petersen argues that Haggai may have tried to include all the people in his audience because he "recognizes who must actually do the work of temple reconstruction." David L. Petersen, *Haggai and Zechariah 1–8* (OTL; Philadelphia: Westminster, 1984), 56. Meyers and Meyers maintain that it may be unwarranted to "accept a specialized theological intent for

were not particularly alarmed that the Temple was lying in ruins should be evidence enough that the prophet does not refer to a qualitatively superior subgroup. The term "remnant" is probably used here to communicate the decimated state of this community.[9]

Haggai clears up the matter in his second oracle when he specifies exactly who constitutes his audience. The text reads: "Yet now take courage, O Zerubbabel, says the Lord; take courage, O Joshua, son of Jehozadak, the high priest; take courage, all you people of the land, says the Lord; work, for I am with you, says the Lord of hosts, according to the promise that I made you when you came out of Egypt (2:4-5a). According to the prophet, the audience is all the people of the land, all the descendants of the tribes that came out of Egypt. One effect of the use of Exodus is the rhetorical unification of the audience. By going to the past, the prophet avoids the thorny division of the present between returnees and "remainees."[10] He wants to inspire collaboration and thus he invokes a story they all have in common. To help achieve the rebirth of the nation, he invokes the foundational story of its birth.

If the in-group consists of all the people in Yehud, who is in the out-group? Haggai opts for a very traditional understanding as he uses an old story that aligns him naturally with past definitions of the outsider: "I am about to shake the heavens and the earth, and to overthrow the throne of kingdoms; I am about to destroy the strength of the kingdoms of the nations, and overthrow the chariots and their riders; and the horses and their riders shall fall, every one by the sword of a comrade" (2:21b-22). It should come as no surprise that the definition of the out-group is construed along the lines of the events of Exodus. The prophet seems to continue his earlier

---

the compiler." They add that "Haggai himself does not appear to distinguish between segments of the Yehudite population." Meyers and Meyers, *Haggai, Zechariah 1–8*, 34.

9. The term "remnant" here applies to the covenantal community as that was established in the fabled events of the Exodus. Haggai does not make any claim for a purified or special status of the postexilic community. To the contrary, he describes the work that "this people and this nation" offer as unclean, in 2:14. Petersen argues that this is contact defilement as opposed to innate defilement. He explains that the agricultural produce was becoming unclean upon placement on the altar because the appropriate rituals of cleansing and rededication had not yet been performed. Petersen, *Haggai and Zechariah 1–8*, 83-85. Meyers and Meyers believe that this defilement results from the people's failure to act in accordance with the will of God. Meyers and Meyers, *Haggai, Zechariah 1–8*, 58.

10. Japhet concludes that Haggai does not discriminate against the returned exiles; instead he focuses on the people of Judah and the returned exiles, who "are for him an integral part of the community." Japhet, "People and Land," 106.

train of thought (in 2:5).[11] Here the Other is the enemy: the political and military powers that decimated his community and reduced it to the status of a remnant. However, YHWH is going to administer justice by causing the enemies to wage mutually destructive war. Foreign powers with their superior military power had been in a position to dictate the fate of his people in the past, but not anymore. In the Exodus story, YHWH faces an enemy with superior military abilities and is victorious. Another effect of Haggai's decision to use the Exodus exemplar is the impression of a sense of continuity with the past and certainty concerning the future among his audience. The matter will be settled in his time as it was settled in the past.

Nevertheless, to the extent that Haggai's pressing objective was to get the Temple rebuilt, the military defeat of the enemy was of ancillary significance. His audience seemed to have faced enough obstacles trying to make ends meet. The tight fiscal situation should have rendered the Temple rebuilding prohibitive. Their poverty is another trait that separates the people of Yehud from the nations. The prophet proposes a solution: "I will shake the heavens and the earth and the sea and the dry land; and I will shake all the nations, so that the treasure of all nations shall come, and I will fill this house with splendor, says the LORD of hosts. The silver is mine, and the gold is mine, says the LORD of hosts" (2:6b-8).

In this oracle the Other is the one who possesses what YHWH's people do not, that is, material wealth. Living in destitution, the people in Yehud perceive their difference from those around them not on the basis of ancestral descent, religious beliefs, or cultic practices, but of financial prosperity. Furthermore, the acknowledgment of this difference seems to come with some resentment, since, as the prophet declares, the gold and the silver belong to YHWH. For this reason, God in his capacity as the ultimate ruler of the cosmos will bring the treasure of nations to Jerusalem and rectify this imbalance.[12]

I would argue that Haggai's construction of the out-group along the

---

11. Kessler maintains that the fall of horse and rider is a quasi-fixed expression derived from the deliverance in the Sea of Reeds in Exodus. He adds that Haggai may also allude to the presence of this theme in Darius's Behistun Inscription. Kessler, *Book of Haggai*, 224.

12. Petersen observes that, even though the language used here is borrowed from Israel's theophanic tradition, it is here used in a distinctive way because the scope of the quaking includes the entire cosmos, not just the mountains, and because it is linked not to an appearance of YHWH but to a new activity of YHWH on behalf of his people. Petersen, *Haggai and Zechariah 1–8*, 67.

lines of the oppressing enemy and the wealthy neighbor can be explained in two ways. First, groups among the prophet's audience were at odds with each other, and his foremost task was to build group solidarity. Anthropologists have observed that there is a direct link between intergroup conflict and cohesion. Sumner has put it as follows: "The relation of comradeship and peace in the we-group and that of hostility and war towards other groups are correlative of each other. The exigencies of war with outsiders are what make peace inside, lest internal discord should weaken the we-group for war."[13]

Therefore, Haggai constructs the relation with the out-group in terms of a hostile confrontation in order to establish the in-group cohesion that would elicit commitment to the rebuilding of the Temple. Second, social psychologist Ruppert Brown maintains that "biased intergroup attitudes may be functional in assisting the group to achieve its objectives."[14] This seems to be the case in situations in which the relationship between groups is conflictual; i.e., when one group's loss means another group's gain. The construction of the Other as the wealthy rival who handles foreign money and who is going to be forced into an involuntary financial contribution is unnerving for the contemporary reader. However, it can be explained as a common biased attitude associated with in-group behavior that seeks to achieve a goal. The rebuilding requires funds that are scarce in Yehud. Thus the ethnically unspecified Other is constructed as the one who has these funds in abundance, yet illegitimately. The resulting antagonism is meant to secure the in-group's commitment to rectifying this wrong by rebuilding the Temple despite the adversity.

---

13. William G. Sumner, *Folkways: A Study of the Sociological Importance of Usages, Manners, Customs, Mores and Morals* (Boston: Ginn, 1906), 12. Other researchers have also confirmed this connection. See Muzafer Sherif, *In Common Predicament: Social Psychology of Intergroup Conflict and Cooperation* (Boston: Houghton Mifflin, 1966), chapter 6. Another group of researchers conducted a study showing that intergroup competition leads to improved work relations in the group, higher self-esteem, lower anxiety, and greater satisfaction with the conditions of group life. James W. Julian, Doyle W. Bishop, and Fred E. Fiedler, "Quasi-Therapeutic Effects of Intergroup Competition," *Journal of Personality and Social Psychology* 3 (1966): 321-27. They also observed that "the quality of interpersonal relations improves in task-related aspects" in the group (p. 326).

14. Ruppert Brown, *Group Processes: Dynamics Within and Between Groups* (Oxford: Blackwell, 1988), 260.

III. The Other in Zechariah 1–8

Proto-Zechariah was a contemporary of Haggai and focused largely on the same issues, albeit with a different style.[15] He also ruminates on the subject of Self and Other but he paints a more complex picture than Haggai. This complexity reveals differences in point of view. Proto-Zechariah seems to adopt a strategy that prevents him from drawing impenetrable barriers between his in-group and the out-group.

The questions raised by the destruction of the kingdom and the exile mark his point of departure. Like Haggai, Proto-Zechariah is aware of the disjunction that the events around the exile created. The first wave of returnees may have understood and claimed as theirs the heritage of the destroyed kingdom, since that would have been the purpose of their return, but these were probably the minority of the prophet's audience. The majority were the people who had stayed behind and for whom the importance of bringing back to life the old nation was not immediately apparent. After all, they were already set in a way of life that did not require any such revival.

The prophet attempts to forge anew the broken link by a short history lesson. In his first chapter he offsets what had happened before with what should take place in his time. He uses the designation "your ancestors" in every verse of his introduction in order to connect the people present in his audience with the past of preexilic Israel.[16] In the process he also connects the returnees and those who stayed behind by impressing upon both parties a common heritage. The motif of connecting the past with the present is a constant in Proto-Zechariah and appears in many forms, the most frequent of which is the connection between earlier prophets and himself. Like Haggai, he understands as his community everybody who happens to be in Yehud at this point in time. This becomes

---

15. Chapters 1–8 are traditionally divided in three sections according to different genres of material: a prologue, a cycle of eight visions, and the oracles. Even though their provenance is not identical, the opinions expressed in these units are congruent with one another. See Petersen, *Haggai and Zechariah 1–8*, 125, and Meyers and Meyers, *Haggai, Zechariah 1–8*, li-lii.

16. Zech. 1:2, 1:3, 1:4, 1:5 and 1:6. He also reprises this device in 8:14. Petersen notes that this device does three things: first, it summarizes past relationships between YHWH and Israel; second, it establishes a link between generations; and last, it allows for a distinction between various generations and their relationships to YHWH. Petersen, *Haggai and Zechariah 1–8*, 130.

evident by the charge he receives from YHWH to speak to "all the people of the land."[17]

Unlike Haggai, however, Proto-Zechariah does not seem to think that membership in this community is automatic or unconditional. In his sixth vision, he reveals that anyone who steals and anyone who swears falsely shall be cut off from the community. The objective of this vision is to explain how YHWH is going to purge human sin from the land, and in the process it emphasizes the ethical imperatives that govern membership in the community.

The prophet elaborates on this social contract further in the concluding verses of the framework of the visionary cycle: "These are the things that you shall do: Speak the truth to one another, render in your gates judgments that are true and make for peace, do not devise evil in your hearts against one another, and love no false oath; for all these are things that I hate, says the LORD" (8:16-17). Although Proto-Zechariah wants to establish continuity with the past, he does not want to see the mistakes of the past repeated. Hence, he warns his audience to stay away from patterns of behavior that had led to their demise. Moreover, the prophet wants to go forward with the rebuilding of the Temple, and he seems to think that this project requires not only cultic but moral purity. He seems to insist on the imperative nature of an ethically superior community.

Furthermore, Proto-Zechariah is acutely aware of the fact that not all of his people are in Jerusalem. He admits that YHWH has spread them "abroad like the four winds of heaven."[18] Later the prophet explains that this scattering "among all the nations that they had not known" came as punishment for their insubordination.[19] Therefore, when he uses the phrase "the remnant of this people," he does not simply refer to the decimated state of the community, as Haggai does, but to the community beyond Yehud. For him the Yehudites are not the sum of his people. There are others in faraway

---

17. Zech. 7:5. Petersen notes that this designation moved the discourse from a small audience to the entire community. Petersen, *Haggai and Zechariah 1–8*, 285. Cf. Meyers and Meyers, *Haggai, Zechariah 1–8*, 387.

18. Zech. 2:6. In 8:13 he emphasizes the punitive side of the scattering by stating that this event turned the houses of Judah and Israel into "a cursing among the nations." Meyers and Meyers offer that this scattering took place according to the stipulations of the covenant. Meyers and Meyers, *Haggai, Zechariah 1–8*, 423.

19. Zech. 7:14a. Kessler observes that this is a Deuteronomism found also in Deut. 13:2; 28:36, 64; Jer. 22:28; 8:13; and 8:7 (Kessler, "Diaspora and Homeland," 144). Petersen maintains that the dispersal of the people among the nations without protection was understood to have a social dimension. Petersen, *Haggai and Zechariah 1–8*, 295.

places who have the same rights as the ones in front of him. This becomes clear when the prophet announces the reunification of the people: "Thus says the LORD of hosts: Even though it seems impossible to the remnant of this people in these days, should it also seem impossible to me, says the LORD of hosts? Thus says the LORD of hosts: I will save my people from the east country and from the west country; and I will bring them to live in Jerusalem" (8:6-8a). Even though the addressee of the prophet's message is the people in Jerusalem and its environs, he does not lose sight of the broader picture. He considers the diasporic communities as part of his people. He declares that YHWH, in an act of compassion, will gather and lead them to Jerusalem in the future.

Zechariah is also aware of the economic difficulties plaguing the rebuilding project but, unlike Haggai, he does not expect the nations to supply the missing funds. Instead he mitigates the responsibility of the Yehudites by placing part of the burden on the shoulders of their compatriots abroad: "those who are far off shall come and help to build the Temple of the LORD."[20] He believes that they should play a partnership role in the restoration project. The prophet sounds certain of this return but he is also proactive about it: "Up, up! Flee from the land of the north, says the LORD; for I have spread you abroad like the four winds of heaven, says the LORD. Up! Escape to Zion, you that live with daughter Babylon" (2:6-7).

Zechariah was active around 520 B.C.E.; there were several more waves of returnees to come. He realized that the community in Yehud needed to be strengthened. The restoration project required all the support it could get, and Israelites abroad seem to have been financially better off than the people in the land. He mentions by name three people — Heldai, Tobijah and Jedaiah — who have returned from Babylon with gifts of silver and gold with them. Thus, he makes an appeal to the rest of the exiles to return to Jerusalem so that the nation will be reborn. However, it is not solely financial considerations that motivate the prophet. There seems to be an emotional link with the land of the exiles. It is interesting to notice that Zechariah refers to the city abroad with the designation "daughter Babylon." This designation stands in parallelism with "daughter Zion" a few verses later. The implication is that Babylon is not thought of as completely foreign. Babylon

---

20. Zech. 6:15. The prophet believes that this is a sign and that it will come to pass if the people "diligently obey the voice of the LORD" their God. Petersen adds that the text refers also "to the recognition of the validity of Zechariah's own work as contingent upon the obedience of the populace to the voice of Yahweh." Petersen, *Haggai and Zechariah 1–8*, 280.

has somehow found itself connected to the family tree of Israel. At the end of the visionary cycle, the prophet explicitly hears: "Lo, those who go toward the north country have set my spirit at rest in the north country" (6:8). In the last vision the patrols of the LORD have returned, and the ensuing report states that the spirit of the LORD is at rest in the north country.[21] Whatever the conflict may have been, it has been resolved.[22] Balance has been restored and there are no hard feelings for the north or the people living there.

This peaceful end, however, does not mean that the prophet or the LORD is content with the international situation as it is. There are a few wrongs that have to be rectified first. This brings us to a fairly complex discussion of the "other" in Proto-Zechariah. The scope of his visions is global. It is not accidental that the first and the last vision refer to the report that the LORD's agents submit, having patrolled the entire earth. The underlying message is that YHWH is interested in rectifying the situation not only in Yehud but also in the international scene. At the end of the first vision, the LORD declares his return to Jerusalem and the prosperity of the LORD's cities in Yehud. At the beginning of the second vision, the prophet changes gears and focuses on powers hostile to the people of Judah:

> And I looked up and saw four horns. I asked the angel who talked with me, "What are these?" And he answered me, "These are the horns that have scattered Judah, Israel and Jerusalem." Then the LORD showed me four blacksmiths. And I asked, "What are they coming to do?" He answered, "These are the horns that scattered Judah, so that no head could be raised; but these have come to terrify them, to strike down the horns of the nations that lifted up their horns against the land of Judah to scatter its people." (1:18-21)

It seems that in order for Jerusalem and Yehud to flourish justice needs to be delivered. The foreign powers that inflicted the exile on the Israelites are going to be terrified and stricken down. The trauma of the past is still open, and this sore spot has to be addressed before anything else. It is a matter of balance, and probably a matter of gaining some favor with his audi-

---

21. Meyers and Meyers note that the north country "can represent the political powers of Syria or Mesopotamia that sometimes have conquered Palestine." They add that if the phrase does not refer to a past or future enemy in the context of the visions it probably refers to Persia. Meyers and Meyers, *Haggai, Zechariah 1–8*, 330-31.

22. Petersen observes that "now the universe is ordered," and he adds that "international justice has been corrected." Petersen, *Haggai and Zechariah 1–8*, 271.

ence. Proto-Zechariah makes the same point in his appeal to the exiles: "See now, I am going to raise my hand against them, and they shall become plunder for their own slaves" (2:9a). Again the point seems to be retribution, making the nations experience the events of the exile from the point of view of the victim. The prophet probably wants to satisfy the audience's need for propriety and justice. The seventh vision (5:5-11) also concerns itself with a foreign land. Even though the details around it are puzzling, its objective is fairly clear:

> Then the angel who talked with me came forward and said to me, "Look up and see what this is that is coming out." I said, "What is it?" He said, "This is a basket coming out." And he said, "This is their iniquity in all the land." Then a leaden cover was lifted, and there was a woman sitting in the basket! And he said, "This is Wickedness." So he thrust her back into the basket, and pressed the leaden weight down on its mouth. Then I looked up and saw two women coming forward. The wind was in their wings; they had wings like the wings of a stork and they lifted up the basket between earth and sky. Then I said to the angel who talked with me, "Where are they taking the basket?" He said to me. "To the land of Shinar, to build a house for it; and when this is prepared, they will set the basket down there on its base." (5:5-11)

The point of the vision is to communicate the removal of the guilt from the land and its deposit in the land of Shinar. According to Israelite cult, sin-guilt is objectified and transferable.[23] One cannot erase it but one can displace it. This is the way in which one can dispose of sin and guilt effectively and prevent their accumulation, which can have disastrous results. The question, however, becomes why transfer it to Shinar? It is interesting to note that the Septuagint, Symmachus, and Theodotion all read "Babel" instead of "Shinar." Maybe it would have been incongruous to call it "Babel" having called the city "daughter Babylon" previously.[24] Petersen understands

---

23. As Petersen observes, the same process took place in the fourth vision, where YHWH "removed the taint of transgression from the high priest." Petersen, *Haggai and Zechariah 1–8*, 256.

24. Zechariah depicts "Wickedness" as a woman in his vision, and this depiction raises the question of construing the Other along gender lines in his prophecy. However, the prophet considers both cities, Babylon and Zion, as female also. This seems to suggest that gender does not play a pivotal role in the construction of the Zechariah's Self and Other.

the place name metaphorically, as a place where error was perpetrated. He reads it in conjunction with the story in Genesis 11 where people are sent out of a territory.[25] The result of this displacement, however, creates an imbalance. On the one hand, Israel is purified, but on the other Babylon is contaminated. One way to approach it would be to see this idea as another version of the retribution that the prophet discussed earlier. It could also be viewed as an additional incentive for the exiles abroad to return home. Petersen believes that this movement seeks to achieve a demographic equilibrium, since the visionary calls for the return of the exiles from Babylon to Israel and he reveals the sending of evil from Israel to Babylon.[26] Despite the metaphorical thrust of the vision and the balancing effect that this act may have accomplished, the point remains that it has a negative impact for the Other that happens to live in that land. There is one detail that may serve to mitigate this negativity. The sin-guilt is not dispersed throughout the foreign land or among its people. Instead, it is placed in what could be a temple and it seems to be confined on a base the way a statue would be. Therefore, one gets the impression that this removal leads also to containment.

Nevertheless, this is not all that Zechariah has to say about the nations. In a passage that follows an eschatological trajectory, he declares: "Sing and rejoice, O daughter Zion! For lo, I will come and dwell in your midst, says the LORD. Many nations shall join themselves to the LORD on that day, and shall be my people; and I will dwell in your midst" (2:10–11a). According to this oracle, the prophet props the door wide open to the outsiders who will choose to join YHWH's people. This oracle has a tangible celebratory character. In this festive atmosphere, Proto-Zechariah does away with social categories, in-groups, and out-groups and delivers a welcoming message to anyone willing to affirm the hope and participate in the joy of YHWH's return.[27] One cannot help but wonder what is the source of this inclusivist stance.

---

25. Petersen sees a parallelism between the dispersal of humanity and the removal of error. Petersen, *Haggai and Zechariah 1–8*, 261.

26. Petersen remarks that this movement achieves a demographic and ethical-ritual homeostasis. Petersen, *Haggai and Zechariah 1–8*, 261.

27. Kessler notes that "such language is frequently used in the sixth century for the renewal of the relationship between Yahweh and his people (Jer. 24:7; 31:1, 33; Ezek. 11:20; 36:28; 37:23; esp. Zech. 8:8), but it is also used for the inclusion of foreigners (Ruth 1:16; Isa. 14:1; 53:3, 6; Jer. 50:5; Esth. 9:27)." However, he asserts that "the exact form that this 'becoming the people of Yahweh' would take is not specified." John Kessler, "Diaspora and Homeland," 156. Meyers and Meyers believe that the nations will share in the special arrangement that had heretofore characterized Israel as a people in her relationship with God. Meyers and Meyers, *Haggai, Zechariah 1–8*, 175.

I would argue that Proto-Zechariah's approach is best understood with the help of social identity theory. Social identity theory is helpful in explaining a wide range of intergroup phenomena. It arose out of the observation that groups seek to maintain some positive distinctiveness from each other and that group members seem to show a consistent tendency to favor their own group. Henri Tajfel and John C. Turner, who introduced this theory, argued that by and large people prefer to have a positive self-concept, which they produce through social comparisons.[28] Put differently, groups seek to differentiate themselves positively from the Other because that contributes directly to their own self-esteem. Therefore, identity is maintained through intergroup comparisons. It is my contention that the prophet's choices in his construction of Self and Other can be explained with this theory.

Tajfel asserts that this theory has three dimensions: cognitive (awareness of belonging to the group or self-categorization), evaluative (recognition of the value attached to the group), and emotional (feelings that are produced from the attachment to the group).[29] Steve Hinkle and Ruppert Brown continued Tajfel's work on social identity theory and concluded that this theory works in groups when two conditions are met. First, when the groups can be characterized as "collectivist," that is, when there is an emphasis on intragroup cooperation and achievement; and second, when the groups are "relational," that is, when there is concern for each group's standing and performance in relation to other groups.[30]

I would argue that both of these conditions are met in the early

---

28. Tajfel and Turner state that social identity theory is based on three theoretical principles. First, individuals strive to achieve or to maintain positive social identity. Second, positive social identity is based largely on favorable comparisons that can be made between the in-group and some relevant out-groups. Third, when social identity is unsatisfactory, individuals will try to leave their existing group or make their existing group more positively distinct. Henri Tajfel and John C. Turner, "The Social Identity Theory of Intergroup Behavior," in *Psychology of Intergroup Relations*, ed. Stephen Worchel and William G. Austin (Chicago: Nelson Hall, 1986), 16. J. C. Baker has used this theory to argue that Jer. 31:31-34 attempts to develop a new common in-group identity for the postexilic community. J. Coleman Baker, "New Covenant, New Identity: A Social-scientific Reading of Jeremiah 31:31-34," *The Bible and Critical Theory* 4 (2008): 1-11.

29. Henri Tajfel, "Interindividual Behavior and Intergroup Behavior," in *Differentiation Between Social Groups: Studies in the Social Psychology of Intergroup Relations* (London: Academic Press, 1978), 63.

30. Steve Hinkle and Ruppert Brown, "Intergroup Comparison and Social Identity: Some Links and Lacunae," in *Social Identity Theory: Constructive and Critical Advances*, ed. Dominic Abrams and Michael A. Hogg (New York: Springer, 1990), 48-70.

postexilic social setting. The book of Deuteronomy emphasizes above all intragroup cooperation. The people have to work and behave as one if they are to hold the land. This is a prime example of collectivist thinking, particularly when it comes to the idea of ascribing responsibility. More to the point, however, in the early postexilic period what Proto-Zechariah tries to instigate is intragroup cooperation in order to achieve the realization of the restoration program. His community is in a shambles, and the task before anything else is to create a sense of togetherness. The relational aspect is also present in this time frame. The prophet compares the community in Yehud with the Israelites in diasporic communities and the entirety of his in-group to the nations. As I have shown, Proto-Zechariah tries to draw lines across all these social modalities. It would then seem appropriate to continue with social identity theory in order to explain the prophet's particular view on group relations.

The next step would be to show that all three dimensions of Tajfel's theory are discernible in the prophet's message. I would argue that Proto-Zechariah's attempt to reforge the link between the past and the present of this community was aiming at creating an awareness of belonging. His objective was to anchor his audience to the preexilic tradition and connect them with the history that would provide the raw materials of their identity. This would be the cognitive aspect of his message. The prophet's emphasis on the ethical imperatives that determine membership in this community would reflect the evaluative aspect. According to Proto-Zechariah, this community upholds certain values, which give the in-group its enviable identity. The qualitatively superior status of this community would make his invitation to the remainder of the exiles to return compelling. The same would hold true for his hope that YHWH would eventually gather them back to Yehud and finally open the way for the consenting nations to join. Last, the emotional dimension can be detected in the prophet's feelings towards the insiders and the outsiders, which are generated from his attachment to this group. On the one hand, these feelings lead to the destruction of the foreign powers in the end of the first vision and the desire for administering justice. On the other hand, they lead to the parallelism between "daughter Zion" and "daughter Babylon." There is a lifeline between the two cities, and the prophet cannot turn a blind eye to it. In the end his sentiments about the people he considers to belong to his in-group influence the way he looks at the out-groups. This, I would submit, is a reason why he feels inclined to mitigate his attitude towards the Other. In light of this discussion, I would like to conclude that social identity theory offers a useful explanation of

Proto-Zechariah's more inclusive tendencies. His motivation seems to stem from a causal connection between intergroup discrimination and self-esteem. The prophet, in his effort to facilitate the restoration program, was trying to establish a desirable identity for his fractured in-group. He sought to do so by raising the community's confidence through a multifaceted comparison with the surrounding out-groups.

IV. Conclusion

In the early postexilic period, the prophets Haggai and Proto-Zechariah labored to get the Temple rebuilt. First they had to reconstitute a community that had been fractured and that was striving to survive under adverse circumstances. They both had to build their in-group from the ground up, and they both wanted to include in it everyone present in Yehud. However, they opted to define this group in different ways.

Haggai acknowledges the decimated status of his community and sees their reluctance to undertake the strenuous task of the rebuilding of the Temple. In order to inspire cohesion for his cause, he draws a rigid line between Self and Other. The two modalities are cast in a hostile scenario. Ostensibly his goal is to unite his people against a common enemy, but actually he seeks to unite them for a common cause.

Proto-Zechariah attempts to create the in-group identity via a multifaceted comparison with the out-group rather than plain conflict. His goal is to raise the people's self-esteem and unite them by presenting their group identity as enviable. To this end he urges his audience to accept their heritage by emphasizing the connection between past and present. Then, he underlines that membership in this group is not automatic. There are standards and members have to live up to them. These higher values make membership in this group a lofty goal. Last, given the socio-historical events that led to the exile and the return, there is an emotional aspect to the prophet's message. The guilty parties need to be punished. Once balance has been achieved, the prophet opens the doors to consenting nations, proving that if membership in his community is a worthy objective for the outsider, it should be so much more valuable to the insider.

When the King Is the Other: Nebuchadnezzar's Hibernian Cousin

Naomi S. Jacobs

John Collins's profound insight into the world of ancient Judaism is, as he himself has acknowledged, in no small part owing to his deep connection to the culture and history of his homeland.[1] This piece celebrates this heritage and also evokes the happy memories of studying with him at the University of Chicago, including a memorable class on the book of Daniel. It is also a work of gratitude for the countless ways he has mentored me and furthered my career.

I would like to bring to the attention of biblical scholars a fascinating Middle Irish text that is part of Daniel's reception history. So far as I can tell, its biblical connections have not been explored by Celtic scholars, either. In addition to laying out the biblical parallels, I will make some initial remarks about what we can learn about the transmission of Daniel in the medieval period.[2] Then, with the utmost caution, I will offer a suggestion as to how

---

1. The similarities between the Jews and the Irish are many, including love of learning, persecution, and a tendency toward failed rebellions against imperialistic powers. Declan Kiberd, *Inventing Ireland: The Literature of the Modern Nation* (Cambridge: Harvard University Press, 1995), 30-32, also chronicles how the English viewed the Irish as the ultimate Other: "superstitious, backward and irrational, not unlike the way Jewish people have sometimes been caricatured, a caricature that reaches back to antiquity."

2. Given that Latin was the language of biblical writings in medieval works of western Europe, all passages with parallels have been checked with the Vulgate and the Old Latin material in Pierre Sabatier's 1751 compilation. The complex situation of Daniel's transmission in Latin will be discussed shortly.

When the King Is the Other

the Irish work may help us look at Daniel 4 anew. In particular, I hope to shed light upon debates about its imagery and the nature and background behind Nebuchadnezzar's apparent psychosis.

The story of Nebuchadnezzar's madness is widely reflected in the writings and iconography in the Middle Ages, with special studies on Middle English literature, as well as the so-called "Wild Man" motif.[3] Less, however, has been said about the Irish relationship to this theme.[4] But the *Buile Shuibhne* ("The Frenzy of Suibhne") must undoubtedly be seen as part of this tradition.[5]

Suibhne, also known as Mad Sweeney, is said to be a king of Dal Araidne in Ulster. Like Nebuchadnezzar, Suibhne is cursed by God via a "holy one."[6] Both kings also live apart from humanity on green herbage. Also like his fellow royal, a portion of Suibhne's punishment takes place over a period of time marked by seven. And the imagery of feathers and bent claws in the *Buile Shuibhne* seems to echo the descriptions of Nebuchadnezzar.[7] The overall theme of the acknowledgement of the divine is present in both as well. Initially anti-Christian, Suibhne gradually reaches out to

---

3. Penelope B. R. Doob, *Nebuchadnezzar's Children: Conventions of Madness in Middle English Literature* (New Haven: Yale University Press, 1974); Richard Bernheimer, *Wild Men in the Middle Ages: A Study in Art, Sentiment, and Demonology* (New York: Octagon Books, 1970). The notion of the wild man is important to the recent studies of Gregory Mobley, "The Wild Man in the Bible and the Ancient Near East," *JBL* 116 (1997): 217-33, and Matthias Henze, *The Madness of King Nebuchadnezzar: The Ancient Near Eastern Origins and Early History of Interpretation of Daniel 4* (JSJSup 61; Boston: Brill, 1999). This idea has been contested with an emphasis on Netherworld imagery by Christopher B. Hays, "Chirps from the Dust: The Affliction of Nebuchadnezzar in Daniel 4:30 in Its Ancient Near Eastern Context," *JBL* 126 (2007): 305-25.

4. It has been argued (James Carney, *Studies in Irish Literature and History* [Dublin: Dublin Institute for Advanced Studies, 1955], 129-52) that the madness theme in the Irish work derives from British traditions such as those surrounding Merlin. Regardless of the merit of this contested proposal, Carney nonetheless agrees that the story's current form draws heavily on specifically Irish traditions, e.g., St. Moling (p. 131). Carney is also surely correct that the story presents numerous source-critical and redaction-critical problems.

5. The standard edition is J. G. O'Keeffe, *Buile Shuibhne (The Frenzy of Suibhne), Being the Adventures of Suibhne Geilt: A Middle-Irish Romance* (London: Irish Texts Society, 1904). See also the online resources supplied by the University of Cork, http://www.ucc.ie/celt/published/G302018/index.html for the Gaelic original and http://www.ucc.ie/celt/published/T302018/index.html for an English translation [accessed May 17, 2008].

6. The "holy one" of the *Buile Shuibhne* is a saint. The Vulgate reads *sanctus* for "holy one," which can likewise be rendered as "saint."

7. Vulgate Dan. 4:30.

God and Christ and repents of his sins just as the proud Nebuchadnezzar ultimately acknowledges God's glory.

There are nevertheless some important differences. Whereas the biblical king merely thinks he is an animal, his Irish counterpart actually turns into a kind of human-bird, with, as noted, the imagery of feathers and bent nails seen in Daniel 4. And although Suibhne's reason does return at points and he briefly regains his kingdom, his end is violent, although his soul is secured. The *Buile Shuibhne*'s depiction of madness is also more complex than that of Daniel 4 and includes an extensive appreciation of the beauty of the natural world, especially trees, and the gifts of both prophecy and poetry. Suibhne himself dies as a revered holy man.

First, some remarks about manuscript evidence as well as an abridged summary of the tale (which does not do justice to its poetry). The *Buile Shuibhne*, of unknown authorship, dates to the twelfth century.[8] It is extant in at least three manuscripts.[9] The story may be stated as follows: King Suibhne, angered when he hears the bell of Ronan, a cleric marking out a church, tosses Ronan's psalter into a lake and drags him out of the church. He is interrupted by the need to go to battle at Magh Rath. The cleric curses the king, asking God that just as Suibhne was naked when he expelled Ronan (in his haste the king has run out leaving his garment in his wife's hand), may Suibhne always wander naked, flying everywhere, and die on the point of a spear *(rinn)*.

On the day of the battle, the king (who has worked against Ronan's attempts to bring about peace) finds Ronan and some psalmists *(psalmchetlaidh)*, who sprinkle him with holy water. Mistakenly thinking that this was done in mockery, Suibhne throws his spear at a psalmist, killing him. He tries to kill the cleric in the same way, but the spear is stopped by the bell. Ronan curses him again, praying that God will make the king go high in the air as a bird just as the spear went into the air and that he will die by spear just as the psalmist did.

At the battle, the shouts of both armies along with the sounds of heaven drive Suibhne into a giddy frenzy. Dropping his weapons, he moves like a

---

8. A poem attributed to King Suibhne has been dated to the ninth century or earlier; see Robert Welch and Bruce Stewart, *The Oxford Companion to Irish Literature* (Oxford: Oxford University Press, 1996), 68-69.

9. B IV 1 82a-95b (paper, 1671-74, Royal Irish Academy), 23 K 44 131-180 (paper, 1721-1722, Royal Irish Academy), and Brussels 3410 59a-61b (1629, Royal Library, Brussels). K is independent of B and lacks material found in B. Brussels 3410 is a summary of B and K. This study is based on B; no variants are critical to my argument.

bird, leaving the battle. He flies on throughout the wild parts of Ireland until he goes into a yew tree. (The battle is won by the other side.) Eventually he finds his way to Glen Bolcain, a hangout of Irish madmen, noted for its great natural beauty and its prized watercress *(biorar)*, the favored food of Irish madmen. (Watercress and water are mentioned repeatedly throughout the story.[10]) There he sleeps uncomfortably on the tops of trees. He laments this in a poem, one of many, contrasting his life as a king with his current state.

After an entire seven years *(seacht mbliadhna comhlána)* he comes to his former abode, where he spends the night. He laments how he has had no sleep for seven years, how he eats watercress and drinks water (watercress is mentioned twice), and how his life has otherwise been altered. He also thanks God and acknowledges that it is his own misdeeds that have led to this state. He finds his wife, who, although living with another man, is still devoted to him and would gladly join him in a tree. He replies that she should give her love to the man she is with rather than "to an uncouth and famished madman, horrible, fearful, stark-naked *(do gheilt ghairbh ghortaigh uathaigh, omhnaigh, urnochtaigh)*." Christ, he says, has caused his weakness.

After further adventures, during which he continues to fly around and live in trees, his relation Loingseachan finds him and laments that he should end up without food, drink, or clothing "like a bird of the air *(amail gach n-ethaid n-aéerdha)*"[11] who in misery goes "from wilderness to wilderness *(ó dhíthribh do dhíthribh)*." He then tells Suibhne that his parents, siblings, and children have died. Suibhne falls out of the tree in shock. Loiungseachan puts manacles *(cuibhreach)* on him and informs him it was a trick; the relatives are all alive. After about six weeks of imprisonment, he becomes sane again with his proper shape and is freed.

Unfortunately he is tricked into behaving like a bird again by a devious mill-hag *(cailleach an mhuilinn)*. A few of the notable things he says subsequently include (1) extensive praise of various trees, (2) that his feathers have grown so much that he can overtake a turtledove and flee various wild animals, (3) further acknowledgement of the origin of his suffering, (4) "My mead is my cold water, my kine are my cresses, my friends are my trees,

---

10. The watercress may correspond with the *herba terrae* of Vulgate Dan. 4:12 and *passim*, as *herba* can mean "herb" as well as "grass," although admittedly watercress grows on water, not earth.

11. Compare this with the plural *aves caeli* of Vulgate Dan. 4:18. The equivalent Aramaic phrase is rendered as "birds of the air" by the NRSV. Of course the phrase is not limited to Daniel.

though I am without mantle or smock *(As é mo mhíodh mh'uisci fúar, as é mo bhúar mo bhíorar, as íad mo charaid mo chroinn, ge 'tú gan leann, gan ionar)*" and (5) "Bent are my nails *(Corra mh'ingni-si),*" in addition to his feeble loins, pierced feet, and bare thighs.

Further adventures include a flight to Britain, where he lives with a madman. He also meets a mad woman in Ireland. His wife Eorann rejects him. Lamenting his suffering since he first grew feathers, he calls out to Christ. At this moment reason returns to him. He goes back to his people. When this is revealed to Ronan, the cleric calls upon God to stop Suibhne from ever going toward a church and that he have no relief until he dies. In response, God sends an apparition of five red torsos without heads and five bodiless screaming heads (some of which are those of goats and dogs) that follow the former king and talk about him until he escapes into the sky. Suibhne laments but again acknowledges that he deserves his travails as a result of his wrongdoing.

Suibhne comes at last to St. Moling as the monk is reading from a psalter (echoing Ronan and his psalter). Moling discerns that he is a madman and states that Suibhne will die there (as Suibhne himself has predicted) and be buried with righteous people in the churchyard. From then on Suibhne would continue to fly around but would attend vespers each night by Moling.

This happy arrangement ends when, in a fit of wrongful jealousy, the husband of the cook who feeds Suibhne thrusts a spear into Suibhne as he is eating. (It is also stated that Suibhne instead fell upon a spear that was placed by the husband.) A man sounding the bell for services laments the murder of "the king, the saint, the saintly madman" *(an rígh, an náomh, an náomhgheilt)*. Suibhne makes confession, takes communion, thanks God, and is anointed by the clerics. He says, among other things, "Though goodly ye deem the salt meat and the flesh that are eaten in banqueting houses, I had liefer eat a tuft of fresh watercress in some place without sorrow" *(Gidh maith libh-si i ttighibh óil bhar ccuirm leanna go n-onóir, ferr lium-sa deogh d'uisge i ngoid d'ól dom bais asin tiopraid)*. He falls into a swoon. Moling takes him to the door of the church. Suibhne places his shoulders on the door-post; his spirit goes to heaven; Moling buries him honorably.

Even if the motif of the mad king were not already recognized, the parallels to Daniel 4 (overall theme of downfall and repentance, banishment from humanity, period of seven, bird imagery, vegetation as food) make sense in the context of the story's strong Christian character as well as its wider use of biblical parallels. The introduction is written in biblical style:

There was a certain noble, distinguished holy patron in Ireland, even Ronan Finn, son of Bearach, son of Criodhan, son of Earclugh, son of Ernainne, son of Urene, son of Seachnusach, son of Colum Cuile, son of Mureadhach, son of Laoghaire, son of Niall; a man who fulfilled God's command and bore the yoke of piety and endured persecutions for the Lord's sake.

The various biblical parallels span different parts of the Bible. When Suibhne flees the house leaving his cloak in his wife's hand, he may recall Joseph in Gen. 39:12, who leaves his garment in the hand of Mrs. Potiphar. The king's preference for a watercress without sorrow over the food at banquets is also very similar in spirit to both Prov. 15:17 and Prov. 17:1.[12] A third parallel lies with the story of Saul. Like Suibhne, a raving Saul throws a spear at a "psalmist" (1 Sam. 18:10-11), as David is later known. Moreover David is playing the lyre at the time, an activity that both the Vulgate and a citation from a fourth-century patristic Old Latin source refer to with the verb *psallebat*.[13] Also like Suibhne, Saul's death is given in two separate accounts, one in which he dies directly by the hand of another (2 Sam. 1:6-10), and one in which he dies by falling upon a weapon (1 Sam. 31:4). There are differences, of course, but this remains suggestive.[14]

It is arguable that the *Buile Shuibhne*'s use of biblical allusions goes further than at least some of the writings and art that adopt imagery from Daniel 4. For instance, feather imagery, featured in both the Jewish and Irish stories, is rare in such medieval "Wild-Man" iconography; fur was much more typical. Details that the figure was a king and that his madness was brought on by God, and that it lasted for a period of seven years, some of which are indeed reflected in other literature, are also not central to the more general "Wild-Man" motif.

On the other hand, the Irish work preserves wider traditions that do not have a clear biblical basis. For instance, Suibhne's capture with bonds by

---

12. The contrast between vegetables and meat matches Prov. 15:17, whereas the reference to a banqueting house evokes Prov. 17:1.

13. The source is Lucifer (d. 370/71), bishop of Cagliari.

14. Suibhne's death has also been said to partially reflect a classic threefold death pattern (by spear, by falling, and by drowning); so Carney, *Studies*, 142. But perhaps the possible Saulide parallel is at least equally relevant, particularly as the threefold pattern does not fit here neatly. To be sure, Suibhne's deaths are due to the same person, whereas both of Saul's deaths are either actual or assisted suicide. Saul's deaths are also caused by swords, not spears, although he does reportedly lean upon his spear in 2 Sam. 1:6.

Loiungseachan fits a motif associated with "Wild Men" although the captor is usually a woman. Another aspect that is closer to wider cultural traditions is the fact that Suibhne's metamorphosis into a bird occurs at a battle. This is akin to other traditions of battle frenzy linked with becoming like an animal, most famously among Scandinavian *berserkers*. Finally, the specific transformation into a bird in a story concerned with the coming of Christianity is also found in the Irish *Children of Lir*, although it has been argued that *Lir* is dependent upon the *Buile Shuibhne*.[15] Further thoughts about the nature of Suibhne's madness will be explored later in this paper.

At this point we turn to the transmission of Daniel in the British Isles.[16] The book of Daniel exists in several different versions. The Old Greek is markedly different from the Masoretic Text. The so-called Theodotion version, which was adopted by the Church, is closer to the MT. The Vulgate is closer but not identical to the "Theodotion," but the Old Latin evidence is split between the OG and "Theodotion." With full caution, including the awareness that our tale has many sources, I would like to suggest that whoever was involved in incorporating biblical allusions into the *Buile Shuibhne* (or its sources) may have had access to OL material that goes back to the OG form of Daniel. Unfortunately, according to Ziegler, there is no OL material corresponding to the relevant verses, so we must work with the Greek.[17]

Where the Vulgate speaks of the tree being tied with a band of iron and brass, OG Dan. 4:14a speaks of the tree being *imprisoned* (εἰς φυλακὴν παρεδόθη) and bound by bronze fetters and *manacles* (χειροπέδαις). This corresponds in part with Suibhne's binding with manacles and imprisonment by Loingsechan, although we have noted its presence in "Wild Man" motifs elsewhere. OG Dan. 4:19 speaks of how Nebuchadnezzar has "desolated the house of the living God" (ἐξερήμωσας τὸν οἶκον τοῦ θεοῦ τοῦ ζῶντος) just as Suibhne has disturbed the marking of a church. OG Dan. 4:28 also has Daniel tell this king that his kingdom will be given to another, something that also happens to Suibhne. In addition, with the exception of other mad people, for a

---

15. Carney, *Studies*, 153-58.

16. I hope John Collins will forgive my subsuming Ireland under this type of nomenclature, but the region needs to be understood as possessing some degree of cultural continuity at this time. Chances are good, however, that the biblical embellishments may be Irish in origin, given that they are at times in tension with the force of the larger story. Also, it has been argued that much of Irish literature was composed in monasteries. Further work to address this question would require an examination of all three of the British traditions Carney cites.

17. Joseph Zeigler, *Septuaginta: Vetus Testamentum Graecum 16/2: Susanna, Daniel, Bel et Draco* (Göttingen: Vandenhoeck & Ruprecht, 1954), 36-37.

long time Suibhne does not speak with another human (cf. OG Dan. 4:29). Also in OG Dan. 4:30, the king's flesh (σάρξ) as well as heart changes and he walks around naked (γυμνός), as does Suibhne on both counts. The king of the OG is also more penitential than that of the MT or Vulgate, also in keeping with Suibhne's behavior. In fact, in OG 34b, like Suibhne, Nebuchadnezzar makes a confession (ἀνθομολογοῦμαι), with the difference that his is public and Suibhne's is to Moling.[18] Although, as noted, caution is in order, it may still be worth exploring through other methods the extent to which OL versions of Daniel with OG features were in circulation in Ireland and/or the British Isles more generally during the Middle Ages. Given that the biblical material may be attributed to monks and that monks (certainly Irish ones) were known to travel, a much wider arena may come under discussion.

Just as the transmission history of Daniel in the medieval period is far from simple, the reception history of the biblical story may likewise present a more complex picture. Most scholars would probably agree that much of these medieval traditions, although they adopt biblical imagery, do not derive exclusively from Daniel 4. Rather, the traditions of the Wild Man may draw upon something pre-Christian that was later recognized as akin to the story of Daniel 4 in its various versions. Gregory Mobley and Matthias Henze quite rightly point to Mesopotamian traditions for understanding Daniel, particularly those of Enkidu in the Babylonian version of the *Gilgamesh Epic*. I would like, however, to cast a somewhat wider net.

Celtic scholar Birgit Beneš, writing on the *Buile Shuibhne*, with little to no attention toward the Bible, argues that Suibhne has shamanistic traits.[19] Naturally there are serious methodological problems in speaking of shamanism divorced from a specific culture and from the integral and diverse roles shamans play in a specific community. There are problems as well with applying a term like "shaman" to cultures other than the Siberian from which the word originates. Most seriously, the basis upon which one can responsibly discern "shamanism" in literary documents is exceedingly problematic.[20] But writing in 1960, less than ten years after Eliade's controversial

---

18. One important difference, however, is that in the OG (and Theodotion) the nails are of a lion, not a bird.

19. Birgit Beneš, "Spuren von Schamanismus in der Sage Buile Suibhne," *Zeitschrift für Celtische Philologie* 28 (1960/61): 309-34.

20. For a recent treatment sharing similar concerns, see Alice Beck Kehoe, *Shamans and Religion: An Anthropological Exploration in Critical Thinking* (Long Grove, Ill.: Waveland, 2000). Some of what I say later in this article probably requires further nuance, but I do not think this detracts from the wider claims being made.

tome on the subject, Beneš remains insightful nonetheless. She brings together a set of features that are attested widely among traditional cultures that view the natural world as numinous and for whom it is the job of certain individuals to manage the various spirits of animate and inanimate beings. This would of necessity include dead spirits. Such a job requires being able to access the spirit world, something that is often achieved by means of altered states of consciousness.

Among the features Beneš lists as the attributes of spirit-managers, she includes the transformation into an animal, something that might be understood as getting in touch with the animal's spirit. This is indeed consistently found across many traditional cultures. Beneš also mentions a strong connection with both "the cosmic tree" and deer (cf. "beasts of the field"), which again are widely attested. These features are all present in Daniel. Beneš also comments on bird imagery and reiterates the well-documented linkage of birds to spirits.[21]

Likely, however, by the time these various elements surfaced in the versions of Daniel,[22] or in whatever sources lie behind Daniel, the purport of the imagery had changed. This resulted in the confused melding of tree and bird and beast imagery and the transformation of human into animal (at least mentally) that is no longer part of a ritual supposed to help the wider community (perhaps in hunting, as some think). Instead it has become a punishment. And the entire set of images, in Daniel at least, has been further subsumed to represent Jewish theological aims. We may look at this from a history-of-religions point of view along the lines suggested by Thorkild Jacobsen. Deities may have been originally associated or identified with animals, but they gradually became human with animal "emblems" that may at times reappear.[23] It is a world where nature is becoming increasingly defined against culture, dominated, manipulated and exploited. And yet the old forces are not entirely gone.[24] Even in Babylonian *Gilgamesh,* with its clear nature-culture divide, the taming of Enkidu is described not without a hint of regret. In the *Buile Suibhne,* the ambiguity is arguably greater, as Suibhne,

---

21. Christian iconography in which the Holy Spirit is represented by a dove attests to this ancient tradition.

22. These aspects are interestingly not present in the Prayer of Nabonidus or in the H2 inscription.

23. Thorkild Jacobsen, *The Treasures of Darkness: A History of Mesopotamian Religion* (New Haven: Yale University Press, 1976), 9.

24. This recalls the famous story of an Irish woman interviewed by Yeats about fairies, who replied, "Of course I don't believe in fairies but they're there."

although ultimately in touch with the Church, remains and dies equally in touch with the wild.

Arguably, when Nebuchadnezzar takes upon the features of both wild beasts and birds, creatures that both take their shelter and food from the tree, this may be a way of stating that in political terms he has been lowered to the level of those who depend upon him politically. This mirrors the temporary loss of his kingdom. The image in Dan. 4:12 (MT) of the tree being placed in a fetter of iron and bronze, although it may refer to some genuine custom with trees, seems in this verse to refer to the king, just as the phrase immediately following refers to the eating of grass, which is not a typical behavior for trees. Whether the fetters (and manacles of the OG) are an independent attestation of the motif of binding the "Wild Man" as we see in medieval literature, I cannot say. But the detail may represent a similar idea of overpowering nature (here, in the form of the animalistic human and perhaps also the tree).

As noted already, the *Buile Suibhne* has features such as poetry and prophecy that go beyond the imagery it shares with Daniel, but are equally consonant with the kinds of activities of persons who undergo altered states of consciousness. The combination of poetry, prophecy, and a thin line separating the prophet from sanity in the Hebrew Bible is no accident. To look at this from another direction, consider historical individuals such as Francis of Assisi, William Blake, and Walt Whitman. All three were deeply in touch with the natural world, all wrote about trees in a significant manner, all wrote poetry, and all had a highly developed sense of spirituality; at least some of them have been understood as prophets and holy men. All three, it has been argued, also underwent altered states of consciousness.[25] This close kinship with trees and beasts and birds is probably as old as the dawn of human culture, perhaps even in nonhuman primate cultures or earlier. It is no surprise, therefore, that certain individuals in altered states may be understood as bypassing the veneer of "civilization" in some of their more marked

---

25. Another famous ecstatic prophetic figure and likely song composer was Ann Lee, founder of the Shakers, who was understood by herself and her followers to be a female form of Christ. See http://www.ubu.com/ethno/visuals/shaker06.html for a Shaker tree of heaven (schematic, not arboreal). On the relationship between altered states and religious experience and leadership more generally, see William James, *The Varieties of Religious Experience* (New York: Random House, 1902), and Frederick K. Goodwin and Kay Redfield Jamison, *Manic-Depressive Illness* (New York: Oxford University Press, 1990), 360-62. Gananath Obeyeskere, *Medusa's Hair: An Essay on Personal Symbols and Religious Experience* (Chicago: University of Chicago Press, 1981), supplies useful field data from South Asia.

behaviors. It is also understandable that a more flexible attitude toward altered states, which may or may not correspond with modern understandings of psychosis, is still found today in some more traditional cultures.

The combination of bird, beast, cosmic tree, and animal transformation in Daniel seems to represent something very old indeed, "from before the flood," older than the written word. It does not matter so much what labels we give the combination as much as that it resonates with traditional cultures worldwide. The *Buile Shuibhne* is still in touch with this world in a way that is not as easily discernable in Daniel 4. And while I certainly would not like to press the significance of altered states of consciousness toward understanding Daniel 4, I am not entirely sure that they are totally irrelevant. It is certainly clear, though, that thinking of Nebuchadnezzar's experience purely in quasi-medicalized terms (even with the parallels in material about Nabonidus) does not help us understand the narrative any better.

Whether my arguments are ultimately convincing, I hope to have highlighted one of the many jewels of Irish literature and shown its dependence on the Hebrew Bible. I also have provided preliminary evidence suggesting that Old Greek traditions may lie behind some of the story's Danielic elements. This in turn may help establish the permeation and continued usage of OL manuscripts in Ireland/the British Isles and perhaps elsewhere. Lastly, I have speculated that it may be no accident that "shaman-like" elements found in the *Buile Shuibhne* were viewed by its composer(s) as akin to Daniel 4. I further present the hypothesis that the current use of the imagery in the extant versions of Daniel may be a reconfigured, muted rendition of something much more potent than it may seem at first. I have also shown, I hope, that the debates between scholars studying Daniel 4 who focus on "Wild Man" imagery (Henze and Mobely) and Christopher B. Hays, who stresses that of the Netherworld, may be resolved. However the two elements are understood, both may be seen as pieces of a larger picture. It is essential to be conversant with Mesopotamian imagery in understanding Daniel, but also with the broader webs of human imagination, for which Jacobsen remains essential reading. At any rate, I am pleased to present our honoree with some connections between his magisterial scholarly contributions and his beloved homeland. *Molann an obair an fear.*[26]

---

26. "The work praises the man."

PART TWO

WISDOM

Elusive Wisdom and the Other Nations in Baruch

Karina Martin Hogan

The book of Baruch, which follows Jeremiah in the Septuagint, is generally thought to be a composite work, made up of either three or four independent compositions. An earlier generation of scholars tended to describe the book as highly derivative and full of inconsistencies,[1] but in more recent scholarship both its exegetical originality and its thematic unity have been evaluated more favorably.[2] The first half of the book, which is in prose, consists of a narrative introduction (1:1-14) and a prayer of confession and repentance (1:15–3:8).[3] The second half consists of two poems, of which the first (3:9–4:4) is generally called a wisdom poem and the second (4:5–5:9), a

---

1. Carey A. Moore, *Daniel, Esther and Jeremiah: The Additions, A New Translation with Introduction and Commentary* (AB 44; Garden City, N.Y.: Doubleday, 1977), 259, 261.

2. Anthony J. Saldarini, "The Book of Baruch," in *NIB*, 6:930. Recent favorable treatments include Odil Hannes Steck, *Das apokryphe Baruchbuch: Studien zu Rezeption und Konzentration "kanonischer" Überlieferung* (Göttingen: Vandenhoeck & Ruprecht, 1993), and André Kabasele Mukenge, *L'Unité littéraire du livre de Baruch* (Études Bibliques, NS 38; Paris: Gabalda, 1998).

3. The prayer of confession bears some sort of literary relationship to Dan. 9:4-19, but the direction of influence is disputed, and it is possible that both depend on a common source. See Doron Mendels, "Baruch, Book of," *ABD* 1:618-20; Saldarini, "Book of Baruch," in *NIB*, 6:931.

I dedicate this paper to John J. Collins, my teacher, mentor, and friend, in gratitude for all the encouragement he has given me over the years. While I can only dream of emulating him as a scholar, I hope to be the kind of support to my students that he has been to me.

prophetic poem or a poem of consolation. The entire book was probably written in Hebrew, although that is somewhat less certain for the poetic than for the prose sections.[4] The various parts of the book are unified by the common prophetic message that the people of Israel are in exile because they have disobeyed God's commandments (e.g., 1:13; 1:19-20; 3:10-13; 4:12-13). Like the prophets of the exile, both the prayer of confession and the poem of consolation hold out hope of a return to the promised land if the people repent.

The central poem, 3:9–4:4, promises the more general reward of "life" to those who follow the commandments (3:9, 14; 4:1). The label "wisdom poem" or "eulogy of wisdom" is often attached to this poem because of its extensive use of sapiential terminology, and on account of its allusions to wisdom texts, especially Job 28. "Wisdom" is a notoriously vague genre label, so it would be useful to clarify in what sense this really is a wisdom poem. In one sense, it is an anti-wisdom poem, since it repudiates the universalism of the international wisdom tradition by arguing that the "way of wisdom" is hidden from people of every nation except Israel. On the other hand, it is strongly pro-wisdom, if wisdom is defined as Torah observance and reflection on the sacred traditions of Israel. The type of wisdom the Baruch poem promotes is "covenant wisdom," a term coined by Stephen Geller in an article entitled "Fiery Wisdom: Logos and Lexis in Deuteronomy 4."[5] The wisdom poem in Baruch shares several themes with Deuteronomy 4, including the two ideas that Geller identifies as innovations on the part of the author of Deuteronomy 4: "the identification of covenantal obedience as Israel's wisdom, and the efficacy of repentance in assuaging divine wrath."[6] Although the term "covenant wisdom" can also be applied to the Wisdom of Ben Sira, Ben Sira does not draw the same conclusions as the Baruch poet

---

4. Emmanuel Tov has shown that the prose portions of Baruch were very likely rendered into Greek by the same translator responsible for the Septuagint version of Jeremiah. See his dissertation, *The Septuagint Translation of Jeremiah and Baruch: A Discussion of an Early Revision of the LXX of Jeremiah 29–52 and Baruch 1:1–3:15* (HSM 8; Missoula, Mont.: Scholars Press, 1976), 111-33. David Burke, *The Poetry of Baruch: A Reconstruction and Analysis of the Original Hebrew Text of Baruch 3:9–5:9* (SBLSCS 10; Chico, Calif.: Scholars Press, 1982), has persuaded most scholars that the poetic parts of Baruch were also translated from Hebrew.

5. Stephen A. Geller, "Fiery Wisdom: Logos and Lexis in Deuteronomy 4," *Prooftexts* 14 (1994): 103-39 (here 123). In my book *Theologies in Conflict in 4 Ezra: Wisdom Debate and Apocalyptic Solution* (JSJSup 130; Leiden: Brill, 2008), I use the term "covenantal wisdom" to designate the type of wisdom found in Sirach and Bar. 3:9–4:4.

6. Geller, "Fiery Wisdom," 108.

does from the identification of transcendent Wisdom with the Torah, as a comparison of the ending of the Baruch poem with the ending of Sirach 24 will demonstrate.

The "wisdom poem" label is also problematic in that it has prompted many scholars to analyze Baruch 3:9–4:4 in isolation from the rest of the book and to overlook allusions to biblical texts outside the wisdom corpus. The other parts of Baruch have a more nuanced view of the other nations and of election than the central poem. The apparently ethnocentric message of the wisdom poem is moderated considerably when it is read in the context of the book as a whole. Drawing upon the work of Odil Hannes Steck and André Kabasele Mukenge, both of whom have argued that the book of Baruch is best interpreted as a literary unity, I will draw attention to allusions to non-wisdom texts, especially Deuteronomy and the Prophets, which connect the wisdom poem to the rest of the book.

I. Literary Analysis

The basic rhetorical structure of Bar. 3:9–4:4 consists of an exordium (3:9-14) setting forth the problem, its cause and its solution; the main argument (3:15–4:1), which is divided into a negative answer and a positive one to the question posed in 3:15; and a brief peroration (4:2-4).[7] The poem opens with "Hear, O Israel, the commandments of life," a Deuteronomic-sounding phrase that has no exact parallel in Deuteronomy; the phrase "the commandments of life" is found only in Ezek. 33:15 (חקות החיים), although the similar phrase "the law of life" occurs in Sir. 17:11 and 45:5. The Deuteronomic language of the exordium links the poem to the penitential prayer that precedes it (1:15–3:8), which, like the prayer in Dan. 9:4-19, is steeped in Deuteronomic language and theology. With its continuation, "give ear, to learn insight," the opening verse alludes in a general way to Deut. 4:6, which calls keeping the commandments Israel's "wisdom and understanding" (חכמה and בינה). The Greek text of Bar. 3:9–4:4 uses four terms for wisdom or understanding more or less interchangeably: φρόνησις, σύνεσις, ἐπιστήμη and σοφία (in order of decreasing frequency), while Da-

---

7. My literary analysis of the poem follows the structure proposed by Carey Moore in Anchor Bible 44 and followed by Anthony Saldarini in the *New Interpreter's Bible* and by Kabasele Mukenge; Steck differs only over the placement of 3:14. Moore, *Daniel, Esther and Jeremiah: The Additions*, 303; Saldarini, "Book of Baruch," in *NIB* 6:960; Kabasele Mukenge, *L'Unité litteraire*, 232-33; Steck, *Das apokryphe Baruchbuch*, 125-28.

vid Burke's reconstruction of the Hebrew uses בינה most frequently, followed by חכמה, תבונה and דעת.⁸

The next four verses (3:10-13) are so closely related in theme and language to the prose sections of Baruch and to the poem of consolation that some scholars consider them a redactional addition to the present poem.⁹ It seems more likely that verses 10-13 are original to the poem, however, since they are well integrated into their present context; for example, verse 13 is linked to verse 14 in that both emphasize "peace" (εἰρήνη) as the reward of following the commandments, and verses 11 and 12 are echoed by the ending of 4:1, "but those who abandon her will die." Kabasele Mukenge has shown that verses 9-14 have a chiastic structure, with verse 12 (the only monostich in the poem) at the center: "You have forsaken the spring of wisdom."¹⁰ The phrase "the spring of wisdom" may be an allusion to Prov. 18:4, but the verse as a whole states compellingly the reason for the exile and recalls an image in Jer. 2:13, "My people . . . have forsaken me, the spring of living water."¹¹ Verse 14 both forms an inclusio with v. 9 through the use of the key terms ζωή (life) and φρόνησις (insight or knowledge) and provides a bridge, through an abundance of sapiential terminology, to the main argument of the poem.

The main argument begins with a question about wisdom that alludes loosely to Job 28: "Who has found her place, and who has entered into her treasuries?" (3:15). The first half of the question (in Burke's reconstruction) uses two words that occur several times in Job 28, מצא and מקום.¹² The second half of the verse alludes more generally to the search for treasure that is contrasted with the quest for wisdom in the Job poem. The negative answer

---

8. See Saldarini, "Book of Baruch," in *NIB*, 6:961, and Burke, *Poetry of Baruch*, 78-79.

9. Burke, *Poetry of Baruch*, 22. For example, the comparison in v. 11 of the exiled addressees to the dead who are in Sheol echoes 3:4 in the penitential prayer: "listen now to the prayer of those of Israel who have died"; cf. also 2:17.

10. Kabasele Mukenge, *L'Unité littéraire*, 234.

11. Burke (*Poetry of Baruch*, 66, 83) reconstructs the phrase מקור חכמה in 3:12 by analogy with Prov. 18:4. Jer. 2:13 reads in full (NRSV): "for my people have committed two evils: they have forsaken me, the fountain (מקור) of living water, and dug out cisterns for themselves, cracked cisterns that can hold no water."

12. Burke, *Poetry of Baruch*, 66; Kabasele Mukenge, *L'Unité littéraire*, 258. The word מקום occurs in Job 28:1, 6, 12, 20, and 23; מצא occurs in the Niphal imperfect in verses 12 and 13, and the similar-sounding noun מוצא (from the root יצא) occurs alongside מקום in v. 1. Some commentators have doubted the originality of תמצא in Job 28:12, since it recurs in the next verse and is replaced by תבוא in 28:20, which otherwise parallels 28:12. The ancient versions all reflect תמצא in 28:12, however, so it is likely that this was the reading familiar to the author of the Baruch poem.

to that question in 3:16-31 advances a single argument: the nations other than Israel have not found "the way of wisdom."[13] The Baruch poet draws extensively on Job 28 in making this argument, but in fact aims at a significantly different conclusion, having to do with the election of Israel, a theme that is completely absent from Job 28. Whereas Job 28 contrasts the triumph of human ingenuity in mining precious metals and stones with the futility of the human search for wisdom,[14] Bar. 3:16-19 suggests that the endless scheming to acquire wealth on the part of the "rulers of the nations" is itself futile, because they will die and their wealth will pass to others (cf. Eccles. 2:18-21). Also like Ecclesiastes (e.g., 4:13; 9:14-17), and in agreement with Job 28:15-19,[15] the poet overturns the traditional sapiential view that the acquisition of wealth and power is a result of wisdom (e.g., Prov. 8:15-18).

The description of the rulers of the nations as having dominion over the beasts of the earth and making sport with the birds of the sky (3:16-17) may have a particular referent, appropriate to the exilic setting of the book: Nebuchadnezzar. In Jer. 27:5-7, the LORD says that he is giving all lands, and even the beasts of the field, into the hand of King Nebuchadnezzar, his son, and his grandson — but that in time his land will be made to serve others. The same theme of Nebuchadnezzar's limitless but temporary dominion over all creatures is expressed in Dan. 2:38 and 4:12, and Jdt. 11:7, all of which add the birds of the air to the list of his subjects.[16] Thus verses 16-19 hint at the prophetic theme that the LORD both grants and takes away the power of human rulers, at the same time as they call into question the traditional association of wealth and power with wisdom.

---

13. Walter Harrelson, who divides the poem into shorter stanzas, summarizes the themes of the negative answer with the following stanza headings: "the way to wisdom is hidden," "even the wisest of nations are ignorant of wisdom," and "the greatest of the ancients lacked wisdom." See his essay, "Wisdom Hidden and Revealed according to Baruch (Baruch 3:9–4:4)," in *Priests, Prophets and Scribes: Essays on the Formation and Heritage of Second Temple Judaism in Honour of Joseph Blenkinsopp*, ed. E. Ulrich et al. (JSOTSup 149; Sheffield: JSOT Press, 1992), 158-71 (here 163-64).

14. Stephen Geller calls the first part of the poem "a kind of hymn to human ingenuity." See his essay "'Where Is Wisdom?' A Literary Study of Job 28 in Its Settings," in *Judaic Perspectives on Ancient Israel*, ed. J. Neusner, B. A. Levine, and E. S. Frerichs (Philadelphia: Fortress, 1987), 155-88 (quotation on 167).

15. Geller ("Where Is Wisdom?" 175) considers these verses secondary, since they represent a digression (or "distraction") from the main topic of the poem, "man's relationship to nature and to God."

16. Both Moore (*Additions to Jeremiah*, 298) and Burke (*Poetry of Baruch*, 86) point out the possible allusion to Nebuchadnezzar through these verses.

The next verses, 3:20-23, pick up a third key term of Job 28: the way (דרך) of wisdom. Geller points out that דרכה in Job 28:23 (and, as emended, in 28:13) has a double meaning: both a literal one, "the way or path *to* it" and a figurative one, "its way of acting," i.e., its nature.[17] Bar. 3:20-21, 23 similarly play on both senses of דרך and its synonym נתיבה: the descendents of the "rulers of the nations" did not "discover her paths" and hence "strayed far from her way" (or from their own way, in the LXX), and even the nations renowned for wisdom have not known "the way of wisdom," in the sense of its true nature.

It is significant that the particular nations that are said not to have found the way of wisdom are all, with the exception of Canaan, closely related to Israel through Abraham, Isaac and Ishmael. Teman is synonymous with Edom and famed for its wisdom (cf. Jer. 49:7; Obad. 8-9; and Eliphaz the Temanite in Job); the sons of Hagar are of course the Ishmaelites, whose nomadic lifestyle is here associated with the search for wisdom; the Greek Merran is probably a corruption of Medan, one of Abraham's sons by Keturah (Gen. 25:2), and Tema (which is rendered identically to Teman in the LXX) is a son of Ishmael (Gen. 25:15). Although Israel's relations with the Ishmaelites and Edomites were not always peaceful, the conflicts are rooted in sibling rivalry, according to Genesis, which emphasizes Israel's kinship with these neighboring peoples by including genealogies of Ishmael and Esau at key transition points (25:12-16 and chapter 36). As Joel Kaminsky has recently pointed out, "Ishmael has more markings of election than perhaps any other non-elect person in the whole Hebrew Bible."[18] Similarly, on the grounds of kinship, God commands the Israelites to deal peaceably with the descendants of Esau in Deut. 2:4-6. It is surprising, therefore, for Canaan to be included in this list of "kindred" nations.

As Kaminsky has shown, the biblical concept of election includes three categories of people: the elect, the non-elect and the anti-elect. There are really only a few examples of anti-elect nations, enemies of God whom Israel is called upon to annihilate, but the Canaanites are definitely in this category.[19] Most nations are simply non-elect, and the way God deals with them depends on how they treat Israel (cf. Gen. 12:3). The wisdom poem collapses

---

17. Geller, "Where Is Wisdom?" 166. He points out a similar play on these two senses of דרך in Prov. 30:18-19.

18. Joel S. Kaminsky, *Yet I Loved Jacob: Reclaiming the Biblical Concept of Election* (Nashville: Abingdon, 2007), 34.

19. Only the Canaanites and the Amalekites are clearly anti-elect; the status of the Midianites is ambiguous, according to Kaminsky, *Yet I Loved Jacob*, 111-19.

this distinction, by heading the list of the nations that have not found wisdom with the Canaanites, but also including the Ishmaelites and Edomites, who are the most closely related to Israel of the non-elect nations, according to Genesis.[20] Thus the poem maintains a dualistic view of election that is at odds with the dominant concept of election in the Hebrew Bible. Perhaps there is an implied a fortiori argument here: if even the nations closest to Israel, either geographically (Canaan) or genealogically (Ishmael, Edom, and their descendents), have not found the way of wisdom, how much farther from wisdom are the more distant nations.

That train of thought would account for the apostrophe to Israel that seems to interrupt the argument at this point, "O Israel, how great is the house of God, how vast his domain! It is great and endless; it is high and immeasurable" (3:24-25).[21] The point of this apostrophe becomes clear a couple of verses later, when the issue of election is finally broached directly: "Not these did God choose, nor did he give them the way of knowledge" (3:27). Mentioning the totality of God's sovereignty underscores the significance of God's election of Israel (cf., e.g., Exod. 19:5-6; Deut. 10:14-15; Ps. 33:6-12).

At any rate, the theme of the vastness of the universe provides a transition to the example of the giants, "men of renown, who from of old were

---

20. A number of prophetic books contain oracles against Edom, however; e.g., Isaiah 34, Jer. 49:7-22, Ezekiel 35, Obadiah, Mal. 1:2-5. The Edomites are also treated as enemies in Lam. 4:21-22 and Pss. 60:9-10 (par. 108:10-11), 83:7, and 137:7. See Elie Assis, "Why Edom: On the Hostility towards Jacob's Brother in Prophetic Sources," *VT* 66 (2006): 1-20. He argues that the traditional kinship between Israel and Edom contributed to the enmity towards Edom expressed in exilic and postexilic texts, because the Edomite participation in the destruction of Judah was interpreted by some to mean that God had rejected Israel and chosen Edom in their place. This dynamic is reflected most clearly in Mal. 1:2-5. I am grateful to Joel Kaminsky for drawing my attention to this article and helping me to nuance this point.

21. The phrase "house of God," which ordinarily denotes a sanctuary in the Bible, here clearly refers to the totality of creation, for which the typical biblical designation is "the heavens and the earth." Burke (*Poetry of Baruch,* 96 and 127, note 76) notes that the concept of the universe as the house of God is found in several treatises of Philo of Alexandria (*De Aeternitate Mundi* §112; *De Cherubim* §52; *De Opificio Mundi* §21), but not in any earlier Jewish text. In calling the whole world "the house of God," the author may have been drawing on biblical texts that contrast God's earthly dwelling (the Temple) with the totality of his dominion, such as Solomon's prayer in 1 Kings 8 (par. 2 Chronicles 6; cf. especially 1 Kings 8:27-30; 2 Chron. 6:18-21) or Isa. 66:1. Some scholars have taken this unusual use of "the house of God" as evidence for a post-70 C.E. date of composition, but the fact that the Temple was still standing did not prevent Philo from referring to the whole world as the "house of God" (Burke, *Poetry of Baruch,* 127, note 77).

men of great stature, skilled in war" (3:26). As Gerald Sheppard has pointed out, verse 26 conflates the Nephilim (LXX: γίγαντες) of Gen. 6:4, who were אנשי השם, with their putative descendants, the אנשי־מדות whom the Hebrews faced in their conquest of Canaan (Num. 13:32-33) and wars with the Philistines (2 Sam. 21:18-22; 1 Chron. 20:6-8).[22] The poet is perhaps playing a bit with the idea of the "nations greater and mightier than you," whom God drove out of the promised land in order to give it to Israel (Deut. 4:38; cf. Deut. 1:28, where a similar phrase refers to the size of the individual inhabitants).[23] By also alluding to Gen. 6:4, however, the poet may possibly mean to evoke the myth of the Watchers, in which the union of בני האלהים with בנות האדם resulted not only in the birth of giants, but also in the revelation of improper knowledge to humankind (1 Enoch 6–11).[24] If so, then the subtext may be that knowledge outside the Torah not only is not true wisdom, but may actually lead to destruction, as the knowledge revealed by the fallen Watchers led to the flood. The poet does not need to specify which generation of giants he means in order to make the point that the reason there are no more giants is that they lacked wisdom, and that is because God did not choose them.

The negative phase of the argument culminates in verses 29-31. The opening words of verse 29 — "Who has ascended to heaven and taken her, and brought her down from the clouds?" — echo the skeptical words of Agur in Prov. 30:4, but as Burke puts it, "the primary source for this verse and the next is manifestly Deut. 30:12-13."[25] Just as he alluded to Job 28 to make his own, quite distinct point in 3:16-19, the poet has inverted the meaning of the questions in Deut. 30:12-13 so that they no longer affirm the proximity of the Torah, but rather underscore the theme of the elusiveness of wisdom, unless God chooses to reveal it.[26] Verse 31 concludes the negative answer to the question in 3:15, recapitulating the main argument regarding the other nations: "There is no one who knows her way, no one who recognizes her path."

The poet then returns to Job 28 to offer a positive answer to the question in 3:15, "Who has found her place, and who has entered into her treasuries?" The answer in 3:32, as in Job 28, is God alone: "the one who per-

---

22. Gerald T. Sheppard, *Wisdom as a Hermeneutical Construct: A Study in the Sapientializing of the Old Testament* (BZAW 151; Berlin, New York: Walter de Gruyter, 1980), 85-90.

23. Sheppard, *Wisdom as a Hermeneutical Construct*, 88. Deut. 4:38 has ועצמים ממך and Deut. 1:28, עם גדול ורם ממנו. גוים גדלים

24. Saldarini, "Book of Baruch," in *NIB* 6:966.

25. Burke, *Poetry of Baruch*, 101.

26. Moore, *The Additions to Jeremiah*, 300.

ceives all knows her" (3:32a) alludes to Job 28:24, while "he searched her out with his intelligence" (3:32b) alludes to the end of Job 28:27.[27] As in Job 28:23-27, the relationship between God and Wisdom is set in the context of creation in Bar. 3:32-35, but rather than the creation "in the beginning" (as in Job 28:26-27 and Prov. 8:22-31), the context seems to be God's ongoing work of creation in the present. There are clear allusions in verses 33 and 34 to Job 38:35, התשלח ברקים וילכו ויאמרו לך הננו, although the poet has changed the referent from lightning to light generally in v. 33, and then to the stars in v. 34.[28]

While various commentators have referred to Bar. 3:32-35 as "hymnic," no one (to my knowledge) has pointed out their structural similarity to prophetic doxologies, although Steck has noted a few specific parallels to such passages.[29] Prophetic doxologies such as Amos 4:13, 5:8, and 9:5-6; Jer. 10:12-16; and Isa. 40:25-26, 45:18, and 48:12-13 share certain features with Bar. 3:32-35 besides the claim that God is the creator and sovereign of the universe: they use participial or imperfect verbal forms to indicate God's ongoing creative activity; they include a more or less explicit reference to the incomparability of God; and two of them, Amos 5:8 and Isa. 40:25-26, feature the stars (in the form of constellations or the heavenly host) quite prominently among the works of creation.[30] The mention of stars as God's creations in these doxologies is probably connected to the theme of the incomparability of the LORD, because of the prevalence of astral worship in the ancient Near East (cf. Deut. 4:19).

27. According to Burke (*Poetry of Baruch*, 104-5), the designation for God, ὁ εἰδὼς τὰ πάντα (which he renders רואה־כל), probably derives from Job 28:24, תחת כל־השמים יראה, but a similar idea is expressed in Ps. 151:4 (11QPs^a xxviii, 7-8) and Sir. 15:18. Burke (*Poetry of Baruch*, 105) and Sheppard (*Wisdom as a Hermeneutical Construct*, 95) independently concluded that the most likely Hebrew Vorlage of ἐχεῦρεν αὐτὴν is חקרה, based on Job 28:27.

28. Sheppard, *Wisdom as a Hermeneutical Construct*, 96. For the interchangeability of lightning and stars, cf. *1 Enoch* 43-44.

29. Steck notes the similarity of 3:32-37 with Jer. 10:6-7, and especially 10:12 and 10:16 (*Das apokryphe Baruchbuch*, 132) and later compares 3:34-35 to Isa. 40:26 and Ps. 147:4-5 (ibid., 152).

30. On the common characteristics of prophetic doxologies, see James L. Crenshaw, *Hymnic Affirmation of Divine Justice: The Doxologies of Amos and Related Texts in the Old Testament* (SBLDS 24; Missoula, Mont.: Scholars Press, 1975), 10-17, 141-46. The divine title "YHWH (the God) of Hosts," which also implies the subordination of the stars to God, appears in Amos 4:13; 9:5-6; Jer. 10:16; and a number of related contexts in Jeremiah and Deutero-Isaiah, and also in Amos 5:27, immediately following the mention of astral deities in 5:26. See ibid., 75-92. A similar passage outside the prophets is Ps. 147:4-5.

The emphasis in Bar. 3:34 on the cheerful obedience of the stars to their Maker suggests a third background for these verses, in addition to Job 38:35 and the prophetic doxologies. It was a common topos in early Jewish literature to contrast the order of creation with human disobedience of the divine statutes, and the orderly courses of the heavenly luminaries are often mentioned in these contexts.[31] So, for example, the indictment of sinners in *1 Enoch* 2–5 begins, "Contemplate all his works, and observe the works of heaven, how they do not alter their paths; and the luminaries of heaven, that they all rise and set, each one ordered in its appointed time; and they appear on their feasts and do not transgress their own appointed order" (2:1, Nickelsburg's translation). The motif of the obedience of the heavenly luminaries is appropriate in the context of the present poem, since it contrasts with both the Israelites, who "have forsaken the spring of wisdom" (3:12), and with the other nations, who "have [not] known the way of wisdom, nor remembered her paths" (3:23).

The concluding verse of the doxology, "This is our God [and there is no other], no other can be considered besides him" (3:35; 3:36 in the LXX), clearly draws on the language of Deutero-Isaiah.[32] This is a point of contact with the poem of consolation that follows this poem in Baruch, since the primary source-text for that poem is Isaiah 40–66. By referring to the Creator for the first time as "*our* God," the poet signals a shift to the language of election that dominates the remainder of the poem. The doxology is immediately followed by the declaration that this God, having "searched out the whole way of knowledge" (echoing 3:32), "gave it to his servant Jacob, and to Israel, his beloved" (3:36/LXX 3:37). As Sheppard observes, the parallelism of Jacob and Israel is typically associated with the election motif in the Hebrew

---

31. See Michael E. Stone, "The Parabolic Use of the Natural Order in Judaism of the Second Temple Age," in idem, *Selected Studies in Pseudepigrapha and Apocrypha: With Special Reference to the Armenian Tradition* (SVTP 9; Leiden: Brill, 1991), 457-67; George W. E. Nickelsburg, *1 Enoch 1: A Commentary on the Book of 1 Enoch, Chapters 1–36; 81–108* (Hermeneia; Minneapolis: Fortress, 2001), 152-55. Examples that specifically mention the luminaries include T. Naph. 3:2–4:1, *Pss. Sol.* 18:10-12, 1Q34bis (1QLitPr) 3 2:1-4, *Sifre Deut.* 32:1 (§306), and probably 4Q416 (4QInst) 1 1-9. For the example from 4QInstruction, which is not listed in the above treatments, see Eibert J. C. Tigchelaar, *To Increase Learning for the Understanding Ones: Reading and Reconstructing the Fragmentary Early Jewish Sapiential Text 4QInstruction* (STDJ 44; Leiden: Brill, 2001), 179.

32. The bracketed words in my translation, like Burke's reconstruction of 3:35, are based on the Syriac version: ܘܠܝܬ ܐܚܪܝܢ / [ܘܠܐ ܕܢܬܚܫܒ] ܐܚܪܝܢ ܥܡܗ ܐܠܗܐ (the bracketed words are of dubious authority, but Burke includes them to balance the verse). See Burke, *Poetry of Baruch*, 73, 109-10.

Bible.³³ Calling "Jacob" God's "servant" also evokes Deutero-Isaiah, although the pairing also occurs, less frequently, in Jeremiah and Ezekiel.

Most scholars regard 3:37 (LXX 3:38) as a Christian interpolation, because most of the versions (Latin, Syriac, Coptic and Arabic) render it with a masculine subject (referring to God, the subject of the previous verse), obviously alluding to the Incarnation (cf. John 1:14): "After that he appeared on earth and lived among human beings."³⁴ Even if the unstated subject is taken to be Wisdom (as in the Ethiopic version), however, there are reasons to doubt its authenticity: nowhere else in the poem is wisdom so thoroughly personified; the universal implications of her living "among human beings" contradict the message of the poem that the "way of knowledge" was given only to Israel, and most obviously, it interrupts the poem's train of thought.³⁵ If the last verse of chapter 3 is omitted, then "the whole way of knowledge" that God gave to Israel (3:36) is immediately identified as "the book of the commandments of God, the Torah that endures forever" (4:1a). Like Sir. 24:23, which is parallel in content and syntax, Bar. 4:1 simply makes explicit what has been implicit in the poem up to this point, that, as Sheppard puts it, "the Torah provides the only sufficient source of life-giving wisdom (4:1b)."³⁶

The wisdom poem of Baruch goes in a very different direction from Sirach 24 after identifying the way of wisdom with the Torah, however. Ben Sira, having made explicit the identification of transcendent Wisdom with the Torah in 24:23, proceeds in verses 25-27 to describe the Torah in very universal terms, comparing it to the four rivers that flow out of Eden, plus the Jordan and the Nile, suggesting that it waters the known world. He then adds a temporal dimension to the universality of Torah-Wisdom: "the first man did not know her fully, nor will the last one fathom her" (Sir. 24:28). The

---

33. E.g., Exod. 19:3; Isa. 44:1; Jer. 10:16; Ps. 135:4; and cf. Sir. 24:8. Sheppard, *Wisdom as a Hermeneutical Construct*, 97.

34. In the Greek, the subject is left unstated, and if the verse is original, the implied subject is personified Wisdom, as in Burke's reconstruction (*Poetry of Baruch*, 73-74, 112-13). Harrelson ("Wisdom Hidden and Revealed," 165) points out that the Ethiopic translator, in assuming that the subject was Wisdom, did not understand the verse as a reference to the Incarnation.

35. See the discussion by Steck (*Das apokryphe Baruchbuch*, 153-54), who thinks it is impossible that the verse could be anything other than a Christian interpolation, and by Kabasele Mukenge (*L'Unité litteraire*, 249-51), who thinks the verse is probably redactional, but not necessarily Christian, since it could refer to the giving of the Torah as the moment of Wisdom's appearance on earth.

36. Sheppard, *Wisdom as a Hermeneutical Construct*, 98-99.

Baruch poem, by contrast, concludes by asserting Israel's *exclusive* claim to wisdom and "life" through the gift of the Torah. To be sure, the choice between "life" and "death" presented in Bar. 4:1b is a frequent motif in Proverbs (e.g., 3:18, 8:35-36). Shannon Burkes has shown, however, that the Baruch poet uses the words "life" and "death" here in a Deuteronomic, covenantal sense, to refer to the salvation or destruction of Israel.[37] This becomes clear when one compares 4:1b with the opening verses of the poem: "Hear, O *Israel*, the commandments of *life* . . . why are you reckoned among the *dead*? You have *forsaken* the spring of wisdom."

The peroration in 4:2-4 takes a much more positive tack than the exordium; rather than addressing Israel as metaphorically dead because they are in exile, the final verses underscore the theme of election in 3:35-36 (through the repetition of the names "Jacob" and "Israel") and suggest that the way to salvation is close at hand. The addressees need only "return" (i.e., repent) and "hold fast" (4:2) to the divine gift that sets them apart from the other nations. In light of the allusions to Deutero-Isaiah in 3:35-36, one might optimistically interpret the light imagery in 4:2b as an allusion to the idea of Israel as a "light to the nations" (Isa. 42:6; 49:6), but the next verse presents a much more inward-looking perspective on Israel's election: "Do not give your glory to another, or your advantage to a foreign nation" (4:3). Kabasele Mukenge has pointed out a close parallel between this verse and Sir. 49:4b-5, a passage from the Praise of the Fathers in which Ben Sira comments on the kings of Judah, "for they abandoned the law of the Most High. . . . They gave their power to others, and their glory to a foreign nation."[38] In the context of the Praise of the Fathers, the "foreign nation" is clearly the Neo-Babylonian Empire, and within the fictive setting of Baruch, the referent would be the same.

The Baruch poet appears to be warning his intended audience about a real threat from a foreign nation in his own time, however, and we can infer from the exordium that he sees the current situation of Israel as analogous to the Babylonian exile. Scholarly opinions about the date of Baruch range from the early Ptolemaic period (around 300 B.C.E.) to the Roman period after 70 C.E., but a consensus seems to be emerging that the most likely historical context, at least for the central poem, is in the land of Israel shortly after the Maccabean Revolt, when the Jewish people were unified by the de-

---

37. Shannon Burkes, "Wisdom and Law: Choosing Life in Ben Sira and Baruch," *JSJ* 30 (1999): 253-76 (see especially 271-74).

38. Kabasele Mukenge, *L'Unité litteraire*, 275-76.

feat of the Seleucids and a return to Torah observance after the persecution under Antiochus IV Epiphanes.[39] Such a context would fit the poem's inward-looking view of election, its suspicion of foreign (i.e., Hellenistic) wisdom, its call for repentance, and its glorification of the Torah as Israel's wisdom. While it is impossible to be certain about the historical context of the poem, it does seem likely that it was written later than Ben Sira and in a time of national crisis.

Although the peroration is a summons to repentance, it ends on a triumphant note: "Happy are we, O Israel, because what is pleasing to God is known to us" (4:4). This beatitude recalls Deut. 33:29, the ending of Moses' final blessing on Israel, which begins אשריך ישראל, but the shift to אשרינו ישראל only amplifies the self-congratulatory tone of the peroration. Perhaps the poet was just aiming at an upbeat ending, but the last two verses seem to contradict the prophetic theme announced in the exordium: that Israel has "forsaken the spring of wisdom." The ethnocentrism of the peroration is jarring in the context of a wisdom poem, but it is consistent with the main argument of the poem, that the other nations are devoid of wisdom because God did not choose them for the gift of the Torah. Compared with Sirach 24, Bar. 3:9–4:4 holds a more exclusive view of the Torah, as an advantage Israel holds over other nations, rather than as a source of wisdom that is potentially beneficial to the whole world.

II. Conclusion

The book of Baruch as a whole, however, presents a more nuanced view of the non-elect nations. In the narrative introduction, the exiles ask the people of Jerusalem to pray for long life for Nebuchadnezzar and his son (1:11), echoing the advice of Jeremiah in his letter to the exiles (Jer. 29:7). Although the request is self-interested, since the exiles also ask for prayers that they will find favor in the sight of Nebuchadnezzar and his son (1:12), the attitude toward foreign rulers (and perhaps even toward King Nebuchadnezzar himself, if he is alluded to in 3:16-19) contrasts strongly with that of the wisdom poem. The penitential prayer does in fact include a request that the exiles

---

39. See the review of the possible dates and the arguments for a Maccabean dating by Steck, *Das apokryphe Baruchbuch*, 290-303; and cf. George W. E. Nickelsburg, *Jewish Literature Between the Bible and the Mishnah: A Historical and Literary Introduction*, 2d ed. (Minneapolis: Fortress, 2005), 97.

will find favor with their captors (2:14), and repeats several times that God has commanded the exiles (through Jeremiah, presumably) to "serve the king of Babylon" (2:21, 23, 24; cf. Jeremiah 27).

The consolation poem in 4:5–5:9 has a more complicated attitude toward other nations. On the one hand, it is much more hostile than the prose sections toward the unnamed "enemy" who exiled Israel, at one point promising "you will quickly see his destruction, and will tread upon their necks" (4:25; cf. LXX Deut. 33:29). On the other hand, in the part of the poem in which a personified Jerusalem is the speaker (4:9-29), she twice calls upon the "neighbors of Zion" to witness what has befallen her children (4:9, 14) and also tells her children, "As the neighbors of Zion have now seen your captivity, so they will quickly see your salvation from God" (4:24). The neighboring peoples are portrayed as at least neutral, and perhaps even sympathetic, witnesses to the fate of the chosen people. In the final part of the poem of consolation, addressed to Jerusalem, there are two passages, overlapping in content, that are based on depictions of the return of the exiles in Isaiah 40–66. Since they are similar, I will quote only the second: "Arise, O Jerusalem, and stand upon the height, and look around toward the east, and see your children gathered from west and east at the word of the Holy One, rejoicing at God's remembering [them]. For they went out from you on foot, led away by enemies, but God will bring them back to you, carried with glory, as on a royal throne" (5:5-6; cf. 4:36-37; *Pss. Sol.* 11:2). Although these verses do not specify who will bring Jerusalem's children back to her, they evoke Isaianic depictions of foreign nations returning the exiles to Jerusalem and contributing to her restoration (e.g., Isa. 43:5-9; 49:18, 22-23; 60:4-16; 66:18-21). Although in some cases this motif is accompanied by the abasement of the nations (e.g., Isa. 49:22-23), more often the other nations are portrayed as God-fearing, even worshipful (cf. Isa. 55:5; 56:6-8). Thus a more balanced view of the other nations emerges when the central wisdom poem is read in the context of the rest of the book of Baruch.

A contextual reading of the wisdom poem is justified because it is an integral part of the overall message of the book: that Israel is in exile (and metaphorically dead or dying) because they have forsaken the commandments of God, which are the way of wisdom and life, but once they repent, God will forgive them and return them to Jerusalem. In other words, the poet incorporates the identification of Torah obedience as the way of wisdom (for which he depends on Deut. 4:6-8 and probably also Sir. 24:23) into a conventional prophetic message reminiscent of Deutero-Isaiah and, to a lesser extent, the consolatory parts of Jeremiah and Ezekiel. The creativity of this poet is expressed not in new ideas but in innovative combinations of themes and allusions. Yet the genre label "wisdom poem" has led many commentators to focus on the allusions to wisdom literature, and sometimes those to Deuteronomy, and to overlook the poet's incorporation of prophetic themes, language and forms.[40]

I have attempted to show that the central poem is integrated with the rest of the book through allusions to Deuteronomy, which is the primary background for the prose portion of the book, and to the prophetic literature, especially Isaiah 40–66, which is the main source text for the poem of consolation. Like much Second Temple period literature, the wisdom poem in Baruch weaves together what seem to us diverse strands of tradition, adding to those traditions just mentioned allusions to Genesis and probably Ben Sira and possibly also the *Book of the Watchers*. The wisdom poem in Baruch is an excellent illustration of a point about late Second Temple period literature that John Collins made in the context of a seminal essay on wisdom and apocalypticism: "The forms of wisdom speech are adaptable, and may be used in the service of more than one worldview."[41]

---

40. Shannon Burkes has made a similar point about the Wisdom of Solomon and the tendency of scholars to overlook its apocalyptic themes. See her article, "Wisdom and Apocalypticism in the Wisdom of Solomon," *HTR* 95 (2002): 43-44.
41. John J. Collins, "Wisdom, Apocalypticism and Generic Compatibility," in *In Search of Wisdom: Essays in Memory of John G. Gammie*, ed. L. G. Perdue, B. B. Scott, and W. J. Wiseman (Louisville: Westminster John Knox, 1993), 181.

The Lady Vanishes:
Wisdom in Ben Sira and Daniel

Shannon Burkes Pinette

Lady Wisdom as portrayed in Proverbs is no shy wallflower; she is a strong-willed and opinionated woman who is constantly on the move, wooing people to her path, cajoling and making promises, and seeking followers in the public spaces of the city gates and the crossroads (8:1–9:6). She searches for all the living (8:4), offering them life and God's favor (8:35). For the more philosophically minded in the audience, she also describes herself as God's first creation and the pivot point between the deity and the human race, rejoicing before God while also rejoicing before humanity (8:30-31). The Lady even on occasion becomes fed up with trying to reel in human foolishness and warns the stubborn not to come crying to *her* when trouble finds them (1:20-33). On the whole, a portrait emerges of a vigorous, engaged, and accessible figure who has the attitude of a loving if sometimes annoyed wife or mother. As time passes, however, and the historical ruptures of the Second Temple period progress, Wisdom's status begins to change. A comparison of Ben Sira and Daniel on this point reveals the magnitude of the shift it could undergo in just a brief span of time. Wisdom becomes so occluded that it in essence goes missing and the core of the

---

I offer this modest essay in tribute to my teacher John J. Collins, whose extensive, one might even say comprehensive, scholarship utterly informed my own academic work. As a scholar, teacher, and mentor he has managed to unite both wisdom and hope, a rare and precious quality from the perspective of tightly wound graduate students who certainly believed on occasion that we were on the brink of the End Time! A blessing on his house.

sapiential tradition becomes something distant and mysterious. Wisdom itself becomes Other.

I. Wisdom as Familiar: Ben Sira

Ben Sira is a book that sometimes gets a bad rap as a plodding throwback to older wisdom traditions, written by a man who keeps his head down and slogs forward with unimaginative optimism in a time of upheaval.[1] Generally dated to around 180 B.C.E.,[2] plenty has happened by this point to unseat Jewish composure regarding divine retribution, political stability and cultural survival. A careful reading of the book shows that the author is actually quite well aware of this fact, and while he does attempt to defend his tradition's structural integrity, he does so through a variety of interesting approaches.[3] A running theme throughout is the need to address the concern that divine reward and punishment no longer operates intelligibly in human experience.

Divine retribution does, in the author's opinion, remain reliable, although at times appearances may be deceiving. Ben Sira dwells rather more on the notion of testing than one finds in Proverbs and declares that anyone who serves the Lord should in fact expect to be tested like gold in the fire (2:1-5). No one who *persists* in fear of the Lord has ever been forsaken (2:10). Ben Sira does not argue that the righteous person will never suffer, only that he will be repeatedly rescued (33:1).[4] He admits that the wicked may seem to

---

1. Gerhard von Rad, *Wisdom in Israel* (Nashville: Abingdon, 1972), 238, believes that "nothing has made sufficient impression on him to force him to rethink traditional teaching in the light of Job."

2. Ben Sira's grandson in the prologue helpfully gives the date when he himself came to Egypt as 132 B.C.E. Counting back two generations moves the date roughly fifty years before that, which conforms to the impression given by Ben Sira that he was alive during the high priesthood of Simon II. See Patrick W. Skehan and Alexander A. Di Lella, *The Wisdom of Ben Sira* (AB 39; New York: Doubleday, 1987), 8-10.

3. James L. Crenshaw, "The Problem of Theodicy in Sirach: On Human Bondage," *JBL* 94 (1975): 47-64 (esp. 48-49), writes that Ben Sira's tone is polemical and the result of the need to dispute unknown foes, as the author "felt the threat posed by his antagonists most acutely."

4. Skehan and Di Lella, *The Wisdom of Ben Sira*, 151, point out that for Ben Sira the people's collective history also bears this out. The "experience of the Ancestors and of the upright men and women of Israel's history bears eloquent witness to the truth that trust in the Lord will never be in vain."

thrive, but that is because God is slow to get angry (5:4). While the end of the unrighteous may be unknown to the outside observer, God sees all (9:11-12; 21:10; 23:18-21). God can punish even on the final day of a person's life (11:26-28). In short, the deity still judges everyone according to a person's deeds (16:12-14). In case these arguments are not entirely persuasive, Ben Sira also points to the perfect order of God's creation as further evidence that the cosmic system is still sound (16:26-30; 42:15–43:33).[5] He even suggests that the world will be good or bad according to the nature of the observer; the necessities of life will be good for the godly but turn evil for the wicked (39:26-27).[6]

What the reader cannot help but ask is, on what ground does Ben Sira make these claims? Can he do so while maintaining a traditional view of Wisdom herself? At first glance the answer would seem to be yes. Wisdom is a powerful female figure who gives life to her children, although consonant with Ben Sira's belief that life consists of testing, Lady Wisdom will also try her followers with tortuous discipline until convinced they are true (4:11-19). This is a key theme for Ben Sira's view of Wisdom, and it adds an interesting layer to the earlier personification developed in Proverbs. There, Lady Wisdom is generally not harsh in her manner, and even when she becomes fed up with human foolishness she intends merely to stand back during tribulation, not engage in it. Now, however, she seems rough indeed until she has proven a person's integrity, and in a surprising turn we learn that Wisdom is "like her name; she is not readily perceived by many" (a play on the Hebrew *musar*, which can mean "withdrawn," 6:20-22). With time, however, her fetters and collar will turn into a strong defense and wonderful robes (6:23-31). The authors of Proverbs would agree that wisdom requires discipline, but this notion is not nearly so well developed as in Ben Sira.[7] In

---

5. Leo G. Perdue, *Wisdom and Creation: The Theology of Wisdom Literature* (Nashville: Abingdon, 1994), 264, comments that the regularity of the cosmos is not merely a result of God's governance but obedience to the rules established by God at the creation. See also his *Wisdom Literature: A Theological History* (Louisville: Westminster John Knox, 2007), 217-66. Skehan and Di Lella, *The Wisdom of Ben Sira*, 281, note that the Greek verb *kosmeō* ("to order, arrange") in Sir. 16:27, "[God] arranged his works," is the basis for the noun *kosmos*. The essence of the cosmos is that which is ordered.

6. Skehan and Di Lella, *The Wisdom of Ben Sira*, 461, believe that this chapter's argument intends to offer a theodicy and can therefore be compared with Job and Qoheleth.

7. Núria Calduch-Benages, "Trial Motif in the Book of Ben Sira with Special Reference to Sir 2,1-6," in *The Book of Ben Sira in Modern Research: Proceedings of the First International Ben Sira Conference, 28-31 July 1996, Soesterberg, Netherlands*, ed. P. C. Beentjes (BZAW 255; Berlin: de Gruyter, 1997), 150, writes that God as well as Wisdom tests the seeker throughout life and each "entails a long and arduous road."

Proverbs, Wisdom is trying to find people in the city gates; here, she plays hard to get.[8] Wisdom's gifts can seem as uncertain as God's justice, but only temporarily.[9]

In another shift, Ben Sira's version of Lady Wisdom's speech describing her own creation and nature includes the interesting announcement that God sent her to dwell in Israel (24:8-12), a new and quite specific localizing of the figure.[10] The reader learns that wisdom is none other than the covenant, the law of Moses (24:23). Ben Sira is convinced that Lady Wisdom remains accessible, but he describes her presence differently than the authors of Proverbs did. Just as reward and punishment appear at times not to come as expected, so Lady Wisdom is no longer laying out rich feasts for the asking, but riding her followers hard in order to test their mettle. However, Ben Sira recovers Wisdom's abiding presence in another way, not through daily proofs of justice in one's life, but through the Torah, which depends not on a state or a temple or king, but only on itself. Regarding both justice and Wisdom, so intimately linked in this tradition, Ben Sira does indeed acknowledge tension and even loss, but he rebuilds in a new direction, and Lady Wis-

---

8. James L. Crenshaw, *Old Testament Wisdom: An Introduction*, rev. ed. (Atlanta: John Knox, 1998), 147, observes that "Sirach perceived the *ambiguity* within things much more clearly than the earlier sages seem to have done." Benjamin G. Wright, "The Discourse of Riches and Poverty in the Book of Ben Sira," in *Society of Biblical Literature Seminar Papers, Part Two* (Atlanta: Scholars Press, 1998), 575, suggests that Ben Sira may have felt some dissonance professionally between the respect a sage would deserve in his own society and the disinterest or hostility of foreign rulers. Hence his awareness of life's challenges was perhaps, in spite of his general optimism, not entirely theoretical.

9. The impassioned prayer for deliverance in chapter 36 is one place where somebody's anguish bursts through, whether it be the author's or an unknown person whose composition was absorbed into the book. John J. Collins, *Jewish Wisdom in the Hellenistic Age* (Louisville: Westminster John Knox Press, 1997), 110-11, considers the prayer a later addition, possibly added during the Maccabean crisis. Benjamin G. Wright, "'Put the Nations in Fear of You': Ben Sira and the Problem of Foreign Rule," in his *In Praise of Wisdom and Instruction: Essays on Ben Sira and Wisdom, the Letter of Aristeas and the Septuagint* (JSJSup 131; Leiden: Brill, 2008), 127-46 (esp. 134), believes that the passage is not really inconsistent with the rest of the book although the emotion is more intense. Whether original or not, this section is not characteristic of the author's mood as a whole.

10. George W. E. Nickelsburg and Michael E. Stone, *Faith and Piety in Early Judaism: Texts and Documents* (Philadelphia: Trinity Press International, 1991), 216, write that this is the first time that wisdom is identified with Torah in the tradition (a revised version of this book was published by Fortress in 2009). Gerald T. Sheppard, *Wisdom as Hermeneutical Construct: A Study in the Sapientializing of the Old Testament* (BZAW 151; Berlin: Walter de Gruyter, 1980), 30, notes that the language used here to describe Wisdom is much more typical of theophany traditions, such as God at Sinai.

dom, though not as predictable as one might like, remains firmly present in an evolved form.[11]

Finally, Ben Sira is so confident in the continuing human bond with Wisdom that he believes fresh teaching is still bubbling forth from human vessels. Any devoted student of Wisdom can participate in the flow through study of the law, wisdom, prophecies, and proverbs, through wide travels, and by petitioning the Most High (39:1-5). God willing, that student will pour forth "wisdom of his own" (39:6). This in fact is exactly what Ben Sira considers himself to have done, as he explains when he signs his book near the end.[12] His mind has poured out all this wisdom in order to help others become wise and be equal to anything (50:27-29), a notion confirmed by his grandson and translator in the book's prologue.[13] An especially interesting slice of narrative comes right after Lady Wisdom's long speech in chapter 24. The author has just equated her with Torah and offers a string of river metaphors for her abundance. Then Ben Sira shifts to the first person and begins to compare *himself* to overflowing rivers in his ability to pour forth wisdom (24:30-34; see also 33:16-19; 39:12, 32; 42:15).[14] This is a positive view of wisdom indeed; a human being can still be a trustworthy source of it and in fact mirror Wisdom herself. Ben Sira is not so self-satisfied that he believes a

---

11. Collins, *Jewish Wisdom in the Hellenistic Age*, 88, describes another new element in Ben Sira's presentation of Wisdom, in that he ascribes to Wisdom qualities and actions that were earlier in the tradition restricted to God, while continuing to regard her as immanent in the world. See also Perdue, *Wisdom and Creation*, 268, who comments that for Ben Sira, Wisdom controls both nature and history. For additional discussion see Johannes Marböck, *Weisheit im Wandel: Untersuchungen zur Weisheitstheologie bei Ben Sira* (Bonn: Hanstein, 1971), 174.

12. Collins, *Jewish Wisdom in the Hellenistic Age*, 23, says that revealing one's name as an author like this is extremely unusual in the ancient Jewish wisdom literature. See also Burton L. Mack, *Wisdom and the Hebrew Epic: Ben Sira's Hymn in Praise of the Fathers* (Chicago: University of Chicago Press, 1985), 186-87. Mack comments that in the book as a whole, Ben Sira's self-awareness as an author is marked, especially "where he employs the first person for heightened claims to wisdom or for the introduction of hymnic material" (p. 103).

13. Jan Liesen, "Strategical Self-References in Ben Sira," in *Treasures of Wisdom: Studies in Ben Sira and the Book of Wisdom (Festschrift M. Gilbert)*, ed. N. Calduch-Benages and J. Vermeylen (BETL 143; Leuven: Leuven University Press, 1999), 64, comments on the autobiographical passages that are laced throughout the text, and adds that one finds "a noticeable increase of emphasis on the person of the author towards the end of the book."

14. Randal A. Argall, *I Enoch and Sirach: A Comparative Literary and Conceptual Analysis of the Themes of Revelation, Creation, and Judgment* (SBLEJL 8; Atlanta: Scholars Press, 1995), 92-93, argues that Wisdom's hymn echoes a prophetic commissioning scene and that Ben Sira then links this prophetic wisdom to his own work.

The Lady Vanishes

mere human can have complete knowledge (24:28-29), and in fact he specifically warns against meddling in esoteric matters that are beyond the proper human scope (3:21-24).[15] But it is possible for gifted individuals to study hard, observe the world and hone their senses to the point that they can keep wisdom flowing; one can certainly know enough for a satisfying existence on earth.[16] While Ben Sira develops new facets of Lady Wisdom and her workings in mortal experience, at times striving to reassure the doubters, she is still, both as a great lady and in her human disciples, familiar and present.

II. Wisdom as Other: Daniel

Daniel came together in its final form only a couple of decades after Ben Sira, but the political situation had changed drastically. Antiochus Epiphanes had taken power, and a full-fledged persecution of the Jews was on. An early apocalypse, the book is quite different from Ben Sira's wisdom text in self-evident ways, although not in its central belief that there must be some method for gaining access to wisdom and understanding divine justice. Here the two authors share common ground, and Daniel's creators clearly come from similar, highly literate, sapiential circles. What sets Ben Sira and Daniel apart, however, is Daniel's conviction that justice does not unfold in a human timeframe, and that a complete breakdown of traditional methods for acquiring wisdom has occurred.[17] Wisdom in this world has

---

15. Benjamin G. Wright, "Putting the Puzzle Together: Some Suggestions Concerning the Social Location of the Wisdom of Ben Sira," in *Conflicted Boundaries of Wisdom and Apocalypticism*, ed. Benjamin G. Wright III and Lawrence M. Wills (SBLSymS 35; Atlanta: Scholars Press, 2005), 89-113, writes that this passage is often read as a criticism of studying Greek philosophy, but that it makes more sense as a warning against becoming ensnared in eschatological concerns of the kind found in the Enoch literature. For further evidence he points to 34:1-8, where Ben Sira criticizes anyone who seeks learning in dreams and omens, possibly a sign that the author wants his audience to avoid revelatory sources (pp. 101-2). See also his "'Fear the Lord and Honor the Priest': Ben Sira as Defender of the Jerusalem Priesthood," in *In Praise of Wisdom and Instruction*, 97-126.

16. Ben Sira would at the same time acknowledge the ambiguity of human existence, and not just in the sense that there may be esoteric, heavenly knowledge that is beyond the human purview as in 3:21-24. See Gabriele Boccaccini, *Middle Judaism: Jewish Thought, 300 B.C.E. to 200 C.E.* (Minneapolis: Fortress, 1991), 82, who points to 20:9-12, a passage that shows how seeming good fortune can turn dangerous while bad fortune can lead to gain.

17. John J. Collins, *Daniel* (Hermeneia; Minneapolis: Fortress, 1993), 49, notes that all would agree that Daniel emerges from "wisdom circles," but what Ben Sira repudiates — dreams and visions — forms the core of Daniel. Daniel represents mantic wisdom.

become so obscure, difficult, and finally overwhelming that the figure of Lady Wisdom breaks down completely. She does not rejoice simultaneously before God and before humanity, nor does she dwell in Israel. Wisdom can be had, but not through a relationship with a benevolent or even a disciplinary Lady who is comfortably bound to creation. That Lady is gone. Her disappearance marks the difference between Ben Sira's wisdom and Daniel's revelation.

Daniel's history of composition is more complex than Ben Sira's, but the book consists of a set of court tales in the first half followed by Daniel's visions in the second, which are somewhat later in date and are a response to the persecution of Antiochus IV.[18] The ethos of the book as a whole assumes that the Jews are under foreign domination, but in the tales, although conditions can be precarious or even life-threatening for Daniel and his three friends, the Jews always prevail. Yet in only one case does *human* wisdom save them, when in the opening chapter the palace guard frets because his captives are refusing to eat their impure royal rations. Daniel suggests that they should be tested for ten days with vegetables and water, and when they are fatter and healthier than everyone else after the trial period, the guard lets them follow their own diet (1:8-16). Reasonable argument can provide a solution, but this is the first and only occasion that wisdom of this kind is to be found in the book. At best, human prudence may buy a little time for the purpose of seeking heavenly wisdom (2:14).

A hint of the change appears in this same chapter when one learns that God gave the four Jewish captives knowledge in all manner of literature and wisdom, but that Daniel also had special insight into "visions and dreams" (1:17). More precisely, Daniel is given the ability to receive revelation about visions and dreams from outside himself. Nebuchadnezzar's own advisors tell him that his demands for exposition of a secret dream cannot be met because no one on earth has that power (2:10). This is a rare instance where the Babylonian and Jewish characters of the story are in agreement. Daniel labels the dream a "mystery" that is revealed to him in a night vision (2:18-19). He then explicitly tells the king that no one on earth can provide his answer, only the God who reveals mysteries (2:27-28). "But as for me, this mystery

---

18. Collins, *Daniel*, 35-36, writes that the court tales in chapters 1–6 may have originated in oral form during the Persian period or the Hellenistic era at the latest. Their genre is best understood as examples of the "wisdom court tale," described at length by Lawrence M. Wills, *The Jew in the Court of the Foreign King: Ancient Jewish Court Legends* (Minneapolis: Fortress, 1990). Chapters 7–12 form the apocalypse and are in Hebrew, except for chapter 7 which, like chapters 2–6, is in Aramaic. See Collins, *Daniel*, 54.

has not been revealed to me because of any wisdom that I have more than any other living being" (2:30).[19] Human ability is irrelevant. The wisdom in question here is revelatory and comes from the realm of the divine (4:8-9, 18; 5:11, 14). The king is impressed and at least momentarily declares Daniel's deity the God of gods (2:47), until the cycle repeats itself.

Each time in the court tales the danger passes, though on one occasion Daniel's friends make the ominous comment, "if our God whom we serve is able to deliver us from the furnace . . . let him deliver us," but even if God does not deliver them, they will still refuse to worship the king's golden statue (3:17-18). Unlike Ben Sira, the wise no longer declare with certainty that the just will be saved, even after a period of testing in the fire.[20] As it happens, they are in this instance saved from the fire, but in their view this was only one possible outcome. While the wise must still act with integrity, they no longer know for certain what consequences will unfold from their actions, and the righteous may die unjustly. Whether in the mundane world or the visionary realm, human understanding fails.[21] Wisdom is given from above. Earlier sages would no doubt agree that wisdom must be given by God, or at least the capacity for wisdom, but here there is little interaction between mortal effort and divine gift.

---

19. Susan Niditch and Robert Doran, "The Success Story of the Wise Courtier: A Formal Approach," *JBL* 96 (1977): 179-93 (esp. 190-91), compare this story in Daniel 2 to other folktale types and remark that in contrast to the expected form, "the hero, the wise man, is almost superseded by a more important protagonist, God." See also Pamela J. Milne, *Vladimir Propp and the Study of Structure in Hebrew Biblical Narrative* (Sheffield: Almond Press, 1988), 221, who comments that, in a shift from typical wise courtier tales, the deity gets credit for the hero's success. Collins, *Daniel*, 46, makes a similar argument regarding the conflict tales in Daniel (chapters 3, 5, and 6), that "the heroes attain deliverance not by their own wits or by the connivance of others but by divine intervention."

20. Collins, *Daniel*, 187, reviews the ways various ancient and modern translators have handled the verse. "The conditional form of this sentence has been perceived as a problem from antiquity." In his view, the fact that the friends express uncertainty about their situation reflects the very real uncertainty of postexilic Jewish experience in general. Louis F. Hartman and Alexander A. Di Lella, *The Book of Daniel* (AB 23; Garden City: Doubleday, 1978), 65, comment that Daniel's authors retained their belief even though they acknowledge that by all appearances "God was silent and not at work."

21. John J. Collins, "The Court-Tales in Daniel and the Development of Apocalyptic," *JBL* 94 (1975): 218-33 (esp. 225), comments that these stories "are not designed to display the wisdom or skill of the protagonists." See also W. Lee Humphreys, "A Life-Style for the Diaspora: A Study of the Tales of Esther and Daniel," *JBL* 92 (1973): 211-23 (esp. 220-21), who argues that the characters are passive and delivered predominantly through the intervention of God.

The intimations in the tales of a sea change come to full fruition in the visions of the second half of the book. Now the inherent danger of foreign rule has escalated into a cosmic crisis, and Daniel himself becomes the dreamer who requires interpretation. An angelic intermediary steps forward to unfold the meaning of his bizarre dreams and visions because otherwise they are simply symbolic ciphers. The sage could not possibly have the faintest idea what his visions might mean without otherworldly assistance.[22] In his first experience he has to approach one of the heavenly attendants within the actual dream to find out what it all signifies (7:16, 23-27). Later the angel Gabriel explains to him that "I have now come out to give you wisdom and understanding" (9:22). Gabriel is with Daniel throughout the bulk of the remaining chapters, because without his continuing interpretations the text would remain meaningless. Human wisdom has no role to play in these circumstances, and if anything, Daniel undergoes steps that will actually decrease his own cognitive abilities, although they increase his susceptibility for receiving the revelations. During a three-week period of mourning, he semi-fasts, avoiding any meat or wine, and does not anoint himself (10:2-3). Not surprisingly, he has another visionary experience in this state.[23] The point is repeatedly driven home that Daniel himself has no comprehension of what it is he sees, and long swaths of the narrative are speeches by the angel expounding the interpretations (8:15-17, 19-26; 10:10-14; 10:18–12:4; 12:9-13).[24]

---

22. Such assistance and encouragement can no longer come from an immanent figure such as Lady Wisdom, and Daniel is just one example of sages turning to angelic mediators in this period. See Alan F. Segal, *Two Powers in Heaven: Early Rabbinic Reports about Christianity and Gnosticism* (SJLA 25; Leiden: Brill, 1977), 187.

23. Collins, *Daniel*, 57-58, comments that some in this period may have been having genuine ecstatic experiences, as the practices outlined here commonly appear in other cultures as preparation for a vision. Such an experience causes the seer's self to be ecstatically submerged, quite unlike Ben Sira.

24. Martha Himmelfarb, "Revelation and Rapture: The Transformation of the Visionary in the Ascent Apocalypses," in *Mysteries and Revelations: Apocalyptic Studies since the Uppsala Colloquium*, ed. J. J. Collins and J. H. Charlesworth (JSPSup 9; Sheffield: JSOT Press, 1991), 89, writing not on wisdom literature but prophecy, observes that prophecy in the post-exilic period is complicated by a growing sense of distance between God and humanity; because of this, prophecy tends to become interpretation of visions to be deciphered, as in Zechariah, a move that grows into an important mode of revelation in the apocalypses, where angels are typically the interpreters. Biblical heroes talked with God, while apocalyptic heroes talk with angels. This insight points to something analogous in the wisdom tradition during the same period, especially when one remembers that the apocalypses are inheritors of both the prophetic and sapiential streams of tradition. Just as the biblical characters once talked with God, so did the sages understand their experience to be an interaction with Lady Wis-

Daniel for his part becomes increasingly mute. He simply has no wisdom to expound.

Even with the angelic explanations, he is puzzled by his experiences and can barely hold up physically or psychologically. He often feels terror (7:15, 28; 8:17) and undergoes strong bodily reactions, turning pale (7:28; 10:8), falling prostrate (8:17), entering trances while collapsed on the ground (8:18; 10:9), being overcome and ill for several days (8:27), losing first his strength (10:8) and then his speech (10:15). The angel must revive him by setting him on his feet or at least his hands and knees (8:18; 10:10), and touching his lips so that he can speak once more (10:16). Daniel finally asks Gabriel how he can withstand the upcoming conversation with the angel since the pain of his vision is sapping his strength, leaving him trembling and breathless (10:16-17). Gabriel again touches him to renew his vigor (10:18-19). Daniel's final words in the book are the statement that he hears but cannot understand, with a request for more answers (12:8). Gabriel simply tells him to go about his business because the words are to remain secret until the end (12:9; also v. 4). At that time many will be purified and refined and then the wise will understand (12:10).

Well might Daniel be disturbed. Over and over he is subjected to images of ravenous animals or horns devouring the innocent (7:2-8, 19-27; 8:23-25), making war in heaven (8:10-12), and attacking the Temple (8:11-13; 9:17, 26-27; 11:30-31; 12:10), while the wise fall before the onslaught (11:33-35).[25] Finally the horror will be resolved in a heavenly battle (12:1-3; see also 7:9-12, 26-27; 8:14, 25; 9:27) which will be a time of great anguish (12:1) but will result in deliverance from the beast.[26] Thus the notion that the wise and righ-

---

dom. But she, too, recedes beyond reach in the chaos of the later Second Temple period, and the vacuum is filled for Daniel the sage, just as for Daniel the prophet, by an angel.

25. The perpetrator of these horrors, Antiochus Epiphanes, is no ordinary human in this conception. George W. E. Nickelsburg, *Resurrection, Immortality, and Eternal Life in Intertestamental Judaism*, rev. ed. (HTS 26; Cambridge: Harvard University Press, 2006), 28, notes that the king's actions are like those committed by the "Lucifer" figure in Isaiah 14, and that he must have seemed to the suffering Jews to be an "anti-God." J. C. H. Lebram, "König Antiochus im Buch Daniel," *VT* 25 (1975): 737-72 (esp. 767), writes that Antiochus "verspottet Götter und Kultus, tötet und verfolgt die Heiligen und zerstört die himmlischen Gesetzmässigkeiten."

26. John J. Collins, "The Meaning of 'the End' in the Book of Daniel," in idem, *Seers, Sibyls and Sages in Hellenistic-Roman Judaism* (JSJSup 54; Leiden: Brill, 1997), 157-65 (esp. 163), observes that the book reveals something of a shifting boundary when it comes to the notion of what exactly will happen in the end time. In his view the apocalyptic chapters in the second half of the book were composed over a period of a few years, over which period the

teous can expect to follow Lady Wisdom's "path of life" in their mortal existence is completely rejected. In fact quite the reverse is now the case. Evil prospers (8:12; 11:30, 32; 12:10) while the wise suffer (11:33-35; 12:10). Only after death will the wise and the wicked be certain of justice, in everlasting life or everlasting contempt (12:2-3).[27] Then, in the time of the end, the wise will shine like the stars and lead many to righteousness (12:3, 13). In Proverbs, Lady Wisdom threatened to stand by and let those who ignored her path experience calamity (1:20-33); Ben Sira acknowledged that Lady Wisdom will actively test her followers with trials, but only for a brief time (4:11-19); in the court tales, Daniel's three friends intimate that possibly they will not be saved from their tribulation in spite of their wise actions (3:17-18). In the visions, Daniel learns that not only will the wise not be spared, they are in fact predestined for violent death *because of* their wisdom. Yet the old wisdom image of refinement remains, since the wise are dying as part of a purification process (11:35; 12:10). The difference is that now that process runs right up to and includes the moment of death.

This is the older wisdom worldview turned on its head. Because historical events are predetermined (7:12, 25: 8:14; 9:24-27; 11:1-45; 12:7, 11-12), the wise cannot take any action to change things, chapter nine of Daniel notwithstanding.[28] There is no counsel or exhortation, other than to adhere to the covenant no matter what comes. The angel specifically tells Daniel not to share the wisdom that he has received but to seal it up for a much later time (8:26; 12:4, 9), a move that is contrary to the whole point of traditional wisdom. Ben Sira's reason for existence was to spread wisdom even further through his personal commentary and, as loquacious as he is, the book runs on to a robust length. He proudly signs his writing with his own name, while Daniel, interestingly, is pseudonymous. As an individual Daniel is not a font of further wisdom, but a conduit of information from above that baffles his understanding. The further

---

thinking of the author or authors evolved. The book in its entirety contains a hope for an eschatological kingdom and also personal reward or punishment after death (see Collins, *Daniel*, 56). The two views coexist, and Daniel's author does not bother to sort out exactly how.

27. John E. Goldingay, *Daniel* (WBC 30; Dallas: Word Books, 1989), 308, says that the resurrection appears to function specifically as a vindication for the martyrs and condemnation of their oppressors, while the rest of the dead seem to stay in Sheol.

28. Hartman and Di Lella, *The Book of Daniel*, 12, consider the prayer a later addition because neither the good quality of its Hebrew nor its content fits the context. However, Collins, *Daniel*, 360, believes the prayer was inserted by the original author. At the same time, he says that there is "an implicit rejection of the Deuteronomic theology of history in Daniel 9, although the author does not polemicize against it."

The Lady Vanishes

his book progresses, the *less* he speaks. The only books of much relevance in his view are in heaven, beyond human reach (7:10; 10:11; 12:1).

For all of the wisdom language and Daniel's portrayal as one "versed in every branch of wisdom, endowed with knowledge and insight" (1:4, cf. 1:17, 20; 2:14, 23; 5:11-12, 14; 10:12), his wisdom is curiously passive. At times he is not even described as wise, but as endowed with a holy spirit (4:9, 18; 5:11; 6:3). He cannot understand his own visions without angelic assistance (7:16; 8:15-16; 9:22; 10:21) or unless understanding is given as part of the vision (10:1), and even so he often remains uncomprehending (8:27; 12:8). His one attempt at textual study, a reading of Jeremiah's prediction that Jerusalem would be devastated for seventy years (9:2), turns out to be incorrect. The plain language of the old prophecy is really a symbolic indicator of a mysterious code that Gabriel must explain as seventy weeks of years (9:24-26). If this is true, the traditional sage's training by reflection on past writings is not in itself a path to understanding. In fact, Daniel is receiving angelic wisdom not because he is *wise*, a fact he himself pointed out to Nebuchadnezzar (2:30), but because he is *beloved* (9:23; 10:19).[29] Wisdom is no longer the central feature of the wise man's life.

III. The Lady and the Angel

The book of Daniel reveals the interesting circumstance of the wise man alienated from his own wisdom tradition. Ben Sira knows that Lady Wisdom's rewards and punishments are in some circles regarded as doubtful, but he shows that confidence in the power of human wisdom informed by the Lady, and in her new identity as the Torah, remained possible. What seemed such a clever move in explicitly locating wisdom's heart in the covenant, however, may have provided the crack in the foundation that led to Daniel's pessimism in the worldly order just a few years later when that covenant came under direct attack.[30] From any conceivable earthly perspective

---

29. Humphreys, "A Life-Style for the Diaspora," 220-21, notes that in this setting the courtier is portrayed as utterly devoted to God, and the emphasis lies on piety. "In this stress on the devotion of the hero characteristic elements in the tale of the courtier are submerged."

30. According to Ben Sira, God gave Aaron's descendents an "everlasting covenant" (45:15), and Ben Sira insists that the covenant will last as long as heaven does. Martha Himmelfarb, "The Wisdom of the Scribe, the Wisdom of the Priest, and the Wisdom of the King according to Ben Sira," in *For a Later Generation: The Transformation of Tradition in Israel, Early Judaism, and Early Christianity,* ed. Randall A. Argall et al. (Harrisburg: Trinity

as a Jew, human wisdom was not delivering life, but violent death. This must have created an unsustainable tension in sapiential thinking, where one either accepted that the wisdom tradition was sound but God must be unjust or disengaged or that God's oversight is sound but human wisdom fails. The sage who assembled Daniel chooses God. For God to be reliable and ultimately just from a human perspective, even if that justice must occur at a distant end time and/or in a personal afterlife, the traditional Lady Wisdom who instructs her audience in this-worldly survival skills must go.[31]

A type of wisdom is still possible and no less important, but it is not a wisdom that can be gained from wide travels, from observing the workings of the surrounding environment, or from reading and studying the writings of old. There is no Lady striding around in one's domestic spaces, rejoicing in mundane human accomplishment, or even scolding and arguing with the stubborn. A loving relationship with a divine intermediary no longer creates an interactive bond that nurtures wisdom within the human breast. The sage certainly needs an intermediary, more so than ever as individual intellectual ability fades in the face of radical crisis, but the intimacy of the Lady who in some sense lives within the human realm is replaced with the awesome and overwhelming power of an angel who is most emphatically not of this world, and who can never really make himself understood to the individual trembling before him. Daniel in the here and now of his own time starts out with no understanding of the mysterious visions that describe his world, and he gains little.

The wise man who finds himself estranged from his own wisdom tradition has become an apocalyptist. Wisdom withdraws from the human sphere and becomes something mysterious and other. Relinquishing the Lady, however, creates a space for the suffering sage to retain his confidence in God, and wisdom defers to hope.

Press International, 2000), 95, notes that this phrase is taken from Ps. 89:29 [verse 30 in the Hebrew], which is a line mourning the destruction of the Davidic kingship. Ben Sira is drawing on royal language for the priestly covenant, but the context from which he takes it confronts the end of the dynastic promise. Once the threat to the covenantal promise and the priesthood as protectors of it became acute, the pressure felt by the sages and the educated to explain why no doubt became excruciating.

31. The inexorable distancing of Lady Wisdom from the human realm can be seen in other apocalyptic settings. In *1 Enoch* 42, Wisdom tried to find a dwelling place on earth but failed, so "Wisdom returned to her place and she settled permanently among the angels" (*1 Enoch* 42:1-2). In *4 Ezra* 5:9-10, the angel explains that at the end of all things wisdom will withdraw into its chamber, sought by many but not to be found.

"The Foolish Nation That Dwells in Shechem": Ben Sira on Shechem and the Other Peoples in Palestine

Matthew Goff

Much of Ben Sira's theology can be summarized by the expression "what a wonderful world." At the beginning of his instruction, the sage asserts that God has "poured" out wisdom "upon all his works, upon every living thing (πάσης σαρκός) according to his bounty" (1:9-10).[1] The famous creation hymns at the end of the book (39:12-35; 42:15–43:33) are designed to teach that "the glory of God fills his works" (42:16; cf. 15:10).

It is easy to extol God's creation in general terms. But the devil is in the details. The sage makes several famously (or infamously) off-color remarks about women, such as "better a man's wickedness than a woman's goodness" (42:14).[2] The sage also offers caustic comments towards other ethnic groups, particularly those that live in Palestine. One of the best examples is the numerical proverb in Sir. 50:25-26: "My soul is disgusted by two nations, and

---

1. With occasional modifications, translations are from Patrick W. Skehan and Alexander A. Di Lella, *The Wisdom of Ben Sira* (AB 39; New York: Doubleday, 1987).
2. See further John J. Collins, *Jewish Wisdom in the Hellenistic Age* (OTL; Louisville: Westminster John Knox, 1997), 64-72; Warren C. Trenchard, *Ben Sira's View of Women* (Chico: Scholars Press, 1982); Claudia Camp, "Understanding a Patriarchy: Women in Second Century Jerusalem Through the Eyes of Ben Sira," in *"Women Like This": New Perspectives on Jewish Women in the Greco-Roman Period*, ed. A.-J. Levine (SBLEJL 1; Atlanta: Scholars Press, 1991), 1-39.

I dedicate this essay to John Collins, a sage who will always be my teacher. I also thank Joel Kaminsky, Greg Goering, Karina Martin Hogan, Marko Marttila, and Eibert Tigchelaar for reading earlier drafts of this paper.

the third is not even a people: those who live in Seir and Philistia, and the foolish nation that dwells in Shechem."[3] The placement of this invective in the book as a whole can seem rather strange. Chapter 50 ends in verses 27-29 with what has been called a "postscript" that has the appearance of being the conclusion to the book as a whole, the hymns of chapter 51 being widely considered secondary.[4] The derogatory comments of vv. 25-26 could be considered the last "lesson" of Ben Sira's instruction.

The comment of Skehan and Di Lella that the invective couplet "is in no way related to the preceding section" suggests that Sir. 50:25-26 has not been sufficiently understood in relation to the rest of chapter 50 or the book of Ben Sira in general.[5] While the odd placement of Sir. 50:25-26 could lead one to think that the lines were added later, a good case can be made that these verses are genuine.[6] In this paper I make three points that support this view: (1) The passage is consistent with what can be inferred about opinions regarding Shechem in the time of Ben Sira. (2) These verses accord with a negative attitude Ben Sira exhibits throughout the book towards non-Judean peoples of Palestine, especially in the "Praise of the Fathers." The dis-

---

3. Unless otherwise noted, the Hebrew is from the B text of Ben Sira (the only witness in Hebrew to Sir. 50:25-26). Otto Mulder understands Sir. 50:25-26 as a "Scheltrede." See his *Simon the High Priest in Sirach 50: An Exegetical Study of the Significance of Simon the High Priest as Climax to the Praise of the Fathers in Ben Sira's Concept of the History of Israel* (JSJSup 78; Leiden: Brill, 2003), 223-27. Note also James D. Purvis, "Ben Sira and the Foolish People of Shechem," *JNES* 24 (1965): 88-94. This essay is reprinted in idem, *The Samaritan Pentateuch and the Origin of the Samaritan Sect* (HSM 2; Cambridge: Harvard University Press, 1968), 119-29. Consult further Richard J. Coggins, "Issues in Samaritanism," in *Judaism in Late Antiquity, Part 3. Where We Stand: Issues and Debates in Ancient Judaism*, ed. J. Neusner and A. J. Avery-Peck (Leiden: Brill, 2001), 63-77 (esp. 65); idem, *Samaritans and Jews: The Origins of Samaritanism Reconsidered* (Atlanta: John Knox Press, 1975); Ingrid Hjelm, *The Samaritans and Early Judaism: A Literary Analysis* (JSOTSup 303; Sheffield: Sheffield Academic Press, 2000), 125-46; Pancratius C. Beentjes, *The Book of Ben Sira in Hebrew* (VTSup 68; repr. Atlanta: Society of Biblical Literature, 2006).

4. Skehan and Di Lella, *The Wisdom of Ben Sira*, 556.

5. Ibid., 558.

6. Collins, *Jewish Wisdom*, 107, suspects that the passage may be an interpolation. Scholars of an earlier generation such as G. H. Box and W. O. E. Oesterley understood the contrast between the praise of Simon in the Jerusalem Temple in Sir. 50:1-24 and the dismissive attitude toward the peoples of vv. 25-26 as a rationale to doubt the authenticity of the latter verses. See their commentary on Ben Sira in *Apocrypha and Pseudepigrapha of the Old Testament*, 2 vols., ed. R. H. Charles (Oxford: Clarendon, 1913), 1:511. Several recent scholars have accepted Sir. 50:25-26 as genuine. See, for example, Coggins, "Issues in Samaritanism," 65; Purvis, *The Samaritan Pentateuch*, 123. Consult also Hjelm, *The Samaritans and Early Judaism*, 126.

dain for Shechem in Ben Sira 50, I suggest, can also be profitably understood against the backdrop of early Jewish interpretation of Genesis 34, which tends to praise the violence perpetrated against Shechem in that chapter. (3) Ben Sira's praise of the high priest Simon leading worship at the Jerusalem Temple in 50:1-24 can be understood as prompting him to make an ad hoc slur against the Samaritans, who worship at Mount Gerizim.[7] In terms of genre, Sir. 50:25-26 is quite different from its surrounding material but in terms of content the verses are fully consistent with chapters 44–50. These lines offer a good opportunity for examining Ben Sira's view of the Other in Palestine.[8]

I. Samaritans, Shechem, and Mount Gerizim in the Time of Ben Sira

All three places mentioned in Sir. 50:25-26 — Seir, Philistia and Shechem — are rooted in biblical lore. Seir, a reference to Edom, and Philistia are traditional biblical enemies of Israel. The case of Shechem is more complicated. The city, nestled between two mountains, Gerizim to the south and Ebal to the north, is important in the Hebrew Bible. When Abram leaves Haran for Canaan, he first arrives at the oak of Moreh at Shechem (Gen. 12:6-8; cf. 33:18-20; 35:4). The bones of Joseph are buried in Shechem.[9] Through covenant renewal ceremonies such as Joshua 24, the Bible connects God's covenant with Israel to Shechem long before Jerusalem becomes the city of David (cf. Deuteronomy 27; Joshua 8).

The Samaritans considered (and still consider) themselves to be the

---

7. I follow the consensus view that the Simon of Ben Sira 50 should be understood as Simon II, who was High Priest from 219 to 196 B.C.E. and thus a contemporary of Ben Sira, although he presumably had died before his instruction was written. This Simon may be referred to in *m. 'Abot* 1:2 as "Simon the Just," as Mulder has argued. James C. VanderKam contends that Ben Sira 50 discusses Simon I, a mid-third-century figure (whom Josephus calls "the Just"; cf. *Ant.* 12.43, 157). See his *From Joshua to Caiaphas: High Priests after the Exile* (Minneapolis/Assen: Fortress Press/Van Gorcum, 2004), 137-57; Mulder, *Simon the High Priest*, 345; Ralph Marcus, *Josephus VII: Jewish Antiquities, Books XII-XIV* (Cambridge, Mass.: Harvard University Press, 1936), 732-36.

8. Lawrence M. Wills, *Not God's People: Insiders and Outsiders in the Biblical World* (Lanham: Rowman & Littlefield, 2008).

9. Josh. 24:32 states that the bones of Joseph, which Moses took out of Egypt, were buried in Shechem (cf. Exod. 13:19). See James L. Kugel, *In Potiphar's House: The Interpretive Life of Biblical Texts* (New York: HarperSan Francisco, 1990), 125-55.

descendants of Ephraim and Manasseh, the sons of Joseph.[10] There is also a long-held view that they are ethnically distinct from the Judeans. Second Kings 17 states that after the Assyrians destroyed the northern kingdom of Israel in 721 B.C.E., they settled peoples there. Some are from the ancient Mesopotamian city of Cuth. Hence in rabbinic literature, and in Josephus, the Samaritans are sometimes referred to as the "Cutheans" (כותים), a term that construes them as ethnically foreign (e.g., *m. Giṭ.* 1:5; *Ant.* 9.288-90; 11.302).[11] There is ambiguity whether they are Jews are not. Josephus, for example, writes that the Samaritans would say they were Jews when it was advantageous to do so and, when it was not, they would say they were not.[12] Grouping the "foolish nation" of Shechem with Seir and Philistia suggests that Ben Sira considered its people to be Gentiles rather than heterodox Jews (cf. Jdt. 5:16).

While it is not clear that there was a full-fledged schism between Judeans and Samaritans in the time of Ben Sira, there were probably significant tensions between the two groups during his lifetime.[13] Ben Sira's main

---

10. Menachem Mor, "Samaritan History: The Persian, Hellenistic and Hasmonaean Period," in *The Samaritans*, ed. A. D. Crown (Tübingen: Mohr-Siebeck, 1989), 1-18; Frank M. Cross, Jr., "Aspects of Samaritan and Jewish History in Late Persian and Hellenistic Times," *HTR* 59 (1966): 201-11. Consult also F. Dexinger and R. Pummer, eds., *Die Samaritaner* (Darmstadt: Wissenschaftliche Buchgesellschaft, 1992); C. S. Chang, *The Samaritan Origins and Identity* (Taejon, Korea: PaiChai University Publishers, 2004).

11. It has been argued that 2 Kings 17 should not be interpreted as historically reliable but as religious polemic. See Coggins, *Samaritans and Jews*, 3.

12. They "alter their attitude according to circumstance and, when they see the Jews prospering, call them their kinsmen, on the grounds that they are descended from Joseph and are related to them through their origin from him, but when they see the Jews in trouble, they say that they have nothing whatever in common with them nor do these have any claim of friendship or race, and they declare themselves to be aliens of another race" (*Ant.* 9.290-91; cf. 11.340-41; 12.257). See further Hjelm, *The Samaritans and Early Judaism*, 194; Richard J. Coggins, "The Samaritans in Josephus," in *Josephus, Judaism, and Christianity*, ed. L. H. Feldman and G. Hata (Detroit: Wayne State University Press, 1987), 257-73 (esp. 259).

13. Scholars generally grant that there was a schism between the two traditions, but they disagree on when this took place. Several commentators date the schism to the reign of John Hyrcanus, who destroyed Gerizim in 128 B.C.E. and Shechem in 107 B.C.E. Crown has pushed for an even later dating. According to 2 Maccabees, Judas takes refuge in Samaria when hiding from Nicanor, the Seleucid governor of Judah (14:30; 15:1). Doran has observed that in 2 Macc. 5:22-23 the word "nation" covers both Jerusalem and Mount Gerizim, suggesting that there was not a sharp break between the two communities at the time. Mathias Delcor argued that this took place in the fourth century B.C.E. Consult his "Hinweise auf das samaritanische Schisma im Alten Testament," *ZAW* 74 (1962): 281-91. See Robert Doran, "2 Maccabees 6:2 and the Samaritan Question," *HTR* 76 (1983): 481-85 (esp. 483); Alan D.

interest is not the Samaritans as a people or the entire region of Samaria. The term "Samaritan" is never used by the sage in the Hebrew, although it is in the Greek.[14] The emphasis on Shechem suggests rather that Ben Sira considered the core problem north of Judea to be the temple on Gerizim.[15] A temple did exist on Gerizim in the early second century B.C.E. Itzak Magen has been excavating on the mountain since 1979 and has brought attention to a temple that was constructed, he argues, in the first half of the fifth century B.C.E.[16] Second Maccabees 6:2 mentions a temple there at the time of the Maccabean crisis.[17]

Crown, "Redating the Schism between the Judaeans and the Samaritans," *JQR* 82 (1991): 17-50 (esp. 17, 27); Purvis, *The Samaritan Pentateuch*, 118; Mor, "Samaritan History," 10, and the minimalist position of Coggins, *Samaritans and Jews*, 164. Note also Jonathan Goldstein, *II Maccabees* (AB 41; Garden City, N.Y.: Doubleday, 1983), 495; Seth Schwartz, "John Hyrcanus I's Destruction of the Gerizim Temple and Judaean-Samaritan Relations," *Jewish History* 7 (1993): 9-25 (esp. 12).

14. In the Greek of Sir. 50:26 the first nation is οἱ καθήμενοι ὄρει Σαμαρείας ("those who reside on Mount Samaria"). I examine the significance of this variant below. The text presumably refers to the city of Samaria (which is on a small mountain; cf. 1 Kings 16:24), ten kilometers from Shechem. Alexander the Great, in response to a revolt of Samarian soldiers in his army when they were in Egypt, destroyed the city of Samaria, after which many of its residents fled to Shechem. A garrison of Macedonian soldiers was stationed at the city of Samaria. See Mulder, *Simon the High Priest*, 306; Elias J. Bickerman, *The Jews in the Greek Age* (Cambridge: Harvard University Press, 1988), 10; Mor, "Samaritan History," 10.

15. Jörg Frey, "Temple and Rival Temple — The Cases of Elephantine, Mt. Gerizim, and Leontopolis," in *Gemeinde ohne Tempel*, ed. B. Ego et al. (WUNT 2.118; Tübingen: Mohr-Siebeck, 1999), 171-203; Ingrid Hjelm, *Jerusalem's Rise to Sovereignty: Zion and Gerizim in Competition* (JSOTSup 404; London/New York: T&T Clark International, 2004). For the diversity of groups among the Samaritans (such as the Dositheans), see J. Fossum, "Samaritan Sects and Movements," in *The Samaritans*, 293-389.

16. Itzak Magen, "Mt. Gerizim — Temple City," *Qad* 33 (2000): 74-118 (esp. 97, 114) (Hebrew). See also VanderKam, *From Joshua to Caiaphas*, 77-78; Ingrid Hjelm, "What Do Samaritans and Jews Have in Common? Recent Trends in Samaritan Studies," *CBR* 3 (2004): 9-59 (esp. 19-21); Ephraim Stern and Hanan Eshel, eds., ספר השומרונים (Jerusalem: Yad Izhak Ben-Zvi, 2002).

17. According to 2 Macc. 6:1-2, Antiochus IV has both temples renamed. The passage also states that the Gerizim temple is called Zeus Xenios (Zeus Hospitable) but Josephus gives the new name as Zeus Hellenios. There is some evidence that the priests at Gerizim were from a line of Zadokites who left the Jerusalem temple in the Persian period (Neh. 13:28; *Ant.* 11.306-12). At issue is a son (unnamed in Nehemiah) of the High Priest Joiada who marries Nikaso, a daughter of the Samaritan leader Sanballat. According to Josephus, Sanballat gives his daughter to Manasseh and has a temple built on Gerizim for his son-in-law, whose marriage estranges him from Nehemiah and the Jerusalem leadership. For discussion of this material, see VanderKam, *From Joseph to Caiaphas*, 53, 75-76; Mor, "The Sa-

II. The "Foolish Nation" of Shechem and Genesis 34

The terminology of Sir. 50:25-26 conveys Ben Sira's disdain for Shechem. Shechem, like Seir and Philistia, is described with the word גוי.[18] The word is used by Ben Sira in expressions that describe other peoples in negative terms. For example, he describes the Babylonian destruction of Jerusalem as God giving the glory of Judah's king over to a "foolish foreign nation" (גוי נבל נכרי) (49:5). Ben Sira calls the Canaanites a "doomed nation" (גוי חרם) (16:9).[19] The sage also describes the Canaanites as גוים in Sir. 39:23: "Again, his wrath dispossesses the nations (זעמו גוים יוריש), and turns fertile land into a salt marsh."[20]

In Ben Sira 50 Shechem is called a גוי נבל, a "foolish nation." The expression also appears in Deut. 32:21. Commentators have reasonably suggested that Ben Sira's use of the phrase derives from this verse.[21] Ben Sira's reliance on Deut. 32:21 may suggest, as James Kugel has argued, that the sage understood this verse as referring to Samaria.[22] Ben Sira's disdain for Shechem would then explain why he borrowed the phrase. In Deut. 32:21 God promises to respond to Israel's transgressions: "They made me jealous with what is no god; they provoked me with their idols. So I will make them jealous with what is no people (בלא־עם); I will provoke them with a foolish nation (בגוי נבל אכעיסם)."[23] Deut. 32:21 occurs in the context of God's anger against his chosen people, who have spurned him (vv. 15, 22). They are a "perverse generation" from whom God has hidden his face (v. 20). As a re-

---

maritan History," 4-5; Józef Zsengellér, *Gerizim als Israel: Northern Tradition of the Old Testament and the Early History of the Samaritans* (Utrechtse Theologische Reeks 38; Utrecht: Utrecht University, 1998), 136-38; Robert Doran, "2 Maccabees 6:2," 481-85; Goldstein, *II Maccabees*, 272-73; Coggins, "The Samaritans in Josephus," 265.

18. In the Greek of v. 25 both גוי and עם are translated with the word ἔθνος. V. 26 has the correspondence גוי//λαός. See Mulder, *Simon the High Priest*, 304.

19. In Sir. 46:6 the sage praises Joshua for destroying "every doomed people" (כל גוי חרם). The phrase is not translated in the same way in G 16:9 and 46:6. See Skehan and Di Lella, *The Wisdom of Ben Sira*, 273-74.

20. Ben Sira may have understood this destruction as an application of the curses of the covenant (cf. Deut. 29:22-23). See Skehan and Di Lella, *The Wisdom of Ben Sira*, 460; Collins, *Jewish Wisdom*, 87.

21. Mulder, *Simon the High Priest*, 231-32; Skehan and Di Lella, *The Wisdom of Ben Sira*, 558.

22. James L. Kugel, *The Ladder of Jacob: Ancient Interpretations of the Biblical Story of Jacob and His Children* (Princeton: Princeton University Press, 2006), 62-63.

23. The expression לא־עם from Deuteronomy is similar to עם איננו in Sir. 50:25.

sult, God will punish Israel *with* "what is no people" and "a foolish nation" (v. 21). Since Ben Sira associates the latter phrase with Shechem, it is possible that he interpreted Deut. 32:21 as stating that God brought Gerizim into being, with its apostate temple, as a way to punish the transgressions of his chosen nation Israel.[24]

The term נבל ("fool") was apparently a Judean insult used against Samaritans in the second and first centuries B.C.E. 4QApocryphon of Joseph attests the word "fool[s]" (נבלי[ם]) and then polemically refers to the construction of a temple: "making for themselves a high place upon a high mountain to provoke Israel to jealousy" (4Q372 1 11-12).[25] This has been reasonably understood as a reference to Gerizim.[26] The editors of 4Q372 argue that it is an anti-Samaritan composition.[27] A brief fragment of the War Scroll from Cave 11, 11Q14, attests the phrase "the fooli[sh] nation" (הגוי הנב[ל]) (2 1).[28] The Philistines may be mentioned in line 2 of the fragment.[29] It is possible that the word "Samaritans" is in line 3, but this is not certain.[30]

The reason that the people of Shechem are called "fools" in Ben Sira and 4QApocryphon of Joseph is suggested by the *Testament of Levi*. After stating that the wrath of God came upon the city (6:11), *T. Levi* 7:2-3 reads: "For from this day forward, Shechem shall be called 'City of the Senseless'

---

24. This perspective would provide an explanation why God tolerates the existence of the Gerizim temple. Israel is called a "foolish people that is not wise" (עם נבל ולא חכם) in Deut. 32:6 (cf. v. 15).

25. The word "fool[s]" is supplied on the basis of 4Q371 1 10. The paleography of 4Q371 is dated to 100-75 B.C.E. and 4Q372 to 50 B.C.E. This text is also known as 4QNarrative and Poetic Composition[a-c] (4Q371-373). See Douglas M. Gropp, Eileen Schuller et al., *Wadi Daliyeh II: The Samaria Papyri for Wadi Daliyeh. Qumran Cave 4.XXVIII: Miscellanea, Part 2* (DJD 28; Oxford: Clarendon, 2001), 167-78 (esp. 165); Eileen Schuller, "4Q372 1: A Text about Joseph," *RevQ* 14/55 (1990): 349-76; T. Thordson and M. Thordson, *Qumran and the Samaritans* (Jerusalem: Emerezian Establishment, 1996). For biblical exegesis in 4Q371-373, see the article by Esther Chazon in this volume.

26. One text mentions an "enemy people" (עם אויב) and appears to proclaim their destruction (lines 21-22). Note the phrase "foreign people" (גוי נאכר) in 4Q372 1 11, which is similar to Ben Sira's description of the Babylonians in Sir. 49:5.

27. Schuller, DJD 28, 171; eadem, "4Q372," 371.

28. Florentino García Martínez et al., *Qumran Cave 11.II: 11Q2-18, 11Q20-31* (DJD 23; Oxford: Clarendon, 1998), 249-50. The hand of 11Q14 dates to the turn of the common era. See ibid., 244.

29. The line reads "get up he]ro, take the Phil[istines] (פ[שתים]) prisoner."

30. The letters ונים survive, from which one could reconstruct שומרונים. 11Q14 2 follows praise of God in fragment 1. This accords with Sir. 50:25-26, which comes after praise of God in vv. 1-24 as expressed by worship led by Simon the High Priest.

(πόλις ἀσυνέτων) because as one might scoff at a fool, so we scoffed at them, because by defiling my sister they committed folly (ἀφροσύνην) in Israel." The dating of the *Testaments of the Twelve Patriarchs* is a well-known problem but *T. Levi* preserves numerous exegetical traditions that are attested in Early Jewish literature, as Kugel has demonstrated.[31] *T. Levi* 7 explains the expression "City of the Senseless" through a patent reference to Genesis 34. נבל terminology plays an important role in Genesis 34 itself. When the sons of Jacob learn what happened to their sister, they become incensed because Shechem "had committed an outrage (נבלה) in Israel by lying with Jacob's daughter, for such a thing ought not to be done" (v. 7). The term נבל elsewhere in the Hebrew Bible refers to sexual crimes.[32] When Amnon forces himself upon Tamar, she asks him to stop, saying, "Such a thing is not done in Israel; do not do this folly (הנבלה הזאת)" (2 Sam. 13:12).[33] The term ἀφροσύνη is used to translate the word נבלה several times in the Septuagint.[34] The Aramaic *Vorlage* of *T. Levi* 7 probably contained a form of נבלה.[35] The expression "City of the Senseless" does more than deride the people of Shechem as stupid. They are immoral and degenerate Canaanites who all bear guilt for the rape committed by their eponymous ancestor.[36]

---

31. Kugel, *Ladder of Jacob*, 36-80. See also Robert A. Kugler, *The Testaments of the Twelve Patriarchs* (Sheffield: Sheffield Academic Press, 2001), 31-39.

32. Anthony Philips, "Nebalah — A Term for Serious Disorderly and Unruly Conduct," *VT* 25 (1975): 237-41.

33. In the gruesome story of the Levite and the concubine, the men's desire to sodomize the Levite is called a נבלה by his host (Judg. 19:23). The Levite uses the same term to describe the rape of his concubine and he expressed outrage that this has taken place "in Israel" (20:6, 10; cf. Hos. 2:12). Deut. 22:21 stipulates that a woman who loses her virginity before marriage shall be stoned to death "for she has committed a disgraceful act (נבלה) in Israel" (NRSV; cf. Jer. 29:23).

34. E.g., Deut. 22:21; Judg. 19:23, 24; 20:6, 10. The LXX translation of Gen 34:7 does not use ἀφροσύνη but ἀσχήμων. This is the only time this correspondence is found in the Septuagint.

35. The *Vorlage* of this text may have contained an etiology that explains the insulting nickname for Shechem through wordplay — Shechem is to be called עיר נבליא by asserting that the eponym of the city committed נבלה, referring to Shechem's sleeping with Dinah.

36. Reinhard Pummer, "Antisamaritanische Polemik in jüdischen Schriften aus der intertestamentarischen Zeit," *BZ* 26 (1982): 224-42 (esp. 232); idem, "Genesis 34 in Jewish Writings of the Hellenistic and Roman Periods," *HTR* 75 (1982): 177-88; Hjelm, *The Samaritans and Early Judaism*, 141. No exact parallel to *T. Lev.* 7:2 is available in Aramaic, but the *Aramaic Levi Document* does retell Genesis 34. The fragmentary column A of the Cambridge manuscript from the Cairo Geniza mentions the proposal to have the men of Shechem circumcised. See Jonas C. Greenfield et al., *The Aramaic Levi Document* (SVTP 19; Leiden: Brill, 2004), 56-59, 110-22 (esp. 56); Henryk Drawnel, *An Aramaic Wisdom Text from Qumran*

"The Foolish Nation That Dwells in Shechem"

Ben Sira's disparaging attitude towards Shechem is consistent with the general tenor of Early Jewish interpretations of Genesis 34, which often take an anti-Samaritan turn.[37] In the book of Genesis itself the violence perpetrated by Simeon and Levi against Shechem's family and city in response to the rape is considered excessive. Jacob complains that their actions make him "odious to the inhabitants of the land" who may be incited to attack in response (34:30). In Gen. 49:5-7 the two brothers are rebuked for their cruelty. Later interpreters view the brothers' actions against Shechem much more favorably. According to *Jubilees*, a text generally dated to the second century B.C.E., Levi and Simeon are instruments of divine judgment against Shechem. Their violent acts are reckoned to them as "righteousness" (30:17; cf. *T. Levi* 6:8).[38] The book of Judith, which probably dates to the second century B.C.E. as well, emphasizes that the people of Shechem are foreigners: "O Lord God of my ancestor Simeon, to whom you gave a sword to take revenge on those strangers who had torn off a virgin's clothing to defile her" (Jdt. 9:2; cf. 5:16; *Ant.* 1.341).[39] The epic of Theodotus asserts that the violence of Levi and Simeon is a form of divine judgment against Shechem. While this work has traditionally been understood to have a Samaritan provenance, John Collins argued in the 1980s that this work was written by a Jew with an anti-Samaritan perspective (*Praep. Evang.* 9.22.1-11).[40] Early Jewish exegesis of Genesis 34 often exhibits an anti-Samaritan *Tendenz*.

It is possible to read the combination of the words "Shechem" and נבל

(JSJSup 86; Leiden: Brill, 2004); Émile Puech, "Le *Testament de Lévi* en araméen de la Geniza du Caire," *RevQ* 20/80 (2002): 511-56.

37. Louis H. Feldman, "Philo, Pseudo-Philo, Josephus, and Theodotus on the Rape of Dinah," *JQR* 94 (2004): 253-77; Pummer, "Antisamaritanische Polemik," 225-34; James L. Kugel, "The Story of Dinah in the Testament of Levi," *HTR* 85 (1992): 1-34; idem, *The Ladder of Jacob*, 36-80; John J. Collins, "The Epic of Theodotus and the Hellenism of the Hasmoneans," *HTR* 73 (1980): 91-104 (esp. 96-98); Hjelm, *The Samaritans and Early Judaism*, 138-46; Hans G. Kippenberg, *Garizim und Synagogue: Traditionsgeschichtliche Untersuchungen zur samaritanischen Religion der aramäischen Periode* (Berlin: de Gruyter, 1971), 90.

38. James C. VanderKam, *The Book of Jubilees* (Sheffield: Sheffield Academic Press, 2001), 21; Doron Mendels, *The Land of Israel as a Political Concept in Hasmonean Literature* (Tübingen: Mohr-Siebeck, 1987), 70-72.

39. Benedikt Otzen, *Tobit and Judith* (Sheffield: Sheffield Academic Press, 2002), 134.

40. Collins, "The Epic of Theodotus," 90-95; idem, *Between Athens and Jerusalem*, 2nd ed. (Grand Rapids: Eerdmans, 2000), 57-60; Pummer, "Antisamaritanische Polemik," 236. Michael Daise, "Samaritans, Seleucids and the Epic of Theodotus," *JSP* 17 (1998): 25-51 (esp. 26-27), argues for a Samaritan provenance for the work. The epic gives prominence to Shechem and calls it a "holy city" (frg. 1, l. 16). See also Robert J. Bull, "A Note on Theodotus' Description of Shechem," *HTR* 60 (1967): 221-27; Mendels, *The Land of Israel*, 109-19.

in Ben Sira 50 as an allusion to Genesis 34. The reference to Genesis 34 is admittedly not as explicit as in *T. Levi* 7.[41] Such an allusion in Sir. 50:26 would be consistent with Ben Sira's disdain for the people of Shechem. This would help explain his association of this city with Gentile nations, since in Genesis 34 Shechem is a Canaanite people. None of the texts reviewed above that engage Genesis 34 are clearly earlier than Ben Sira. His opinion of Shechem, however, is consistent with later texts' interpretation of Genesis 34. 4Q371 establishes that second century B.C.E. texts aside from Ben Sira use the word נבל to disparage Samaria. The word was apparently important in the interpretation of Genesis 34 in the Aramaic *Vorlage* of the *Testament of Levi* and occurs in Genesis 34 itself to describe the sexual transgression (v. 7). It is reasonable to think that Ben Sira is alluding to Genesis 34, albeit indirectly.

III. "Not Even a People"

The residents of Shechem, according to Sir. 50:25, are "not even a people" (איננו עם). They should be considered a גוי but not an עם. The latter term is used repeatedly (but not exclusively) by Ben Sira to refer to Israel, God's chosen people.[42] The sage's encomium of the High Priest Simon begins with the assertion that he is "the glory of his people" (תפארת עמו) (50:1). Context indicates that the suffix refers to Simon. The expression "his people" probably refers to the people of Israel, whose special status before God is ratified by their worship at the Jerusalem Temple, with Simon in charge.[43]

---

41. Eibert J. C. Tigchelaar, *Prophets of Old and the Day of the End: Zechariah, The Book of Watchers, and Apocalyptic* (Leiden: Brill, 1996), 202. Note that the word נבל does not refer to sexuality every time it is used in Ben Sira (cf. 4:27; 33[36]:5 [ms E]; 49:5).

42. Sir. 37:25 states that while individual persons are doomed to die, "the people of Israel" (עם ישראל) live forever. According to Ben Sira 45, which praises Moses, Aaron and Phinehas, Moses was given the Torah "to teach the precepts to his people (עמו), and the norms to Israel (בני ישראל)" (v. 17). עמו and בני ישראל are also in parallelism in v. 23. Also note that the expression בני עמו in v. 9 refers to the Aaronid priestly line. Sir. 16:6 describes rebellious Israelites whom God destroyed with fire at Taberah as a "godless people" (גוי חנף) (cf. Num 11:1-3). The word גוי does not always refer to a specific ethnic group in the book. עם can also refer to Gentiles in Ben Sira (36:3; 47:17).

43. Mulder, *Simon the High Priest*, 107. See also Saul M. Olyan, "Ben Sira's Relationship to the Priesthood," *HTR* 80 (1987): 261-86; Benjamin G. Wright III, "'Fear the Lord and Honor the Priest': Ben Sira as Defender of the Jerusalem Priesthood," in idem, *In Praise of Wisdom and Instruction: Essays on Ben Sira and Wisdom, the Letter of Aristeas and the Septuagint* (JSJSup 131; Leiden: Brill, 2008), 96-126.

Since עם often signifies Israel in Ben Sira, his claim that the people of Shechem are "not even a people (עם)" may imply not only that they are not a legitimate people, but that they are not the people Israel and should not be considered part of that entity.[44] Ben Sira describes Simon officiating at the Temple "before the whole assembly of Israel" (50:13; cf. v. 20). The sage believed that all of Israel should revere the Jerusalem temple. There is evidence roughly from his time period that the Samaritans called themselves Israelites. Two inscriptions from the island of Delos were discovered in 1979 that are reasonably attributed to Samaritan authors. Both state that they are written by "Israelites who make offerings to holy Argarizien (Ἀργαριζείν)," a clear reference to Mount Gerizim.[45] One has been dated to 250-175 B.C.E. and the other to 150-50 B.C.E. If adherents of the Gerizim temple were referring to themselves as the people of Israel or considered themselves part of Israel, supporters of the Jerusalem sanctuary such as Ben Sira could have easily understood such language as polemical, whether it was intended that way or not.

IV. Phinehas's "Covenant of Peace" and the History of Israel according to Ben Sira

Ben Sira's account of the history of Israel in his "Praise of the Fathers" is fully consistent with his invective toward Shechem.[46] He writes that Jeroboam, the founder of the northern kingdom, "led Israel into sin" and "brought ruin to Ephraim and caused them to be exiled from their land" (47:23; cf. 48:15). This perspective is firmly in line with 2 Kings 17 — the original inhabitants

---

44. Graham Harvey, *The True Israel: Uses of the Names Jew, Hebrew and Israel in Ancient Jewish and Early Christian Literature* (AGJU 35; Leiden: Brill, 1995); Coggins, "Issues in Samaritanism," 76.

45. Reinhard Pummer, "Samaritan Material Remains and Archaeology," in *The Samaritans*, 135-77 (esp. 150-51); Crown, "Redating the Schism," 19; Philippe Bruneau, "Les Israélites de Délos et la juiverie délienne," *BCH* 106 (1982): 466-504. See also Schwartz, "John Hyrcanus I's Destruction of the Gerizim Temple," 9.

46. Burton L. Mack, *Wisdom and the Hebrew Epic: Ben Sira's Hymn in Praise of the Fathers* (Chicago: University of Chicago Press, 1985); Thomas R. Lee, *Studies in the Form of Sirach 44-50* (SBLDS 75; Atlanta: Scholars Press, 1986); Jeremy Corley, "A Numerical Structure in Sirach 44:1–50:24," *CBQ* 69 (2007): 43-63; Alexander A. Di Lella, "Ben Sira's Praise of the Ancestors of Old (Sir 44-49): The History of Israel as Parenetic Apologetics," in *History and Identity: How Israel's Later Authors Viewed Its Earlier History*, ed. N. Calduch-Benages and J. Liesen (Berlin: de Gruyter, 2006), 151-70; Mendels, *The Land of Israel*, 9-17.

were exiled by the Assyrians because of their transgressions against God. There is a remnant of Joseph, but it is in exile not in the land. Ben Sira envisages the eventual restoration of the twelve tribes through the return of Elijah. Sir. 48:10 states "You are destined, it is written, in time to come to put an end to wrath before the day of the Lord, to turn back the hearts of parents toward their children, to reestablish the tribes of Israel" (cf. 36:11).[47] The grouping of Shechem with the Gentile nations Seir and Philistia in Sir. 50:25-26 implies that the full restoration of the allotment of land to the twelve tribes requires not the repentance or conversion of non-covenant peoples of Palestine but their elimination, although Ben Sira never advocates this.

Ben Sira's Praise of the Fathers singles out the priest Phinehas for special praise: "When, zealous for the God of all, he met the crisis of his people (עמו) and, at the prompting of his noble heart, atoned for the people of Israel (בני ישראל)" (45:23). The elevated language refers to the well-known incident recounted in Numbers 25, in which Phinehas pierces the stomachs of an Israelite man and a Midianite woman with a spear. Phinehas is rewarded for his violence ironically with "my covenant of peace" (ברית שלום), a special bond that Phinehas and his priestly descendants share with God (v. 12).[48] As in Numbers 25 itself, Ben Sira emphasizes this priestly covenant. He goes beyond Numbers, however, by connecting Phinehas's covenant to the Jerusalem temple: "Therefore on him (Phinehas) again God conferred the right, in a covenant of peace (ברית שלום//διαθήκη εἰρήνης) to provide for the sanctuary, so that he and his descendants should possess the high priesthood forever" (45:24). The culmination of his praise of Simon in 50:24 stresses the priest's continuity with Phinehas: "May his (God's) kindness towards Simon be lasting; may he fulfill for him the covenant with Phinehas (ברית פינחס) so that it may be not abrogated for him or for his descendants, while the heavens last."[49]

---

47. Skehan and Di Lella, *The Wisdom of Ben Sira*, 531.

48. In the Septuagint there is no suffix attached to "covenant."

49. V. 23 mentions the "peace" of God, which may allude to the covenant with Phinehas. The verb translated "may he fulfill" in v. 24 is יקם, which is probably a *hip'il*. The imperfect verbs of this section likely have a progressive sense — "may he continue to fulfill." The covenant with Phinehas is never mentioned in the Greek of 50:24. Despite Ben Sira's prayer for this covenant to endure through Simon's descendants as long as the heavens last, his priestly line did not continue beyond his son Onias III. He was assassinated ca. 172 B.C.E. (2 Macc. 4:34). Sir. 50:24 shows no indication that Simon's line has been disrupted. This supports the consensus view that Ben Sira was written before the Maccabean crisis. See Mulder, *Simon the High Priest*, 316, 343; Skehan and Di Lella, *The Wisdom of Ben Sira*, 554.

In 1 Maccabees Phinehas epitomizes intolerance for religious diversity to the point of violence. Mattathias displays, as John Collins has reminded us, the "zeal of Phinehas" when he kills a fellow Jew who makes a sacrifice at a pagan altar (1 Macc. 2:23-26; cf. 4 Macc. 18:12).[50] Ben Sira understands Phinehas in a compatible, if less violent, way. For Ben Sira the covenant of Phinehas combines the biblical Aaronid's disdain for other Palestinian peoples with an assertion of the exclusive legitimacy of Simon's priestly office. The insult of Sir. 50:25-26 makes perfect sense following the covenant of Phinehas mentioned in v. 24.

Ben Sira's connection of Simon to Phinehas may be a polemical adaptation of Samaritan tradition, although this cannot be proven. If so, this would be another reason why the slur of Sir. 50:25-26 follows the praise of Simon. The Samaritans believe that their high priests were of Phinehas's line until the seventeenth century.[51] In the *Tolidah* ("Genealogy"), often called the *Samaritan Chronicle,* Phinehas and his perpetual covenant is an important motif.[52] The Samaritan reckoning of the calendar is, for example, attributed to this priest.[53]

V. Judean Nationalism in the Hasmonean Period

Neither Ben Sira nor the Judean leaders of his day wielded enough political power to give concrete expression to any animosity towards the Samaritans

---

50. John J. Collins, "The Zeal of Phinehas: The Bible and the Legitimation of Violence," *JBL* 122 (2003): 3-21. See also idem, *Does the Bible Justify Violence?* (Minneapolis: Fortress, 2004).

51. The end of the book of Joshua situates Phinehas in Ephraim. After mentioning the burial of the bones of Joseph in Shechem, Josh. 24:33 states that they buried Eleazar son of Aaron "at Gibeah, the town of his son Phinehas, which had been given him in the hill country of Ephraim."

52. One section of this text reads "Now our father Phinehas was the possessor of the covenant of the high priesthood, which is our inheritance forever, and after the children of Israel had entered the land of Canaan and were settled there securely, our father, Phinehas, tested this calculation [of the years] on the side of the holy Mount Gerizim." This knowledge, the text states, was handed down from Shem, Noah, Seth, Adam, the angels and God. Shem, Seth and Adam are mentioned in Sir. 49:16, just before the praise of Simon begins. See John Bowman, *Samaritan Documents Relating to Their History, Religion and Life* (Pittsburgh: Pickwick, 1977), 39.

53. The main manuscript of the *Samaritan Chronicle* is from the twelfth century C.E. but preserves traditions that are much older. See P. Stenhouse, "Samaritan Chronicles," in *The Samaritans,* 218-65 (esp. 219).

or other traditional Palestinian peoples. This changed in the Hasmonean period. All three groups mentioned in Sir. 50:25-26 were attacked by either the Maccabees or Hasmonean kings (1 Macc. 5:65-68).[54] Emboldened by the death of the Syrian king Antiochus VII Sidetes in 129 B.C.E., John Hyrcanus (135/4-104 B.C.E.) expanded the existing borders of Judah. He destroyed the temple on Mount Gerizim in 128 B.C.E. and the city of Shechem in 107 (*Ant.* 13.254-58, 275-81; *J.W.* 1.62-65).[55] John Collins has suggested that the anti-Samaritan epic of Theodotus gives expression to the militant Judean nationalism of this period.[56] Ben Sira provides an impression of pre-Maccabean Judean disdain for other Palestinian groups. He exhibits an attitude that would underpin the later violent nationalism of the Hasmoneans. The replacement of "those who live in Seir" with "those who reside on Mount Samaria" in the translation of Sir. 50:26 by Ben Sira's grandson may reflect an increase of anti-Samaritan sentiment during the reign of Hyrcanus.[57] The translation is generally dated to sometime between 132 and 117 B.C.E.[58] It is

---

54. The Edomites (Idumeans) may have resettled some Judean areas after the Babylonian devastation of Judah. 1 Esdras (3 Ezra) claims that they wrongfully held Judean villages in the Persian period (4:50). After the exile the Edomites apparently moved northward and, according to 1 Macc. 5:65 and Josephus (*Ant.* 12.353), Judas Maccabee pushed them out of Hebron and the surrounding area (cf. 1 Macc. 14:33). 1 Maccabees continues by claiming that Judas marched into Philistine territory, which he attacked and returned to Judah (5:66-68). See Hjelm, *The Samaritans and Early Judaism*, 127. Some manuscripts incorrectly read "Samaria" instead of "Marisa" in 1 Macc. 5:66. See Emil Schürer, *The History of the Jewish People*, rev. ed., ed. G. Vermes, F. Millar and M. Black (Edinburgh: T&T Clark, 1973-87), 1:165; Seth Schwartz, *Imperialism and Jewish Society, 200 B.C.E. to 640 C.E.* (Princeton: Princeton University Press, 2001), 33-42; Mendels, *The Land of Israel*, 70.

55. The archaeological excavations of Itzak Magen support this general timeframe for these military actions. See his "Gerizim, Mount," in *The New Encyclopedia of Archaeological Excavations in the Holy Land*, 4 vols., ed. E. Stern et al. (Jerusalem: Israel Exploration Society, 1993), 2:484-92 (esp. 487); idem, "Mt. Gerizim — Temple City," 118. Cf. Frey, "Temple and Rival Temple," 183-84; Schürer, *The History of the Jewish People*, 1:207; Zsengellér, *Gerizim als Israel*, 164-65; Schwartz, "John Hyrcanus I's Destruction of the Gerizim Temple," 19.

56. In Theodotus, Jacob urges the people of Shechem to become Jews through circumcision (frg. 4). See Collins, "The Epic of Theodotus," 101.

57. It is possible that his grandson is distinguishing the residents of Samaria (the first nation of the insult) from those of Shechem (the third nation). Since, as mentioned above, the city of Samaria is ten kilometers from Gerizim, one wonders how great a distinction Ben Sira was trying to make between the two locales. See Mulder, *Simon the High Priest*, 304.

58. 132 B.C.E. is when the grandson went to Egypt, the thirty-eighth year of King Euergetes (Ptolemy VII Physkon Euergetes II), who is mentioned in the prologue by Ben Sira's grandson. 117 B.C.E. is the year this king died. See further Skehan and Di Lella, *The Wisdom of Ben Sira*, 8-9.

thus quite possible that G Sir. 50:25-26 was written shortly after Hyrcanus destroyed Gerizim. The Greek addition of the Samaritans to the insult in these verses is consistent with the rise of anti-Samaritan views in this period represented by Hyrcanus's policies. His destructive actions resonate with Ben Sira 36, which advocates violence toward non-Jews to an extent not found in the rest of the book. It should probably be considered a later addition for this reason.[59]

VI. Conclusion: The Elect and the Enemy Nations

Ben Sira asserts that all of humankind is made in the image of God (17:3). Sirach 17:8 claims that when God created human beings he placed fear of him, a major topos in the book, within them (cf. 10:19-22; 24:6). In principle all peoples can know and revere God. Ben Sira teaches that the one who studies Torah should also travel abroad (39:4). His positive anthropology and openness to other cultures do not accord with his attitude towards the inhabitants of Shechem or other Palestinian groups. The only non-Jewish nation in the region of Palestine that Ben Sira casts in a positive light is Lebanon, and this apparently has more to do with its trees than its people.[60] One way to understand the issue of Israel vis-à-vis other peoples is through

---

59. Wright and Marböck have argued that Ben Sira 36 is authentic and was written after the death of Simon II in 196 B.C.E. when Onias III, who had Ptolemaic sympathies, became high priest. This is possible, but the upheaval of the Maccabean crisis is much greater than that which followed the death of Simon II. This suggests that the poem is more plausibly dated to the Maccabean crisis, or sometime afterward, rather than during any turmoil that followed Simon's death in 196. See Gregory Goering, *Wisdom's Root Revealed* (JSJSup 139; Leiden: Brill, 2009); Benjamin G. Wright III, "'Put the Nations in Fear of You': Ben Sira and the Problem of Foreign Rule," in idem, *In Praise of Wisdom and Instruction*, 127-46; Johannes Marböck, "Das Gebet um die Rettung Zions, Sir. 36,1-22 (Gr. 33,1-13a; 36,16b-22) im Zusammenhang der Geschichtsschau Ben Siras," in *Memoria Jerusalem: Freundesgabe Franz Sauer zum 70. Geburtstag*, ed. J. B. Baer and J. Marböck (Graz: Akademische Druckverlagsanstalt, 1977), 93-116; Samuel L. Adams, *Wisdom in Transition: Act and Consequence in Second Temple Instructions* (JSJSup 125; Leiden: Brill, 2008), 164-69; M. C. Palmisano, "*Salvaci, Dio dell'Universo!*" *Studio dell'eucologia di Sir 36H,1-17* (AnBib 163; Rome: Pontifical Biblical Institute, 2006).

60. Both Simon and Woman Wisdom are compared to a cedar in Lebanon (24:13; 50:12; cf. v. 8). This form of praise is probably not related to an admiration for the Phoenicians but to the tradition that Solomon's temple was constructed out of cedars from Lebanon (1 Kings 5). The image of a "cedar in Lebanon" in the Psalms symbolizes abundance and strength (37:35; 92:12; 104:16). See Mulder, *Simon the High Priest*, 157-58.

the categories of Joel Kaminsky, who makes a distinction between the anti-elect and the non-elect.[61] The former comprises the enemies of Israel and those of the latter category are "fully part of the divine economy."[62] This is an important corrective to the view that the election of Israel has negative implications for all non-Israelites. But, if one restricts the focus to the all-important region of Palestine, it is not clear that the "non-elect" category comes into play at all. Israel's unique inheritance is bestowed to the detriment of neighboring groups, as Kaminsky stresses. Ben Sira frankly says: "Some he blesses and makes great . . . others he curses and brings low, and expels them from their place" (33:12). When Ben Sira discusses humankind in general terms he is often quite positive. But when he names specific other groups, particularly those of Palestine, he often has nothing good to say.

---

61. Joel Kaminsky, "Did Election Imply the Mistreatment of Non-Israelites?" *HTR* 96 (2003): 397-425; idem, *Yet I Loved Jacob: Reclaiming the Biblical Concept of Election* (Nashville: Abingdon, 2007). See also Robert Goldenberg, *The Nations That Know Thee Not: Ancient Jewish Attitudes Towards Other Religions* (New York: New York University Press, 1998).

62. Kaminsky, "Did Election," 399.

Poverty and Otherness in Second Temple Instructions

Samuel L. Adams

In one of his more colorful statements on financial matters, the Jewish sage Ben Sira describes a typical group reaction to wealth and poverty: "The rich person speaks and all are silent; they extol to the clouds what he says. The poor person speaks and they say, 'Who is this fellow?' And should he stumble, they even push him down" (Sir. 13:23). Such a scenario captures a timeless truth about the relationship between money and status. All societies have some form of stratification, and the rich usually have a number of intrinsic advantages. For the period being considered in this volume, for the cultural world of Second Temple Judaism, financial inequality became a topic of central concern. The fluid economic climate is attested in multiple sources, from the Zeno papyri, to Josephus, to the instructional literature from this period.[1] Not only do sapiential authors like Ben Sira speak out against corrupt practices and unfair aspects of the system, but they bring a palpable specificity to their charges, offering a glimpse of the financial structure and various responses to it.[2]

A related development occurred during this period, one that fundamentally altered the wisdom tradition and, in certain respects, the larger cul-

---

1. For a classic treatment of the economic and political landscape during this period, see Victor Tcherikover, *Hellenistic Civilization and the Jews* (Philadelphia: Jewish Publication Society, 1959; repr., Peabody, Mass.: Hendrickson, 1999).

2. On Ben Sira's discussion of financial matters, see Benjamin G. Wright and Claudia V. Camp, "'Who Has Been Tested by Gold and Found Perfect?': Ben Sira's Discourse of Riches and Poverty," *Hen* 23 (2001): 153-74.

ture. Less privileged persons, like the struggling fellow in Ben Sira's illustration, began to engage in sapiential discourse. These were not individuals who collected proverbs as part of the royal bureaucracy, as with the book of Proverbs, nor did they depend on the priestly authorities for their livelihood, as we find with Ben Sira.[3] Texts like 4QInstruction, the longest sapiential document from the Dead Sea Scrolls corpus, and the *Epistle of Enoch*, reflect a more peripheral authorship and audience.[4] The target audience for 4QInstruction struggles to remain on solid financial footing, and they are repeatedly reminded of their challenging situation (e.g., the "you are poor" refrain), with little possibility for improved status in the future.[5] The traditional promise of earthly rewards for virtuous behavior, found in texts like Proverbs and Ben Sira (and in the Egyptian instructions), does not square with the economic circumstances for such individuals. They are distinctively Other in relation to the more affluent sectors of society, and the content of 4QInstruction demonstrates that they do not expect to become part of the elite classes.[6]

---

3. Michael V. Fox, "The Social Location of the Book of Proverbs," in *Texts, Temples, and Traditions: A Tribute to Menahem Haran*, ed. M. V. Fox et al. (Winona Lake, Ind.: Eisenbrauns, 1996), 239, makes a convincing argument about the editorial process for the book of Proverbs. Even if some of the sayings originated in rural areas among diverse sectors of the society, "Learned clerks, at least some of them the king's men, were the membrane through which principles, sayings and coinages, folk and otherwise, were filtered. The central collections of Proverbs are their filtrate, an essentially homogeneous one." Regarding Ben Sira's social location as a member of the retainer class of scribes, reliant on the upper classes, including the priests, for their livelihood, see Benjamin G. Wright, "'Fear the Lord and Honor the Priest': Ben Sira as Defender of the Jerusalem Priesthood," in *The Book of Ben Sira in Modern Research: Proceedings of the First International Ben Sira Conference, 28-31 July 1996, Soesterberg, Netherlands*, ed. P. C. Beentjes (BZAW 255; Berlin: de Gruyter, 1997), 189-222.

4. 4QInstruction is preserved in 1Q26; 4Q415-418, 423, and there are at least six copies. For the primary edition of the text, see John Strugnell and Daniel J. Harrington, *Qumran Cave 4.XXIV: Sapiential Texts, Part 2. 4QInstruction (Mûsār Lĕ Mēvîn): 4Q415ff. With a Re-edition of 1Q26* (DJD 34; Oxford: Clarendon Press, 1999). On a second-century B.C.E. date and the provenance for the *Epistle of Enoch*, see George W. E. Nickelsburg, *1 Enoch 1: A Commentary on the Book of 1 Enoch, Chapters 1–36; 81–108* (Hermeneia; Minneapolis: Fortress, 2001), 425-29.

5. 4QInstruction has a refrain that underscores the addressee's difficult situation: "You are poor." See 4Q415 6 2; 4Q416 2 ii 20; 4Q416 iii 2, 8, 12, 19; 4Q418 177 5. In addition, many of the topics in the text underscore the precarious circumstances of the persons being addressed (e.g., 4Q416 2 ii 9-15 and the danger of working for a difficult overseer).

6. Many instructions from this period depict a binary contrast between wealth and poverty and categorize the poor as a distinct class of persons who can be manipulated and swindled by the wealthy. Because of this dichotomy, the language of Otherness is appropriate.

This situation of Otherness led to increasingly diverse perspectives during the late Second Temple period and a movement beyond longstanding typologies for reward and punishment. The marginal locations of certain authors and audiences forced a modification of the traditional association between virtue and success.[7] Economic and social realities prohibited less privileged groups from being able to claim that "The reward for humility and fear of the Lord is riches and honor and life" (Prov. 22:4). Consequently, the idea of an "inheritance" (4Q416 2 iii 8) that includes eternal life became a compelling alternative to the longstanding earthly framework for retribution. The promise of individual immortality for the righteous offered a radical, neat application of the act-consequence understanding found in the ancient Near Eastern wisdom tradition, an otherworldly version of the *Tun-Ergehen-Zusammenhang*. The reasons for the shift to an eschatological understanding are complex and beyond the scope of the present discussion.[8] What is relevant here is that the transition to an otherworldly framework led to divergent perspectives on wealth, poverty, and Otherness.

This paper will consider where the open acknowledgment of poverty and belief in the afterlife as the "inheritance" of faithful living, found in texts like 4QInstruction, leaves the status of material wealth as a reward for "fear of the Lord." For struggling individuals, does wealth itself become anathema and an impediment to one's eschatological reward, or can the righteous elect continue to pursue earthly riches? In a text like 4QInstruction, does poverty create solidarity among marginalized persons, since they share in a more significant spiritual "inheritance"? This discussion will demonstrate a variety of responses to such questions among authors and groups during the Second Temple period, as they negotiated complex financial dynamics, apocalyptic ideas, and the assumptions of an established wisdom tradition. Certain texts, including 4QInstruction, continue to affirm wealth as a sign of favor from God, while others, such as the *Epistle of Enoch*, do not. A primary reason for the reluctance in abandoning the longstanding model is that it meant a jettisoning of one of the core assertions of the tradition: that wealth

---

7. For a classic treatment of causality in the instructions, especially Proverbs, see Klaus Koch, "Is There a Doctrine of Retribution in the Old Testament?" trans. T. H. Trapp, in *Theodicy in the Old Testament*, ed. J. L. Crenshaw (IRT 4; Philadelphia: Fortress Press, 1983), 57-87; originally published as "Gibt es ein Vergeltungsdogma im Alten Testament?" *ZTK* 52 (1955): 1-42.

8. For a study of this development in sapiential literature from this period, see Samuel L. Adams, *Wisdom in Transition: Act and Consequence in Second Temple Instructions* (JSJSup 125; Leiden: Brill, 2008).

stems from righteous living and the pursuit of wisdom (e.g., Prov. 24:3-4). Challenges to this assumption coincided with the involvement of new participants in the writing of instructions and a fluid economy. When examining the relationship between poverty and Otherness in the extant instructions from the Second Temple period, it becomes clear that various sages continued to struggle with an appropriate response to material holdings, especially the longstanding association between divine favor and material success.

I. The Perspectives of Earlier Sages

In clarifying this development within the wisdom tradition, it is helpful to examine the content of the book of Proverbs, since this anthology represents an earlier perspective on poverty and Otherness. Many sayings in this book surely date from the preexilic period, when the monarchy was a viable institution, and scribal sages like the "men of Hezekiah" (Prov. 25:1) gathered and edited proverbial clusters.[9] Despite arguments to the contrary, the final form of Proverbs was probably reached during the Persian period, especially since there is no awareness of a major reassessment of death and retribution such as one finds in Qoheleth and Ben Sira. Unlike Proverbs, these latter sages struggle mightily with death and the cessation of earthly possibilities.[10]

Even if the book of Proverbs reflects complex perspectives on financial issues, as studies in recent years have shown, a few generalizations are possible.[11] First, wealth is frequently associated with virtuous behavior (i.e., the "act-" or "character-consequence" paradigm). For example, the figure of Wisdom promises material rewards for faithful, industrious pupils: "Riches and honor are with me, enduring wealth and prosperity" (Prov. 8:18).[12] De-

---

9. The content of Proverbs 28–29 points to an actual dynamic between the ruler and his subjects. There are many sayings elsewhere in the book with an implied royal setting (e.g., 14:35; 17:7; 19:12).

10. On such a date for Proverbs and additional reasons for it, see Richard J. Clifford, *Proverbs* (OTL; Louisville: Westminster John Knox Press, 1999), 3-6; Adams, *Wisdom in Transition*, 62-68.

11. See Timothy J. Sandoval, *The Discourse of Wealth and Poverty in the Book of Proverbs* (Leiden: Brill, 2006).

12. Cf. Prov. 13:21-22; 22:4; 28:10, 25-26. This type of saying frequently equates industrious behavior with wealth and laziness with poverty: "The hand of the diligent will rule, while the lazy will be put to forced labor" (12:24).

spite such optimism, the editors of Proverbs are not naïve about mistreatment of the poor or the possibility of the wicked prospering (e.g., 14:20; 18:23; 22:7; 28:12).[13] Moreover, these sages express concern for the plight of the oppressed, especially in the section that is reliant on the Egyptian *Instruction of Amenemope*. For those who are trampled upon, "the Lord pleads their cause" (22:23; cf. 17:5). Moreover, as proponents of the "folk" hypothesis have shown, many sayings in the book cannot be categorized as royal or elitist.[14] For example, "Better is a dry morsel with quiet than a house full of feasting with strife" (17:1). The book of Proverbs also conveys the superiority of wisdom over wealth: "Happy are those who find wisdom, and those who get understanding, for her income is better than silver, and her revenue is better than gold" (3:13-14; cf. 15:16).

Yet there is no idealization of poverty among the scribal sages who compiled this collection, but more of an outsider's observation of its effects. Penury is an unfortunate state, which in many instances is cited as the result of slothfulness (e.g., 6:10-11). According to these sages, to be "poor" is to be "other," and to be "other" is to be lonely. In this respect, Proverbs does little to acknowledge communal solidarity among the lower classes.[15] For example, "Wealth brings many friends, but the poor are left friendless" (19:4). Moreover, these sayings do not offer immortality as consolation for difficult circumstances, and in fact there is no indication of a belief in the afterlife.[16] "Fear of the Lord" may bring present treasures and contentment, including a good name, but the sages responsible for Proverbs do not fret over the fact that their belief system has all persons proceeding to the same fate, thereby forfeiting all of their material holdings.

The book of Ecclesiastes/Qoheleth, which is dated to the Ptolemaic period by most commentators, also addresses the power of material wealth, the repercussions of inequality and corruption, and the loneliness of poverty.[17]

---

13. See R. N. Whybray, *Wealth and Poverty in the Book of Proverbs* (JSOTSup 99; Sheffield: JSOT Press, 1990).

14. For an endorsement of a non-elite setting for Proverbs, see Friedemann W. Golka, *The Leopard's Spots: Biblical and African Wisdom in Proverbs* (Edinburgh: T&T Clark, 1993).

15. See J. David Pleins, *The Social Visions of the Hebrew Bible: A Theological Introduction* (Louisville: Westminster John Knox, 2001), 467-70. He contrasts the wisdom literature and the prophets on this point.

16. No statement in Proverbs offers hope for individual immortality. See Bruce Vawter, "Intimations of Immortality and the Old Testament," *JBL* 91 (1972): 158-71; Adams, *Wisdom in Transition*, 93-96.

17. On a date for Qoheleth during the third century, see James L. Crenshaw, *Ecclesiastes* (OTL; Philadelphia: Westminster Press, 1987), 49-50.

Regarding the advantages of riches, Qoheleth cites the following saying in chapter 10: "Feasts are made for laughter; wine gladdens life, and money meets every need" (v. 19). By including such proverbs, this sage affirms Israel's wisdom tradition through the assertion that wealth and the ability to enjoy it are a gift from God. At the same time, Qoheleth alludes to the unsavory practices that can occur in the pursuit of plenty. For example, he seems to cite a network of corruption under the Ptolemies: "If you see in a province the oppression of the poor and the violation of justice and right, do not be amazed at the matter; for the high official is watched by a higher, and there are yet higher ones over them" (5:8).[18] In addition, Qoheleth shares with the book of Proverbs a belief in the unenviable situation of Otherness among the impoverished. Their difficulty in becoming respected members of society is clearly illustrated in chapter 9, which describes a poor man's deliverance of a city through his sage counsel. The act is quickly forgotten: "Wisdom is better than might; yet the poor man's wisdom is despised, and his words are not heeded" (9:16). In his incisive commentary throughout this work, Qoheleth provides a dramatic characterization of isolation and hardship for the less fortunate (e.g., 4:1-3) and a marked frustration that all earthly gains are lost when a person descends to Sheol (e.g., 2:18-21).[19]

Similarly, Ben Sira acknowledges the Otherness of poverty and speaks out against dishonesty in the marketplace. This figure, writing in the early second century B.C.E., tries to maintain at several points that the insights of the commoner will be heard: e.g., "The poor are honored for their knowledge, while the rich are honored for their wealth" (10:30). Yet his hard-nosed assessments throughout the instruction seem to reflect life on the ground in Judea, as Ben Sira describes the ruthless arena in which commercial transactions take place and his ambivalence about such activities.[20] Since he is a member of the retainer class, as Wright and others have argued, Ben Sira does not reprimand the elite directly. Because of his reliance on the privileged classes for income and support, his sayings reflect a delicate balancing

---

18. Thomas Krüger, *Qoheleth*, trans. O. C. Dean (Hermeneia; Minneapolis: Fortress, 2004), 113-14, posits a specifically Ptolemaic background for these verses. For the understanding of גבה ("high official") as a "payment taker" in Qoh. 5:7, see James Kugel, "Qohelet and Money," *CBQ* 51 (1989): 36-38.

19. Shannon Burkes, *Death in Qoheleth and Egyptian Biographies of the Late Period* (SBLDS 170; Atlanta: Society of Biblical Literature, 1999), explicates the centrality of death in Qoheleth's writings.

20. A representative statement can be found in 27:2: "As a stake is driven firmly into a fissure between stones, so sin is wedged in between selling and buying."

act. Even as he implores his audience to practice almsgiving, avoid corruption, and lend to a neighbor, the sage does not vilify actual assets.[21] The reason for such reticence is not just pragmatism, since Ben Sira considers financial gains to be a divine gift and an attainable goal for his young charges. He declares that "Riches are good if they are free from sin" (13:24). Based on his discourses throughout the book, however, he considers the combination of wealth and "fear of the Lord" to be a very remote possibility.[22] Nevertheless, Ben Sira encourages his students to soak up the pleasures that their resources allow them, since death eventually overtakes every person. Like Qoheleth, this sage places no hope in a beatific afterlife: "Give, and take, and indulge yourself, because in Hades one cannot look for luxury" (14:16).

In all of these instructional texts, we find significant continuities that have bearing on our discussion of poverty and Otherness: the belief in wealth as a reward for Wisdom; a *carpe diem* mentality, especially since there is no hope for individual immortality; a distaste for blatant corruption and mistreatment of the poor; much advice directed towards scribal retainers and more affluent members of the society; and the remarkably consistent conclusion that poverty is a desolate, unenviable state. Perhaps the most pointed description of Otherness in this regard is Ben Sira's understanding of the life of a beggar: "When one looks to the table of another, one's way of life cannot be considered a life" (Sir. 40:29).

II. The Change with 4QInstruction

Such assumptions were reassessed by the authors of 4QInstruction, the *Epistle of Enoch*, and other figures from this period, as individuals and groups with more modest backgrounds offered their own maxims. In the available fragments of 4QInstruction, the "pupil" in this text (the מבין/*mēvîn*) is repeatedly reminded of his financial challenges and presented with situations that differ markedly from those envisioned in Proverbs and Ben Sira. An illustrative example appears in 4Q417 2 i 17-19: "And you, when you lack food, [br]ing your lack and your surplus [together; wh]en you have surplus, bring (it) to his place of business, and take your portion from him, and do not take

---

21. For Ben Sira's treatment of almsgiving, corruption, and the need for generosity, see Wright and Camp, "'Who Has Been Tested by Gold and Found Perfect?'" 155-61.

22. See 31:8-9: "Blessed is the rich person who is found blameless, and who does not go after gold. Who is he, that we may praise him? For he has done wonders among his people."

any mor[e.]²³ Rather than observing the impact of poverty, such advice is directed to those experiencing it. Contrary to certain arguments about these statements, the financial terminology in 4QInstruction generally refers to present material difficulties for the recipients of this advice rather than to some sort of spiritual lack. The "you are poor" refrain seems to reflect actual circumstances and not "metaphorical" poverty.²⁴ In support of this interpretation, references in the extant fragments depict the specific situations of farmers, low-wage artisans, and poor families facing the risk of debt-slavery.²⁵ Certain passages indicate a level of self-sufficiency among some of the recipients of this advice (e.g., 4Q416 2 iii 3 and the placement of a deposit/loan with the addressee), but such persons need to live prudently so that destitution does not strike them and their families.²⁶ Several statements in 4QInstruction suggest that indentured servitude is a distinct possibility for these individuals.²⁷

In facing this chronic situation of "barely getting by," the audience for 4QInstruction is encouraged to take solace in their mutual solidarity as members of an elect class, especially their access to the secrets of the universe

---

23. On the proper translation for these lines, see Eibert J. C. Tigchelaar, "הבא ביחד in 4QInstruction (4Q418 64 + 199 + 66 par 4Q417 1 i 17-19) and the Height of the Columns of 4Q418," *RevQ* 18 (1998): 589-93. This advice refers to prudent business transactions and not to the יחד of the rulebooks. For the translation of מחוז חפצו as "his place of business," see Matthew J. Goff, *Discerning Wisdom: The Sapiential Literature of the Dead Sea Scrolls* (VTSup 116; Leiden: Brill, 2007), 55, n. 84. The context is the buying and selling of goods with another individual. Unless otherwise noted, subsequent translations of 4QInstruction are from the *DSSSE*.

24. Benjamin G. Wold ("Metaphorical Poverty in '*Musar leMevin*,'" *JJS* 58 [2007]: 140-53) views much of the poverty language in this text to be symbolic and related to the inferiority of human beings vis-à-vis the angels. In contrast, Benjamin G. Wright III ("The Categories of Rich and Poor in the Qumran Sapiential Literature," in *Sapiential Perspectives: Wisdom Literature in Light of the Dead Sea Scrolls, Proceedings of the Sixth International Symposium of the Orion Center for the Study of the Dead Sea Scrolls and Associated Literature, 20-22 May, 2001*, ed. J. J. Collins et al. [STDJ 51; Leiden: Brill, 2004], 112) claims that the references to the addressee's poverty should for the most part be taken as real descriptions. The latter position is more persuasive: even if some of the economic vocabulary is symbolic (e.g., "an inheritance of glory" [ובנחלת כבוד] in 4Q416 2 iii 11-12), this does not negate the references to actual financial struggles throughout the text.

25. For example, see 4Q416 2 ii 4-6 and the advice about borrowing and lending.

26. For historical background on this issue of debt-slavery, see David A. Fiensy, *The Social History of Palestine in the Herodian Period: The Land Is Mine* (Lewiston, N.Y.: Edwin Mellen, 1991).

27. See, e.g., 4Q416 2 ii 17.

and their eternal "inheritance." Even if circumstances are precarious, these individuals are to commit to upright, sensible behavior: "Honor your father in your poverty (ריש), and your mother in your steps" (4Q416 2 iii 15-16). If they develop the correct behavioral patterns, including proper management of financial resources, *and* reflect on heavenly matters, 4QInstruction promises "eternal joy" (4Q417 2 i 12) for its audience. For the righteous category, God will act "to lift up the head of the poor ones [. . .] with eternal glory and everlasting peace" (4Q418 126 ii 7-8). It is noteworthy that the elect group is designated as "poor ones" (דלים) in this fragment and contrasted with the "wicked."[28] These individuals who are favored by God, also referred to as the "spiritual people" (4Q417 1 i 13-18) in 4QInstruction, are supposed to reflect on the רז נהיה/*raz nihyeh* concept (usually translated as "mystery that is to be") that lies at the heart of the didactic process in this text.[29] Through their access to the *raz nihyeh* and upright conduct, such persons can expect eschatological reward. As many commentators have argued, perhaps the most noteworthy feature of 4QInstruction is the combination of mundane advice with apocalyptic eschatology.

One of the more interesting features of the advice in 4QInstruction is that even with this apocalyptic background, mystery concept, and the use of economic terms such as נחלה to describe eternal rewards, the pursuit of profit is never discouraged, and poverty is not lifted up as a desirable state. Although the daily situation of the addressee might be burdensome, money is not an object of scorn in 4QInstruction. In fact, the author of this text encourages the enjoyment of one's resources. One of the most important examples of this perspective can be found in a statement on the possibility of sudden financial gain: "If he (the subject here is most likely "God") restores you in glory, walk in it" (4Q416 2 iii 9).[30] In another fragment, the text warns, "Do not take pride in your want when you are poor, lest you despise your life" (4Q416 2 ii 20-21). In these and related examples from 4QInstruction, poverty is not an ideal, not something about which a person should boast.

---

28. 4Q418 126 ii 7: "to lock up (ולסגור) wicked ones." Cf. 1QH 11:18.

29. For a thorough treatment of scholarly discussion on the *raz nihyeh*, see Matthew J. Goff, *The Worldly and Heavenly Wisdom of 4QInstruction* (STDJ 50; Leiden: Brill, 2003), 51-79; idem, *Discerning Wisdom*, 13-17.

30. Wright, "The Categories of Rich and Poor," 115, argues that the subject of the singular verb ישיבכה is God, despite the use of the plural form (יושיבוכה) in the overlap in 4Q418 9 7. If this reading is correct, the statement would be underscoring the belief that all things are possible with God, rather than suggesting that a sudden windfall is likely for the addressees of 4QInstruction.

Significantly, this text warns against assuming an intrinsic connection between poverty and election: "You are poor, (but) do not say, 'I am poor and (therefore) I canno[t] seek knowledge.' Bring your shoulder under all discipline" (4Q416 2 iii 12-13, translation mine). Moderation is mentioned in several admonitions (4Q416 2 ii 18-20), as is the pooling of resources when a person comes into difficult straits. Yet the marginal status of the audience for 4QInstruction does not lead to a glorification of penury *or* a polemic against the upper classes. In this respect, 4QInstruction is consistent with most ancient Near Eastern instructions.

In contrast, the *Epistle of Enoch* makes frequent, strident statements about financial inequality and the fact that the rich do not acknowledge the responsibility that comes with their considerable holdings. The *Epistle* elevates the poor, called the "pious ones" in this text, as the recipients of a unique eschatological gift. A series of woe statements offers a clear contrast, in language that is evocative of Amos and some of the other prophets: "Woe to you, rich, for in your riches you have trusted; and from your riches you will depart, because you have not remembered the Most High in the day of your riches" (*1 Enoch* 94:8).[31] Unlike 4QInstruction, this section of the Enochic corpus portrays a polemical separation between social classes and guarantees punishment for the wicked, who are specifically identified as wealthy. In an address to the "pious ones," the speaker declares, "Take courage, then; for formerly you were worn out by evils and tribulations, but now you will shine like the luminaries of heaven; you will shine and appear, and the portals of heaven will be opened for you" (*1 Enoch* 104:2). The *Epistle* offers a promised reversal here, guaranteeing ultimate deliverance for those faithful persons who have suffered economic oppression during their earthly existence. We find a similar assessment of poverty in certain gospel passages from the New Testament, particularly the Sermon on the Plain in Luke (6:17-49) and the parable of the rich and foolish farmer (Luke 12:13-21).[32]

The question then becomes why 4QInstruction does not denigrate the accumulation of earthly treasures in the manner of a text like the *Epistle of Enoch*. 4QInstruction does raise the specter of torment in Sheol for the unfaithful (referred to as the "fleshly spirit"), but it does not specifically

---

31. This paper follows the translation of George W. E. Nickelsburg and James C. VanderKam, *1 Enoch: A New Translation* (Minneapolis: Fortress, 2004).

32. For further discussion on the relationship between these two texts on financial matters, see George W. E. Nickelsburg, "Revisiting the Rich and Poor in 1 Enoch 92–105 and the Gospel according to Luke," *The Society of Biblical Literature 1998 Seminar Papers*, 2 vols. (SBLSP 37; Atlanta: Scholars Press, 1998), 2:579-605.

threaten punishment *on the basis of financial holdings*. Although the addressee has an "inheritance of glory" awaiting him (4Q416 2 iii 11-12), he can pursue his livelihood in the marketplace, trying to eke out a living and perhaps enjoy moderate success. In accounting for this feature of the text, Matthew Goff makes the following assertion: "The depiction of the addressee's elect status as a type of wealth explains why 4QInstruction exhibits none of the hatred of the rich that is characteristic of the *Epistle of Enoch*." According to Goff, the elect status of the audience in 4QInstruction does not "highlight class tension but mitigates it."[33] Similarly, Catherine Murphy notes that the pupil of this text is told to meditate on the elliptical *raz nihyeh* that lies at the heart of 4QInstruction, and he is promised immortality in exchange for his faithful contemplation of the mystery. Murphy claims that such a framework for learning "may also explain why there is no critique of sudden riches *per se* in Instruction...."[34]

Both of these statements are valid, and it is beyond dispute that the author of 4QInstruction offers comfort to the individuals receiving this advice by highlighting their elect status. Future reward provides consolation and fortitude for precarious circumstances in the present. One important fragment in this regard is 4Q417 2 i 10-11, where the addressee is told to "[Gaze upon the mystery] that is to be, and grasp the birth-times of salvation, and know who will inherit glory and who ini[qu]ity."[35] Another key passage is 4Q416 2 iii 7-8, where the author warns against embezzling money given by a stranger. If the advice is followed, "Then you may lie down with the truth, and when you die your memory will blos[som for ev]er, ואחריתכה will inherit joy." John Collins has argued that ואחריתכה should be read as "your hereafter," so that the text connects prudence in financial decisions with the promise of eternal life.[36] In the passage about shutting the door on the wicked and raising the head of the poor, "in glory everlasting and peace eternal" (4Q417 1 i 7-8), the designation of the elect group as "poor ones" (דלים) and the fact that they are juxtaposed with the wicked (רשעים) demonstrate

---

33. Goff, *Worldly and Heavenly Wisdom*, 151.

34. Catherine M. Murphy, *Wealth in the Dead Sea Scrolls and in the Qumran Community* (STDJ 40; Leiden: Brill, 2002), 191.

35. On the best translation for these lines, see Goff, *Worldly and Heavenly Wisdom*, 60, n. 112.

36. John J. Collins, "The Mysteries of God: Creation and Eschatology in 4QInstruction and the Wisdom of Solomon," in *Wisdom and Apocalypticism in the Dead Sea Scrolls and in the Biblical Tradition*, ed. F. García Martínez (BETL 168; Leuven: Leuven University Press/Peeters, 2003), 294.

that the addressees should take solace in their eschatological reward, especially since they do not enjoy the privileges of the elite classes. In a sense, the extension of this hopeful promise is the *raison d'être* of 4QInstruction.

Yet this factor alone does not fully explain why the author of 4QInstruction is reticent about highlighting his listeners' situation of Otherness as a means of speaking out against social inequality and casting wealthier citizens as likely candidates for the depths of Sheol. There must be additional reasons for the disparity on this point between 4QInstruction and a text like the *Epistle of Enoch*. I would suggest several additional factors at work in the more cautious approach.

As a Wisdom text, even if one written by non-elite persons, 4QInstruction still holds wealth to be a gift from God, for whom all things are possible. Although sapiential figures like Ben Sira speak out against social injustices during the Second Temple period, they also affirm the status quo. The author of 4QInstruction does not serve the retainer classes, but he does tilt towards standard sapiential caution in assuming that wealth is a sign of divine favor, and one should live properly within the social structure. Several statements affirm the longstanding assumption of the wisdom tradition that all things, including food and wealth, derive from God. For example, 4Q417 2 i 19-20: "for the storehouse [of God] has no lack, [and on] his command everything will be." Such an affirmation is one of the primary reasons we do not find class warfare in this text. Even as it depicts an otherworldly framework for retribution, 4QInstruction does not dispense with God's capacity to offer present blessings, however remote such an occurrence might be for some of the recipients of this advice.

Another factor is simply variation among different authors. Just as Qoheleth and Ben Sira respond to the debates of their day with divergent conclusions, one should not homogenize the sapiential perspectives at the margins of society. Collins has aptly described works like the *Epistle of Enoch* and 4QInstruction as an "exercise in bricolage, piecing together a new view of the world that drew motifs and ideas from many sources."[37] Within such a framework, conclusions on poverty and Otherness would naturally vary. During this fluid period in which the Enochic traditions were gaining notoriety and more marginal voices like the one responsible for 4QInstruction were beginning to engage in sapiential discourse, it is logical to assume a multiplicity of perspectives.

---

37. John J. Collins, "The Eschatologizing of Wisdom in the Dead Sea Scrolls," in *Sapiential Perspectives*, 63.

This issue of course raises the questions of provenance, date, and authorship. Such questions are notoriously difficult to assess for a sapiential text like 4QInstruction, largely because it is so fragmentary and devoid of historical markers. Most commentators understand the more open society depicted in this text to preclude identification with the undisputed sectarian literature of the Dead Sea Scrolls corpus. 4QInstruction does not presume common ownership of property, refers to the *raz nihyeh* and not the Torah as the primary source of authority (contrast 1QS 5:8), and never mentions the Teacher of Righteousness. The extant fragments are in Herodian script, but they seem to preserve an earlier document. While many scholars place this text prior to the Maccabean Revolt, 4QInstruction could just as easily date from the latter portion of the second century B.C.E., as the Enochic texts and Daniel were continuing to develop and gain popularity. The author(s) of 4QInstruction is a scribe of some sort, but he does not seem to be writing for a tightly configured sect, and he does not draw attention to his own personality. These admonitions and longer discourses presume a variety of individuals as the recipients of this advice, and the extant fragments suggest that the author, editors, and the addressees were familiar with the changing economic and social landscape of second-century Judea.[38] This author, a marginal scribe, advises a group of individuals who do not have the same opportunities as the "son" in Proverbs or the scribal retainers in Ben Sira. Their daily experiences are far from the corridors of power.

As previously mentioned, meditation on the "mystery that is to be" remains the key to enlightened existence for such an audience, and in the final analysis, financial holdings are of little consequence. One should live properly in the world and maintain the necessary comportment, and extravagance is specifically condemned. What ultimately matters, however, is the addressee's focus on the esoteric "mystery" and his ability to distinguish himself from the "fleshly spirit" before the final judgment. The available fragments of 4QInstruction evince no concern for the poor as a class of people; the text offers solace for the current situation of the elect, but neediness itself does not affect one's salvation.

Finally, the economic situation addressed in 4QInstruction is varied, and the author probably had to be careful about vilifying those enjoying modest financial success. In certain fragments, the advice is pragmatic and

---

38. For helpful background, see Jack Pastor, *Land and Economy in Ancient Palestine* (London: Routledge, 1997); Seth Schwartz, *Imperialism and Jewish Society, 200 B.C.E. to 640 C.E.* (Princeton: Princeton University Press, 2001).

could just as easily be found in the book of Proverbs. For example, "Be an advocate for your own business interests" (4Q417 2 i 12, translation mine). 4QInstruction presumes a diversity of occupations, with no common control over the purse strings. Some of the individuals mentioned in this text, especially those involved in agricultural production, undoubtedly had favorable seasons and periods of trading, which would have provided a certain degree of prosperity (e.g., 418 103 ii 3, and the reference to a harvest). 4QInstruction allows such an individual to support his family and trade for other goods. These individuals are warned to look out for oppressive creditors and avoid the practice of surety, but there is no indication that minor or even major financial gains are an impediment to favorable status with God or future rewards.[39] An explicit polemic against financial gain is simply not part of the agenda in this text.

III. Conclusions

One of the hallmarks of texts like 4QInstruction is that they combine the cautious ethic of earlier wisdom with a belief in otherworldly retribution. J. Z. Smith defines apocalypticism as *"wisdom lacking a royal patron,"* and this certainly fits the perspective found in this text.[40] If Proverbs and Ben Sira affirm the possibility of present justice and prosperity among righteous disciples, including a potential windfall, the author of 4QInstruction and his audience have a different socioeconomic background and therefore require another framework for retribution. The promise of eschatological reward allowed such individuals to cope with more desperate circumstances than their counterparts with more abundant resources.

Yet one of the more interesting features of 4QInstruction is that it does not endorse poverty as a preferential state. Like the wisdom tradition of which it is a part, this text squarely acknowledges financial hardship as burdensome and undesirable. In one of the better known fragments, the following question is posed: "For what is more trivial than a poor man?" (4Q417 2 i 10). Even though subsequent statements in this fragment provide comfort for the addressees by discussing the *raz nihyeh* and the eschatological reward of the elect group, this text does not endorse the Otherness of poverty as a

---

39. On the issue of surety and how it is addressed in 4QInstruction, see Goff, *Worldly and Heavenly Wisdom*, 140-45.

40. J. Z. Smith, *Map Is Not Territory* (Chicago: University of Chicago Press, 1978), 81.

necessary path to salvation. The addressee's "inheritance of glory" does not mean that he should reject industrious behavior as a means of achieving earthly success and security for his offspring. 4QInstruction certainly demonstrates a reassessment of core assumptions within the wisdom tradition, but it also shows that sapiential views about wealth, poverty, and the reward for virtue continued to be as complex as ever.

Transcending Death: The Reasoning of the "Others" and Afterlife Hopes in Wisdom 1–6

Daniel J. Harrington, S.J.

I have known John Collins for over forty years and have marveled at his many excellent books and articles on Second Temple Judaism and at the remarkable positive influence he has had on younger scholars in our field. His very early essay on apocalyptic eschatology as transcendence of death has particularly interested me since its publication in 1974.[1] In that article he defined the distinctive character of apocalyptic eschatology as hope for the transcendence of death. He argued that in apocalyptic eschatology present experience and future hope are intrinsically connected and mutually interdependent. In this view fear of ultimate loss in death is countered by hope for a form of life that transcends death. And this hope in turn gives the freedom needed to respond properly to the demands of wisdom and righteousness in the present.

In this essay honoring John Collins on his sixty-fifth birthday, I want to apply and develop the thesis of his early article with reference to the first part of the book of Wisdom (chaps. 1–6). Written in Alexandria in the first century B.C.E., the Wisdom of Solomon (as it is also known) combines biblical concepts and motifs with Greek philosophical ideas, and so it marks an early stage in what is called Hellenistic Judaism.[2] By its presence in the Catholic and Orthodox Christian Bibles, it has been a major factor in the great intel-

---

1. John J. Collins, "Apocalyptic Eschatology as the Transcendence of Death," *CBQ* 36 (1974): 21-43.

2. For general treatments of the book of Wisdom, see Collins, *Jewish Wisdom in the Hellenistic Age* (Louisville: Westminster John Knox, 1997), 178-95; and Daniel J. Harrington, *Invitation to the Apocrypha* (Grand Rapids: Eerdmans, 1999), 55-77.

lectual project of integrating the Bible and Greek philosophical ideas that has been at the heart of Christian theology throughout the centuries.

Here I want first to focus on the "reasoning" of the "Others" in Wisdom 2, and to place it in the context of the author's argument in Wisdom 1–6. Then I want to explore how this section of the book of Wisdom joins Greek notions of immortality and Jewish eschatology so as to produce a hope for transcending death and how it serves as a bridge between the two Testaments in the Christian Bible. I am especially proud to note that the very first time (in the fall of 1970) I ever taught a class on the book of Wisdom, John Collins was present as a student.

I. The Reasoning of the Others in Wisdom 1:16–2:24

According to the author of Wisdom, the "reasoning" (see 2:1a, 21) of the Others goes something like this: Since physical death is the absolute end of human existence, true happiness consists in enjoying oneself in the present. Moreover, this pursuit of personal happiness might involve oppressing the weak and useless, and doing violence to the "righteous," who prove to be an annoyance and inconvenience in the pursuit of pleasure.

Efforts at specifying the identity of these Others with a particular ancient philosophy such as Epicureanism or with the biblical book of Qoheleth/Ecclesiastes have never been entirely successful.[3] Given the historical context of the book of Wisdom in first-century B.C.E. Alexandria, the Others may have been real or potential apostates from the local Jewish community who were being seduced by various philosophical currents in the wider cultural discourse of that great cosmopolitan center in the ancient world. However, it is possible to find in their statements the positions of materialist and secularists in many different ages. Indeed, the fact that such views are increasingly well represented in our own "secular age" makes this text especially relevant in the current philosophical and religious context.[4]

The Author's Preface (1:16–2:1a). In the brief introduction to the discourse of the Others, the author characterizes them as "ungodly" *(asebeis)* and accuses them of reasoning "unsoundly." Their fundamental mistake, as we will see, concerns their understanding of death. They think only in terms of physical death and regard it as the absolute end of human existence. They

---

3. David Winston, *The Wisdom of Solomon* (AB 43; New York: Doubleday, 1979), 114. Winston's commentary provides a full catalogue of ancient parallels to the book of Wisdom.
4. Charles Taylor, *A Secular Age* (Cambridge, Mass.: Belknap Press, 2007).

reject the concept of life after death and fail to recognize the possibility of eternal life with God for the wise and righteous and of ultimate death for the foolish and godless.

The author accuses the Others of regarding death as their "friend" and even of making a "covenant" with death. They fail to recognize what Michael Kolarcik has described as "the ambiguity of death."[5] That is, they do not understand that besides the physical death that is natural and common to all humans, there is also an ultimate death — a death after death or a "second death" that awaits persons like themselves, as well as an eternal life "in the hand of God" that is the appropriate reward for those who have loved righteousness, sought God, and lived wisely. The author's short commentary that prefaces his version of the discourse of the Others is already a negative assessment of their reasoning and is meant to influence how we read their words.

The Covenant with Death (2:1a-5). The philosophical assumption of the Others' viewpoint is that physical death is the absolute end of human life.[6]

> 1For they reasoned unsoundly, saying to themselves,
> Short and sorrowful is our life,
> and there is no remedy when a life comes to its end,
> and no one has been known to return from Hades.
> 2For we were born by mere chance,
> and hereafter we shall be as though we had never been,
> for the breath in our nostrils is smoke,
> and reason is a spark kindled by the beating of our hearts;
> 3when it is extinguished, the body will turn to ashes,
> and the spirit will dissolve like empty air.
> 4Our name will be forgotten in time,
> and no one will remember our works;
> our life will pass away like the traces of a cloud,
> and be scattered like mist
> that is chased by the rays of the sun
> and overcome by its heat.
> 5For our allotted time is the passing of a shadow,
> and there is no return from our death,
> because it is sealed up and no one turns back.

---

5. Michael Kolarcik, *The Ambiguity of Death in the Book of Wisdom: A Study of Literary Structure and Interpretation* (AnBib 127; Rome Editrice Pontificio Istituto Biblico, 1991).

6. All biblical quotations are from the New Revised Standard Version.

Their basic position is stated in 2:1a and restated in 2:5: Death is the end, and no one returns from death. Birth is only by chance, and after death it is "as though we had never been" (2:2). The OT idea that there is immortality through one's "name" — whether through physical offspring or a good reputation — is dismissed as an illusion. In making the case for the Others' position about the absolute character of death, the author piles up many images pointing to the transitory character of human existence: smoke, spark, ashes, empty air, cloud, mist, rays of the sun, and passing shadow. The descriptions of the breath of life as "smoke" and of reason as "a spark kindled by the beating of our hearts" in 2:2 represent a thoroughgoing materialist conception of human life. The absolute significance given to death in the worldview of the Others justifies the author's introductory comment that they have in effect "made a covenant" with death (much as ancient Israel made a covenant with YHWH) and thus have assigned a kind of divine status to death insofar as it shapes everything they think and do.

The Search for Pleasure (2:6-9). Those Others who have made a covenant with death constitute a kind of a community, and so the rest of their discourse is marked with many Greek verbs in the hortatory subjective ("Let us . . ."). This section is a call to pleasure-seeking or hedonism on the part of the Others:

> 6Come, therefore, let us enjoy the good things that exist,
> and make use of the creation to the full as in youth.
> 7Let us take our fill of costly wine and perfumes,
> and let no flower of spring pass us by.
> 8Let us crown ourselves with rosebuds before they wither.
> 9Let none of us fail to share in our revelry;
> everywhere let us leave signs of enjoyment,
> because this is our portion, and this our lot.

The call to enjoy the good things of life in 2:6 can be found elsewhere in the Hebrew Bible from Genesis 1 ("and God saw that it was good") to Ecclesiastes 11:9 ("Follow the inclination of your heart and the desire of your eyes"). This is not in itself worthy of condemnation. But the context presupposed in 2:1-5 and the development in what follows in 2:7-9 turn what may have been innocent and praiseworthy in other circumstances into something pernicious. The images of costly wine, perfumes, and crowns of rosebuds attest to both materialist extravagance and the fleeting character of the pleasures that such things bring. These extravagances are characterized correctly as "signs of enjoyment," or to use a modern sociological term "conspicuous consumption." In the author's view, they cannot bring true happiness because they concern only appearances rather than realities.

Permission to Commit Injustice (2:10-11). While there are parallels to Epicureanism and to the book of Ecclesiastes/Qoheleth in the first two parts of the Others' discourse, the third section, which assumes the right of the Others to oppress the most vulnerable in society, probably belongs more to the realm of history than philosophy:

> 10Let us oppress the righteous poor man;
> let us not spare the widow
> or regard the grey hairs of the aged.
> 11But let our might be our law of right,
> for what is weak proves itself to be useless.

In the OT world the poor, the widows, and the aged were regarded as among the most defenseless members of society. And so they are the objects of special concern in the social legislation of the Torah and the discourses of the Prophets. The truly wise and righteous man was expected to be the benefactor of such persons, as Job's remembrance of his past benefaction so eloquently shows (see Job 29). The author here accuses the Others not only of disregarding the needs of these persons but also of actively oppressing and harming them on the ground that "might makes right" with respect to those who are "weak" and "useless." The transition from the covenant of death and the pursuit of pleasure to such active injustice is not inevitable. Whether the author had in mind some concrete historical evidence for this development, or merely assumed it to be true as a convenient part of his polemic against materialism and the culture of death, is not clear. What is clear is that the annoyance caused by the weak and useless in society becomes personalized in the "righteous man" in the remainder of the Others' discourse.

The Scandal of the Righteous Man (2:12-20). In the Bible a *skandalon* is first and foremost an obstacle or stumbling block that interrupts an otherwise smooth journey. In the final section of their discourse, the Others find their chief "scandal" to be the anonymous figure called "the righteous man." The language of their complaint is expressed with the repeated use of "we/us" and "he/him" terminology that contributes to the sense of their hostility toward him. Some of the words and phrases are reminiscent of the Suffering Servant passage in Isaiah 53. But while the sufferings of the Servant in Isaiah 53 have an expiatory or atoning value for others, what is emphasized in Wisdom 2 is the good example of the righteous person that has a maddening effect on the Others.

> 12Let us lie in wait for the righteous man,
> because he is inconvenient to us and opposes our actions;
> he reproaches us for sins against the law,
> and accuses us of sins against our training.
> 13He professes to have knowledge of God,
> and calls himself a child of the Lord.
> 14He became to us a reproof of our thoughts;
> 15the very sight of him is a burden to us,
> because his manner of life is unlike that of others,
> and his ways are strange.
> 16We are considered by him as something base,
> and he avoids our ways as unclean;
> he calls the last end of the righteous happy,
> and boasts that God is his father.

The charge that the righteous one reproaches the Others for their "sins against the law" (2:12) suggests that the Others are or were Jews, either loosely observant or perhaps even apostates. His claim to be a "child" or "servant" (the Greek word *pais* can be translated either way) of God in 2:13 is echoed by mention of his boast that "God is his father" in 2:16. The Others find his way of life to be different from theirs, and thus a rebuke and an offense against them personally. What really sets him apart from them is his conviction about life after death: "he calls the last end of the righteous happy" (2:16; see also 2:20). The implication is that his beliefs about life after death, divine judgment, and rewards and punishments shape his conduct in the present and distinguish him from the Others in word and deed.

According to 2:17-20, the plan of the Others is to test the righteous one by having him condemned to death. Their assumption is that his convictions about life after death will fall away under pressure, and that he will be exposed as like themselves in recognizing that physical death is the absolute end of life.

> 17Let us see if his words are true,
> and let us test what will happen at the end of his life;
> 18for if the righteous man is God's child, he will help him,
> and will deliver him from the hand of his adversaries.

> 19Let us test him with insult and torture,
> so that we may find out how gentle he is,
> and make trial of his forbearance.
> 20Let us condemn him to a shameful death,
> for, according to what he says, he will be protected.

The Others' reference to the righteous one as "God's child" (or, "servant") as well as their apparently mocking statements about God helping and protecting him in 2:18 and 20 find parallels in the NT accounts about the crucifixion of Jesus (see Mark 15:27-32 par.). It is not clear whether we are to assume that the Others ever get to carry out their plan, or we are to regard it only as a fantasy illustrating their foolish reasoning.

The Author's Concluding Comment (2:21-24). From the author's closing observations, we are to understand that the Others have failed to grasp "the secret purposes of God," which include eternal life with God as the reward for wise and righteous behavior ("the wages of holiness . . . the prize for blameless souls," 2:22). The Others understand death only in material or physical terms. But since God made humankind in his own image and likeness (see Gen. 1:27), and since God is eternal, so according to the author's reasoning God must also have "created us for incorruption" (2:23). The author attributes the reality of physical death not to God but rather to the devil's "envy" (presumably at humankind's immortality) and his success in enticing Adam and Eve to disobey God's command about eating from the tree in the garden (see Gen. 3:1-24). This confirms what the author stated previously in 1:13: "God did not make death, and he does not delight in the death of the living." What the Others fail to see is that there is a difference between physical death and ultimate death, and between temporary human existence on earth and eternal life in the hand of God.[7]

II. The Reasoning of the Author in Wisdom 1:1–6:21

The author of the book of Wisdom clearly regards the "reasoning" of the Others to be fallacious, and he includes it only to refute it. To do so, he places it in the context of his own "logical" argument in chapters 1–6.

The three main parts of the book of Wisdom concern righteousness and immortality (chaps. 1–6), the nature of wisdom (chaps. 7–9), and wisdom's role in the early history of Israel (chaps. 10–19). The language and

---

7. Kolarcik, *The Ambiguity of Death*, 76-81.

Transcending Death

style of the book indicate that all three parts were written by the same author, though not necessarily at the same time. They may well have originated as separate lectures or essays. Nevertheless, the three parts are now linked together so that it is possible to take chapter 6 as the end of Part 1 or the beginning of Part 2, and chapter 10 as the end of Part 2 or the beginning of Part 3. The third part consists of seven comparisons designed to show that in the exodus God used the same elements to help the Israelites and to harm the Egyptians. Between the first and the second comparisons there are excursuses on God's justice and mercy (11:15–12:27) and on the folly of idolatry (13–15).[8]

Various outlines have been proposed for the reasoning contained in Wisdom 1–6. One that is both complex and simple is the concentric outline developed by Michael Kolarcik.[9] It is complex in that it takes account of the roles of keywords, inclusions, links, and other rhetorical devices. It is simple in that it lays bare the author's reasoning. There is first an exhortation to seek justice in the Lord (1:1-15). Next comes the discourse of the impious Others treated above (1:16–2:24). Then at center there are four comparisons between the just and the wicked (3:1–4:20). Next the wicked Others recant their first speech (5:1-23). Finally there is another exhortation, this time to seek wisdom in the Lord (6:1-21). The result is a neat (perhaps too neat) concentric structure: A — exhortation to righteousness; B — the Others' first speech; C — comparisons of the righteous and the wicked; B' — the Others' second speech; and A' — exhortation to wisdom.

(A) The exhortation to seek righteousness or justice in 1:1-15 is directed to "you rulers of the earth." The two references to rulers (1:1; see also 6:21) mark an inclusion for the first large part of the book. However, it was more likely intended for young Jewish intellectuals at Alexandria who may have been turning away from their ethnic-religious heritage and distinctive Jewish practices toward pagan ways of thinking and acting. The term "righteousness" or "justice" that brackets the first unit (see 1:1 and 1:15) is used in its biblical sense of right relationship with God and right behavior toward others. The author links righteousness with wisdom, which he portrays as a kind of world soul: "For wisdom is a kindly spirit . . . the spirit of the Lord has filled the world, and that which holds all things together knows what is said" (1:6-7). While suspicious of the attractions of Hellenism, the author uses some of its terms and concepts to communicate with his Diaspora Jew-

---

8. Harrington, *Invitation to the Apocrypha*, 55-57.
9. Kolarcik, *The Ambiguity of Death*, 62.

ish audience. He denies that God made death and that God delights in death (1:13). The death to which he refers here does not seem to be merely natural physical death. Rather, in 1:12 he implicitly introduces the concept of ultimate death (death after physical death) by warning about the evil consequences of "the error of your life" (bad behavior) and "the works of your hands" (idolatry; see chaps. 13–15). He also links righteousness with immortality, and declares in conclusion that "righteousness is immortal" (1:15). The idea seems to be that righteousness (and wisdom; see chap. 6) is a necessary condition for enjoying eternal life with God.

(B) The discourse of the Others in 2:1b-20 has already been treated in detail. With his prefatory remarks in 1:16–2:1a the author has accused the Others of making a covenant with death, and suggests that their misguided views about death and life are at the root of their unsound reasoning. Likewise in his concluding comments in 2:21-24 the author has traced the Others' erroneous thinking to their failure to appreciate what he describes as "the wages of holiness" and "the prize for blameless souls" (2:22) — the divine gift of immortality for truly righteous and wise persons.

(C) At the center of the author's argument in the first part of his work are four comparisons between the righteous and the wicked in chapters 3 and 4. The most famous verse in the book of Wisdom appears at the beginning: "But the souls of the righteous are in the hand of God, and no torment will ever touch them" (3:1). The passage that these words begin (3:1-9) is often used today at Catholic funerals as the OT reading. Having dismissed as unsound the reasoning of the Others, the author now develops his own positive views about life after death by four comparisons.

The first comparison (3:1-12) picks up the theme of appearance and reality from the discourse of the Others. While righteous persons may seem to have died with their physical death, they are in fact now "in the hand of God" and "their hope is full of immortality." On the contrary, the ungodly (= the Others) will be punished "as their reasoning deserves," since they have rebelled against God and despised wisdom, and so "their hope is vain." The second comparison (3:13-19) contrasts the final destinies (at the Day of Judgment) of two despised figures — the barren woman and the eunuch — who are nonetheless righteous and wise with the miseries that "children of adulterers" (perhaps apostates or idolaters; see also 4:6) endure both in this life and "on the day of judgment." The third comparison (4:1-6) contrasts the fates of those who are childless "with virtue" and "the prolific breed of the ungodly" when God examines them, and thus denies that immortality can be won merely through the procreation of children. The fourth comparison

(4:7-20) contrasts the righteous who may die young with the wicked who may live a long life on earth, and warns that at the divine judgment "the righteous who have died will condemn the ungodly who are living" (4:16). In these four comparisons the theme of the divine judgment after death plays an increasingly important role, and the righteous become not only the recipients of a favorable verdict but also the judges who condemn the wicked.

(B') The Others' second speech in 5:4-13 takes back much of what they said in their first speech (2:1a-20). Facing the prospect of divine judgment, the Others now recognize the error of their ways. At the judgment they see that those whom they regarded as mad and undergoing shameful death will be included among the children of God and share the lot of the saints, while they will still belong to the lot of death (see 1:16; 2:24). They admit their fundamental mistake: "So it was we who strayed from the way of truth, and the light of righteousness did not shine on us" (5:6). They observe that their neglect of the Lord's way as well as their arrogance and pursuit of material wealth have proven fruitless (5:7-8). The folly of their obsession with transitory and fragile material goods is developed with the help of similes in which they admit that what they imagined was important is comparable to a shadow, a rumor, a ship sailing in the sea, a bird in flight, and an arrow shot at a target (see 2:2-5). Their final self-assessment is that from their birth they were as good as dead, and they confess that "we had no sign of virtue to show, but were consumed in our wickedness" (5:13). The author rounds off the second speech of the Others with four more comparisons — like chaff, a light frost, smoke, and a guest who stays only one day — to characterize once more the insubstantial nature of what the Others once thought was so important. By contrast, in 5:15-23 the righteous are said to have been granted eternal life and divine protection: "But the righteous live forever, and their reward is with the Lord; the Most High takes care of them" (5:15).

(A') The exhortation to seek wisdom in 6:1-21 parallels the instruction to seek righteousness in 1:1-15. Indeed, both wisdom and righteousness are needed if one is to be granted eternal life with God. After calling on the rulers (6:1; see 1:1; 6:21) to pay attention, the author reminds them that the God who gave them power will also demand a strict accounting from them. The threat of divine judgment leads to an invitation to learn wisdom in 6:9-11, since wisdom and righteousness go together. What follows in 6:12-21 is a transition to the second major part of the book, which concerns the nature of wisdom. After describing in 6:12-16 wisdom's attractive qualities in terms of Proverbs 8, the author traces the quest for wisdom in a chain (sorites) with seven links: the beginning of wisdom, desire for instruction, love of wisdom, keeping wisdom's law, assurance of immortality, nearness to God, and a kingdom. The "kingdom" is most likely the fullness of eternal life with God. The first major part of the book ends as it began, with another address to rulers to "honor wisdom, so that you may reign forever" (6:21).

III. The Book of Wisdom and Apocalyptic Eschatology

If an apocalypse is a narrative about a dream or a vision pertaining to the heavenly world and/or the end of human history as we know it, the book of Wisdom is clearly not an apocalypse in the sense of a literary genre.[10] But in the content of its first six chapters it does use many Jewish apocalyptic concepts and is especially concerned with the transcendence of death and immortality/eternal life with God. The speech of the Others in chapter 2 serves as a foil to the author's argument about righteousness and wisdom as the keys to hope for immortality, and about beliefs in life after death, divine judgment, and rewards and punishments as the proper context for pursuing righteousness and wisdom in this life.

The book of Wisdom was surely composed in Greek. The author displays some familiarity with Greek philosophical terminology ("soul," "immortality," etc.), was conversant with the Stoic concept of the world soul (which he identifies as wisdom in 1:6-7), and uses Greek rhetorical devices (sorites, allegory, etc.) in developing his arguments. However, he did not know anywhere near as much Greek philosophy as Philo did, and his philosophical references are not sufficiently developed to link him or what he opposes to any specific philosophical school.

Nevertheless, one of the author's most original contributions was to have integrated Greek philosophical concepts and biblical thought (and apocalyptic eschatology in particular). Foundational to his theological position and logical arguments in chapters 1–6 are early Jewish apocalyptic beliefs about life after death, divine judgment according to one's deeds, and appropriate rewards and punishments. His description of the blessed as shining forth and running "like sparks through the stubble" in 3:7 evokes the picture of the astral immortality of the wise envisioned in Dan. 12:3. The increasing significance given to the theme of divine judgment in chapters 3–5 reflects the central motif of divine justice in Jewish apocalyptic. The detailed

---

10. Collins, "Introduction: Toward the Morphology of a Genre," *Semeia* 14 (1979): 1-20.

description of God as a warrior in 5:17-20 and the catalogue of cosmic portents in 5:21-23 would be quite at home in a Palestinian Jewish apocalypse. The scattered references to the "law" (2:12; 6:4, 18c) reflect the typically Jewish connection between wisdom and the Torah.

At the same time, some of the "hard edges" in Palestinian Jewish apocalyptic eschatology are softened. While there can be no doubt about the author's identity as a Diaspora Jew, he makes his implied audience into the rulers of earth (even though the real audience was more likely young Jewish males) and displays little explicit Jewish nationalistic concern in chapters 1–6 (though he does mock the Egyptians in chaps. 11–19). It is hard to find clear references to bodily resurrection, and we are never sure whether the judgment is the one and only Last Judgment, or a particular or occasional divine judgment. At the same time, he roots the hope for immortality not in the nature of the human person and the immortal soul (as some Greeks did) but rather insists (as other Jews did) on blessed immortality as a gift from God granted to the wise and righteous. The wicked Others must endure punishments and ultimate death (which seems to be annihilation).

Immortality as the transcendence of death in Wisdom 1–6 has great ethical and theological significance. It provides purpose and direction to human ethical effort, since eternal life with God is the reward for wise and righteous living. It also offers a solution to the problem of innocent suffering — a major topic underlying the speech of the Others in chapter 2 and the author's argument in Wisdom 1–6. In this approach (see also Daniel, 2 Maccabees, some Qumran texts, etc.) the definitive manifestation of God's power and justice is deferred until the Last Judgment. The sufferings that the wise and righteous undergo in the present serve as a test of their virtue and/or as a source of discipline by which they come to adhere more closely to the way of wisdom and righteousness. And in the end they will be vindicated and rewarded, and the foolish and wicked will be exposed as fools and punished (as in 5:4-14).

The treatment of immortality in Wisdom 1–6 marks an important moment in the history of biblical afterlife expectations. The earlier documents (Proverbs, Psalms, etc.) speak at best about a shadowy afterlife existence in Sheol, the abode of the dead. Real life is here on earth. Physical death is viewed as the natural end of life, while premature death is often regarded as a just punishment for evildoing on someone's part. In Sheol there is only darkness, and no one can praise God there (see Ps. 88:10-12). Job is so overcome with despair in his suffering that the prospect of Sheol had become attractive to him (Job 3:13-19) — that is how bad it got for Job.

However, with the book of Daniel (see 12:1-3), we meet the first clear biblical reference to the resurrection of the dead: "Many of those who sleep in the dust of the earth shall awake, some to everlasting life, and some to shame and everlasting contempt" (12:2). Belief in the resurrection of the body is prominent in the story of the seven sons and their mother in 2 Maccabees 7. Clear references to belief in life after death appear in many of the OT Pseudepigrapha and Qumran scrolls, where there are even a few tantalizing references to what may seem like bodily resurrection (1QH^a 14:34-35; 4Q521). In Jesus' time, the Pharisees had become the great proponents of life after death among the Jewish sects, and Jesus in Mark 12:18-27 and parallels agrees with them against the Sadducees.[11]

While the New Testament writers shared the early Jewish belief in a blessed life after death for the wise and righteous, they based their hope primarily on the resurrection of Jesus Christ as "the firstborn from the dead" (Col. 1:18).[12] In Johannine theology Jesus becomes the point of "crisis" or decision for all. In John 6:40, he proclaims that his Father's will is that "all who see the Son and believe in him may have eternal life; and I will raise them up on the last day." Eternal life has already begun for those who believe in Jesus. The pivot in all this is the idea that Jesus' resurrection is the preview and guarantor of the resurrection of believers. In him and through him believers have already begun to experience eternal life and can expect something even better at the general resurrection and the Last Judgment.

In Rom. 6:3-9 (which is the earliest theological reflection on Christian baptism), Paul focuses on the link between baptism and Christ's death and resurrection. Through baptism believers enter into both the death of Jesus and the eternal life of the risen Christ. Baptism involves dying with Christ in order to live with Christ. The water of baptism at once symbolizes death (by drowning) and life (without water life is impossible for humans). Baptism means receiving the Holy Spirit, which is the power of God to live a virtuous and fruitful life in the present and to enjoy eternal life in the age to come.

While the NT approach to life after death is thoroughly christological, there are some texts that sound like what we find in Wisdom 1–6. In writing

---

11. For full surveys of the ancient Near Eastern and Jewish evidence, see Alan F. Segal, *Life after Death: A History of the Afterlife in the Religions of the West* (New York: Doubleday, 2004); and Jon D. Levinson, *Resurrection and the Restoration of Israel: The Ultimate Victory of the God of Life* (New Haven: Yale University Press, 2006).

12. For full treatments, see R. Bieringer, V. Koperski, and B. Lataire, eds., *Resurrection in the New Testament: Festscrift J. Lambrecht* (BETL 165; Leuven: Peeters, 2002); and Jaime Clark-Soles, *Death and Afterlife in the New Testament* (New York: Continuum, 2006).

from prison to the Philippians, Paul debates with himself whether it is better for him "to depart and be with Christ" or "to remain in the flesh" (Phil. 1:23-24). And in 2 Cor. 5:1-10, Paul assumes a Greek (Platonic)–sounding anthropology ("the earthly tent") and envisions his being "away from the body and at home with the Lord," while noting that "all of us must appear before the judgment seat of Christ, so that we each may receive recompense for what has been done in the body, whether good or evil" (5:10). In the great judgment scene in Matt. 25:31-46, Christ as the glorious Son of Man serves as the judge, and invites the wise and righteous to share eternal life with him and condemns the "goats" (the Matthean equivalent of the wicked Others in Wisdom 1–6) for failing to recognize him in "the least" ones.

PART THREE

APOCALYPTICISM

The Apocalyptic Other

Lorenzo DiTommaso

> *When the stars threw down their spears*
> *And water'd heaven with their tears:*
> *Did he smile his work to see?*
> *Did he who made the Lamb make thee?*
>
> William Blake, "The Tyger," from
> *Songs of Innocence and of Experience*

Apocalypticism asserts that a transcendent reality, concealed from casual observation yet operative on a grand scale, defines and informs existence beyond human understanding and the normal pale of worldly experience. It reveals a cosmos that is structured by two forces, good and evil, which have been in conflict since the dawn of history. It discloses the necessity and imminence of the final resolution of the conflict at the end of time, and the truth about human destiny.

This worldview — potent, persistent, and pervasive — has informed the ideologies of cults, communities, nations, and empires. It has inspired the production of *apocalyptica* both biblical and secular.[1] And it has insti-

---

1. *Apocalyptica* refers to all artifacts that are constitutionally informed by the apoca-

Research for this paper has been funded in part by a 2008-2011 Research Grant from the Social Sciences and Humanities Research Council of Canada. Biblical quotations are drawn from the NRSV. I am indebted to Michael E. Stone for his comments and suggestions.

gated the formation of apocalyptic groups ranging from the Qumran sectarians and the earliest Christians in the ancient world, to Heaven's Gate and Aum Shinrikyō in the modern one.

Apocalypticism makes sweeping claims about time, space, and human existence.[2] One of the most important is the existence of the Other. By this I first mean the constitutive Other, or that *genus* of persons who appear and act in immutable ways, and who are considered to be as intrinsically different from their opposites as tigers are from lambs. The concept of apocalyptic otherness is not restricted to this application, as we shall see, but this is its most common form. Of course the early apocalypticists did not have in mind a notion that was first used by Hegel and later developed by Lacan, Levinas, and Buber, and there are several key differences. But the underlying idea is basically the same.

This paper explores the epistemological basis of apocalyptic otherness, describes the ways in which the concept is expressed, and concludes with some thoughts as to its relevance today. It is informed throughout by the studies of John J. Collins.[3] Distinguished by a profound appreciation of early Judaism, and anchored by a taxonomy featuring an elegant, parsimonious definition of the genre that is sensitive to the evidence and not imposed on it, Collins's studies overthrew the prevailing understanding of "apocalyptic"

---

lyptic worldview. Literary examples include formal apocalypses such as Daniel and Revelation, as well as apocalyptic oracles, homilies, commentaries, physiognomies, testaments, sermons, speculative fiction, and even quasi-fictional works like the *Left Behind* novels. Nonliterary examples include apocalyptic manuscript illumination, paintings, engravings, manga, and graphic novels, as well as apocalyptic motion pictures, music, and anime. The category's inclusive nature permits it to function as a barometer of apocalypticism in a culture regardless of the prevailing media, as well as a measure of the worldview's development through history or within a tradition. Naturally, any text, painting, or motion picture can be apocalyptic and something else at the same time, while some vehicles (medieval manuscript books and the Internet) can contain both literary and nonliterary expressions of the worldview. On biblical and secular apocalypticism, see below, note 10.

    2. See L. DiTommaso, "Apocalypses and Apocalypticism. III. Judaism," in *Encyclopedia of the Bible and Its Reception*, ed. H.-J. Klauck, B. McGinn et al. (Berlin: de Gruyter, 2009), 2: cols. 325-40; and idem, *The Architecture of Apocalypticism*, vol. 1: *From Antiquity to Armageddon*, forthcoming from Oxford University Press.

    3. A quarter-century along, Collins's *Apocalyptic Imagination* (New York: Crossroad, 1984; 2d ed. Grand Rapids: Eerdmans, 1998) remains the finest study of the subject. See also his magisterial Hermeneia commentary on Daniel (Minneapolis: Fortress, 1993), his indispensable handbook on *Apocalypticism in the Dead Sea Scrolls* (London: Routledge, 1997), and his numerous *opera minora*, many of which have been reprinted in *Seers, Sibyls and Sages in Hellenistic-Roman Judaism* (Leiden: Brill, 1997).

that had long impoverished the appreciation of apocalyptic literature.[4] With his work, the study of apocalypticism became a scientific endeavor, one that for the first time accurately reflected the nature of its subject.

I. The Epistemology of Apocalyptic Otherness

Apocalyptic otherness, as well as apocalypticism generally, works from the interaction of two epistemological poles, the rational and the emotive.[5] The worldview's ability to propose a simplistic yet global explanation for human destiny, which depends in part on its conception of otherness, forms a major part of its historical persistence, which is to say its ability to express ideas from different ages and diverse cultures and societies.

The rational pole is articulated by an internally consistent logic, comprehended along the dimensions of space, time, and human existence. Apocalypticism addresses the ontological discord between the world as it is and the world as it ought to be. To some degree this is true for every religion and philosophy. However, there are certain propositions which are axiomatic to the worldview and logically underwrite the concept of the apocalyptic otherness.

One proposition is that human existence is structured by a pervasive dualism. Everyday binaries of male/female, day/night, fall/spring, water/earth, chaos/order, and death/life disclose themselves in myriad patterns great and small. The dualistic perspective is one among a small handful of imaginative constructs which by virtue of their comprehensive and comprehensible nature are able to satisfy, to quote François Jacob, the "requirement of the human brain to put order in the universe."[6] Apocalypticism extends

---

4. J. J. Collins, ed., *Apocalypse: The Morphology of a Genre* (*Semeia* 14; Atlanta: Scholars Press, 1979). The ground for the new understanding of apocalypses and related phenomena had been prepared by P. D. Hanson, K. Koch, P. von der Osten-Sacken, and M. E. Stone.

5. For C. O'Regan, the epistemic axis of the "space of apocalyptic" turns on "how full is the disclosure of divine reality and its relation to the world and history and how directive is it of specifically Christian practices and forms of life." *Theology and the Spaces of Apocalyptic* (Milwaukee: Marquette University Press, 2009), 27. Without subjecting his view to a detailed analysis, it may be said here that the self-limiting nature of his description renders it inappropriate to an examination of the worldview beyond the specifically Christian manifestations.

6. F. Jacob, "Evolution and Tinkering," *Science* n.s. 196, no. 4295 (10 June 1977): 1161-66 at 1161.

this dichotomy to the otherworldly or ultra-mundane plane, whereupon angelic figures, powers or spirits, and so-called "inclinations" are understood to be either good or evil.[7] There is not much middle ground in dualistic worldviews as a class, and none at all in apocalypticism.

Another proposition is the existence of a transcendent reality. It is not a shadow reality or a parallel universe, or an external world of forms. Instead, it is the veritable reality; ours by contrast is subordinate and transitory. This perspective, while not unique to apocalypticism, acquires in the worldview its distinctive eschatological character. It insists that the present world is so imperfect as to be beyond redemption and soon must be annihilated.[8] We live in the winter of history, anxiously awaiting the approaching end.[9]

In the biblical form of apocalypticism, the transcendent reality is inseparable from the notion of a good and just God.[10] Hence any attempt to justify the veracity of the transcendent state naturally takes the form of theodicy: the endeavor to exonerate God for evil or suffering, or to explain these things so

---

7. *Angelic figures:* the classic biblical texts are Dan. 10:13, 20, which speak of Israel's angelic protectors, including Michael, and their struggle against the heavenly princes of Persia and Greece, and Rev. 12:7-12. Of course angels and demons are not in themselves apocalyptic: 2 Macc. 10:29-30 (which is not an apocalyptic text) records that five angelic riders helped Judas Maccabaeus defeat Timothy and his mercenaries; the Qumran *War Rule* describes a final battle in which both angelic figures and humans participate. *Powers or spirits:* e.g., the two ways or spirits of 1QS iii 23–iv 26. *Inclinations:* e.g., the good and evil inclinations *(Yetzer ha-Tov/ha-Ra)* of ancient and medieval Judaism, which in contemporary popular culture visibly appear as cartoon manifestations of one's angelic and demonic sides, arguing with the self as to an appropriate course of action.

8. "Since the antidote to what is wrong in the world does not lie in the world, the point of departure — on the apocalyptic landscape — from which there can be movement to set things right cannot be found in the world." J. L. Martyn, "The Apocalyptic Gospel in Galatians," *Interpretation* 54 (2000): 248-66 at 255. This statement reflects a profound understanding of apocalypticism on the part of its author.

9. On the imminent end as a proposition of the worldview or as derivation from its propositions, inasmuch as it is part of its chief function, see further DiTommaso, *Architecture of Apocalypticism*.

10. *Biblical apocalypticism* is the worldview of *1 Enoch,* Daniel, and Revelation, and their late-antique, medieval and modern manifestations, Jewish, Christian, and Muslim (along with their syncretistic variants). Its influence on Western civilization has been profound. See *The Encyclopedia of Apocalypticism,* 3 vols., ed. J. J. Collins, B. McGinn, and S. J. Stein (New York/London: Continuum, 1998). *Secular apocalypticism,* which derives from the biblical form but is a product of ideas originating in the Renaissance and the Enlightenment, is most associated with modernity. I highlight the biblical form of the worldview in this and the next paragraph because the notion of transcendent reality in secular apocalypticism is more complicated.

as to demonstrate their ultimate utility. Consequential to the belief in a good God is the conviction that, despite the evidence of present-day problems, the helm of history remains under divine control. His is the hand that steers history to its foreordained climax, and the world to its appointed end.

Apocalypticism purports to disclose God's hidden plan for humanity.[11] It accomplishes this by means of a rational, well-formed historiography, or the way that history — the record of human activity — is conceived.[12] Despite the war and destruction that are popularly associated with the end of the world, the God of apocalypticism is a deity of order, not chaos. His purposes, so it is believed, manifest themselves in the orderly structures of space and time. This theology of history would later come to frame the deism of the Enlightenment *philosophes* and their vision of the divine watchmaker of the universe.

The preceding considerations reveal the rational basis of apocalyptic otherness. There is no room within the logic of the worldview for anything resident between the two absolutes of good and evil, at least within the bounds circumscribed by the historical age/mundane world, that is, the state in which humans presently live. This is the foundation for otherness in its spatial sense.[13] As for its temporal sense, apocalyptic historiography is always linear, teleological, and salvation-oriented. The resolution of the conflict between good and evil is understood to transpire after the historical age, which is to say it is eschatological. It is usually envisioned as a last great bat-

---

11. The pattern is hidden because, from the standpoint of human awareness, the transcendent reality is a mystery. See L. DiTommaso, "The Development of Apocalyptic Historiography in Light of the Dead Sea Scrolls," in *Celebrating the Dead Sea Scrolls: A Canadian Collection*, ed. P. W. Flint, J. Duhaime, and K. Baek (SBLEJL; Atlanta: Society of Biblical Literature; Leiden: Brill, 2010).

12. See A. Funkenstein, "A Schedule for the End of the World: The Origins and Persistence of the Apocalyptic Mentality," in *Visions of Apocalypse: End or Rebirth?* ed. S. Friedländer et al. (New York/London: Holmes & Meier, 1985), 44-60, esp. 47-50; U. Rappaport, "Apocalyptic Vision and Preservation of Historical Memory," *JSJ* 23 (1992): 217-26; L. DiTommaso, "History and Apocalyptic Eschatology: A Reply to J. Y. Jindo," *VT* 56 (2006): 413-18; and M. E. Stone, *New Perspectives on Ancient Judaism* (Grand Rapids: Eerdmans, forthcoming), chapter 3.

13. That apocalypticism might have a spatial dimension was first proposed by M. E. Stone in "Lists of Revealed Things in the Apocalyptic Literature," in *Magnalia Dei: The Mighty Acts of God. Essays on the Bible and Archaeology in Memory of G. Ernest Wright*, ed. F. M. Cross et al. (New York: Doubleday, 1976), 414-52, and expanded most notably by J. C. VanderKam, *Enoch and the Growth of an Apocalyptic Tradition* (CBQMS 16; Washington, D.C.: Catholic Biblical Association, 1984). Cf. Stone, "Three Transformations in Judaism: Scripture, History, and Redemption," *Numen* 32 (1985): 218-35.

tle (Armageddon), inasmuch it pertains to nations and kingdoms, and as a final judgment, inasmuch it pertains to individuals. At the same time, the worldview's radical dualism demands that the focus of the historiography remain on its special object, the One (also: the elect, chosen, or saved) and its relationship with the Other (also: the enemy or the damned). History thus becomes a series of milestones marking the long road of the conflict between good and evil. Any salvation-history tends to streamline the past. Apocalyptic dualism simplifies it an additional degree, to the point where there are two kinds of everything — *now and until the end of time.*

The emotive pole relies on the worldview's logic for its reference points, but is subject to elements beyond intellection. In the apocalyptic mode, the belief that tigers cannot change their stripes, or leopards their spots, is not falsifiable. We may disagree with its premises, object that it neglects the exercise of free will, or observe that sometimes tigers can act like lambs (or *vice versa*). But such explanations are foreign to the intuitive process, which is influenced by traditional sayings and stories,[14] and driven by powerful emotions.

---

14. Stories in every culture echo the truism. Who does not recall the tale of the teenage Achilles? Prophecy foretold his death if he went to fight at Troy. Seeking to prevent this, his immortal mother Thetis sent him to the court of Lycomedes disguised as a girl. Odysseus exposed the ruse by concealing a spear and shield among a collection of "feminine" gifts for the daughters of the king. A false alarm having been sounded, Achilles alone reached for the weapons, thereby revealing his true identity and sealing his destiny (Statius, *Achilleis* i 269; Apollodorus iii 13). A similar message underwrites the tale from India of an orphaned tiger cub who was raised by a herd of goats. An older tiger happened on the scene. He led the cub to a river, showed him his striped face reflected in the water, and gave him some freshly killed goat to eat. With these things, the tiger cub recovered his true identity with a mighty roar; see H. Zimmer, *Philosophies of India* (Bollingen Series 26; Princeton: Princeton University Press, 1951), 5-7. The efficacy of traditional sayings and stories is limited only in that they do not normally explain *why* the tiger is known by its stripes or the lamb by its nature. This is the province of general theories and worldviews. The ancient science of physiognomy tended not to include the supporting logic (exception: 4Q186), but its modern congeners propose various mechanisms. One example will suffice. In 1876 Cesare Lombroso published *L'uomo delinquente*, the first major work on the new science of criminal anthropology. It proposed that criminality is biological and reveals itself physiologically and in social behavior. Criminals could be identified by their facial features or cranial profiles, or from the designs of their tattoos. Such individuals, Lombroso argued, were throwbacks to a more primitive stage of humanity, unable to escape their biological legacies or criminal destinies. Like the tigers of the story, criminals are indelibly marked by their nature. See S. J. Gould, *The Mismeasure of Man* (New York: Norton, 1981), and D. G. Horn, *The Criminal Body: Lombroso and the Science of Deviance* (New York: Routledge, 2003).

Apocalyptic logic marshals these emotions, and gives them direction and intellectual sustenance.[15] We long to validate those whom this world tramples. We desire an antidote to despair and anomie and hunger to console and exhort those who must endure oppression and the menace of death. We pursue the hope of sanctuary and the dream of utopia. We seek a reality greater than ourselves, a high destiny with sublimity and purpose, which accords to life a meaning beyond the oblivion of the grave.

Apocalypticism channels the baser emotions equally well. Musing on the Whore of Babylon in Revelation, D. H. Lawrence scoffs:

> Splendid she sits, and splendid is her Babylon. How the late apocalypticists love mouthing out all that gold and silver and cinnamon of evil Babylon! How they *want* them all! How they *envy* Babylon her splendor, envy, envy! How they love destroying it all! The harlot sits magnificent with her golden cup of the wine of sensual pleasure in her hand. How the apocalypticists would have loved to drink of her cup! And since they couldn't: how they loved smashing it![16]

This is a sophisticate's view — apocalypticists consider evil anathema, not attractive. But there is some truth in its hyperbole. The heart does not always obey the rule of heaven. The lure of the siren-call of forbidden fruit echoes in the apologies of moralistic religious leaders past and present.

The belief that a hidden reality governs existence can nurture feelings of paranoia and xenophobia, particularly when one's lifestyle (*lege* identity) is threatened.[17] This plays to the fact that persons tend to be most at ease with

---

15. In their classic study *When Prophecy Fails* (Minneapolis: University of Minnesota Press, 1956), L. Festinger et al. explain the conflict between expectation and reality among members of a modern doomsday group in terms of "cognitive dissonance." In no way does the model account for the motivations of every movement that expects an imminent end of the world, and other cases do not confirm its predictions regarding group reactions to unfulfilled expectations. But its basic concept describes apocalyptic sociology well. On the application of the model to new religious movements (and the problems associated with it), see G. S. McGhee, "A Cultural History of Dissonance Theory," in *War in Heaven/Heaven on Earth: Theories of the Apocalyptic*, ed. S. J. O'Leary and G. S. McGhee (London/Oakville, Conn.: Equinox, 2005), 197-219, and the sources cited therein, and the essays in *Millennium, Messiahs, and Mayhem*, ed. T. Robbins and S. J. Palmer (New York/London: Routledge, 1997), and J. R. Stone, ed., *Expecting Armageddon: Essential Readings in Failed Prophecy* (New York/London: Routledge, 2000).

16. D. H. Lawrence, *Apocalypse* (New York: Viking, 1932), 139, italics original.

17. J. F. Rinehart, *Apocalyptic Faith and Political Violence: Prophets of Terror* (New

their own lifestyles and beliefs, even if these are in constant flux or even incompatible.[18] Alternately, persons are less likely to understand, accept, or even tolerate lifestyles and beliefs other than their own. That this is true for nearly every person is not a point of dispute. Apocalypticism, though, amplifies every distinction, and brings it into high relief. This is due partly to the internal logic of the worldview, and partly to a feedback loop that results from a dearth of external data and social stimuli. The latter phenomenon, known as social encapsulation, develops spontaneously or is cultivated by charismatic leaders.[19] It can affect any group espousing a totalizing worldview, but is typical of apocalypticism, whose social setting is frequently (but not always) that of small groups under oppression, real or perceived. In this setting it induces a condition that may be described as *apocalyptic narcosis*.

At the same time, the fabrication of clearly defined enemies strengthens group identity and solidarity ("Whoever is not with me is against me," Matt. 12:30). Group cohesion is further reinforced by the memory of grievances and shared suffering. Neither of these processes is wholly explainable by rational argument. From here it is only a short step to the conviction that misfortunes that befall enemies are self-inflicted or deserved. Bad trees, after all, bear bad fruit (Luke 6:43; par. Matt. 7:17-18). We are speaking in very broad terms, but this is the sea in which such emotions swim.[20]

Fear and terror beget hatred and revenge. Rationally, we recognize there is no profit in reprisal, only the illusion of satisfaction. The past cannot be altered, or time regained:

> *tempus edax rerum, tuque, invidiosa vetustas,*
> *omnia destruitis vitiataque dentibus aevi*
> *paulatim lenta consumitis omnia morte!*
> (Ovid, *Metamorphoses*, 15.234-36)

York: Palgrave Macmillan, 2006), esp. 143-48. Yet apocalypses are not conspiracy literature, *contra* M. Barkun's fine study, *A Culture of Conspiracy: Apocalyptic Visions in Contemporary America* (Berkeley: University of California Press, 2003).

18. A classic study remains S. Lieberman, "The Effect of Changes in Roles on the Attitudes of Role Occupants," *Human Relations* 9 (1956): 385-402.

19. See L. L. Dawson, *Comprehending Cults: The Sociology of New Religious Movements*, 2d ed. (New York: Oxford University Press, 2006), 162-66, and the sources cited therein.

20. The process of national reconciliation carries this logic one step farther: after the time of troubles, the people who had been temporarily led astray by leaders or misrouted by events are assumed to have regained their true identity and reintegrated into their natural group.

The crow is black, the crane white, the willow green, and flowers red. (Hakuin)[21]

In reality, though, few things motivate like the sting of injustice and the thirst for retribution. Apocalypticism gives full rein to revenge fantasies, facilitated by a historiography that justifies the reasons and guarantees the results. Violence is an inbuilt feature of the system. Neither benevolent coexistence nor tolerant accommodation is an outcome. Lawrence is correct: what cannot be assimilated must be smashed. It is either conversion or annihilation — the little death or the great death — nothing in between.

For a worldview whose classic literature is typically pseudonymous, apocalypticism is rarely anonymous. The enemy is always known.[22] Often it is the hated oppressor. Other times it is a historic adversary, an equal, since the worldview also lends its voice to mighty religions and sprawling empires.[23] Sometimes it is simply the alien, either the foreigner beyond the gates or the enemy within,[24] stereotypically delineated with thick brushstrokes and bold colors. Medieval Christian manuscripts of the Apocalypse are richly illuminated with princes, popes, Saracens, and Jews — enemies destined to spend eternity in torture and torment. This is only one example of a general phenomenon.[25] Even when the fine details of the apocalyptic

---

21. P. B. Yampolsky, trans., *The Zen Master Hakuin* (New York: Columbia University Press, 1971), 104.

22. Clarity of friend and foe is demanded by the logic of the worldview, despite the fact that the often cryptic and allusive descriptions to historical figures and events in apocalyptic texts frequently defy modern identification. Contemporary audiences had to be able to recognize their enemies, historical or eschatological, in order to locate themselves in history, and thus bring their relationship to its end. See DiTommaso, *Architecture of Apocalypticism*.

23. B. McGinn, *Visions of the End: Apocalyptic Traditions in the Middle Ages*, 2d ed. (New York: Columbia University Press, 1998), 28-36. The apocalyptic oracles of Byzantine Christians and Arab Muslims typically consider the Other as the great enemy.

24. "In the apocalypticist's world, the Christian is the historical here-and-now foe, while the Jew is the metahistorical foe." D. Cook, *Studies in Muslim Apocalyptic* (Princeton: Darwin Press, 2002), 31.

25. Modern apocalyptic movements paint their enemies with the same stereotypical brush. See P. Boyer, *When Time Shall Be No More: Prophecy Belief in Modern American Culture* (Cambridge, Mass.: Belknap Press of Harvard University Press, 1992), esp. 167-69. Examples include Aum Shinrikyo, which saw the world through the lens of biblical prophecy and Japanese nationalism, and the Nation of Islam, whose theology radically reworks the biblical accounts of creation and redemption as part of a perceived historic struggle among the races. On the Nation, see M. Lieb, *Children of Ezekiel: Aliens, UFOs, the Crisis of Race, and the Advent of the End Time* (Durham: Duke University Press, 1998). Similarly race-defined

picture are left to the imagination, retribution remains the vanishing point of the worldview that provides its perspectival frame. Pastors and theologians who seek to denature apocalypticism misunderstand its essential drives. At stake is nothing less than existence itself.

II. Apocalyptic Otherness

Quantum theory proposes that certain objects in the universe are so intimately linked that they cannot be described without reference to their complements. The textbook example of the phenomenon, known as quantum entanglement, involves a subatomic property called "spin." Consider a pair of identical elementary particles, spins unknown. If an observer measures the spin of one particle to be "up," the spin of the other particle immediately resolves itself as its opposite value, or "down."[26] Neither particle exists independently. The spin of one particle automatically determines that of the other, while the spins of both particles ultimately depend on external measurement.

Apocalyptic Otherness functions in much the same manner. It expresses itself trilaterally as: (1) the constitutive Other, the enemy; (2) the One, the opposite of the enemy but at the same time inseparable from it; and (3) the transcendent reality, which stands in an extramural yet definitional relationship to the One and the Other, and which in the classic biblical form of the worldview is God.

The first expression is the traditional *Other* — the opposite, the negative, the enemy. The code-words used to identify it — Babylon, Rome, Gog/Magog, the army of Darkness, the forces of Satan, the Evil Empire — are part of the vocabulary by which the grammar of apocalypticism has shaped Western notions of history, politics, and culture. The idea evolved from the "oracles against the nations" of Israelite prophecy. Time and again the

---

are the apocalyptic scenarios of the groups known loosely as Christian Identity; see M. Barkun, *Religion and the Racist Right: The Origins of the Christian Identity Movement* (Chapel Hill: University of North Carolina Press, 1994); A. L. Apple and B. A. Messner, "Paranoia and Paradox: The Apocalyptic Rhetoric of Christian Identity," *Western Journal of Communication* 65 (2001): 206-27, and the sources cited therein. The intersection of apocalypticism and race is not limited to religions; see A. M. Soltysik, "Evolutionary Narratives and American Ideological Tropes: The End of Progress," in *Apocalypse,* ed. F. Gysin (Swiss Papers in English Language and Literature 12; Tübingen: Gunter Narr, 2000), 41-59.

26. This occurs no matter the distance between the two particles, which indicates a transfer of data faster than the speed of light, or else the need to revise the framework by which we understand this phenomenon to occur.

prophets of old identified their adversaries in blanket fashion, usually along national-ethnic lines, e.g., Ethiopia, Egypt, and Babylon (cf. Amos 1:3–2:3, Isaiah 13–23; Jeremiah 46–51; Zephaniah 2). It is one thing for the prophets to identify these nations qua nations, subject to anticipated woe and catastrophe. But they were also asserting that Ethiopians qua Ethiopians were destined to suffer because of the circumstances of their birth. "Can Ethiopians change their skin, or leopards their spots?" asks the prophet Jeremiah (13:23). His rhetorical question, posed over 2,500 years ago, still encapsulates for many people today what common sense suggests, experience verifies, and tradition confirms: destiny and design are two sides of the same coin.

Apocalypticism added supra-historical and ultra-mundane dimensions to the prophetic message by realigning its elements along the temporal and spatial axes of the cosmic struggle between good and evil.[27] One of John Collins's key contributions to the field was to recognize that these dimensions, reified in the expectation for individual postmortem judgment, define apocalyptic eschatology and distinguish it from other eschatologies.[28] The supra-historical dimension was applied to Israel's enemies or, as was often the case in early Judaism, to the enemies of those who believed themselves to be the true Israel. Hostile nations and peoples were now commonly expected to congregate at the end of days under the oriflamme of evil.

This leads us to the second expression of apocalyptic otherness — *the One*, also known as the chosen, the elect of God, or equivalent terms. Apocalyptic logic requires that everything in the historical age have its opposite: the "up" spin and the "down" spin, the lamb and the tiger, the saved and the damned. One part is entangled with the other; neither is autonomous. By nature Otherness is complementary.[29]

Whether or not it is framed by the apocalyptic worldview, the construction of the Other is always an exercise in self-definition. Then as now,

---

27. For example, the "two ways" of Deut. 30:19 and Jer. 21:8 acquired cosmic scope and eschatological significance in its apocalyptic formulation. Cf. DiTommaso, "Development of Apocalyptic Historiography."

28. See J. J. Collins, "Prophecy, Apocalypse and Eschatology: Reflections on the Proposals of Lester Grabbe," in *Knowing the End from the Beginning: The Prophetic, the Apocalyptic and Their Relationships*, ed. L. L. Grabbe and R. D. Haak (JSPSup 46; London/New York, 2003), 44-52, and other studies.

29. P. Geach, *Logic Matters* (Oxford: Blackwell, 1972), 238-47; H. Deutsch, "Identity and General Similarity," *Philosophical Perspectives* 12 (1997): 177-200; H. Noonan, *Objects and Identity: An Examination of the Relative Identity Thesis and Its Consequences* (Boston: Kluwer, 1980); idem, "Relative Identity," in *A Companion to the Philosophy of Language*, ed. B. Hale and C. Wright (Oxford: Blackwell, 1997), 634-52.

persons define themselves as much by the negation or the absence of qualities as by the presence of them. The flaws with such reasoning should not obscure its power and appeal.

With its radical dualism and eschatological horizon, apocalypticism accentuates such contrasts and amplifies their meaning.[30] When Ezra Pound wrote that it is useless to determine the value of an object by comparing it with similar or degenerate forms, he meant that we discover its limits, and hence its nature, only by contrasting it with something different.[31] In literature as in art: the darker the shade, the more brilliant the sun. The effects are most intensely experienced in graphic depictions of the Apocalypse — in manuscript illuminations certainly, but also in the works of Hieronymus Bosch, Albrecht Dürer, Jean Duvet, and John Martin.[32] The terrified figures in Michelangelo's *Last Judgment*, tormented by oar-wielding demons while ferried to Hell across the River Styx: who could mistake them for anything but doomed souls?

In this fashion the inability of the worldview to include the enemy Other in its calculus of empathy is exposed. Consider two *apocalyptica*, separated in time by twenty centuries but linked by a common perspective. The first, the Revelation of John, describes the destruction of Babylon/Rome in almost elegiac tones. Kings, merchants, and sailors witness the event from afar, awestruck by its magnitude (18:1–19:10). The second, a painting of the Rapture by Charles Anderson, depicts Jesus Christ floating high above the white skyscrapers of a modern metropolis.[33] In the foreground, wrecked automobiles litter the city's highways. In the distance, a jet airliner crashes into one of the buildings. From the vehicles and a nearby cemetery, the souls of the faithful rise heavenward.

---

30. See, more generally, A. Sen, *Identity and Violence* (New York: Norton, 2006).

31. Ezra Pound, *ABC of Reading* (New York: New Directions, 1960), 59-60.

32. F. Carey, ed., *The Apocalypse and the Shape of Things to Come* (Toronto/Buffalo: University of Toronto Press, 1999). On medieval art specifically, see G. Vezin, *L'Apocalypse et la fin des temps* (Paris: Editions de la Revue Moderne, 1973); F. van der Meer, *Apocalypse: Visions from the Book of Revelation in Western Art* (New York: Alpine Fine Arts, 1978); L. Seidel, "Apocalypse and Apocalypticism in Western Medieval Art," in *Encyclopedia of Apocalypticism*, vol. 2, ed. B. McGinn, 467-506; H. Mayr-Harting, "Apocalyptic Book Illustration in the Early Middle Ages," in *Apocalyptic in History and Tradition*, ed. C. Rowland and J. Barton (JSPSup 43; London: T&T Clark, 2003), 172-211; and the essays in Part II of R. K. Emmerson and B. McGinn, eds., *The Apocalypse in the Middle Ages* (Ithaca, N.Y.: Cornell University Press, 1992).

33. Reproduced in D. Wojcik, *The End of the World as We Know It: Faith, Fatalism, and Apocalypse in America* (New York: New York University Press, 1997), pl. 6.

The population of Rome, the greatest city of the ancient world, was around one million persons at the time when John wrote his apocalypse. John's attitude to the fate of Rome and its inhabitants is not in question:

> Hallelujah! Salvation and glory and power to our God, for his judgments are true and just; he has judged the great whore who corrupted the earth with her fornication, and he has avenged on her the blood of his servants. (19:1b-2)

One assumes that the metropolis over which the returned Christ looms in Anderson's painting was similarly populated. One also assumes that the artist and his audience considered those whom the Rapture has "left behind" — the inhabitants of the city, the passengers on the doomed jet, and the occupants of the building it struck — as deserving their fate, just like the terrified figures en route to Hell in the *Last Judgment*.

Such comparisons additionally reveal the multivalent character of apocalyptic Otherness. *A posteriori* revision occurs when an apocalyptic schema is expanded to include present events; *a priori* revision refers to the interpretation of current events in light of an extant schema.[34] For Daniel the earthly adversary is the Seleucid Empire. For the Revelation of John the enemy is Rome, and for Pseudo-Methodius it is the Muslim Arabs. Enemies in modern *apocalyptica* are different still. It is true that the persistence of Judaism, Christianity, and Islam has occasioned a measure of stability to their opponents — real, anticipated, or extrapolated. It is also true that exceptionally oppressive states or virulent figures can acquire a posthumous half-life of their own. Even so, recurring elements like Babylon/Rome or Nero Caesar appear in later *apocalyptica* in the present tense, their historic identities overwritten by current circumstances. John used Babylon, the scourge of an earlier era, to describe Rome, the imperial bane of his time. Nearly 2,000 years later, David Berg and his Children of God redefined Babylon/Rome to identify their apocalyptic enemy, America and its godless lifestyle. These are only two among many scores of examples. It is a sublime irony that although each apocalyptic timetable presumes that it alone correctly divulges the details of the historical record and the time of the end, multivalence only

---

34. McGinn, *Visions of the End,* esp. 33-36. The transcendent reality, the third Other, is also subject to multivalent interpretation. Apocalyptic UFO religions such as the Heaven's Gate movement can envision God and Jesus as intergalactic beings from the "Evolutionary Level Above Human," and the enemy Other as evil space aliens. See the group's website, http://www.heavensgate.com/, which as of September 2009 remained on the Internet.

works from the failure of all earlier predictions, and in this way unintentionally provides the worldview with the ideal mechanism to ensure its ongoing application. "Apocalypse," as Frank Kermode observes, "can be disconfirmed without being discredited."[35]

The third expression of apocalyptic Otherness is the *transcendent reality* itself. In biblical apocalypticism this reality is God. It is difficult to recall an apocalyptic text that uses the language of Otherness to describe the transcendent reality. But the logic of the worldview, and the manner in which it is articulated in the media, are such that it is *de facto* impossible for it to be otherwise.

The otherness of the transcendent reality does not preclude movement between it and the mundane world. In the apocalyptic way of thinking, humans discover the true nature of space, time, and existence through access to data from the other realm. This information is essential, because without it we remain unaware of the radical dualism that structures and in fact defines all things, including Otherness. Sometimes it is channeled through visions or dreams, and remains incoherent, even to the seer, without angelic interpretation. Other times the data are transmitted by heavenly tablets or hidden books,[36] or by pneumatic phenomena such as the Holy Spirit. Intersection between the realities is also presumed by the logic of the worldview. It may imagine the higher reality as existing before, after, and apart from the historical age, but God still plays the critical role in history. Likewise, New Testament apocalypticism conceives of Jesus in terms of invasive movement into our reality.[37]

---

35. F. Kermode, *The Sense of an Ending: Studies in the Theory of Fiction with a New Epilogue* (Oxford/New York: Oxford University Press, 2000 [orig. 1967]), 8.

36. Cf. *Jub.* 3:10, 31; 4:5; 1QH ix 21-24, etc. See R. A. Kraft, "Scripture and Canon in Jewish Apocrypha and Pseudepigrapha," in *Hebrew Bible/Old Testament: The History of Its Interpretation. I, 1: From the Beginnings to the Middle Ages (Until 1300)*, ed. M. Sæbø (Göttingen: Vandenhoeck & Ruprecht, 1996), 199-217, esp. 205-9; and A. A. Orlov, *From Apocalypticism to Merkabah Mysticism* (JSJSup 114; Leiden: Brill, 2007), 109-31.

37. Martyn, "Apocalyptic Gospel"; D. Harink, *Paul among the Postliberals: Pauline Christianity beyond Christendom and Modernity* (Grand Rapids: Brazos: 2003), 68. The apocalyptic worldview, freighted by a Christian gnostic theology, informs the final, quasi-autobiographic trilogy of the science-fiction writer Philip K. Dick. The novels work from the premise that the historical age began in 70 C.E. and ended in 1974, and that an orbital satellite, the Vast Active Living Intelligence System (VALIS), transmits coherent information to persons on Earth about God, Jesus, and another reality in the form of lost writings, pink beams of light, incarnated wisdom figures, and other phenomena. The title of the second novel is *The Divine Invasion*.

All the same, God remains the ultimate Other, despite the permeable boundary between the realities. In the conclusion to his *Gnostic Religion*, Hans Jonas wrote, "The beginning and the end of the paradox that is gnostic religion is the unknown God himself who, unknowable on principle, because the 'other' to everything known, is yet the object of a knowledge and even asks to be known."[38] Apocalypticism is not gnosticism, nor is it mysticism, but it seems to me that the essential idea of transcendental Otherness is common to all three worldviews, as it also is to many other religions, and, *mutatis mutandis*, to secular or quasi-religious philosophies as well. The final section of this paper explores the implications of transcendental Otherness as it applies to apocalypticism today.

III. Apocalypticism Now

In a seminal essay published in 1971, Amos Wilder argued that despite common themes and a shared vocabulary, biblical and contemporary expressions of apocalypticism are fundamentally dissimilar. As he saw it, modern secular "apocalyptic" is unable to engage the ultimate crisis, which involves the fate of all life and creation, or to offer answers which derive from the hope of world renovation and affirmation. By contrast, the ancient literature, being a total existential response induced by the manifestation of God in the world, displays what he calls the "healthy function of genuine transcendental apocalyptic."[39]

---

38. H. Jonas, *The Gnostic Religion*, 2d ed. (Boston: Beacon Press, 1963), 288. Jonas wrote before the bulk of the Nag Hammadi texts were published, and many of his views are now out of step with the evidence. But his view on the God of Gnosticism — taking "gnosticism" in the sense of a general worldview and not as a group definition — remains relevant. Even now the links among apocalypticism, gnosticism, and mysticism remain to be explained clearly.

39. A. Wilder, "The Rhetoric of Ancient and Modern Apocalyptic," *Interpretation* 25 (1971): 436-53 at 440. His essay is one of several important studies on contemporary apocalypticism precipitated in part by the cultural ferment of the 1960s. See also Kermode, *Sense of an Ending*; R. Alter, "The Apocalyptic Temper," *Commentary* (June 1966): 61-66; E. Rovit, "On the Contemporary Apocalyptic Imagination," *The American Scholar* 37 (1968): 453-68; N. A. Scott, Jr., "'New Heav'ns, New Earth' — The Landscape of Contemporary Apocalypse," *Journal of Religion* 53 (1973): 1-35; and J. V. Schall, "Apocalypse as a Secular Enterprise," *Scottish Journal of Theology* 29 (1976): 357-73. See also R. J. Bauckham, "The Year 2000 and the End of Secular Eschatology," in *Called to One Hope: Perspectives on the Life to Come*, ed. J. Colwell (Carlyle, UK: Paternoster Press, 2000), 240-51.

This opinion is bankrupt.[40] Apocalypticism is an *unhealthy* worldview, particularly in its biblical form. It is inimical to a mature vision of human destiny, or any social order founded on humanistic ideals. It is hostile to life on Earth, especially in light of the nature and needs of contemporary society.

Apocalypticism cannot be salvaged. It cannot be allegorized, spiritualized, or sanitized into what it is not. It cannot be made healthy by quarantining the unpalatable passages[41] or by resetting its timetables.[42] There is no pristine version of the worldview that can be recovered from antiquity, before a later century or an alien religion corrupts it or transforms it into something else. If some of the earliest apocalyptic literature appears more sophisticated in its outlook, less vicious in its exhortations, or less virulent in its assumptions, the worldview itself is inherently poisonous. Its core axioms have not changed for over two thousand years. Indeed, they are what have allowed it to stay relevant for so long and to so many cultures.

Apocalyptic Otherness, and the worldview from which it derives, are an adolescent reply to the nuances and ambiguities of modern life. This is expressed in the basic simplicity of the worldview and, more significantly, in the notion of transferred or abrogated responsibility that it engenders.

Complexity is not a prerequisite of profundity, but simple philosophies, which can be quite profound, may be distinguished from simplistic ones. There is a saying, attributed to Clemenceau: *N'être pas socialiste à vingt ans preuve d'un manque de coeur; l'être après trente ans est preuve d'un*

---

40. Wilder's view of the superficiality of modern apocalypticism is essentially correct, however. See Y. Sherwood, "'Not with a Bang but a Whimper': Shrunken Eschatologies of the Twentieth Century — and the Bible," in *Apocalyptic in History and Tradition*, 94-116; L. DiTommaso, "At the Edge of Tomorrow: Apocalypticism and Science Fiction," in *End of Days: Essays on the Apocalypse from Antiquity to Modernity*, ed. K. Kinane and M. Ryan (Jefferson, N.C.: McFarland, 2009), 221-41. I see the superficiality of modern apocalypticism to be apparent in *both* its secular and biblical varieties.

41. Cf. J. Dey's list of sermons designed to prepare congregations for the Second Coming: "Armageddon Anxiety and Satan's Six-Pack: A Pastoral Response," in *Apocalypticism and Millennialism: Shaping a Believers Church Eschatology for the Twenty-First Century*, ed. L. L. Johns (Kitchener, Ont.: Pandora Press, 2000), 386-94.

42. Beside the fact that no apocalyptic timetable has yet proven to be accurate, the issue of when the historical age precisely begins and ends (which in the biblical variety of the worldview usually correlates with the origin of evil and its final overthrow) is irrelevant to the logic of the worldview. The date of the end could vary even within a single book, as it does with the double dates of Dan. 12:11-12. The same rationale applies, *mutatis mutandis*, to the types of millennialism (pre-, post-, and a-millennialism).

manque de tête.⁴³ On one hand there is a wistful, romantic aspect to youthful attempts to better the world or to rectify injustice. This is balanced in its antistrophe by the recognition that ideologies which explain the world in blanket categories are inadequate responses to modern problems. It is of profound significance that totalizing worldviews such as Marxism and apocalypticism comprehend history schematically and deterministically, and both rely on hidden-hand mechanisms to make their case.⁴⁴

In its streamlining of past events and inability to accept historical causality based on the interaction of circumstance, happenstance, and human decision, apocalypticism is a reaction to pluralism. As such, its binary simplicity renders it incompatible with contemporary society on several levels. For example, in imposing the stark polarity of apocalyptic Otherness on the diversity and richness of life, the worldview can arrest the full development of the individual in its modern liberal contexts.⁴⁵ Apocalypticism is also unable to operate in spheres that require a common realist dialogue, such as foreign policy, since it considers Otherness to derive from the revelation of unimpeachable knowledge imparted by a transcendent reality.⁴⁶ More could be said about

---

43. Apparently the aphorism was first uttered, with *républicain* as its subject, by François Guizot, prime minister of France (1847-48), and was thereafter recycled by others, including, most famously, Clemenceau — *"le Tigre."*

44. The hidden hand of Marxist historiography asserts a degree of determinism with respect to class struggle and history, a claim invalidated most famously by the universal voting of war credits in 1914.

45. "Few of us can be saints," wrote the anthropologist and humanist Loren Eiseley, "[but] few of us are total monsters. To the degree that we let others project upon ourselves erroneous or unbalanced conceptions of our natures, we may unconsciously reshape our own image to less pleasing forms." *The Unexpected Universe* (New York: Harcourt, Brace & World, 1964), 182.

46. "Such beliefs, dependent as they are upon revelation thought to be divine and peculiar to specific religious communities, are simply not a viable basis for the foreign policy of a multicultural democracy in a pluralistic world." W. Martin, "With God on Their Side: Religion and U.S. Foreign Policy," in *Religion Returns to the Public Square: Faith and Policy in America*, ed. H. Heclo and W. M. McClay (Washington, D.C.: Woodrow Wilson Center Press, 2003), 327-59 at 355. Note also the curious phenomenon of Christian Zionism. It should not be understood, however, as a monolithic force motivated solely by apocalyptic expectations; see M. Durham, "Evangelical Protestantism and Foreign Policy in the United States after September 11," *Patterns of Prejudice* 38 (2004): 145-58; and S. Spector, *Evangelicals and Israel: The Story of American Christian Zionism* (Oxford/New York: Oxford University Press, 2009). Nor should apocalypticism be equated automatically with fundamentalism: although apocalypticism is fundamentalist by inclination, not all apocalypticism is fundamentalist, and not all fundamentalist movements are apocalyptic.

the effects of apocalyptic simplicity,[47] but that would divert us from the main point, which is the consequences of transferred responsibility.

Few biblical scholars today would agree with Martin Buber, who set prophecy against apocalypticism as the "old philosophical quarrel between indeterministic and deterministic views of the world."[48] Every hidden-hand historiography — prophetic, apocalyptic, or secular — sidetracks human agency to some degree, and therein minimizes human responsibility. Apocalypticism merely amplified prophecy's implicit determinism, and grafted a supra-historical horizon onto it.[49]

At issue are the role and degree of free will within a system. No doubt apocalyptic logic can accommodate free will. Bernard McGinn observes that most apocalyptic writings have a built-in moral component that declares itself in the choice to persevere in the good or persist in evil.[50] Early Jewish apocalypses like Daniel and *2 Baruch* make more determined attempts to integrate human decision with divine design. Similarly, the Christian *Apocalypse of Peter*, hardly special in this regard, correlates prior behavior with future punishment:

---

47. "We are not like the social insects. They have only the one way of doing things and they will do it forever, coded for that way. We are coded differently, not just for binary choices, *go* or *no-go*. We can go four ways at once, depending how the air feels: *go, no-go*, but also *maybe*, and *what the hell let's give it a try*. . . . We can build structures for human society never seen before, thoughts never thought before, music never heard before. Provided that we do not kill ourselves off . . . there is no end to what we might do on or off this planet." L. Thomas, *Late Night Thoughts on Listening to Mahler's Ninth Symphony* (New York: Viking, 1983), 62-63, italics original.

48. M. Buber, "Prophetie und Apokalyptik," in idem, *Sehertum: Anfang und Ausgang* (Cologne: J. Hegner, 1955), 49-74. Reprinted as "Prophecy, Apocalyptic, and the Historical Hour," in *Pointing the Way: Collected Essays*, ed. and trans. M. S. Friedman (New York: Harper and Row, 1957), 192-207.

49. Although the classic Israelite prophets placed much stock in Israel's ability to alter its behavior on the basis of its memory of God's mighty deeds, this did not dilute the determinism of their forecasts of doom for the nations. Alternately, some early apocalypses maintain that individual Jews still have to keep the covenant's strictures; see Collins, *Apocalyptic Imagination*, 221-22, and the text below. In the case of MT Daniel, its combination of individual free will and corporate determinism is more a result of the history of its composition rather than design, although its final redactor deliberately retained the free will that marks the earlier court tales.

50. B. McGinn, "Introduction: Apocalyptic Spirituality," in *Apocalyptic Spirituality: Treatises and Letters of Lactantius, Adso of Montier-en-Der, Joachim of Fiore, the Franciscan Spirituals, Savonarola*, ed. and trans. B. McGinn (The Classics of Western Spirituality; New York: Paulist, 1979), 1-16 at 12.

And I saw the murderers and their accessaries [sic] cast into a gorge full of venomous reptiles and tormented by those beasts, and thus writhing in that torture, and worms oppressed them like dark clouds. But the souls of those who had been murdered stood and watched the punishment of those murderers and said, *"O God, righteous is thy judgment."*[51]

Several obstacles, however, collaborate to minimize the meaningfulness of free will in the apocalyptic mode. First, the worldview assumes an impending radical change, ascribed to an omnipotent agency. Any historiography based on these premises will incline to determinism, free will notwithstanding. Second, the worldview's radical dualism and the power it accords to the transcendent reality generate hypertrophic expectations. End-time punishments and rewards are invariably extreme. Events and objects are equally exaggerated: witness the monumental New Jerusalem of Revelation 20–21 and the sociopolitical utopias of secular apocalypticism.[52] Such expectations cultivate a climate incommensurate with human-scale causality. Third, apocalyptic texts seldom outline the mechanism, kenotic or otherwise, by which free will is perceived to interact with the hidden hand of history. Daniel and Revelation, the paradigm apocalypses, are notoriously deficient here. The first half of Daniel assumes right action will be rewarded; the second half is resolutely deterministic. Likewise, Revelation might warn, "Repent then. If not, I will come to you soon and make war against them with the sword of my mouth" (2:16), but it is difficult to square this with the march of history that is described in the rest of the book. The lack of meaningful integration inevitably isolates free will from the main line of thought. For these reasons, even in the earliest apocalyptic literature we find the deadening sense of historical determinism that would become one of the worldview's defining characteristics.[53]

---

51. Akhmimic version, §25 (cf. Rev. 19:2 and 16:7), in R. McL. Wilson, trans. and ed., *New Testament Apocrypha, Volume Two: Writings Related to the Apostles; Apocalypses and Related Subjects* (Cambridge/Louisville: James Clarke/Westminster John Knox, 2003), 629, italics original.

52. E. J. Hobsbawm, *Primitive Rebels: Studies in Archaic Forms of Social Movements in the 19th and 20th Centuries* (Manchester: Manchester University Press, 1959); J. Gray, *Black Mass: Apocalyptic Religion and the Death of Utopia* (New York: Doubleday, 2007); and J. R. Hall, *Apocalypse: From Antiquity to the Empire of Modernity* (Cambridge, Mass.: Polity, 2009).

53. See L. DiTommaso, "Biblical Genre, Form, and Function in the Post-Biblical Historical Apocalyptica," in *The Reception and Interpretation of the Bible in Late Antiquity*, ed. L. DiTommaso and L. Turcescu (BAC 6; Leiden/Boston: Brill, 2008), 145-61, and the apocalyptic oracles and political prophecies in McGinn, *Visions of the End*.

Most critically, however: even if a text or a tradition stresses the consequences of what it imagines to be free will, there is no real choice when there are only two options. The worldview preselects the choices: either One or the Other, neither ambiguous, nothing in between. Apocalyptic free will is nothing more than an extension of the binary minimalism of apocalyptic otherness.[54]

The toxicity of the system is patent. A belief in the transitory nature of the world and the assurance of an imminent and otherworldly resolution of its problems, rising as it does from the worldview's axioms and resting in no small part on its conception of Otherness, establish a framework of transferred responsibility. Apocalypticism is an adolescent worldview not only because it comprehends the problems of the world simplistically, but most importantly because it considers their solutions to reside elsewhere — and with someone (or something) else. In biblical apocalypticism, this Other is God. In the secular variety of the worldview, it can be an idealized or divinized humanity, a hidden-hand "force" or "law," or a superhuman (but not supernatural) agency. In all cases, the abrogation of responsibility to the degree obliged by the worldview's logic and function leads to *moral hazard*. In economics, this refers to a state where a party insulated from financial risk might act in a different way than it would if it were exposed to that risk. As it refers to apocalypticism, it sanctions believers to act in ways that absolve them of personal accountability.

The ramifications can be catastrophic. Most palpable is the use of the worldview as a justification to promote a present agenda in light of a future forecast. Although not unique to apocalypticism, this feature finds its quintessential expression in the worldview's singular amalgam of dualism, extremism, and determinism. Its radical Otherness permits no ambiguity as to the destiny and design of adversaries. At the same time, its propensity to determinism and its claim to disclose the panoramic view of history blur the distinction between present and future states. These features underwrite situations where, as representatives of mysterious and sinister cosmic forces, members of the eschatological Other are subject to prejudice or persecution in the present.

A prime example is the dehumanization of the Other. This action involves a spectrum of responses ranging from the automatic classification of

---

54. Hence, rather than an act of free will, conversion in apocalypticism is nearly always a predestined eschatological event, whereupon the Gentile nations will come to know God, the Jews will convert to Christianity, etc.

individuals (all tigers look and act the same) to their deliberate demonization as a group (all tigers are monsters).⁵⁵ The imbrutement of apocalyptic enemies, freighted by pseudo-scientific theories from physiognomy to Social Darwinism, is most conspicuous in medieval texts, with deep roots in the teratological speculation of the era. Christians assigned to Jews, Ethiopians, and Muslims the same barbaric social customs used to describe the monstrous races that were thought to inhabit the world's frontiers.⁵⁶

History teaches that apocalyptic trajectories typically follow this route, despite the best intentions. We might admire the attempts of Augustine and his intellectual heirs to liberate apocalypticism from the chains of its logic through symbolism or allegory.⁵⁷ But the relatively minuscule number of

---

55. Although the monster is an "Other," it is not necessarily an apocalyptic "Other." Cf. the definition of the monster in J. J. Cohen, "Monster Culture (Seven Theses)," in *Monster Theory: Reading Culture,* ed. J. J. Cohen (Minneapolis: University of Minnesota Press, 1996), 3-25.

56. D. Strickland, *Saracens, Demons and Jews: Making Monsters in Medieval Art* (Princeton: Princeton University Press, 2003). A related trajectory saw the association of the enemy Other with Gog/Magog and the armies of the eschaton, which, imprisoned behind a massive gate at the edge of the world, waited for the appointed time when the gate would be opened and the final battle joined. See A. R. Anderson, *Alexander's Gate, Gog and Magog, and the Inclosed Nations* (Monographs of the Medieval Academy of America 5; Cambridge, Mass.: The Medieval Academy of America, 1932); and A. C. Gow, *Red Jews: Antisemitism in an Apocalyptic Age, 1200-1600* (Studies in Medieval and Reformation Thought 55; Leiden: Brill, 1995).

57. B. E. Daley, *The Hope of the Early Church: A Handbook of Patristic Eschatology* (Peabody, Mass.: Hendrickson, 2003), 127-50; B. McGinn, "The Emergence of the Spiritual Reading on the Apocalypse in the Third Century," in *Reading Religions in the Ancient World: Essays Presented to Robert McQueen Grant on His 90th Birthday,* ed. D. E. Aune and R. Darling Young (NovTSup 125; Leiden: Brill, 2007), 251-72. The influence of the Augustinian interpretation of Revelation remains strong in some circles. W. Klaassen, for example, writes that the "litany of destruction and death discourages many honest Christians from reading [Revelation]. In its scope and terror, it rivals anything available on the evening television news ... [but] we must remember that we are not dealing with a description of what will literally happen" (*Armageddon and the Peaceable Kingdom* [Waterloo, Ont.: Herald Press, 1999], 245). But literal interpretations were (and remain) dominant everywhere else. They appear in nearly every other context in Western medieval Christianity (see below, note 58, and the dozens of texts in McGinn, *Visions of the End*), in eastern Christianity, medieval Judaism, and medieval Islam, in the post-medieval variants of these religions, and in the later secular variations of the worldview. Even within its limited circles in the Western tradition the Augustinian view was overwritten by later developments; see E. L. Tuveson, *Redeemer Nation: The Idea of America's Millennial Role* (Chicago: University of Chicago Press, 1968). We must not confuse a resistance to millennialism in the West with a wholesale disinterest in literal interpretation, or impose Augustinian nonliteralism onto earlier texts. Hence on this

nonliteral interpretations bears little on the nature of the worldview or how it has been understood. There are no roads that lead away from literal interpretation,[58] or from the binary simplicity of apocalyptic Otherness and the notion of transferred responsibility. All end in the license for abuse. As the Tiburtine Sibyl promises, "Whoever does not adore the cross of Jesus Christ will be punished by the sword." Any group considered less than human will be treated inhumanely.

No less harmful are the indirect consequences of transferred responsibility. For example, detailed descriptions of end-time scenarios are hardly innocuous compositions. Instead, they can create and sustain the social climate which legitimates policies such as the dehumanization of enemies and exclusion by assimilation or elimination.[59] But there is a more vital factor that needs accounting in light of the thesis concerning the hostility of apocalypticism to life on Earth today.

Sigmund Freud was famously fond of saying that the three most important revolutions in the history of science share the quality of having deflated humanity's sense of superiority. Copernicus demonstrated that the Earth does not occupy the center of the solar system. Darwin described how humans are not the culmination of created life forms living in a Panglossian world. Freud himself undermined the idea of humans as fully rational beings. General relativity, quantum physics, plate tectonics, the discovery of

---

last point I cannot concur with J. Niewiadomski that Mark 13:22 provides grounds to say that Augustine remained faithful to Jesus' understanding of apocalypticism. See Niewiadomski, "'Denial of the Apocalypse' versus 'Fascination with the Final Days': Current Theological Discussion of Apocalyptic Thinking in the Perspective of Mimetic Theory," in *Politics and Apocalypse*, ed. R. Hamerton-Kelly (East Lansing: Michigan State University Press, 2007), 51-67 at 60.

58. Apocalyptic *multivalence* (the ability of an apocalyptic timetable to be reinterpreted time and again in response to present-day events) and *polyvalence* (the ability of *apocalyptica* to permit several yet not necessarily contradictory readings simultaneously) admit multiple interpretations of a text, insofar as they may be supported by its internal data. But the logic of the worldview and the corollaries that may be rigorously derived from its axioms do not permit the sort of non-literal readings that address the difficulties that some scholars and theologians have found with literal interpretations of these texts or with the propriety of the apocalyptic worldview in a post-Enlightenment world. Nor do we find many texts that are designed to be read non-literally, or, on balance, audiences reading them this way, the point being that apocalyptic literature is almost always written to be understood literally, a fact that these audiences, whose reaction we can determine from their own commentaries and art, seemed to have grasped with perfect clarity. See also above, note 57.

59. M. Volf, *Exclusion and Embrace: A Theological Exploration of Identity, Otherness, and Reconciliation* (Nashville: Abingdon, 1996), esp. 74-75.

DNA — none of these has transformed our self-conception in precisely the same manner.[60]

A fourth revolution is presently underway. Unlike the revolutions of Copernicus, Darwin, and Freud, it is not associated with a single name, although it has many godparents: John Muir, Sir Albert Howard, Aldo Leopold, Rachel Carson, Masanobu Fukuoka, and Michael Pollan, among others. Like the three prior revolutions, the new revolution is changing the way we perceive ourselves and our relationship to the universe. It is the environmental revolution. It presumes that human activity has perilously altered the environment, and that only human activity can ameliorate or rectify the situation. So long as we view the planet as a place where we and our children will live, and where our actions, for better or worse, will have a measureable if not always predictable effect on its life forms, then we have not abrogated our responsibility to it, or transferred this responsibility to another agency. The risk is ours.

Apocalypticism is incompatible with this perspective.[61] The tension stems less from a hostility to the environment on the part of believers (although this is not absent) than it does from a lack of concern that derives from the worldview's purposes and premises, including the anticipation of an imminent and inevitable end to history, which devalues all historical objects, including life.

A timely illustration of this phenomenon is the trend among evangelical Christians in the United States to downplay or ignore environmental crises on the basis that creation will be redeemed in a very short time.[62] Rather than discrete events with human causes, ecological calamities are comprehended alongside natural disasters and political upheavals as part of a fore-

60. The Turing revolution might eventually have the same profound effect on humanity's hubris, albeit (if the science-fiction writers are correct) one that might be imposed on us by artificial intelligences.

61. See J. T. Sanders, *Ethics in the New Testament* (Philadelphia: Fortress, 1975), 112-15, on Revelation specifically.

62. See, e.g., B. Moyers, "A Question for Journalists: How Do We Cover Penguins and the Politics of Denial?" keynote address, annual convention of the Society of Environmental Journalists, Austin, Texas, 1 October 2005 (http://www.sejarchive.org/confer/austin/PenguinsandthePoliticsofDenial.pdf), retrieved September 2009, and G. Scherer, "Christian-Right Views Are Swaying Politicians and Threatening the Environment," *Grist*, 27 October 2004 (http://www.grist.org/article/scherer-christian/), retrieved August 2009. Less overt but equally disturbing is the attitude of Mother Teresa: "Why should we care about the Earth when our duty is to the poor and sick among us? God will take care of the earth" (reported in J. Lovelock, *The Revenge of Gaia* [London: Penguin, 2007], 3).

ordained series of signs of the approaching end.⁶³ The *eschatologization of the environment* reflects the apocalyptic stance on time and history, and illustrates the full effects of transferred responsibility:⁶⁴

> For the creation waits with eager longing for the revealing of the children of God; for the creation was subjected to futility, not of its own will but by the will of the one who subjected it, in hope that the creation itself will be set free from its bondage to decay and will obtain the freedom of the glory of the children of God. We know that the whole creation has been groaning in labor pains until now. (Rom. 8:19-22)

> [B]y the word of God heavens existed long ago and an earth was formed out of water and by means of water, through which the world of that time was deluged with water and perished. But by the same word the present heavens and earth have been reserved for fire, being kept until the day of judgment and destruction of the godless. . . . [The] day of the Lord will come like a thief, and then the heavens will pass away with a loud noise, and the elements will be dissolved with fire, and the earth and everything that is done on it will be disclosed. (2 Pet. 3:5-10)

Neither stewardship nor spirituality is the answer.⁶⁵ Both are indentured to a worldview that regardless of its form — ancient or modern, bibli-

---

63. Boyer, *When Time Shall Be No More*, 301-2, 331-37. It is not always possible to isolate this viewpoint from others contributing to the same effect. A general denial of scientific theory and method can lead to conflicts with pro-environmental policies where they are at variance with theology. Similarly, on the basis of social issues "green" conservatives might support a candidate with platforms indifferent or hostile to ecological issues.

64. The phrase also describes the mindset of apocalyptic environmental groups; see M. F. Lee, *Earth First! Environmental Apocalypse* (Syracuse: Syracuse University Press, 1995); L. A. Lorrentzen, "Phallic Millennialism and Radical Environmentalism: The Apocalyptic Vision of Earth First!," in *The Year 2000: Essays on the End*, ed. C. B. Strozier and M. Flynn (New York: New York University Press, 1997), 144-53; D. Wall, *Babylon and Beyond: The Economics of Anti-Capitalist, Anti-Globalist, and Radical Green Movements* (London/Ann Arbor: Pluto Press, 2005), and the sources cited therein.

65. These options are often but not always affiliated. On stewardship, see, e.g., the Evangelical Environmental Network (EEN), which seeks "to educate, inspire, and mobilize Christians in their effort to care for God's creation, to be faithful stewards of God's provision, and to advocate for actions and policies that honor God and protect the environment" (http://www.creationcare.org/about.php, retrieved September 2009). The EEN also publishes *Creation Care: A Christian Environmental Quarterly*. "Spirituality" is a well-defined term, but I mean it here to express what the historian of medieval science Lynn White, Jr.,

cal or secular, literary or graphic, active or latent — subordinates nature to purposes informed by the transcendent reality.[66] Thus nature is similarly excluded from the empathy that the worldview is constitutionally unable to extend to others.

Nature is the fourth Other. This is the singular tragedy of apocalypticism today. After the flood, God blessed Noah and his sons, telling them to multiply and fill the earth. As part of his new covenant with humanity, God promised Noah:

> The fear and dread of you shall rest on every animal of the earth, and on every bird of the air, on everything that creeps on the ground, and on all the fish of the sea; into your hand they are delivered. (Gen. 9:2)

Although not apocalyptic in itself, this passage forms the basic ideological platform on which the apocalyptic view of the environment rests, mediated by the broader worldview. This view, anchored by the idea of the corruption of creation[67] and the binary simplicity of apocalyptic Otherness, prompts some to hasten the apocalypse by actions destructive to the environment. It allows the grotesque hubris of labeling eschatological devastation as recycling, since the new earth is "regenerated out of the old."[68] It encapsulates

---

identifies as the "animism" that Christianity had supplanted (and via the industrial and scientific revolutions reinforced the notion that "nature has no reason for existence save to serve man"), and to which the theology of Francis of Assisi provides a close Christian analogue. See Lynn White, Jr., "The Historical Roots of Our Ecologic Crisis," *Science* n.s. 155, no. 3767 (10 March 1967): 1203-7. In the same vein, but a slightly different light, see W. Berry, *A Continuous Harmony* (New York: Harcourt Brace Jovanovich, 1972), 6-7: "perhaps the greatest disaster of human history is one that happened to or within religion: that is, the conceptual division between the holy and the world, the excerpting of the Creator from the creation. . . . If God was not in the world, then obviously the world was a thing of inferior importance, or no importance at all. Those who were disposed to exploit it were thus free to do so." On the notion that all pre-industrial societies were ecologically sound, see the multiple examples to the contrary discussed in J. Diamond, *Collapse: How Societies Choose to Fail or Succeed* (New York: Viking Penguin, 2005).

66. Its secular variants range from the cold calculations of utopian visions that consider others as tools in service of a transcendent vision, to the casual amorality of popular culture, wherein continents are ravaged by calamities both natural and artificial in the service of a plotline.

67. H. A. Hahne, *The Corruption and Redemption of Creation: Nature in Romans 8.19-22 and Jewish Apocalyptic Literature* (LNTS 336; London/New York: T&T Clark, 2006).

68. E. Adams, *The Stars Will Fall from Heaven: Cosmic Catastrophe in the New Testament and Its World* (London/New York: T&T Clark, 2007), discussing K. D. Dyer, "When Is

every injustice that has been perpetrated against the other inhabitants of this planet. It permits humans to speak for all other life forms.

The alternative is obvious. The great naturalist John Muir wrote, "I have never happened upon a trace of evidence that seemed to show that any one animal was ever made for another as it was made for itself."[69]

> Even the broken grass, or the fallen tree, or the cut stone gives us sorrow, because we feel they are in our minds. (Ōshio Heihachirō [Chūsai])[70]

---

the End Not the End? The Fate of Earth in Biblical Eschatology (Mark 13)," in *The Earth Story in the New Testament,* ed. N. C. Habel and V. Balabanski (The Earth Bible 5; Sheffield: Sheffield Academic Press, 2002), 44-56.

69. J. Muir, "Wild Wool," *The Overland Monthly* (April 1875), reprinted in W. Cronon, ed., *John Muir: Selected Writings* (Library of America; Penguin Putnam, 1997), 589-606 at 602-3.

70. Trans. R. H. Blyth, *Haiku,* Volume 1: *Eastern Culture* (Tokyo: Hokuseido Press, 1949), 78.

Apocalypticism as the Rejected Other: Wisdom and Apocalypticism in Early Judaism and Early Christianity

Sean Freyne

John Collins has been more influential than any other contemporary scholar in bringing to our attention the importance and variety of the wisdom and apocalyptic writings of the Second Temple period. His work has particular importance in the field of New Testament studies also. As is well known, the issue of the relationships between these two genres continues to play an important role in discussions about the historical Jesus and early Christian writings, especially the Q document. Collins's detailed, yet measured treatment of the literature in a highly impressive list of monographs and articles is based on his engagement with a whole range of texts and his ability to situate them in the social and religious worlds of Palestinian and Diaspora Judaism as well as the broader Mediterranean and ancient Near Eastern contexts. While he is widely read in modern literary and sociological theories, Collins never allows these to set the agenda for his own investigations. Ideal types or pure genres will for him always have to give way to the counter evidence of the mixed genres and complex social and political situations as these operate in both the real and textual worlds with which he deals.

In this paper I would like to offer some reflections on the importance of apocalypticism within early Judaism and early Christianity, especially in view of the negative attitude towards it in some recent writings. Indeed, so strong are these reactions in some quarters that it has been suggested that something more is at stake than merely a difference of opinion about literary tropes and genres.¹ In such circumstances there is a danger that the Other can be constructed in such a way that vilification rather than appreciation becomes the norm. I propose, therefore, to examine the ways in which wisdom and apocalypticism are interwoven in two writings, namely, 1 Corinthians and Mark's gospel. I shall begin, however, by exploring the background of some of the current unease among certain scholars with the "Otherness" of apocalyptic thought to modern sensibilities. My second step will be to report on the work of those, including John Collins, who have been studying the pertinent Jewish writings, including the recently published 4QInstruction, in order to demonstrate the complexity and the richness of the relationship between the two genres. Finally, I hope to offer some closing hermeneutical reflections arising from the previous discussions as an attempt to retrieve the rejected Other of the Judeo-Christian heritage.

I. Apocalypticism in Recent Scholarly Discussion

Foremost among those adopting a negative position towards apocalypticism is the late Robert Funk, the founder and leading member of the Jesus Seminar. He called for apocalypticism "to be exorcized" from the Christian religious vocabulary because of its world-denying and vindictive features.² These sentiments are echoed by the question John Dominic Crossan poses for his readers, namely, whether apocalypticism is about divine mercy or divine revenge. His own conclusion is that it is about the latter. This opinion helps to explain, if not vindicate, Crossan's curious decision to opt for a sapiential rather than an apocalyptic understanding of Jesus' preaching about the kingdom of God, given the nature of the evidence he produces for his claims with regard to Jesus.³

Feminist literary critic Tina Pippin is more frank and more autobiographical in articulating her difficulties with apocalypticism, as she reflects on her life in the American South surrounded by the signs of violence and

---

1. Melanie Johnson-Debaufre, *Jesus among Her Children: Q, Eschatology and the Construction of Christian Origins* (Cambridge, Mass.: Harvard University Press, 2005), 6-7.

2. Robert Funk, *Honest to Jesus: Jesus for a New Millennium* (San Francisco: HarperSanFrancisco, 1996), 314.

3. John D. Crossan, *The Birth of Christianity: Discovering What Happened in the Years Immediately after the Execution of Jesus* (New York: HarperCollins, 1998), 586; idem, *The Historical Jesus: The Life of a Mediterranean Peasant* (New York: HarperCollins, 1991), 292-97 and 340.

racial hatred, often buttressed by images and language drawn from apocalyptic literature. While refusing to read apocalypticism as "an acceptable ethical narrative," she rejects the Funk-Crossan solution of excising apocalyptic discourse, thereby "cleaning up" the mess, as it were. Adopting a postmodern stance to the so-called little apocalypse of Mark 13, and reading it intertextually with Flannery O'Connor's short story "A Good Man Is Hard to Find," she fails to find any trace of hope here, only the violence and meanness of an apocalyptic God and Jesus' participation with him, as he warns his hearers to be watchful, promising that Paradise will await them if they remain responsible. For Pippin, it would seem, the only ethics of apocalyptic eschatology is its refusal to yield to our utopian dreams of human well-being and fulfillment. Rather it reminds us that life is like that and we can so easily and readily become co-conspirators with the violent God, enabling global disasters and mass genocide.[4]

Mention of genocide is a reminder that this struggle with the language of the New Testament and the failures of Christian theology to deal adequately with it had its own tragic consequences a century ago. Faced with the challenges of the European Enlightenment in the nineteenth century, German New Testament scholars found themselves grappling with a similar issue. Whereas liberal theologians such as Albert Ritschl and Adolf van Harnack sought to present Jesus as a universal teacher of ethics, espousing their own liberal ideas of human freedom and responsibility, others such as Johannes Weiss and Albert Schweitzer insisted on Jesus as a preacher of an apocalyptic kingdom of God, following the History of Religions approach.[5] Once more it was a matter of either abandoning the apocalyptic dimension of the text, thereby making Jesus relevant, or opting for a Jesus of his own time who had little to offer to the contemporary world, since his apocalyptic dream had failed.

We may well ask with Tertullian: what has Athens to do with Jerusalem, faced with this modern unease with apocalypticism and its worldview? Central to the problem are the theodicy that is presupposed and the nature and function of the religious language that is employed. Responsible scholarship would seem to suggest that if we must choose between Pippin and Funk-Crossan, the former has taken the better part. In dealing with the nineteenth-century crisis, Rudolf Bultmann, whose own approach to the

---

4. Tina Pippin, "A Good Apocalypse Is Hard to Find," *Semeia* 72 (1995): 153-71.

5. John Riches, *A Century of New Testament Study* (Cambridge: Lutterworth, 1993), 14-30.

New Testament was a combination of a History of Religions methodology and existentialist philosophical categories in explicating the message for his contemporaries, opted for a program of demythologization as a way of dealing with the problem. This meant that he was taking religious language seriously, while recognizing its cultural limitations and the discredited worldview that it represented. Before addressing this issue head on, however, we must take the necessary detour of examining the results of recent studies of Second Temple literature, in order to see whether or not our problem may have arisen at an earlier stage still, and if so how it was negotiated.

II. Wisdom and Apocalypticism in Second Temple Literature

Whatever the ancient origins of apocalypticism and wisdom in terms of divine combat myths and court advisors, it is surely significant that both worldviews and their related genres came to the surface in the postexilic period. Judean society had gone through the experience of exile and return, but was faced with having to live under the control of various imperial powers — Persian, Greek, and Roman. Even a nodding acquaintance with postcolonial theory would suggest that this situation would inevitably give rise to external pressures to conform and internal tensions to dissent. The brief period of self-rule that was achieved in the second century B.C.E. with the rise of the Hasmonean state is illustrative of these pressures. On the one hand, we see the ruling elites taking on Hellenistic trappings in terms of language, architecture, coins, use of mercenaries, and so forth; on the other hand, we see them engaging in a culture war against the surrounding peoples, especially the Greek city-states in the region.

This hybridity inevitably brought to the surface the deep divisions within the society that went back to the return from exile. The rise of the various Jewish "philosophies" — the Essenes and the Pharisees in particular — indicates the concern for traditional values, even when the two groups adopted quite different strategies. A glance into the ongoing and varied literary output among the Qumran Essenes is indicative of the differing points of view, both among the sectarians and more generally.

The publication of 4QInstruction, to the elucidation of which John Collins and his students have contributed significantly, is a good example of this atmosphere. The fact that six or seven copies of the text have been found shows its importance, though Collins is of the opinion that it was not addressed to Jewish society at large but to those who are familiar with "the mystery that is to come," the *raz nihyeh*. Yet the nature of the instructions dealing with such everyday realities as family, money matters (loans and sureties), and farming points to an audience that is wider than the community at Qumran, though still regarding itself as chosen and therefore privy to the deeper understanding of things, based on their knowledge of the mystery that is to be.[6]

Notwithstanding its fragmentary nature, the reconstructed document has a consistency of theme similar to what one finds in Proverbs and Sirach. The addressees are repeatedly reminded that they are poor, yet poverty is not an ideal to be espoused, but rather a fact of life to be accepted. Equally, should prosperity come one's way it should not be rejected. One detects behind these instructions and admonitions the social situation of the Hellenistic age, marked by both increased opportunities for some, but likewise the danger of sliding into poverty for others. Yet despite this aspect of practical wisdom based on the biblical laws, 4QInstruction differs markedly from the wisdom book because of the repeated (over twenty times in all) use of the phrase *raz nihyeh* ("the mystery that is to be") which gives the work the quality of a revelatory text, indicative of apocalyptic literature.[7]

Thus the addressee is admonished "to gaze upon," "to examine," "to mediate on," and "to grasp" this mystery. He is to honor his parents because it was they who first "opened his ear" to the mystery. This terminology might appear to suggest that the phrase simply refers to the acquisition of wisdom, similar to Sirach's description of the ideal scribe (Sir. 38:1-3). However, even though there is no mention of an interpreting angel of the sort found in classic apocalyptic writings, further consideration of the scope of this mystery within the document clearly suggests an apocalyptic worldview. This includes knowledge of the future mysteries concerning the ways of truth and iniquity, the birth-time of salvation, the inheritance of everything that lives, and who is to inherit glory and iniquity. The fact that the *raz nihyeh* appears to be identified with wisdom's role in creation in laying down the foundations of truth suggests an Urzeit/Endzeit pattern, by which the revelatory power of the mystery with regard to the things that are to be is based on prior knowledge of the way things really are. In the judgment of Matthew Goff, whose studies of the text are the most

---

6. John J. Collins, *Jewish Wisdom in the Hellenistic Age* (London: Routledge, 1997), 120.

7. Daniel Harrington, "The *Raz Nihyeh* in a Qumran Wisdom Text (1Q26, 4Q 415-418, 423)," *RQ* 6(1996): 549-52; Collins, *Jewish Wisdom*, 121-25.

comprehensive to date, 4QInstruction is best described as "a sapiential work but with an apocalyptic worldview."[8]

This understanding of the relationship between the worldviews of wisdom and apocalyptic in the Qumran writings concurs with the finding of a ten-year consultation in the Society of Biblical Literature Symposium on Wisdom and Apocalypticism in the Second Temple period.[9] George Nickelsburg's discussion set the agenda by reviewing the relevant literature.[10] He begins the discussion by outlining what he considers to be established points of consensus with regard to the apocalyptic genre, namely, only those writings in which revelation is a significant component should be so classified. On this criterion six works can definitely be listed, among them 1 *Enoch* and Daniel being the prime examples. Yet a perusal of these two works quickly indicates that from a literary point of view they are quite different in terms of the material that each draws on, which includes both visionary and wisdom elements. In contrast, those books with practical instruction for living, often based on the Torah, are usually classified as wisdom books, foremost among which is the book of Proverbs. Other books that would come under the same rubric, such as Tobit, Sirach, and Baruch, all show a high regard for prophetic traditions, including interest in the future. On this sampling both apocalypticism and wisdom are flexible categories of classification, demonstrating a broad scope of "generic compatibility," as Collins has argued.[11] Thus, it would seem that notions of pure genres should be avoided, since ideal types do not correspond to the realities of the extant literature, nor should their worldviews be regarded as opposing, no matter how much we moderns have difficulty in identifying what it is that makes such compatibility possible.[12]

The notion of revealed wisdom, which John Ashton has labeled "remote" in contrast to "accessible" wisdom makes the bridge between these

---

8. Matthew Goff, "Discerning Trajectories: 4QInstruction and the Sapiential Background of the Sayings Source Q," *JBL* 124 (2005): 657-73, esp. 655; idem, *Discerning Wisdom: The Sapiential Literature of the Dead Sea Scrolls* (VTSup 116; Brill: Leiden, 2007), 17 and 297-308.

9. Ben Wright and Larry Wills, eds., *Conflicted Boundaries in Wisdom and Apocalypticism* (SBL Symposium 35; Atlanta: SBL Publications, 2005).

10. George Nickelsburg, "Wisdom and Apocalypticism in Early Judaism: Some Points for Discussion," in Wright and Wills, eds., *Conflicted Boundaries*, 17-38.

11. John J. Collins, "Wisdom, Apocalyptic and Generic Compatibility," in idem, *Seers, Sibyls and Sages in Hellenistic-Roman Judaism* (JSJSup 54; Leiden: Brill, 1997), 385-404.

12. Jonathan Z. Smith, "Wisdom and Apocalyptic," in *Religious Syncretism in Antiquity: Essays in Conversation with Geo. Windengren*, ed. Birger Pearson (Chico, Calif.: Scholars Press, 1975), 131-56.

Apocalypticism as the Rejected Other

two types of literature. This latter relies on observation and skill in various crafts (Sirach 38, 11), but even these can easily be cloaked with the aura of "the eternal secrets, which were made in heaven" (*1 Enoch* 9:6). Remote wisdom, on the other hand, finds its most complete expression in the idea of personified Wisdom as a female figure, which makes its appearance in a series of poems in which she describes her closeness to God, and therefore claims to be privy to the deepest secrets of the created world (Prov. 8:22-31; Job 28; Sirach 24; Wisdom 9). The earliest of these poems, that of Proverbs 8, is introduced in the LXX translation by the statement: "If I explain earthly things to you, I will also remind you to remember the things of eternity" (Prov. 8:21a). It is as though the author perceives the transition from one form of wisdom to the other and feels the need to relate them.[13]

Because of this connection the sage/teacher can appear as an inspired spokesperson for God insofar as he too is privy to the secrets of the cosmos because of his concentration on wisdom. Even Sirach, the most self-consciously scribal in character of the books mentioned, can profile the ideal scribe (presumably a self-portrait of the author) in language that is not far removed from that of 4QInstruction, as was mentioned earlier. The scribe is concerned with prophecies, preserving the sayings of the famous and penetrating the subtleties of parables and the hidden *(apokrypta)* meaning of proverbs. Furthermore, just like Enoch before receiving his dream vision (*1 Enoch* 11–16), Sirach's ideal scribe communes with the creator in morning prayer and may expect to receive a spirit of understanding and direction from the Lord "as he meditates on the mysteries" (Sir. 39:7). The identification of Torah with personified Wisdom, who decided to take up her abode in Zion, means that as Torah teacher the scribe must also acknowledge that for proper understanding he requires divine assistance and inspiration.

If, then, wisdom is by no means incompatible with revelation, apocalypticism can show an interest in earthly things, drawing on wisdom tropes to convey its revealed message.[14] Thus, the content of *1 Enoch* is repeatedly described as wisdom (5:6; 37:1; 92:1; 93:10). The focus is on creation and cosmos rather than the Mosaic Torah, which seems to have been replaced by Enoch's ("the scribe of righteousness") books, as the repository of heavenly wisdom (*1 Enoch* 81:1–82:4 in contrast to Sirach 24 and Baruch 1). The instruc-

---

13. John Ashton, "The Transformation of Wisdom," in idem, *Studying John* (Oxford: Clarendon, 1994), 8-17.

14. Randall L. Argall, *1 Enoch and Sirach: A Comparative Literary and Conceptual Analysis of the Themes of Revelation, Creation, and Judgment* (Atlanta: Scholars Press, 1995).

tional material in *1 Enoch* 92-105 is heavily dependent on the prophetic tradition, particularly with regard to the teaching on wealth and its abuse. In the *Book of the Watchers,* Enoch's ascent to heaven is cast in terms of a prophetic call, whereby he must return and communicate their fate to the Watchers, who had asked him to plead for them (*1 Enoch* 12-16). By contrast, wisdom in Daniel seems to be more circumscribed in that it is mainly concerned with the interpretation of dreams in the opening chapters. Yet, a consideration of Daniel's own prayer suggests that it has a much broader scope, as he gives thanks for the gift of being able to "uncover depths and mysteries to things only known to God alone" (Dan. 2:20-23). This range explains the opening description of Daniel as "proficient" *(maśkîl)* in all wisdom, thus preparing him for his role as prototype for the *maśkîlîm* in the second half of the book, to whom the message of God's eventual triumph over evil in the visionary chapters is directed (Dan. 11:33; 12:2-3).

The discussion thus far underlines the need to have a much more fluid understanding of what constitutes both wisdom and apocalypticism, in view of the range of common themes and tropes, even when one or the other genre functions as the controlling type. Nevertheless, there is need for some precision if the two categories are not to become totally meaningless. As mentioned already, the character of revelatory literature gives apocalypticism some distinctive features, all of which need not be present in every apocalypse, but which assist in establishing generic boundaries. These include interest in otherworldly regions, angels and demons, eschatological judgment and the promise of rewards for the faithful.[15] In the case of wisdom literature there would appear to be a greater variety and less definition as to what are the common features within this group of writings that would make it identifiable as a separate genre, yet practical wisdom and proverbial advice combined with a sense of the mysterious nature of the world are the predominant features.

This suggests that "worldview" may be a useful category in deciding on commonalities and differences between the two types of writings. Even here, however, there is the danger of creating an oppositional dualism such as world-affirming or world-denying that does not correspond to the range of human experience that this literature is attempting to address.[16] Insofar as

---

15. Sarah Tanzer, "Response to George Nickelsburg, 'Wisdom and Apocalyptic in Early Judaism,'" in *Conflicted Boundaries,* 39-50, esp. 43; John J. Collins, ed., *Apocalypse: The Morphology of a Genre* (*Semeia* 14; Atlanta: Scholars Press, 1979), 21-59.

16. Richard Horsley argues for a distinction between wisdom scribes, who affirm the status quo, and those of an apocalyptic mentality, who were disaffected and called for radical

the proverbial or gnomic is based on human experience of the world and its ways, it would seem that it is markedly different from full-blown apocalypticism, which is so interested in another world and deems the present to be irreversibly evil and chaotic. But that is the extreme position that can easily be turned into caricature, and is not representative of the point of view of the literature of the Second Temple generally.

The introduction of personified Wisdom as the source and legitimation of proverbial wisdom elevates human observation and experience to a different plane. Knowledge of the hidden secrets of the world and God's purpose for the creation is now available to humans, not through an attempt to claim it as of right and autonomously, as in Eden, or by human reason alone, but through the generous gift of God's emissary. Even human achievements in the natural and human sciences, as these were known and practiced, can come under the purview of wisdom. While human agency still had a more pronounced place than in apocalypticism, Lady Wisdom's role as instructress is not so far removed from that of the interpreting angel who explains the significance of the dream or vision with regard to the divine plan. Wisdom too has its own form of dualism that differentiates between the wise and the foolish, with ultimate consequences for those who reject the invitation to follow the path of righteousness. However we are to deal with the more strident aspects of apocalyptic rhetoric that make it the rejected Other, it would seem that if we are to expunge it from our theological language, much else will have to be sacrificed as well!

III. Wisdom and Apocalypticism in Paul and Mark

Narrative accounts of Jesus' life and letters as instruments of communication with various churches are the dominant types of early Christian literary production, yet the idiom of these writings participates fully in this world of Jewish wisdom and apocalyptic speculation we have been describing. Paul's letters represent our earliest written documents from the Jesus movement, and it is generally agreed that his thinking was, and continued to be, shaped within a thoroughly apocalyptic framework, even when other strands of thought of a Hellenistic coloring enter. With regard to his overall worldview,

---

change. See his article "The Politics of Cultural Production in Second Temple Judea: Historical Context and Political-Religious Relations of the Scribes who Produced 1 Enoch, Sirach, and Daniel," in *Conflicted Boundaries*, 123-45.

it is noticeable, however, that a shift of emphasis occurs already between his two earliest letters, 1 Thessalonians and 1 Corinthians. In the former the framework is dominated by apocalypticism, as the author describes the soon return of Christ in order to save the Thessalonian converts from the wrath to come (1 Thess. 1:9-10; 4:13-18). Without abandoning this framework of imminent expectation of the return of Christ, Paul introduces the notion of wisdom to explain the scandal of the cross to the Corinthian believers (1 Cor. 7:29-31; 11:26; 15:51-56; 16:22).

In all probability he had inherited the idea of Christ as the wisdom of God from an earlier stage of the tradition already on the basis of the communal creedal statement that he introduces at 1 Cor. 8:2-4: "For us, there is One God. . . ." Here we see a wisdom-inspired Christology being introduced into the Jewish Shema; the one God and Father is described as the originating and end cause of everything (the prepositions *ek* and *eis*), and the title Lord is transferred from God to Jesus, who is described as the instrumental cause of everything (preposition *dia*). Behind this formulation is the image of personified Wisdom as God's partner in creation (Prov. 8:22-31). For both Jews and Greeks, Paul's preaching of the cross was deemed folly and scandalous, but on the basis of the inherited formulation he is able to contrast the Wisdom of God with the folly of this present age, thereby utilizing sapiential motifs within a thoroughly apocalyptic framework. For those who believe, Jesus is both the power of God and the wisdom of God (1 Cor. 1:18-25), and perception of this transcendent reality takes place not through human reasoning, but through the heavenly mode of revelation that is granted through the gift of the Spirit. Creation and eschatology are interwoven in this formulation; each informs the other within the framework of Paul's Jewish upbringing and belief system with regard to the origins and ultimate destiny of God's world.[17]

Turning to the Markan framework, it is interesting to note that the Pauline formula "Christ the power of God and the wisdom of God" recurs, not directly as a Christological designation but as reactions to Jesus' activity as teacher and healer. With subtle Markan irony, the townspeople of Nazareth are reported to have enquired: "From what source *(pothen)* does this one get these things? What is this *wisdom (sophia)* that is given to him that such *mighty deeds (dynameis)* are done by his hands?" (Mark 6:2). They go

---

17. Henrik Tronier, "The Corinthian Correspondence between Idealism and Apocalypticism," in *Paul beyond the Judaism/Hellenism Divide*, ed. Troels Engberg-Peterson (Louisville: Westminster John Knox, 2001), 165-96, esp. 182-84.

on to describe Jesus as a *tektōn*, a description which recalls Sirach's contrast between the learned scribe and the craftsman *(tektōn)* engaged with his labors night and day (Sir. 38:24-27).[18] The unanswered question is ironic in its intent, relating to Mark's theory of the messianic secret and summoning the ideal readers to supply the correct answer in the light of the information one has already been given as to the source of Jesus' power and wisdom.

A similar scenario occurs in the Capernaum synagogue on the first day of the ministry, as described by Mark. The episode is introduced by a general statement that Jesus taught in their synagogue, giving rise to the excited reaction of the crowd: "This man *teaches* with authority *(kath' exousian)* and not as the scribes and Pharisees." Again, at the close of the episode, the people respond enthusiastically in the form of the unanswered question: "What is this, a new *teaching* with authority?" Both reactions stress Jesus' teaching, yet no example is given, only the successful exorcism. Deed and word, *sophia* and *dynamis*, are combined, since Jesus' *dabar* (word and deed) has its source in God's spirit for the struggle against human blindness and demonic presence (Mark 1:27).

It is generally accepted that the parable chapter (chap. 4) is crucial within Mark's overall dramatic narrative, functioning as it does as a miniplot that foreshadows the main plot's outcome,[19] namely, the mysterious messiah, whose true identity, like that of the kingdom of God which he proclaims, is not properly recognized until the end. In this context the three so-called growth parables, contrasting as they do small and unlikely beginnings with the miracle of harvest and the triumph of completion, function as metaphors for the way in which God's kingdom as preached by Jesus manifests itself. The description of this process as "the mystery of the kingdom" which is entrusted to the unwitting disciples (vv. 10-11), provides an apocalyptic coloring to the whole chapter, while the parables that are used as illustrative of this process are thoroughly sapiential in both theme and tone. The first and third focus on everyday experiences of the farmer's life, sowings, losses and gains, waiting for the harvest and reaping the rewards that constitute the mysterious cycle, while the second draws attention to the wondrous side of nature, namely, the most unlikely of outcomes for the smallest of seeds.

---

18. Adela Yarbro Collins, *Mark: A Commentary* (Hermeneia; Minneapolis: Fortress, 2006), 290.

19. Mary Ann Tolbert, *Sowing the Gospel: Mark's World in Literary-Historical Perspective* (Minneapolis: Fortress, 1989).

While presenting the reader with these everyday images, Mark gives a subtle twist to each which points to the strangeness of the processes being described, giving them the quality of a *mashal* or enigmatic riddle that not everybody will comprehend. Thus, the repeated failure of the sowing is in stark contrast to the superabundance of the eventual harvest; the small seed does not yield a great tree, as we might expect, but a mere shrub. Yet it is a shrub that can function to protect the birds of the air, thereby subverting but at the same time realizing the purpose of an eschatological image (Ezek. 17:2-24): humans' inability to affect the growth process, which remains hidden and mysterious, as mother earth answers the call first issued in the creation story: "let the earth bring forth. . . ." Yet for all the mysterious and hidden nature of the process, and the separation between insiders and outsiders that the giving of the mystery to the chosen ones creates, Mark is clear that this is a temporary, if necessary step in the process of proclaiming the kingdom: "Nothing is hidden except that it might be revealed, nor is anything secret except that it may be brought out into the open" (Mark 4:22).

The accessible wisdom associated with the everyday struggles of life can become the pointer to the remote wisdom of the kingdom, to borrow Ashton's terminology. As the proverb puts it: "It is the glory of God to conceal things and the glory of kings to search things out" (Prov. 25:2). Mark's wisdom examples are not taken from the life of the royal court but from the struggles and observations of the simple peasant. There is an open invitation to explore for everyone: "those who have ears to hear let them hear" (Mark 4:23). As the story line progresses, many outsiders become insiders and no one who asks to be included is turned away, whether it be the Syro-Phoenician woman, the unnamed exorcist, the well-meaning scribe, the blind Bar Timaeus, the centurion at the foot of the cross, or the Galilean women. Those in greatest danger of being left behind are those to whom the mystery was given! The elect that the angels of the Son of Man will gather come from the ends of the earth.

Had Tina Pippin focused on the whole gospel of which Mark 13 is an integral part, one wonders if she might not have been able to find a more positive note in Mark's apocalyptic worldview, even if her less well informed neighbors in the South were happy to live with their distorted version of an envious and destructive God. Concentrating solely on the "little apocalypse" of chap. 13 and its rhetoric creates the danger of not "getting the whole picture." Embedded as it is in a larger narrative, chap. 13 has a particular role to play in the unfolding drama of the gospel as a whole, especially since Mark chose not to give a closing reassurance to the community of the disciples being reunited with the resurrected Christ, a lacuna that the other evangelists felt the need to fill. Thus chap. 13 is not simply a preparation in advance of the reader for the shock of the trial and crucifixion just ahead, as some have suggested. It is addressed rather to the Markan community of the postresurrection period, exhorting them not to fall away in time of crisis and reassuring them of the soon return of the Son of Man to gather his elect.[20] If the emphasis in chap. 4 was on wisdom, albeit hidden and remote, more than on apocalypticism, this latter mode of discourse takes over in chap. 13, revealing to the chosen ones the eventual outcome of the drama. As they await the imminent unfolding of this event, their sapiential wisdom is not to be ignored. They are advised to learn a lesson from the fig tree as to the time of his return, and their prudential wisdom should teach them to be both vigilant and prepared as they await expectantly.

IV. Some Hermeneutical Afterthoughts

My purpose in this essay is to suggest that sapiential and apocalyptic motifs and themes are so interwoven into the warp and woof of both early Jewish and early Christian writings that to attempt to excise the apocalyptic elements in the name of modernity's sensibilities is both historically distorting and hermeneutically short-sighted. That is not to minimize the interpretative task that we are confronted with in dealing responsibly with the more troubling aspects of the rhetoric, not least the use of violent imagery. Perhaps the cosmic challenges we are currently facing can predispose us to think once more about the enduring possibilities, or otherwise, of these difficult dimensions of our foundational texts, without allowing them to be commandeered for justifying the most unethical behavior, in both the political and personal realms.

Faced with various doomsday scenarios, real or contrived, it has been an ongoing temptation for many to take apocalypticism's totalizing language literally and apply it uncritically in order to bring the final solution to some seemingly intractable problems. Millenarian expectations based on various apocalyptic scenarios have time and again been subsequently disconfirmed, yet this "failure" of the alleged predictions has in no way inhibited the appeal

---

20. Robert Fowler, *Let the Reader Understand: Reader Response Criticism and the Gospel of Mark* (Minneapolis: Fortress, 1991), 82-87.

of the genre, as John Collins has noted more than once.[21] No doubt it is this uncritical fascination that has caused the negative reactions to apocalypticism from the liberal theologians and critics already discussed. However, in rejecting apocalypticism entirely, they are unwittingly, it would seem, adopting the literalist approach to texts that they so vehemently oppose in others. One can hardly expect to win the battle if one opts to withdraw from the fray and cede the ground to the fundamentalists. Instead what is required is a determination to fight the war on the proper grounds, namely, the nature and limitation of all religious language and the need to understand its symbolic rather than literal meaning if we are not to engage in a form of verbal idolatry. In this regard it is not only the apocalyptic rhetoric and imagery of the Bible that causes the problem. Many other facets of the biblical record are equally troubling, not least the story of Israel's origins and the treatment of the neighboring peoples, the more so should any of these conquest narratives be used to legitimate military aggression in today's world.[22]

In a particularly perceptive essay, literary critic William A. Beardslee has tackled the issue of some of the more bizarre features of apocalyptic rhetoric, while at the same time retrieving the enduring aspects of the message it seeks to convey.[23] For Beardslee it is the ongoing struggle between the forces of spontaneity and order that the apocalyptic imagination is seeking to explore. In order to achieve its aim, apocalypticism breaks with many of the normal patterns of language and imagery, thereby suggesting unease with the existing patterns and the need to subvert them. To achieve this purpose, recourse is had to ancient mythical images, such as those of the holy war, or sea monsters invading the earth. These are often represented as distorted and unreal, with the aim of jolting the hearers'/readers' imagination to let go of the existing order and prompting them to imagine alternatives, where freedom and spontaneity can replace domination and grinding constraint. The existing order is often presented by its keepers as being both natural and immutable, and it is this perception that needs to be challenged. It is for this reason that the apocalyptic imagination has a particular resonance in situations of oppression and domination, and the vio-

---

21. John J. Collins, *Encounters with Biblical Theology* (Minneapolis: Fortress, 2005), 155-68; idem, "Apocalyptic Theology and the Dead Sea Scrolls: A Response to Jonathan Wilson," in *Christian Beginnings and the Dead Sea Scrolls*, ed. John J. Collins and Craig A. Evans (Grand Rapids: Baker Academic, 2006), 129-34.

22. John J. Collins, *Does the Bible Justify Violence?* (Minneapolis: Fortress Press, 2004).

23. William A. Beardslee, *Literary Criticism and the New Testament* (Philadelphia: Fortress, 1971), 53-62.

lence of the language and imagery must be judged and evaluated against that background.

Beardslee concludes his essay with the thought that while a situation of pure spontaneity might be considered the ideal that many would aspire to, in fact "apocalyptic[ism] was able to make an impression on the imagination of later times in a form that kept the centrifugal, spontaneous elements in dynamic tension with the centripetal, form-building elements." He wonders whether or not contemporary apocalyptic style might be able to maintain this tension. It has been the argument of this paper that to ignore as secondary or, worse still, to jettison one element of that polarity would indeed be a serious mistake. In terms of this discussion, the tension of which Beardslee speaks was expressed through the interlocking aspects of wisdom and apocalypticism as these found expression in the literature of Second Temple Judaism. These categories were deemed appropriate by Jesus' first followers also to express his liberating message, suitably modified by his particular stance towards the use of violence against one's enemy, real or perceived. It will undoubtedly be part of the enduring legacy of John Collins's scholarship that these dimensions of the Jewish and Christian literary traditions can neither be ignored nor excised.

The We and the Other in the Worldview of 1 *Enoch*, the Dead Sea Scrolls, and Other Early Jewish Texts

George W. E. Nickelsburg

The Other in the biblical world and late antiquity has been the subject of considerable discussion over the past two and a half decades, bracketed by the publication of three major works — at the beginning by the broad-ranging Brown University conference volume edited by Jacob Neusner and Ernest S. Frerichs, *"To See Ourselves as Others See Us": Christians, Jews, "Others" in Late Antiquity*, and at this end by the Groningen Qumran congress volume edited by Florentino García Martínez and Mladen Popović, *Defining Identities: We, You, and the Other in the Dead Sea Scrolls*, and by Lawrence M. Wills's provocative new book, *Not God's People: Insiders and Outsiders in the Biblical World*, which performs the all-too-infrequent service of placing the academy's work in the context of the world in which we work.[1] With the publication of the present volume it is obvious that the topic is not disappearing from the scholarly agenda.

In this brief essay I shall epitomize and elaborate my own forays into

---

1. Jacob Neusner and Ernest S. Frerichs, eds., *"To See Ourselves as Others See Us": Christians, Jews, "Others" in Late Antiquity* (Scholars Press Studies in the Humanities; Chico, Calif.: Scholars Press, 1985); Florentino García Martínez and Mladen Popović, eds., *Defining Identities: We, You, and the Other in the Dead Sea Scrolls: Proceedings of the Fifth Meeting of the IOQS in Groningen* (STDJ 70; Leiden: Brill, 2008); Lawrence M. Wills, *Not God's People: Insiders and Outsiders in the Biblical World* (Lanham, Md.: Rowman & Littlefield, 2008), which cites several articles in the Brown volume. See also John J. Collins, "The Zeal of Phinehas: The Bible and the Legitimation of Violence," *JBL* 122 (2003): 3-21.

the topic as it pertains to the literature of Second Temple Judaism.² From the selection of texts under consideration, I shall illustrate how, in a variety of ways, their authors seem to find it necessary to describe reality as they perceive it precisely in terms of the counterposition and interaction of the We and the Other — a phenomenon that is by no means limited to our literature or to *homo religiosus*.³ Usually the contrast is drawn in black and white, with one group depicted as the foil or negative image of the other. Occasionally, and sometimes surprisingly, the contrast finds some resolution. A much longer treatment would demonstrate the extent to which the polarization of the We and the Other permeates the Jewish literature of this period, and it would identify some other exceptions.

I. *1 Enoch*

1 Enoch is a collection of Jewish apocalyptic writings composed incrementally between the late fourth century B.C.E. and the turn of the era. Each of its component parts depicts the situation of its author(s) in terms of a clash between opposing groups and portrays the Other in a way that seemed appropriate to the specifics of the respective situation.

The Myth of the Watchers (1 Enoch 6–16)

In the collection's core myth (chaps. 6–11) and its primary exposition (chaps. 12–16), the villains are truly of another order. Heavenly beings rebel against the Deity by taking mortal women for wives.⁴ According to chaps. 6–11, the

---

2. George W. E. Nickelsburg, "Revealed Wisdom as a Criterion for Inclusion and Exclusion: From Jewish Sectarianism to Early Christianity," in *To See Ourselves*, 73-91; idem, "Religious Exclusivism: A World View Governing Some Texts Found at Qumran," in *Das Ende der Tage und die Gegenwart des Heils: Begegnungen mit dem Neuen Testament und seiner Umwelt: Festschrift für Heinz-Wolfgang Kuhn zum 65. Geburtstag*, ed. M. Becker and W. Fenske (AGJU 44; Leiden: Brill, 1999), 45-67, reprinted in *George W. E. Nickelsburg in Perspective: An Ongoing Dialogue of Learning*, 2 vols., ed. J. Neusner and A. J. Avery-Peck (JSJSup 80; Leiden: Brill, 2003), 1:139-61; idem, "Polarized Self-Identification in the Qumran Texts," in *Defining Identities*, 23-31.

3. Gordon Allport, *The Nature of Prejudice* (Garden City, N.Y.: Doubleday, 1958); and Bernard Lewis, *The Jews of Islam* (Princeton: Princeton University Press, 1984), 19-20, cited by Neusner and Frerichs, *To See Ourselves*, xi; and Wills, *Not God's People*, vii-viii.

4. On these chapters, see George W. E. Nickelsburg, *Jewish Literature between the Bi-*

offspring of this illegitimate mating of spirit and flesh is a race of bellicose giants who devastate the earth and its human and animal populations and then begin to cannibalize one another. In addition, the Watchers reveal forbidden secrets that include astrology and similar mantic arts; magic and related pharmacology; and the technologies of metallurgy and mining that facilitate warfare and sexual seduction (weapons, jewelry, and cosmetics).

By attributing this broad spectrum of evils to supernatural intervention, the myth asserts that these evils cannot be reduced to the sinful deeds of the humans who carry them out — generals and their armies, sorcerers and prognosticators, craftsmen and fornicators. They are the functions of a malevolent demonic realm that is bent on the destruction of God's creation and created order. In the wake of the wars waged by the Hellenistic kings and the penetration of Hellenistic culture, the poets who created these mythic materials experienced reality with an intensity that led them to posit a force qualitatively greater and other than the humans who perpetrated these evils.[5] The human individuals and groups that warred against them and threatened them in many ways were the real presence of a nonhuman Other. Anything less than the activity of an ontologically other realm of evil failed to do justice to the intensity of the evils that they experienced. Thus, in the exposition of the myth in chaps. 12–16, when the giants destroy one another in a war of mutual extermination, the result of the heavenly rebellion is the generating of a hoard of demons — the spirits of dead giants — that plague humanity in a multitude of ways from the time of the flood to the eschaton (15:8–16:1).

Not only did the creators of this mythic material posit the existence of a demonic realm to account for the evils that were plaguing them, they also sought a solution to these problems in the realm of the Other. Evil of demonic proportions must be countered by supernatural agents, namely, the four archangels, Sariel, Raphael, Gabriel, and Michael. These highest of the holy ones were the appropriate antidote to those watchers who had given up their holiness to rebel against "the Great Holy One." Deliverance from the Other could be found in no human quarter (e.g., a Davidic Messiah), but only among the ranks of the Other.

Although the myth depicts the Gentile warriors as oppressors of Israel

---

ble and the Mishnah, 2d ed. (Minneapolis: Fortress, 2005), 47-51; and in more detail, idem, *1 Enoch 1: A Commentary on 1 Enoch 1–36, 81–108* (Hermeneia; Minneapolis: Fortress, 2001), 165-72, 229-32.

5. For a possible reference here to the wars of the Diadochoi, see Nickelsburg, *1 Enoch 1*, 170.

and as the agents of demonic powers, it does not issue a blanket condemnation of the Gentiles as the Other. In its portrayal of the end-time, where it singles out the righteous of Israel, who are end-time antitypes of primordial Noah (10:1-3, 17-20), it anticipates the conversion of "all the sons of men" (10:21), that is, the Gentiles who do not fall under the judgment that is the latter-day counterpart to the flood.

The Animal Vision (1 Enoch 85–90)

Composed, at least in its present form, during the time of Judas Maccabeus (ca. 163 B.C.E.), this allegorical account of human history from creation to the eschaton also tells its story with reference to the counterposition of humans and the supernatural Other.[6] The primordial history is dependent on the myth of the Watchers, who create havoc for the human race and who, along with their offspring, are exterminated by the four archangels (chaps. 86–88). As the narrative moves beyond the flood, humanity bifurcates into Israel, which is depicted as white sheep, and the Gentiles, who are portrayed as wild beasts and birds of prey that harass the sheep (see 89:9-12 and then most of the remainder of the vision). This generic distinction, which reflects the known facts of life in the animal world, brings the difference between the Israelites and the Gentiles into high relief. The opposition of victim and victimizer that is central to the myth of the Watchers here finds its counterpart in the predators' violence on their prey.

But although the Gentiles are Israel's violent Other, the victims are hardly innocent, as they are, by and large, in the myth of the Watchers. From the time of Israel's wilderness wandering to the author's own time, the Israelite sheep are depicted as uniformly blind, that is apostate, and up to roughly the time of Manasseh, the nation's predators are the agents of divine punishment for its sins.

Then the scenario changes (89:59-64). The Lord of the sheep appoints seventy angelic shepherds who are to tend the flock during their respective periods of responsibility, but who fail to live up to that responsibility. Thus, from this point on, it is the shepherds' negligence that facilitates the nation's victimization by their predators. In this sense, with the focus once more on the polarity of the human and the angelic, the seventy shepherds function

---

6. On my discussion of these chapters, see Nickelsburg, *1 Enoch 1*, 346-63. On the date, see ibid., 360-61.

like the demonic victimizers in the myth of the Watchers. Gentile oppression is enabled by evil supernatural powers that constitute a qualitatively different Other. Highlighted by the devastation of Jerusalem in 587 B.C.E. (89:65-67) and the violence of the Hellenistic kings, notably the Seleucids (90:2-19), the events of this period are perceived by this author as the functions of a rebellious supernatural Other. There is, however, a new twist. Contrasted with the blind apostate sheep is a new generation of lambs, who begin to open their eyes and who call on the recalcitrant sheep to turn from their erring ways (90:6-7). It is a motif that appears in the myth of the Watchers only in the reference to Noah (10:1-3) and in the eschatological section (10:17-19). But here, the violence of the Gentiles reaches its peak in the slaughter of a leader of the newly awakened pious (90:8). The universal suffering of the human race depicted in the myth of the Watchers has become the innocent suffering of the righteous.

As in chaps. 6–11, the evil demonic Others have their opposites in the realm of the Other. The seven archangels function as God's agents — to punish the Watchers of old (88:1-3; 90:20-21), to act as witnesses of the violence during the period of the seventy shepherds (89:61-64, 70-72, 76-77; 90:20), and to drive the negligent shepherds and the apostate Jews to their everlasting perdition (90:21-27). The beasts who have been the human oppressors of Israel have already been annihilated (90:17-19).

With the supernatural villains of the story, their human Gentile agents, and the apostates of Israel removed from the scene, the *Vision's* portrayal of the end-time concludes as the whole of humanity — the Israelite sheep and the Gentile beasts and birds who have survived the judgment — are restored to their primordial, pristine unity (90:30-38). With the *Endzeit* recapitulating the *Urzeit*, there is no longer a threatening Other.

The Epistle of Enoch (1 Enoch 92–105)

These chapters of *1 Enoch* were composed in the second century B.C.E. as an exhortative conclusion to an earlier form of the Enochic corpus.[7] Thematically and in its literary forms, the section is shot through with contrasting portraits of the righteous and their opposite numbers, who are dubbed "the sinners." The interactions between the two groups are of two kinds,

---

7. See Nickelsburg, *1 Enoch 1*, 416-29, and in shorter form, Nickelsburg, *Jewish Literature*, 110-14.

summarized in the so-called *Apocalypse of Weeks* as "violence and deceit" (93:4; 91:11). These interactions are thoroughly antagonistic and the charges against the sinners are embedded in strings of woes that conclude with threats of damnation.

One set of the sinners are the rich and powerful, who oppress "the righteous." They are said to hold slaves (98:4; cf. 103:11, 15), burden the peasants, perhaps through high taxation and overwork (103:11-13; cf. 96:5), hoard up silver and gold acquired by unjust means (97:8; cf. 103:5), commit physical violence (103:15), and manipulate the legal system by lying in court, rendering unfair verdicts (95:6), taking bribes (94:7), and ignoring the pleas of those who have been wronged (103:14-15).[8]

Interlaced with these recitations of social and economic oppression are other strings of woes that depict *religious* conflict between those of the author's persuasion and others whose false and deceitful teaching "lead many astray" (98:15). The antagonism here is between the true and false understanding and practice of Israelite religion:

> Woe to those who alter *(exalloiountes)* the true words
> and pervert *(diastrephontes)* the everlasting covenant
> and consider themselves to be without sin;
> they will be swallowed up in the earth. (99:2)

A similar charge occurs at the end of the Epistle, where Enoch contrasts the wisdom of his books with the writings of those who pervert the truth:

> And now I know this mystery
> that sinners will alter *(exalloiousin)* and copy the words of truth,
> and pervert *(allassousin)* many and lie and invent great fabrications,
> and write books in their own names. (104:10)

> And again I know a second mystery,
> that to the righteous and pious and wise
> my books will be given for the joy of righteousness and much wisdom. (104:12)

In these passages the antagonism is between Enoch, the transmitter of divinely revealed truth and wisdom, and those who pervert this truth. The lat-

---

8. Nickelsburg, *1 Enoch 1*, 426.

ter are literally the Other because they "change" the truth as it is understood by the author into something other (Greek *exalloiousin, allassousin*, related to *allos*). This alleged behavior, moreover, parallels the aforementioned charges of violence and victimization, since false teaching leads those whom it deceives down the path to damnation.

One striking difference from the myth of the Watchers and the *Animal Vision* is the *Epistle*'s almost complete lack of reference to the demonic Others that play a central role in those texts. Indeed, according to 98:4, "lawlessness was not sent upon the earth; but humans created it by themselves." A hint of the existence of a demonic realm appears only in 99:14, according to which those who reject inherited law are pursued by "a spirit of error." Thus, this text presumes and emphasizes human responsibility and does not depict humans as the victims of demonic interference. The supernatural Others in this section of 1 Enoch are the angelic helpers of the righteous, who function as witnesses who will testify in the final judgment (97:6; 99:3; 100:10; 102:3; 104:1-3, 7-8).

Although the *Epistle* features a sharp social polarity between the righteous and the sinners and some severe inner-Jewish squabbles over Torah, like chap. 10 and the conclusion of the *Animal Vision*, this text anticipates, paradoxically, an eschatological turnabout for the Gentiles who survive the judgment and accept the wisdom of Enochic Torah (91:14; 100:6; 105:1-2).

The Parables of Enoch (1 Enoch 37–71)

Dating from the decades around the turn of the era, these chapters are probably the latest part of the Enochic corpus.[9] The cast of characters resembles that in the myth of the Watchers, the *Animal Vision*, and to some extent the *Epistle of Enoch*. Counterpoised against each other are the righteous and the chosen and the kings and the mighty — the foreign powers that oppress them. The kings and the mighty are the Other, both because they are labeled "the sinners" as opposed to "the righteous and the chosen" and because they are the oppressors of the oppressed and the executors of power over against the powerless.

Parallel to this antagonism that is played out between groups of humans on earth is the opposition of good and evil superhuman forces: Azazel and his hosts of rebel angels and the Chosen and Righteous One, also called God's Anointed and the Son of Man. The relationship between the demonic

---

9. On this section, see Nickelsburg, *Jewish Literature*, 248-56.

forces and the kings and the mighty is not as clear as it is in the myth of the Watchers and the *Animal Vision,* where the giants are the offspring of the Watchers and the Gentile beasts operate in the vacuum created by the negligence of the angelic shepherds. Only two passages in the *Parables* allude to the rebel angels' mating with human women (39:1; 69:4-5), and the latter may belong to a later, redacted form of the *Parables*. Instead, Azazel and his angels are revealers of forbidden secrets that lead humanity astray (54:1-6; 56:1-4; and 65:6-7; 67:5-7; 69:6-12, passages that are more or less likely to be secondary to the *Parables*). However one resolves the redactional issue, the *Parables* in their final form and also in an earlier form depict the righteous and chosen as the victims of violence and other evils brought on by powerful figures of another order: the Gentile rulers of the earth and a horde of demonic instigators of evil. As in the myth of the Watchers and the *Animal Vision,* however, the righteous and chosen have their heavenly champions, the Chosen One and the angels of punishment, who will carry out the judgment that the Chosen One enacts on the kings and the mighty and the rebel angels.

In one important respect, the *Parables* differ from the *Epistle of Enoch,* especially. Although the text identifies the victims of the kings and the mighty as the righteous and the chosen and never as humanity in general — and the double term implies a distinction from humans (and Israelites) who are not righteous and chosen — such a distinction is not a major issue in the *Parables*.[10] The *Parables* speak from the point of view of the community of the righteous and chosen, and the principal polarity in the book is between them and their oppressors, the kings and the mighty and the hordes of demons, whose revelations wreak havoc on earth.

Finally, like the other parts of *1 Enoch,* their excoriation of the kings and the mighty notwithstanding, the *Parables* anticipate the conversion of Gentiles who abandon their idols (50:2-4).

Summary of 1 Enoch

Major components of *1 Enoch* frame their exposition in terms of the (asymmetrical) clashing of opposing groups. Human beings in general or the righteous in particular are the helpless victims of the mighty and the rich, sometimes those in power, sometimes bellicose foreign overlords who ravage the

---

10. It may be implied in an occasional use of "the sinners" to refer to persons other than the kings and the mighty.

land and its inhabitants. On the historical level, the Otherness of these oppressors lies in their economic status, in the power of their social and political standing, and in their role as oppressors of the oppressed. In two of the four sections reviewed (chaps. 6–16; 85–90), their Otherness lies in their status as the offspring, or at least the agents of malevolent or negligent supernatural powers at war with the high Deity. In one telling of the story, these demonic forces wreak havoc on many aspects of human life (chaps. 6–16). Yet another scenario depicts false teachers, who are pitted against the revealers of truth, and who pervert divine law and victimize those who fall into their clutches by leading them astray on the path of eternal perdition. It is a black and white world, and from the point of view of these writers and their communities, daily experience involves the dangerous encounter with the Other — whether human or demonic — and its resultant threat of historical misery or eternal damnation. The authors proclaim, however, that deliverance will also come from the realm of the Other, through the intervention of the archangels, others who function as witnesses, and God's Anointed One, the Chosen One and Son of Man.

Alongside the polarity of humans and demons, the powerful and the oppressed, the wise and the false teachers, one finds some softening of these authors' black and white world. They anticipate the salvation of Gentiles who have not oppressed Israel and who turn to the worship and obedience of the true God.

II. The Qumran Sectarian Scrolls

The sectarian documents in the Qumran collection that have survived reasonably intact attest both forms of the polarizing worldview that we have seen in *1 Enoch:* the Other as oppressor or conqueror and, especially, the Other as religious opponent.[11]

The Pesharim

Among the *pesharim,* whose form lends itself well to historical reference, one finds mention of military conquest, violence, and political and social op-

---

11. In this section on the scrolls, I summarize and expand my discussion in Nickelsburg, "Polarized Self-Identification," in *Defining Identities,* 23-31, which, in turn, summarizes and expands on my "Revealed Wisdom," in *To See Ourselves,* 73-91 and "Religious Exclusivism," in *Das Ende der Tage,* 45-67.

pression at points where the biblical text invited the exegete to interpret it in this manner. The Habakkuk *pesher* describes the fearful might of the Roman army and the widespread carnage and devastation left by their horses and troops (1QpHab 2–6). The Psalms *pesher*^{a} (4Q171) focuses on the oppression of the community and its leader at the hands of "the Wicked Priest" (4:5-10; cf. 2:12-18). The Nahum *pesher* refers to Alexander Jannaeus's crucifixion of eight hundred of his opponents (4Q169 3 + 4 i 6-8). Texts like these provide a glimpse of the violent world in which these authors of the first century B.C.E. lived and demonstrate how they turned to the prophetic Scriptures for the symbols that would depict a stage on which victims and their victimizers played major roles.

But if these texts provide such a glimpse, they and other of the sectarian texts are dominated by the *religious* polarization that plays a significant, albeit less important role in the *Epistle of Enoch.* Thus the Habakkuk *pesher* pits the Teacher of Righteousness, the inspired interpreter of the Torah and the prophets (1QpHab 8:1-3; 7:1-5), against "the Man of Lies" (2:1-2; 5:10-11), "the Dripper of Lies" (10:9), and "the Wicked Priest" (8:8; 9:9; 11:4; 12:2, 8). In the Nahum *pesher* we hear of "the slippery interpreters" *(dwršy ḥlqwt),* who "lead many astray" with their "false teaching, lying tongue and perfidious lip" (4Q169 3 + 4 ii 8; cf. i 7; ii 2, 4; iii 3, 6-7; *1 Enoch* 98:15). The Psalms *pesher* speaks of "the Man of Lies, who had led many astray through words of deceit because they chose worthless things and did not lis[ten] to the Mediator of Knowledge" (4Q171 i 26-27). In each of these cases (although only implied in the Nahum *pesher*), the otherness of the villains relates to the fact that they take a position that opposes that of the authors and their group. It is a matter of falseness and lies over against the truth and knowledge. Moreover, we should note that terms like "lies" and "falsehood" — even when not explicitly contrasted with "truth" — imply their opposite and thus indicate their Otherness in a way, for example, that red does not imply yellow or blue and "up" need not imply "down."

The Hodayot

Written in the first person singular, the compositions contained in the Qumran *Hymn Scroll* (1QH^a) express an especially strong version of the polarization I have been describing. One defines oneself and the Other negatively in terms of each other. The Other is what I am *not*, and I am what the other is *not*. I take as my example 1QH^a 12:5–13:4, one of the so-called hymns of the teacher. In it the author explicitly contrasts the revelation he has received and the teaching that he dispenses with the false teaching of his opponents. God has brightened his face with his covenant, enlightened him like the perfect dawn (12:5-6) and made known to him the wondrous divine mysteries (12:27), engraving the Torah in his heart (12:10), and thus effecting everlasting salvation for those who listen to him (12:21-24). By contrast, his opponents ridicule and belittle him (12:8-22), perverting the Torah and giving vinegar rather than the drink of knowledge. They are: deceitful interpreters who lead others astray and whose actions evidence folly; deceitful seers who exchange the Torah for smooth things and go astray; and prophets of falsehood who draw others into error. This polemical vocabulary echoes the *Epistle of Enoch,* and as in the *pesharim,* these terms are employed for the purpose of contrasting the teacher and his opponents. They are the opposite of what he is and, therefore, the Other, as black is other than white and cold, the opposite of hot. In his situation the teacher finds himself unable to define himself without reference to the Other. The stakes are as high as they can get. His teaching leads to salvation, while his opponents who stray and those whom they lead are headed for damnation when God's judgment takes place (see 12:18-22 for the explicit contrast between the fates of the two groups). Where this hymn differs from the *Epistle of Enoch,* at least from its emphasis, is in its explanation of the opponents' false teaching: they are agents of the demon Belial (12:13 twice), while he is the mouthpiece of God (12:5-6). What two entities could be more Other than God and the Devil (cf. 2 Cor. 6:14-15)?

The polarity between good and evil, truth and falsehood, salvation and damnation found in this hymn of the teacher is sharpened and extended in two hymns that focus on the individual and his relationship to the community (11:20-37; 19:3-14). This community is the realm of salvation, and entrance into it involves a resurrection or ascent from destructive Sheol, the sphere of death, to heaven, the place of eternal life and communal praise with the angelic chorus.

The Community Rule (1QS 3:13–4:26)

The existential *Auseinandersetzung* that dominates the Qumran hymn finds its "doctrinal" counterpart in the two-spirits/two-ways passage in the 1QS version of the *serek hayaḥad.* As in the *Hodayot,* with its language of leading astray and its references to Belial, 1QS 3–4 describes human actions in terms of the two ways and ascribes these actions to the two opposing angels that act as guides on the two paths. That these two spirits are the opposites of one another is indicated by their association with light and darkness (see again 2 Cor. 6:14-15). The present passage differs from 1QH^a 12–13 in that it absolutizes the opposition. It encompasses all of humanity in its scope and not just the antagonism between the teacher and his group and his opponents and their group(s). Nonetheless, from within the enlightened *yaḥad*, the rest of Israel — to say nothing of humanity — constitutes the Other, as darkness is other than light. Moreover, this opposition is worked out in detail in the liturgy and many of the regulations that constitute a large part of the *serek*, even if 3:13–4:26 is an interpolation into an earlier form of the document.

These texts and others like them derive from a sectarian community whose members consider themselves to be exclusively Israel, the chosen of God. Enlightened by the revelation received and expounded by their leaders, they alone are the recipients of eternal life. By contrast, those who are not so enlightened are excluded from the pale of salvation. As such they are the epitome of the Other.

III. "Apocryphal Psalm" (11QPs^a xviii)

This noncanonical psalm largely preserved in the *Psalms Scroll* from Qumran Cave 11 (11QPs^a) celebrates the status and activities of "the congregation of the pious" (*qhl ḥsydym;* v. 12) and the benefits that YHWH bestows on them.[12] If we presume some retroversion at the beginning and end from a Syriac version of the psalm (vv. 1-2, 17b-20), the pious are also described as "the congregation of the many," *qhl rbym* (v. 1); "the multitude of the upright," *rwb yšrym* (v. 2); "the faithful," *'mwnym* (v. 2); "the good ones," *ṭwbym* (v. 3); "the righteous," *ṣdyqym* (v. 11); "the humble" (or "poor"), *'ny* (v. 18); and "the blameless" *(tmymym)* (v. 3; [v. 18]).

As in all of the aforementioned texts, the righteous and pious have their counterparts, who are of two sorts. Toward the end of the psalm they are identified as "the wicked" (*rš'ym,* v. 15; [v. 18]) and "the haughty" (*zdym,*

---

12. For the text, see James A. Sanders, *The Psalms Scroll of Qumrân Cave 11* (DJD 4; Oxford: Clarendon, 1965), 64-70. Versification follows the poem (including lines reconstructed from the Syriac) on p. 64 of Sanders's edition. Citations in brackets signify reconstructed text.

v. 15 and possibly [v. 18]).[13] The wording of verse 18, as attested in the Syriac, suggests that these persons are oppressors of some sort: "[Blessed is] YHWH, who redeems the poor from the hand of <the haughty> [and deliv]ers [the blameless from the hand of the wicked]." In any event, the terms "wicked" and "haughty" stand in opposition respectively to "the pious, the righteous, the upright, the good, the blameless," and to "the poor" or "humble." Thus, the terminology parallels "the sinners"/"the rich" in the *Epistle of Enoch* and "the sinners"/"the kings and the mighty" in the *Parables of Enoch*.

The second group of Others differs notably from the second group in the *Epistle of Enoch* and from the opponents in 1QH^a 12–13, as is evident from the relationships between the two groups described in 11QPs^a 18:4-8. The activity of the pious and righteous in vv. 1-14 is cultic or liturgical. Enabled by the wisdom that is revealed (literally, "given") to them (v. 5),[14] they glorify God, recount God's deeds, sing praise in the assembly, where they eat and drink in community and meditate on the Torah of the Most High. Related to this, however, is their responsibility to "make known" God's "might" and "majesty" to "all the simple" *(pwt'ym)* (v. 4) and to "make wise those lacking judgment" (v. 7). That is, the Others here described, while in some sense outsiders ("those far from her gates, those who stray from her portals"), are neither false teachers or irredeemable. The difference between the two groups is between those who are wise and study and understand God's Torah, and those who are in some sense ignorant, unlearned, naive and lacking in judgment. And part of the responsibility of the former, and an element in their proclamation of God's mighty and wondrous deeds, is to make these known to the latter. Thus different from the Qumran sectarian texts, the outsiders are not to be cursed, shunned, and excluded; they are to be invited to shed their Otherness and become insiders. And in no sense are they seen to be in league with a demonic realm, as in the Qumran hymn. The dichotomy resembles that of *the Epistle of Enoch,* and the spirit of the text with its openness to outsiders is somewhat reminiscent of the Enochic texts, although the outsiders here are Israelites rather than Gentiles and the atmosphere is not eschatological.

13. The Syriac presumes *zrym* ("strangers"), and the barely perceptible upper fragments of the first two letters are read thus by Sanders in his transcription (DJD 4, 64). However, given the word pair *rš'ym/zdym* in v. 15, I suggest *zdym* here to complement *rš'ym* restored from the Syriac of v. 18. Sanders suggests this as a possibility in his comment on v. 18 (ibid., 67).

14. For the idiom "wisdom is given," see Nickelsburg, *1 Enoch 1,* 162.

IV. The Psalms of Solomon

The psalms in this collection were composed in Palestine in the first century B.C.E. in a community that considered itself to be "the righteous" *(dikaioi = ṣdyqym)* and "(the congregation of) the pious" (*[synagōgē/synedrion] hosiōn = [qhl] hsydym*).[15] Their opposites are usually dubbed "the sinners" *(hamartōloi = ršʿym)*.[16]

The sinners are of several types. They are the Gentiles who threaten Israel or, especially, who have invaded Jerusalem and its Temple (*Pss. Sol.* 1, 2, 8, 17). In keeping with a motif found in some of the Qumran texts (e.g., CD 4:16–5:11), the sinners are also the priests whose sexual halakah has polluted the Temple cult (*Ps. Sol.* 8:12; cf. 2:3) and others whose adultery and incest brought on the Roman invasion (2:11-13; 8:9-10; cf. 4:5-12).

Striking a major motif in the collection — partly in these examples, but mainly in half of the rest of the psalms — are the juxtaposition of, and the contrast between the personal conduct and attitudes of, the righteous and the sinners (2:11-13; 8:8-10; psalms 3, 4, 10, 12-16). Here the issue is not the sinners' oppressing or outright threatening the life and religion of the pious. Rather one compares the two types, their religious attitudes, their actions, and the consequences that follow from them when God exacts "righteous judgment." *Psalms of Solomon* 3:3-12 is perhaps the most explicit example:[17]

> The righteous remember the Lord at all times,
>> when they confess and declare the Lord's judgments to be just.
> The righteous one does not despise the chastisement of the Lord;
>> his good pleasure is always before the Lord.
> The righteous one stumbles and considers the Lord to be just;
>> he falls and he looks to see what God will do to him;
>> he watches whence his salvation will come.
> The faithfulness of the righteous (comes) from God their savior;
>> sin upon sin does not lodge in the house of the righteous.
> The righteous one continually searches his house,

---

15. On the *Psalms of Solomon* in their setting, see Kenneth Atkinson, *I Cried to the Lord: A Study of the Psalms of Solomon's Historical Background and Social Setting* (JSJSup 84; Leiden: Brill, 2004); and in summary, Nickelsburg, *Jewish Literature*, 238-47.

16. For *ršʿ* as frequently translated by *hamartōlos*, see Edwin Hatch and Henry A. Redpath, *A Concordance to the Septuagint* (Grand Rapids: Baker Books, 1998), 64-65.

17. Translation from George W. E. Nickelsburg and Michael E. Stone, *Faith and Piety in Early Judaism: Texts and Documents,* 2d ed. (Minneapolis: Fortress, 2009).

> to remove the iniquity of his transgression.
> He makes atonement for (sins of) ignorance through fasting and the humiliation of his
> soul; and the Lord cleanses every pious man and his house.
> The sinner stumbles and curses his life,
> the day of his birth and his mother's birth pangs.
> He adds sin upon sin in his life;
> he falls — for evil is his fall — and he does not rise again.
> The destruction of the sinner is forever;
> and he will not be remembered when the righteous is visited.
> This is the lot of the sinners forever.
> But those who fear the Lord will rise to everlasting life;
> and their life will be in the light of the Lord and will never fail.

The difference between the righteous and the sinners is a matter of both actions and attitudes. The righteous are not sinless, but they are concerned about their sins and attend to them through acts of cultic piety. The sinners, by contrast, could not care less. As a result God deals with the two types in contrasting ways: the righteous are chastened so that they may repent and eventually rise to everlasting life, while the sinners face damnation at God's judgment. Neither this psalm nor the closely related psalms 13-15 identify the specific sins of concern to their author(s). The issue is, rather, the contrast between the two types of persons (gross, callous sinners and sinful individuals whose piety of attitude and action makes them "righteous") and the two ways in which the divine Judge responds to them. In these respects "the sinners" are Others — foils to "the righteous."

If the aforementioned psalms speak in generalizations, elsewhere some specific sins of the sinners come into focus: the arrogance of the Gentile oppressor (2:22-31; 17:11-14); the usurping of the Davidic throne (17:4-7); cultic pollution (2:3-5; 8:12, 22); slander (12:1-4); hypocrisy (4:2-8, 20); and perhaps preeminently, sexual sins (2:11-13; 4:3-12; 8:12; perhaps 1:7; cf. 4:5).[18] In most of these instances, the sinners are precisely the Other. The Gentiles are the Others par excellence vis-à-vis the Israelites. The Hasmoneans are non-Davidites who usurp David's throne. Cultic pollution is, at least in part, a function of halakah that does not agree with ours (8:12). The slanderer victimizes the innocent. The hypocritical adulterer is Other in two respects. He is the opposite of what he claims to be, and, as such, he sits in the community of the pious.

---

18. See Theorem 5 in Wills, *Not God's People*, 13.

The psalms' constellation of sexual sins is especially interesting because the Others who perpetrate these sins may be the shadow side of the authors, who do not.[19] The author of psalm 4 is nervous about the adulterer's presence in the council of the pious, while the author of psalm 16 admits to a dangerous attraction to "the evil woman." If, in fact, he escaped her clutches, the near miss was too close for comfort. There is ambiguity here. Even if he did, in fact, survive the encounter, he acknowledges that he was in danger of becoming what he is determined not to be. Conversely, however, his speech betrays him: "every evil woman seduces the foolish" and "the beauty of a criminal woman" can "deceive me." The fault lies with the woman, who is the Other — the one who is the subject of the verbs denoting the gross sinner who victimizes the pious one.

This last point raises the issue of the cause and responsibility for sin. With respect to personal piety or the lack of it, psalm 9 is clear:

Our works are in the choosing and power of our souls,
  to do right and wrong, in the works of our hands. (v. 4)

Thus God's judgment, for better or for worse, which is so central to these psalms, is a corollary of human free will. One cannot claim that "the devil made me do it." The demonic dimension may not be totally lacking in the psalms, however.

Pompey's arrogance is similar to that attributed to Antiochus (Epiphanes) and his prototype, the king of Babylon (Dan. 8:10-11; cf. Isa. 14:12-14). The language of *Pss. Sol.* 2:25-29 is apparently informed by the parallel passage in Ezek. 28:1-10. The description of Pompey as a "dragon" refers to the mythological motif of the chaos monster. A similar combination of the dragon motif with the arrogant anti-god figure is also found in Rev. 12:7-9.[20] Thus, the author of this psalm may see the enemy as an agent of a demonic power.

Finally, although these psalms emanate from a group whose members identify themselves as "the congregation of the pious," unlike the psalm discussed in the previous section, there is no evidence in this text that "the righteous" and "the pious" have a responsibility to communicate with "the sinners." As in the Qumran literature, the sinners are, by and large, the unredeemable, polar-opposite Others, who are to be left to their own devices.

---

19. See Theorem 3 and 4 in Wills, *Not God's People*, 13.
20. Nickelsburg, *Jewish Literature*, 239.

V. Conclusions

The texts that we have discussed illustrate the degree to which Jewish authors of the Second Temple period saw and described their world in terms of an interaction, or at least a contrast, between polar opposites. Over against the We was the Other. The broad spectrum of these opposites included: Jews and Gentiles; humans and superhuman beings of benevolent and malevolent character; rich and powerful oppressors and their victims; revealers and guardians of truth and purveyors of perverted religion; the righteous and pious and the sinners. More often than not the interactions and contrasts between the We and the Other are explicit; occasionally they are implicit. What is striking in my view is the degree to which the We are defined not in their own right, but with reference to the Other, and how often this contrasting definition is explicit. That is, there must be an Other in order for Us to understand who We are. This is clear in the Qumran sectarian literature. But it is evident also in the *Psalms of Solomon,* where in the same psalm one describes the actions, attitudes, and fates of not only the righteous but also the sinners — even when the latter are not interacting with the former. Since these compositions are in-group literature, the function of this kind of contrasting is perhaps best seen as a kind of self-justification. This interpretation, however, should not be taken as an affirmation of outmoded stereotypes of Judaism vs. Christianity. A study of New Testament texts reveals similar contrasting type-casting, often with a strong "sectarian" bent — even if the issues differ sometimes from those in the Jewish texts, as I have noted elsewhere and as is documented in Wills's study.[21]

More often than not, the opposition between the We and the Other is eliminated through the divine judgment that will bring blessing or salvation to Us and condemnation and destruction to the Other. Occasionally, the opposition is ameliorated when the outsiders become insiders and the Other are included among the Us. It is worth noting that this transformation is a consistent feature in the various strata of *1 Enoch,* an apocalyptic text that features a powerful We/They worldview. At the same time, we should note that the collapse of the opposites occurs not through what we might call "negotiation," but when the Other comes to accept Our terms and becomes one of Us.

---

21. Nickelsburg, "Revealed Wisdom," 82-89; Wills, *Not God's People,* 101-209.

Monsters and the Crippled Cosmos: Construction of the Other in *Fourth Ezra*

Rebecca Raphael

> . . . aut monstra mihi vocis imaginem . . .
>
> 4 Ezra 5:37

The Jewish apocalypse known as *Fourth Ezra*, scholars often note, is not like the others. If I may once use the term "apocalyptic" in the colloquial sense that confuses it with what scholars call the *eschaton*, *4 Ezra* is a postapocalyptic apocalypse: one of a handful of works written after the concrete structures — city and temple — that centered on the author's world were, in fact, destroyed.[1] The apocalypse's more salient atypical features include an unusual choice of persona for pseudepigrapha,[2] an idiosyncratic fusion of wis-

---

1. In this essay, I take the current consensus on a late-first-century date and basic unity of authorship as well-established premises. For full discussion and bibliography on both matters, see Michael E. Stone, *Fourth Ezra: A Commentary on the Book of Fourth Ezra* (Hermeneia; Minneapolis: Fortress, 1990), 9-35. Regarding the issue of centrality, this is not to suggest that Jerusalem and the Temple were the *axis mundi* in the book's mythology, explicit or implicit. K. William Whitney finds the idea of Zion as *axis mundi* in other late Jewish apocalypses, but not in *4 Ezra* (*Two Strange Beasts: Leviathan and Behemoth in Second Temple and Early Rabbinic Judaism* [HSM 63; Winona Lake, Ind.: Eisenbrauns, 2006], 31-91). Rather, the book represents Zion as the *axis animi*; i.e., the central point of psychological orientation and identity.

2. Stone (*Fourth Ezra*, 37) notes that Ezra is a unique persona among extant Jewish apocalypses, although Christian authors, following this initial appropriation, continued to use the figure.

dom elements with numerous other genres of Hebrew literature,[3] Ezra's persistent identification with the lost,[4] a marked reticence about the goodness of this creation,[5] and, beyond a mere cataclysmic transformation, the widely noted, actual destruction of the cosmos, punctuated by seven days of silence.[6]

For all that, its most touching atypical feature may be something John Collins saw in its troubled protagonist: a keen sense of limitation coupled with "a humane spirit."[7] In addition to these features, *4 Ezra* also employs profligate body imagery, attributed both to human beings and to the cosmos itself. Much of this imagery has been appreciated separately: the decrepit cosmos draws on and amplifies earlier myths of world ages; the various bizarre human phenomena have been discussed as traumatic eschatological signs; the monsters amplify their predecessors in Daniel and elsewhere; and, once all is over, the pristine post-destruction, post–new creation bodies of the righteous have been discussed under the heading of eschatology. In this essay, I set aside these conventional categories under which the body imagery is compartmentalized (dismembered?) and instead analyze it in its own right, with the critical tools of contemporary disabilities studies and monster theory. This approach discloses that, beyond mythical parallels and literary embellishment, images of anomalous bodies provide a major means by which the text constructs the Other.

I. Varieties of Anomalous Bodies

In the past twenty years, disability studies and monster theory have both emerged primarily within literary criticism. From somewhat different angles,

---

3. Michael A. Knibb, "Apocalyptic and Wisdom in *4 Ezra*," *JSJ* 13 (1982): 56-74.

4. Alden L. Thompson, *Responsibility for Evil in the Theodicy of IV Ezra* (SBLDS 29; Missoula, Mont.: Scholars Press, 1977), 127-34; Walter Harrelson, "Ezra Among the Wicked in 2 Esdras 3–10," in *The Divine Helmsman: Studies on God's Control of Human Events, Presented to Lou H. Silberman*, ed. James L. Crenshaw and Samuel Sandmel (New York: Ktav, 1980), 21-39.

5. Richard J. Clifford and John J. Collins, "Introduction: The Theology of Creation Traditions," in *Creation in the Biblical Traditions*, ed. Richard J. Clifford and John J. Collins (CBQMS 24; Washington, D.C.: The Catholic Biblical Association of America, 1992), 1-15; see p. 15 for their remarks on *4 Ezra*.

6. Arthur J. Ferch ("The Two Aeons and the Messiah in Pseudo-Philo, *4 Ezra*, and *2 Baruch*," *AUSS* 15.2 [1977]: 135-51) finds the silence exceptional.

7. John J. Collins, *The Apocalyptic Imagination: An Introduction to Jewish Apocalyptic Literature*, 2d ed. (Grand Rapids: Eerdmans, 1998), 212.

both approaches study the ideological construction of bodies, "normal" and not. The field of disability studies encompasses the history of disabled persons, the variety of ways in which disability has been defined, the interaction between actual bodies and socially constructed environments, literary representations, and philosophical questions related to embodiment.[8] Although it emerged in contemporary sociology and literary criticism over the latter half of the twentieth century, its arrival in biblical studies has been the work of the past two decades.[9] Disability studies scholars have been careful to avoid a completely social constructivist view of disability, which undeniably involves real differences in embodied experience. Nevertheless, societies do select and value, or devalue, bodily differences, and in doing so, define Self and Other.

---

8. Major works include Lennard J. Davis, *Bending Over Backwards: Disability, Dismodernism, and Other Difficult Positions* (New York: New York University Press, 2002); idem, *Enforcing Normalcy: Disability, Deafness, and the Body* (London: Verso, 1995); idem, ed., *The Disability Studies Reader*, 2d ed. (New York: Routledge, 2006); Rosemarie Garland Thomson, *Extraordinary Bodies: Figuring Physical Disability in American Culture and Literature* (New York: Columbia University Press, 1997); David T. Mitchell and Sharon L. Snyder, *Narrative Prosthesis: Disability and the Dependencies of Discourse* (Ann Arbor: University of Michigan Press, 2000); Anita Silvers, David T. Wasserman, and Mary B. Mahowald, eds., *Disability, Difference, Discrimination: Perspectives on Justice in Bioethics and Public Policy* (Lanham, Md.: Rowman & Littlefield, 1998); Sharon L. Snyder, Brenda Jo Brueggemann, and Rosemarie Garland Thomson, eds., *Disability Studies: Enabling the Humanities* (New York: Modern Language Association of America, 2002).

9. To list only monographs that most directly address disability, in order of publication: Lynn Holden, *Forms of Deformity* (JSOTSup 131; Sheffield: JSOT Press, 1991); Nancy L. Eisland, *The Disabled God: Toward a Liberation Theology of Disability* (Nashville: Abingdon, 1994); Hector Avalos, *Illness and Health Care in the Ancient Near East: The Role of the Temple in Greece, Mesopotamia, and Israel* (HSM 54; Atlanta: Scholars Press, 1995); Judith Z. Abrams, *Judaism and Disability: Portrayals in Ancient Texts from the Tanach through the Bavli* (Washington, D.C.: Gallaudet University Press, 1998); John Wilkinson, *The Bible and Healing: A Medical and Theological Commentary* (Grand Rapids: Eerdmans, 1998); Hector Avalos, *Health Care and the Rise of Christianity* (Peabody, Mass.: Hendrickson, 1999); Tzvi C. Marx, *Disability in Jewish Law* (London: Routledge, 2002); Mikeal Parsons, *Body and Character in Luke and Acts: The Subversion of Physiognomy in Early Christianity* (Grand Rapids: Baker Academic, 2006); Jeremy Schipper, *Disability Studies and the Hebrew Bible: Figuring Mephibosheth in the David Story* (New York: T&T Clark, 2006); Hector Avalos, Sarah J. Melcher, and Jeremy Schipper, eds., *This Abled Body: Rethinking Disabilities in Biblical Studies* (SemeiaSt 55: Atlanta: The Society of Biblical Literature, 2007); Joanna Dorman, *The Blemished Body: Disability and Deformity in the Qumran Scrolls* (Ph.D. diss., Rijksuniversiteit Groningen, 2007); Saul M. Olyan, *Disability in the Hebrew Bible: Interpreting Mental and Physical Differences* (Cambridge: Cambridge University Press, 2008); and Rebecca Raphael, *Biblical Corpora: Representations of Disability in Hebrew Biblical Literature* (New York: T&T Clark, 2008).

Rebecca Raphael

These categories mutually depend on each other; indeed, one of the key insights is that the ideologically "normal" body is often constructed indirectly, by contrast with a more explicit "disabled" body.[10] This overlay of significance on human bodies attempts to make matter cohere with ideology. One common contemporary example, pertaining to disease rather than disability, can be found in remarks that someone did not "deserve" to become ill. This kind of statement implies the concept of "deserved" illness, often, even today, credited to one's own behavior. Although one might insist, correctly, that some behaviors increase the risks of some diseases, we tend to oversimplify probability into causality. In any case, cultures have strata of powerful, often unstated, notions of how bodies ought to fit ideas. Matter that does not or cannot so cohere thus signifies a threat, even an existential one, to order. Leslie Fiedler has perhaps given this dynamic its most sweeping expression: "the strangely formed body has represented absolute Otherness in all times and places since human history began."[11]

While disability studies focus on the human body, they do not exhaust the role of bodily anomaly in human culture. I note in passing the different valuations of animals, which play a role in the imaginative generation of those morphological hybrids that we call monsters. On the basis of his survey of both world mythology and previous scholarship, anthropologist David Gilmore lists the following characteristics of monsters: morphological hybridity or grotesqueness, large size, malice (often consumption of human beings), and ultra-mundane or geographically marginal provenance.[12] He concludes: "[The monster] embodies the existential threat to social life, the chaos, atavism, and negativism that symbolize destructiveness and all other obstacles to order and progress, all that which defeats, draws back, undermines, subverts the human project. . . ."[13] Timothy Beal uses the term *unheimlich* to express the monster's uncanny quality, and further notes that "we" feel the existential threat, not just to our mundane social order, but to

---

10. See Lennard J. Davis, "Constructing Normalcy," in *The Disability Studies Reader*, 3-16.

11. Leslie A. Fiedler, "Foreword," in *Freakery: Cultural Spectacles of the Extraordinary Body*, ed. Rosemarie Garland Thomson (New York: New York University Press, 1996), xiii-xviii. The quotation, on p. xiii, summarizes Fiedler's book *Freaks: Myths and Images of the Secret Self* (New York: Simon and Schuster, 1978). The freak body and the disabled body are not necessarily the same, but both play Other to the Normal, and there is some overlap.

12. David D. Gilmore, *Monsters: Evil Beings, Mythical Beasts, and All Manner of Imaginary Terrors* (Philadelphia: University of Pennsylvania Press, 2003), 1-10.

13. Ibid., 12, brackets mine.

the cosmic order of the gods.[14] Hence the prominent role of monsters in pre-creation combat myths and eschatological myths, where divine order is defined by the violent removal of chaos.[15] Literary critic Jeffrey Cohen succinctly captured why a hybrid or anomalous body should *mean* existential threat: "The monster is difference made flesh."[16] Cohen observes that monsters come during crises, when order and identity, both personal and national, seem threatened.[17] (His observations can also be applied to apocalypses.) The monster embodies the fragments of self that do not cohere with the desired order, and are therefore refused in the construction of a Self. As parts of the self, however, they cannot be truly eliminated and also tend to attract desire.[18] In short, with due attention to cultural specificity, our monsters are ourselves:[19] they embody primitive and aggressive impulses, or they simply take on the features of whatever is not desired as part of the Self.

These critical approaches can be fruitfully applied to biblical and cognate literatures. They are particularly apt for apocalyptic literature, with its plethora of divine beings, disabled or "cured" human beings, mythical revenants, and political-satirical hybrids. Regarding *4 Ezra*, I shall employ the synthetic category "anomalous body" to encompass the disabled, freak, or monstrous bodies that recur throughout the text.

---

14. Timothy K. Beal, *Religion and Its Monsters* (New York: Routledge, 2002), 6.

15. Beal discusses this theme in several places. From a large literature, see, with particular reference to biblical apocalypticism, Hermann Gunkel, *Creation and Chaos in the Primeval Era and the Eschaton: A Religio-Historical Study of Genesis 1 and Revelation 12*, trans. K. William Whitney, Jr. (Grand Rapids: Eerdmans, 2006); trans. of *Schöpfung und Chaos in Urzeit und Endzeit* (Göttingen: Vandenhoeck & Ruprecht, 1895); Adela Yarbro Collins, *The Combat Myth in the Book of Revelation* (HDR 9; Missoula, Mont.: Scholars Press, 1976; repr. Eugene, Ore.: Wipf and Stock, 2001); George Aichele and Tina Pippin, eds., *The Monstrous and the Unspeakable: The Bible as Fantastic Literature* (Playing the Texts 1; Sheffield: Sheffield Academic, 1997).

16. Jeffrey J. Cohen, "Monster Culture (Seven Theses)," in *Monster Theory: Reading Culture* (Minneapolis: University of Minnesota Press, 1996), 3-25; quotation on p. 7.

17. Ibid., 6, 10.

18. Ibid., 19-20. Cohen refers to Kristeva's concept of abjection, on which more below.

19. Gilmore, *Monsters*, 174-94; Beal, *Religion and Its Monsters*, 193-96; Cohen, "Monster Culture," 19-20. Gilmore and Beal independently used this phrase as a subject heading. Since these authors deal with both ancient and contemporary monsters, I should note their common observation that ancient monsters tend to be animal-human hybrids that embody fear of reversion to the animal. In the postmodern world, anxiety fixates instead on the human-machine boundary. The cyborg, a machine-human hybrid, becomes the paradigmatic monster. This anxiety probably arises from the conflict between our high valuation of individuality and our great dependence on machines. Film cyborgs tend to be deficient in individuality and identity, although it is not at all obvious why machine parts would have this effect.

II. The Anomalous Bodies of *4 Ezra*

The book contains a variety of anomalous bodies: human, monstrous, and, arguably, cosmic. To begin with the general human condition, *4 Ezra* paints a picture of current and increasing deterioration. In particular, the image of the evil heart *(cor malignum)* occurs in several passages. In the first unit, Ezra asks why human life is so fragile and fleeting (4:23-25). Uriel's reply integrates physical debility, moral decline, and cosmic processes: "For it will not be able to bring the things that have been promised to the righteous in their appointed times, because this world is full of sadness and infirmities *[plenum maestitia . . . et infirmitatibus]*. . . . For a grain of evil seed was sown in Adam's heart from the beginning . . ." (4:27b, 30a).[20] In his comment on this passage, Stone notes the correlation between the heart and the world, and thus the necessity, in terms of the book's cosmology, for re-creations of both.[21] It would be easy to read the notion of an "evil heart" as a metaphor for moral corruption, but the text also links it to disease and death (3:21-22, 7:48).[22] Although Ezra laments the ravages of present existence (e.g., 4:11b-12), he and Uriel agree about cosmic and human decrepitude, so we can reliably take this view as a major part of the text's cosmology.

Taken by themselves, these passages would provide only a modest imagination of embodiment. Beyond death itself as a physical instantiation of metaphysical corruption, *4 Ezra* details progressive human bodily anomaly as an important locus for cosmic ills and also for the re-creation. As the end approaches, human physical decline and monstrosities appear as omens. This idea of the universe as a body takes several forms. Uriel compares a woman's childbearing ability to cosmic processes in various ways, among them the notion that just as older women bear weaker children, the older cosmos produces weaker inhabitants (5:51-55).[23] Although earlier Mediterra-

---

20. All English quotations of *4 Ezra* are from Stone, *Fourth Ezra*. All quoted Latin text is from A. Frederik J. Klijn, *Der Lateinische Text der Apokalypse des Esra* (Berlin: Akademie-Verlag, 1983). In a few places, I have also consulted the earlier Latin text by Bruno Violet, *Die Esra-Apokalypse (IV. Esra)*, vol. 1, *Die Überlieferung* (GCS 18; Leipzig: Hinrichs, 1910).

21. Stone, *Fourth Ezra*, 94.

22. In 3:21, a passive construction introduced the evil heart; the reticence about agency has been widely noted by scholars. See Thompson, *Responsibility for Evil*, 337 for this passage and its parallels. See also Stone, *Fourth Ezra*, 63. Stone (*Fourth Ezra*, 74) contrasts this idea with the concept of the Two Spirits found in 1QS. For Ezra, all are subject to the evil inclination, whereas 1QS tends to divide people into two groups.

23. Stone notes variation in the Latin MSS on "stature" versus "strength" *(statu, statura)* and sees no way to resolve the question. Either case implies the idea of decline from

Monsters and the Crippled Cosmos

nean and Near Eastern literature used the idea of deteriorating human types or empires, the notion of the cosmos itself as an entity that undergoes life stages is distinct from these earlier ideas.[24] This image places the typical eschatological signs in new context: they become an inherent part of the cosmic aging process. Human physical and cognitive disability (5:9b-10) is one symptom of a much larger disease.[25]

Fourth Ezra's strong connection between the human and cosmic bodies can also be seen in one of its less typical eschatological signs. Two passages describe anomalous births. In the first unit, Uriel speaks of a cosmic decay that includes the usual astronomical disturbances, geological disruptions and failures, moral collapse — and the birth of monsters *(monstra)* to human women (5:1-13, esp. v. 8).[26] The passage does not give further details about the monstrosities. Most of these signs are typical of similar lists, but the detail about monstrous births is not widespread in Second Temple Jewish literature.[27] There are two likely sources for this notion in Second Temple Jewish literature. Some Assyro-Babylonian texts list birth omens, that is, in-

---

a more valued norm. He also observes that the Babylonians had the opposite view of the relationship between maternal age and infant strength, and that both opinions are medically incorrect (Stone, *Fourth Ezra*, 153).

24. The earliest text with a historical scheme of human races is Hesiod, *Works and Days*, 106-201. Daniel 2:31-45 and 7 describe successions of world empires. For a full discussion of this motif, see Arnoldo Momigliano, "The Origins of Universal History," in *On Pagans, Jews, and Christians* (Middletown, Conn.: Wesleyan University Press, 1987), 31-57. Momigliano notes that classical Greek historical schemes did not apply the idea of biological decline to world history or to the cosmos, and Stone suggests that this motif originated in Second Temple Judaism (*Fourth Ezra*, 152-53).

25. Although this essay focuses on body imagery, *4 Ezra*'s frequent references to intelligence and its loss also lend themselves to a disability analysis.

26. Violet conjectured Greek *terata* behind the Latin *monstra* because it has the same range of meanings. See Bruno Violet, *Die Apokalypsen des Esra und des Baruch in deutscher Gestalt* (GCS 32; Leipzig: Hinrichs, 1924), 27. Knibb remarks on this detail, "But the word used really conveys the idea that the children born will be signs or portents of what is to come" (R. J. Coggins and M. A. Knibb, *The First and Second Books of Esdras* [CBC; Cambridge: Cambridge University Press, 1979], 133). He seems concerned to rule out women giving birth to chimeras or similar mythical monsters, but fails to say why some births were regarded as portents: the infants were physically anomalous, disabled, deformed, or otherwise too divergent from a cultural norm.

27. Other "signs" passages in Jewish literature include *Testaments of the Twelve Patriarchs* (*T. Levi* 4:1 and *T. Judah* 21:7–22:1); *Jub.* 23:11-25; *1 Enoch* 80:2-4; 91:6-7; 99:4-9; 100:1-3; *Sib. Or.* 2:154-73; 3:796-807; 5:74; *Apoc. Abr.* 30:1-8; *2 Bar.* 26:1-35; 48:30-41; 70:2-3. None of these passages uses specific terms for monstrosity, but *Jub.* 23:25 and *Sib. Or.* 2:55, both of which parallel features of Hesiod's fifth race, present close parallels to *4 Ezra* 6:21.

terpretations of the portentous qualities attributed to specific physical differences.[28] Early Roman interest in unusual births as portents would be a more temporally proximate source.[29] Such portents included not only physically different infants but also statues manifesting lifelike qualities, intrasexuals, and unusual meteorological and astronomical phenomena.[30] Both the Assyro-Babylonian and Roman material treat such births, among other omens, as matters of public concern, that is, as indicating events that would affect many people. Thus the scale is larger, compared to a belief that physically different infants were divine punishments for their parents' sins.[31] *Fourth Ezra* greatly expands the scale, from the community to the whole cosmos. This expansion fits with the book's depiction of the cosmos itself as ill and disabled in the last phase of its determined life cycle.

The second passage with an anomalous birth motif occurs in the second unit: "Infants a year old shall speak with their voices, and women with child shall give birth to premature children at three or four months, and these shall live and dance *(scrirtiabuntur)*" (6:21).[32] The image combines opposite extremes, for the exceptionally weak (premature infants) can perform feats of exceptional ability (talking and dancing). Such a combination characterizes monsters, for it has both their hybrid quality and their typical disproportion, relative to the ideological norm.[33] The parallel passage in *Jubi-*

---

28. See, for instance, "Birth Omens" and "City Omens" in *Prophets and Prophecy in the Ancient Near East*, ed. Martti Nissinen et al. (SBLWAW 12; Atlanta: Society of Biblical Literature, 2003), 189-92.

29. Robert Garland contrasted Greek and Roman attitudes on this topic and concluded that Greeks regarded such births as punishments of the parents, but did not otherwise take religious countermeasures. Romans in the late Republican period, on the other hand, took a public interest in portents, which waned once the Empire was established. See Robert Garland, *The Eye of the Beholder: Deformity and Disability in the Graeco-Roman World* (London: Duckworth, 1995), especially chapter 4, "The Deformed and the Divine," 59-72. See also Robin Lorsch Wildfang and Jacob Isager, *Divination and Portents in the Roman World* (Odense: Odense University Press, 2000), for a discussion of major Roman sources.

30. Wildfang and Isager, *Divination*, 11. Except for intrasexuals, the items are similar to Second Temple "sign" lists. For the intense interest Romans took in intrasexuals, see also Garland, *Eye of the Beholder*.

31. The individual and public meanings are not mutually exclusive; the disciples' question about the congenitally blind man in John 9:2 suggests that individualized interpretations of disability were present in popular consciousness.

32. Stone (*Fourth Ezra*, 170) comments that this image is the logical extreme of a shortening life span.

33. Gilmore, *Monsters*, 6-9. As Stone notes (*Fourth Ezra*, 170), this detail may or may not come from the same tradition as the one in 5:8.

lees has grey-haired children and aged infants (23:25).³⁴ Grey-haired infants also appear in *Sibylline Oracle* 2:155, in a context of the usual plagues and wars.³⁵ In turn, Hesiod's tale of the five kinds of human beings has two parallels to *4 Ezra*. Grey-haired children are to appear in the narrator's future, as the end of the fifth race approaches (*Works and Days*, 131). The second race, however, featured a century-long infancy characterized by rampant foolishness (*Works and Days*, 130). This motif parallels *4 Ezra*'s detail about the eschatological loss of wisdom and intelligence (5:9b-10).³⁶ In any case, Hesiod gives these two characteristics to different races, whereas *4 Ezra* allocates them to human beings of the same cosmic life phase. Finally, all of these parallels give infants the anomalous quality of grey hair, but not speech and precocious dancing ability. Whatever the sources of 6:21 or 5:8, the author selected and arranged them to link physical-moral corruption to the common motifs of Jewish creation myths, and then sustained the association such that corruption of the human body mirrors corruption of the cosmic order. The result is a representation of the progressive physical, mental, and emotional disability of human beings as integral parts of a cosmos that grows progressively disabled and strange.

III. Monsters and Others

The descriptions of human and cosmic anomaly in the first three units prepare the stage for the book's proper monsters. Monstrosity of the non-human variety appears in two major forms: the mythical monsters present at the creation and the eschaton, and the visionary monsters that depict (and mythologize) historical enemies. Regarding the first, *4 Ezra*'s retelling of the Hexaemeron (6:38-54) refers to Behemoth and Leviathan, present at the origin and to be consumed at the end: "Then thou didst preserve two living creatures which you created . . . Behemoth and . . . Leviathan . . . and thou hast kept them to be eaten by whom thou wilt, and when thou wilt" (6:49, 52b). The parallels have long been noted, and apparently indicate a Second

---

34. See *Jubilees*, trans. O. S. Wintermute, in *The Old Testament Pseudepigrapha*, ed. James H. Charlesworth, 2 vols. (New York: Doubleday, 1983-85), 2:101. Stone comments that the detail is embedded in a larger system (*Fourth Ezra*, 170).

35. In a note to his translation of the *Sibylline Oracles* in *The Old Testament Pseudepigrapha* (1:349), Collins notes the apparent earliest occurrence of the grey-haired infant motif in Hesiod, *Works and Days*, 181.

36. See note 25 above.

Rebecca Raphael

Temple tradition, later taken up in rabbinic literature, that serves these monsters as the main course at the eschatological banquet in the world to come.[37] Their treatment in *4 Ezra* has some unusual features. Stone notes the disproportionate amount of space they take up in the Hexaemeron, for he regards their presence as incidental to the author's main point in the passage. In a monograph on these monsters, Whitney further observes that God, rather than Adam, names these two, a detail that marks them as special.[38] The explicit text makes them primordial elements of chaos that inhabit marginal realms, both key monster characteristics. Their presence calls up an old mythical motif, not explicit in *4 Ezra*, of chaos monsters defeated by God at the creation, to be defeated again at the end.[39] Further, the mode of their final defeat alludes to but reverses that unfortunate monster habit of eating humans: in the end, human beings get to eat them.[40] This passage is their only appearance in *4 Ezra*;[41] they represent an element of monstrosity present at the creation and in the cosmos until the new creation.

Even if Leviathan and Behemoth do not appear again by name, *4 Ezra* does have an eschatological monster, commonly called "the eagle," an animal term that hardly does justice to its monstrous qualities. This vision, the fifth unit, occurs after the seer's major transformation in the fourth unit, which I shall treat in more detail below. After consuming the field flowers, Ezra sees a multi-headed, multi-winged eagle arise from the sea (11:1-3). This is no ordinary eagle, nor does it reflect Roman representations of the eagle. As if three heads were not bad enough, one of them is disproportionately large; the "eagle" produces a voice that does not appear to come from anywhere,

---

37. Cf. *2 Bar.* 29:4, *1 Enoch* 60:7-10. The monsters are mentioned several times in the Hebrew Bible (Isa. 51:9; Pss. 74:13-14; 89:10-11; Job 7:12; 26:12-13; and 40–41), but not in the context of a banquet. For the development of the whole complex of tradition in the Second Temple period, see Whitney, *Two Strange Beasts*, 31-58. For later rabbinic sources, see Stone, *Fourth Ezra*, 187.

38. Whitney, *Two Strange Beasts*, 37.

39. Gunkel, *Creation and Chaos*, 21-77.

40. Whitney isolated a tradition in which Leviathan is a major threat to the *axis mundi* itself, a role conceived as both pre-creation and post-eschatological. It is possible that mention of Leviathan in *4 Ezra* alludes to, or would remind a contemporary reader of, this tradition. His main source texts are the *Apocalypse of Abraham* and the *Ladder of Jacob*. Whitney, *Two Strange Beasts*, 59-91.

41. Stone sees this as evidence that the author had not fully integrated the monsters into his eschatology (*Fourth Ezra*, 183). However, I contend that monstrosity, as a term to describe a variety of different motifs including these two monsters, is indeed integrated thematically.

certainly not from a head as one would expect (11:10); and it has a penchant for partial self-cannibalism (11:28-32). It produces speech by unusual means, speaking "from the midst of its body" rather than from a mouth in a head (11:10).[42]

Of course it signifies Rome; scholarship has thoroughly dissected the possible political associations.[43] But let us consider the eagle *as* a monster. It shows extreme size (11:2), morphological hybridity (11:1, 10, 12ff), disproportion (11:4), an appetite for the wrong things, extreme destructiveness, and an uncanny ability to control natural forces (11:2). Generally, monsters physically instantiate evil, imagined as an anomalous body with extreme appetites. Physical anomaly encodes negative value, just as physical "rightness," however defined, encodes positive value. Here, through monster imagery, a specific series of historical events with specific players has taken on mythic proportions, or disproportions. In effect, this move places all players outside the realm of the mundane limitations and on to a cosmic plane of essential goodness or evil. This move is fairly typical of apocalyptic mythologizing, which sees in the mundane world evidence of supra-mundane forces in conflict.[44] In terms of monster theory, it is an axiom that monsters represent the Other or the Abject:[45] the eagle's intention either to rule or to destroy the world (monsters are notoriously unclear on the difference between these) is directly incompatible with the seer's belief, however disturbed by events, that the world was created for Israel (6:55-59). For the author, history cannot simultaneously harbor Roman imperialism and a Judeo-centric cosmology. Hence Rome is an existential threat, not just to actual Jewish lives and sacred spaces, but to Judaic identity and mythos. By treating Rome as a monster,

---

42. Knibb comments, "because the Roman Empire itself is speaking, not one of the emperors" (*First and Second Books of Esdras*, 240). This is correct as far as it goes, but misses the sheer creepiness of voices that do not come from a mouth, an image that goes far beyond the demand to corporatize Rome.

43. The still-leading interpretation relates the heads to the Flavians (Stone, *Fourth Ezra*, 9-10; cf. Collins, *Apocalyptic Imagination*, 195-96), but there is widespread disagreement on what all the wings signify. Recently, DiTommaso has raised serious objections to this interpretation. He agrees with the consensus dating of *4 Ezra* to the late first century C.E., but argues that the details of the wing passage fit better with the Severans and thus indicate a later redaction of this one passage. See Lorenzo DiTommaso, "Dating the Eagle Vision of *4 Ezra*: A New Look at an Old Theory," *JSP* 20 (1999): 3-38.

44. See John J. Collins, "Apocalyptic Eschatology as the Transcendence of Death," in idem, *Seers, Sibyls and Sages in Hellenistic-Roman Judaism* (JSJSup 54; Leiden: Brill, 1997), 84.

45. These are not quite the same. See the conclusion.

4 Ezra both effectively taps the binary quality of deity-monster, order-chaos myths, and also subsumes (consumes?) the historical opponent into the author's myth.

Mythically, there is one right way to kill a monster: redundantly. The eagle is destroyed piecemeal, in a fashion reminiscent of dismemberment, by several different means: disappearance (11:13ff; *non + appareo*), self-cannibalism (11:31-35, *devoro*, not the most pleasant term for "eat"), and burning (12:3a, *incendo*, passive). The first two occur as unexplained processes, as if disappearance were simply a feature of the body parts. The third manner of destruction happens after the lion has appeared and spoken to the eagle. After a rehearsal of his crimes, the lion says: "Therefore you will surely disappear, you eagle, and your terrifying wings and your most evil little wings, and your malicious heads, and your most evil talons, and your whole unjust body *(omne corpus tuum vanum)*" (11:45).[46] As if the specific crimes listed were not enough, this closing passage dwells on each detail of the eagle's body, emphasizes the evil quality of every part, and wraps up with this condemnation of the whole. This conclusion underlines a connection between evil actions and bodily form, an association that occurs with all monsters, and which is also in keeping with the book's close linkage of physical and ethical qualities. Surely the complete destruction that follows this speech is no accident (12:3a). Then, through means not made clear, the lion presides over the eagle's final dismemberment and burning. From context, it seems that the lion's speech is the agent of the eagle's destruction, just as God's speech was emphasized as the means of creation in *4 Ezra* 6.[47] Even so, the passive lends a touch of inevitability, as if such evil monsters simply self-destruct, unable to sustain their own chaos. Organic bodies — the kind we find in actual history — do not have to be destroyed in redundant, supernatural fashion. In addition to the wonderful image of a polity in self-destructive conflict, the bizarre morphology encodes cosmic corruption that can only be eliminated from *existence*, not reformed or cured in continuity with the status quo.

---

46. The NRSV and NEB come closer to *vanum:* "worthless." The term echoes the nothingness of the nations earlier in the book (6:56-57). Stone seems to prefer *iniustum*, from the Armenian version.

47. The Man's speech plays a similar role in 13:9-10.

IV. Bodies, Primordial and Eschatological

These monsters have their opposites in representations of pristine, "right" bodies, human and divine. Since neither the term "norm" nor "ideal" seems appropriate to this material, I shall use a capitalized Right to indicate the ideologically correct body, the one that embodies the text's values, as opposed to the monsters that not only do not embody the text's values but are actually inimical to them. In addition to its "wrong" bodies, *4 Ezra* contains other passages that represent Right embodiment and equate it with the text's insiders, i.e., with the Self. The creation Hexaemeron, the post-eschatological body, and the messianic figures all contribute to this construction.

In the third unit's sensuous rewriting of Genesis 1, Ezra recapitulates the cosmogony, to use an Eliadic phrase. Scholars have noticed several important divergences from the source myth. Stone observes that the passage omits closing formulae in favor of opening formulae ("On the X day, thou didst . . .").[48] Cook analyzes the importance of this omission: God never says that anything is good.[49] Both link the addition of purposive clauses ("Y so that Z") to the book's claims about divine determinism of the cosmos and history. Although some commentators remark on one or two details of the sensory imagery, it has not been treated as an overall part of *4 Ezra*'s revision of Genesis 1.[50] The passage emphasizes and enhances sensual elements. On the first day, Ezra contrasts primordial silence with the post-cosmogonic human voice (6:39). Then a "ray of light" comes forth from the heavenly storehouses, in order to make God's work visible (to whom?) (6:40). On the second day, the "spirit of the firmament" is positively kinetic, moving the waters up and down (6:41). The third day's fruit comes in "endless abundance and of varied appeal to the taste; and flowers of inimitable color, and innumerable beautiful trees and inexpressible fragrances" (6:44). Visual and gustatory elements predominate, along with a hint of the ineffable, of a sensory experience at the limits of the much-vaunted human speech to describe. The light of the heavenly bodies gets two statements (6:45), but is not

---

48. Stone, *Fourth Ezra*, 180.

49. Joan E. Cook, "Creation in *4 Ezra:* The Biblical Theme in Support of Theodicy," in *Creation in the Biblical Traditions*, 129-39.

50. Stone and Myers both note the "fragrances" (Stone, *Fourth Ezra*, 186; Jacob M. Myers, *I and II Esdras* [AB 42; Garden City, N.Y.: Doubleday, 1974], 229). Stone and Cook both observe the use of silence, which they interpret as underscoring the significance of speech (Stone, *Fourth Ezra*, 184; Cook, "Creation," 132-33). Cook goes farthest in noticing the overall sensual quality, but she does not detail it or interpret it in its own right (p. 133).

otherwise amplified. On the fifth day, living creatures emerge from water; the latter is described as "dumb and lifeless" *(muta et sine anima)*, an interesting conjunction. Does the author mean that the water was lifeless before the fifth day, and now is full of life? If so, then "dumb" is a subtle analogy by which the creatures are what the water speaks. Behemoth and Leviathan, treated above, follow. Finally, the animals and Adam appear on the sixth day, and receive virtually no description (6:54).[51] In short, the Hexaemeron employs frequent and rich sensory images as one of its main variations on Genesis 1. Compared to its source, this cosmos is far more embodied and addresses itself to embodied beings. In particular, the terms assume human embodiment and sensory capacities. *Fourth Ezra* depicts the cosmos as an orthosomatic body geared to the perceptions of a central perceiver. Adam perhaps gets short shrift because the author sees humans as the perceivers, not as the perceived. It is also possible that he withholds a positive assessment of the human body because of the inherent defects that time will advance. Even so, human beings start with a deficit of sensory richness, at least as they are represented by this text.[52]

Thus the original Right body of the cosmos is more natural than human. In the eschatological future, *4 Ezra* depicts a restored, even improved, mode of the human body. Ezra has asked Uriel what happens to souls between the deaths of their bodies and the general re-creation. After discussing the fate of the wicked, Uriel describes the future condition of the righteous. In addition to a beatific vision of God, the righteous see what their future remade bodies will be like: faces will "shine like the sun," bodies will be "made like the light of the stars, being incorruptible" (7:96-97). I see no reason to take this as an intentional metaphor: the text envisions the remade human body as a light-giving form not subject to decay. Since the stars were thought to be the bodies of heavenly spirits, the text seems to expect that the righteous shall become what the star-spirits already are.[53] Indeed, a later passage

---

51. Stone finds the Adam passage disproportionately short (*4 Ezra*, 180).

52. I shall leave Ezra's main question, to which all this leads, for the conclusion. Suffice to say for the present that Adam is the progenitor not just of individual human beings but of national groups (6:54). The nations of the text's contemporary world are then represented as productions of Adam's body; Israel are descendants proper, whereas the nations (especially the Romans) come from Adam but are spit (6:56), i.e., literally abjects from the proper body. For a discussion of the possible sources of this motif, see Stone, *Fourth Ezra*, 189.

53. There is a long tradition connecting two or more of the following elements: shining light, the sun, the stars, angels, and the righteous. For extensive references in biblical,

specifically notes the absence of physical ailments as a feature of the world to come: "The root [i.e., of evil] is sealed up from you, illness is banished from you, and death is hidden" (8:53-54, brackets original). The association of light with incorruptibility makes intuitive sense, for light cannot be damaged as organic bodies can, nor could anyone in the ancient world observe the material of which stars are composed, let alone their deaths. Thus, in the beginning, we have a pristine cosmos, except possibly for the underdescribed Adam, and at the end, the righteous are reembodied as incorruptible light. This eschatological body is the human Right Form, both achievement and reward, but not inherent in this creation. It is not too strong to say that the book turns the human body into a universal clock: one can tell cosmic time by reading anomalous human bodies.

Finally, let us turn to the eagle's opposite numbers, the various messianic figures. They take two forms, that of the lion in the fifth unit and that of the man from the sea in the sixth.[54] The first figure is introduced as "a creature like a lion," but the simile does not recur. He comes from the forest, appropriately roaring, and can also speak with a human voice (11:37). Like the eagle, the lion also embodies a kind of human-animal hybridity, but his hybrid features are represented as right. Like a prophet, he speaks for God (11:38). Like a sage, he is a fine exegete, addressing the eagle as the fourth beast of Daniel's vision (11:39), an interpretation later elaborated by Uriel (12:11). His one unusual ability seems to be making monsters self-incinerate on hearing his voice (12:1-3). Although animal imagery occurs in other apocalypses, and the lion image has a long history, here the lion draws on the repertoire of this cosmos to present a messiah in a right form, while avoiding, at first presentation, the human form that has taken much criticism from both Ezra and Uriel. Through the lion image, the text also associates the messiah with Judah (cf. Gen. 49:9-10).

The second time around, Ezra sees an anthropomorphic figure. The sixth unit reverses the order in which the combatants appear on stage, with the

---

apocryphal, and rabbinic literature, see Stone, *Fourth Ezra*, 244, and Myers, *I and II Esdras*, 238-39. For a discussion of this motif in apocalyptic eschatology, see John J. Collins, "Cosmos and Salvation: Jewish Wisdom and Apocalypticism in the Hellenistic Age," in *Seers, Sibyls and Sages*, 317-38, especially 330-32.

54. Uriel's earlier reference describes generally what the messiah does, but not who he is or what he looks like (7:28-29). Shannon Burkes (*God, Self, and Death: The Shape of Religious Transformation in the Second Temple Period* [JSJSup 79; Leiden: Brill, 2003], 200) notes that the three messianic figures are not necessarily identical and seem to have different functions.

man from the sea arising first (13:1-2). This like-a-man has some interesting properties: he flies (13:3), his gaze provokes trembling in anything (13:3), and his voice can melt other bodies (13:4). These abilities would be monstrous in, say, a dragon, but in a heroic figure, they appear as superpowers. His opponents in this passage are human rather than monstrous (13:5), and he defeats them by breathing a combination of three different fiery substances blended together into one toxic mixture (13:10-11).[55] Although this vision features anthropomorphic combatants on both sides, the triple redundancy of the man's attack abilities taps into the monster motif of redundant destruction. Heroes must have multiple means by which to destroy monsters that must be multiply killed. Moreover, bodily substances, projected out, provide the mode of attack; Ezra draws attention to the man's lack of weapons (13:9). This detail only furthers the integration of the messiah's body with his mode of destroying enemies: he fights with what he is, not with what he can use.[56]

V. Reembodiment and Eschatological Transformations

All are agreed that the fifth and sixth units form an eschatology that reconciles Ezra to the ways of God. But why does this disclosure provide a satisfying answer, or least quietus, to his questions? The fourth unit, the Vision of Zion, has long been recognized as the turning point, at which Ezra abandons his relentless questioning of God's justice and accepts his new prophetic role. Here, Ezra encounters a woman weeping in the field, chides her for her private griefs when the communal ones are direr, and finds himself spouting the angel's party lines. She then transforms into the city of Zion. Ezra collapses at the sight, gains some explanation from Uriel, and is invited to enter the city. At that moment, the narrative leaves him, to resume after this experience. Humphrey has divided scholarship into two camps, one favoring the conversation with the woman, and the other the vision of the city, as the pivotal moment.[57] Humphrey sensibly argues that both portions play a role, for

---

55. Stone (*Fourth Ezra*, 386) provides a full discussion of the earlier motifs of divine speech, breath, and judgment by fire. He does not, however, reflect on the embodied quality of these powers.

56. The angel does not interpret these details.

57. Edith McEwan Humphrey, *The Ladies and the Cities: Transformation and Apocalyptic Identity in Joseph and Asenath, 4 Ezra, the Apocalypse, and the Shepherd of Hermas* (Sheffield: Academic Press, 1995), 57-81. See pages 59-69 for her thorough discussion of the scholarship.

the vision discloses the identity of the mourning woman with the extant Zion. The role-reversal view has merit, along the lines suggested by Collins: he compares the vision to juridical parables in the Hebrew Bible.[58] Nevertheless, the two figures' griefs are asymmetrical. Ezra did not harbor a private grief, but the public and communal one (10:11). Second, he does not try to persuade the woman out of grief per se, but merely out of her private grief (10:16). In fact, he tries to talk her *into* the communal grief for Zion (10:20). By contrast, the angel tried to persuade Ezra out of grief per se, and especially out of his most general grief for the human condition. Finally, when Ezra is rewarded with a vision of Zion, the angel does not grade him on how well he performed the angel's task, but rather on the depth of his grief for Zion (10:50).[59] As for the visionary experience as pivot, Stone argues that Ezra undergoes a religious conversion, after which he emerges with a new sense of mission.[60] Breech sees the author making "grief itself . . . the basis for community," and the visions provide consolation for this communal grief.[61] Humphrey, trying to pinpoint why this vision should be so transforming for Ezra, makes a case for the identity of suffering Zion and glorious Zion as the crucial new perception.[62]

The scene's double reembodiments can provide further insight into how such vision changes Ezra. The woman's physical presentation gets his attention and elicits his advocacy of the communal grief (10:38-40). Her transformation into Zion is a reembodiment, analogous to the bodies of the righteous: "her face suddenly shone exceedingly, and her countenance flashed like lightning . . . she suddenly uttered a loud and fearful cry, so that the earth shook at her voice" (10:25-26).[63] That physical similarity is fleeting, for Ezra finally sees "an established city" (10:27, *civitas aedificabatur*). The woman-city provides analogous modes of embodiment for the righteous and for Jerusalem itself, not just in the radiant quality, but also in the transformation to incorruptible form.[64] Three key sensory images, intense light,

---

58. Collins, *Apocalyptic Imagination*, 206.

59. Pointedly observed by Humphrey, *Ladies and the Cities*, 64.

60. Stone, *Fourth Ezra*, 315-39.

61. Earl Breech, "These Fragments I Have Shored against My Ruins: The Form and Function of 4 Ezra," *JBL* 92.2 (1973): 267-74; p. 272 for this quotation.

62. Humphrey, *Ladies and the Cities*, 71-76.

63. The parallels to 6:13ff. and 7:125 have been noted by Stone (*Fourth Ezra*, 327) and others, albeit not in the context of systematic study of body imagery.

64. Stone rightly dismisses the question whether this Jerusalem is heavenly or eschatological; the point is simply that it exists and that Ezra has seen it (*Fourth Ezra*, 335).

intense sound, and solid order, dominate the description of a supra-sensual experience, reminiscent of the Hexaemeron.

In turn, Ezra's vision of the city precipitates his change of mind and body. To be sure, the vision does not answer the questions he raised earlier, or provide a discursive theodicy. Those questions sought to understand how the destruction of Jerusalem was compatible with a just and powerful God who has a special concern for Israel. Theodicy is, by nature, directed to the past: no one worries a great deal about the injustice of God's *future* actions. But what explication of the past, however perspicuous, could possibly satisfy? Without logical solution, only redirection is possible. The vision thus redirects (or, less charitably, distracts) Ezra's attention by answering questions he has *not* asked: "What next? Where do we go from here?" There is a mutual lack of fit between two sets of questions and answers. Even if theodicy were possible, it would not give one direction for future action. Conversely, the will to act in the present and future does not conform the past to the logical demands of theodicy. Redirection gives one something to do, and this something cannot be arbitrary. Uriel does not persuade Ezra that God is just. He sees the city whole, and she persuades him that he still has something for which and toward which to act.

Ezra's own reembodiment follows. Extreme physical and emotional distress preceded his first three visions (3:1-3; 5:20b-21; 6:35-37).[65] In unit four, he collapses to the point of death (10:30), experiencing sensory overload both before and after the collapse (10:27a-30; 10:56-57). Such disturbances do not preface the fifth through seventh units. Indeed, the last unit begins with commands directed at two distinct areas of activity: instructing the people and preparing for his own removal. Both of these contain elements of bodily representation. Ezra's remaking into the New Moses is explicit (14:1-6). Before he undertakes the task of rewriting the lost scriptures, his heavenly interlocutor explains, "I will light in your heart the lamp of understanding, which shall not be put out until you finish what you are about to write" (14:25). Once away with his five scribes, Ezra hears a voice that gives him something to drink: "Then I opened my mouth, and behold, a full cup was offered to me; it was full of something like water, but its color was like fire. And I took it and drank; and when I had drunk it, my heart poured forth understanding and wisdom increased in my breast, and my spirit retained its memory" (14:39-40).

---

65. On cross-cultural visionary techniques applied to apocalyptic literature, see Adela Yarbro Collins, *Cosmology and Eschatology in Jewish and Christian Apocalypticism* (JSJSup 50; Leiden: Brill, 1996), 17, 88.

This passage represents inspiration as a highly embodied process. First, Ezra must imbibe a drink. Whatever it is, it transforms his heart and breast, the seats of interiority. The mind *(sensus),* so highly valued by the earlier Ezra, is not mentioned in the physicality of inspiration. So this experience rearranges Ezra's own modus operandi. Second, the focus on the heart echoes the "evil heart" of corrupt human nature, yet remakes this organ at least in Ezra himself. Finally, if we compare this kind of inspiration to hearing a voice or seeing a vision, we obtain a distinction between these two long-range senses and an extremely intimate operation whereby scripture, both exoteric and esoteric, is embodied by Ezra. His final transformation, like his earlier entry into Zion, is not described (14:50). However, the detail about Ezra going to others "who are like him" has physical as well as ethical and spiritual ramifications. After all, the reason for his departure was that he should not continue to inhabit the physically crippled cosmos (14:13-14). This final unit intertwines Mosaic motifs with Ezra the scribe such that Ezra's presentation of the (redefined) Torah does not merely accompany the reconstruction of Jerusalem, but becomes the *means* by which the real Jerusalem shall be achieved. The book invites its readers to imbibe scripture, i.e., the cultural production of the lost city, in order to make themselves conduits of the city's future realization, as the center of communal identity and reconstruction in a new key — in a new cosmos.

VI. Conclusion

The book's prodigious body imagery lines up a certain way. Anomalous bodies — monsters and ill or disabled human bodies — do not participate in the new cosmos. Indeed, as I have argued, the monsters and the increasing human anomalies are inseparable from the cosmos' own progressive decline. Corrupt humans, specific monsters, and the crippled cosmos are all instances of the same thing, and all are done away with in the end. The text suggests by analogy, if not overtly, that that current cosmos itself *is* the chaos monster that God must defeat before another creation. In this light, we can discern various levels at which monstrous representations operate. Within the current cosmos, Rome as a monster is a specific case of body imagery constructing the Other. More generally, Leviathan and Behemoth, given so much detail at the creation and consumed at the end by the righteous, represent generic forces of chaos literally planted by God in the cosmic structure. Finally, this cosmos itself displays its decay by monstrous signs, cannot support a reward for the righteous, and must be utterly destroyed rather than reworked. All of these binaries — Rome-Jerusalem, Chaos Monster–God, Old Cosmos–New Cosmos — are analogous, with the difference that the last binary undoes the very matrix of the first two.

In short, *4 Ezra* abjects the cosmos. Julia Kristeva differentiates between the object and the abject thus:

> The abject has one quality of the object — that of being opposed to *I*. If the object, however, through its opposition, settles me within the fragile texture of a desire for meaning, which, as a matter of fact, makes me ceaselessly and infinitely homologous to it, what is *abject*, on the contrary, the jettisoned object, is radically excluded and draws me toward a place where meaning collapses.[66]

That is, Kristeva locates Self-Other opposition within an already established system of representations. By contrast, the abject is what is thrown out *prior* to the constitution of a clear Self, an ego. In our text, Rome-Jerusalem is a Self-Other construction; this cosmos, the monster, is abject. It is telling, for instance, that although the author incorporates, as a penultimate phase, a traditional messianic eschatology that does not abject this cosmos, he found this cosmos to be inadequate material for re-making and proposed instead its complete destruction.[67] If we ask why it was inadequate, I find the best hints in the Vision of Zion: Ezra experiences this world as meaningless because Zion could not go on existing in it, and his vision of a nevertheless existing Zion points him out of this world and any futures or heavens it may hold. The post-eschatological state has no monsters, no anomalous bodies, and no enemies of Israel.[68] The whole monster dies in the end, and for *4 Ezra*, the whole monster is this cosmos.

The structure of abjection is integral to that major concern of apocalypticism, the transcendence of death. On that subject, John Collins writes:

---

66. Julia Kristeva, *Powers of Horror: An Essay on Abjection,* trans. Leon S. Roudiez (New York: Columbia University Press, 1982), 1-2. Tina Pippin has employed Kristeva's thought in her monograph *Apocalyptic Bodies: The Biblical End of the World in Text and Image* (New York: Routledge, 1999), which focuses on New Testament apocalypticism.

67. On the messiah's limited role in *4 Ezra*, see Michael E. Stone, "The Question of the Messiah in *4 Ezra*," in idem, *Selected Studies in Pseudepigrapha and Apocrypha with Special Reference to the Armenian Tradition* (SVTP 9; Leiden: Brill, 1991), 317-32.

68. Who, exactly, constitutes Israel is another question.

Apocalypticism still deals with a communal context, whether it be the nation or, more often, the just, but its concern has extended to the life of the individual. By its focus on heavenly, supernatural realities it provides a possibility that human life can transcend death, not merely by the future generations of the nation but by passing to the higher, heavenly sphere.[69]

4 Ezra shows this layering of the national, the just, and the individual. Posthumous judgment and admission to the new cosmos seem to be mainly individual, with the messiah's mainly national activity subsumed in a larger framework. Further, Ezra's final retransmission of the Torah and the esoteric books reflects some role for the national project, although membership in the community is no assurance for anyone.[70] However, focus on transcendence of death by itself neglects crucial features of apocalypticism's construction of Self and Other. First, merely not dying is not enough for the apocalypticist; the righteous must not-die in a certain way. Second, the significance of the apocalypticist's transcendence also rests on some things that do *not* get to transcend death. Body imagery provides the key to both aspects of transcendence.

The elect of *4 Ezra* obtain new bodies that have properties in addition to immortality. Some of these properties — e.g., radiance like the stars — may reflect underlying beliefs about the nature of stellar bodies and their incorruptibility. This association highly values light, associating it with knowledge. Light is, after all, an important means of obtaining knowledge for sighted beings. Disease and disability no longer exist, although it is not obvious that one could not be (say) immortal and deaf. But the text dissociates the members of the elect (dismembers them, if you will) from their current bodies. Without attempting to untangle "physical" and "spiritual" bodies, we can say that the body's qualities change significantly, and that this change is integral to the author's particular concept of transcendence.

Further, the absence of the wicked constitutes one of the valued features of the new cosmos. Transcendence of death is thus a both-and proposition: both that Self transcends, and Other does not. But why does Self's transcendence entail Other's nontranscendence? At the least, *4 Ezra* constructs *membership* in its conceptual Self and Other based on prospects for the next cosmos. It also represents the next cosmos as being in continuity with this

---

69. Collins, "Apocalyptic Eschatology as the Transcendence of Death," 84.
70. See Shannon Burkes's assessment of this question in *God, Self, and Death*, 225.

one, if not "physically" (whatever that would mean in cosmic cases), then narratively. This apocalypse does not present righteous individuals as random elements who just happen to make it because a quirky cosmic process works that way; it tells a story in which these righteous and their God are the protagonists, a story that is all about them, no matter how things look now. The psychology is easy enough to understand, and scholars have long considered the role of narrative as a response to oppression. I suggest that narrative in *4 Ezra* is also a means of transcending death, not only because the story represents such a state, but because the narrative itself attempts to transcend its own possible cultural defeat. *Fourth Ezra* represents the story of Israel as still true, and as transcendent of observable circumstances. This observation dovetails with the solution that the book offers its readers. By concluding with the retransmission of scripture (and then some) and Ezra's departure from this world, it tries to persuade the audience to recenter identity on the study of scripture, and therefore of scripture's mythos. In that respect, it shares a significant feature of rabbinic Judaism.

Thus the new cosmos that this abjection enables represents more than transcendence of death for individuals or for the group. Whether Israel survives as a people is not clear, but it does transcend death in two ways: as the implicitly defined Right-Bodied Self (over against the Monstrous Other) a community of the few who are righteous gains the new existence. Beyond this, Israel's *story* transcends death on the rocks and shoals of history: like the righteous feasting on Leviathan and Behemoth, the text of *4 Ezra* consumes the Roman imperial narrative and re-narrates Israel's historical defeats as moments in a larger drama, one in which the text's Right-Bodied Self bears into the next world the story of Israel and its God. Thus, concealed under the overt concern with theodicy, *4 Ezra* is a covert mythodicy (to make a little monster of my own): the author has not only provided a way for a few individuals to transcend death, but he has also projected the story beyond the events that could kill it in this world. This shift underlies the redirection of attention away from discursive theodicy and toward emotive, and motivating, mythodicy. This kind of achievement does not logically solve the problems of theodicy, but instead reinforces the psychological investment in a particular interpretive framework — and in the framework itself, rather than in the process by which such things are made.

Theologian John Shea provides another, perhaps more accessible, way into the special qualities and difficulties of *4 Ezra*. He recounts a conversation with his fellow theologian and priest Bill Carroll, who said about the brain cancer that would eventually kill him, "God is not in any of the meanings, but in the deeper darkness that keeps us making all the meanings. I don't want to talk about it anymore."[71] The destruction of a city, one's *axis animi*, is a deep darkness indeed. Ezra's troubled questioning comes from this place where the event has collapsed the possibilities of meaning. But even there, the text already represents that cosmos not as "the close and holy darkness," to use Shea's interpretation of Dylan Thomas,[72] but as a decrepit and yet devouring monster that must be destroyed. The author does not remain in the abyss long enough to see its radiance, or at least does not allow Ezra to come to this awareness. To shift the metaphor from sight to sound, the author keeps talking, and serves up authoritative language for consumption, as if that would remove the silence before and after all meanings. The silence, of course, remains on the spatio-temporal horizons. To shore up the mythos, *4 Ezra* consigns silence to extra-cosmic pauses, and thus cannot hear it as the uncanny moment that drives us to make meaning.

71. John Shea, *Starlight* (New York: Crossroad, 1993), 157.
72. Shea, *Starlight*, 155-59.

Idolatry and Alterity:
Israel and the Nations in the
Apocalypse of Abraham

Daniel C. Harlow

Among ancient religions, Judaism stood out by virtue of its monotheism, the touchstone of which was monolatry — the exclusive and imageless worship of the one God, the creator of heaven and earth, who called Abraham and created a people of his descendents; who entered into a covenant with them at Mt. Sinai; and who gave them his instruction, his Torah, to guide their life and their witness to him among the nations. Already in the preexilic period, Israelite beliefs about their God underwent some crucial developments. A significant movement took place in the Deuteronomic reforms of Hezekiah and Josiah in the seventh century B.C.E., when worship was centralized in Jerusalem and restrictions on how the God of Israel could be represented were imposed. A major transition occurred during the Babylonian exile of the sixth century B.C.E., when Second Isaiah pushed the henotheism that had characterized Israelite faith toward a monotheism that not only asserted the supremacy of the God of Israel over all other gods but denied the very existence of those gods: "I am the LORD, and there is no other; besides me there is no god" (Isa. 45:5 and often; cf. Deut. 32:39). Another noteworthy trend got underway in the third and second centuries B.C.E., when their encounter with Hellenism led Jewish thinkers to import Greek philosophical categories into their reflections on God.

These movements in monotheism occurred in tandem with developments in the perception of monolatry's opposite — idolatry, from εἴδωλον + λατρεία, "worship of idols." As Moshe Halbertal and Avishai Margalit have documented in an inquiry ranging from the Hebrew Bible to Maimonides, the two have always exercised a reciprocal influence on one another. Just as changing conceptions of God gave rise to different notions of idolatry, so differing ideas about idolatry shaped the Jewish understanding of God. In the history of Judaism, idolatry has been variously conceived as a betrayal of the divine-human relationship, as the ultimate metaphysical error, as misguided devotion to one or another of God's attributes or intermediaries, and as *avodah zerah* — strange (foreign) worship. Each of these understandings of idolatry presumes and promotes different conceptions of God, from the more immanent and anthropomorphic to the more transcendent and abstract.[1]

In the Greco-Roman world, avoidance of idolatry served as a way of defining what it meant to be a Jew over against the Other, functioning alongside circumcision, Sabbath and *kashrut* as a social identity and boundary marker. Both literary and nonliterary evidence from the Second Temple age suggest several practical ways in which their steering clear of idolatry impinged on the daily life of Jews. It dictated the food, oil, and wine they bought as well as what and with whom they ate. It determined whether they used Gentile coins in the marketplace, and whether they frequented the baths, took in athletic games, and engaged in other cultural pursuits. It even affected the freedom with which they moved through public spaces, especially in cities that were full of images, statues, and inscriptions devoted to pagan deities.[2]

By the first century C.E. Jews had developed a repertoire of responses to the "idolatry" of Gentiles and a variety of rhetorical techniques for assailing it — from mild satire, to crude caricature, to philosophical polemic. The tools of their trade came out of the Hebrew Bible but also from Greek philosophers, who had been critiquing popular religion for centuries. Jews writing in Greek and even in Hebrew availed themselves of these resources, employing them to denounce, *inter alia*, the pagan use of images made by human hands to represent the divine.[3]

---

1. Moshe Halbertal and Avishai Margalit, *Idolatry*, trans. Naomi Goldblum (Cambridge, Mass.: Harvard University Press, 1992). On the difficulty of formulating a general definition of idolatry, see Naomi Janowitz, "Good Jews Don't: Historical and Philosophical Constructions of Idolatry," *HR* 47 (2007): 239-52.

2. See Mark Bonnington, "Fleeing Idolatry: Social Embodiment of Anti-Idolatry in the First Century," in *Idolatry: False Worship in the Bible, Early Judaism and Christianity*, ed. Stephen C. Barton (London: T&T Clark, 2007), 107-19.

3. See further Yehoshua Amir, "Die Begegnung des biblischen und des philosophischen Monotheismus als Grundthema des jüdischen Hellenismus," *EvT* 38 (1978): 2-19; and Johannes Tromp, "Critique of Idolatry in the Context of Jewish Monotheism," in *Aspects*

Daniel C. Harlow

On the border between Israel and the other nations in the matter of monolatry and idolatry stands the figure of Abraham. In Jewish tradition, Abraham has always been regarded as the first monotheist, even though the book of Genesis portrays him as more of a henotheist. In both early and rabbinic Jewish literature he is literally an iconoclast — a smasher of idols.[4] His reputation in this regard is rooted in the story of how he renounced the idols of his father's house. The story was evidently quite popular in the Second Temple period, showing up in various forms in the book of *Jubilees*, the writings of Philo and Josephus, Pseudo-Philo's *Biblical Antiquities*, and the *Apocalypse of Abraham*.[5] Rather surprisingly, though, it has no basis at all in Genesis. Instead, it seems to have been inspired by a passing reference to Abraham in Josh. 24:2-3,

> And Joshua said to all the people, "Thus says the LORD, the God of Israel: Long ago your ancestors — Terah and his sons Abraham and Nahor — lived beyond the Euphrates and served other gods. Then I took your father Abraham from beyond the River and led him through all the land of Canaan and made his offspring many."

As James Kugel has intuited, early Jewish interpreters concluded from this passage that there was a reason why God singled out Abraham and called him: he was different from his father and brother in that he did not serve other gods.[6]

The most extensive narrative treatment of Abraham's renunciation of idolatry comes in the *Apocalypse of Abraham*.[7] In this paper I would like to

---

of Religious Contact and Conflict in the Ancient World, ed. P. W. van der Horst (Utrecht: Falculteit der Godgeleerdheid, 1995), 105-20.

4. On Abraham traditions in early Judaism, see James E. Bowley, "Compositions of Abraham," in *Tracing the Threads: Studies in the Vitality of Jewish Pseudepigrapha*, ed. J. C. Reeves (SBLEJL 6; Atlanta: Scholars Press, 1994), 215-38; and James L. Kugel, *Traditions of the Bible: A Guide to the Bible As It Was at the Start of the Common Era* (Cambridge, Mass.: Harvard University Press, 1998), 243-350.

5. It also features in rabbinic midrashim — *Gen. Rabb.* 38:19 (on Gen. 11:28), *Tanna debe Eliyahu* 2:25, and *Midrash ha-Gadol* on Genesis (ed. Schechter, 189-90) — in patristic sources, and in the Qur'an. See G. Nathanael Bonwetsch, *Die Apokalypse Abrahams* (Leipzig: Deichert, 1897), 45-55; and G. H. Box with J. I. Landsman, *The Apocalypse of Abraham* (London: SPCK, 1918), 88-94.

6. James L. Kugel, *The Bible As It Was* (Cambridge, Mass.: Belknap Press of Harvard University Press, 1997), 134.

7. There are two main critical editions of the work: Belkis Philonenko-Sayar and Marc

explore idolatry and Otherness as an integral theme in this work. I wish not only to show that a concern for false vs. true worship runs throughout the narrative, but to clarify how closely connected this theme is with the text's other major preoccupations, among them the problem of evil, the relation of determinism and free will, and the destruction of the Temple. In my study of this document, as in so many things, I have learned the most from John J. Collins, my beloved mentor and friend.[8]

The *Apocalypse of Abraham* survives only in late Slavonic manuscripts transmitted by Christians, but it is an early Jewish pseudepigraph that was probably composed, in Hebrew, in the land of Israel in the late first or second century C.E. before being translated into Greek and thence into Slavonic.[9] It offers a fascinating blend of early Jewish midrashic exegesis, mystical speculation, and apocalyptic imagination. The work falls into two main parts: a haggadah of Abraham's conversion from idolatry to monotheism (chaps. 1–8) and an apocalypse of his ascent to heaven and vision of history (chaps. 9–32). Both sections are narrated in the first person and are carefully integrated with several textual details. With the theme of false vs. true worship in view, I will offer a close reading of the text in five movements: Abraham's separation from false worship (chaps. 1–8); his preparation for true worship (chaps. 9–14); his ascent for true worship (chaps. 15–18); his vision

---

Philonenko, *L'Apocalypse d'Abraham: Introduction, texte slave, traduction et notes* (*Semitica* 31; Paris: Librairie d'Amérique et d'Orient Adrien-Maisonneuve, 1981); and Ryszard Rubinkiewicz, *L'apocalypse d'Abraham en vieux slave: Introduction, texte critique, traduction et commentaire* (Lublin: Société des Lettres et des Sciences de l'Université Catholique de Lublin, 1987). English translations with introductions and notes are available in Box and Landsman, *Apocalypse of Abraham;* R. Rubienkiewicz and H. G. Lunt, "The Apocalypse of Abraham," in *OTP,* vol. 1 (1983), 681-705; H. F. D. Sparks and A. Pennington, "Apocalypse of Abraham," in *AOT* (1984), 361-91; and Alexander Kulik, *Retroverting Slavonic Pseudepigrapha: Toward the Original of the Apocalypse of Abraham* (Atlanta: Society of Biblical Literature, 2004). In this study, I will be using Kulik's translation with slight modifications for English style. His clarifying additions appear in square brackets, mine in parentheses.

8. See the chapter on the *Apocalypse of Abraham* in John J. Collins, *The Apocalyptic Imagination: An Introduction to Jewish Apocalyptic Literature,* 2d ed. (Grand Rapids: Eerdmans, 1998), 225-32. I would also like to thank Andrei Orlov for offering comments on my paper and helping me with the Slavonic.

9. On the original language of the work, see Arie Rubinstein, "Hebraisms in the Slavonic 'Apocalypse of Abraham,'" *JJS* 4 (1953): 108-15; Ryszard Rubinkewicz, "Les sémitismes dans l'Apocalypse d'Abraham," *Folio Orientalia* 21 (1980): 141-48; Horace G. Lunt, "On the Language of the Slavonic Apocalypse of Abraham," *Slavica Hierosolymitana* 7 (1985): 55-62; Rubinkiewicz, *L'apocalypse d'Abraham en vieux slave,* 33-37; Kulik, *Retroverting Slavonic Pseudepigrapha,* 1-3.

of false worship (19:1–29:13); and his vision of true worship restored (29:14–31:12).[10] I will conclude with some brief comments on the message, setting, and function of the work.

I. Separation from False Worship

The apocalypse opens with Abraham recounting how he left his father's house, in a midrashic expansion of Gen. 12:1. The first eight chapters juxtapose three episodes of satire (chaps. 1–2 and 5) with two scenes of reflection (chaps. 3–4 and 6–7) in a chiastic arrangement:

  A. Fall of Mar-Umath and the five idols (chaps. 1–2)
    B. Reflections on the powerlessness of idols (chaps. 3–4)
      C. Fall of Bar-Eshath and reflections thereon (chap. 5)
    B'. Reflection on gods, natural elements, and luminaries (chaps. 6–7)
  A'. Abraham's departure and the fall of Terah's temple (chap. 8)

In the initial verses of chap. 1, Abraham tells how he was "destroying"[11] the gods of his father Terah and those of his brother Nahor while serving as a junior priest in his father's temple. The idea that Terah was a manufacturer and priest of idolatry derives from God's command in Gen. 12:1 ("Abram, go . . . from your father's house") read midrashically in light of Josh. 24:2 ("Terah, the father of Abraham and Nahor . . . served other gods"). The verb "serve" in Joshua 24 was taken by our author to mean "serve *as a priest,*" and the word "house" in Genesis 12 was understood as "temple." Terah's temple, it should be noted, is the first of three temples in the apocalypse; the other two are the Jerusalem Temple and the new or renewed temple of the coming age. Like Terah's temple, the Temple in Jerusalem is doomed to destruction for its being implicated in idolatry.

Satirical polemics against idolatry of the sort found in the *Apocalypse of Abraham* appear already in the Hebrew Bible and are elaborated in Second

---

    10. For a different and more elaborate analysis of the structure, see R. Rubinkiewicz, "La vision de l'histoire dans l'Apocalypse d'Abraham," *ANRW* II.19.1 (1979): 144-46; idem, *L'apocalypse d'Abraham en vieux slave,* 28-32.

    11. The word "destroying" translates насмръзами, a *hapax legomenon* whose root is debated. Kulik takes the root to be **strig* and proposes that it renders the Greek ἐπικείρω (*Retroverting Slavonic Pseudepigrapha,* 9). Rubinkiewicz translates "guarding" from the root **sterg;* Box and Landsman have "planed," from **strug.*

Temple texts.[12] The first of three rather humorous incidents in the apocalypse has Abraham entering Terah's temple and finding a fallen idol, one Mar-Umath, whose name means "Lord of the Nation." When he and his father try to lift the idol back into place, the head falls off. No problem: Terah carves a new torso for the old head. The scene recalls the fate of the Philistine god Dagon in 1 Sam. 5:3-5, who keeps falling down in the presence of the Ark of the Covenant and ends up losing his head and both his hands.

The second incident involves five idols that Terah has told Abraham to sell in town. Abraham meets up with some Syrian merchants interested in purchasing them, but one of their camels bellows so loudly that Abraham's donkey smashes three of the idols. Not at all put off, the three merchants proceed to purchase the two remaining idols, going so far as to include in their payment the price of the smashed ones.

The third incident showcases the destruction of a small god named Bar-Eshath, whose name means, ironically, "Son of the Fire." Here the author dramatizes the sort of polemic we find in Isaiah 44 and Wisdom of Solomon 13, ridiculing idolatry in a narrative *reductio ad absurdum* that offers no apologies for the caricature, no acknowledgment that for most ancients images were not deities but only objects representing or mediating the presence of the deity. Abraham discovers Bar-Eshath among a pile of woodchips his father has sent him to collect for cooking supper. By now disenchanted with idols, he sets Bar-Eshath next to the hearth and says sarcastically, "Bar-Eshath, make sure the fire does not go out before I come back. If the fire does go out, blow on it to make it flare up" (5:7). True to his name, the little fellow keeps the home fires burning — by falling backwards and being consumed. When Abraham returns, he praises the idol: "Bar-Eshath, you certainly are able to kindle fire and cook food!" And when serving his father's meal he says, "Father Terah, do not bless your god Mar-Umath; do not praise him. Praise rather your god Bar Eshath, because in his love for you he threw himself into the fire in order to cook your food!" (5:14). In response, Terah, who is no brighter than the Syrian merchants, exclaims, "Great is the power of Bar-Eshath! I shall make another today, and tomorrow he will make my food!" (5:17).

Interspersed among these parodies of idolatrous devotion are reflec-

---

12. Note esp. Isa. 44:9-20, Jer. 10:1-16, and Ps. 115:3-8. Prominent examples in early Jewish literature include Bel and the Dragon, Epistle of Jeremiah, *Joseph & Asenath* 13, *Jubilees* 11–12, 20, 22, *Letter of Aristeas* 134–138, *Sibylline Oracles* 3:29-53, *Wisdom of Solomon* 13–15, and Philo, *De Decalogo* 52–81.

tions by Abraham, both to himself and in dialogue with his father. His introspections become increasingly philosophical. In chap. 3 he begins by considering the origin of his father's gods, posing rhetorical questions to himself:

> What is the profit of labor which my father is doing? Is not he rather a god of his gods, since by his sculpting, carving, and skill they come into being? It would be more fitting for them to worship my father, since they are his work.... If it is thus, how then can my father's god ... save a man or hear a man's prayer and reward him? (3:2-4a, 8)

The last verse cited (3:8) foreshadows exactly what will happen to Abraham later in the story: God will hear his prayer, rescue him from his father's house, and reward him with a promise of descendents and a vision of their history. In chap. 4, when he tries to persuade Terah of the folly of idolatry, Abraham exteriorizes his earlier thoughts: "Hear, Terah, [my] father! It is the gods who are blessed by you, since you are a god to them, since you have made them, since their blessing is perdition, and their power is vain" (4:3).[13]

From these basic doubts, Abraham moves to a different mode of critique. In pondering his father's folly, he graduates from his rather pedestrian puzzlings — "How can a statue made by my father be his helper?" — to more philosophical musings, in a manner reminiscent of Philo's Platonic anthropology: "Why," he asks, would my father "subordinate his body to his soul, his soul to his spirit, and then his spirit to folly and ignorance?" (6:3).[14] These considerations then impel Abraham to employ an alternate strategy of persuasion; having failed to convince his father of the futility of idols, he tries to convince him at least to give up the gods of his own house. His argument takes the form of a parodic taxonomy of idols based on the relative superiority or inferiority of their constitutive materials, a common trope in Jewish and Greco-Roman philosophical polemics against images.[15] So Terah's god Mar-Umath is inferior to his son Nahor's god Zoukh, because

---

13. A similar passage is found in *Jub.* 12:2-5.

14. Cf., e.g., Philo, *Leg. Alleg.* 1.12-13 on the tripartite nature of the soul, and Kulik, *Retroverting Slavonic Pseudepigrapha*, 85.

15. See, e.g., *1 Enoch* 99:7; *Jub.* 22:18; *Epistle of Jeremiah* 3; *Sib. Or.* 3:11-14, 57-59, 586-90; *Sib. Or.* 5:82-83; *Ep. Arist.* 135; Wis. 13:10; 14:21; Philo, *De Decalogo* 66; Josephus, *Ag. Ap.* 2.252; Pseudo-Philo, *Bib. Ant.* 2:9. For Greco-Roman critiques of the inferior materials of handmade idols, see, e.g., Heraclitus B frg. 5 (in Diels-Kranz, *Die Fragmente der Vorsokratiker*); Pseudo-Heraclitus, *Epistula* 4; Plutarch, *De Iside et Osiride* 71; Epictetus 2.8.13-14; Juvenal, *Satirae* 13; 14; Horace, *Satirae* 1.8.1-3; Lucian, *Philopseudes* 20.

the former is made of stone and the latter of gold. Bar-Eshath is less noble than Youvan, because the one is made of wood and the other of silver. Bar-Eshath's fate is particularly pathetic because he began life, so to speak, as a beautiful tree "with branches, and flowers, and beauties" only to be cut down with an ax; "he has dried up, and his sap is gone"; he "has been burned up by the fire, and turned to ashes and is no more" (6:11-17).

Reflection on the fiery fate of the god whose name means "Son of the Fire" then inspires Abraham to put on the mantle of a naturalist and astronomer (chap. 7). He formulates a hierarchy of the natural elements and principal luminaries. Fire is ostensibly the noblest of elements because of its destructive power, but it cannot be a god because water can extinguish it. Water, though, cannot be a god because it runs beneath the earth. Yet since the earth can be dried up by the sun, it cannot be a god. But even the sun cannot be a god since its course can be obscured by the night and by clouds. And the same is true of the moon and stars: they too can be darkened. With this hierarchical ranking, the author is filling out the profile of Abraham the astrologer and natural philosopher already in the making in *Jubilees* and further developed in Philo, Josephus, and rabbinic midrashim.[16]

It is this process of elimination that finally pushes Abraham toward monotheism. "Listen, Terah, my father," he says. "I shall seek in your presence the God who created all the 'gods' we suppose to exist" (7:11, my trans.).

> For who is it, or which one is it,
> Who colored heaven and made the sun golden?
> Who has given light to the moon and the stars with it?
> Who has dried the earth in the midst of the waters?
> Who set you yourself among the elements?

---

16. *Jub.* 12:16-21; Josephus, *Ant.* 1.155-157; Philo, *De Abrahamo* 68–80. The hierarchical ordering of natural elements in *Apoc. Abr.* 7 resembles a tradition recorded in *Gen. Rab.* 38:13, in which Terah turns Abram over to Nimrod, whom Abram then taunts: "He [Nimrod] said to him [Abram], 'Bow down to the fire.' He said to him, 'We should rather bow down to water, which extinguishes fire.' He said to him, 'Bow down to water.' He said to him, 'We should rather bow down to the clouds, which hold the water.' He said to him, 'Then let us bow down to the clouds.' He said to him, 'We should rather bow down to the winds, which scatter the clouds.' He said: 'Then let us bow down to the wind.' He said to him, 'We should rather bow down to human beings, who can withstand the wind.' He said, 'You are just throwing words around. We will worship nothing but fire. Behold, I will cast you into it, and let your God whom you adore come and save you from it'" (my translation).

> And who now has chosen me in the distraction of my mind? —
> (If only) he would reveal himself by himself to us (as) the (only) God! (7:12)[17]

At precisely this moment, the voice of the Almighty comes down from heaven in a stream of fire that calls to Abraham: "Abraham, Abraham.... In the wisdom of your heart you are searching for the God of gods and the Creator. I am he! Leave Terah your father, and leave the house, so that you too are not slain for the sins of your father's house" (8:1, 3-4; cf. Gen. 12:1). Abraham gets no farther than the courtyard when a "sound of thunder" burns Terah and his house to the ground (8:6).

II. Preparation for True Worship

Now that Abraham has renounced idolatry and left his father's house, he is ready to begin learning what true worship means and how false worship has bedeviled the history of the world and of the people to come from him. Chapters 9–14 function to depict Abraham undergoing a process of ritual consecration and preparation for worship of God. Together with the chapters narrating Abraham's ascent, the plot in this section unfolds structurally in another chiasm:

> A. Preparation for true worship (chap. 9)
>   B. Yahoel the chief priest (chaps. 10–11)
>   C. Journey to Horeb for sacrifice (chap. 12)
>   B'. Azazel the fallen priest (chaps. 13–14)
> A'. Ascent for true worship (chaps. 15–18)

As chapter 9 opens, Abraham is called by God to offer a sacrifice (9:1-5). Here the author jumps from his haggadic biblical base in Gen. 12:1 to a new one in Gen. 15:7-21, the covenant between the pieces ceremony, which opens with the words, "I am YHWH who brought you out of Ur [taken here to mean "fire," Hebrew 'ûr[18]] of the Chaldeans" (Gen. 15:7).[19] In 9:3 God calls

---

17. The last line is my translation. Kulik renders it, "Will he reveal himself by himself to us? — [He is] the God" (*Retroverting Slavonic Pseudepigrapha*, 15).
18. Earlier narrations of Abraham's escape from Ur — the fire — of the Chaldeans, appear in *Jub.* 12:12-14 and Pseudo-Philo, *Bib. Ant.* 6.
19. For other midrashic treatments of Genesis 15 in Second Temple texts, see Christo-

Idolatry and Alterity

himself "the primordial and mighty God who initially created the two luminaries of the world," a self-designation that knits the present scene nicely to Abraham's reflections on the luminaries at the end of chap. 7. The command to sacrifice in 9:5 follows the wording of Gen. 15:9 closely, but a new, nonbiblical element comes in the next verse with God's claim,

> And in this sacrifice I shall set before you the ages
> and make you know secrets,
> and you will see great things which you have not seen,
> since you loved to search for me,
> and I called you "my friend." (9:6)

The idea that God revealed divine secrets to Abraham has a basis in those verses in Genesis 15 that describe the LORD putting Abraham to sleep and predicting Israel's slavery in Egypt, the exodus, and the conquest of Canaan (Gen. 15:12-21). Early Jewish interpreters of this numinous nocturnal vision (Gen. 15:1 uses the word מחזה) sensed that God must have revealed to Abraham more than this — not only Israel's destiny but also heavenly and eschatological mysteries.[20]

Before Abraham can perform the sacrifice, however, he must prepare for it by separating himself ritually from the defiling idolatry he has renounced. This is the narrative logic of God commanding Abraham in the areas of eating, drinking, and anointing: "But for forty days abstain from every food which issues from the fire, and from the drinking of wine, and from anointing [yourself] with oil" (9:7). Because Abraham is about to carry out the services of a priest, he must consecrate himself by abstaining from three staple items that were used in pagan sacrifices. Interestingly, Abraham's fasting represents an inversion of Levi's feeding in the (Christian) *Testament of Levi*, where the visionary is anointed with oil by angels and fed bread and

---

pher Begg, "Rereading the Animal Rite of Genesis 15 in Early Jewish Narratives," *CBQ* 50 (1988): 36-46.

20. Three examples, from sources roughly contemporaneous with *Apoc. Abraham*: (1) *4 Ezra* 3:14 depicts Ezra saying to God, "you loved [Abraham] and to him you revealed the end of the times, secretly by night." (2) Pseudo-Philo, *Bib. Ant.* 23:6 has the LORD recount, "I . . . put before [Abraham] the place of fire where the deeds of those doing wickedness against me will be expiated, and I showed him the torches of fire by which the just who have believed in me will be enlightened." (3) In *2 Baruch* 4:3-4 God informs the seer that he showed the heavenly temple to Adam before he sinned, to Moses on Mt. Sinai, and also "to my servant Abraham in the night between the pieces of the victims."

holy wine as part of his priestly investiture (8:4-5). Later, in chap. 12, when Abraham journeys to Mt. Horeb in the company of the angel Yahoel, we learn that God not only tended to Abraham's need for nourishment but also provided the animals to be sacrificed (a detail inspired no doubt by Gen. 22:13-14, where God provides a ram for Abraham to sacrifice at the Binding of Isaac):

> And we went, the two of us alone, together, forty days and forty nights. And I ate no bread and drank no water, because [my] food was to see the angel who was with me, and his speech with me was my drink.... And I looked behind me. And behold all the prescribed sacrifices were following us: the calf, the she-goat, the ram, the turtledove, and the pigeon. (12:1-2, 6)

The patriarch's fasting for "forty days and nights" marks one of several places in the apocalypse where the author models Abraham's experience on Moses' (Exod. 34:28). It also links Abraham with other heroes of early Jewish tales such as Daniel, Judith, Eliezar, and Joseph, who abstain from Gentile food, wine, and oil to avoid defilement.[21]

In chap. 10, the angel Yahoel appears and offers his services as mentor and guide, enabling Abraham to render true worship to God. Many apocalypses feature a principal angel, and in ascent apocalypses they typically serve as heavenly tour guides.[22] The chief biblical precedent for such figures is the "angel of the LORD" in the Pentateuch (e.g., Gen. 16:7-14; 22:11-18; Exod. 14:19-20). Here in the *Apocalypse of Abraham*, Yahoel performs essentially the same functions of angelic viceregent and heavenly choirmaster that Enoch-Metratron does in the Hekhalot literature.[23] Abraham hears the voice

---

21. Daniel in the book of Daniel 1; Judith in Jdt. 10:5; 12:19, where she brings her own oil and bread into Holophernes' camp; Eliezar in 2 Macc. 6:18-31; and Joseph in *Jos. & Asen.* 7:1; 8:5-7. According to Josephus, the Essenes avoided oil because they considered it defiling (*J.W.* 2.8.3). Rabbinic law regards meat, wine, and oil as vulnerable to defilement because of their possible origins in idolatrous contexts (e.g., *m. Ḥagiga* 3:4; *t. Ḥagiga* 3:30-32; *b. Ḥagiga* 25a; *b. 'Aboda Zara* 36a; *b. Sanhedrin* 17b).

22. Various angels, including Uriel, guide Enoch on his tour of the inaccessible regions of the earth in the *Book of the Watchers* (1 *Enoch* 17–36); so also in the *Similitudes of Enoch* (1 *Enoch* 37–71) and in 2 *Enoch*, which features Michael prominently in chap. 22 (recensions A and J). An unnamed angel interacts with Levi in *Testament of Levi* 2–5. In 3 Baruch the *angelus interpres* is Phamael/Phanuel; in the *Apocalypse of Zephaniah* it is Eremiel.

23. See, e.g., 3 *Enoch* (*Seper Hekhalot*); also *b. Ḥagiga* 15a. For a detailed analysis, see Andrei A. Orlov, *The Enoch-Metatron Tradition* (TSAJ 107; Tübingen: Mohr-Siebeck, 2005).

of God announce, "Go, Yahoel, the namesake of the mediation of my ineffable name, sanctify this man and strengthen him" (10:3). As soon as Yahoel shows up, he introduces himself to Abraham:

> I am Yahoel, named by him who shakes those that are with me on the seventh vault, on the firmament. I am a power in the midst of the Ineffable who put his names in me. I am appointed according to his commandment to reconcile the rivalries of the living creatures of the cherubim, and teach those who bear him [to sing] the song in the middle of man's night, at the seventh hour. I am made in order to rule over the Leviathans, since the attack and the threat of every reptile are subjugated to me. I am ordered to unlock Hades and to destroy those who worship dead things. I (was) ordered to burn your father's house with him, for he honored dead things. I am sent to you now to bless you and the land which the Eternal One, invoked by you, has prepared for you. (10:8-13)

Yahoel bears the names of YHWH God in a combination of the two theophoric elements *yah-* and *-el*. This makes him the midrashic embodiment of what God promised the people of Israel at Mt. Sinai: "I am going to send an angel in front of you, to guard you on the way and to bring you to the place that I have prepared. Be attentive to him and listen to his voice . . . for my name is in him" (Exod. 23:20-21).

Significantly, Abraham is not tempted even for a moment to fall down and worship Yahoel, as the visionaries in other apocalypses are inclined to do, only to be rebuked by their angelic guides.[24] This is the case even though features of Yahoel's appearance resemble those attributed to God in biblical theophanies. His head looks like a man's, but his torso looks like that of an eagle or griffin, and in this respect he resembles the angel Serapiel in *3 Enoch*.[25] Yet his body is also "like sapphire," a detail that recalls the sapphire pavement under God's feet in Exod. 24:10 and Ezek. 1:26; and his hair is white as snow, like the Ancient of Days' in Dan. 7:9. Yahoel's clothing, moreover, indicates that he is the heavenly high priest: he wears a "turban on his head like the appearance of the bow in the clouds," his garments are purple, and he has a golden staff in his hand (11:2). These elements evoke the ward-

---

24. Cf., e.g., Rev. 19:10; 22:8-9; *Asc. Isa.* 7:18-23; 8:1-10, 15; *2 Enoch* 1:4-8; *3 Enoch* 1:7; *Apoc. Zeph.* 6:11-15. The theme also appears in works that are not apocalypses (e.g., Tobit 12:16-22; *Jos. & Asen.* 15:11-12). See Loren T. Stuckenbruck, *Angel Veneration and Christology* (WUNT 70; Tübingen: Mohr-Siebeck, 1995), 75-103.

25. Kulik, *Retroverting Slavonic Pseudepigrapha*, 19, 83.

robe and accoutrement of Aaron (Exodus 28; Numbers 17). That Abraham never prostrates himself before Yahoel gives one measure of how strict the author's monotheism is: it rejects the giving of undue veneration to God's angelic intermediaries, dispensing completely with the widespread worship-refusal tradition.

After they have journeyed and fasted together, Abraham and Yahoel arrive on Mt. Horeb. Genesis 15 does not identify the site of the covenant of pieces ceremony; its association with Horeb (the name for the holy mountain in the Elohist and Deuteronomic traditions of the Pentateuch) reflects another attempt to assimilate Abraham's experience to that of Moses. In chap. 12, Yahoel acts like a senior priest showing a junior priest the ropes as he instructs Abraham: "Slaughter and cut all this, putting together the two halves, one against the other. But do not cut the birds" (12:8). The detail of leaving the birds uncut derives from Gen. 15:10. The author seized on this unexplained detail in the biblical text and exploited it for his purposes: the birds remain uncut so that Yahoel and Abraham can fly to heaven on them, Yahoel mounting the left wing of the turtledove and Abraham the right wing of the pigeon (12:10; 15:2). In this act of preparation, Yahoel is assisted by other angelic priests, who appear on the mountain to receive the divided parts of the animals that have been cut (12:9; 13:1).

In chap. 13 Yahoel's nemesis arrives on the scene — the fallen angel Azazel, who in early Jewish literature is best known from the *Book of the Watchers* (1 Enoch 1–36, esp. chaps. 6–16).[26] Azazel appears as an "impure bird" swooping down on the animal carcasses, a description inspired by Gen. 15:9-11. He has come not only to halt the sacrifice but to block Abraham's ascent to heaven:

> What are you doing, Abraham, on the holy heights, where no one eats or drinks, nor is there upon them food for men? But these (sacrifices) will be consumed by fire and they will burn you up. Leave the man who is with you and flee! If you ascend to the height, they will destroy you. (13:4-5)

Clearly Azazel recognizes an adversary in Abraham, whose going without food already makes him resemble the angels. Azazel knows that Abra-

---

26. See further Robert Helm, "Azazel in Early Jewish Tradition," *AUSS* 32 (1994): 217-26; Lester L. Grabbe, "The Scapegoat Tradition: A Study of Early Jewish Interpretation," *JSJ* 18 (1987): 152-68.

ham is a heavenly-priest-in-training and that his participation in the angelic liturgy (chap. 17) will mark his attainment of angelic status. The scene is reminiscent of Zechariah 3, where the *śāṭān* attempts to disqualify Joshua from serving as high priest.[27] This theme of rivalry between angels and humans gets developed at great length in Merkabah mysticism, and here we have one of the best and earliest examples of it.[28] It seems to represent an imaginative attempt to work through generational and priestly rivalries by projecting them into the heavenly realm. At a deeper level the theme uncovers a nexus of theological tensions: the presence of good and evil in humanity, the paradox of fate and free will, and the justice and mercy of God. These tensions are hinted at in Yahoel's rebuke of Azazel:

> Reproach is on you, Azazel! For Abraham's portion is in heaven, and yours is on earth, since you have chosen it and desired it to be the dwelling place of your impurity. . . . For behold, the garment that was formerly yours in heaven has been set aside for him, and the corruption that was on him has gone over to you. (13:7-8, 14)

Although Abraham does not undergo any experience of transformation that turns him into an angel — as, for example, Enoch does in the *Similitudes of Enoch, 2 Enoch,* and *3 Enoch (Seper Hekhalot)* — here he proleptically assumes his angelic status and displaces Azazel.[29] Azazel, the now fallen priest, has abused his free will as one of God's heavenly creatures by choosing earth as the arena to "scatter the secrets of heaven and conspire against the Mighty One" (14:4). Abraham, by contrast, has freely chosen to renounce the impurity and corruption of idolatry and is therefore fit to worship God in heaven as a newly consecrated priest. Accordingly, Yahoel teaches Abraham a kind of exorcistic spell to drive Azazel away (14:5-7; cf. Gen. 15:11, "And when birds of prey came down on the carcasses, Abram drove them away").

---

27. George W. E. Nickelsburg, *Jewish Literature between the Bible and the Mishnah*, 2d ed. (Minneapolis: Fortress, 2005), 285-86.

28. The book to read on this subject is Peter Schäfer, *Rivalität zwischen Engeln und Menschen* (SJ 8; Berlin: de Gruyter, 1975).

29. For more on the transformation and priestly investiture of apocalyptic visionaries, see Martha Himmelfarb, *Ascent to Heaven in Jewish and Christian Apocalypses* (Oxford: Oxford University Press, 1993), 29-46 (and 61-66 on the *Apocalypse of Abraham*).

III. Ascent for True Worship

The beginning of chap. 15 returns to the biblical base in Genesis 15, to the verse where the sun sets and the smoke and fire appear (Gen. 15:17). The author incorporates a detail from the Sinai theophany in Exod. 19:18 ("the smoke went up like the smoke of a kiln") to depict the angelic priestly attendants ascending in the smoke. Yahoel and Abraham themselves ascend by mounting the uncut birds left over from the sacrifice. Instead of passing through a numbered series of lower heavens, as is typical in ascent apocalypses, the two travelers go directly to the highest heaven. On arrival Abraham is frightened by the sight of a crowd of man-like figures (angels) running, being transformed, bowing, and shouting in an unearthly language. Sensing his fear, Yahoel comforts Abraham with the promise, "He whom you will see going before both of us in a great sound of sanctification is the Eternal One who has loved you; his very self, (though), you will not see" (16:3).[30]

Once in the highest heaven (15:4–17:3), Abraham and Yahoel bow and worship God, whose presence is signaled with fire and "a sound in the fire like many waters" (17:1). Significantly, throughout the passage the author resists depicting God in anthropomorphic terms, as some of the early Jewish apocalypses do (e.g., *1 Enoch* 14, Daniel 7, and *2 Enoch* 39).[31] Yahoel then teaches Abraham a song which they recite together (17:4-21). No doubt this is the same song referred to earlier when Yahoel introduced himself to Abraham (10:9). The only other early apocalypses to give the lyrics of celestial songs are the *Similitudes of Enoch* (*1 Enoch* 39:10-14) and the book of Revelation (4:8, 11; 5:9-10, 13; 7:12; 15:3-4). The lyrics here are longer than their apocalyptic parallels, and with their piling up of titles and predicate adjectives for God they show a greater affinity with those in the Hekhalot literature.[32] The first lines of the song unwind a string of abstract attributes in praise of God:

---

30. The final clause is my translation; Kulik renders it "whom himself you will not see" (*Retroverting Slavonic Pseudepigrapha*, 22).

31. The anti-anthropomorphic tendencies and "aural mysticism" of the *Apocalypse of Abraham* are discussed brilliantly by Andrei A. Orlov, "Praxis of the Voice: The Divine Name Traditions in the Apocalypse of Abraham," *JBL* 127 (2008): 53-70.

32. For some examples, see Gershom Scholem, *Major Trends in Jewish Mysticism*, 3d rev. ed. (New York: Schocken, 1961), 57-63. Abraham's song also resembles the song of Jacob in the *Ladder of Jacob* (2:6-22), a work of uncertain date that survives only in Slavonic. A song of Abraham himself is mentioned (though without the lyrics) in *Genesis Rabbah* and the *Haggadah on the Song of Songs*. The exegetical stimulus for the song may be an apocalyptic rewriting of Gen. 14:22; so Steven Weitzman, "The Song of Abraham," *HUCA* 65 (1994): 21-33.

> O, Eternal, Mighty, Holy El, God Autocrat,
> Self-begotten, incorruptible, immaculate, unbegotten, spotless, immortal,
> Self-created, self-illuminated, without mother, without father, without genealogy,
> High, fiery,
> Wise, lover of men, favorable, generous, bountiful,
> Jealous over me, patient, most merciful
> Eli, eternal, mighty, holy Sabaoth, most glorious El, El, El, El, Yahoel,
> You are he whom my soul has loved, the guardian
> Eternal, fiery, shining, light formed, thunder-voiced, lightning-looking, many-eyed.... (17:8-14)

The succeeding lines become more discursive and speak to Abraham's rescue from the metaphysical error of idolatry, praising God as the one who "releases those who are in the midst of the impious, those who are confused among the unrighteous of the inhabited world in the corruptible life.... Accept my prayer, and let it be sweet to you, and also the sacrifice which you yourself made to yourself through me who searched for you" (17:17, 20). The overwhelming rhetorical effect of Abraham's song is to underscore how wholly Other the true God is in comparison with false gods worshipped as idols.

The climax of the heavenly liturgy comes in chap. 18 with Abraham's vision of the throne-chariot. The details of the Merkabah scene draw extensively on Ezekiel 1 and 10 (cf. also *1 Enoch* 14): Abraham sees the fire under the throne, the many-eyed wheels, and the four living creatures.[33] Yet the passage departs from Ezekiel in two striking respects. First, there is no anthropomorphic description of God, even though Ezekiel (1:26) describes God as having "the likeness of a human form" (דמות כמראה אדם). The four living creatures are there under the throne, but God is not seated above it; evidently, he has vacated it — but not to make room for Yahoel or Abraham.[34] This is so because God invisibly inhabits not only the highest heaven but *all* of the heavens, as we learn a bit later (19:3). Abraham hears the sound

---

33. See further David Halperin, *The Faces of the Chariot: Early Jewish Responses to Ezekiel's Vision* (TSAJ 16; Tübingen: Mohr-Siebeck, 1988), 103-14.

34. Contrast Ezekiel the Tragedian's second-century B.C.E. drama *Exagōgē*, which depicts a dream of Moses in which God vacates the throne and invites Moses to sit upon it, whereupon heavenly beings prostrate themselves before him. See Pieter W. van der Horst, "Moses' Throne Vision in Ezekiel the Dramatist," *JJS* 34 (1983): 21-29.

of the four creatures' "*qedushah* like the voice of a single man" (18:14) but never sees the Holy One in the form of a man. Throughout the scene, fire and sound communicate God's presence and act as surrogates for any corporeal manifestation of the deity (16:3; 17:1; 18:1-2). Surely this studied avoidance of anthropomorphism says something about the author's monotheism, and it throws in the sharpest of relief Terah's pathetic man-like idol Mar-Umath with his decapitated head.

Second, the *Ḥayyot* in Abraham's vision, unlike those in Ezekiel's, threaten one another and need to be tamed:

> And as they were finishing singing, they looked at one another and threatened one another. And it came to pass when the angel who was with me saw that they were threatening each other, he left me and went running to them. And he turned the face of each living creature from the face that was opposite it so that they could not see each other's threatening faces. And he taught them the song of peace, that everything belonged to the Eternal One. (18:8-11)

This remarkable scene was foreshadowed back in the presentation of Yahoel's angelic portfolio in 10:9. It implies that even heavenly creatures have a free will that must be kept in check by their fellow creatures; otherwise, fallen angels like Azazel can invade earth and infect its human creatures with idolatry. We are led to recall how two free wills — Abraham's and Azazel's — collided earlier on Horeb, at the midpoint between heaven and earth. Abraham has renounced the rebellion of idolatry and so ascended to heaven, whereas Azazel has refused to join in the angelic song and so descended to earth in order to spread "demonic idolatry" (26:3). The unruly forces of creation represented by the Leviathans that threaten and attack each other on earth (10:10) have their counterparts in heaven, the home of angels who must sing the song that tames.

IV. Vision of False Worship

Abraham's visions of history commence in chap. 19, in a panorama of idolatry that has a progressively narrow spatial and temporal focus: from the upper heavens to the earth to the underworld, from the history of humanity to the destiny of Israel, from the destruction of the Temple to the advent of a false messiah.

From the highest heaven, Abraham looks down on the seventh, sixth, and fifth heavens, which are full of different classes of angels but empty of any gods.[35] The utter absence of gods is emphasized twice, once by God in 19:3 and then by Abraham in 19:8; in the former verse, God speaks to Abraham from the midst of the fire and says, "Look at the levels that are under the expanse on which you are brought, and see that on no single level is there any other but the one whom you have searched for or who has loved you." With this revelation, so poignantly expressed, Abraham receives definitive proof that the so-called gods whom mortals worship as idols do not even exist. He also learns that God invisibly inhabits not only the highest heaven but all the other heavens as well.

On the fifth level of heaven, Abraham sees the stars carrying out their assigned tasks as mere created objects and not destiny-controlling deities (19:9). In the following verses, 20:1-3, the author returns to his biblical base and paraphrases Gen. 15:5 ("He brought Abram outside and said, 'Look toward heaven and count the stars, if you are able to count them'") to read, "And the Eternal Mighty One said to me, 'Abraham, Abraham! . . . Look from on high at the stars that are beneath you and count them for me and tell me their number!'" (20:1, 3). The word *outside* in Gen. 15:5 is made to mean not *out of doors* but *outside the firmament*.[36] Further, God's promise at the end of Gen. 15:5 — "So shall your descendants be" — is elaborated with wording drawn from Gen. 17:4-6 to read, "As the number of the stars and their host, so shall I make your seed into a company of nations, set apart for me in my lot with Azazel" (20:5).

This verse (20:5) has been identified as an interpolation made by the Bogomils, a medieval dualist sect in the Balkans that considered the God of Israel an evil deity.[37] Yet the verse — and others that mention Azazel and

---

35. On the number of heavens, see John C. Poirier, "The Ouranology of the Apocalypse of Abraham," *JSJ* 35 (2004): 391-408.

36. Cf. Ps.-Philo, *Bib. Ant.* 18:5, "And he [the Lord] said to him [Balaam]: 'Is it not concerning this people that I spoke to Abraham in a vision saying, "Your seed will be like the stars of heaven" [Gen. 22:17], when I lifted him above the firmament and showed him the arrangements of all the stars?'" Note also *Gen. Rab.* 44:12 on Gen. 15:5, "And he brought him outside [Gen. 15:5]. R. Joshua said in the name of R. Levi, Did he bring him outside of the world, so that it says, 'And he brought him outside'? It means that he showed him the open spaces of heaven, as it says, While as yet he had not made the earth nor the open spaces [Prov. 8:26]. R. Judah b. R. Simon in the name of R. Yoḥanan: He brought him above the vault of heaven; therefore he says to him, 'Look toward heaven,' and 'look' means 'look down from above.'"

37. Rubinkiewicz, "La vision de l'histoire," 139-41; idem, *L'apocalypse d'Abraham en vieux slave*, 66-69.

God in the same breath — can be read as integral to the text. That God's "lot" is with Azazel need not mean that God and Azazel are working on the same side but that they are striving toward the same goal from opposite sides. They are competing for the devotion — the worship — of human beings. Azazel's designs, however, fall completely within God's power, so in that sense they may be said to share a common lot, which is humanity at large. Abraham, however, does not understand just how Azazel can operate within the sovereign will of God, and so he asks, "Behold, before you led me up, Azazel abused me. Why, then, while he is not before you, have you set yourself with him?" (20:7).

Like Job in the book of Job, Abraham receives no direct answer to his question; instead, in the following chapter (chap. 21) he gets a vision of the natural world and of human history. The latter is telescoped in a series of vignettes framed in a great picture that is divided into left and right halves.[38] The left side is inhabited by a "multitude of tribes who were before and who are destined to be after you, some for justice and judgment, others for revenge and perdition at the end of the age" (22:4). The right side is occupied by the people of Israel — "the people set apart for me from the people with Azazel. These are the ones I have destined to be born of you and to be called my people" (22:5).

Chapter 23 then describes the sin of Adam and Eve, who are seduced by Azazel. The three of them appear in a *ménage à trois,* the man and woman entwined in an erotic embrace, the fallen angel in serpentine guise feeding them grapes. In terms evocative of Philo's Platonic anthropology, God identifies Adam with the principle of "reason" in humanity and Eve with the faculty of "desire" (23:10).[39] The hybrid, serpentine man he identifies as "the impiety of their pursuits for destruction, Azazel himself." Abraham and God then engage in a question-and-answer session, which restates the query regarding Azazel posed in 20:7 but now in refined terms:

> And I said, "Eternal Mighty One! Why then did you adjudge to this one such power to destroy humankind by his works on earth?" (23:12)
>
> And he said to me, "Hear, Abraham! Those who desire evil and whom I have hated as they are doing these works, over them I gave him power and he is to be loved by them." (23:13)

---

38. Box and Landsman (*Apocalypse of Abraham,* xix-xxi) thought that this feature reflected Gnostic influence, but there is nothing distinctly Gnostic about it.

39. See, e.g., Philo, *De Opificio Mundi* 165; *Quaestiones et Solutiones in Genesim* 1.45-48; *Legum Allegoriarum* 2.10.14; *Quis Rerum Divinarum Heres Sit* 11.

Eternal Mighty One! Why did you will to do so, that evil is desired in the heart of man? Since you are angry at what was willed by you, who (can be said to do) a bad thing (when it is) according to your design? (23:14)[40]

The answer to this last question does not come until chapter 26; it is postponed until after Abraham has received further visions that impress upon him the full extent of humanity's idolatrous rebellion against God. Human iniquity is treated very briefly, beginning with the mere mention of Adam and Eve and Cain and Abel (24:1-4) and ending in a short list of vices that include fornication, defilement, jealousy, and corruption — terms often used in the Bible in discourse on idolatry (24:6-9).[41]

The sins of Israel are revealed next, in a vision of the Jerusalem Temple and its altar being desecrated by cultic abominations centered on an "idol of jealousy" that is worshiped by a man and before which youths are slaughtered (25:1-6). The idol of jealousy comes from Ezekiel 8, and the child sacrifice recalls the sin of King Manasseh, which in the Deuteronomic view was the last straw that led to Judah's conquest by Babylon (2 Kings 21:10-15). The idol has the "likeness of a craftsman's [work] such as my father made, and its statue was of shining copper" (25:1). So a figure similar to those that Terah made has been installed in the Temple! That the statue is made of copper may owe to the fact that copper was the only metal mined in first-century Palestine.[42] The scene implies no criticism of the Temple as such — indeed, God calls the Temple "my image of the sanctification of the name of my glory" (25:4) — and there is no overt criticism of the priesthood. The author no doubt regarded the Second Temple as defiled in some sense, whether morally, cultically or both, but the portrait here is hardly a description of what was actually transpiring in the Temple in the first century. The idol that provokes God's jealousy functions instead as a symbol for the cumulative sins of Israel's entire history, a representation of idolatry in all its forms. Indeed, one might say that all sin is at root an act of idolatry — a rebellious self-assertion that assigns ultimate value to created things (including one's own inordinate desires) instead of to the Creator.

40. The words in parentheses are my clarifying additions; Kulik translates the last part of the verse thus: "who does a bad thing according to your design" (*Retroverting Slavonic Pseudepigrapha*, 28).

41. E.g., Hos. 5:3; Jer. 2:20-24; Ezek. 22:3-4; Ps. 106:39.

42. Fabian E. Udoh, "Economics in Palestine," in *The Eerdmans Dictionary of Early Judaism*, ed. J. J. Collins and D. C. Harlow (Grand Rapids: Eerdmans, 2010), 557-61.

Daniel C. Harlow

The mere fact of God's showing Abraham this vision convinces him of God's sovereignty, but it also raises again the problem of God's complicity, which is addressed in a final round of questions and answers that make up chap. 26:

> And I said, "Eternal Mighty One! Why did you ordain it to be so? Take back these testimonies!" (26:1)

> And he said to me, "Hear, Abraham, and understand what I tell you, and answer whatever I ask you. Why did your father Terah not listen to your voice and abandon the demonic idolatry until he perished, and all his house with him?" (26:2-3)

> And I said, "Eternal Mighty One! Evidently because he did not will to listen to me, nor did I follow his deeds." (26:4)

> And he said to me, "Hear, Abraham! As the will of your father is in him, as your will is in you, so also the will desired by me is inevitable in coming days. . . ." (26:5)

Not many will find God's answer to Abraham any more satisfactory than his answer to Job, but the answer itself (which was common in Jewish and Christian antiquity) is clear enough: free will and divine sovereignty are both operative in human affairs. God has ordained that human beings who do not align their will with his should be led astray and suffer divine punishment. Sin, epitomized as idolatry, is a matter of human choice, but human history proceeds nonetheless according to God's plan, a plan that includes the machinations of Azazel, which function to put people to the test and to provoke a pledge of allegiance.

The next scene in Abraham's vision focuses on the destruction of the Temple (chaps. 27–28). Four hosts enter the Temple, burning and plundering it (27:3).[43] To Abraham's query "Why?" God replies, "Listen, Abraham, all that you have seen will happen because of your seed who will provoke me, because of the idol and the murder that you saw in the picture in the temple

---

43. Other readings in the manuscripts call for various translations: "entrances," "exits," "ascents," "descents." The four hosts have been taken to refer to the successive invasions of Jerusalem by Nebuchadnezzar, Antiochus IV, Pompey, and Titus; so Robert G. Hall, *Revealed Histories: Techniques for Ancient Jewish and Christian Historiography* (JSPSup 6; Sheffield: Sheffield Academic Press, 1991), 76-77, note 3.

Idolatry and Alterity

of jealousy" (27:7). Abraham accepts the justice of God's judgment, now asking only about its duration (28:1–29:3). In reply he is given two overlapping chronologies: the four hosts he has seen entering the Temple represent four hundred-year periods, each of which is also one of twelve hours allotted to the impious age (28:5; 29:1-2). The presentation of such a schema makes the *Apocalypse of Abraham* unique among the ascent apocalypses, none of which includes a review and periodization of history as historical apocalypses do.[44]

Verses 4-13 of chapter 29 depict false worship being given to a false messiah who leads both Israel and the other nations astray by accepting their worship. The passage also mentions in passing a true messiah, a man from Abraham's seed whom God's people will eventually accept but without worshiping. The false messiah is described in these terms:

> 4And I looked and saw a man going out from the left side of the heathen. Men and women and children, great crowds, went out from the side of the heathen and they worshiped him. 5And while I was still looking, those on the right side went out, and some shamed this man, and some struck him, and some worshiped him. 6And I saw that as they worshiped him, Azazel ran forward and worshiped, and having kissed his face he turned and stood behind him. (29:4-6)

The interpretation of the vision follows:

> 8Listen, Abraham, the man whom you saw shamed and struck and again worshiped is the laxity[45] of the heathen for the people who will come from you in the last days, in this twelfth hour of the age of impiety. 9And in the [same] twelfth period of the close of my age I shall set up the man from your seed which you saw. 10Everyone from my people will [finally] admit him, while the sayings of him who was as if called by me will be neglected in their minds. 11And those you saw going out from the left side of the picture and those worshiping him, this [means that] many of the heathen will hope in him. 12And those of your seed you saw on the

---

44. Collins, *Apocalyptic Imagination*, 225.
45. The Slavonic word translated here as "laxity" is the word ослаба *(oslaba)*. Kulik, *Retroverting Slavonic Pseudepigrapha*, 32, 51, notes that its likely Greek counterpart, ἔκλυσις or παράλυσις, can have a negative connotation and may refer to laxity (רפיון) in matters of Torah (cf. *Lam. Rabb.* 1:4: רפיון התורה; *Midr. Tanhuma, Beshalah* 25: רפיון ידים מן התורה). Rubinciewicz ("Apocalypse of Abraham," in *OTP*, 1.703 and note e) takes the word's Greek counterpart to be ἄδεια or ἄνεσις, and translates it "liberation."

right side, some shaming and striking him and some worshiping him, many of them will be misled on his account. 13And he will tempt those of your seed who have worshiped him. (29:8-13)

Many scholars regard this passage as an interpolation concerning Christ that was made by a Bogomil scribe in the Middle Ages.[46] However, a few interpreters have tried to salvage the passage by reading it (or at least most of it) as part of the original Jewish work. Robert G. Hall has argued that only verse 9b — the verse that identifies the man who is worshiped as one of Abraham's seed — need be taken as a gloss, since only it contradicts verse 4a, which says that the man was going out from the left side of the heathen.[47] Hall is on the right track, especially since the vision and its interpretation continue the theme of false worship that runs throughout the apocalypse. However, instead of regarding verse 9b as an interpolation, I am inclined to follow Alexander Kulik in recognizing verses 9-10a as an original description of a true messiah.[48] Doing so requires accepting Kulik's new translation of the troublesome verse 10.

Yet there is a problem (not noted by Kulik) with the phrase "the man from your seed which you saw" in verse 9: in the vision Abraham sees only the man from the heathen side and not the man from Abraham's seed. This problem, though, may be solved by recognizing that the syntax of the relative pronoun "which" (Slavonic ero) in verse 9 is ambiguous; grammatically, it can have its antecedent in either the masculine noun "man" (муж) or the neuter noun "seed" (семени). If verses 9-10a do refer to a true messiah, then the antecedent of the pronoun "which" would have to be the word "seed" — "I shall set up the man from your seed, which (seed) you saw." Or perhaps the words "which you saw" in verse 9b, and they alone, are a gloss.

Hall proposes that the man from the heathen is the emperor Hadrian, who identified himself with Jupiter and built a temple to himself and one to that deity in Jerusalem. But the messiah pictured in the passage bears an uncanny resemblance to Jesus of Nazareth and hardly suits Hadrian. The man is alternately shamed, struck, worshiped, and kissed by Azazel. The shaming

46. So, e.g., Rubinkiewicz, who is followed by Collins and Himmelfarb. Bonwetsch was noncommittal on the passage's origin (*Apokalypse Abrahams*, 64). Box and Landsman regarded the passage as a Jewish-Christian interpolation (*Apocalypse of Abraham*, 78, n. 1).

47. Robert G. Hall, "The 'Christian Interpolation' in the *Apocalypse of Abraham*," *JBL* 107/1 (1988): 107-12.

48. Kulik, *Retroverting Slavonic Pseudepigrapha*, 51-52.

and striking call to mind Jesus' passion; the worship given by the heathen, Gentile veneration of Jesus; and Azazel's kiss, Judas Iscariot's betrayal of Jesus. A Jewish writer of the late first or early second century could have written all this; there is no reason to invoke a Bogomil interpolator.

The man's "going out" from the left side of the heathen may not be a denial of Jesus' Jewishness but an allusion to the success of the Jesus movement among Gentiles. If the Jewishness of Jesus *is* being denied, then the statement would join a small handful of texts and traditions from the first and second century C.E. that cast aspersions on his Jewish pedigree or regard him as an apostate.[49] The mention of the false messiah's "sayings" in verse 10 would be a reference to the teachings of Jesus. If this is plausible, then the author would be suggesting that the Devil led many Gentiles and even some Jews astray by getting them to venerate Jesus — who wasn't really a (true) Jew — but then betrayed Jesus with a kiss though Judas.[50]

---

49. When in John 8:41 "the Jews" say to Jesus, "We are not illegitimate children (ἐκ πορνείας οὐ γεγεννήμεθα)," the implied subtext may be *unlike you*. Some of the arguments made by the unnamed Jewish informant in books 1 and 2 of Origen's *Contra Celsum* reflect Jewish polemics of the first and second century C.E.: Jesus' Jewish pedigree is suspect; the story of his virgin birth was fabricated; and his father was a Roman soldier named Panthera (*C. Cels.* 1.28, 32, 69). Origen wrote the *Contra Celsum* in ca. 248 C.E.; Celsus's now lost work, *On the True Doctrine*, was written ca. 177-180 C.E.; and the Jewish traditions on which it drew go back earlier still. The Panthera stories may originally have centered on an otherwise unknown figure of the second century, but Jewish tradition wasted no time in relating them to Jesus. The name Panthera itself may have been chosen as a pun on the Greek word for "virgin," πάρθενος. See further Henry Chadwick, *Origen: Contra Celsum* (Cambridge: Cambridge University Press, 1953), 31, n. 3. There is no mention of Jesus in the Mishnah or other tannaitic literature, only in late Talmudic passages and in the medieval tract *Toledot Yeshu*. For a recent assessment of the former, see Peter Schäfer, *Jesus in the Talmud* (Princeton: Princeton University Press, 2007). Interestingly, the *Toledot Yeshu* has a detail that brings to mind Azazel's prostration before the man in *Apoc. Abr.* 29:6, "[Yeshu] entered the Temple with his three hundred and ten followers. One of them, Judah Iskarioto, apprised the Sages that Yeshu was to be found in the Temple, that the disciples had taken a vow by the Ten Commandments not to reveal his identity, but that he would *point him out by bowing to him*. So it was done and Yeshu was seized" (trans. Morris Goldstein, *Jesus in the Jewish Tradition* [New York: Macmillan, 1950], 152, emphasis mine).

50. According to Luke 22:3, "Satan entered into Judas." Similarly John 13:2, 27: "the Devil had already put it into the heart of Judas son of Simon Iscariot to betray him.... After he received the bread, Satan entered into him." Also in the Gospel of John, "the Jews" accuse Jesus of leading the people astray ("he is deceiving the crowd," 7:12), having a demon (7:20; cf. 8:48); being a Samaritan (8:48); and committing blasphemy ("It is not for a good work that we are going to stone you but because you, though only a human being, are making yourself God," 10:33; cf. 5:18).

Admittedly the wording of 29:10 is difficult, and the wider passage may be textually corrupt in places.[51] Nevertheless, I think that Kulik has made the presence of two messianic figures here a real possibility. Only the false messiah appears in the vision, but the true messiah is mentioned in the vision's interpretation. That there is a true messiah in the apocalypse becomes clear near the end of the work, when God tells Abraham, "Then I shall sound the trumpet from the sky, and I shall send my chosen one, having in him the measure of all my power, and he will summon my people blamed among the heathen" (31:1). What makes the figure a true messiah is not simply that he comes from Abraham's line but that he neither invites nor accepts worship.

V. True Worship Restored

The closing chapters of the apocalypse envision eschatological salvation as both a reward for true worship and a restoration of it. On the flip side, eschatological justice demands the destruction of those who have abandoned worship of the true God by following after idols:

> And I shall burn with fire those who mocked [my people] ruling over them in this age . . . since I have destined them to be food for the fire of hell, and ceaseless soaring in the air of the underground depths, the contents of a worm's belly. . . . And those who followed after the idols and after their murders will rot in the womb of the Evil One — the belly of Azazel; they will be burned by the fire of Azazel's tongue. (31:2-3, 5)

To add insult to the injury of the heathen, the righteous will see and "rejoice with joy" at their eternal damnation (31:4).

The glory that awaits the righteous is a new or renewed Temple and sacrificial cult in which all God's people have assumed the status of priests:

---

51. Kulik himself admits that his rendering of the final clause in 29:10 is no more than an "alternative proposal, although based on the new understanding of the whole chapter" (*Retroverting Slavonic Pseudepigrapha*, 52 n. 12). Rubinkiewicz ("Apocalypse of Abraham," *OTP*, 1:703) translates 29:9-10 as follows: 9"In the last days, in this twelfth hour of impiety, in the twelfth period of the age of my fulfillment, I will set up this man from your tribe, the one whom you have seen from my people. 10All will imitate him . . . (you) consider him as one called by me . . . (they) are changed in their counsels." In a note on the word *changed* at the end of v. 10, he comments, "This clause is corrupt, and omissions must be assumed."

"And they will live, being sustained by the sacrifices and the offerings of justice and truth in the age of justice" (29:18). It is unclear whether the author is spiritualizing the notion of sacrifice. The phrase "sacrifices and offerings of justice and truth" may refer either to bloodless offerings or to animal sacrifices offered rightly and truly. In any event, the priestly status of the chosen people in the new age is hinted at in the statement that they will be "*sustained* by the sacrifices and offerings" — just as priests in the Jerusalem Temple had been. Abraham's assumption of the office of the fallen priest Azazel in chap. 13 now shows itself to be an anticipation of the status that all the righteous will enjoy. Those who mock God instead of mocking idols, as Abraham did when he left his father's house, will suffer the same fate that the idols and house of Terah did — destruction by fire — whereas those who turn and remain true to the living God will attain the same status of heavenly priest that Abraham achieved in his ascent.

The apocalypse ends with a prophecy of the Hebrew enslavement in Egypt and the exodus. God says, "Therefore, hear Abraham and see! Behold your seventh generation will go with you. And they will go out into an alien land. And they will be enslaved and distressed for about one hour of the impious age. And of the people whom they will serve I am the judge" (31:9-12). On the face of it, this may seem like a rather anticlimactic ending, following as it does on the picture of eschatological salvation. Yet the ending is appropriate in two respects. First, it returns to the covenant of pieces ceremony in Genesis 15 (15:13-14), which was the biblical launch pad for Abraham's ascent. Second, by ending with a prophecy of the exodus, the work points to *the* historical event that became the foundation of Israel's covenantal obligation toward YHWH, expressed most succinctly in the opening words of the Decalogue: "I am the LORD your God, who brought you out of the land of Egypt, out of the house of slavery; you shall have no other gods before me" (Exod. 20:2). Israel's rescue now resembles that of Abraham, whom the LORD brought out of the land of Chaldea, out of the house of idolatry, because he had no other gods before Him.

VI. Message, Setting, Function

Many of the details in the *Apocalypse of Abraham* are supplied by midrashic interpretations of Genesis 12 and 15. But as John Collins has rightly emphasized, "the text is not generated by exegetical concerns. The problem addressed is not that of the meaning of the texts in Genesis but that of the prominence of evil in the world, especially in the form of idolatry."[52] Indeed, the work epitomizes evil in the world as idolatry — evil in its various forms amounts to false worship. Only when Abraham has renounced idolatry and been ritually separated from it, and only once he has overcome and displaced Azazel as a heavenly priest and been taught proper worship by Yahoel, is he ready for a vision of God and of history's course and climax. When the people of Israel commit idolatry, they align themselves with the very nations that have oppressed them. They place themselves under the dominion of Azazel and will share the same fate as the heathen and their idols.

The *Apocalypse of Abraham* conceives of idolatry not as Israel's betrayal of YHWH the jealous husband but as a universal error in metaphysics. Moreover, in its portrait of God the work resists the anthropomorphizing found in the book of Ezekiel and in apocalypses inspired by it. And in its portrayal of Abraham's interactions with Yahoel, it rejects the granting of undue veneration to God's angelic intermediaries.

The apocalypse relates the issue of Israel's election among the nations to the even larger one of free will and predestination, affirming that the two coexist. Sin is a matter of human choice, but history nevertheless unfolds according to God's plan. Azazel is at large in the world, but he operates within God's sovereign will.

The apocalypse does not finally overcome the opposition of Israel and the nations, at least not clearly. On the one hand, some of the nations are destined for "judgment and justice," others for "revenge and perdition" (22:4) — phrases whose parallelism may be antithetical instead of synonymous. On the other hand, God's judgment is said unequivocally to fall upon "the heathen" (29:14), who will suffer ten plagues as the Egyptians of old did (29:15; 30:2-8). The antinomy of Israel vs. the other nations is modulated insofar as the coming age is reserved not for all of Abraham's descendents but only for a select number who have been preserved by God because they aligned their wills with his: "And then from your seed will the righteous be left, kept by me by number" (29:17). The righteous are said to include "those who do justice, who have chosen my will and clearly kept my commandments" (31:4). The only commandment the work emphasizes, however, is the exclusive and imageless worship of the one God. Avoidance of idolatry is a universal moral requirement. The just among the heathen — if there are any at the close of the age — are not expected to accept the ritual requirements

---

52. Collins, *Apocalyptic Imagination*, 227.

of the Mosaic covenant, not even circumcision, which is conspicuous by its absence in a work with Abraham as its protagonist.

The destruction of the Temple and the issues of theodicy it raises feature prominently in the *Apocalypse of Abraham*, as they do at much greater length in the work's contemporaries *4 Ezra* and *2 Baruch* The tragedy of the year 70 may have provided the immediate occasion for the work's (final) composition,[53] but it neither opens nor closes the work, nor is it the work's only or chief preoccupation. Beyond the Temple's demise, it is hard to know whether any specific incident(s) prompted the author to write. In the decades leading up to the First Revolt, Jewish aniconic scruples took on a renewed urgency. During his reign (37-4 B.C.E.) Herod had erected temples and statues in his territory in honor of Augustus, the goddess Roma and other deities, in cities such as Caesarea, Sebaste, and Paneion. On three notable occasions the Jews of Jerusalem resisted the introduction of Roman images into the Holy City: shortly before Herod's death, two Torah teachers in Jerusalem were executed for pulling down a golden eagle that Herod had hung over the main entrance of the Temple (Josephus, *J.W.* 1.648; *Ant.* 17.6.3); during his tenure as prefect of Judea (26-36 C.E.), Pontius Pilate brought into the city Roman military standards with the bust of the emperor Tiberius attached to them (Josephus, *J.W.* 2.169-74; *Ant.* 18.55-59) and/or shields with the name of the emperor inscribed on them (Philo, *Legatio* 299-305);[54] and in the year 39, Caligula gave orders to have an image of himself installed in the Jerusalem Temple, an order that, fortunately, was never carried out (Philo, *Legatio* 30.203).

It is tempting to associate the idolatry and murder in the Temple (chap. 25) with the bloodshed perpetrated by the rival Jewish factions that vied for control of Jerusalem during the First Revolt, and in particular with the Zealot occupation of the inner court of the Temple in 69-70 C.E. Or the author may have been a disenfranchised priest who regarded the Temple, as the Qumran sect had, as defiled and deserving of destruction because it was

---

53. See James R. Mueller, "The Apocalypse of Abraham and the Destruction of the Second Jewish Temple," *SBLSP* 21 (1982): 341-49.

54. Philo and Josephus may be recounting two separate episodes or different versions of the same incident. See Daniel R. Schwartz, "Josephus and Philo on Pontius Pilate," in *Josephus Flavius: Historian of Eretz-Israel in the Hellenistic-Roman Period*, ed. U. Rappaport (Jerusalem: Yad Ben Zvi, 1982), 217-36 (in Hebrew; English version in *The Jerusalem Cathedra* 3 [1983]: 26-45); Helen K. Bond, "Standards, Shields and Coins: Jewish Reactions to Aspects of the Roman Cult in the Time of Pilate," in *Idolatry: False Worship in the Bible, Early Judaism and Christianity*, 88-106.

being run by the wrong people. But these are only possibilities, none of which is required by a text that is allusive and therefore elusive.

We can only infer the work's intent and only guess at its early reception. It is conceivable that the apocalypse was intended, or taken, as a call for iconoclastic zeal in face of the growing idol trade in Palestine. A half century ago, Ephraim Urbach noted that in the decades following the destruction of the Temple Jewish artisans had to compete with Gentile craftsmen in meeting a rising demand for images among the increasing number of non-Jews settling in the land of Israel. It was hard for Jewish craftsmen and merchants to avoid making and trading in idols.[55] This change in the socioeconomic situation of Jews gave rise in rabbinic circles to the principle of "nullification" (בטול), according to which one could annul the defiling character of an idolatrous object by mentally denying it sanctity. Some devout Jews destroyed idolatrous objects; others used them but only after desecrating them or disfiguring them. In the view of some sages, though, not even desecration was necessary; the function of an object and the meaning one attached to it were sufficient to render it innocuous. So, for instance, since "images on common vessels are purely decorative and nothing more," their use for menial tasks "destroys any thought of the sanctity of their images."[56] This accommodation made it possible for Jews to manufacture and sell idols without being tainted by idolatry. Second-century sages disagreed over whether Jewish artisans and merchants could take part in the idol business, and as the century wore on rabbinic rulings on this matter became more rigorous even as the broader principle of nullification became more lenient.[57] In such a context, the *Apocalypse of Abraham* could have been read as a manifesto against Jews trafficking in idols, with the eponymous hero of the tale serving as exemplar.

Again, this is only a possibility. All we can say with confidence is that the author of the *Apocalypse of Abraham* saw in one potentially seductive aspect of Greco-Roman culture a threat to Jewish monotheism and a temptation to idolatry, and that he wished to reaffirm Israel's uniqueness — its Otherness — among the nations.

---

55. Ephraim E. Urbach, "The Rabbinical Law of Idolatry in the Second and Third Centuries in the Light of Archaeological and Historical Facts," *IEJ* 9 (1959): 156-58, 229-33.

56. Gerald Blidstein, "Nullification of Idolatry in Rabbinic Law," *JSJ* 5 (1974): 8. Note, e.g., *m. 'Aboda Zara* 3:3-4, which records opinions attributed to R. Gamaliel (usually identified with R. Gamaliel of Yavneh, ca. 90 C.E.) and his son R. Simeon b. Gamaliel.

57. Blidstein, "Nullification of Idolatry," 20-27.

… PART FOUR

THE DEAD SEA SCROLLS

Religious Epistemology and the History of the Dead Sea Scrolls Community

Shane Berg

The tendency of human communities to differentiate themselves from the groups and individuals around them can be found in all cultures in all times. The notion of the Other is especially prominent in sectarian groups, and such groups go to great lengths to create and maintain boundaries between themselves and these "others." John Collins has carefully examined this sectarian impulse as manifested in the Second Temple Jewish group known as the Essenes, shedding light on both the social structures and the underlying patterns of thought that allowed its members to draw sharp distinctions between their community and other Jewish groups.

In several recent essays, Collins has turned his attention to the social patterns of organization of the Essene movement.[1] In "Forms of Community in the Dead Sea Scrolls," he points out the diversity of patterns of social organization attested in the scrolls, a point that he expands in "The Yaḥad and the Qumran Community" by showing that the term *yaḥad* refers not exclusively to the group at Qumran but to the entire network of local groups of

---

1. Collins has now shaped his essays on this topic into a monograph: *Beyond the Qumran Community: The Sectarian Movement of the Dead Sea Scrolls* (Grand Rapids: Eerdmans, 2009).

I am grateful for the opportunity to offer the ideas and suggestions in this paper in honor of John Collins, my teacher and doctoral advisor. John is a wonderful teacher and mentor whose drive for scholarly excellence and whose commitment to collegial interaction have become models for me.

members ("cells").² Collins also argues that the group that settled at Qumran may have been an elite group that was set aside for special training.³ Finally, Collins suggests in "Sectarian Consciousness in the Dead Sea Scrolls" that the scrolls that do not refer to sectarian social structures may nonetheless be considered sectarian if in their theological ideas and patterns of thought they give evidence of a separatist self-consciousness.⁴

Related to Collins's interest in the nature and history of the community are his reflections on the difficult task of dating the *floruit* of the Teacher of Righteousness. His essay "The Time of the Teacher: An Old Debate Renewed" is an incisive critique of the consensus view that dates the Teacher to the middle of the second century B.C.E.⁵ Collins persuasively argues that any attempt to link securely the Teacher to historical events and figures of the Hasmonean era is destined to fail due to lack of evidence.

The goal of this essay is to provide a new angle of vision for the question of the history of the community and the role of the Teacher within it that supplements and builds on Collins's insights. Though it might seem puzzling at the outset, I hope to show that attending to questions of religious epistemology can prove fruitful for thinking about the history of the community and the rise of the Teacher. A dramatic transformation regarding how claims about knowledge about and from God are constructed and legitimated suggests a significant set of developments in the history of the Dead Sea Scrolls community. The key document for demonstrating this shift in religious epistemology is the *Hodayot*.

---

2. John J. Collins, "Forms of Community in the Dead Sea Scrolls," in *Emanuel: Studies in the Hebrew Bible, Septuagint, and Dead Sea Scrolls in Honor of Emanuel Tov*, ed. S. M. Paul et al. (VTSup 94; Leiden: Brill, 2003), 67-82; idem, "The Yaḥad and the 'Qumran Community,'" in *Biblical Traditions in Transmission: Essays in Honor of Michael A. Knibb*, ed. C. Hempel and J. M. Lieu (JSJSup 111; Leiden: Brill, 2006), 81-96.

3. For a discussion of this possibility taking its cue from Collins, see Shane Berg, "An Elite Group within the יחד," in *Qumran Studies: New Approaches, New Questions*, ed. B. A. Strawn and M. T. Davis (Grand Rapids: Eerdmans, 2007), 161-77.

4. John J. Collins, "Sectarian Consciousness in the Dead Sea Scrolls," in *Heavenly Tablets: Interpretation, Identity, and Tradition in Ancient Judaism*, ed. L. LiDonnici and A. Lieber (JSJSup 119; Leiden: Brill, 2007), 177-92.

5. John J. Collins, "The Time of the Teacher: An Old Debate Renewed," in *Studies in the Hebrew Bible, Qumran, and the Septuagint Presented to Eugene Ulrich*, ed. P. W. Flint, E. Tov, and J. C. VanderKam (VTSup 101; Leiden: Brill, 2006), 212-29.

Religious Epistemology and the History of the Dead Sea Scrolls Community

I. Two Religious Epistemologies in the *Hodayot*

Since its publication, scholars have noted that the hymns in the *Hodayot* tend to fall into two major groups. Some of the hymns are expressed in a first-person singular "I" that seems to reflect a general human perspective while others are articulated in a first-person singular "I" that seems to represent a unique, personal experience. The first type, or "community" hymns, is clustered in columns 3-9 and 18-27, while the second type, or "teacher" hymns, is found in columns 10-17.

This division of the *Hodayot* hymns into two groups, which is based on their literary characteristics, just happens to match their division into two groups based on their religious epistemology. Many scholars have noticed the striking claims to authority and to the mediation of divine revelation made by the speaker of the "teacher" hymns. A study of the religious epistemology of the *Hodayot* reveals two different patterns of thought that correspond to this division into "community" and "teacher" hymns. One of the religious epistemologies of the *Hodayot* — residing in the so-called "community" hymns — has similarities to the wisdom-based epistemology of 4QInstruction and the Discourse on the Two Spirits, while the religious epistemology of the so-called "teacher" hymns reflects a prophetic-type epistemology that differs from these other texts in key ways.[6]

Several threads related to religious epistemology run through the community hymns of the *Hodayot*, 4QInstruction, and the Discourse on the Two Spirits.[7] An emphasis on the submission of all creation — past, present, and future — to God's fixed plan is a key element in each text.[8] In 4QIn-

---

6. The claims in this essay concerning the religious epistemology of the *Hodayot*, as well as 4QInstruction and the Discourse on the Two Spirits of the *Community Rule*, are discussed in detail in my recent dissertation supervised by John Collins: "Religious Epistemologies in the Dead Sea Scrolls: The Heritage and Transformation of the Wisdom Tradition" (Ph.D. dissertation, Yale University, 2008). What follows is an overview and summary of the results of the close textual work that is carried out in the dissertation.

7. Matthew Goff identifies some important similarities between 4QInstruction and the *Hodayot* in the areas of determinism, creation, and election, all of which are quite relevant to this topic, in his article "Reading Wisdom at Qumran: 4QInstruction and the Hodayot," *DSD* 11 (2004): 263-88.

8. Armin Lange has very helpfully articulated the general thesis that there is a notion of a preexistent cosmic sapiential order underlying a variety of Dead Sea Scrolls, including 4QInstruction, the Discourse, and the *Hodayot*. See his *Weisheit und Prädestination: Weisheitliche Urordnung und Prädestination in den Textfunden von Qumran* (STDJ 18; Leiden: Brill, 1995).

335

struction the term רז נהיה is employed as a sort of shorthand for this divine plan and also points to its revealed character.[9] One of the most important elements of the divine plan in 4QInstruction for religious epistemology concerns the "moral architecture" of the cosmos, a blueprint according to which qualities like good and evil, truth and falsehood, and wisdom and folly come to expression in the world.[10] The recognition of this determined pattern for moral attributes is stressed by the sage as a crucial task for the faithful pupil. Knowing that there is a deterministic divine plan at work in the cosmos and possessing a working acquaintance with its basic character are regarded by the sage as of the utmost importance.[11]

This same concern for knowledge of how God's deterministic plan unfolds in the world is a prominent theme in the Discourse on the Two Spirits as well. Good and evil, truth and falsehood, and justice and injustice are manifest in the cosmos according to a divinely determined pattern.[12] The major difference is that in the Discourse these moral attributes are directly linked to the presence and activity of good and evil spirits that carry out their respective tasks according to God's plan. There is thus a "spiritual architecture" that governs the presence of good and evil in the cosmos with which members of the group must become familiar through formal instruction at the hands of the *Maskîl*.[13]

This same sort of deterministic divine plan is found in the community hymns of the *Hodayot* as well.[14] Because the emphasis in the hymns is extolling what God has done for the hymnist and not on laying out the content of instruction, references to the operations of this deterministic plan are less frequent and more subtle than in 4QInstruction and the Discourse. Despite this generic difference, though, the divine plan and structure of the cosmos in the community hymns is clearly of the same kind and nature as in the other two texts.

Beyond the fact that the three texts share a deterministic divine plan, it can be further noted that this plan seems to be patterned after the orderly ac-

---

9. See Matthew Goff, *The Worldly and Heavenly Wisdom of 4QInstruction* (STDJ 50; Leiden: Brill, 2003), 51-79, for a definitive treatment of this important term.

10. See 4Q417 1 i 6-13.

11. For a full treatment of this point, see Berg, "Religious Epistemologies," 39-68.

12. See 1QS 3:19 and 4:2-14.

13. 1QS 3:13: למשכיל להבין וללמד כול בני אור בתולדות כול בני איש, "It is the role of the *Maskîl* to instruct and teach all the sons of light concerning the history of all the sons of man." See the discussion in Berg, "Religious Epistemologies," 99-118.

14. See 1QH^a 9:7-20; this passage is analyzed in Berg, ibid., 173-78.

count of creation in Genesis 1.[15] While the Genesis account is centered on the creation of the physical world, 4QInstruction, the Discourse and the community hymns use language evocative of that account to describe the structured cosmos that reflects God's design and becomes the mechanism by which his plan becomes actualized.[16]

Another major thread that ties the three texts together is an anthropology that is rooted in creation and has profound implications for religious epistemology.[17] In 4QInstruction the two creation accounts in Genesis 1–2 are taken to refer to the creation of two types of humanity, one of which is not privy to divine revelation and thus is not able to discern between good and evil.[18] The author clearly regards himself and his pupil as members of the elite group that has been granted the ability to discern between good and evil. The interpretation of the Genesis creation accounts takes a different shape in the Discourse on the Two Spirits, where there is not the creation of different kinds of humans but rather different kinds of spirits; the anthropological divide in humanity is thus not rooted in the creation of the human, as in 4QInstruction, but in the creation of the spirits who are at work within humans.[19]

The anthropology of the community hymns of the *Hodayot* appropriates creation ideas in yet a different way that is relevant for religious epistemology. Drawing on a constellation of prophetic and wisdom texts as well as Genesis 2–3, the hymnists construct the human as essentially ignorant of

---

15. For a discussion of the role of Genesis 1–3 in Ben Sira and the Dead Sea Scrolls, see John J. Collins, "Wisdom, Apocalypticism, and the Dead Sea Scrolls," in *"Jedes Ding hat seine Zeit . . .": Studien zur israelitischen und altorientalischen Weisheit; Diethelm Michel zum 65. Geburtstag,* ed. A. A. Diesel et al. (Berlin: de Gruyter, 1996), 19-32; republished in John J. Collins, *Seers, Sibyls and Sages in Hellenistic-Roman Judaism* (JSJSup 54; Leiden: Brill, 2001), 369-84. See also Goff, *4QInstruction,* 116-23.

16. See especially 4Q417 i 6-13; 1QS 3:13-17; 1QH^a 9:7-20.

17. For a wide-ranging survey and discussion of anthropological issues in the Dead Sea Scrolls, see Hermann Lichtenberger, *Studien zum Menschenbild in Texten der Qumrangemeinde* (SUNT 15; Göttingen: Vandenhoeck und Ruprecht, 1980). The volume treats 1QS and 1QH^a extensively but was published before the appearance of 4QInstruction.

18. The group that is cut off from revelation is characterized as רוח בשר ("fleshly spirit," a metonymy for "fleshly people"), while the other group is the עם רוח ("spiritual people"); see 4Q417 1 i 16-18. See the discussion by Collins in "In the Likeness of the Holy Ones: The Creation of Humankind in a Wisdom Text from Qumran," in *The Provo International Conference on the Dead Sea Scrolls: Technological Innovations, New Texts, and Reformulated Issues,* ed. D. W. Parry and E. Ulrich (STDJ 30; Leiden: Brill, 1999), 609-18. There is also an excellent treatment of this issue in Goff, *4QInstruction,* 94-116.

19. See 1QS 3:17–4:16; for a discussion see Berg, "Religious Epistemologies," 111-27.

God's plans and purposes because of the vulgar nature of the dust, clay, and other raw materials from which it is made.[20] This way of representing the human condition means that only God is able to overcome this ignorance and grant knowledge, a claim that is used in the service of sectarian ideas.

A third and final red thread common to all three texts is the agency of spirits in the reception of religious knowledge. 4QInstruction has the least developed notion of spirits, but even so at a crucial point in its mini-treatise on epistemology (4Q417 1 i) humanity is divided into two groups — one of which has access to revelation while the other does not — based on the presence or absence of spirit(s).[21] This shows that even at an early stage of development, the concept of spirit is tied to both religious epistemology and sectarian tendencies.

The agency of spirits of course finds its most robust expression in the Discourse on the Two Spirits. Like 4QInstruction, these spirits are decisive for the question of religious knowledge and also function as the governing forces of whether one is an insider ("son of light") or an outsider ("son of darkness").

The community hymns also place spirits in a central role, though they are not so systematically presented as in the Discourse,[22] nor is there as much emphasis on evil spirits and their operative role in the life of the wicked. The spirits in the community hymns function primarily to overcome the ignorance that is inherent in the human by enabling the knowledge of God's will and purposes.[23]

One final area of common ground in these texts is rich engagement with Torah.[24] All three texts incorporate, allude to, and creatively interpret

---

20. While employing a wide range of such images to describe the deplorable material constitution of the human being, the community hymns especially emphasize the claim that the human is composed of "dust" (עפר) and "clay" (חמר), often, though not always, occurring in tandem. See 1QH^a 11:20-21; 18:4, 12; 19:3; 20:24, 25, 26; 21:6, 14, 18; 22:8, 11; and 23:9. A full discussion of the anthropology of the community hymns can be found in Berg, "Religious Epistemologies," 161-72.

21. 4Q417 1 i 16-18.

22. A less systematic presentation of theological ideas is to be expected given the genre (hymnic compositions rather than instruction).

23. See the discussion of this epistemological agency of spirits in the community hymns in Berg, "Religious Epistemologies," 173-83.

24. For an orientation to the use of biblical texts in wisdom texts, see George Brooke, "Biblical Interpretation in the Wisdom Texts from Qumran," in *The Wisdom Texts from Qumran and the Development of Sapiential Thought*, ed. C. Hempel, A. Lange, and H. Lichtenberger (BETL 159; Leuven: Leuven University Press, 2002), 201-20.

Religious Epistemology and the History of the Dead Sea Scrolls Community

biblical texts. What is very significant, though, is that Torah, while pervasive and influential, is not marked in the rhetoric of these texts as a source of revelation. The knowledge of God's plan comes through the mediation of a structured, determined cosmos and the epistemological agency of spirits. There is not to be found in these texts the notion of "Scripture" or "the Bible" in the sense of a revelatory document to which one appeals as a source of knowledge from God. Such appeals are central to some prominent texts among the Dead Sea Scrolls, but in the three important texts under discussion there is no such notion of revelatory texts.

This absence of the idea of sacred texts as revelatory in 4QInstruction, the Discourse and the community hymns is most plausibly linked to the influence of the wisdom tradition and to sapiential ways of knowing, which in the biblical wisdom tradition do not ground knowledge claims in revealed texts. Knowledge claims are rather grounded in a conception of God's wisdom as immanent in creation. When this notion of God's immanent wisdom was brought into relation to apocalyptic ideas such as God as the creator and revealer of mysteries[25] and divine control over history and the eschaton,[26] the result, found in various forms in the texts examined in this study, is a notion of revealed wisdom that is made known through divine agency rather than being universally available. It is not difficult to imagine why texts that feature revealed wisdom also tend to have sectarian overtones.

In the turn to the teacher hymns of the *Hodayot*, a striking difference in religious epistemology becomes apparent. Absent is the epistemological agency of spirits, a prominent feature in the community hymns, the Dis-

---

25. That is, mantic wisdom; see H.-P. Müller, "Mantische Weisheit und Apokalyptik," in *Congress Volume: Uppsala, 1971* (VTSup 22; Leiden: Brill, 1972), 268-93, as well as John J. Collins's discussion of Müller in relation to von Rad's views on wisdom and apocalypticism. See his "The Court Tales in Daniel and Development of Apocalyptic." *JBL* 94 (1975): 218-34.

26. The intertwining of wisdom and apocalypticism in Second Temple Judaism has been the subject of considerable scholarly attention in the last thirty years. John Collins has addressed this issue in a number of articles and essays, including: "Wisdom Reconsidered, in Light of the Scrolls," *DSD* 4 (1997): 265-81; "Wisdom, Apocalypticism, and the Dead Sea Scrolls," in *"Jedes Ding hat seine Zeit . . . ,"* 19-32; "Wisdom, Apocalypticism, and Generic Compatibility," in *In Search of Wisdom: Essays in Memory of John G. Gammie*, ed. L. G. Perdue, B. B. Scott, and W. J. Wiseman (Louisville: Westminster John Knox, 1993), 165-86; "The Root of Immortality: Death in the Context of Jewish Wisdom," *HTR* 71 (1978): 177-92; "Cosmos and Salvation: Jewish Wisdom and Apocalypticism in the Hellenistic Age," *HR* 17 (1977): 121-42. With the exception of the first, all of these articles are also available in Collins, *Seers, Sibyls and Sages*.

course on the Two Spirits and 4QInstruction; absent as well is the sort of dualism created by spirits in those texts. Also lacking in the teacher hymns are an emphasis on a divine plan for the cosmos and an interpretation of the Genesis creation account that is employed in an epistemologically significant way. These differences are a clear signal that the epistemology of the teacher hymns is constructed in a different fashion than that of 4QInstruction, the Discourse on the Two Spirits, and the community hymns of the *Hodayot*.

In the teacher hymns one finds an epistemology in which God provides unmediated revelation to an elite individual. By means of a rich set of metaphors and images, the hymnist repeatedly asserts God's active role in supplying him with knowledge and understanding.[27] The hymnist has drawn to himself a group of dedicated followers, but these disciples do not have the same sort of unmediated access to God's revelation that the hymnist enjoys. They rather form a community around their teacher and receive God's knowledge and instruction through him. The dominant image for this social reality is that of a water source like a fountain or spring (= the teacher) that provides irrigation to soil and plants (= the disciples).[28]

The hymnist of the teacher hymns is thus an intermediary figure who has direct access to God's revelation and in turn shares this revelation with an elect community. As the recipient of unmediated divine revelation and the one who disseminates that revelation, the hymnist occupies a social role that evokes the prophets of the biblical tradition. The religious epistemology of the teacher hymns is so different from the wisdom-based epistemology of the other texts examined in this study that it warrants its own designation as a prophetic-type epistemology.

Michael C. Douglas, building on earlier insights, argues that the teacher hymns of the *Hodayot* constitute a unified literary composition whose authorship differs from that of the community hymns.[29] The observations made here buttress Douglas's claims insofar as they suggest that the two sets of hymns in the *Hodayot* exhibit different religious epistemologies.

---

27. E.g., 1QH^a 15:26-27; 12:27-29; 13:11-12. The rich variety of metaphors employed for direct revelation from God to the hymnist is discussed in Berg, "Religious Epistemologies," 212-28.

28. E.g., 1QH^a 10:13-15, 17-19; 16:16. A treatment of the hymnist as mediator can be found in Berg, "Religious Epistemologies," 228-37.

29. Michael C. Douglas, "Power and Praise in the Hodayot: A Literary Critical Study of 1QH 9–18:14" (Ph.D. dissertation, University of Chicago, 1998). See also his "The Teacher Hymn Hypothesis Revisited: New Data for an Old Crux," *DSD* 6 (1999): 239-66.

II. Implications of the Two Epistemologies

The presence of two distinct religious epistemologies in the *Hodayot* prompts three related questions: (1) What can be said about the authorship of each set of hymns? (2) Are there other texts among the Dead Sea Scrolls in which one can find the sort of prophetic-type epistemology exhibited in the teacher hymns? and (3) Can the relative chronology of the two sets of hymns be determined?

The Question of Authorship

The significant differences in religious epistemology between the community hymns and the teacher hymns would tend to rule out common authorship of the two sets of hymns. While some suggestions can be made about the authorship of the teacher hymns, the authorship of the community hymns is a much more difficult question. Given their generality, it is unlikely that a specific historical person or a figure known from elsewhere in the Dead Sea Scrolls could ever be identified as the author. Even the issue of whether there was a single author or multiple authors remains an open question.³⁰ The sorts of literary studies that would be necessary to address the question have not yet been undertaken. What this study has shown is that the community hymns exhibit a fairly consistent religious epistemology, which perhaps suggests but in no way demonstrates that a single author lies behind the bulk of them, a suggestion that in no way precludes the possibility of subsequent editorial shaping.³¹

With the teacher hymns the question of authorship is considerably more intriguing. In his thorough literary study and a follow-up article, Michael Douglas argues compellingly that the teacher hymns reflect the work of a single author.³² Furthermore, the author of these hymns represents

---

30. Angela Kim Harkins very helpfully lays out the issues related to the literary complexity of the community hymns and discusses the thorny questions of authorship and editing. See her "Observations on the Editorial Shaping of the So-Called Community Hymns from 1QHª and 4QHª (4Q427)," *DSD* 12 (2005): 233-56.

31. E.g., Harkins, building on Puech, argues that the recurrence of למשכיל in the community hymns (1QHª 1:1 [hypothetical], 5:21, 7:21 [reconstructed], 20:7 [reconstructed], 25:34) indicates editorial groupings of similar hymns and even the inclusion of so-called "floating" hymns that differ from the majority of the hymns. See her "Observations," 234-39.

32. Douglas, "Power and Praise," 15-238; idem, "The Teacher Hymn Hypothesis," 239-66.

himself as an authoritative figure with special access to revelation from God who is surrounded by a community of faithful disciples whom he leads and teaches. Such a figure quite obviously calls to mind the Righteous Teacher, who in the *Damascus Document*, the *pesher* on Habakkuk, and other texts is portrayed as an authoritative teacher who makes unique claims concerning divine revelation.[33] At various times scholars have argued that the Righteous Teacher wrote all or part of the *Hodayot*,[34] but Michael Douglas's contention that the Righteous Teacher wrote the teacher hymns is the most nuanced and persuasive argument for this position.[35] While it is difficult to pin down the historical identity of the Righteous Teacher,[36] it is reasonable to assert that the figure who is rhetorically presented in texts like the *Damascus Document* and the Habakkuk *pesher* matches up well with the self-presentation of the hymnist in the teacher hymns of the *Hodayot*.[37] It is quite plausible to regard the author of the teacher hymns as the pivotal figure from the community's past known from other texts as the Righteous Teacher. The prophetic-type epistemology identified in the teacher hymns fits very well with such a charismatic figure.

33. CD 1:10-17; 20:33; 1QpMic 8-10 6; 1QpHab 1:13; 2:2; 7:4; 8:3; 9:9-10; 11:5; 4QpPs^a 3:15, 19; 4:8, 27; 4QpPs^b 2 2. Elsewhere he is called "the Teacher of the Yaḥad" (CD 20:1, 14) or simply "the Teacher" (CD 20:28). Other epithets that likely refer to this same figure are "the Interpreter of the Torah" (CD 6:7; 4Q174 1:12), "the Interpreter" (1QS 8:12), and "the Priest" (4QpPs^a 3:15; 1QpHab 2:8).

34. This position was argued most forcefully by the so-called "Göttingen School": Gert Jeremias, *Der Lehrer der Gerechtigkeit* (SUNT 2; Göttingen: Vandenhoeck & Ruprecht, 1963); Jürgen Becker, *Das Heil Gottes: Heils- und Sündenbegriffe in den Qumrantexten und im Neuen Testament* (SUNT 3; Göttingen: Vandenhoeck & Ruprecht, 1963); Heinz-Wolfgang Kuhn, *Enderwartung und gegenwärtiges Heil: Untersuchungen zu dem Gemeindeliedern von Qumran* (SUNT 4; Göttingen: Vandenhoeck & Ruprecht, 1963).

35. Douglas, "Power and Praise," 308-51.

36. There have been myriad attempts to identify the Righteous Teacher with known figures from the Second Temple period, especially priestly figures from the early Hasmonean period. Representative scholarship includes: Jerome Murphy-O'Connor, "The Essenes and Their History," *RB* 81 (1974): 215-44; and William Brownlee, "The Wicked Priest, the Man of Lies, and the Righteous Teacher — The Problem of Identity," *JQR* 73 (1982): 1-37. More recently the case for the mid-century date has come under scrutiny; see Michael O. Wise, "Dating the Teacher of Righteousness and the Floruit of His Movement," *JBL* 122 (2003): 53-87, and esp. John J. Collins, "The Time of the Teacher," in *Studies in the Hebrew Bible*, 212-29. See now the essay by James VanderKam in this volume.

37. Douglas, "The Teacher Hymn Hypothesis," 257-66, echoing the sentiments of Jeremias, Becker, and Kuhn, points out the improbability of two different early leaders in the community making these sorts of exclusive claims.

Religious Epistemology and the History of the Dead Sea Scrolls Community

A Prophetic-type Epistemology in Other Texts?

The presentation of the Righteous Teacher as an intermediary figure in the Habakkuk *pesher* is interesting in light of the prophetic-type religious epistemology of the teacher hymns of the *Hodayot*. The following fragmentary passage illustrates this way of representing the Teacher:

> [This passage refers to] the traitors together with the Man of the Lie, because they did not [. . . the words of?] the Righteous Teacher from the mouth of God (מפיא אל). (1QpHab 2:1-3)

While a couple of key words are lost in the lacuna, the overall thrust is able to be discerned — the Righteous Teacher claims to speak for God, and that claim is rejected by some. The intermediary role of the Teacher is made very clear in another passage:

> Then God told Habakkuk to write everything that would come upon the latter generation, but God did not make known when the time would be fulfilled. Concerning the saying, "in order that someone might read it": *its interpretation concerns the Righteous Teacher to whom God made known all mysteries of the words of his servants the prophets* (פשרו על מורה הצדק אשר הודיעו אל את כול רזי דברי עבדיו הנבאים). (1QpHab 7:1-5)

Note that the religious epistemology of this well-known passage has significant points of contact with the prophetic-type mode of revelation found in the teacher hymns. The Righteous Teacher is portrayed as the recipient of unique, unmediated divine revelation that is characterized by the term "mysteries."[38] What is different, however, is that the "mysteries" in this passage are further specified as "the words of his servants the prophets." The revelation that God provides to the Righteous Teacher includes the correct interpretation and understanding of the written words of prophetic books.[39] As presented here in the Habakkuk *pesher*, the religious epistemology that

---

38. Cf. 1QH^a 12:27-28: כי הודעתני ברזי פלאכה, "for you made known to me your wondrous mysteries"; 15:27: וברזי פלאכה הודעתני, "and you made known to me your wondrous mysteries."

39. Cf. also 1QpHab 2:6-10: "They are enemi[es of the covena]nt who disbelieve when they hear everything that will come upon the latter generation that comes from the mouth of the Priest in wh[ose heart] God granted [underst]anding to interpret all the words of his servants the prophets." The "Priest" here is almost certainly the Righteous Teacher.

undergirds this inspired exegesis is an extension of the sort of prophetic-type epistemology found in the teacher hymns of the *Hodayot* — God, in an unmediated fashion, reveals knowledge to a unique and authoritative figure. In this particular case, the content of that revealed knowledge pertains to the interpretation of prophetic books.[40]

What is intriguing is that in the Habakkuk *pesher* there are two levels of inspired exegesis. In passages like the one cited above, the Righteous Teacher is portrayed as divinely enabled to read the mysteries of the prophetic books. But at the same time, the author of the Habakkuk *pesher* himself is carrying out precisely the same sort of reading of Habakkuk, that is, explaining the contemporary and local "meaning" of the text of Habakkuk.[41] The pesherist is doing what he describes the Teacher as having himself done. It is thus clear that inspired exegesis, while highlighted as one of the particular gifts of the Teacher, is not his exclusive prerogative in the community's life and history.

This fact does not necessarily mean, however, that inspired exegesis could be carried out by any member of the community. There are some references to biblical interpretation in the Dead Sea Scrolls that suggest that particular individuals in leadership roles took primary responsibility for such interpretation. In the *Damascus Document*, for example, a figure called "the interpreter of the law" (דורש התורה) establishes the proper "statutes" by which the community is to "walk" before God. It is possible but not certain that the "interpreter of the law" is the Righteous Teacher who is men-

---

40. Alex Jassen argues persuasively for the influence of modified models of biblical prophets and prophecy on the *pesharim*. In his concluding reflections on the Habakkuk *pesher*, Jassen writes: "Pesher Habakkuk indicates that the community viewed the Teacher of Righteousness as the inspired interpreter of the hidden meaning of the ancient prophetic announcements. This process involved the Teacher's uncovering of the 'true' meaning of prophetic Scripture while in a state of inspiration. This process, according to pesher Habakkuk, reflects the Teacher's receipt of the divine message 'from the mouth of God'. This expression points to the prophetic understanding of the Teacher's activity. Unlike the classical prophecy of the Hebrew Bible, however, prophetic revelation has become a literary experience." See Alex Jassen, *Mediating the Divine: Prophecy and Revelation in the Dead Sea Scrolls and Second Temple Judaism* (STDJ 68; Leiden: Brill, 2007), 362.

41. For discussions of the hermeneutical approaches found in the *pesharim*, see especially George Brooke, "Qumran Pesher: Toward the Redefinition of a Genre," *RevQ* 10 (1979-81): 483-503; Shani Berrin, "Qumran Pesharim," in *Biblical Interpretation at Qumran*, ed. M. Henze (Grand Rapids: Eerdmans, 2005), 110-33; and Jutta Jokiranta, "Pesharim: A Mirror of Self-Understanding," in *Reading the Present in the Qumran Library: The Perception of the Contemporary by Means of Scriptural Interpretation*, ed. K. de Troyer and A. Lange (SBLSymS 30; Atlanta: Society of Biblical Literature, 2005), 23-34.

tioned elsewhere in the *Damascus Document*.⁴² There is also a reference to a unique "interpreter" in the *Community Rule*:

וכול דבר הנסתר מישראל ונמצאו לאיש הדורש אל יסתרהו מאלה
מיראת רוח נסוגה

> And every matter that is hidden from Israel but brought forth by the interpreter shall not be hidden from these (men) out of a fear of a disloyal spirit. (1QS 8:11-12)

It is again possible but in no way certain that this "interpreter" is the Righteous Teacher. It is not important to reach a firm conclusion on the relationship between the "Righteous Teacher" and the "Interpreter"; what is important is to note that in these examples, inspired biblical interpretation is especially linked to a unique individual. This pattern is significant in considering the relationship between a prophetic-type epistemology — which features a uniquely inspired individual with unmediated access to divine revelation — and inspired exegesis, which in some key texts is linked to just such an elite figure who functions as an intermediary between God and the community with respect to biblical interpretation.

The *pesher* on Habakkuk thus helps illustrate the link between the prophetic-type epistemology of the teacher hymns of the *Hodayot* and the religious epistemology of the *pesharim*. Other texts, such as the *Community Rule* and the *Damascus Document*, give evidence of similar interpretive approaches and the elite figures associated with them. It is thus fair to suggest that "inspired exegesis" is undergirded by the extension of a prophetic-type epistemology to biblical texts.⁴³ It represents a significant development in the interpretation of the Bible in Second Temple Judaism.

The Chronology of the Two Epistemologies

The remaining question concerns what, if anything, can be said about the relative chronology of the two types of religious epistemology found in the *Hodayot*.

---

42. See note 33 above for all the references in CD to the Righteous Teacher. It should be pointed out that 4Q174 1:12 (4QFlorilegium) also refers to an "interpreter of the law," but the epithet in this instance seems to refer to a future figure rather than someone in the community's past or present.

43. This is an argument developed at length by Jassen in his discussions of the turn to "literary prophecy" in the Second Temple period. See Jassen, *Mediating*, 197-240, 343-62.

1QH^a reflects significant editorial activity.[44] Although on the basis of what look like inclusions or elaborations in the teacher hymns of themes from the community hymns one might tentatively conclude that the community hymns predate the teacher hymns, such a conclusion cannot be proven on textual grounds alone.[45]

If the relative chronology of the two sets of hymns cannot be determined with any certainty through textual criticism, it is nonetheless possible to make some more general suggestions about the relative chronologies of the two types of epistemologies found in them. Since 4QInstruction would seem to be safely regarded as being composed before both the Discourse on the Two Spirits and the community hymns of the *Hodayot*, one would not consider the community hymns a pioneering text with respect to a wisdom-based epistemology; it has at least one significant precursor among the Dead Sea Scrolls.[46]

On the other hand, there is no clear precursor among the Scrolls to the teacher hymns and the prophetic-type epistemology found within them. The teacher hymns can be plausibly attributed to the Righteous Teacher, and the texts that contain a similar kind of religious epistemology — most importantly the *pesharim* — clearly post-date the Teacher, some even making reference to him. It thus seems plausible that the Righteous Teacher, as a charismatic and innovative figure who claimed authority from God to read biblical texts in bold new ways, was responsible for the rise to prominence of "inspired exegesis" and the prophetic-type epistemology that supports it.

This is not to say that the Teacher invented the inspired interpretation of biblical texts out of the blue. There were to be sure a variety of complex developments over long periods of time in diverse communities that led to the emergence of the idea of "scripture" as a source of revelation.[47] But such

---

44. See the discussions in Harkins, "Observations," 233-56, as well as Douglas, "Power and Praise," 204-38.

45. Douglas discusses this issue in ibid., 177-78.

46. I.e., 4QInstruction. It is difficult to determine the relative chronology of the Discourse and the community hymns, though one is tempted to place the Discourse later in light of its high degree of systematization of themes and motifs found in less ordered forms in 4QInstruction and the community hymns.

47. The emergence of Torah in the exilic, Persian, Hellenistic, and early Roman periods is a burgeoning field of research. For helpful guides to this area of scholarship, see Frank Crüsemann, *The Torah: Theology and Social History of Old Testament Law*, trans. A. W. Manke (Minneapolis: Fortress Press, 1996); Gary N. Knoppers and Bernard M. Levinson, eds., *The Pentateuch as Torah: New Models for Understanding Its Promulgation and Acceptance* (Winona Lake, Ind.: Eisenbrauns, 2007).

an observation does not preclude dramatic developments or radical innovations with respect to biblical interpretation on the part of a charismatic visionary and a devoted band of followers.[48] In fact, such a hypothesis fits the data from the texts found at Qumran fairly well.

It is thus possible to claim that the inspired exegesis attested in the Dead Sea Scrolls was accompanied by — maybe even enabled by — a particular kind of religious epistemology associated with the prophetic tradition. Other religious epistemologies, such as the wisdom-based variety, continue to exist, but it appears that they tend to get contextualized alongside the increasingly ascendant model of inspired exegesis. The Discourse on the Two Spirits, for example, is contextualized within the *Community Rule,* where it is brought into relation with texts that emphasize the inspired interpretation of biblical texts, and the community hymns of the *Hodayot* are brought alongside the hymns of the teacher. The implications of bringing these two religious epistemologies into immediate proximity within a single document warrant further reflection and research.

III. Religious Epistemology and the History of the Dead Sea Scrolls Community

One might attempt to trace the developments of religious epistemology in the Dead Sea Scrolls in the following way. In the early period of the community, authors grounded their religious knowledge in ways that were largely informed by the wisdom tradition, but at the same time they were increasingly influenced by apocalyptic ideas and worldviews. 4QInstruction is a fairly early representative of this tendency to wed wisdom and apocalyptic traditions, while later examples are the Discourse on the Two Spirits (in its independent form) and the community hymns of the *Hodayot*. The interpretation of biblical books plays an important role in these texts, but explicit claims about divine revelation are not made on the basis of such interpretation.

With the advent of the Teacher within the community, a striking new way of reading scripture found forceful expression. The inspired exegesis of

---

48. For general discussions of biblical interpretation in the Dead Sea Scrolls, see George Brooke, "Formation and Renewal of Scriptural Tradition," in *Studies in the Hebrew Bible,* 39-59; in the same volume, James VanderKam, "To What End? Functions of Scriptural Interpretation in Qumran Texts," 302-20; Armin Lange, "Interpretation als Offenbarung," in *Wisdom and Apocalypticism in the Dead Sea Scrolls and in the Biblical Tradition* (BETL 168; Leuven: Leuven University Press/Peeters, 2003), 17-33.

biblical texts became a means of divine revelation. The *pesharim*, the *Damascus Document*, and 1QS 5–11 are some examples that bear witness to this phenomenon. The older way of accessing God's secrets — an epistemology with roots in the wisdom tradition — was profoundly transformed by the emergence of this innovative religious epistemology. Texts like 4QInstruction continued to be copied, and a freestanding treatise like the Discourse on the Two Spirits could be preserved and taken up into a work such as the *Community Rule*. The community hymns could be placed alongside the teacher hymns in a text like the *Hodayot*. But it seems clear that while such older texts were preserved and valued, the ongoing life of the community was increasingly sustained by the robust inspired exegesis of the scriptures.

Such an account of the history of religious epistemology found in these important texts maps quite well onto Collins's sketch of the history of the community and its social patterns of organization. Prior to the rise of the teacher, intellectual religious life in the Dead Sea Scrolls community was dominated by an epistemology that had its roots in the wisdom tradition. Their key texts — such as 4QInstruction, the Discourse on the Two Spirits and the community hymns of the *Hodayot* — reflect a separatist self-consciousness but not necessarily separatist patterns of communal organization.[49] John Collins succinctly captures this stage of the community's life:

> It does appear, however, that 4QInstruction[50] reflects a stage of spiritual separatism that was not yet embodied in social action. The "spiritual people" were aware of their need to separate from "the spirit of flesh," but they had not yet found their Teacher. They had not yet developed the kind of systematic focus on Torah interpretation that we find in the "mature" sectarian scrolls from Qumran, and they had not yet set up the social structures that would enable them to separate themselves from the multitude of the people.[51]

When this group did find its Teacher, he was the catalyst for a significant shift in religious epistemology that had its roots in prophetic ways of making claims about divine revelation and made biblical texts a key locus of

---

49. An observation that makes sense in light of the assertion by Collins, "Forms of Community," 85, that the membership of the *yaḥad* lived among the general Jewish population and came together in small local cells for fellowship, study, and worship.

50. I would also add the Discourse on the Two Spirits and the community hymns of the *Hodayot*.

51. Collins, "Sectarian Consciousness," 192.

Religious Epistemology and the History of the Dead Sea Scrolls Community

God's ongoing revelatory activity. Texts that reflect this innovative religious epistemology — such as the teacher hymns of the *Hodayot*, the *Community Rule*, the *Damascus Document* and the *pesharim* — show not only a separatist self-consciousness but signs of separatist patterns of communal organization and accompanying conflict with outside groups and individuals. It is not difficult to imagine that this was the period in which some select group within the *yaḥad*, led by the Teacher, settled the site at Qumran.[52] The Teacher would thus not only have brought to the community new ways of making claims about divine revelation but also engendered new and more complex patterns of communal organization.

---

52. Quite obviously attention to religious epistemology, while making it possible to chart a major shift in the history of the Dead Sea Scrolls community, has not been able to address the vexed and much-debated question of *when* the Teacher arose within the group (e.g., in the priesthood of Jonathan [152-43 B.C.E.] or during the reign of Alexander Jannaeus [103-76 B.C.E.]). John Collins is certainly correct when he opines that the issue is "likely to remain controversial until either new evidence is found or a trustworthy prophet should arise" ("The Time of the Teacher," 229).

The Wicked Priest Revisited

James C. VanderKam

The Wicked Priest (הכוהן הרשע) is mentioned five times (8.8; 9.9; 11.4; 12.2, 8) in *Pesher Habakkuk*[1] and once in *Pesher Psalms*ª. Since the *Commentary on Habakkuk* was one of the first texts made available, attempts to identify the Wicked Priest began almost as soon as Qumran research started. The most widely adopted solution has been that just one person was the Wicked Priest, and experts early on suggested various candidates: in 1951 Mathias Delcor proposed Alexander Jannaeus,[2] in 1953 Karl Elliger suggested Aristobulus II,[3] and in the same year Geza Vermes offered a detailed defense of the Hasmonean high priest Jonathan as the Wicked Priest.[4] A number of other

---

1. The epithet may have occurred in col. 1.13 (on Hab. 1:4) as the scriptural lemma refers to the wicked one and the righteous one, while the preserved part of the commentary mentions the Teacher of Righteousness. However, one cannot be sure because, while in 4.8-12 (on Hab. 1:13) the lemma again mentions the wicked and righteous, the commentator interprets the righteous one as the Teacher but takes the wicked one to be the Liar. The simple designation הכוהן for the Wicked Priest occurs in 1QpHab 8.16; 9.16; and 11.12. Håkan Bengtsson (*What's in a Name? A Study of Sobriquets in the Pesharim* [Uppsala: Uppsala University, 2000], 52) notes that the uses of "the Priest" are sandwiched between full references to the Wicked Priest (cf. Karl Elliger, *Studien zum Habakuk-Kommentar vom Toten Meer* [BHT 15; Tübingen: Mohr-Siebeck, 1953], 208). The full title also occurs in 4QpIsaᶜ frg. 30, line 3 (the first two letters must be supplied), but so little of the context survives that it will not figure in the present study.

2. See, for example, "Le Midrash d'Habacuc," *RB* 58 (1951): 521-48.

3. *Studien zum Habakuk-Kommentar vom Toten Meer*, 266-74.

4. *Les manuscripts du désert de Juda*, 2d ed. (Paris: Desclée, 1954), 92-100 (the first edi-

scholars came to the conclusion that there was a Wicked Priesthood occupied by at least two individuals. Already in 1950 André Dupont-Sommer had argued for Hyrcanus II and Aristobulus II as the Wicked Priests;[5] and in 1952 William Brownlee held that several priests were meant by the title (especially John Hyrcanus, Aristobulus I, and Alexander Jannaeus).[6] Much later Adam Simon van der Woude was to argue that six high priests were included under the successive uses of the title in *Pesher Habakkuk*, a proposal that became part of the Groningen Hypothesis.[7]

It is understandable that the problem of identifying the Wicked Priest attracted the attention it did because it seemed to offer a relatively firm point in the debates about the time when the scrolls community existed. The Wicked Priest and the Teacher of Righteousness were contemporaries who came into conflict with each other; therefore, fixing the date of one would determine that of the other as well. The Wicked Priest appeared to be the

---

tion appeared in 1953). Vermes notes that he was following a suggestion by H. Bardtke, *Die Handschriftenfund am Toten Meer* (Berlin, 1952), 142. Vermes thought some traits fit Jonathan, some Simon, and that *the Liar* is another epithet for the Wicked Priest. J. T. Milik also advocated Jonathan as the Wicked Priest (e.g., *Ten Years of Discovery in the Wilderness of Judaea* [SBT 26; London: SCM, 1959], 64-87).

5. *Observations sur le Commentaire d'Habacuc découvert près de la Mer Morte* (Communication lue devant l'Académie des Inscriptions et Belles-Lettres le 26 Mai 1950; Paris: Librarie Adrien-Maisonneuve); "Le 'Commentaire d'Habacuc découvert près de la Mer Morte," *RHR* 137 (1950): 162-71.

6. "The Historical Allusions of the Dead Sea Habakkuk Midrash," *BASOR* 126 (1952): 10-20 (he acknowledges that Bo Reicke had earlier identified the Wicked Priest as a superindividual or false priesthood ["Die Ta'amire-Schriften und die Damaskus-Fragmente," *ST* 2 (1949): 608]). Igor R. Tantlevskij ("The Two Wicked Priests in the Qumran Commentary on Habakkuk," *QC* 5 [1995]: Appendix C, 1-2) and Bengtsson (*What's in a Name?* 54-63) survey many publications defending the more than twenty identifications proposed. The hypotheses making New Testament characters into the Wicked Priest are vastly unlikely, since most references to the Wicked Priest come from what appears to be a pre-Christian text. For the AMS dating of 1QpHab, see A. Jull et al., "Radiocarbon Dating of Scrolls and Linen Fragments from the Judean Desert," *Radiocarbon* 37 (1995): 11-19 (1σ 104-43 B.C.E.); for the dates according to the 1997 calibration, see Greg Doudna, "Dating the Scrolls on the Basis of Radiocarbon Analysis," in *The Dead Sea Scrolls after Fifty Years: A Comprehensive Reassessment*, 2 vols., ed. J. VanderKam and P. Flint (Leiden: Brill, 1998, 1999), 1:469: 1σ 88-2 B.C.E.; 2σ 160-148 or 111 B.C.E. [49 B.C.E.]–2 C.E.

7. "Wicked Priest or Wicked Priests? Reflections on the Identification of the Wicked Priest in the Habakkuk Commentary," *JJS* 33 (1982): 349-59. This version of the multiple Wicked Priest theory has received strong criticism — and rightly so — as an implausible reading of the text. See, e.g., Timothy Lim, "The Wicked Priests of the Groningen Hypothesis," *JBL* 112 (1993): 415-25.

more likely candidate for associating with a known historical figure, as the Teacher of Righteousness was proving impossible to identify in a convincing manner. Since the title was probably a polemical play on the official title הכוהן הראש, it seemed likely that the Wicked Priest was a high priest.[8] The inference considerably narrowed the field of candidates from any priest to one of the small group of men who held the supreme position. Moreover, since the Teacher was generally thought not only to have been the founder of the group that went to Qumran but also its leader there, the chronology suggested by the archaeological investigations of the site provided a means for further delimiting the list of high priests who could have been so designated. The site was first occupied not far from 130 B.C.E. according to the conclusion reached by Roland de Vaux;[9] as a result, the Wicked Priest was a high priest who served no later than that time and probably not a long time before it.

As scrolls studies progressed, the candidate suggested by Vermes, Jonathan (152-42 BCE), became widely accepted in the literature, though others continued to attract attention. But in more recent times, the situation in Qumran studies has changed noticeably and now the picture looks rather different. For one, more recent analysis of the still incompletely published archaeological data points toward a later date for the initial sectarian occupation of Khirbet Qumran than the one de Vaux had proposed. Jodi Magness has argued that there is no evidence for de Vaux's period 1a; on the contrary, the site was first reused by sectarians between 100 and 50 B.C.E.[10] If, once all the evidence is available, her dating still stands, then it may have important implications for the time of the Teacher and thus of the Wicked Priest. If the Teacher was the founder of the group that used the Qumran installations and was actually present there, then it becomes chronologically difficult to hold that he was already a prominent leader of the group in the 150s or 140s B.C.E. when Jonathan was the high priest and when the two men

---

8. The suggestion was made by Elliger, *Studien zum Habakuk-Kommentar vom Toten Meer*, 198.

9. De Vaux published preliminary reports after the various seasons of excavation, with the fullest statement eventually appearing in his Schweich lectures of 1959. A French version of the lectures was published in 1961; the revised English version is *Archaeology and the Dead Sea Scrolls: The Schweich Lectures 1959* (London: Oxford University Press, 1973). Some of the earliest identifications of the Wicked Priest, therefore, had little to do with the archaeological evidence, since it was largely unavailable at the time.

10. *The Archaeology of Qumran and the Dead Sea Scrolls* (Studies in the Dead Sea Scrolls and Related Literature; Grand Rapids: Eerdmans, 2002).

opposed each other. Of course, if one does not think the Teacher was ever at Qumran (though his followers were), the chronology is not problematic for the hypothesis that Jonathan was the Wicked Priest.

In addition, several scrolls experts have maintained that the earlier scholars who worked on the problem of identifying the Wicked Priest failed to appreciate the nature of the language the pesharim use to deride leading opponents of the group. The earlier students of the scrolls wrote minutely detailed and impressively thorough treatments of the Wicked Priest passages, but they assumed that the expressions used by the commentator(s) reflected historical reality, when in fact they are often phrased in generic language that was stereotypical for defaming an enemy.[11] As is often the case in the texts found in the caves, the language in the commentary sections of the pesharim is scripturally conditioned; it should not, in the first instance, be assumed to contain historical details about the priest in question. The rhetoric chosen by the expositor may have been selected because it was a standard way in which to vilify someone important. The earlier studies remain valuable in many respects, but that value is hedged by the failure of their authors fully to appreciate the language of the texts for what it is.[12]

Correctly identifying the Wicked Priest remains an important goal, though it may now be more difficult to attain. The method for handling the issue here will be to collect the descriptions of the Wicked Priest in the passages about him, compare the language with scriptural and other samples to test whether it is traditional, and use only what is left after removing the stereotypical or generic items for the purposes of historical identification.[13]

---

11. Some of these earlier studies are Gert Jeremias, *Der Lehrer der Gerechtigkeit* (SUNT 2; Göttingen: Vandenhoeck & Ruprecht, 1963), 36-78; Hartmut Stegemann, *Die Entstehung der Qumrangemeinde* (Bonn: privately printed, 1971), 95-115. Both thought Jonathan was the Wicked Priest. To be fair to them, both Jeremias and Stegemann show some sensitivity to the nature of the language used in the pesharim. Note for example Jeremias, ibid., 73, where he observes that charges against the Wicked Priest could be stereotypical, as the ones against heretics in early Christianity at times were.

12. Bengtsson, *What's in a Name?* 62-63; Rick Van De Water, "The Punishment of the Wicked Priest and the Death of Judas," *DSD* 10 (2003): 395-419.

13. A further methodological issue should be noted. Questions have arisen about whether it is justified to derive historical information about individuals designated by epithets in the pesharim. *Pesher Nahum* proves that the genre could be a vehicle for referring to historical individuals, but the question is how far the evidence permits one to go with titles such as Wicked Priest. Philip R. Davies (*Behind the Essenes: History and Ideology in the Dead Sea Scrolls* [BJS 94; Atlanta: Scholars Press, 1987], 90-92) acknowledged the implication of the names Demetrius and Antiochus, two Seleucid monarchs, in *Pesher Nahum* but cau-

The approach is not foolproof since it may no longer be possible to identify every case of traditional language and, even if a phrase is stereotypical, it may have a historical referent; but the procedure has the advantage of paying attention to and honoring the ways chosen by the commentator(s) to describe an archenemy. I should note up front that I accept the explanation that הכוהן הרשע is a word play on a high-priestly title and that the Wicked Priest was therefore a high priest.

I. Pesher Habakkuk

Almost all of the extant references to the Wicked Priest occur in the *Commentary on Habakkuk* from Cave 1, and all of them are bunched between 8.8 and 12.10. It is worth noting that the places where Habakkuk contrasts the righteous one with a wicked individual (1:4, 13) do not occur in the section in question. The expositor concentrates references to the Wicked Priest in his explanations of Hab. 2:5-17, verses belonging to the Lord's reply (2:2-20) to the prophet's complaint (his second one [see 1:2-4]) regarding how God tolerates the triumph of the wicked over the righteous (1:12-17) and the prophet's announcement that he is waiting at his watch post for an answer (2:1). The deity's response opens with a call for patience and an assurance that the appointed time, the end, will surely come though for the prophet it seems unduly delayed. He states that a vision relating to the future will be

---

tioned: "The way forward at this point seems to be as follows: wherever there is presented as an interpretation of a biblical text information which is not derivable from the text but seems gratuitous, then that information may be regarded as potentially of historical value. At least, it must be regarded as having a basis independent of the biblical text" (p. 92). His approach presupposes that the modern reader can determine what the ancient exegete could and could not derive from the scriptural text. Even if we could distinguish the exegetical from the gratuitous, how would we know that the one is likelier than the other to contain historical information? Timothy Lim (*Pesharim* [Companion to the Qumran Scrolls 3; London/New York: Sheffield Academic Press, 2002], 69-70), although he does not entirely avoid the dubious term *gratuitous*, phrases the matter more satisfactorily: "It is better to consider 'gratuitous' information or textually independent material in the pesherist comment as most probably containing historical data, but not to exclude other material that can also be derived directly or indirectly from the scriptural texts. It is in the nature of pesherite exegesis to read into the scriptural text allusions to contemporary figures and events. To disqualify categorically comments that are related to the biblical lemma is to exclude information that may be potentially significant. Each passage needs to be examined on its own merits for what historical information they can and cannot yield."

given and that Habakkuk is to record it clearly and wait for it to happen. During the time of waiting the righteous person is to remain faithful; the one who is proud will not endure (2:2-4). "Still, the content of the vision itself is not revealed; instead, one finds the description of a third kind of response to life, that of the grasping, arrogant man who trusts in his amassed wealth rather than in God's vision for life. His object of trust will prove far less reliable than the vision Habakkuk is to record."[14] The person intended in the deity's answer might be Nebuchadnezzar.[15]

That arrogant, grasping man brought the Wicked Priest to the pesherist's mind. He understood most of the prophetic text to be describing one person, not a series of individuals with assorted dubious traits. The verses that he did not apply to the Wicked Priest are 2:12-14 and 2:18-20. The second of these units clearly has to do with idolatry; the commentator did not think vv. 18-20 described a fault of the Wicked Priest. Roberts characterizes most of vv. 13-14 as a set of marginal glosses.[16] They are, of course, treated in the pesher because they were in the base text, but they break the flow of the description of the arrogant man. The commentary acknowledges the different nature of the verses by not attaching them to the Wicked Priest. Habakkuk 2:12, which pronounces a woe on the one who builds a city with blood and iniquity (or falsehood), the expositor interprets as condemning the Spouter of Lies, who seems to be a different target of verbal abuse.[17]

The other sections in the pericope relate to the Wicked Priest according to *Pesher Habakkuk*. He is understood to be the arrogant man who amasses wealth from the nations but who loses his unreliable support when they turn against him and take revenge on him for the way in which he has treated them. That is the fundamental portrait of him in the pesher: he is not only a grasping man but also one who had the power to despoil nations and

---

14. J. J. M. Roberts, *Nahum, Habakkuk, and Zephaniah: A Commentary* (Louisville: Westminster John Knox, 1991), 81.

15. Ibid., 117.

16. Ibid., 122-24.

17. At least, this seems a likely conclusion; see Jeremias, *Der Lehrer der Gerechtigkeit*, e.g., 77-89, who showed the Wicked Priest and the Spouter of Lies or the Liar have rather different functions. Others have argued that the Wicked Priest and the Liar were the same (e.g., Vermes, see above). Barbara Thiering, with a different notion of how to read the commentary, also thinks the two are titles for the same person; she considers the abhorred individual to be, not one of the high priests, but a former member of the group who left and became the leader of a rival party ("Once More the Wicked Priest," *JBL* 97 [1978]: 191-205).

one who was finally punished by those nations.[18] The general portrait adds support to the idea that the Wicked Priest was a powerful military leader in addition to being a priest — a combination that rules out any of the pre-Hasmonean high priests.[19] Among the specific traits and actions of this individual as depicted in Habakkuk are:

- He is arrogant (v. 5, developed in vv. 5-8).
- He gets evil gain (v. 9, expanded in vv. 9-11).
- He builds a town with bloodshed (v. 12, expanded in the remainder of v. 12).
- He makes his neighbor drink (v. 15, expanded in vv. 15-17).

The first two and the last of these descriptions, the pesherist claims, apply to the Wicked Priest. His seeming greatness preceded his downfall — a sequence that documents the point of Habakkuk and the interpreter that the evil one is punished even as the righteous person endures faithfully. The fate of the Wicked Priest serves as a word of comfort that Habakkuk's prophecy was being realized in contemporary events.

a. 8.8-13[20]

The lines comment on Hab. 2:5-6 (quoted in 8.3-8) which speak about an insatiable, arrogant person who gathers the peoples to himself; he will become the object of taunts for amassing what does not belong to him. The key term in the lemma is הון, the reading in the commentary (8.3), not the MT's היין. The reference to deceptive wealth then drives several sentences in the interpretation. Also, the commentator reads the word משל as a verb for ruling

---

18. Stegemann (*Die Entstehung der Qumrangemeinde*, 98-100) found three basic motifs in the descriptions of the Wicked Priest in *Pesher Habakkuk* and 4QpPsalms[a]: violent procedures against the Teacher and his group, cultic failings, and God's judgment that hangs over him because of the first two. The first and third, he observed, are shared with the Liar and the group called Manasseh in 4QpNahum. But Stegemann's enumeration misses the all-important theme of plundering the nations, one that is vital for identifying who the Wicked Priest might have been.

19. The adjective רשע appears to be too general in meaning to support Stegemann's suggestion that it should be translated *illegitimate* (*Die Entstehung der Qumrangemeinde*, 109). See also Brownlee, "The Wicked Priest, the Man of Lies, and the Righteous Teacher — the Problem of Identity," *JQR* 73 (1982): 17; Bengtsson, *What's in a Name?* 65.

20. On the passage, see Jeremias, *Der Lehrer der Gerechtigkeit*, 41-42.

rather than as a term for a byword.²¹ Perhaps the participle expressing betrayal (בוגד) in the scriptural text implied for the expositor that there was a time when the person under discussion had not possessed the wealth that led to his corruption. *Betrayal* is also applied to his relationship with God — the Wicked Priest forsook God and his precepts for the sake of wealth. Those from whom he stole his wealth were the men of violence who had also rebelled against God. The priest took wealth from peoples to increase his own wickedness — perhaps a word play involving הון and עון. At this point the writer elaborates on the עון of the Wicked Priest: "heaping sinful iniquity upon himself. And he lived in the ways of abominations amidst every unclean defilement" (8.12-13) — traits that are the opposite of proper priestly characteristics.²²

In this passage, the traits of the Wicked Priest are:

- He was good/truthful until wealth that came to him as a ruler of all Israel deceived him.
- He forsook God for wealth.
- He rebelled against the statutes for wealth.
- He robbed the wealth of violent people who had rebelled against God.
- He took the wealth of nations (עמים) so that he increased his guilt.
- He acted in abominable ways with great impurity.

All of the verbs of which the Wicked Priest is the subject are in the perfect tense or are converted imperfects. This is the case, though in one instance — ישאו — the lemma has an imperfect form. Hence, none of the characteristics attributed to him here are predicted and thus not related to the past. Also, none of the traits, except perhaps his impure actions, is formulated in traditional derogatory language. Bengtsson points especially to

---

21. Stegemann adduced evidence to show that the verb points to exercise of non-kingly political power, not to a priestly function; it is a more general verb for ruling than מלך but, in Qumran parlance, would not be employed for another ruler who was subordinate to a king (*Die Entstehung der Qumrangemeinde*, 101-6). Bilha Nitzan (*Pesher Habakkuk: A Scroll from the Wilderness of Judaea [1QpHab]* [Jerusalem: Bialik Foundation, 1986 (in Hebrew)]), in her impressive section on the Wicked Priest (132-36), who she thinks is Alexander Jannaeus, and in her comment on 1QpHab 8.9-10 (p. 178), makes no mention of the verb used for his rule and its implications. Since Jannaeus was a king, it would be inappropriate to use משל for him.

22. Translations of scrolls come from Geza Vermes, *The Complete Dead Sea Scrolls in English* (New York: Penguin, 1997).

the much discussed אשר נקרא על שם האמת בתחלת עומדו as very likely indicating a historical connection. The language is not stereotypical, and it is difficult to imagine why the pesherist would admit the Wicked Priest was highly regarded at first if this was not the case.²³ Moreover, a priest amassing wealth from nations does not appear to be a generic charge.²⁴

Suspicions could be aroused by the presence here of what may be two of the three nets of Belial mentioned in CD 4:14-19.²⁵ In the *Damascus Document* they are identified as הון, זנות, and טמא המקדש. The reference to wealth in *Pesher Habakkuk* was conditioned by the scriptural lemma, and, while it and impurity are two of the three nets, at least wealth is not imported into the scriptural context as נדת טמאה is. The latter is a scriptural expression and the words are paired in sundry ways in several places (Lev. 18:19; see also Lev. 15:24, 26; Ezek. 36:17); it is also a Qumran phrase.²⁶ Its frequency in the scrolls entails it may be traditional, not shaped to a specific situation, although this is not necessarily so. A priest inevitably was affected by purity concerns, and debates about their intricacies are important in the texts. In addition, interpretation of purity laws was an issue between the community and those in control of the Temple (as in 4QMMT). But *specifically* what is meant by the impurity charge in the pesher is not clear.

b. 8.16–9.2 (or 8.16–9.12)

The passage is a continuation of the preceding one, since the scriptural unit on which it comments (2:7-8) is the direct sequel of the one for the pesher in

---

23. *What's in a Name?* 70.

24. Brownlee ("The Historical Allusions," 12-13) thought the passage referred to John Hyrcanus. It is now difficult to believe, of course, that the sectarians would have thought he began well when he was allied with the Pharisees, their archenemies.

25. There is a series of similarities between CD 4 and this section of *Pesher Habakkuk*. In addition to the nets of Belial in a passage that is called a pesher (CD 4.14), note the occurrence of "ones called of the name" (here a designation for the sons of Zadok [4.3-4]), מעמדם in line 5, and justifying the righteous and condemning the wicked in line 7. Also, the notice about each man standing on his post in 4.11-12 uses one of Habakkuk's words for where he stands awaiting God's answer in Hab. 2:1 (in CD the form מצודו should be read with a *resh*, as is generally recognized). For other similarities between *Pesher Habakkuk* and the *Damascus Document*, see Phillip R. Callaway, *The History of the Qumran Community: An Investigation* (JSPSup 3; Sheffield: JSOT Press, 1988), 146-50.

26. See 1QS 4.10; CD 12.2; 1QM 13.5; 4Q274 1 i 7; 277 1 ii 5, 6; 286 7 ii 4; 381 69, 2 (twice); 511 2 ii 8; cf. 512 1-6, 9; 11Q19 45.10; 48.16-17. For נדה and תועבה together in Qumran texts, see 1QHᵃ 19.11; 4Q511 43, 7.

8.8-13. Also, as there is a re-citation of the first part of Hab. 2:8 in 1QpHab 9.2-4, one could include 9.2-7; and, with the last part of 2:8 forming the basis for the pesher in 9.7-12, a sizable and indeed very instructive unit is formed. All of the biblical statements are again interpreted as referring to the Wicked Priest.

That is, all of them at one level pertain to the Wicked Priest. Whenever he is the subject under consideration, the commentator uses perfect tense verbs or converted imperfects. As we have seen, this was the case in 8.8-13, though the lemma used one imperfect form. In Hab. 2:7-8 (MT) there are three imperfect tense verbs (ישלוך, ויקצו, יקומו) and one converted perfect (והייתה); as the lemma appears in the pesher, all three of the imperfect forms have *vav* prefixed to them so that they may be converted forms, while what appears to be a converted perfect could indeed be one but in the context is more likely to be taken as a past-tense form. In the exposition only past-tense verbs figure.

1QpHab 9.2-7 is especially interesting on this point. It begins with a re-citation of part of Hab. 2:8, and this time the commentator seems to understand the scriptural words as future in meaning: both verbs in the pesher section are imperfect forms. Yet he does not relate the text to the Wicked Priest but to the last priests of Jerusalem. The fact that to this juncture the pesherist has used only past tense verbs for the Wicked Priest should prove helpful in looking at the next passage.

In this lengthy section there is a little more uncertainty than in 8.8-13 because the text is broken near the beginning of the pesher section. It is probable that the Wicked Priest (he is simply *the Priest* here) suffers at the hands of the nations whom he had pillaged, but too little of 9.17 is available to secure the point. The following are said to be traits of the (Wicked) Priest:

- Some group made him suffer.
- The punishments they inflicted on him included:
  - chastisement
  - judgments of wickedness
  - evil diseases
  - physical mistreatment.
- He wronged the Teacher and his group.
- For this God gave him over to his enemies (not identified) who humbled/afflicted him.

While expressions such as "chastisement" and "judgments of wickedness" may be too vague to provide any detail and could be dismissed as clichés, the references to evil diseases and physical mistreatment may be more specific. As noted above, the ones who inflicted various ills on the Wicked Priest may have been the nations whom he had relieved of their loot — the straightforward implication of the lemma, Hab. 2:7-8a. Others have advanced differing interpretations that strongly affect the meaning of and consequences drawn from the passage.

Brownlee thought one should render the scriptural term נשכיך as "ones who bite you" and that these biters should be understood as "angels of pain" (as in 1QS 4.12). The Wicked Priest, then, was handed over to punishing angels — something the pesher would have indicated in the lost section at the bottom of col. 8. Brownlee translated the segment in question: "T[he prophetic meaning of the passage conce]rns the priest who rebelled [and abroga]ted the ordinances of [[God; but He raised up pain-inflicting angels who attac]]ked him in [[order]] to plague him. In recompense for (his) wicked laws and abominable acts, they inflicted evil diseases upon him and vengeful acts on his body of flesh."[27] He regarded the verb ויקיצו as related to the hollow root קוץ, meaning "to be sick" and in the hiphil "to sicken."[28] The scriptural verb as read in the pesher would then have given rise to the reference to "evil diseases" in the commentary. The terms מחלה and נגע are paired elsewhere, and נגע can have the meaning of disease.[29] Van De Water, who approves of Brownlee's inferences, concludes with him that the passage claims "the Wicked Priest has been handed over to the spiritual forces of evil as the agents of his physical suffering."[30]

The argument is burdened by a series of implausible elements. Both in the context of Habakkuk and in the pesher, נשך should have its meaning of "to be a creditor, debtor," since the issue is that the arrogant person has taken wealth from the nations. Those nations, who lost their goods to him, are now going to take their revenge on him. "Biting" is unsuited to the context, and importing "angels of pain" to do the biting and other harmful acts is arbitrary. It is more likely in the context that the subject of עשו in 1QpHab 9.2

---

27. *The Midrash Pesher of Habakkuk: Text, Translation, Exposition with an Introduction* (SBLMS 24; Missoula, Mont.: Scholars Press, 1979), 145. The double brackets indicate restorations that are more uncertain than the ones enclosed in single brackets (see p. vii). In "The Historical Allusions," 13, he presented his view that the passage describes the death of Aristobulus I.

28. Ibid., 146.

29. Ibid., 150-51. It can, of course, also refer to *blows* or *strokes* of various kinds (e.g., 2 Sam. 7:14; DCH 5.611-12).

30. "The Punishment of the Wicked Priest," 409.

is the nations who have suffered at the Wicked Priest's hands. At least no other subjects are mentioned as enemies of the arrogant hoarder in the surviving stretches of text.

Those who object to identifying Jonathan as the Wicked Priest have pointed to the diseases in this passage as a counterargument because there is no indication in 1 Maccabees that Jonathan suffered any diseases during his presumably terrible end (13:12-24).[31] The phrasing of the passage raises the question of what is meant by the "evil diseases" because it is difficult to imagine how the peoples would have punished the Wicked Priest by inflicting sicknesses on him, and bad ones at that. Unless there is a surprisingly early reference to germ warfare here, one could take the lines as using figurative language for punishment (see *Jub.* 23:13 which uses such rhetoric for eschatological woes). The fact that they (that is, the nations) also took vengeance on his flesh makes one think the first two lines in col. 9 are not distinguishing different kinds of punishment but are simply stating forcefully that the nations took a harsh approach to him.[32]

The next segment mentioning the Wicked Priest may cast the first part of col. 9 in a clearer light. 1QpHab 9.8 cites Hab. 2:8b and 9.9-12 contain the pesher. The scriptural words "because of human bloodshed, and violence to the earth, to cities and all who live in them" suggested the Wicked Priest: because of the wrong he did to the Teacher of Righteousness and his group, God gave (past tense) him into the hand of his enemies "that he might be humbled by means of a destroying scourge,[33] in bitterness of soul, because he had done wickedly [past tense] to his Elect." Vermes's "destroying scourge" renders בנגע לכלה, that is, for a second time the term נגע (with a slightly different spelling) appears in this general part of

---

31. See, for instance, Brownlee, "The Wicked Priest," 7-9. As he puts it, "To examine references to the doom of the Wicked Priest . . . is to open a Pandora's box of evil plagues which are fatal to any theory of only a single priest, for they cannot be made to fit a single person, least of all Jonathan" (pp. 7-8).

32. Jeremias (*Der Lehrer der Gerechtigkeit*, 45) thinks the passage indicates he was tortured and probably lost his life in that way. Taking a somewhat different approach, Tantlevskij ("The Two Wicked Priests," 7) writes: "the 'evil diseases' (or, 'pain') inflicted on the Wicked Priest (*ex hypothesi* Jonathan) by his enemies may have been a consequence of the cruel treatment of him in captivity."

33. Brownlee (*The Midrash Pesher of Habakkuk*, 153) has a different translation: "to afflict with blows and to waste away. . . ." Since there is no conjunction before לבלה, that can hardly be the meaning; the context favors taking the word with the preceding בנגע. His translation allowed him to avoid the possible implication of the passage that the blow was mortal (see p. 156).

James C. VanderKam

1QpHab. The wording suggests the blow led to destruction or death — the enemies struck him a mortal blow. Yet, the common reading כלה is, as Brownlee correctly noted, very much in doubt; the first letter of the word looks more like a *bet* than a *kaph*. In the manuscript the scribe does not always distinguish as sharply as one might like between *bet* and *kaph* (see the *bet* in בו in 9.2; the *bet* could be mistaken for a *kaph*), but the letter in question does more nearly resemble *bet* (see the form with *kaph* in 12.5).[34] Hence, the blow under consideration may be one intended "to wear out, consume"[35] — possibly resulting in a meaning similar to the term with *kaph*.[36] In speaking of this passage and the one at the beginning of the column, F. M. Cross wrote: "Regularly the author describes the death in hyperbolic images. The priest is struck down by a divine blow, suffers the pangs of the damned, etc. None of these figures can be made to walk on all fours. In effect, all point to a violent death at the hand of enemies, and we can say little more."[37] Van De Water thinks the enemies in 1QpHab 9.10 are the same as the ones at the beginning of the column ("angels of pain" for him) and that the blow in 9.11 is sickness caused by these angels as in 9.1.[38] The implausibility of the interpretation here rivals that at the beginning of the column. The enemies in 9.10 are indeed very likely to be the same as the ones meting out punishment in 9.1-2, but they are probably the nations of

---

34. A *bet* is read by Nitzan, *Pesher Habakkuk*, 183, and by M. Abegg in *Exegetical Texts*, ed. D. Parry and E. Tov (The Dead Sea Scrolls Reader 2; Leiden: Brill, 2004), 88. Much earlier, Avraham M. Habermann, *The Scrolls from the Judean Desert, edited with Vocalization, Introduction, Notes and Concordance* (Israel [sic]: Machbaroth Lesifruth, 1959), 47 (in Hebrew) had also read a *bet*. Eugene Ulrich, who kindly examined the letter with me, reports that in 1QIsa[b] a lack of rigor in distinguishing *bet* and *kaph* is apparent at times (see his note on col. 22.17 in his forthcoming DJD edition of the scroll); the same seems to be the case in 1QpHab. For an interchange of the two verbs in a biblical verse, see Job 21:13, where the form with *bet* is the *ketiv* and the one with *kaph* is the *qere*.

35. *DCH* 2.176. See Sir. 14:17.

36. Jeremias (*Der Lehrer der Gerechtigkeit*, 46-47) considered the passage extraordinarily important for identifying the Wicked Priest because the number of them tortured to death by their enemies was, of course, not large. He did read the debated word as כלה.

37. *The Ancient Library of Qumran and Modern Biblical Studies* (Westport, Conn.: Greenwood, 1976 [reprint of the 1958 edition]), 108-9, n. 68 = *The Ancient Library of Qumran*, 3rd ed. (Minneapolis: Fortress, 1995), 111, n. 1.

38. "The Punishment of the Wicked Priest," 410-12. He points to some of the curses in Deuteronomy 28 and to Ps. 31:9, 16, but the language in these passages is not the same and the curses in Deuteronomy are inflicted by God himself. The imagery of God handing one to one's enemies is, of course, traditional, but apart from it the Psalms passages offer little help in reading the pesher.

the scriptural text,[39] not angels who are nowhere mentioned in the lemma or commentary.

The subsequent passages that mention the Wicked Priest add little of use to the assortment of evidence for identifying him. A new element in them is that they use future tense forms regarding the Wicked Priest, but they do so in connection with punishments that God will impose on him. As a number of commentators have noted, these appear to be future punishments, not the ones at the hands of the nations described in the preceding passages.[40] A few comments are in order:

c. 9.12-17; 10.1-5

1QpHab 9.16-17 contains the damaged beginning of a pesher on Hab. 2:9-11. Although only the first two letters and the last are visible, the word הכוהן does appear to be the correct reading in 9.16. In this respect the passage parallels the beginning of the pesher in 8.16, where the Wicked Priest is also called simply *the Priest*. The scriptural passage is therefore understood as pointing to the familiar villain, but how far the pesher relating to him extends is unclear since the immediate sequel is lost. When col. 10 picks up, the interpretation of Hab. 2:9-11 is continuing, but line 2 then offers a re-citation of a part of Hab. 2:10. The pesher on it contains four instances of a third-person, masculine-singular suffix without explaining to whom it refers. It is reasonable to think all of them stand for the Wicked Priest, although it is not a necessary conclusion in the case of a re-citation. If, however, one assumes the Wicked Priest is meant, then one has the first instance in *Pesher Habakkuk* in which he appears with future tense verbs. There are also four of these, and in each case God, not the Wicked Priest, is the subject. The clear association between God as subject and future tense verbs with the Wicked Priest as the object has led scholars to conclude that, in addition to the historical abuse the priest suffered at the hands of his enemies, an eschatological judgment by God awaited him. Language such as ובאש גופרית in 10.5 also favors the inference.[41]

---

39. Cf. Elliger, *Studien zum Habakuk-Kommentar vom Toten Meer*, 204-6. Van der Woude ("Wicked Priest or Wicked Priests?" 356) thought the passage is the only one in which Jonathan functions as the Wicked Priest. The earlier sections about the Wicked Priest described first Judas and then Alcimus (353-56).

40. Ibid., 208.

41. E.g., Stegemann, *Die Entstehung der Qumrangemeinde*, 114-15; Van De Water, "The Punishment of the Wicked Priest," 412-14. Jeremias (*Der Lehrer der Gerechtigkeit*, 48-49)

The remaining sections featuring the Wicked Priest supply interesting information about his relations with the Teacher and his followers but say little that can be related to documented historical events and that would thus be pertinent to the quest to identify him.

d. 11.4-8

The commentary on Hab. 2:15 (11.2-3) is a familiar passage in which the Wicked Priest attacks the Teacher of Righteousness and his community on their day of fasting. The passage was, of course, vital in the early determination that the Teacher's group organized their festivals by a calendar that differed from the one used by the Wicked Priest,[42] but for the present purposes the noteworthy item is that in the two instances in which the Wicked Priest is the subject of verbs (11.5, 7), they are perfect tense forms (רדף and הופיע).

e. 11.12-16 (?)

The pesher on Hab. 2:16 (cited in 11.8-11) finds the Wicked Priest adumbrated in the person who was filled with disgrace more than honor. In 11.12 the perfect tense גבר appears, and in line 13 two more past tense forms are used with him as subject. When God functions as subject of a verb in line 15, the form is imperfect (תבלענו). The charge that the Wicked Priest failed to circumcise the foreskin of his heart sounds stereotypical, but the charge about his walking "in the ways of drunkenness" has made some experts think of the High Priest Simon's execution at a banquet where he had become inebriated.[43]

---

thinks "the condemned house" or house of judgment refers to the final judgment and that at that time God will make the Wicked Priest like the nations by judging him among them — an expression of the contempt they felt for him. Van der Woude ("Wicked Priest or Wicked Priests?" 356-57) believed the passage describes Simon but, oddly, did not conclude from the imperfect tenses that he was alive when the commentator wrote — contrary to his argument that imperfects later in the text indicate that the Wicked Priest then (Alexander Jannaeus) was alive when *Pesher Habakkuk* was written.

42. Shemaryahu Talmon, "Yom Hakkippurim in the Habakkuk Scroll," *Bib* 32 (1951): 549-63. For van der Woude, the Wicked Priest here is John Hyrcanus, a conclusion he reached on the basis of de Vaux's dating of phase I*a* at Qumran to his reign ("Wicked Priest or Wicked Priests?" 357).

43. It, too, has a good chance of being a stock charge. See Van De Water, "The Punish-

f. 11.17–12.10

The pattern continues into col. 12. The commentator claims that Hab. 2:17 (quoted in 11.17–12.1) relates to the Wicked Priest, who serves as the subject of two perfect tense verbs in lines 3 and 6 (גמל and זמם). God, however, is the subject of ישופטנו in line 5. The contents of the passage concern the Wicked Priest's relations with community members and cannot be associated with known historical events. When a section of Hab. 2:17 is re-cited in 12.6-7 the expositor again ties the text to the Wicked Priest, against whom he levels charges like those in 1QpHab 8.8-13: he committed (פעל) abominable acts (מעשי תועבות) in Jerusalem, defiled the Temple (ויטמא את מקדש אל), and robbed the possessions (הון) of the community members (12.8-10). The acts of the past may be general accusations; at any rate, they do not help in establishing a historical identification of the Wicked Priest.

II. *Pesher Psalms*ᵃ 3–10 iv 8-10

The single reference to the Wicked Priest in the first copy of *Pesher Psalms* adds little of relevance to the topic at hand, though it is important for perceiving the relations between him and the Teacher of Righteousness. In commenting on Ps. 37:32-33 (cited in iv 7), the interpreter sees the Wicked Priest as the one the Psalm calls simply a wicked person, while the Teacher is the righteous one of the verse. No complete verbal form of which the Wicked Priest is the subject survives in the broken text (apparently the Teacher is the subject of שלח in line 9), but when God is the subject of the verb in line 9 it is imperfect in form. Although little in the battered passage is certain, it may be that the divine punishment of the Wicked Priest *will* be executed by the violent of the nations. God's handling of the Wicked Priest is once more in the future as it is in *Pesher Habakkuk*.[44]

---

ment of the Wicked Priest," 413. Jeremias (*Der Lehrer der Gerechtigkeit*, 58) had made the same point — an example, incidentally, of his sensitivity to the language in the pesher. Van der Woude found Alexander Jannaeus and his excessive drinking in the passage and maintained the future tense verbs showed he was alive when the expositor wrote ("Wicked Priest or Wicked Priests?" 358-59).

44. The first letter of what may be the only other finite verb in line 9 is not preserved, so that one cannot determine its tense. Obviously, as Van De Water points out, the passage should not be used to say the nations made the Wicked Priest suffer in the past ("The Punishment of the Wicked Priest," 415). However, that point was made in 1QpHab 8–9, so that

III. Identifying the Priest

The traits of the Wicked Priest, as the writers of the two pesharim saw him, are numerous and almost all decidedly negative. Many of them are too vague or stereotypical to provide any solid information on the basis of which to identify him when these data are compared with the limited historical information available in 1 Maccabees or elsewhere. The ones that are sufficiently specific, nongeneric, or unexpected are:

- He had a good reputation before he ruled all Israel and became evil.
- He plundered the wealth of other nations, who eventually took their revenge on him in the past.

No text explicitly mentions his death, but 1QpHab 9.1-2 and 9.9-11 are certainly consistent with it and may indeed imply it. As we have seen, the suggestion that sickness is meant in these places has no firm evidence to support

this passage is not necessary for the argument. The tenses of the verbs employed in the Wicked Priest sections have been explained variously. There are 29 finite verbs in all; 23 are past tense forms, the remaining six are future. The Wicked Priest is the subject only of past tense forms (21 of them). The subjects of the other two are the nations (or so it is argued here, 9.2) and God (9.10). God is the subject of all six imperfect-tense verbs (four examples in 10.3-5; 11.15; 12.5). In 1952 Brownlee, who assumed that the interpretations in *Pesher Habakkuk* came from the Teacher (based on his understanding of 7.4-5), proposed that events which occurred before the Teacher's death were expressed in the past tense while events subsequent to it are presented as predictions that he made ("The Historical Allusions," 16). It is apparent, however, that the tenses are mixed in the text and do not follow a sequential order of first past-tense forms and then future ones. Future-tense forms appear in 10.3-5 while past-tense verbs figure not only before this passage but also after it (ten of them), with two future forms mixed in. As we have seen, van der Woude thought the future-tense forms indicated the Wicked Priest was still alive but he applied the principle inconsistently ("Wicked Priest or Wicked Priests?" 356-59). Tantlevskij, while not following van der Woude's theory entirely, thinks there are two Wicked Priests (Jonathan and Alexander Jannaeus [in Hab. 2:16 גם אתה marks the change from one priest to the other, in his opinion — an implausible suggestion]); the imperfect tense forms from 11.15 on show Jannaeus was alive when the commentary was written ("The Two Wicked Priests in the Qumran Commentary on Habakkuk," 2-12; but he thinks 9.12–10.5, where some future forms occur, describes the eschatological destiny of the Wicked Priest). None of these theories is convincing because the authors do not properly distinguish the subjects of the verbs. It is simpler and more consistent with the text to identify a single Wicked Priest who suffered punishment in the past (and God was involved in it as well [9.10]) and will be punished in the future when God again uses the nations for the purpose. Tantlevskij argues that the text, with others found at Qumran, presupposes a resurrection.

it. *Pesher Habakkuk* in a variety of ways says that the nations treated the Wicked Priest in a very rough way, and it may entail that they killed him.

These traits fit Jonathan better than they do any other high priest who ruled in Israel. If one compares them with those reported for the Hasmonean high priests (the only high priests who also ruled over all Israel and controlled an army), one can quickly eliminate several. If משל entails political rule but not that of a king, then one can probably exclude Aristobulus I, Alexander Jannaeus, Hyrcanus II and Aristobulus II, and Antigonus — all of whom are called kings in the sources. It is difficult to know whether the commentator in *Pesher Habakkuk* would have thought some of the Hasmoneans had a good reputation at first, so it is not a helpful criterion. As for plundering nations, Jonathan, Simon, John Hyrcanus, probably Aristobulus I, and Alexander Jannaeus all could qualify; it would be more difficult to claim this trait for Hyrcanus II and Aristobulus II and Antigonus. But the criterion of the nations taking revenge on the ruling high priest does not fit Simon, John Hyrcanus, Aristobulus I, Alexander Jannaeus, or Hyrcanus II. It could apply to Aristobulus II and to Antigonus, who was abused before being executed by the Romans. Jonathan, nevertheless, is the only one who could qualify on all counts.

If this kind of argumentation — combining information from different kinds of sources — is valid, it points to Jonathan as the Wicked Priest and hence to his time as the period when the Teacher was active and influential — so influential that a ruling high priest thought he was worth pursuing and attacking. If so, and if the dating of the earliest sectarian occupation of the Qumran site to 100-50 B.C.E. is correct, it is unlikely the Teacher was at Qumran.

Poetry of the Heavenly Other:
Angelic Praise in the *Songs of the Sabbath Sacrifice*

Eric D. Reymond

Jewish texts of the Second Temple Period and of the early first millennium C.E. characterize Judah/Israel as separate and apart from other nations within a matrix of complementary oppositions and dichotomies. The opposition between humanity and divinity is one of these and is an essential component to Jewish identity of this era. In these texts, God and the angels are represented as fundamentally distinct from humanity through, among other measures, their obscure and sometimes paradoxical expression. Examples of the esoteric angelic idiom, or allusions to it at least, are found in at least two nonbiblical texts: the *Testament of Job* and the *Songs of the Sabbath Sacrifice*, known from the Dead Sea Scrolls.

Relatively early in his career, John Collins addressed the former work, the *Testament of Job*, showing how it can meaningfully be read as a coherent whole.[1] In that text, the daughters of Job are presented in the last chapters as singing in angelic dialects to Job and to those around his death bed. The author of the work (or, of this last portion of it) not only mentions what dialects each daughter sang in but also names the titles of the songs or hymns and then the titles of the extra-textual sources where these poetic texts can be found. As all commentators recognize, the poems and the extra-textual

---

1. J. J. Collins, "Structure and Meaning in the Testament of Job," in *Society of Biblical Literature: 1974 Seminar Papers*, ed. G. MacRae (Cambridge, Mass.: Society of Biblical Literature, 1974), 1:35-52; idem, "Testaments," in *Jewish Writings of the Second Temple Period*, ed. M. E. Stone (Assen: Van Gorcum, 1984), 349-54.

sources in which they were collected never existed; they are, rather, imaginary hymns and books that were invented by the author for the purposes of his narrative. As I have endeavored to demonstrate elsewhere, the naming of the books in which the hymns can (supposedly) be found, the mention of the angelic dialects in which they were written, and the other details of their copying down by Job's brother serve several functions within the narrative: most importantly, they demonstrate the reality of the heavenly world and the daughters' access to it (and, by extension, Job's access to it).[2] The fact that the daughters' texts are not quoted functions, among other things, to underline the Otherness of their poetry, that it is of a character totally different from the more human poems and dirges uttered by other characters within *T. Job*.[3]

Angelic poetry is also of concern in the *Songs of the Sabbath Sacrifice* (4Q400-407, Mas1k, 11Q17) (= *Songs*). As in *T. Job*, in the *Songs* the hymns of the angels are referred to but never fully quoted, and this has an effect similar to that in the pseudepigraphal testament; the absence of the hymns (one possible blessing notwithstanding) underlines the fact that they are completely different from human expressions of praise.[4] In other ways, too, the *Songs* incorporate paradox in descriptions of the angelic hymns.[5] I wish to explore the expression of one of these in the following pages.

---

2. See my article, "Imaginary Texts in Pseudepigraphal Literature: The Angelic Hymns of Job's Daughters in *The Testament of Job*," *Henoch* (forthcoming). As Collins observed in his early work on this text, *T. Job* seeks to assert the reality of the heavenly world ("Structure and Meaning," 44).

3. In addition, the absence of the poems themselves reflects a tension running throughout *T. Job*, where Job has the knowledge to explain certain fundamental mysteries of the world due to his exclusive knowledge, but refuses to do so, or is not inclined to do so.

4. Dale C. Allison suggests that this absence perhaps reflects the belief that it was not possible for the angels' language to be represented "on paper" ("Silence of the Angels: Reflections on the Songs of the Sabbath Sacrifice," *RevQ* 13/49-52 [1988]: 190). Allison connects this absence with the paradoxical references to the angels' "sound of quiet stillness" (4Q405 19ABCD, 7) and "stillness of divine blessing" (4Q405 20-22 ii 13), writing that such references "probably indicate an awareness that the words of this world cannot plumb the depths of the Godhead. Because the divine realm transcends human understanding, its nature cannot be adequately grasped or conveyed by language" (ibid., 194).

5. Aside from the text presented in this paper, consider the paradoxical quiet praise offered to God by the angels (mentioned in passages cited in the note above), and the curious description of the angelic praise in 4Q403 1 i 32-33: "Because in the splendor of praises (is) the glory of his kingdom (מלכותו); in it (i.e., his kingdom) are the praises of all the divine ones, together with the splendor of [his] king[dom] (מלכותו)." One interpretation of this passage is reflected in this more idiomatic rendering: "Because the glory of heaven (is)

The paradoxical expression is found at the end of the sixth Sabbath Song, in 4Q403 1 i 28:

ברוך [ה]אד[ו]ן מל[ך ה]כול מעלה לכול ברכה ות[שבחות]
Blessed be [the] Lo[r]d, ki[ng] of all, (who is) above all blessing and p[raise].[6]

The blessing represents the only possible quotation of angelic words in the *Songs*. The idea that this blessing is uttered by the angels seems to be implied by Newsom's description of the sixth song's structure: "Lines 10-29 [of 4Q403 1 i] contain an account in highly formulaic language of the blessings of the seven chief princes."[7] Ra'anan Abusch is more explicit, writing that the blessing is "the only portion of either of the hymns of song 6 formulated in direct discourse."[8] Similarly, Bilhah Nitzan describes this phrase as pre-

---

within splendorous praise; in it (i.e., heaven) are the praises of all the divine ones, together with the splendor of hea[ven]." If we follow the idiomatic translation offered above and assume the text makes logical sense, it seems that the first clause is asserting that one aspect of heaven is contained implicitly within the praise offered to God, while the next clause insinuates that the heavenly glory within the praise is due to the fact that the angels praise God in heaven. If this interpretation is correct, then the text would seem to suggest that by praising God one experiences something of the heavenly realm.

6. The Hebrew text here and in what follows is based on the readings of Carol A. Newsom, "Shirot 'Olat Hashabbat," in *Qumran Cave 4, VI: Poetic and Liturgical Texts, Part 1*, ed. Esther Eshel et al. (DJD 11; Oxford: Clarendon, 1998), 257. The same author has also presented her transcriptions (as well as translations and commentary) in *Songs of the Sabbath Sacrifice: A Critical Edition* (HSS 27; Atlanta: Scholars Press, 1985) and in *Angelic Liturgy: Songs of the Sabbath Sacrifice* (The Dead Sea Scrolls: Hebrew, Aramaic, and Greek Texts with English Translations 4B; Tübingen: Mohr-Siebeck; Louisville: Westminster John Knox, 1999). Another text (4Q291 1 5-6), although fragmentary, seems to contain a similar phrase: ברוך אתה {אל} [ ]/[מ]עלה לכל ברכ[ה].... See Bilhah Nitzan, "Works Containing Prayers," in *Qumran Cave 4, XX: Poetical and Liturgical Texts, Part 2*, ed. Esther G. Chazon et al. (DJD 29; Oxford: Clarendon, 1999), 10; eadem, "Prayers for Peace in the Dead Sea Scrolls and the Traditional Jewish Liturgy," in *Liturgical Perspectives: Prayer and Poetry in Light of the Dead Sea Scrolls, Proceedings of the Fifth International Symposium of the Orion Center for the Study of the Dead Sea Scrolls and Associated Literature, 19-23 January, 2000*, ed. Esther G. Chazon (Leiden: Brill, 2003), 114.

7. Newsom, *Songs of the Sabbath Sacrifice*, 195. Esther Chazon, citing pp. 195-96 and 206 of Newsom's work, asserts that this is Newsom's interpretation ("Liturgical Communion with the Angels at Qumran," in *Sapiential, Liturgical and Poetical Texts from Qumran: Proceedings of the Third Meeting of the International Organization for Qumran Studies, Oslo 1998, Published in Memory of Maurice Baillet*, ed. Daniel K. Falk et al. [STDJ 35; Leiden: Brill, 2000], 101, n. 19).

8. Ra'anan Abusch, "Sevenfold Hymns in the *Songs of the Sabbath Sacrifice* and the

serving the words of angelic praise.⁹ Philip Alexander expresses the same idea somewhat more cautiously.¹⁰ Daniel Falk and Esther Chazon, on the other hand, believe that the *Songs* contain no quotation of angelic words and argue that the above blessing is uttered by human worshipers.¹¹ But, even if the blessing represents the words of human worshipers, it is clear that it is uttered in the community of angels and that, therefore, it in some way still reflects angelic expression or, at least, what angels can understand.

The blessing would appear to be an adaptation of Neh. 9:5 or a phrase like it.¹² Neh. 9:5 reads:

ויברכו שם כבודך ומרומם על־כל־ברכה ותהלה
May your glorious name be blessed and (may it be) exalted above all blessing and praise.

Considering the differences between the Nehemiah passage and the blessing of 4Q403, one notices that the paradox in the Dead Sea text is amplified and emphasized through (1) its use of the passive participle rather than the impersonal plural construction (which might also be construed with an active meaning: "they blessed");¹³ (2) its direct reference to God rather than to an attribute ("the Lord, king of all" versus "your glorious name"); (3) the ab-

---

Hekhalot Literatures: Formalism, Hierarchy and the Limits of Human Participation," in *The Dead Sea Scrolls as Background to Postbiblical Judaism and Early Christianity: Papers from an International Conference at St. Andrews in 2001*, ed. James R. Davila (STDJ 46; Leiden: Brill, 2003), 235.

9. Bilhah Nitzan, "Harmonic and Mystical Characteristics in Poetic and Liturgical Writings from Qumran," *JQR* 85 (1994): 177, n. 39.

10. He writes: "apart, possibly, from one brief benediction at 4Q403 1 i 28 . . . , we are not given the wording of any of the psalms and blessings which the angels utter" (Philip Alexander, *Mystical Texts* [Library of Second Temple Studies 61; London: T&T Clark International, 2006], 113).

11. Daniel K. Falk, *Daily, Sabbath, and Festival Prayers in the Dead Sea Scrolls* (STDJ 27; Leiden: Brill, 1998), 147-48; and Esther Chazon, "Liturgical Communion with the Angels at Qumran," 101.

12. The affinity between the *Songs'* blessing and that of Neh. 9:5 was first noted by E. Qimron ("A Review Article of *Songs of the Sabbath Sacrifice: A Critical Edition*, by Carol Newsom," *HTR* 79 [1986]: 367-68). Even if the two passages emerged independently, our understanding of the 4Q403 blessing is enhanced by consideration of the biblical text. Note also the recent discovery of a Nehemiah text (Neh. 3:14-15) among the Dead Sea Scrolls (James H. Charlesworth, "Announcing a Dead Sea Scrolls Fragment of Nehemiah," n.p. [cited 17 August 2008]. Online: http://www.ijco.org/?categoryId=28681, and to be published in a forthcoming issue of *Maarav*).

13. On this construction in Hebrew (more common in Aramaic), see GKC §144g.

sence of any conjunction or relative pronoun; (4) its use of a prepositional phrase rather than a participle + prepositional phrase (... מרומם על־כל).[14] The Nehemiah passage, itself, seems to play on more straightforward statements, like that in Ps. 57:6 and 12: "Be exalted, O God, beyond the heavens." In this verse from Psalm 57 (as in Neh. 9:5) the verb רום is modified by the על preposition.[15] Since רום indicates (in its most basic sense) "to be high" and the heavens are a place high above, the statement in Ps. 57:6, 12, although intended figuratively, makes sense in a concrete way and does not seem paradoxical. The Nehemiah text expresses a more abstract idea by (among other things) replacing the location "heavens" with abstract words "blessing and praise."[16] In the Nehemiah text, the על preposition no longer indicates position ("above the sky") but rather suggests, together with מרומם, superiority or "preeminence."[17] The *Songs'* text presents a terser expression and allows a more complex interpretation.

The blessing from 4Q403 does not include the verb רום and relies only on the expanded preposition/adverb מעלה ל to indicate superiority and preeminence. With fewer words, the redundancy between the verb ברך and the noun ברכה is thrown into sharper relief. At the same time, there is less clarity as to what the prepositional phrase is modifying; it might be God, blessing, or an implicit verb.[18]

Due to the fact that the 4Q403 blessing uses the typical *qal* passive participle (and not the comparatively more obscure impersonal plural construction found in Neh. 9:5), the text represents the more usual formula for blessing. This stereotypical blessing, however, is unusual in that it seems to

---

14. It is difficult, of course, to be certain to what degree any writer is influenced by another text. Even if the *Songs'* writer did not think specifically of the passage from Nehemiah when writing the blessing in 4Q403, it seems likely to me that the writer had something like this in mind.

15. The Hebrew reads: רומה על־השמים אלהים.

16. Note that the meaning of ברכה as "praise of God" is unusual; more commonly it indicates the conferring of prosperity or divine favor. Under the definition of "praise," BDB lists only this verse from Nehemiah (though it also has this meaning in Ps. 21:7).

17. See BDB, 755 (sub על, def. II.3) and *DCH*, 6:398 (sub על, def. 29h).

18. A similar syntactic ambiguity is found in another liturgically important biblical passage, Isa. 6:3, where the Hebrew phrase מלא כל־הארץ כבודו is translated in most versions as though "all the earth" is the subject of the verb ("the whole earth is filled with his glory"); nevertheless one could understand "his glory" as the subject just as easily ("his glory fills all the earth"). One should note that the syntactic ambiguity of Isa. 6:3 does not generate ambiguity on the semantic level the same way that the syntactic ambiguity of the blessing of 4Q403 does.

question the relevancy and/or the power of the blessing itself. This is not simply a case of two contradictory assertions being juxtaposed ("God is blessed" and "God is beyond blessing"). Instead, the very function of blessing seems to be undermined. A blessing is a performative utterance, that is, it is "a speech act that, when uttered, alters some state of affairs in the world."[19] Thus, the statement "God is blessed" (when accompanied by a specific context) accomplishes the action of blessing. But, in 4Q403, this speech act is immediately undermined by the following prepositional phrase, or so it would at first appear.[20] Importantly, the blessing is not void or unsuccessful as a speech act; rather, the prepositional phrase, by implying the blessing's lack of effectiveness and worth, means to express the piety of the one blessing or, alternatively, the sincerity with which the blessing is made.[21] This interpretation is relevant whether the prepositional phrase modifies "Lord" or "blessed," though the nuances of the paradox differ for each of these interpretations.

As mentioned above, the syntax of the passage is unclear. The prepositional phrase might modify "Lord," the verb "blessed," or some implicit verb (like "exalted"). Each of these possibilities results in a slightly different translation. The first is implied in the translation offered above, after the text's transcription. The second might be translated: "May the Lord, King of all, be blessed beyond blessing and praise." In this case, we might assume that the writer or speaker (whether human or angelic) intended a comment on his or her own ability in blessing. Paraphrased, the blessing would say: "May the Lord be blessed beyond my (or, our) ability to bless and praise." Alternatively, we might also imagine the author of the blessing intended us to understand a word "exalted," like that which is present in the Nehemiah passage; this results in a translation essentially the same as that for the blessing in Neh. 9:5.

Determining the likelihood of these interpretations depends on our understanding of מעלה and how it functions in the sentence. The word itself, although technically a substantive, מַעַל (to which has been added an adver-

---

19. B. G. Szuchewycz, "Blessings," in *The Encyclopedia of Language and Linguistics*, ed. R. E. Asher, 10 vols. (Oxford: Pergamon, 1994), 1:370-71; repr. in *The Encyclopedia of Language and Linguistics*, ed. E. K. Brown and A. Anderson, 14 vols., 2d ed. (Amsterdam: Elsevier, 2006), 2:71.

20. Although a similar contradiction may be present in Neh. 9:5, it is less obvious there due to that text's more explicit syntax and the fact that the prepositional phrase containing ברכה does not directly modify יברכו.

21. Speech acts are typically not described as true or false, but rather as felicitous or infelicitous, successful or void.

bial *heh*), functions like a preposition when combined with a following *lamedh* preposition.²² This represents an innovation in the Hebrew of the Dead Sea Scrolls since in the Bible מעלה is used exclusively as an adverb and is never followed by another preposition.²³ In biblical Hebrew the word sometimes appears with a preceding *lamedh* preposition (למעלה) and sometimes even with a *lamedh* and *min* preposition (מלמעלה). In these cases, too, the phrases are used as adverbs and are never accompanied by a following *lamedh*. In the Hebrew of the Dead Sea Scrolls, however, these words can also be combined with a following *lamedh* or *min* and be used, themselves, as prepositions.²⁴ These phrases in the Dead Sea Scrolls are used in ways that overlap with the way the shorter preposition על is used in the Bible; that is, these phrases are used in contexts that indicate not only position ("above"), but also in contexts that imply (among other things) comparison and the su-

22. The combination of מעלה with a following *lamedh* preposition occurs in 4Q378 6 ii 5 (4QapocrJoshᵃ), though the text is fragmentary:]מעלה לראשי["above my (or, our) head." See C. A. Newsom, "Apocryphon of Joshua," in *Qumran Cave 4, XVIII: Parabiblical Texts, Part 3*, ed. George Brooke et al. (DJD 22; Oxford: Clarendon, 1996), 248-49. The same phrase occurs in 11Q5 22, 12 (11QPsᵃ), within a poem titled "Apostrophe to Zion" by that text's first editor, James A. Sanders: מעלה לכול תבל. See J. A. Sanders, ed., *The Psalms Scroll of Qumran Cave 11 (11QPsa)* (DJD 4; Oxford: Clarendon, 1965), 86; and James A. Sanders, J. H. Charlesworth, and H. W. L. Rietz, "Non-Masoretic Psalms (4Q88 = 4QPsᶠ, 11Q5 = 11QPsᵃ, 11Q6 = 11QPsᵇ)," in *Pseudepigraphic and Non-Masoretic Psalms and Prayers*, ed. J. H. Charlesworth and H. W. L. Rietz (The Dead Sea Scrolls: Hebrew, Aramaic, and Greek Texts with English Translations 4A; Tübingen: Mohr-Siebeck; Louisville: Westminster John Knox, 1997), 202. Although the editors of another version of the "Apostrophe to Zion" (in 4Q88) maintain that this construction is an error (for either מִמַּעַל or מֵעַל), it seems, rather, that this is a quite legitimate construction in the Hebrew of the Dead Sea Scrolls based on the several examples of מעלה, למעלה, and מלמעלה with a following *lamedh*. See Patrick W. Skehan, Eugene Ulrich, and Peter W. Flint, "Psalms," in *Qumran Cave 4, XI: Psalms to Chronicles*, ed. Eugene Ulrich et al. (DJD 16; Oxford: Clarendon, 2000), 100. The frequency of all of these similar constructions suggests, furthermore, that מעלה is not a *hophal* participle, as some early commentators to 11Q5 22, 12 had asserted (Jean Starky, "Les Psaumes apocryphes de la grotte 4 de Qumrân (4QPsᶠ VII-X)," *RB* 73 [1966]: 363).

23. In only one case in the Bible is מעלה followed immediately by a noun, in Ezra 9:6; in another case it is followed by the compound preposition מֵעַל (2 Chron. 34:4). It is not clear, however, that the adverb is being used together with the compound preposition as one expression; it seems more likely that מעלה is used as an adverb and it is simply juxtaposed to a prepositional phrase with מֵעַל.

24. There are two cases from the Dead Sea Scrolls where למעלה ל functions as a preposition, 4Q216 5, 13 (4QJubᵃ) and 4Q393 3, 6 (4QCommunal Confession), and one sure case where מלמעלה מן functions as a preposition, 11Q19 10:11 (11QTemple) (see *DCH* 5:402-403 [sub מעל, def. 3 and 5]).

periority of one thing over another.²⁵ In this flexibility, these phrases are similar to the compound preposition מֵעַל, which is used in late biblical Hebrew and in the Hebrew of the Dead Sea Scrolls in a wide variety of contexts.²⁶ The phrase ממעל ל, made up of the *min* preposition + substantive מַעַל + *lamedh*, is not so flexible in the Bible or in the Dead Sea Scrolls; in both corpora it primarily appears in contexts related to position and is often translated "above."²⁷ With this information, we may now consider the likelihood of the above interpretations based on precedents from the Bible and the scrolls.

The first interpretation of the blessing, presented under the transcription above, presumes that the prepositional phrase is modifying "Lord" or "King." A similar kind of syntax is found in other passages of the *Songs*, like 4Q405 20-22 ii 8-9:

תבנית כסא מרכבה מברכים ממעל לרקיע הכרובים
[והו]ד רקיע האור ירננו ממתחת מושב

The image of the chariot throne do they bless (which is) above the platform of the *cherubim*. / [And the splendo]ur of the luminous platform do they sing (which is) beneath His glorious seat.²⁸

---

25. The context of superiority is found in 4Q393 3, 6, quoted below.

26. See BDB, 759 (sub עַל, def. IV.2.d and e) and *DCH* 6:398 (sub עַל, def. 29h). The compound preposition מֵעַל is found, for example, in a context associated with pre-eminence in Ps. 108:5 [108:4], which the NRSV translates: "For your steadfast love is higher than the heavens, and your faithfulness reaches to the clouds." The Hebrew reads: כי־גדול מעל־שמים חסדך ועד־שחקים אמתך. *DCH* also list Esth. 3:1. A similar sense to the compound preposition is that of "excess, comparison," cited as definition 29g in *DCH*, found in Qoh. 5:7; Ps. 119:14; and Prov. 14:14. It should also be mentioned that in late biblical Hebrew sometimes the compound preposition is further extended with a following *lamedh* preposition. Although this looks superficially closer to מעלה ל, and although this biblical phrase also overlaps in function with עַל, it is used only in contexts indicating spatial relationships.

27. It might be mentioned in passing that Martin Abegg's *The Dead Sea Scrolls Concordance* (Leiden: Brill, 2003) confuses, in some instances, the compound preposition (מֵעַל) (listed under מִן) and the substantive with preceding *min* preposition (מִמַּעַל) (listed under מַעַל). For example, it lists under the entry מַעַל two instances where the substantive is not preceded by the *min* preposition, 4Q385a 6, 3 and 4Q403 1 i 33; these are, rather, examples of the compound preposition and should be listed under the entry מִן. Similarly, although the same concordance lists five instances of ממעל under the entry מִן (from 4Q317 1+1a ii 28; 4Q403 1 i 44; 4Q404 5, 2; 4Q405 20-22 ii 8; 4Q406 1, 2), they should all be understood as the preposition *min* + the substantive מַעַל and listed under the entry for the adverb מַעַל; listing them under מִן implies the underlying structure *min* + *min* + '*al*, which is perhaps possible due to reanalysis, but less likely than the adverb.

28. Newsom, DJD 11, 345, 347.

Although it is grammatically ambiguous, the most likely interpretation of this passage is that the prepositional phrases (ממעל ל and מתחת) are modifying the preceding nouns, not the preceding verbs.[29] In relation to the 4Q403 blessing, it should also be mentioned that interpreting the prepositional phrase as modifying the preceding noun ("Lord" or "king") presumes a syntax similar to that in the later Kaddish prayer.[30] According to this interpretation of the 4Q403 blessing, the prepositional phrase, on the surface, seems to diminish the worshiper's act of blessing; since God is superior to even his own praise, the human or angelic worshiper who praises God performs an act that seems redundant or superfluous. Curiously, however, this is not the effect of the qualification; rather, by adding that God is "beyond blessing," the worshiper presumably intends to recognize his own humility and inferiority to God.

The second interpretation offered above presumes that the prepositional phrase of the blessing modifies the passive participle ברוך. A precedent for this verb being modified by a prepositional phrase is not hard to find. Consider, for example, Deut. 7:14, in which the preposition *min* (in its comparative sense) complements the participle: "blessed you will be more than all the peoples."[31] These comparative expressions are significant since the interpretation "blessed beyond blessing" in 4Q403 implies a comparison itself. A precedent for ברך being modified by מעלה ל is found only in the similarly phrased blessing from 4Q291 i 5-6.[32] All the same, the semantically similar רום (in the *polal* and *hithpolel* conjugations) is modified by על

---

29. In this passage the cherubim are the subjects of the verbs. Although they are depicted as moving, it seems less redundant to assume that the prepositional phrase that includes mention of the cherubim modifies "throne," not the verb. Furthermore, Newsom has demonstrated that this passage is based on Ezek. 1:26, where the דמות כסא is described in relation to the רקיע (DJD 11, 351).

30. The affinity between the 4Q403 blessing and that of the Kaddish is mentioned by Qimron ("Review Article," 367-68). Note that the Kaddish prayer (in Aramaic) seems in some ways syntactically closer to the blessing in 4Q403 than it does to the blessing in Neh. 9:5. Like the blessing in *Songs*, the blessing in the Kaddish does not contain a relative particle before the prepositional phrase, nor does it contain a conjunction or another predicate like מרומם. It reads: יתברך... שמה די־קדשא בריך הוא לעלא מן־כל־ברכתא; "Blessed . . . be the Name of the Holy One, blessed be He; though he be high above all the blessings. . . ." Translation by Joseph H. Hertz, *The Authorised Daily Prayer Book, Revised Edition* (New York: Bloch, 1960), 236-37.

31. See also Deut. 33:24. It also seems conceivable, from a grammatical standpoint, that Ezek. 3:12 might be interpreted in a similar way, with *min* indicating comparison, rather than a relationship in space.

32. Nitzan, DJD 29, 10. For the phrase, see note 6 above.

and למעלה in both the Bible and in the Dead Sea Scrolls. I have already quoted above Neh. 9:5, in which a prepositional phrase with על modifies רום in the *polal* conjugation. Another example with a similar verbal rection is found in Dan. 11:36,[33] which itself seems to influence a similar phrase among the scrolls that uses למעלה ל, in 4Q393 3, 6 (4QCommunal Confession): ויתרוממו למעלה לכול ("and they exalted themselves above everything").[34] Given these parallels, it does not seem unreasonable that an ancient reader would understand the prepositional phrase as modifying the verb ברוך. The most likely way of understanding this reading of the blessing, it seems to me, is as a wish that God be blessed beyond (the human or angelic capacity) to bless. Here again, the prepositional phrase does not void the preceding blessing; God is still blessed by its utterance. The purpose of adding this complement is not to question the act of praise or blessing, but rather to emphasize the limits on the worshiper's (whether human or angelic) language and knowledge.

The third interpretation offered above presumes the elision of a verb (or predicate), perhaps even the *polal* participle of רום. Such elision of a word in heightened or artistic writing is not that uncommon, especially when the elided verb is a verb of motion.[35] Here, it would result in a translation essentially identical to that of Neh. 9:5: "Blessed is the Lord, king of all, (exalted) above every blessing and praise." As in Neh. 9:5, there seems to be less paradox in this expression, given the fact that the concrete sense of "exalted" is "raised high." Nevertheless, this entire utterance can still be interpreted as paradoxical in the way that it blesses God with words that assert God is greater than his own praise.

Intentionally or not, the author of the *Songs* has produced a blessing that can be interpreted in several different ways. Whichever way one chooses to interpret the blessing's syntax, it still expresses a paradox. As stated above, the prepositional phrase does not void the blessing or render it unsuccessful as a speech act. Curiously, it would seem that qualifying the blessing with a prepositional phrase that on the surface insinuates the blessing's ineffectiveness or its diminished worth actually implies the piety of the worshiper,

---

33. The Hebrew reads: ויתרומם ויתגדל על־כל־אל.

34. This passage is listed in *DCH* as 4QConfess 2.6 (5:402 [sub מעל, def. 3]). The Hebrew transliteration is found in D. Falk, "Works of God and Communal Confession," DJD 29, 53.

35. On the construction, see Bruce K. Waltke and M. O'Connor, *An Introduction to Biblical Hebrew Syntax* (Winona Lake, Ind.: Eisenbrauns, 1990), 224. These authors cite GKC§ 119ee and Dennis Pardee, "The Preposition in Ugaritic," *UF* 8 (1976): 246, 248.

which implication would presumably make the blessing that much more powerful or relevant. In being expressed in this way, the blessing also reveals the more general paradoxical situation confronting both humans and angels in praising and blessing God; God's creations never succeed in sufficiently praising or blessing him, though these same actions represent the acme of their existence.

This paradox is also represented in other, related literature. Both humans and angels are presented in postexilic literature as unable to praise God sufficiently. One example of this is found in the Sirach poem conventionally titled "Hymn to the Creator" (Sir. 42:15–43:33). In that poem, the speaker emphasizes the limited abilities of his own perception and praise and even cites the angels' incapacities at praise (42:17): "(Even) God's holy ones do not (fully) succeed/in recounting all his (i.e., God's) wonders."[36] In some cases, individuals (human and angelic) suggest that they receive the words of praise from God himself, in essence implying that God praises himself (e.g., 1QH^a 9:27-31; *Odes Sol.* 26:8, 10-11; and *Apoc. Abr.* 17:20).[37]

Although the ability of the angels in praising God is never explicitly qualified in the preserved portions of *Songs,* their limits of expression are implied in certain passages, like 4Q400 2, 3: "they recount the splendor of

---

36. See my translation and interpretation of the entire poem in *Innovations in Hebrew Poetry: Parallelism and the Poems of Sirach* (SBLStBL 9; Leiden: Brill, 2004), 60-78.

37. This paradox is mentioned by James L. Kugel in relation to David and medieval scholars' comments on Psalms ("Poets and Prophets: An Overview," in *Poetry and Prophecy: The Beginnings of a Literary Tradition,* ed. James L. Kugel [Ithaca, N.Y.: Cornell University Press, 1990], 10). The various explanations of these medieval scholars are mentioned by Uriel Simon, *Four Approaches to the Book of Psalms: From Saadiah Gaon to Abraham Ibn Ezra,* trans. Lenn J. Schramm (Albany: State University of New York Press, 1991; first published in Hebrew in 1982), 8, 44 n. 15, 189. The text of 1QH^a 9:27-31 can be translated: "You created breath on the tongue, and know its words. You determined the fruits of lips before they were. You set words in verse, so lips' breath flows in a measured way. You elicit verses according to their mysteries, and breath's fluency according to its design, to declare your glory, recount your miracles, with all your honest deeds, your just [verdicts], to praise your name through every mouth of those who know you; according to their insight they bless you forever [and ever.]" In the *Apocalypse of Abraham* (from the first or second century C.E.), an angel is recorded praising God in these words: "Accept my prayer and delight in it, and (accept) also the sacrifice which you yourself made to yourself through me as I searched you" (trans. R. Rubinkiewicz, "Apocalypse of Abraham," in OTP, 1:697). From approximately the same period there emerges another implicit expression of the poet's role as a vehicle for God's words, this from *Odes Sol.* 26:10-11: "Who is (so) at ease concerning the Most High, that he speaks from his own mouth? Who is able to translate the wonders of the Lord? For he who translates melts away, but what (would be) translated survives."

heaven (lit., his kingdom) according to their knowledge."[38] The last words imply limits to the knowledge of the angels, just as the similar phrase in the Hodayot implies the limits of humanity in thanking God.[39] Similar limitations are the subject of another passage, attested (with varying degrees of completeness) in three texts: 4Q402 4, 14-15 = Mas 1 k II, 4-7 = 4Q406 1, 2. Newsom translates the passage in its first occurrence:

> [And there are none among those who have knowledge who] can discern [His wondrous revelations] before [He] ac[ts. And when he acts, (even) the god-like ones cannot comprehend/that which He purposes. For th]ey are [part of His glorious works;] before [even they existed, they were part of His plan.[40]

Here, it is clear that the angels ("those who have knowledge") are part of God's works of creation.[41] They do not exist outside of God's designs. Just as the angels cannot know beforehand what God intends to do because they are pieces of a larger design, so it seems likely that the angels are, for the same reasons, also not able to sufficiently praise or bless God. Furthermore, we might assume that what praise they do offer is dependent on God himself.

The findings of this brief study may now be summarized. This study demonstrates, tangentially, how מעלה (made up of the substantive + adverbial *heh*) in combination with a following *lamedh* preposition (and sometimes also a preceding *lamedh* or *min*), functions as a preposition among the texts of the Dead Sea Scrolls. This represents a development from the biblical

---

38. יספרו הוד מלכותו כדעתם (DJD 11, 187). In her various publications, Newsom offers three different interpretations of the phrase הוד מלכותו: "His royal splendor" (*Songs of the Sabbath Sacrifice*, 111); "His regal majesty" (DJD 11, 188); "the majesty of his kingship" (*Angelic Liturgy*, 21). In conjunction with these translations, she cites comparable phrases from the Bible, הוד מלכות (1 Chron. 29:25) and הדר מלכות (Dan. 11:20) (DJD 11, 189). Much more appropriate, it seems to me, are two passages from Ps. 145:11-12 where the psalmist says: "the glory of your kingdom (כבוד מלכותך) they [i.e., all God's creations] will speak . . . in order to declare . . . the glory of his kingdom's splendor (כבוד הדר מלכותו)." The idea that מלכותו in the *Songs* refers to heaven is further confirmed by the parallel passages to this phrase among the Dead Sea Scrolls that James R. Davila cites, in *Liturgical Works* (Eerdmans Commentaries on the Dead Sea Scrolls; Grand Rapids: Eerdmans, 2000), 125.

39. See 1QHª 9:27-31, quoted in note 37, especially the concluding phrase: "according to their insight they bless you forever [and ever]."

40. Newsom, DJD 11, 229.

41. Newsom cites 1QHª 11:13-14 as a passage where "Those who have knowledge" refers to the angels (DJD 11, 232).

usage where מעלה does not occur with following prepositions and is used exclusively as an adverb. The fact that this complex of related phrases (מלמעלה, למעלה, מעלה) occurs several times throughout the scrolls followed by a *lamedh* preposition, and in each case, used as a preposition, suggests that these were legitimate constructions, not mistakes or errors for ממעל ל.

Perhaps of more interest, this study demonstrates that the blessing from 4Q403 1 i 28, which comes at the end of the sixth Sabbath song, can be interpreted syntactically in one of several ways. Whichever interpretation is followed, the blessing is phrased in what seems to be an intentionally paradoxical way, more so than the similar expression in Neh. 9:5. Both passages play on the semantic overlap between the verb and noun ברך and ברכה, but the blessing of 4Q403 emphasizes this redundancy by limiting itself to one verb (the passive participle), by referring directly to God, and by not using any conjunction that might distance the cognate verb and noun. In addition, the blessing in 4Q403 would seem to undermine its function by asserting that God transcends the speech act itself. In its context, however, this contradiction suggests the piety of the person blessing or the sincerity with which the blessing is uttered. Furthermore, the blessing reflects the paradox facing God's creations (both angels and humans) in blessing God. Nothing about the blessing's expression can prove that it represents the words of angels and not humans. If it does represent an angelic blessing, then it is another example of the way angelic poetry or praise is portrayed as different from normal human language. Even if the blessing represents the words of humans, the paradoxical nature of the phrase presumably intends to convey that these words are uttered among the angels, in a way that angels would understand. Thus, although the *Songs of the Sabbath Sacrifice* is like the pseudepigraphal text *T. Job* in its general reticence to quote angelic words, it finds other ways to suggest the strangeness and otherness of heavenly communication; one of these is through the paradoxical blessing of 4Q403.

"At the Crossroads": Anti-Samaritan Polemic in a Qumran Text about Joseph

Esther Chazon with Yonatan Miller

It is a pleasure and an honor to dedicate this piece to my colleague and friend John Collins on the occasion of his sixty-fifth birthday. One of John's many areas of expertise is biblical interpretation in ancient Judaism, and this was precisely the topic of his seminar, taught with Steven Fraade, in which I participated during my sabbatical at Yale in spring 2007. With this delightful experience and John's contributions to this field in mind, I have chosen to present a case study of biblical use and interpretation for this volume in his honor. In keeping with the theme of this volume, the example that I have selected also shows how this particular use of the Bible is pressed into the service of a tendentious portrayal of "the Other in Second Temple Judaism."

I will focus on the deployment of a unique biblical expression in the narrative introduction to Joseph's prayer in 4Q371-373 (4QNarrative and Poetic Composition[a-c]), formerly called "A Text about Joseph."[1] The question I wish to address is: what of the biblical context is transmitted along with the biblical allusion and to what rhetorical effect? This question is posed against the background of significant developments in the study of biblical allusions in the psalms, hymns and prayers found at Qumran from the pioneering

---

1. Eileen Schuller and Moshe Bernstein, "371-373 4QNarrative and Poetic Composition[a-c]," in *Wadi Daliyeh II: The Samaria Papyri from Wadi Daliyeh and Qumran Cave 4 XXVIII, Miscellanea, Part 2* (DJD 28; Oxford: Clarendon, 2001), 151-204; Eileen Schuller, "4Q372 1: A Text about Joseph," *RevQ* 14 (1989/90): 349-76. This text is also known as 4QApocryphon of Joseph.

work on the *Hodayot* by Bonnie Kittel to the recent monograph by Julie Hughes.[2] My analysis is inspired most immediately by Adele Berlin's work on the lament literature from Qumran, in which she demonstrates how the juxtaposition of biblical allusions in a new composition creates new meanings as well as how the allusions transfer meaning from the biblical context to the new one.[3]

In an earlier exploration of the broad question posed here, I arrived at four criteria that gauge the degree to which a biblical allusion accesses its larger biblical context.[4] These are: (1) the presence of a clearly identifiable quotation from or allusion to a specific biblical passage that establishes a link between the two texts; (2) an additional qualitative or quantitative marker that flags that particular passage and makes it virtually impossible for the biblically acquainted reader/listener to miss it — for example, a rare word, sustained allusion, or long quotation; (3) a concentration of multiple intertextual allusions to the same biblical context that focuses attention on that particular context; and (4) continuity between the new work and its biblical source in matters of genre, content, and/or context. Continuity engages the biblical context and imports it into the new composition not only where the two are harmonious[5] but also where the later work pointedly sets up a dissonance with the biblical context to which it alludes in the service of its own rhetorical aims.[6] The case examined in the present study offers a

---

2. Bonnie Kittel, *The Hymns of Qumran: Translation and Commentary* (SBLDS 50; Chico, Calif.: Scholars Press, 1981), 48-55; Julie A. Hughes, *Scriptural Allusions and Exegesis in the Hodayot* (STDJ 59; Leiden: Brill, 2006), 41-55, and see the literature cited there.

3. Adele Berlin, "Qumran Laments and the Study of Lament Literature," in *Liturgical Perspectives: Prayer and Poetry in Light of the Dead Sea Scrolls, Proceedings of the Fifth International Symposium of the Orion Center, 19-23 January 2000*, ed. E. Chazon (STDJ 48; Leiden: Brill, 2003), 1-17.

4. Esther G. Chazon, "The Use of the Bible as a Key to Meaning in Psalms from Qumran," in *Emanuel: Studies in Hebrew Bible, Septuagint, and Dead Sea Scrolls in Honor of Emanuel Tov*, ed. S. Paul et al. (VTSup 94; Leiden: Brill, 2003), 85-96.

5. An example of harmonious continuity, which I previously termed "continuity of identity," is found in the noncanonical psalm entitled *Tehillah* of the Man of God (4Q381 24 4-12). This *Tehillah* quotes extensively from Psalm 18 (= 2 Samuel 22) and continues that biblical psalm's theme of crying out in distress for deliverance throughout the new psalm, even in the freely composed lines (Chazon, "Use of the Bible as a Key," 86-89, 95-96).

6. Berlin has shown a similar phenomenon in the so-called laments from Qumran, 4Q179 and 4Q501, in which the allusions to the book of Lamentations are conflated with other allusions to different biblical contexts that set up a dissonance with, undercut, and recontextualize the verses from Lamentations thereby producing "poems of (current) alien-

stellar example of such "continuity of dissonance" in addition to meeting the first and second criteria for establishing that the allusion in question accesses its larger biblical context.[7]

The case under consideration is the use of the expression אם הדרכים, "crossroads," in 4QNarrative and Poetic Composition (4Q372 1 9), which clearly relies on and alludes to the biblical phrase אם הדרך in Ezek. 21:26 (MT; English 21:21).[8] The utilization of this singular collocation, a *hapax legomenon* in the Hebrew Bible, functions as a qualitative marker that isolates the quoted verse and links it to the new composition. The singularity of this biblical turn of phrase provides an excellent opportunity to assess the extent of the scriptural context pulled into the new literary work and the concomitant rhetorical effect.

I begin by summarizing the biblical context of the unique expression אם הדרך. Ezekiel 21 relates that the king of Babylon stopped at a crossroads that branched off in two different directions — one to Rabbah of the Ammonites, the other to Jerusalem — at which he performed divinations in order to decide which of the paths to follow in his westward journey (vv. 23-27).[9] Lying in the balance were the conquest of Judah and Jerusalem, the destruction of the Temple, and the deportation of the Jews to Babylon — cataclysmic events brought by God upon the Jewish people because of their misdeeds (vv. 28-29).

The new composition, with its use of the phrase אם הדרכים, summons up this image of the same fateful crossroads and the historical consequences of the Babylonian king's choice of the road to Jerusalem. The latter

---

ation" rather than of mourning for the past destruction and desolation of Jerusalem. For instance, 4Q501 6 conflates Lam. 5:10 and Ps. 119:53 so that the new poem says, "We are physically devastated . . . like the Jerusalemites in Lamentations, not by famine but by wicked people who have abandoned the Torah" (Berlin, "Qumran Laments," 13-14). Similarly, 4Q179 1 ii 9-13 juxtaposes allusions to Lam. 4:1-5 with allusions to the luxurious finery in Ezek. 16:13, 27:24 that turn Lamentation 4's "sympathy (for the impoverished) into a critique of the (fancily-dressed) Jerusalemites (who) had turned away from God while things were still good" (ibid., 7-8).

7. An earlier version of this example was published in my Hebrew article, "Dialogue with Scripture in Hymns and Prayers from Qumran," *Meghillot: Studies in the Dead Sea Scrolls* 1 (2003): 59-70.

8. Schuller, "A Text about Joseph," 359. The plural for "roads" in the Joseph text might reflect the author's interpretation of the single form of the noun in the biblical expression or an already existing scribal gloss like that found in MT (NJPS translation), "at the fork of the road, where two roads branch off." See Schuller and Bernstein, DJD 28, 174.

9. Moshe Greenberg, *Ezekiel 21–37* (AB 22A; New York: Doubleday, 1997), 426-28.

383

image is underscored by the grim depiction of the desolation and destruction of Jerusalem portrayed in the lines that immediately precede the crossroads scene in the Qumran text:[10]

4 עליון ויתנם ב̇יד הגוים ל[ויפץ]
5 אתם בכל הא̇רצות ובכל[הגוים יבזרם ♦   ל̇א יב̇או   [
6 ישראל וישמד אתם מארץ̇[ ]ץ̇[ממקום י̇   ל̇א יניחו להם]
7 הגוים יתֿד̇ עומדת בגי החזון ו[י]ס̇   ציון ויעשו   וישימו את]
8 ירושלי̇ם לעיים ואת הר אלהי לבמות יע̇[ר___
9 וגם יהודה יחד עמו והוא על אם הדרכים י̇עמוד לעׂ̇ן̇ש̇ות

4. the Most High, and he gave them into the hand of the nations l[he scattered]
5. them in all the lands, and among all[the nations he dispersed them   they did not come]
6. Israel. And he destroyed them from the land[ ]Ṣ[from the place of y   ]   the nations[did not leave for them]
7. a peg standing in the valley of the vision and [y]s[Zion and they did   and they made]
8. Jerusalem into ruins and the mountain of my God into wood[ed] heights[.
9. also Judah (was) together with him, and he stood at the crossroads to d[o   ].

The author has strategically placed the unique biblical term for crossroads against the backdrop of the foregoing depiction of devastation. Hanan Eshel contends that this biblical allusion continues the description of the Babylonian exile in the Qumran text in accordance with the original context of Ezekiel 21.[11] I would argue, however, that the author of the new composition exploited the historical context of Ezekiel 21 in order to turn the tables and conjure up a new image of Judah's return from exile on the very same path. The key to the latter interpretation is the reversal of the characters depicted as standing at the same crossroads: in Ezekiel, the king of Babylon stands at the אם הדרך, whereas in the Qumran text it is Judah who stands at the אם הדרכים. Furthermore, in Ezekiel the king sets his eyes on conquering Jerusalem and bringing about the exile of Judah to Babylon,

---

10. All quotations are taken from the most complete manuscript, 4Q372, as published in Schuller and Bernstein, DJD 28, 167-70. Underscoring indicates the overlapping text in 4Q371. For the variants between 4Q371 and 4Q372, the reconstruction of this passage and its additional biblical allusions, notably to Isa. 22:25, Ps. 79:1, and Mic. 3:12 in lines 7-8, see Schuller, "A Text about Joseph," 358-59; Schuller and Bernstein, DJD 28, 173-74. For the identification of the figure who appears with Joseph in line 9, see note 13 below.

11. Hanan Eshel, "The Prayer of Joseph, a Papyrus from Masada, and the Samaritan Temple on ΑΡΓΑΡΙΖΙΝ," *Zion* 56 (1991): 125-36; idem, "The Samaritans in the Persian and Hellenistic Periods: The Origins of Samaritanism" (Ph.D. dissertation, Hebrew University of Jerusalem, 1994), 180-83 (in Hebrew).

whereas the new composition portrays Judah at that same crossroads but in the opposite direction — on the return path from Babylon to the land of Judah and to Jerusalem.[12]

I concur with the interpretation offered by Eileen Schuller and Moshe Bernstein, the editors of 4QNarrative and Poetic Composition[a-c], that the words והוא על אם הדרכים יעמוד, "and he stood at the crossroads" (line 9), not only describe Judah's return to Zion but also serve to accentuate the contrast with Joseph, who is described in the next line (lines 10-11a) in Jeremian exilic language (Jer. 16:13; cf. 22:26-28) as still "cast into lands he did not k[now . . .] among a foreign nation."[13] This contrast is reinforced by the repetition of the last statement as an *inclusio* at the end of the passage (see below). I would add yet one more refinement: the crossroads mentioned that leads either to Rabbah of the Ammonites or to Jerusalem must be situated to the northeast of the former.[14] While in the Qumran text Judah is indeed on a path of return to his land, he nonetheless remains outside of its borders at a location from which he could attest his own — and, more poignantly, Joseph's — presence in Gentile lands, thereby exposing the fallacy of the Sa-

---

12. On this point see also Michael A. Knibb, "A Note on 4Q372 and 4Q390," in *The Scriptures and the Scrolls: Studies in Honour of A. S. van der Woude on the Occasion of His 65th Birthday*, ed. F. García Martínez et al. (VTSup 49; Leiden: Brill, 1992), 164-77 (esp. 168).

13. Schuller and Bernstein, DJD 28, 170-72, 174; Schuller, "A Text about Joseph," 359, 370-76. 4Q372 1 9-11a reads:

⁹וגם יהודה יחד עמו והוא על אם הדרכים יעמוד ל[ע]שות] ¹⁰להיות יחד עם שני אחיו
ובכל זה יוסף מוטל בארצות לא י[ו]דע[¹¹בגוי נא̇כ̇ר ובכל תבל מפצפצים]

⁹also Judah (was) together with him, and he stood at the crossroads to d[o] ¹⁰to be together with his two brothers. And in all this, Joseph was cast into lands he did not k[now] ¹¹among a foreign nation and dispersed in all the world.

Line 9 mentions Judah explicitly, and its third-person masculine-singular independent pronoun apparently refers to him. The two brothers referred to in line 10 are presumably Levi and Benjamin, both of whom are named with Judah in line 14 of this fragment; one of them would be the individual said to be together with Judah at the beginning of line 9.

14. This specific location suits the description in Ezek. 21:24-26, the route of the Babylonian king's journey, and our knowledge of historical crossroads. The reference may plausibly be to one of the crossroads on the King's Highway or *Via Maris* in the vicinity of Damascus. I thank Hanan Eshel for providing information on these routes. See Yohanan Aharoni, *The Land of the Bible: A Historical Geography*, trans. A. F. Rainey (Philadelphia: Westminster, 1979), 45-57; Y. Aharoni et al., *The Carta Bible Atlas* (Jerusalem: Carta, 2002), 123-28. For the various theories regarding the exact location of the crossroads, see Walther Zimmerli, *Ezekiel 1* (Philadelphia: Fortress, 1979), 443.

maritan claim to their Josephite lineage and attendant entitlement to residence in Joseph's lot in the land of Israel.

Most scholars agree that the trenchant pronouncement that "in all this, Joseph was cast into lands he did not k[now]" constitutes a broadside attack against the aforementioned Samaritan claim and is well integrated with other manifestations of a polemic against the Samaritans in this composition, including those in the immediately following lines:[15] "[and fools were dwelling in their land] and making for themselves a high place upon a high mountain[16] to provoke Israel to jealousy . . . and they acted terribly with the words of their mouth to revile against the tent of Zion . . . [and all] words of deceit they spoke to provoke Levi and Judah and Benjamin with their words" (lines 11-14). In addition, the reiteration of the pronouncement that "in all this, Joseph [was given/cast] into the hands of foreigners" (ובכל זה יוסף [נתן] ביד בני נאכר, lines 14-15, compare lines 10-11) at the conclusion of this polemical passage and as the transition from the narrative to Joseph's prayer drives home the message of his continuing exile.[17] It also cues the reader/listener to the fact that Joseph's release from the crushing hand of

---

15. Schuller, "A Text about Joseph," 371-76; Schuller and Bernstein, DJD 28, 170-72; Eshel, "Prayer of Joseph." For an alternative interpretation of the anti-Samaritan polemic that emphasizes the theological importance of the continuing exile of the northern tribes (= Joseph), see Matthew Thiessen, "4Q372 1 and the Continuation of Joseph's Exile," *DSD* 15 (2008): 380-95. See also Ferdinand Dexinger, "Samaritan Origins and the Qumran Texts," in *Methods of Investigation of the Dead Sea Scrolls and the Khirbet Qumran Site: Present Realities and Future Prospects*, ed. M. O. Wise et al. (Annals of the New York Academy of Sciences 722; New York: The New York Academy of Sciences, 1994), 231-49 (esp. 244). A different approach is taken by Robert A. Kugler, who views the lines cited here as additional manifestations of the Qumran community's execration of the "apostate practice of the Jerusalem cult"; see his article "Joseph at Qumran: The Importance of 4Q372 frg. 1 in Extending a Tradition," in *Studies in the Hebrew Bible, Qumran, and the Septuagint Presented to Eugene Ulrich*, ed. P. W. Flint et al. (VTSup 101; Leiden: Brill, 2006), 261-78 (esp. 272-76).

16. The reference is almost certainly to the Samaritan temple; moreover, the present participle, which insinuates that the Samaritan temple is still standing, leads Schuller and Bernstein, DJD 28, 154, 174-75, to assert that "this section must have been written before the attack of John Hyrcanus on Shechem." The words "fools were dwelling (ונבלים ישבים)" are supplied here in the lacuna from the overlapping text, 4Q371 1 10, and are remarkably similar to the derogatory remark against "the foolish nation that dwells in Shechem" in Sir. 50:26 (וגוי נבל הדר בשכם, ms B). For the designation of the Samaritans as "fools" and the strategic position of this slur against them right after Ben Sira's praise of Simon, the great high priest officiating at the Jerusalem Temple, see the article by Matthew Goff in this volume.

17. Furthermore, the polemical language of the narrative in lines 11-14 is repeated in Joseph's prayer itself (lines 19-21) according to Elisha Qimron, "Observations on the Reading of 'A Text about Joseph,'" (4Q372)," *RevQ* 15 (1992): 603-4.

the foreigners and the answer to his prayer for deliverance will only be secured in an appointed time in the future, designated by the pregnant language, "until the time of the end for him" (עד עת קץ לו).[18]

The foregoing analysis of the crossroads scene in 4QNarrative and Poetic Composition[a-c] has demonstrated how this text bolstered its anti-Samaritan polemic through its clever invocation of the *hapax legomenon* אם הדרך alongside other biblical allusions. This unique biblical collocation pulls along with it the prophetic context of the fateful crossroads on the road from Babylon to Judah and its destructive consequences, but the transposition of the figure standing at the crossroads and the reversal of the direction of travel create a dissonance with the biblical context that serves the polemical, anti-Samaritan message of this new composition discovered at Qumran. This test case thus provides a fine example of a particularly sophisticated type of allusive continuity with the biblical context: it is a continuity that, at one and the same time, both invokes the biblical context and turns it on its head in order to serve the new agenda of the new composition. This allusive strategy is highly suited to inner-religious disputes between groups laying claim to the same authoritative text and effectively casts the reviled, fraternal group as the Other. As seen in the case of the Joseph narrative and prayer, it is a potent weapon in the arsenal of the polemic against the Samaritans.

---

18. See Dan. 8:17; 11:35; 12:4; Schuller and Bernstein, DJD 28, 176.

PART FIVE

JEWS AMONG GREEKS AND ROMANS

Romans, Jews, and Christians on the Names of the Jews

Martin Goodman

It is a curious fact that by the end of the Second Temple period Jews had inherited from their shared biblical tradition a number of different ways to refer to their nation. They, and others, could describe the people as Jews (using *yehud* and related words, such as *yehudim, ioudaioi* [in Greek], *iudaei* [in Latin], or as Hebrews *[ivri, hebraios, hebraeus])*, or as Israel *(yisrael, Israelites)*. What, if anything, was the significance of a choice to use one name rather than another?

The question has been asked before, and a variety of answers proposed. "Israel" may sometimes be an archaizing name in contrast to "Jew," used for contemporaries. "Israel" may be an insider term, "Jew" the name used by outsiders. "Israel" may be prescriptive — the name of the ideal nation — in contrast to "Jew," which describes the nation as it actually is. "Israel" may refer to the nation as a religious community, "Judeans" to their location or geographical origins. "Jews" may be defined as an ethnic or political group, "Hebrews" as the users of a distinctive language.[1] It is not my

---

1. For previous general discussions, see J. Juster, *Les Juifs dans l'Empire Romain*, vol. 1 (Paris: Paul Geuther, 1914), 172-76; S. Zeitlin, "The Names Hebrew, Jew and Israel," *JQR* 44 (1953): 365-79; A. Arazy, "The Appellations of the Jews" (Ph.D. dissertation, New York University, 1977); P. J. Tomson, "The Names Israel and Jew," *Bijdragen* 41 (1986): 120-40; G. Harvey, *The True Israel* (Leiden: Brill, 1996); D. Goodblatt, "From Judaeans to Israel: Names of Jewish States in Antiquity," *JSJ* 29 (1998): 1-36; Shaye J. D. Cohen, *The Beginnings of Jewishness* (Berkeley: University of California Press, 1999), chapter 3; D. Goodblatt, *Elements of Ancient Jewish Nationalism* (New York and Cambridge: Cambridge University Press,

intention to take issue with these interpretations, which are not mutually exclusive. Each of them can indeed help to explain the usage of particular texts. But (as many of these earlier studies recognize) it is important to avoid ascribing essential meanings to words, since words derive their meanings from the context in which they are used,[2] and the specific issue on which I shall concentrate is the shifting connotations of the names used to refer to the Jews during the first two centuries C.E., when Jews came into violent and disastrous conflict with the Roman state.

It is a familiar fact that the overtones of equivalent names for Jews in European languages have undergone considerable change over the past two centuries. For English Jews to refer to themselves as "Hebrews," as they did with pride in the nineteenth century, would now sound odd. French Jews now think of themselves as *juifs* rather than *Israelites*. There has been a comparable shift in Italian, from *ebrei* to *giudei*. It is worth noting that even in Hebrew there could be uncertainty in more recent years: the name to be given to the modern State of Israel was decided only at 11 p.m. on 12 May 1948 by the committee convened to deal with crucial issues on the last days before the declaration of independence on 14 May.[3] Changes in meaning can be rapid: in contemporary usage names used to refer to minority groups can often become politically incorrect at remarkable speed (and what was politically incorrect can become socially acceptable). It is thus at least a reasonable hypothesis that there might have been a similar shift in the connotations of names used to refer to the Jews in reaction to the destruction of the Temple in Jerusalem in 70 C.E. and the marginalization of the Jews in the Roman world which was a product of that catastrophe.[4] The specific usages I shall seek to explain are the consistent use of *iudaei* or *ioudaioi* by the Roman state to refer to the Jews, and their lack of use of the term "Israel" in any

---

2006). I hope that this new study may seem an appropriate tribute to John Collins, whose scholarship has so greatly enriched our knowledge of the complex nature of Jewish self-understanding in the Hellenistic and Roman worlds.

2. Note the classic study by James Barr, *The Semantics of Biblical Language* (London: Oxford University Press, 1961).

3. On uncertainty over the name of the modern state, see Z. Sharef, *Three Days* (London: W. H. Allen, 1962), 128, 123 (name decided after debate between "Israel" and "Zion"); D. Kurzman, *Ben Gurion: Prophet of Fire* (New York: Simon and Schuster, 1984), 22-23 (rejection of Judea); B. C. I. Ravid, in S. Ravidowicz, *Studies in Jewish Thought* (Philadelphia: Jewish Publication Society of America, 1974), 34, 410 (on Ravidovicz's opposition to "Israel" for the state).

4. M. Goodman, *Rome and Jerusalem: The Clash of Ancient Civilizations* (London: Allen Lane, 2007), chapter 12.

form, in contrast to the lack of use of any term related to "Jew" by the Jewish rebel states in 66-70 and 132-135 C.E. when they referred to themselves; and I shall suggest, albeit tentatively, that the unwillingness of Gentile Christians after 135 C.E. to allow the name of the Jews to be applied to them, despite their appropriation to themselves of the ancient history of the Jews, may be related to this usage by the Roman state.[5]

It will be best to begin by noting the sheer variety of names for the Jews found in ancient sources between 200 B.C.E. and 300 C.E., and the quite distinctive patterns which emerge from different contexts and sources. Both Hasmonean and Herodian rulers in Jerusalem referred consistently to their subjects as "Jews" *(yehudim, ioudaioi, iudaei)*. Hasmonean coins bore the legend *hever haYehudim*,[6] and the Hasmoneans seem never to have called their people "Israel" — the hypothesis that this usage reflected adoption by the dynasty of a Gentile Greek perspective[7] is not impossible, but it may be simpler to explain the name of the Hasmonean kingdom as a continuation of the name of the Persian province of Yehud.[8] According to Josephus, Herod in 40 B.C.E. was made by the Romans "king of *ioudaioi*";[9] whether it is significant that his grandson Agrippa I was made king of Judea (the place) rather than *iudaei* (the people) is uncertain,[10] but that neither Herod nor his descendants referred to their realm as "Israel" seems clear. The usage of Philo, contemporary of Agrippa I, is in contrast. Philo does indeed use *ioudaios* and *Ioudaia* to denote the people and the place,[11] but he makes curiously little use of what might have seemed his quite suggestive allegorical meaning of "Judah" as "confession of praise to the Lord,"[12] whereas "Israel," meaning "he who sees God," is used both to refer to Jews as a people and as the ideal to which all, including pious non-Jews, should aspire.[13] Philo is aware of the term *ebraios*, particularly as a descriptor of Abraham, but de-

---

5. Goodman, *Rome and Jerusalem*, chapter 13, gives this argument in a much more general form.

6. Y. Meshorer, *A Treasury of Jewish Coins from the Persian Period to Bar Kokhba* (Jerusalem: Yad ben Zvi Press, 2001).

7. Tomson, "The Names Israel and Jew."

8. For a fine discussion, ending with cautious agnosticism, see Goodblatt, *Elements*, 140-59.

9. Josephus, *J.W.* 1.282.

10. Goodblatt, *Elements*, 160-65.

11. Philo, *Legatio ad Gaium* 200-201.

12. Philo, *De Plantatione* 134; cf. Harvey, *True Israel*, 43-46.

13. See Philo, *Legum Allegoriarum* 4; in general E. Birnbaum, *The Place of Judaism in Philo's Thought* (Atlanta: Scholars Press, 1996).

spite the attractions of allegory ("Hebrew" means "migrant," hence one who progresses from sense perception to mind), Philo uses the term only rarely.[14]

The dates of composition of the sectarian scrolls from Qumran span (at least) the Hasmonean and Herodian periods. They use both *Yehudah* and *Yisrael* quite frequently to refer both to all Jews and to the sect (including those who sin), but the use of *yehudim* is rare.[15] The Roman state (as I have remarked above) uses only names related to Judea to denote Jews, apparently without variation in different media.[16] Rather more variation is to be found in non-official pagan writings of all kinds. The names *ioudaios* and *iudaei* are indeed frequent, and, as in usage by the state, "Israel" appears unused,[17] but curious is the increasing use of *hebraios* and *hebraeus* from the last quarter of the first century C.E.[18] It is noteworthy that many of these authors — such as the Greeks Plutarch, Ptolemy Chennus, Charax of Pergamum, and the Latin writer Tacitus — had some connection with the city of Rome in this period, and that Statius, also writing in Rome under the Flavians, seems to have been the first Latin writer to call Jews *hebraei*. It is tempting to explain this development as a reaction to the arrival after the fall of Jerusalem in 70 into the city of Rome, which had long sheltered a Greek-speaking Jewish population, of a large influx of Jewish slaves who spoke Hebrew (or Aramaic) or perhaps pronounced Greek with a markedly "Hebrew" accent.[19]

No word related either to "Jew" or to "Hebrew" seems ever to have been adopted by the rebel Jewish states of 66-70 and 132-135 C.E.[20] The rebels preferred "Israel" as a self-designation, opting occasionally also for "Jerusalem" and rarely (on bronze coins of the second year of the rebellious state of 66-70 C.E.) for "Zion."[21] The hypothesis that the rebels wished thereby to

14. Philo, *De Migratione Abrahami* 20.
15. Harvey, *True Israel*, chapters 3 and 10.
16. See, for example, F. W. Madden, *History of Jewish Coinage* (London: no publisher recorded, 1864), chapter 8, on the Roman coinage after 70 C.E.
17. M. Stern, *Greek and Latin Authors on Jews and Judaism*, 3 vols. (Jerusalem: The Israel Academy of Sciences and Humanities, 1974-84).
18. Stern, *Greek and Latin Authors*, 2:161.
19. Cf. also E. J. Bickerman, *Studies in Jewish and Christian History*, vol. 2 (Leiden: Brill, 2007), 1015, on "Hebrew" in Pausanias as the name of the inhabitants of Palestine, where the language is spoken.
20. For an excellent discussion of the terminology used by these states, see now Goodblatt, *Elements*, chapters 5-7.
21. On the many difficulties involved in interpreting the Zion coins, see D. Goodblatt, "Ancient *Zionism*? The Zion Coins of the First Revolt and Their Background," *International*

distance themselves from the earlier Jewish states of the Hasmoneans and Herodians is attractive, but in light of the Roman state terminology just noted a desire to signify a clear break from the colonial power may provide a better explanation: it is worth noting, for instance, that the rebel coinage shows considerable continuity with (in particular) the design and types of Hasmonean coins (including the use of paleo-Hebrew script), whereas it is, apparently deliberately, strikingly dissimilar to Roman coins (in contrast to rebel coinage produced elsewhere in the empire, which tended to mimic imperial issues, presumably as a way to reassure those who used it that it could safely be treated as of comparable value).[22]

In light of this marked contrast between the terminology of the Jewish rebels and that used by Romans, the choices made by Josephus, who had himself participated as a rebel leader but was writing about the revolt for Romans in Rome, take on a greater significance. In much of his writings *ioudaioi* is of course standard, hence his own references to the revolt as "the Jewish war,"[23] and he explains the name in the *Antiquities* as the standard term, derived from the tribe of Judah, by which Jews have been known "from the time when they went up from Babylon."[24] Josephus uses *hebraios* to refer to the language and territory of the Jews, and (quite frequently in the first ten books of the *Antiquities*) to the Jews in biblical times, but he also (unusually) designates himself as a *hebraios* when he introduces himself to his readers in the preface to the *Jewish War*.[25] Such usage would be familiar, or at least make sense, to his Roman readers. Josephus refers often to "Israel" and "Israelite" in his paraphrase of the biblical narrative in the first half of the *Antiquities*, but he never uses such terminology for Jews of his own day, and he does not seem to make references of any kind to "Zion." The terminology adopted by the rebels is totally ignored. In the case of Josephus, who must have known the propaganda of the Jewish state in which he had been a

---

Rennert Guest Lecture Series 8 (2001): 1-36; U. Rappoport, "Who Minted the Jewish War's Coins?" *INR* 2 (2007): 103-16, who argues that the bronze Zion coins were minted by Simon bar Giora's party and present a specifically messianic and nationalistic message quite separate from the messages of the silver coinages minted by the Temple authorities.

22. M. Goodman, "Coinage and Identity: The Jewish Evidence," in *Coinage and Identity in the Roman Province*, ed. C. Howgego, V. Heuchert, and A. Burnett (Oxford: Oxford University Press, 2005), 163-66.

23. See in general P. Bilde, *Flavius Josephus between Jerusalem and Rome: His Life, His Works, and Their Importance* (Sheffield: Sheffield Academic Press, 1988), 71-73.

24. Josephus, *Ant.* 11.173.

25. Josephus, *J.W.* 1.3 (but note that this designation is not found in all manuscripts); cf. Harvey, *True Israel*, 124-29.

leader, such silence was surely deliberate.²⁶ Whether the same is also true of the other diaspora Jews whose names for their people are preserved on inscriptions is much more difficult to ascertain; in the epigraphic record, "Jew" is the most common designation, "Hebrew" is more common in Rome than elsewhere, and "Israel" is very rare indeed,²⁷ but the inscriptions are spread over so long a period, and many are so hard to identify securely as Jewish or to date, that it is difficult to come to any very clear conclusions about their significance.²⁸ It is, however, worth contrasting the standard use of *Yisrael* in tannaitic texts, and the rarity in such texts of *yehudi* and *ivri*, both of which are confined to legal formulae.²⁹

In Christian writings the standard term used to refer to Jews is *ioudaioi* or *iudaei*. In writings firmly dated to before 70 C.E. (essentially, the Pauline epistles), the word "Jew" has no negative overtones, but after 70 C.E. some Christians literature, such as the Gospel of John,³⁰ is intensely hostile to the *ioudaioi*, and after 135 C.E. it can confidently be asserted that the name "Jew" in most Gentile Christian texts "defines the other,"³¹ although the danger of circular argument has to be faced: alongside the numerous Christian texts which use the name "Jew" as either neutral or a term of abuse are a few, such as the *Clementine Recognitions* and *Apostolic Constitutions*, which imply that to be a real Jew is to be pious (that is a Christian),³² and it may only be with hindsight that such "Jewish Christian" texts are commonly treated as outside the mainstream³³ (although the incompatibility of such positive images of Jews with the negative image to be found in a writer such as Justin Martyr, whose writings were to become mainstream in due course, is not in doubt).³⁴

---

26. For Josephus's avoidance of the term "Zion" as deliberate, see Goodblatt, *Elements*, 187-89, 202.

27. See the indices to D. Noy, *Jewish Inscriptions of Western Europe*, 2 vols. (Cambridge: Cambridge University Press, 1993-95).

28. R. Kraemer, "On the Meaning of the Term 'Jew' in Greco-Roman Inscriptions," *HTR* 82 (1989): 35-53.

29. S. Stern, *Jewish Identity in Early Rabbinic Writings* (Leiden: Brill, 1994).

30. On the term *ioudaioi* in the Gospel of John, see J. Ashton, "The Identity and Function of the *Ioudaioi* in the Fourth Gospel," *Novum Testamentum* 27 (1985): 40-75.

31. J. M. Lieu, *Image and Reality: The Jews in the World of the Christians in the Second Century* (Edinburgh: T&T Clark, 1996).

32. *Clementine Recognitions* 5.34; *Apostolic Constitutions* 2.60.3; cf. J. Juster, *Les Juifs dans l'Empire romain* (1914), vol. 1, p. 260, note.

33. On the difficult notion of "Jewish Christianity," see J. M. Lieu, *Christian Identity in the Jewish and Graeco-Roman World* (Oxford: Oxford University Press, 2004), 3.

34. Lieu, *Image and Reality*, 136-40, 177-82.

The pattern of other terminology for Jews in early Christian texts is more complex. Paul called himself polemically both "Hebrew" and "Israelite" when asserting his Jewishness,[35] and both terms continued to be used occasionally to refer to non-Christian Jews in Christian literature after 70 C.E., although "Hebrews" generally seems to refer primarily to language use,[36] and the lack of any terminology for the Jews (just "them," compared to "us") in the *Epistle of Barnabas* may reflect unease about which terminology to use.[37] In light of the appropriation of "Hebrews" and (especially) "Israel" by some Gentile Christians in the second century (see below), continuing references to non-Christian Jews under this name in second-century Christian texts referring to ancient biblical history[38] or, as in Melito, *Peri Pascha*, to the Gospel narratives of Christ's passion, read strangely: "An unprecedented murder has occurred in the middle of Jerusalem, the city of the law, in the city of the Hebrews, in the city of prophets, in the city accounted just.... This man has been murdered! And where was he murdered? In the heart of Jerusalem. By whom? By Israel."[39]

Any lack of clarity in the names used by Christians in the first two centuries to refer to Jews may be explained in part both by the vagaries of the specific local tensions which gave rise to much early Christian literature (I do not wish to minimize the crucial role of the social and religious self-definition of local church communities in the separation of Christianity from Judaism[40]) and by the vagueness among Christians about how best to refer to themselves: the nomen *Christianum* seems to have been an outsiders' term and only rarely used in internal Christian literature before the end of the second century despite its value in the declarations of martyrs as portrayed in martyr acts.[41] But also significant was the adoption by Gentile Christians for themselves of some of the names which had been used for Jews. This was not a usage imposed on Christians from outside. It is true that Christian writings sometimes portray the Roman state as treating Christians in the first generations as types of Jews. Acts portrays Paul and Silas at

---

35. 2 Cor. 11:22; Phil. 3:5.

36. Cf. Acts 6:1, on *Hebraioi* in Jerusalem.

37. J. Carleton Paget, *The Epistle of Barnabas: Outlook and Background* (Tübingen: Mohr-Siebeck, 1994), 41, 52.

38. Justin, *First Apology* 53.

39. Melito, *Peri Pascha* 505-8, 693-95.

40. For my view on the complex issue of the "parting of the ways," see M. Goodman, *Judaism in the Roman World: Collected Essays* (Leiden: Brill, 2007), chapter 15.

41. Cf. J. M. Lieu, *Christian Identity*, 250-59.

Philippi being accused of being "Jews ... advocating customs which it is illegal for us Romans to adopt and follow,"[42] but in reporting the accusation against Christians of responsibility for the fire in Rome in 64 C.E. neither Tacitus nor Suetonius called Christianity a type of Judaism. On the contrary, it was a *superstitio* specifically denigrated because it was new.[43] It is possible that the distinction between Christians and Jews had in fact been less clear in the time of Nero, and that this clear separation had come about only by the time Tacitus and Suetonius were writing, in the early second century. Neither the younger Pliny (in his discussion of the trials of Christians)[44] nor Roman governors as portrayed in Christian martyr acts[45] ever refer to Christians as Jews of any kind, and it is possible that the nonpayment of the special tax to the *fiscus Judaicus* imposed on all Jews (but not on Gentile Christians) after 70 C.E. helped to clarify the distinction in the eyes of the state.[46] This was the case not least because Jews (who paid the tax) could evidently avoid punishment if accused of nonparticipation in pagan sacrificial worship, whereas Gentile Christians evidently could not. Pagan authors know that the movement of the Christians started in Judea[47] and that they worship the same God as the Jews,[48] but they were in no danger of confusing the two groups.[49]

What about Christians themselves? For Christians to define their faith as the true Judaism was not obviously impossible, and the author of Revelation in the late first century seems to imply that a true Jew is someone with right belief, and therefore a Christian: "And unto the angel of the church in Smyrna write: 'These things says the first and the last, which was dead, and is alive: I know your works, and tribulation, and poverty (but you are rich), and I know the blasphemy of them which say they are Jews, and are not, but are the synagogue of Satan.'"[50] But by the time of Tertullian in the early third

---

42. Acts 16:19-23.

43. Tacitus, *Annals* 15.44.2-8; Suetonius, *Nero* 16.

44. Pliny, *Epistles* 10.96.

45. H. A. Musurillo, *The Acts of the Christian Martyrs* (Oxford: Clarendon Press, 1972).

46. M. Goodman, "Nerva, the *Fiscus Judaicus* and Jewish Identity," *JRS* 79 (1989): 41-44.

47. Tacitus, *Annals* 15.44.3.

48. Celsus, in Origen, *Contra Celsum* 5.59.

49. Note that Julian, *Contra Galilaeos*, 253A, was writing as an apostate Christian when he noted that "the Galileans [i.e., Christians] say that, though they are different from the Jews, they are still, precisely speaking, Israelites in accordance with their prophets."

50. Rev. 2:8-9.

century, Judaism could be described by at least some Christians as the religion they had left behind:

> But having asserted that our religion is supported by the writings of the Jews, the oldest which exist, though it is generally known, and we fully admit that it dates from a comparatively recent period — no further back indeed than the reign of Tiberius — a question may perhaps be raised on this ground about its standing, as if it were hiding something of its presumption under shadow of an illustrious religion, one which has at any rate undoubted allowance of the law, or because, apart from the question of age, we neither accord with the Jews in their peculiarities in regard to food, nor in their sacred days, nor even in their well-known bodily sign, *nor in the possession of a common name, which surely ought to be the case if we did homage to the same God as they.* . . . But we are neither ashamed of Christ . . . nor do we differ from the Jews concerning God![51]

Instead, Christians portrayed themselves as the true Israel. Already in the writings of Paul the claim seems to be found that the followers of Christ Jesus are the "Israel of God,"[52] and the notion was picked up later in the first century in *1 Clement*,[53] but it appears most explicitly as a polemical assertion against Jewish claims to be Israel in the report of the dialogue of Justin Martyr with the Jew Trypho:

> "What, then?" says Trypho, "are you Israel? And speaks He [God] such things of you?" "If, indeed," I replied to him, "we had not entered into a lengthy discussion on these topics, I might have doubted whether you asked this question in ignorance; but since we have brought the matter to a conclusion by demonstration and with your assent, I do not believe that you are ignorant of what I have just said, or desire again mere contention, but that you are urging me to exhibit the same proof to these men." And in compliance with your assent expressed in his eyes, I continued. . . .[54]

There are not to be found in Christian texts of the second and third centuries as many explicit assertions that the Church is the True Israel as one

---

51. Tertullian, *Apology* 21.2.
52. Gal. 6:15-16.
53. 1 Clement 29.1-2.
54. Justin Martyr, *Dialogue with Trypho the Jew* 123.9.

might have expected from the title of the justly celebrated book by Marcel Simon,[55] but the notion had become sufficiently commonplace by the end of the second century for Clement of Alexandria to adopt Philo's etymology for "Israel" ("he who sees God") when describing Christians for pagan readers.[56]

What are the implications of all this for the parting of the ways between Judaism and Christianity? Christian self-definition had encouraged separation of Gentile Christians from Jews already in the first century, and by the second century some texts expressing hostility to Jews from those times, such as the Gospel of John, had become authoritative within some Christian communities. As a result it is probable that the main audiences at which Gentile Christian writings were aimed in the second century were other Christians or pagans rather than non-Christian Jews, although it is an interesting question whether this was true also for Justin Martyr's *Dialogue with Trypho*. By the mid-second century, for any Christians just to ignore the relationship of the Church to Judaism had become difficult, not because of anything Jews did or thought but because of the immensely influential doctrine asserted by the Christian "heretic" Marcion that Christ, as the Savior God, had nothing in common with the wicked Creator God of the Jews.[57] The reaction to Marcion, an assertion by what became the Christian mainstream of the continuity of the Church with the Jewish past, was further encouraged by the need to claim antique origins, and hence respectability, in a pagan world which viewed new religious movements as suspect simply on the grounds of their novelty.[58] On the other hand, some in that pagan world, and especially in the city of Rome where Marcion preached and opposition to him was most necessary, would be unimpressed by any movement that laid claim to the name of the Jews, which was seen as so hostile to the Roman state that after 135 C.E. even the name "Judea" had been stripped from the Jewish homeland.[59]

The danger that hostility directed at Jews might also be directed at Christians was real enough. As Tertullian noted, the slur in his day that Christians worship an ass's head had been derived by pagans from the accu-

---

55. M. Simon, *Verus Israel: Study of the Relations between Christians and Jews in the Roman Empire (135-425)* (Oxford: Littman Library, 1986).

56. Clement of Alexandria *Paedeia* 1.7; *Stromata* 1.5; cf. also Origen, *De Principiis* 3.8.

57. On Marcion, see still A. Harnack, *Marcion: Das Evangelium von fremden Gott*, 2d ed. (Leipzig: Hinrichs, 1924).

58. See in general M. Beard, J. North, and S. Price, *Religions of Rome*, 2 vols. (Cambridge: Cambridge University Press, 1998), 1:226.

59. W. Eck, "The Bar Kokhba Revolt: The Roman Point of View," *JRS* 89 (1999): 89.

sation by Tacitus that Jews worship an ass, because "Christianity is nearly allied to Judaism."[60] It was therefore a great advantage for Christians that they could adopt ancient biblical history back to the time of Abraham without advertising to the pagan world that this had anything whatever to do with the Jews, because the name "Israel," even though it had been used by the Jewish rebels as the name of their state both in 66-70 and in 132-135, apparently meant nothing whatever to pagan Greeks and Romans until it began to be proclaimed by Christians as theirs. It is perhaps a separate question, and one less susceptible to a satisfactory answer, whether, impelled either by an apologetic desire to protect themselves against accusations by pagans of hostility to others,[61] or a missionary impulse to win over pagans to the faith,[62] Christians did not just reflect the general denigration of Jews in the Roman world after 135 C.E. but manipulated it in order to distance their own communities from the odium heaped upon the Jews.[63]

---

60. Tertullian, *Apology* 16.

61. On Christian apologetic in these centuries, see the contributions by Tessa Rajak, Frances Young, Simon Price, and Mark Edwards in *Apologetics in the Roman Empire: Pagans, Jews and Christians,* ed. M. Edwards, M. Goodman, and S. Price (Oxford: Oxford University Press, 1999), chapters 4, 5, 6, and 9.

62. On the (not very extensive) evidence for Christian mission in this period, see M. Goodman, *Mission and Conversion: Proselytizing in the Religious History of the Roman Empire* (Oxford: Clarendon Press, 1994), chapter 5.

63. So Goodman, *Rome and Jerusalem,* 583.

Jews and Greeks as Philosophers: A Challenge to Otherness

Erich S. Gruen

Identification of the Gentile as the Other has a long record in Jewish history. The biblical narrative reinforces the idea with regularity. Israelite identity goes hand in hand with demonizing the foe. Canaanites are stigmatized from the start in the tale of Noah's drunkenness and nakedness, culminating in a mighty curse upon his grandson Canaan (innocent though he be in the story) as one doomed to be the lowliest slave to his brothers (Gen. 9:18-27). Application of the curse plainly foreshadowed and legitimized the eventual Israelite conquest of Canaanite land, rendering its people the quintessential Other.[1] Moabites and Ammonites suffered similar stigma. Deuteronomy forbids those nations from entering the congregation of the Lord forever. Edomites and Egyptians are slightly better off. Their ban extends only to the third generation (Deut. 23:4-9). The blemish, however, endured. The *War Scroll* from Qumran brands the Edomites, Moabites, Ammonites, and Philistines as enemies of Israel (1QM 1:1-2). One need hardly mention the condemnation of exogamous marriages with Canaanites, Ammonites, Moabites, and others in Ezra-Nehemiah (Ezra 10:1-2; Neh. 10:29-31; 13:1-3, 23-30). Resistance to commingling with the alien appears repeatedly in Second Temple texts like *Jubilees*, the *Testament of Levi*, the *Testament of Job*,

---

1. On Canaanites as the Other, see R. L. Cohn, "Before Israel: The Canaanites as Other in Biblical Tradition," in *The Other in Jewish Thought and History*, ed. L. Silberstein and R. L. Cohn (New York: New York University Press, 1994), 74-90. See now also the essay by Katell Berthelot in Part One of this volume.

Jews and Greeks as Philosophers

Tobit, and *Joseph and Asenath*. It constitutes a standard motif.[2] And it became enshrined in the celebrated prayer of thanksgiving in the Mishnah: "Thank you, O Lord, for not making me a slave, for not making me a woman — and for not making me a goy!"

That is not, however, the whole story. The Hellenistic period witnessed a far more complex and ambivalent relationship between Jews and Gentiles (first and foremost, Greeks) than conventional dualities would suggest. Scholarship in the past generation has moved beyond the simplistic bifurcation of "Judaism" and "Hellenism," recognizing that, while distinctions still mattered, they were fuzzier and more tangled than previously assumed. Scholars have in recent years increasingly questioned the dichotomy and challenged the very notion of a *Kulturkampf*. John Collins, of course, has been a central figure in this scholarly shift.[3] The idea that Jews could have regarded Greeks as the Other at a time when they were enmeshed in Hellenic culture and part of the society of Hellenisitic cities seems singularly off the mark.

Jews and Greeks did indeed view each other through their own peculiar lenses. But they did not do so with the presupposition that the object of their gaze was an alien people whose idiosyncratic characteristics served only to set off and underscore the distinctiveness of the superior culture. Quite the contrary. A noteworthy and fascinating instance of this deserves exploration: the interest that both peoples exhibited in the concept of philosophy. The issue here is not that of the influence of Greek philosophy upon Jewish thinking. That subject has had extensive treatment and, at least along broad lines, is uncontroversial. That Hellenic philosophical tenets made their way into Jewish writings from Qohelet to Philo does not need to be argued here. A rather different topic claims attention: the reciprocal set of perceptions (or constructs) in which Greeks understood Jews as philosophers and Jews viewed Greek philosophers as dependent on Jewish lore. This double lens, however distorted its refractions, seriously complicates the concept of Otherness.

---

2. See, e.g., the articles collected in Silberstein and Cohn, *The Other in Jewish Thought and History*. Also E. Benbessa and J.-C. Attias, *The Jew and the Other* (Ithaca, N.Y.: Cornell University Press, 2004); cf. R. M. Schwartz, *The Curse of Cain* (Chicago: Chicago University Press, 1997), 120-42. A more balanced statement can be found in F. Spina, *The Faith of the Outsider: Exclusion and Inclusion in the Biblical Story* (Grand Rapids: Eerdmans, 2005), 1-13.

3. See especially John J. Collins, *Between Athens and Jerusalem: Jewish Identity in the Hellenistic Diaspora*, 2d ed. (Grand Rapids: Eerdmans, 2000); idem, *Jewish Cult and Hellenistic Culture: Essays on the Jewish Encounter with Hellenism and Roman Rule* (Leiden: Brill, 2005). See also the review of scholarship, stemming from the classic work of Hengel, by J. K. Aitken, "Review Essay on Hengel, *Judaism and Hellenism*," *JBL* 123 (2004): 331-41.

Erich S. Gruen

I. Greek Authors on Jews as Philosophers

Theophrastus

A fragment of Theophrastus, the most celebrated pupil of Aristotle and his successor as head of the Peripatetics, demands notice in this connection. Writing as he did in the late fourth and early third century, Theophrastus belongs to the very beginning of the Hellenistic period and is thus unlikely to have had much (if any) acquaintance with Jews, their customs, or their principles. And his comments on Jewish sacrificial practices reflect that lack of comprehension. The fragment comes from Theophrastus's *Peri Eusebeias,* as transmitted by Porphyry, and reflects his hostility to the institution of animal sacrifice. Jews are mentioned in this connection as a people among the Syrians who sacrifice animals in a way repellent to Greeks, for they do not eat the victims but burn them whole, pouring honey and wine upon them so that the deed is finished quickly and at night lest this terrible thing be witnessed under the sun. And they proceed to fast on intervening days. Theophrastus goes on to claim that Jews were the first to conduct human as well as animal sacrifices.[4]

A puzzling passage. Just what it was that Theophrastus found objectionable in nighttime holocausts remains obscure. Holocausts were not uncommon in antiquity and were often done at night. References to honey, wine, refraining from meat, and fasting evidently derive from erroneous or confused information. As for human sacrifice, Theophrastus is more concerned to excuse than to condemn: the Jews did this, according to him, out of compulsion rather than zeal. Nor does he suggest even that they maintain this practice in his own day.

The segment has given rise to tortured and ingenious interpretations. Most of them focus on the question of whether Theophrastus had a positive or a negative impression of Jews.[5] That issue has occupied too much scholarly energy. It is not likely to be resolved, it appears irrelevant to Theophrastus's

---

4. Porphyry, *De Abstinentia,* 2.26 = M. Stern, *Greek and Latin Authors on Jews and Judaism,* vol. 1 (Jerusalem: Israel Academy of Sciences & Humanities, 1974), 10.

5. E.g., Stern, *Greek and Latin Authors,* 1:8; J. Mélèze-Modrzejewski, "L'Image du Juif dans la pensée grecque vers 300 avant notre ère," in *Greece and Rome in Eretz Israel,* ed. A. Kasher et al. (Jerusalem: Yad Izhak Ben-Zvi, 1990), 107-10; L. H. Feldman, *Jew and Gentile in the Ancient World* (Princeton: Princeton University Press, 1993), 7-8, 203-4; B. Bar-Kochva, *The Image of the Jews in Greek Literature: The Hellenistic Period* (Berkeley: University of California Press, 2009).

Jews and Greeks as Philosophers

objectives, and it bears only marginally on our purpose. The passage demonstrates little more than that the author retailed misinformation, had only marginal familiarity with Judaism, and was prepared to embrace unreliable reports. Ignorance rather than ideology seems paramount.

More to the point are Theophrastus's remarks elsewhere in that fragment. He calls the Jews "a nation of philosophers" who converse with one another about God, gaze at the stars and speculate about them, and summon the divinity through their prayers.[6] Here again Theophrastus's knowledge of the Jews has distinct limitations. The description as star-gazers appears to equate them with astrologers, an attribution that he would not have drawn from a knowledgeable source. That they discuss God among themselves and call upon him with prayers suggests priestly responsibilities, as if all Jews were priests, a characterization that could hardly be based on serious research. Theophrastus relied on surmise and inference rather than trustworthy authorities (or perhaps any authorities).

That does not, however, render the surmise any less significant. How did Theophrastus reach the conclusion that Jews were a nation of philosophers? A number of possibilities have been proposed, none of them exclusive of the others. Perhaps Theophrastus knew of Jews as monotheists and inferred that those who speculated about a solitary divinity must be philosophers by nature.[7] Or he was impressed by Jewish aniconism, which he associated with a strong Greek philosophical tradition rejecting anthropomorphic representations of the divinity.[8] Or he reckoned Jews as a philosophic caste within the Syrians.[9] Or he confused the priestly class in Judea with the people as a whole.[10] Embrace of any of these propositions has to come with considerable caution. Nothing in the passage alludes to monotheism or aniconism.

---

6. Porphyry, *De Abstinentia*, 2.26 = Stern, *Greek and Latin Authors*, 1:10: ἅτε φιλόσοφοι τὸ γένος ὄντες, περὶ τοῦ θείου μὲν ἀλλήλοις λαλοῦσι, τῆς δὲ νυκτὸς τῶν ἄστρων ποιοῦνται τὴν θεωρίαν, βλέποντες εἰς αὐτὰ καὶ διὰ τῶν εὐχῶν θεοκλυτοῦντες.

7. W. Jaeger, "Greeks and Jews: The First Greek Records of Jewish Religion and Civilization," *Journal of Religion* 18 (1938): 131-34; Stern, *Greek and Latin Authors*, 1:11; E. Gabba, "The Growth of Anti-Judaism or the Greek Attitude Towards the Jews," in *The Cambridge History of Judaism*, vol. 2, *The Hellenistic Age*, ed. W. D. Davies and L. Finkelstein (Cambridge: Cambridge University Press, 1989), 619; Mélèze-Modrzejewski, "L'Image du Juif," 107-8.

8. M. L. Satlow, "Theophrastus's Jewish Philosophers," *JJS* 59 (2008): 15-19.

9. So J. Bernays, *Theophrastos' Schrift über Frömmigkeit* (Berlin, 1866), 111, in the classic work on Theophrastus. Similarly Stern, *Greek and Latin Authors*, 1:10; Feldman, *Jew and Gentile*, 525; Bar-Kochva, *Image of the Jews*, who prefers the term "community" to "caste".

10. Satlow, "Theophrastus's Jewish Philosophers," 13-14.

The denotation of the Jews as a people of the Syrians refers to their sacrificial customs, not to their philosophic character.[11] And the conclusion that Theophrastus might have conflated Jewish priests with Jews as a whole, turning them into philosophers as well, is hardly an obvious one. The root of Theophrastus's tangled description cannot be recovered. On any reckoning, however, he regarded Jews as a nation of philosophers, a people whose conception of divinity involved them in rational discussions among themselves, thus plainly seeing them in the light of Greek philosophical tradition. It is pointless and immaterial to argue about whether this puts Theophrastus into the camp of those who viewed Jews positively.[12] In all probability, he, like his younger contemporaries Clearchus and Megasthenes (see below), viewed them as among Eastern nations whose wise men presided over practices and beliefs that seemed akin to Greek philosophical inquiry. Later Hellenic writers regularly cast legendary or semi-legendary religious figures of the East together in comparative schemata. Moses thus found his place with Orpheus, Musaeus, Amphiarius, the Magi in Persia, and the gymnosophists in India.[13] Theophrastus may have been among the first to set Jews on a plane with other Eastern nations to whom Greek writers imputed an "oriental wisdom" that they found to resonate with Greek philosophy.

Clearchus of Soli

A fragment from yet another pupil of Aristotle belongs in this category. Clearchus, from the Cyprian city of Soli, produced a work (now lost) entitled *On Sleep*, from which Josephus quoted a choice item.[14] The Jewish historian

---

11. Bar-Kochva, *Image of the Jews*, combines these and has Theophrastus regard the Jews as a community of philosopher-priests among the Syrians.

12. Bar-Kochva, *Image of the Jews*, maintains that the identification of Jews as philosophers does not outweigh the critical character of his comments on their sacrificial practices. Satlow, "Theophrastus's Jewish Philosophers," 1-2, rightly questions the value of categorizing Greek thinkers in terms of their supposedly positive or negative opinions of Jews.

13. See, e.g., Strabo, 16.2.39; cf. 16.1.68, 16.1.70. Cf. H. Lewy, "Aristotle and the Jewish Sage According to Clearchus of Soli," *HTR* 31 (1938): 216-21; A. Momigliano, *Alien Wisdom: The Limits of Hellenization* (Cambridge: Cambridge University Press, 1975), 85-86; Gabba, "Growth of Anti-Judaism," 618-24; Feldman, *Jew and Gentile*, 7-9. In the view of Satlow, "Theophrastus's Jewish Philosophers," 10-11, Greeks blurred the line between Eastern philosophers and ritual experts.

14. On Clearchus's work and career, the evidence is assembled by F. Wehrli, *Die Schule des Aristoteles*, Vol. III: *Klearchos* (Basel: Schwabe, 1948). See also the discussions by Lewy,

utilizes the passage as part of his lengthy argument that Greek writers knew of Jews from an early period and found much to admire. Clearchus's text (or Josephus's extract from it) served this purpose very conveniently.[15] Clearchus described a chance encounter in Asia Minor between his master Aristotle and an unnamed Jew from Coele-Syria. He puts the narrative into the mouth of Aristotle, although the tale itself may have been a concoction of the pupil.[16] Whether fictitious or not, it offers a striking instance of a Greek intellectual's depiction of a learned Jew. According to the anecdote, the man mightily impressed Aristotle. He admired in particular the man's remarkable endurance and self-restraint. He describes him as a Jew τὸ γένος from Coele-Syria.[17] The Jews, evidently unfamiliar to Clearchus's presumed readership, then receive a fuller description. They are descendants of philosophers in India, men called Calanoi by the Indians but Jews by the Syrians. This particular individual, so notes Clearchus in the voice of Aristotle, was a frequent guest among many Greeks in Asia on his visits from the highlands to the coastal places, for he was Greek not only in his speech but in his very soul.[18] When he encountered Aristotle and other scholars in Asia, he tested their wisdom and, in view of his having dwelled with many people of παιδεία, he was rather able to impart something of his own.[19] "Aristotle" went on to recount in detail the Jew's great and astounding endurance and the self-restraint he exhibited in the conduct of his life, but Josephus chose not to repeat all of that, encouraging his readers to look up Clearchus's book themselves.[20] Such is the account.

"Aristotle and the Jewish Sage," 205-35, and now, most importantly, Bar-Kochva, *Image of the Jews*.

15. Josephus, *Ag. Ap.* 1.176-83; cf. Clement of Alexandria, *Stromateis* 1.15.70.2.

16. Whether the anecdote is historical has properly been doubted by Jaeger, "Greeks and Jews," 130-31; Bar-Kochva, *Image of the Jews*.

17. Josephus, *Ag. Ap.* 1.179. The term τὸ γένος, employed twice by Clearchus and also by Theophrastus in reference to Jews as philosophers τὸ γένος, does not readily lend itself to precise translation. Here it appears to mean something like "by origin." So Bar-Kochva, *Image of the Jews*; J. M. G. Barclay, *Flavius Josephus: Translation and Commentary*, vol. 10: *Against Apion* (Leiden: Brill, 2007), 104, prefers "by ancestry" or "by descent." But since Clearchus proceeds to speak of Jews as descendants of Indian philosophers, this seems inappropriate. Satlow, "Theophrastus's Jewish Philosophers," 13-14, chooses "race" for Clearchus but leans toward "caste" for Theophrastus, which would be a highly unusual rendering.

18. Josephus, *Ag. Ap.* 1.180: Ἑλληνικὸς ἦν οὐ τῇ διαλέκτῳ μόνον, ἀλλὰ καὶ τῇ ψυχῇ.

19. Josephus, *Ag. Ap.* 1.181: ἐντυγχάνει ἡμῖν τε καί τισιν ἑτέροις τῶν σχολαστικῶν πειρώμενος αὐτῶν τῆς σοφίας. ὡς δὲ πολλοῖς τῶν ἐν παιδείᾳ συνῳκείωτο, παρεδίδου τι μᾶλλον ὧν εἶχεν. On the meaning of μᾶλλον here, not "more" but "rather," see Barclay, *Against Apion*, 105; Bar-Kochva, *Image of the Jews*.

20. Just why Josephus elected to omit the rest has been the subject of much fruitless

Here again, the question of whether Clearchus sought to deliver a favorable assessment of Jews misses the point. He had his own agenda. And his portrait plainly imposes an *interpretatio Graeca*. For Clearchus, the skills of the cultivated Jew came not from being steeped in biblical texts but from his time spent in the company of numerous learned Greeks, the men of παιδεία. The esteem felt for him expresses itself as praise for his Greekness. The ability to hold his own in philosophical dialogue exhibited the Hellenic soul. The "Greek" qualities serve as the measuring rod. Nevertheless, characterization of the Jew in those terms is a telling fact. Clearchus elevates him by making him a philosopher.[21]

But more than "Greekness" is involved here. Clearchus has Aristotle bring in Indian wise men. And not incidentally. He introduces Jews themselves as a people descended from philosophers in India. Indeed they are philosophers in their own right, called Jews among Syrians on a par with those called Calanoi among Indians.[22] Clearchus evidently reckons Jews as a philosophic sect. They hold that place among Syrians, as Calanoi do among Indians. Confusion, as well as invention, permeates this text. Calanoi, as such, do not exist. Clearchus has simply and erroneously extrapolated from the figure of Calanus, the celebrated Indian gymnosophist noted for his sparring with Alexander the Great.[23] But the connections he evokes are significant. Clearchus elsewhere in his corpus claims that Indian gymnosophists descended from Persian *magi*. And others conjectured that Jews themselves had *magi* as ancestors.[24] As the philosophic elite of Persia, *magi* stood with Chaldeans in Babylon, and gymnosophists in India.[25] Clearchus placed the

---

speculation. For Stern (*Greek and Latin Authors*, 1:52) Josephus did not have access to Clearchus's text but only a later compilation that included parts of it. Bar-Kochva, *Image of the Jews*, suggests that, by ascribing the virtues of καρτερία and σωφροσύνη to the Jews, he really transferred to them characteristics of the Indian gymnosophists, the principal focus of his attention, and Josephus omitted the details because he recognized them as inapplicable to Jews. The idea is ingenious but implausible. Josephus was not averse to ascribing καρτερία and σωφροσύνη to Jews; *Ag. Ap.* 2.146, 2.170; see Barclay, *Against Apion*, 106.

21. Nothing in the text supports the interpretation of Bar-Kochva, *Image of the Jews*, that praise for the Jew signified only surprise that a member of a "barbarian" nation had managed to acquire Greek speech and learning.

22. Josephus, *Ag. Ap.* 1.179: οὗτοι δ' εἰσιν ἀπόγονοι τῶν ἐν Ἰνδοῖς φιλοσόφων, καλοῦνται δέ, ὥς φασιν, οἱ φιλόσοφοι παρὰ μὲν Ἰνδοῖς Καλανοί, παρὰ δὲ Σύροις Ἰουδαῖοι.

23. On Calanus, see Arrian, *Anabasis* 7.2-3; Strabo, 15.1.61-68; Plutarch, *Alexander* 65, 69.

24. Diogenes Laertius 1.9.

25. Diogenes Laertius 1.1; Clement of Alexandria, *Strom.* 1.15.71.4.

Jews in that category. These speculative fantasies, however remote from reality, offer insight into what passed as plausible perceptions of Jews in the early Hellenistic period. They belonged to the wise men of the East. Characterization as philosophers allowed them to combine Eastern wisdom with Hellenic παιδεία. The associations counted for more than any Otherness.

Megasthenes

The notion of Jews as philosophers certainly went beyond the school of Aristotle. The erudite Megasthenes served as envoy of Seleucus I at the court of the Indian ruler Chandragupta on one or more occasions and dwelled in India for a number of years, whether on several visits or an extended one. At some point, perhaps in the 290s, he composed a major study of that land and its people, the *Indica,* cited and quoted by several later Greek and Roman writers, evidently a classic work on the subject. Only one preserved fragment refers to the Jews, but it is a most intriguing one, particularly in light of the comments of Theophrastus and Clearchus, his slightly earlier but near contemporaries. The passage appears in the *Stromateis* of Clement of Alexandria who was eager to find parallels between Greek philosophy and Eastern learning, and thereby to establish that Hellenic precepts were derivative from the older wisdom of the east. To that end Clement quotes Megasthenes as witness to the antiquity of Jewish philosophy, its priority to and influence over the Greeks. In the segment quoted, Megasthenes asserted that everything said about nature by the ancient Greeks can also be found among those outside Greece who philosophize, some of the views held by the Brahmans in India, some by those called Jews in Syria.[26]

The passage is often misconstrued. It does not show that Megasthenes himself gave priority to Jewish learning (or to Indian learning) over that of the Greeks — even though Clement used it to that purpose. Megasthenes seems in fact to employ Greek views as the touchstone of the argument, with the others seen by comparison with it. Strabo quotes Megasthenes at greater length on the Brahmans and the parallels he found with Hellenic opinions about nature. The quotation significantly contains Megasthenes' remark that

---

26. Clement of Alexandria, *Strom.* 1.15.72.5 = Stern, *Greek and Latin Authors,* 1:46: ἅπαντα μέντοι τὰ περὶ φύσεως εἰρημένα παρὰ τοῖς ἀρχαίοις λέγεται καὶ παρὰ τοῖς ἔξω τῆς Ἑλλάδος φιλοσοφοῦσι, τὰ μὲν παρ' Ἰνδοῖς ὑπὸ τῶν Βραχμάνων, τὰ δὲ ἐν τῇ Συρίᾳ ὑπὸ τῶν καλουμένων Ἰουδαίων.

some of the Brahmans' ideas rest on myths and suffer from simplicity because Brahmans are better at deeds than words. That would hardly qualify them as sages from whom Greeks drew their philosophy.[27] The approach once again suggests an *interpretatio Graeca*. The Hellenic vantage point is paramount. How far Megasthenes may have researched or written about Jewish beliefs is beyond our knowledge. What parallels he discerned, if any, with the Brahmans also elude conjecture. The sole surviving passage implies that Jewish and Brahman beliefs, at least in some respects, diverged.[28] More importantly, however, both overlapped with Greek ideas and both engaged in philosophizing, the central point of Megasthenes' text. He refrains from making a genealogical connection, as does Clearchus. But Jews are once again bracketed with Indian wise men and their opinions associated with Greek philosophers. The juxtaposition carries meaning. Hellenic thinkers seemed quite comfortable in ascribing to Jews conceptualizations that coincided with their own and reckoning them as part of Greek philosophical tradition.

II. Jewish Authors on Greek Philosophy

Letter of Aristeas

This was not, however, a one-sided proposition. Hellenistic Jews who had drunk deep (or even shallow) at the springs of Greek philosophy could turn the relationship around to their own advantage. The celebrated *Letter of Aristeas*, a Jewish composition, is a striking case at point. The work purports to tell of the translation of the Hebrew Bible into Greek. But it contains much more than that. The narrative has significant implications for the place of Jewish intellectuals in the culture of Hellenism.

Familiarity with Greek philosophy pervades the text. The Jewish author has Demetrius of Phaleron, Athenian philosopher and statesman, now counselor to Ptolemy II of Egypt, advise the king to commission the translation. In doing so, Demetrius commends the legislation contained in the Scriptures for its particularly philosophical character.[29] Hellenic virtues like justice, piety, self-restraint, and philanthropy gain repeated mention as Jewish quali-

27. Strabo, 15.1.59. See the valuable discussion of Bar-Kochva, *Image of the Jews*.
28. So, rightly, Bar-Kochva, *Image of the Jews*. See Clement of Alexandria, *Strom*. 1.15.72.5 = Stern, *Greek and Latin Authors*, 1:46: τὰ μὲν ... ὑπὸ τῶν Βραχμάνων ... τὰ δὲ ... ὑπὸ τῶν καλουμένων Ἰουδαίων.
29. *Ep. Arist.* 31: φιλοσοφωτέραν.

ties.³⁰ The high priest in Jerusalem, in recounting the significance of Jewish dietary prescriptions, explains them in good Greek style either as having a rational basis or as requiring allegorical interpretation.³¹ Jewish legislation on food and drink, as he puts it, is an expression of "right reason."³²

The central exhibit on this score is the extended symposium recorded by the *Letter of Aristeas*. In this scenario the king interrogates each of the seventy-two Jewish sages who had come from Jerusalem to Alexandria for the task of rendering the Bible into Greek.³³ The episode occupies fully one third of the whole work, something to which the author evidently sought to call attention.³⁴ The banquet with intellectual exchange is a quintessentially Greek institution, familiar from Plato's *Symposium*, and the format of a king asking questions of sages appears in Plutarch's *Symposium of the Seven Wise Men*. Ptolemy, over a period of a week, asks each of the Jewish elders in turn a question, receives a reply, and (without fail) praises the speaker. A large proportion of the questions involve the proper means for a monarch to govern his realm, thus putting this segment in a genre similar to that of Hellenistic treatises on kingship. And a substantial number of the responses stem from Greek philosophy or political theory, each one, however, punctuated by reference to God as ultimate authority. But the divinity often appears in mechanical, even irrelevant, fashion. The context is strictly philosophical rather than theological. To the question of what constitutes the strongest form of rule, for instance, the Jewish interlocutor replies "to control oneself and not be carried away by passions" — standard Stoic ideology.³⁵ Ptolemy's queries to the Jews included the Socratic one of whether wisdom can be taught, though the term τὸ φρονεῖν refers to practical wisdom rather than theoretical wisdom. The response looks like a clever side-step: if the soul's receptivity to all that is good is guided by divine power, this would hardly amount to being taught.³⁶ To one guest Ptolemy actually poses the direct question of

---

30. E.g., *Ep. Arist.* 2, 131, 147, 189, 208, 209, 237, 292.

31. *Ep. Arist.* 128-71.

32. *Ep. Arist.* 161. See also *Ep. Arist.* 244.

33. On the banquet scene, see O. Murray, "Aristeas and Ptolemaic Kingship," *JTS* 18 (1967): 344-61; P. M. Fraser, *Ptolemaic Alexandria*, vol. 1 (Oxford: Clarendon, 1972), 701-3; F. Parente, "La lettera di Aristea come fonte per la storia del Giudaismo Alessandrino durante la prima metà del 1 secolo a.C," *Annali della Scuola Normale Superiore de Pisa, Classe di Lettere e Filosofa* 2.1-2 (1972): 549-63.

34. *Ep. Arist.* 184-296.

35. *Ep. Arist.* 222; cf. 211.

36. *Ep. Arist.* 236.

"What is philosophy?" — indicating that the answer would best come from a Jew. The response was little different from those delivered several times in various forms by the guests: to deliberate with reason and resist passions, a perfectly good Stoic formulation in the mouth of the Jew.[37]

The relationship with Greek philosophy, however, takes a more complex and ambiguous turn. The author of the *Letter of Aristeas* has a mischievous side. Greek philosophers appear directly in the narrative, appointees of the king and members of the court, playing a supportive role that sets off the wisdom of the Jews by comparison and contrast. When Ptolemy completed his first round of questioning and hailed each of the Jewish scholars for the acuity of their answers, he turned to his own sages asking for confirmation of his opinion. Their spokesman Menedemus of Eretria, who gained repute as a significant thinker in the early third century B.C.E., responded appropriately, endorsing the king's assessment and praising the Jewish guests for their focus upon God.[38] Menedemus's approbation of the Jews, solicited by Ptolemy, and Ptolemy's immediate assent to his remarks in turn imply a staged event, an implication that the author perhaps offers with a wink and a nod. At the conclusion of the next day's interrogation, the king, having once more commended every answer, however banal or commonplace, looked again to his entourage for assent. All responded on cue and joined in the approbation — especially the philosophers.[39] The author surely did not inject this item fortuitously. His portrait of Greek intellectuals, prompted by the king, acknowledging their own inferiority through what were doubtless clenched teeth, has to be deliberate whimsy. And he underscores the point by adding in his own voice that the Jewish wise men, in their conduct and speech, far outpaced the philosophers.[40] At the end of the seven-day banquet, "Aristeas" gives high marks to the Jewish scholars who had supplied such prompt, careful, and acute answers to difficult questions that should have required lengthy deliberation. He concludes the section by reiterating his earlier message: everyone admired the Jews' replies, especially the philosophers.[41] The repetition here gives a satiric edge to the author's treatment.

---

37. *Ep. Arist.* 256.
38. *Ep. Arist.* 200-201. Menedemus served at the court of Antigonus Gonatas; Diogenes Laertius 2.125-44. Both his dates and his service with the Macedonian king make it improbable that he would become a confidant of Ptolemy II in Alexandria. "Aristeas" may have imported him into the text simply as a philosopher whose name might be known to his readership.
39. *Ep. Arist.* 235: μάλιστα δὲ τῶν φιλοσόφων.
40. *Ep. Arist.* 235: ταῖς ἀγωγαῖς καὶ τῷ λόγῳ πολὺ προέχοντες αὐτῶν ἦσαν.
41. *Ep. Arist.* 295-96.

Jewish sages, though fresh from Jerusalem, had fully absorbed the tenets of Greek philosophy, better than the Greek professionals themselves. The playful character of the exchange is hard to miss.[42] The oblique mockery does not represent a challenge to the caliber of Hellenic learning. But it reminds the readership that Jewish thinkers had assimilated it, shaped it to their own purposes, and even improved upon it. Once again, and this time from the Jewish side, the links take precedence over any sense of alienation.

Aristobulus

Other Hellenistic Jews took the matter further and on a different track. They made Greek philosophers dependent upon Jewish text and tradition. First and foremost among perpetrators of that endeavor was the gifted and inventive intellectual Aristobulus, probably an Alexandrian of the second century B.C.E.[43] Like the author of the *Letter of Aristeas*, a treatise perhaps contemporary or nearly so, Aristobulus offered an engagingly imaginative presentation of Jewish involvement with Greek philosophy.[44] He had or at least was purported to have had philosophical credentials. Clement of Alexandria and Eusebius, who preserve the extant fragments of his work, designate him a Peripatetic.[45] The characterization need not, strictly speaking, mean that he was a follower of the Aristotelian school. It signifies more general philosophical interests or even wider intellectual leanings. He certainly had a familiar-

---

42. For this interpretation of the *Letter of Aristeas* more generally, see E. S. Gruen, *Heritage and Hellenism: The Reinvention of Jewish Tradition* (Berkeley: University of California Press, 1998), 206-22; idem, "The Letter of Aristeas and the Cultural Context of the Septuagint," in *Die Septuaginta — Texte, Kontexte, Lebenswelten*, ed. M. Karrer and W. Kraus (Tübingen: Mohr-Siebeck, 2008), 134-56.

43. Specific provenance and date remain somewhat disputed. But few will challenge the conclusion that Aristobulus was a Jewish intellectual of the mid-Hellenistic period. The most important study remains that of N. Walter, *Der Thoraausleger Aristobulos* (Berlin: Akademie, 1964), 13-123. On the lengthy debate, see the valuable summary of C. R. Holladay, *Fragments from Hellenistic Jewish Authors*, vol. 3: *Aristobulus* (Atlanta: Scholars Press, 1995), 49-75. Further bibliography in E. S. Gruen, *Diaspora: Jews Amidst Greeks and Romans* (Cambridge, Mass.: Harvard University Press, 2002), 337, n. 55. See now also the essay by Patricia D. Ahearne-Kroll in this volume.

44. The relative dates of Aristobulus and the *Letter of Aristeas* and the question of who influenced whom have long been debated, with no consensus; see, e.g., Walter, *Aristobulos*, 88-103; Holladay, *Aristobulus*, 64-65, 86, n. 90, with bibliography. Each could easily have drawn on the same tradition.

45. Clement of Alexandria, *Strom.* 1.15.72.4; Eusebius, *Praep. Evang.* 9.6.6; 13.11.3.

ity with a range of Greek philosophical traditions.⁴⁶ Aristobulus, purportedly a tutor to Ptolemy VI of Egypt, produced an extensive composition, either a commentary on or a substantial exegesis of the Torah, of which only a few fragments survive.⁴⁷ They suffice, however, to disclose a notable agenda. Aristobulus undertook the task of establishing that the Hebrew Bible lay behind some of the best of Greek philosophical thought.

The author reached back to a famed and fabled figure: Pythagoras of Samos, the sixth-century philosopher, scientist, and religious thinker around whom legends collected and a pseudonymous literature accumulated. In Aristobulus's formulation, Pythagoras borrowed heavily from the books of Moses and incorporated them into his own doctrines.⁴⁸ Whether he had actually read any Pythagoras may be doubted. But the aura of Pythagoras's mystique invited a fictive association — especially one in which Jews got the credit. Aristobulus pressed the point with regard to an even more celebrated figure, Plato, who, in his view, followed the precepts of the Jewish lawgiver and worked assiduously through every detail of the laws.⁴⁹ He added Socrates, too, to that lineup, alluding to his famous "divine voice" and putting him in the company of Pythagoras and Plato, who claimed that they heard the voice of God when they observed the form of the universe so meticulously created and sustained by him and used Moses' words to affirm the fact.⁵⁰ Nor did Aristobulus stop with the ancient philosophers. He saw fit also to cite the Hellenistic poet Aratus of Soli, who had studied with the Stoic master Zeno and whose astronomical poem, the *Phaenomena*, suffused with Stoicism, served his purposes nicely. Aristobulus seized upon the opening lines of the poem in which Aratus offered a pantheistic vision of God not only as father of all but as permeating every corner of the universe. By the simple device of altering Aratus's terminology from Δίς or Ζεύς to θεός, he underlined the debt owed by the Stoic poet to Jewish ideas.⁵¹ In case anyone missed the point, Aristobulus added a still more sweeping statement that a

---

46. See Walter, *Aristobulos*, 10-13.
47. Eusebius, *Praep. Evang.* 7.13.7; 7.32.16; *Chronicle* 151; Clement, *Strom.* 5.14.97.7; cf. Holladay, *Aristobulus*, 74, 92-94.
48. Clement of Alexandria, *Strom.* 1.22.150.3; Eusebius, *Praep. Evang.* 9.6.8; 13.12.1.
49. Clement of Alexandria, *Strom.* 1.22.150.1; Eusebius, *Praep. Evang.* 13.12.1.
50. Clement of Alexandria, *Strom.* 5.14.99.3; Eusebius, *Praep. Evang.* 13.12.4. Cf. Y. Gutman, *The Beginnings of Jewish-Hellenistic Literature*, vol. 1 (Jerusalem: Bialik, 1958, in Hebrew), 192-94, who sees the proposition as a plausible one.
51. Clement of Alexandria, *Strom.* 5.14.101.4b; Eusebius, *Praep. Evang.* 13.12.6-7; Gutman, *Beginnings of Jewish-Hellenistic Literature*, 195-96.

consensus holds among all (Greek) philosophers about the necessity of maintaining reverent attitudes toward God. And that conviction, he notes, is most prominently promoted in the Jewish school of philosophy.[52] Indeed, Mosaic law enshrines the principles of piety, justice (righteousness), self-restraint, and all other qualities that are genuinely good.[53] It is hardly an accident that Aristobulus cites those virtues that became standard traits in Greek philosophical thought. The creative writer had no hesitation in framing Hellenic philosophy as an expression of Jewish tradition.

Indeed, he needed to be creative. Pythagoras, Socrates, and Plato lived long before the composition of the Septuagint. Unless they miraculously gained a command of Hebrew, they could hardly have had access to the laws of Moses. Aristobulus did not resort to conjuring up miracles, but he did the next best thing. He got around the problem by compounding the fiction: Greek translations of at least parts of the Bible, he claimed, had been available some centuries before the compiling of the Septuagint. So Pythagoras, Plato, and others could have studied the Scriptures in an accessible language to their heart's content.[54] The idea, of course, is preposterous. How many people might actually have believed it can be left to the imagination. One might indeed suggest that Aristobulus concocted the idea with tongue largely in cheek. A certain playfulness exists in his whole contrived scenario not only of Greek philosophers poring over biblical texts but also of numerous Greek poets and dramatists reproducing the lessons of the Bible.[55] But whether serious or not, Aristobulus's imaginative fabrications set Greek philosophy into the framework of the Jewish intellectual and religious achievement — the reverse of "othering."

---

52. Eusebius, *Praep. Evang.* 13.12.8: ὃ μάλιστα παρακελεύεται καλῶς ἡ καθ' ἡμᾶς αἵρεσις. Use of αἵρεσις here is noteworthy, for the term regularly denotes a Greek philosophical school.

53. Eusebius, *Praep. Evang.* 13.12.8.

54. Clement of Alexandria, *Strom.* 1.22.150.2; Eusebius, *Praep. Evang.* 13.12.1.

55. For this interpretation, see Gruen, *Heritage and Hellenism*, 246-51; idem, *Diaspora*, 221-24. Other scholars take Aristobulus's endeavor as an altogether serious enterprise. E.g., Gutman, *Beginnings of Jewish-Hellenistic Literature*, 186-220; Walter, *Aristobulos;* M. Hengel, *Judaism and Hellenism*, vol. 1 (London: SPCK, 1974), 163-69; E. Schürer, *The History of the Jewish People in the Age of Jesus Christ*, vol. 3, rev. ed., ed. G. Vermes, F. Millar, and M. Goodman (Edinburgh: Clark, 1986), 579-87; J. M. G. Barclay, *Jews in the Mediterranean Diaspora: From Alexander to Trajan (323 BCE–17 CE)* (Edinburgh: T. & T. Clark, 1996), 150-58; Collins, *Between Athens and Jerusalem*, 186-90.

Erich S. Gruen

Philo of Alexandria

Aristobulus's work heralded a long tradition of Jewish claims to the priority of their teachings and the indebtedness of Hellenic philosophers. This edifying inference found its way into the works of the great Jewish philosopher and exegete Philo of Alexandria, where it appears in various forms and in numerous scattered places of his vast corpus. Philo, like Aristobulus, traced the effects of Jewish learning back to the pre-Socratics. Greeks had claimed that Heraclitus first hatched the idea that only the contemplation of opposites leads to understanding of the whole. Philo dismissed that claim: Moses had propounded the notion long before Heraclitus.[56] Even Heraclitus's famous statement regarding the soul's death as entombment in the body and its release to life when the body dies merely follows the teaching of Moses.[57] Philo duly acknowledges the persuasiveness of Plato's cosmology that sees the world as created and indestructible. But, although some ascribe the origin of this view to Hesiod, Philo asserts that one can find it already in Genesis, thus to the credit of Moses.[58] The Jewish philosopher also paraphrases with approbation Plato's famous dictum that states can only reach their potential if kings become philosophers or philosophers become kings. But he points out that Moses had long since blended both kingship and philosophy in his own person — not to mention his roles as lawgiver, priest, and prophet.[59] So, the Scriptures again supplied precedent for Plato.

Hellenistic philosophy, for Philo, owes a similarly heavy debt to the teachings of the Scriptures. He cites with high praise the thesis of Zeno the Stoic with regard to the necessity of subjecting the intemperate to the wise, but adds the conjecture that he must have got this idea from Isaac's command in Genesis that Esau serve his brother Jacob.[60] Stoic doctrine held that the wise man alone, no matter his material circumstances, is true ruler and king and that virtue has unassailable authority. Philo, however, finds this principle already enshrined in a passage of Genesis wherein the Hittites (Canaanites) hail Abraham as a Prince of God among them.[61] Philo elsewhere allows himself a rather gratuitous bit of one-upmanship. He notes

---

56. Philo, *Quis Rerum Divinarum Heres Sit* 207-14.
57. Philo, *Legum Allegoriarum* 1.105-8.
58. Philo, *De Aeternitate Mundi* 13-19.
59. Philo, *De vita Moysis* 2; cf. Plato, *Republica* 5.473D.
60. Philo, *Quod Omnis Probus Liber Sit* 53-57; cf. Gen. 27:40.
61. Philo, *De Mutatione Nominum* 152; *De Somniis* 2.244; cf. Gen. 23:6.

that Greek philosophers regarded those who first applied names to things as sages. But Moses had the better of them on that, for he had the distinction of naming Adam![62] Philo rarely shows flashes of humor. But this just might be an instance of it. And one can perhaps find another in his arresting claim that Socrates' thoughts about God's fashioning of body parts that perform excretory functions drew on Moses![63] Philo's powers of invention were not negligible. In re-creating the education of Moses, he performs a neat and surprising twist on the interpenetration of Greek and Jewish learning. Philo has Moses not only learn arithmetic, geometry, music, and hieroglyphics from erudite Egyptians, but progress through the rest of the curriculum, presumably rhetoric, literature, and philosophy, with Greek teachers.[64] Just where Moses might have found itinerant Greek schoolmasters in late Bronze Age Egypt Philo leaves to the imagination. This, too, may have been no more than a half-serious flight of fancy. But it attests to a continuing by-play of *interpretationes Graecae* and *interpretationes Iudaicae*.

Josephus

A generation after Philo, the idea that Greek philosophers hewed closely to the concept of God obtained from acquaintance with the Books of Moses still made the rounds. The Jewish historian Josephus retailed the notion in his last — and most contrived — treatise, the *Contra Apionem*.[65] Josephus interestingly forbears, as he puts it, to make the case that the wisest of the Greeks learned their doctrines about God from the formulations of Moses. The idea could by that time be taken for granted. He affirms indeed that Greek philosophers have long since testified to the excellence and suitability of Jewish formulations with regard to the nature and glory of God. He cites Pythagoras, Anaxagoras, Plato, and the Stoics as witnesses to the fact. But why stop there? Josephus extends the point to encompass nearly all philosophers, since they hold similar views about the nature of God. And he gives the advantage to Moses on more than just priority. The Greeks philosophized to a small circle; Moses spoke with both actions and words not only to his contemporaries but

---

62. Philo, *Legum Allegoriarum* 2.15.
63. Philo, *Quaestiones et Solutiones in Genesim* 2.6.
64. Philo, *De vita Moysis* 1.23.
65. On the contrived character of the work, see E. S. Gruen, "Greeks and Jews: Mutual Misperceptions in Josephus' Contra Apionem," in *Ancient Judaism in Its Hellenistic Context*, ed. C. Bakhos (Leiden: Brill, 2005), 31-51.

to all future generations.⁶⁶ The historian makes a similar point elsewhere: the first imitators of Mosaic laws were Greek philosophers who, although ostensibly observing the practices of their native lands, actually in their deeds and their philosophizing followed the precepts of Moses.⁶⁷ Josephus can also become more specific. He cites two principles of Plato, that citizens should study their laws assiduously with precision and that they restrict the introduction of foreigners so as to limit the state to those who adhere to its laws. On both those counts, he maintains, Plato took his cue from Moses.⁶⁸ For the Jewish readership of Josephus, like that of Philo, such claims were evidently uncontroversial. They had been around a long time.

For how long? As we have seen, Greek writers had already made connection between Jewish sages and Greek philosophy in the late fourth century B.C.E. The assertion that Greeks owed philosophical doctrines to the Jews, on the other hand, appears, as one might expect, in Jewish texts, stemming at least from Aristobulus in the mid-second century B.C.E. This bifurcation, however, is crossed by a fascinating passage from a Hellenic author with no obvious Jewish axes to grind, one who precedes any extant Jewish texts on the matter. Hermippus of Smyrna, a pupil of Callimachus in Alexandria, composed a wide range of works, including a biography of Pythagoras, some time in the late third or early second century B.C.E.⁶⁹ This puts him approximately a half century earlier than Aristobulus. Yet Hermippus included the arresting statement that Pythagoras imitated and adapted the views of Jews and Thracians. Coming from a Greek at so early a date, this striking remark demands attention.

The quotation comes from Josephus's *Contra Apionem,* which has as one of its chief aims a demonstration that Jews were held in esteem by eminent Greeks familiar with their writings. Josephus indeed has an axe to grind. But that does not itself cast suspicion upon the accuracy of Hermippus's remarks that he conveys. A curious story about Pythagoras appeared in the first book of Hermippus's biography, as reported by Josephus. The phi-

---

66. Josephus, *Ag. Ap.* 2.168-69. Josephus refers to Pythagoras's knowledge of Jewish matters also at *Ag. Ap.* 1.162.

67. Josephus, *Ag. Ap.* 2.281: πρῶτοι μὲν γὰρ οἱ παρὰ τοῖς Ἕλλησι φιλοσοφήσαντες τῷ μὲν δοκεῖν τὰ πάτρια διεφύλαττον, ἐν δὲ τοῖς πράγμασι καὶ τῷ φιλοσοφεῖν ἐκείνῳ κατηκολούθησαν; cf. 1.175.

68. Josephus, *Ag. Ap.* 2.257: Πλάτων μεμίμηται τὸν ἡμέτερον νομοθέτην.

69. On the life and works of Hermippus, see the discussion, with testimony and bibliography, by J. Bollansée, *Hermippos of Smyrna and His Biographical Writings: A Reappraisal* (Leuven: Peeters, 1999), 1-20; also Bar-Kochva, *Image of the Jews.*

losopher spoke about the death of one of his followers, Calliphon of Croton, whose soul then accompanied him day and night. He urged that one ought not to cross a spot where an ass sank to its knees, to avoid any thirst-producing water, and to refrain from all blasphemy.[70] An odd combination of precepts. To this point, Josephus appears to be paraphrasing Hermippus. He then quotes him directly as saying that Pythagoras acted upon and spoke about such matters by imitating and adapting to himself the views of Jews and Thracians.[71] And in his own voice Josephus adds that Pythagoras is rightly said to have brought into his philosophy many of the precepts found among the Jews.[72]

The passage is noteworthy. One will not be surprised to learn that some scholars have seized upon this information to argue that Hermippus falls into the category of those Greek intellectuals who had a positive appreciation of the Jews and that he embraced the idea of a Jewish influence upon Greek philosophy even before the Jews did.[73] But, as usual, the matter is not so simple. Hermippus's writings gained popularity — enough to warrant epitomes of them for a wider readership already in the second century B.C.E. by Heraclides Lembus.[74] But the popularity did not arise from sober, scholarly monographs. Hermippus earned the reputation of a lively storyteller, noted for parody, fantasy, and rather caustic comments on the subjects of his works.[75] His depiction of Pythagoras falls into that category. It was no laudatory one. Fragments of the biography suggest sarcasm, innuendo, and mockery.[76] Nor was Hermippus the first. Pythagoras was a controversial figure who drew considerable criticism from philosophers and others.[77] That puts a very different slant on the passage conveyed by Josephus.

---

70. Josephus, *Ag. Ap.* 1.164. Whether the advice comes from Pythagoras or from the soul of Calliphon is ambiguous in the text. See Bar-Kochva, *Image of the Jews*. A decision is not required for our purposes.

71. Josephus, *Ag. Ap.* 1.165: ταῦτα δὲ ἔρατπε καὶ ἔλεγε τὰς Ἰουδαίων καὶ Θρακῶν δόξας μιμούμενος καὶ μεταφέρων εἰς ἑαυτόν.

72. Josephus, *Ag. Ap.* 2.165. See below.

73. E.g., Gabba, "Growth of Anti-Judaism," 623-24; Feldman, *Jew and Gentile*, 201-2.

74. On the subsequent reputation of Hermippus, see Bollansée, *Hermippos of Smyrna*, 104-16.

75. See Bollansée, *Hermippos of Smyrna*, 118-53; Bar-Kochva, *Image of the Jews*.

76. Examples in Bar-Kochva, *Image of the Jews*. See, e.g., Diogenes Laertius 8.41. Cf. Bollansée, *Hermippos of Smyrna*, 44-52, who, however, takes far too generous a view of Hermippus's bias.

77. E.g., Diogenes Laertius 5.1, 8.7, 8.36, 9.1, with the discussion of Bar-Kochva, *Image of the Jews*.

The particulars ascribed to Pythagoras appear, under this lens, to border on the ludicrous. The story of Calliphon's spirit dwelling night and day with the philosopher looks like an ironic comment on his doctrine of the immortality of the soul.[78] And the three prohibitions that he prescribed hardly suggest earnest guidance to his followers. Avoidance of a spot where an ass sank to his knees and refraining from salty or sugary water recall a host of Pythagorean pronouncements that few outside his sect (or perhaps even within) would take seriously.[79] The ban on blasphemy looks more solemn. But it is one so widely shared among creeds and sects that it might have been included for its banality rather than its solemnity.[80] Hermippus was having some fun with the superstitions and ritual taboos associated with Pythagoreanism.

What then are we to make of Hermippus's statement (here in a direct quote by Josephus) that Pythagoras both asserted and practiced these precepts in imitation of Jewish and Thracian doctrines? It certainly constituted no compliment to Jews or Thracians. A search for Jewish parallels for the three prohibitions leads nowhere, let alone guesswork as to which may have been Thracian and which Jewish.[81] On the other hand, it does not follow that Hermippus was denigrating Jews and Thracians together with Pythagoras. The philosopher was said to have been conversant with and influenced by various Eastern traditions, including those of Egyptians, Chaldeans, and *magi*.[82] It would be logical enough to add Jews to that company. As for Thracians, a people usually regarded as on the periphery of civilization, one might be tempted to infer that Hermippus inserted them as yet another sardonic jab at Pythagoras. He did not, however, invent the connection. Biographical references to the sage include one that has his slave bring Pythagorean teachings to the Thracians.[83] More important perhaps is the association of Pythagoras with Orphism.[84] Since legend has Orpheus, the father of Hel-

---

78. Cf. Diogenes Laertius 8.32; Barclay, *Against Apion*, 96; Bar-Kochva, *Image of the Jews*.

79. H. Jacobson, "Hermippus, Pythagoras, and the Jews," *REJ* 135 (1976): 145-49, makes a laudable but ultimately unsuccessful attempt to find biblical prescriptions behind Hermippus's statements. Similarly, P. Gorman, "Pythagoras Palestinus," *Philologus* 127 (1983): 33-36. See the criticisms of Bar-Kochva, *Image of the Jews*.

80. Bar-Kochva, *Image of the Jews*, goes further to argue that Greeks did not worry about blasphemy anyway except at a sacred shrine — an extreme position.

81. So, rightly, Barclay, *Against Apion*, 97-98; Bar-Kochva, *Image of the Jews*.

82. Diogenes Laertius 8.3; Porphyry, *Vita Pythagorae* 6, 11-12.

83. Herodotus 4.95; Strabo 7.3.5; Iamblichus, *Vita Pythagorae* 14-15.

84. Cf. Iamblichus, *Vita Pythagorae* 146; Barclay, *Against Apion*, 97.

lenic song and poetry, as a Thracian, the suggestion of influence from Thrace upon Pythagoras need not itself be a hostile one. But it is easy enough to imagine that Hermippus might have turned the relationship to his own purpose in comic fashion.

Josephus's own comments go well beyond what might be inferred from the Hermippus fragment. The historian introduces the subject by stating that Pythagoras, a figure of great antiquity, preeminent among philosophers in wisdom and piety, not only knew about Jewish matters but was a most eager emulator of them.[85] And he closes the segment by affirming that Pythagoras is correctly said to have imported many Jewish precepts into his own philosophy.[86] This plainly embellishes and enhances the information in Hermippus. It is picked up and further amplified by Origen, who cites Hermippus for the view that Pythagoras transferred his own philosophy from Jews to Greeks.[87] Those sweeping assertions have more to do with the objectives of Josephus and Origen than with the more cynical intent of Hermippus.

This does not, however, obviate the main point. There is no reason to doubt that the association of Pythagoras with Jewish ideas and traditions was already current in the time of Hermippus. Even if he alluded to the presumed connection only in order to mock Pythagoras, he attests to its existence. It matters not whether Josephus had access to Hermippus's text, to an epitome of it, or even a reference to it in a Jewish author. Hermippus's affirmation that Pythagoras was influenced by Jewish beliefs can hardly be sheer invention.[88] It reflects both the Hellenic conceptualization that links Eastern

---

85. Josephus, *Ag. Ap.* 1.162: σοφίᾳ δὲ καὶ τῇ περὶ τὸ θεῖον εὐσεβείᾳ πάντων ὑπειλημμένος διενεγκεῖν, τῶν φιλοσοφησάντων, οὐ μόνον ἐγνωκὼς τὰ παρ' ἡμῖν δῆλός ἐστιν, ἀλλὰ καὶ ζηλωτὴς αὐτῶν ἐκ πλείστου γεγενημένος.

86. Josephus, *Ag. Ap.* 1.165: λέγεται γὰρ ὡς ἀληθῶς ὁ ἀνὴρ ἐκεῖνος πολλὰ τῶν παρὰ Ἰουδαίοις νομίμων εἰς τὴν αὐτοῦ μετενεγκεῖν φιλοσοφίαν.

87. Origen, *Contra Celsum*, 1.15.334. Cf. also Porphyry, *Vita Pythagorae* 11.

88. Bar-Kochva, *Image of the Jews,* whose dissection of the text is decidedly superior to other treatments, nevertheless takes a minimalist approach. His conclusion that Hermippus made no allusion to Jews except for the three precepts actually recorded by Josephus is implausible. A similar view is in Schürer, *History of the Jewish People,* 3:696. Gorman ("Pythagoras Palestinus," 32-33), Barclay (*Against Apion*, 98), and Bar-Kochva (*Image of the Jew*) propose that Josephus based his broader statement about Jewish influence upon Pythagoras strictly or largely on Aristobulus (Eusebius, *Praep. Evang.* 13.12.1). The language is indeed similar (though not identical). But many Jewish writers, now lost, may have conveyed parallel information. Josephus nowhere cites Aristobulus. To infer that he simply adopted Aristobulus's formulation about Jewish impact upon Pythagoras and ascribed it to

wisdom with Greek philosophy and the Jewish construct that has Greek philosophers derive their ideas from Jewish learning. The overlap and interconnection leave a deep impression.[89]

III. Conclusion

The reciprocation has a long history. Two striking passages provide a coda to underscore it. Philo in the mid–first-century C.E. comments that the world contains multitudes of rich, eminent, and pleasure-seeking individuals, but very few who are wise, just, and virtuous. He then specifies important examples of the latter category: the seven sages of Greece, the Persian *magi*, the Indian gymnosophists, and the Jewish Essenes.[90] The Jewish philosopher, therefore, echoes a linkage between Hellenic savants and Eastern wise men (including Jews) that goes back more than three centuries to Greek thinkers like Megasthenes, Clearchus, and Hermippus.[91] And as late as the second half of the second century C.E., the Platonist philosopher Numenius of Apamea (whom some referred to as a Pythagorean) reiterated the affinities of Plato and Pythagoras with the teachings of Brahmans, Egyptians, *magi*, and Jews.[92] Numenius has the signal distinction of uttering the most celebrated remark on this entire subject: "For what is Plato, but Moses speaking in good Attic Greek?"[93] As Philo the Jew mirrors the constructed interconnections first formulated by Greeks, so Numenius the Greek mirrors the conceit of Jewish origins for Greek philosophy first formulated by Jews. The mutual regard stands out. There is no sign of Otherness here.

Hermippus without any basis except the three precepts is highly questionable. Bar-Kochva's view that Origen's statement is a mere paraphrase of Josephus also stands on shaky ground. Whereas Josephus cites Hermippus's *Life of Pythagoras*, Origen drew his information from Hermippus's work *On Lawgivers; Contra Celsum*, 1.15.334. Bar-Kochva's conclusion that the information simply passed from Aristobulus to Josephus to Origen, denying any role to Hermippus, is unpersuasive.

89. Note also the comment of Josephus that Essenes borrowed their way of life from Pythagoras! *Ant.* 15.371.

90. Philo, *Quod Omnis Probus Liber Sit* 72-75.

91. The presumed parallels were still very much alive among Greek thinkers in the time of Strabo; see 16.1.39.

92. Eusebius, *Praep. Evang.* 9.7.1.

93. Eusebius, *Praep. Evang.* 9.6.9: τί γάρ ἐστι Πλάτων ἢ Μωσῆς ἀττικίζων. Other references in Stern, *Greek and Latin Authors*, 2:210.

The Persecution of Judeans by Antiochus IV: The Significance of "Ancestral Laws"

Robert Doran

"Das eigentliche und einzige Rätsel der Geschichte des seleukidischen Jerusalem," declared Elias Bickermann about the persecution of the Jews by Antiochus IV.[1] The statement was later echoed by Fergus Millar: "There seems no way of reaching an understanding of how Antiochus came to take a step so profoundly at variance with the normal assumptions of government in his time."[2] Since Bickermann's magisterial work, various attempts have been put forward to explain this enigma. Bickermann himself held that the main proponents of the persecution were Hellenized Jews who wished to reform and bring up-to-date the Jewish religion.[3] In this he was followed by Martin Hengel, and more recently by J. Scurlock.[4] In response to this religious motivation of the persecution, Victor Tcherikover formulated his own lapidary statement: "It was not the revolt which came as a response to the persecution, but the persecution which came as a response to the revolt."[5] Tcherikover saw the revolt as an uprising of the poor against the rich elites who had imposed the transformation of Jerusalem into a

---

1. Elias Bickermann, *Der Gott der Makkabäer* (Berlin: Schocken, 1937), 92.
2. Fergus Millar, "The Background to the Maccabean Revolution," *JJS* 29 (1978): 16-17.
3. Bickermann, *Gott der Makkabäer*, 126-33.
4. Martin Hengel, *Judaism and Hellenism: Studies in Their Encounter in Palestine in the Early Hellenistic Period*, 2 vols. (Philadelphia: Fortress, 1974); J. Scurlock, "167 BCE: Hellenism or Reform?" *JSJ* 32 (2000): 126-61.
5. Victor Tcherikover, *Hellenistic Civilization and the Jews* (Philadelphia: Jewish Publication Society, 1959), 191.

*polis.*⁶ Jonathan Goldstein reverted to the religious interpretation of Bickermann but identified Antiochus IV as the cause. Aware of the Roman attacks on the followers of Bacchus, Antiochus sought to distinguish between the present, depraved Judaism and that of the original tradition.⁷ Klaus Bringmann looked more to political factors, the desire of Menelaus to gain control, and the support given by Antiochus IV to crush Menelaus's rivals.⁸ Erich Gruen, in a masterful overview of the question, pointed to the need for Antiochus IV, after the humiliation of the "day of Eleusis," to show that he was still a force with which to reckon.⁹ In his recent analysis of the persecution edict, Peter Franz Mittag concluded that the divergent details of the edict from all the sources made it well nigh impossible to reconstruct the edict in detail.¹⁰

All of these suggestions have been prompted by the firm conviction that religious persecution was unthinkable in the Hellenistic world: "Such direct interference in the ancestral cults of a nation was unheard of in the Greek-speaking world from immemorial times," as Arnaldo Momigliano stated.¹¹ I would like to test that assumption. Part of the confusion has arisen from the existence of five accounts of the persecution (perhaps six if one includes 4Q248): 1 Maccabees, 2 Maccabees, Josephus's *Jewish War* (1.31-35), Josephus's *Antiquities of the Jews* (12:239-254), and the book of Daniel (11:28-30). There are difficulties with the accounts in Daniel and Josephus, as well as with 4Q248. The account in 1 Maccabees has Antiochus IV attack Jerusalem in 143 Seleucid Era, that is, 170-169 B.C.E., after his first expedition into Egypt. Antiochus despoils the Temple and takes away numerous vessels. After two years, with no mention of a second attack on Egypt by Antiochus and his repulse by the Romans, Antiochus again sends a large force into Jerusalem and a garrison is installed in the Acra (1 Macc. 1:29-35). Then Antiochus orders the whole Seleucid kingdom to give up their particular

---

6. Tcherikover, *Hellenistic Civilization,* 187-203.

7. Jonathan A. Goldstein, *I Maccabees* (AB 41A; Garden City, N.Y.: Doubleday, 1976), 104-60.

8. Klaus Bringmann, *Hellenistische Reform und Religionsverfolgung in Judäa* (Göttingen: Vandenhoeck & Ruprecht, 1983), 126-35.

9. Erich S. Gruen, "Hellenism and Persecution: Antiochus IV and the Jews," in *Hellenistic History and Culture,* ed. Peter Green (Berkeley: University of California Press, 1993), 262-64.

10. Peter Franz Mittag, *Antiochos I. Epiphanes: Eine politische Biographie* (Berlin: Akademie, 2006), 267-68.

11. Arnaldo Momigliano, *Alien Wisdom: The Limits of Hellenization* (Cambridge: Cambridge University Press, 1975), 100.

customs (1 Macc. 1:41). Interestingly, no motivation is given for Antiochus's attack on Jerusalem. He is depicted simply as a powerful bully who takes what he wants (1 Macc. 1:20: ἐν ὄχλῳ βαρεῖ; cf. 1:17, 29). Also, no reason is given for his sending someone to cause further slaughter. The final notice that he wanted everyone in his kingdom to be the same and this is why he abrogated the polity of the Jews is not borne out by what we know of Antiochus IV from other sources.

The narrative of events in 2 Maccabees, while at times cryptic, is much more coherent in its outline of events. What I intend in this essay is to concentrate on the rhetorical persuasiveness of this account.

I. The Outline of Events

During the second invasion of Egypt by Antiochus IV in 168 B.C.E., a rumor spread that Antiochus IV had died. How this arose and whether it is connected to the "day of Eleusis" is a matter of dispute.[12] The text of 2 Maccabees makes no mention of Antiochus's forced retreat at the Roman threat and simply claims that there was such a rumor. On the basis of this rumor, the former high priest Jason attempted to gain control of Jerusalem and oust Menelaus. Hearing of the revolt, Antiochus marched on Jerusalem, the rebellion was quashed and the Temple pillaged (2 Macc. 5:1-16). Antiochus's response to the revolt is harsh: he attempted to depopulate the city and install a garrison (2 Macc. 5:24-26).[13] More importantly, he considered the city "spear-won" (5:11: δοριάλωτον) and his to do with as he chose. He no longer had to allow the city, as his father Antiochus III had,[14] to be governed by its ancestral laws (πολιτευέσθωσαν . . . κατὰ τοὺς πατρίους νόμους) and polity, but sent an Athenian named Geron "to compel the Jews to change from their ancestral laws and not to be governed by the laws of God" (2 Macc. 6:1: μεταβαίνειν ἀπὸ τῶν πατρίων νόμων καὶ τοῖς τοῦ θεοῦ νόμοις μὴ πολιτεύεσθαι). Later, possibly before his march towards the East in 165 B.C.E., Antiochus IV favorably listened to a request from Menelaus to change his decision. Antiochus granted full permission "for the Jews to use their own customs and laws as

---

12. See the comments of M. Gwyn Morgan in response to Erich Gruen's essay in *Hellenistic History and Culture*, ed. Green, 265-66.

13. Either colonists (Tcherikover, *Hellenistic Civilization*, 194-95; Bringmann, *Hellenistische Reform*, 87-89, 127) or simply a garrison (Bezalel Bar-Kochva, *Judas Maccabaeus* [Cambridge: Cambridge University Press, 1989], 438-44).

14. Josephus, *Ant.* 12.142.

formerly" (2 Macc. 11:31: χρῆσθαι τοὺς Ἰουδαίους τοῖς ἑαυτῶν διαιτήμασι καὶ νόμοις καθὰ καὶ τὸ πρότερον).[15] The language of his son on accession to the throne is similar: "We have heard that the Jews do not consent to our father's change to Greek customs (τῇ τοῦ πατρὸς ἐπὶ τὰ Ἑλληνικὰ μεταθέσει) but prefer their own way of living (τὴν ἑαυτῶν ἀγωγὴν αἱρετίζοντας) and ask that their own customs (τὰ νόμιμα) be allowed them" (2 Macc. 11:24).

II. The Rhetoric

The king is therefore depicted in 2 Maccabees as having the power to allow a city to follow its ancestral laws or to change them. Note the consistent use of πάτριος, πατρῷος, πατρίς. What is striking in the accounts of persecution is the emphasis on the ancestral laws as opposed to the newly imposed laws. The Jews could not keep the Sabbath nor observe the ancestral festivals (πατρῷοος ἑορτάς) nor, in sum, proclaim that they were Jews (6:6). Throughout the narrative of the mother and her seven sons, the first of the sons proclaims that they are ready to die rather than transgress the ancestral laws (7:2: τοὺς πατρίους νόμους). When the seventh son comes forward, Antiochus promises to enrich him if he changes from the ancestral ways (7:24: μεταθέμενον ἀπὸ τῶν πατρίων), but the son answers that he, like his brothers, hands over body and soul for the sake of the ancestral laws (7:37: περὶ τῶν πατρίων νόμων). The mother and brothers use their ancestral voice in responding (7:8, 27: τῇ πατρίῳ φωνῇ). At a crucial battle, Judas cries out in his ancestral voice and they prevail (12:37). Also, the ancestral voice is used in triumph at the defeat of Nicanor (15:29). The author of the condensed narrative, in fact, holds that the beginning of the problem was the rejection by the priests of the ancestral honors in favor of the Hellenic honors (4:15: καὶ τὰς μὲν πατρῴους τιμὰς ἐν οὐδενὶ τιθέμενοι, τὰς δὲ Ἑλληνικὰς δόξας καλλίστας ἡγούμενοι). Jason and Menelaus are described as traitors to the fatherland (5:15).

III. The Slogan "Ancestral Laws"

By casting Antiochus's persecution as an attack on ancestral laws, the author of 2 Maccabees appealed to the deeply rooted patriotism of individuals

---

15. See Christian Habicht, "Royal Documents in 2 Maccabees," in idem, *The Hellenistic Monarchies: Selected Papers* (Ann Arbor: University of Michigan Press, 2006), 114, 120.

in local cities.¹⁶ As Erich Gruen has said, ancestral law, like freedom (today's democracy?), was a slogan that carried great emotional appeal. Opposing parties would both claim that they were the upholders of πάτριοι νόμοι (ancestral laws). At the time of the Peloponnesian War, in the conflict between the democratic party and the anti-democratic opponents at Samos, Thucydides recounts how the democrats argued that, even if the antidemocratic opposition at Athens had done wrong in abolishing the ancestral laws (τοὺς πατρίους νόμους καταλύσαντες), they themselves would try to preserve these and force the government at Athens to do likewise (Thucydides 8.76.6). When Andokides was on trial for impiety, he cited the earlier Decree of Teisamenos, which began: "The Athenians shall conduct their public affairs in the traditional manner (πολιτεύεσθαι Ἀθηναίους κατὰ τὰ πάτρια)."¹⁷ In his study of the ancestral constitution, Alexander Fuks concluded that the phrase "ancestral laws" referred not to some archaizing originalism, but to the laws currently in existence and to the existing constitution.¹⁸

There are other instances where the ancestral laws of cities were changed after they were captured. Polybios relates how those cities who had been compelled (ἠναγκασμένους) to join the Aetolian League against their will were reinstated in their ancestral form of government (εἰς τὰ πάτρια πολιτεύματα) and that they could use their ancestral laws (νόμοις χρωμένους τοῖς πατρίοις).¹⁹ After Seleucus, son of Antiochus III, had taken Phocaea, their ancestral constitution must have been changed, since later the Romans restored to them their ancestral constitution (τὸ πάτριον πολίτευμα).²⁰ Cleomenes changed the Spartan constitution to a tyranny, but later Antigonos restored their ancestral polity to them.²¹ A decree of the Chersonnites authorized a golden crown to be sent to the people of Athens because they had been the cause of all the great benefits (πάντων τῶν μεγίστων ἀγαθῶν παραίτιος) in freeing them from Philip and restoring their fatherlands, their

---

16. Daniel R. Schwartz notes that "every Greek reader knew how reprehensible it was to violate or suppress [ancestral laws]." See his *2 Maccabees* (Berlin: Walter de Gruyter, 2008), 275.

17. Andokides I.83. See the commentary by Douglas MacDowell, *Andokides On the Mysteries* (Oxford; Clarendon, 1962).

18. Alexander Fuks, *The Ancestral Constitution: Four Studies in Athenian Party Politics at the End of the Fifth Century B.C.* (London: Routledge and Kegan Paul, 1953), 40.

19. Polybios 4.25.7.

20. Polybios 21.6; 21.45.7; see Livy 37.11.15.

21. Polybios 2.47.3; 2.70.1.

laws, their freedom, and their sanctuaries (τὰ ἱερά).²² Finally, Antiochus III seems to have taken away the ancestral polity of Apollonia of Rhyndacos, but Eumenes II restored it at the request of Korragos, governor of the Hellespont. Eumenes gave back "the laws and the ancestral polity, the sacred precincts and the money towards the temples and the financial administration of the city, the oil for the *neoi* and the other things which belonged to the people from the beginning" (ἀποδοθῆναι τούς τε ν[ό]μους καὶ τὴν πάτριον πολιτείαν καὶ τὰ ἱερὰ τεμένη καὶ εἰς τὰ ἱερὰ καὶ πόλεως διοίκησιν ἀργύριον καὶ τὸ τοῖς νέοις ἔλαιον καὶ τὰ ἄλλα ἅπερ ἐξ ἀρχῆς ὑπῆ[ρ]χεν τῶι δήμωι).²³ Here change of laws and polity does seem to have had an effect on the sacred precincts and so on the religious life of the city. Given the number of laws that each city would pass on religious matters within that city,²⁴ one would suspect that, when ancestral laws were changed, there would also be some effect on sacred laws. It is particularly interesting that one finds two instances where the rituals are said to belong to the ancestral laws. In an inscription from Cos dating to the third century B.C.E., instructions are given "so that the purifications and the purificatory offerings and the sacrifices be celebrated in accordance with the ancestral laws (κατὰ τοὺς ἱε]ροὺς καὶ πατρίους nĒmouv)."²⁵ From Ephesus in the third century C.E. comes an inscription entitled "Summation of Ancestral Law" (κεφάλαιον νόμου πατρίου). The summation begins with the chief magistrate being required to light a fire on all the altars and to offer incense.²⁶ An interesting combination is found in the letter of Hadrian to Narkya from 137/138. Hadrian states that no one will dispute that the Narkyians "have a *polis* and the rights of a *polis*, seeing that . . . you have a council, magistrates, priests, Greek tribes."²⁷ Here cult and council go hand in hand.

What exactly a change in ancestral laws meant as regards cult is not clear: Polybius only mentions the change from democracy to tyranny. Inscriptional evidence, since inscriptions are put up to honor some individual or the city, will probably yield only tangential evidence, as in the case of

---

22. Decree cited in Demosthenes, *De Corona* 92.

23. Thomas Corsten, *Die Inschriften von Prusa ad Olympum* (Bonn: Rudolf Habelt, 1993), 2.85-91 (#1001).

24. See the inscriptions collected by F. Sokolowski: *Lois sacrées des cités grecques* (Paris: Boccard, 1969); idem, *Lois sacrées des cités grecques. Supplément* (Paris: Boccard, 1962).

25. Sokolowski, *Lois sacrées des cités grecques*, #154, lines 5-6 (p. 263).

26. Sokolowski, *Lois sacrées des cités grecques. Supplément*, #121, lines 2-4 (p. 203).

27. See Christopher P. Jones, "A Letter of Hadrian to Narkya (Eastern Locris)," *Journal of Roman Archeology* 19 (2006): 151-62.

Korraghos, for damage done to a city's cult. One change probably would be that the conquered would have instituted honors for the new king, including perhaps cultic honors for the king. In his excellent discussion of the relations between kings and cities in Asia Minor, John Ma gives numerous examples, among them Smyrna,

> which multiplied cultic honours for the Seleukids. Months received Seleukid names: Antiocheon, Stratonikeon, and Laodikeon, implying festivals for their namesakes (attested in the case of the Antiocheia). Cults are specifically documented for Antiochos I ("god and saviour"), Antiochos II, Stratonike (under the title "Aphrodite Stratonikis"; the main civic shrine of Aphrodite now associated a Seleukid to the goddess), and Seleukos II.[28]

What other changes other Greek cities would have undergone is unknown.

IV. Significance for Jerusalem

Under the new laws imposed on Jerusalem was the cultic celebration of the birthday of Antiochus IV (2 Macc. 6:7). What we do know is that Greek customs and laws (2 Macc. 11:24: τὰ Ἑλληνικά) were imposed on Jerusalem. Fergus Millar summed up the situation this way: "By our most detailed evidence, II Macc. shows precisely that a number of altars and sacred precincts were established, and specifically that rites in honour of Dionysus were required. In short, what was imposed was paganism."[29] The term Millar chose, "paganism," is instructive, for it highlights the problem of imposing Greek laws on a monotheistic society whose laws were given by their one God. The notion that Antiochus IV instigated a religious persecution is flawed because it assumes that, at this time, religion and politics are separate. It assumes, for example, that circumcision and eating kosher food are part of religion, quite distinct from societal rules. However, circumcision is part of the ancestral laws of Judaism. It is how one becomes a member of Jewish society. "Any uncircumcised male who is not circumcised in the flesh of his foreskin shall be cut off from his people; he has broken my covenant" (Gen. 17:14). Particu-

---

28. John Ma, *Antiochos II and the Cities of Western Asia Minor* (Oxford: Oxford University Press, 1999), 37.

29. Fergus Millar, "The Background to the Maccabean Revolution," *JJS* 29 (1978): 20.

larly important is the description of the first martyrs who do not choose to change to Greek customs (2 Macc. 6:9: μεταβαίνειν ἐπὶ τὰ Ἑλληνικά) in 2 Macc. 6:10. Throughout the verse, stress is on the "city." The women are led publicly (δημοσίᾳ) through the city (τὴν πόλιν) and thrown down from the wall, an edifice set up to protect and defend the city. Like the later charades put on by the Romans, when criminals like the Christians were displayed publicly in the amphitheater,[30] here two women are put on public display. They are childbearing women, their babies hung at their breasts, the very symbol of fertility. At 1 Macc. 1:61, the babies are hung from the women's necks, a much more practical suggestion. But the author of 2 Maccabees emphasizes the women's fertility. Cities in the ancient world survived through childbearing, yet here childbearing women are presented and paraded as antithetical to the values that Antiochus IV espoused for the city. By prohibiting circumcision, the new government in Jerusalem was excluding new Jews from being in the city. It is important to note also that, for the Greeks, circumcision was a mutilation. The prepuce was an ornament provided by nature,[31] and circumcision seen as arising from superstition.[32] Philo, even while dismissing the notion, recognized that circumcision was ridiculed by many people.[33] To be circumcised was thus not appropriate for a member of a Greek city.[34]

The second incident involving Sabbath observance takes place away from the city (2 Macc. 6:11). The group gathers in secret, out of public view, in caves, not in civilized dwellings. Here the city has been symbolically abandoned. However, even secret ritual actions are destroyed. Plato had argued that no one should possess shrines in private houses and that anyone who disobeyed was to be executed.[35] Plato recognized how religion is a central part of city life, as did Aristotle.[36] Private shrines suggested anti-public, anti-political activity.[37] They are alien rites. In Jerusalem under Antiochus IV's

---

30. K. M. Coleman, "Fatal Charades: Roman Executions Staged as Mythological Enactments," *JRS* 80 (1990): 44-73.
31. Galen, *De usu partium corporis humani* 11.13.
32. Strabo, *Geography* 16.4.5.
33. Philo, *Special Laws* 1.1.2.
34. On this whole question, see Frederick M. Hodges, "The Ideal Prepuce in Ancient Greece and Rome: Male Genital Aesthetics and Their Relation to *Lipodermos*, Circumcision, Foreskin Restoration, and the *Kynodesme*," *Bulletin of the History of Medicine* 75 (2001): 375-405.
35. Plato, *Laws* 10.909-910d.
36. Aristotle, *Politics* 1322b, 1328b.
37. The Roman senator Postumius argued that the rites of Dionysos be suppressed in

new rules, Jewish rituals are attacked as anti-polis, as a threat to the state, and as if they were foreign. The irony is that the audience knows that the observance of the Sabbath is part and parcel of Jewish ancestral tradition and that Philip, the Phrygian (5:22), is the foreigner. Sabbath observance was part of the ancestral law: "You shall keep the Sabbath, because it is holy for you; everyone who profanes it shall be put to death; whoever does any work on it shall be cut off from among the people" (Exod. 31:14).[38]

Kosher regulations are also part of the ancestral law (Leviticus 11), particularly the eating of blood: "I will set my face against that person who eats blood, and will cut that person off from the people" (Lev. 17:10). The narrative about the death of Eleazar appears to take place at a meal setting with Eleazar among his "friends." As a prominent member of society, Eleazar has been invited to a meal, but this "Greek" meal involves a sacrifice to the gods. His friends suggest that next time he eats with them he can bring his own food and pretend to eat non-kosher flesh (2 Macc. 6:21). The author emphasizes that Eleazar is of the same social status as his meal companions, and the story is a debate among equals about how to behave. Like any well-brought-up gentleman, Eleazar rejects pretense. However, if he is to maintain his status in society, it is required that he participate in such meals. The story of the mother and her seven sons is quite different in character. Here they are brought before the king at a trial. The highly emotional quality of the narrative does not allow one to conclude anything about what really happened.

That circumcision and kosher laws could be considered part of "ancestral law" is suggested also by Josephus's attack on Apion. In response to Apion's denunciation of the Jews for not eating pork and for practicing circumcision, Josephus pointed out that Egyptian priests were circumcised and abstained from eating swine's flesh.[39] He concludes: "I cannot, therefore, but regard the penalty which Apion paid for the blasphemy towards his ancestral laws (εἰς τοὺς πατρίους αὐτοῦ νόμους) as just and appropriate. An ulcer on

---

Rome in 186 B.C.E. because they were secret/hidden rites performed at night. Livy 39.15.2-3; 39.16.6-9. Cf. Cicero, *De Natura Deorum* 1.56; 2.71; *De Divinatione* 1.132. For a brilliant analysis of the affair, see Erich Gruen, "The Bacchanalian Affair," in idem, *Studies in Greek Culture and Roman Policy* (Berkeley: University of California Press, 1990), 34-78.

38. The phrase "cut off from among the people" is also found at Exod. 12:15, 19; Num. 9:13 (Passover ritual); Lev. 23:29 (Yom Kippur); Lev. 7:20, 21; 22:3; Num. 19:13, 20 (state of impurity); Lev. 7:25; 19:8 (sacrificial mistakes); intentional sin (Num. 15:30); Lev. 7:27 (eating blood).

39. Josephus, *Ag. Ap.* 2.137-42.

his person rendered circumcision essential; the operation brought no relief, gangrene set in, and he died in terrible tortures."[40]

What I am suggesting, therefore, is that the narrative found in 2 Maccabees 5–7 provides a coherent account of what happened in Judea under Antiochus IV. Thinking the city was in revolt, Antiochus IV took it by storm and abrogated the gift of allowing the city to live by its ancestral laws, as his father had done formerly to Apollonia at Rhyndacos. The new "Greek" laws imposed on the city included cultic celebration of the birthday of the king, sacrifices to Zeus, and processions in honor of Dionysos. The ancestral laws abrogated included circumcision, Sabbath observance, and kosher regulations. It appears that these were attacked not because Antiochus IV was persecuting the Jewish religion, but because circumcision affected citizenship, Sabbath observance affected the civic economy, and kosher regulations affected cultic meals — they were part of the ancestral law that was being abrogated.

V. What Really Happened?

What I have been proposing so far is that this is the intent of the author of the condensed version. He was drawing on a traditional *topos* to affect the emotions of his audience. Is this really what happened? The author has structured his narrative to suit his own rhetorical aims and is not concerned about "history" as we are. He does not take into account, for example, the shame inflicted on Antiochus by the Roman Popillius Laenas. One can see Antiochus's determination to regain prestige by his elaborate staging of the games at Daphne in Antioch in 166 B.C.E. to honor his victory in Egypt.[41] Gruen is right to argue that the psychological effect of the "Day at Eleusis" led to Antiochus wanting to show that he was still a force to be reckoned with. Earlier scholars were also right to point to the unusualness of the events. However, I would suggest that one should also take into account that what happened in Jerusalem was the result of Antiochus IV following the same principles as his father in dealing with rebellious cities: he would not allow them to follow their own ancestral laws, but instituted others. The tragedy was that, in his ignorance, he did not know that the ancestral laws of Jerusalem were quite different from those in other cities in that they were the

40. Josephus, *Ag. Ap.* 2.143.
41. Polybius 30.25.1–30.31.3.

laws of the one God. Not knowing Jewish society, he did not foresee the consequences of his actions. This accounts for the unusualness of what happened. When it became apparent what those consequences were, he did not hesitate to change his position.

Constructing Jewish Identity in Ptolemaic Egypt: The Case of Artapanus

Patricia D. Ahearne-Kroll

In recent years, some scholars have been rethinking the origin of noncanonical literature and questioning previous scholarship's designation of some of this literature as "Jewish."[1] Many of the proponents of this position argue that Christian scribes produced the textual evidence that preserves noncanonical texts,[2] and so we should first analyze this literature as "Christian" and more cautiously determine whether or not Jewish authors initially composed these texts. In principle, this approach raises an important point: if a particular literary text is preserved in a Christian manuscript, the rhetoric and purpose of that manuscript should receive considerable attention before we hypothesize about the origin of the literary text. Unfortu-

---

1. Robert A. Kraft has articulated this problem in "The Pseudepigrapha in Christianity," in *Tracing the Threads: Studies in the Vitality of Jewish Pseudepigrapha*, ed. John C. Reeves (SBLEJL 6; Atlanta: Scholars Press, 1994), 55-86; idem, "The Pseudepigrapha and Christianity Revisited: Setting the Stage and Framing Some Central Questions," *JSJ* 32 (2001): 371-95. Building on Kraft's observations, James R. Davila proposes a set of guidelines for this type of analysis in *The Provenance of the Pseudepigrapha: Jewish, Christian, or Other?* (Leiden: Brill, 2005), but see critiques by Marinus de Jonge (review in *JSJ* 38 (2007): 101-3) and Sabrina Inowlocki (*RBL*, 28 October 2006).

2. "Noncanonical texts" simply refer to pseudepigrapha, apocrypha, and other writings that are generally ascribed to Jewish or Christian audiences of the Greco-Roman period but are not within modern religious canons (or "bibles") that consist of literature dated to the same ancient period. "Literary text" stands for a clearly identifiable, independent written work, and "manuscript" or "textual witness" refers to the actual evidence that preserves literary texts; any given manuscript/witness can preserve more than one literary text.

nately, the evidence for much noncanonical literature complicates this approach. Any particular literary text may be partially preserved or may exhibit slight variations in several manuscripts,[3] and some literary texts are attested with extreme variations in the textual witnesses.[4] There is also the matter of the production and use of manuscripts, which raises the issue of distinguishing between scribal reception and transmission, on the one hand, and the origin of a literary text, on the other.[5]

These complications notwithstanding, the critique raised by these scholars challenges us to take more seriously the manuscript evidence and to articulate more explicitly the criteria that are used in identifying a text as "Jewish." I will apply these considerations to a related issue: Artapanus's presentation of Moses in his work entitled *On the Jews*.[6] Ever since Freudenthal's work on Polyhistor, most discussions of Artapanus's writings conclude that Artapanus was Jewish, but not without qualifications;[7] reservations about his "Jewishness" remain, as Howard Jacobson has recently argued.[8]

---

3. See, for example, the manuscript evidence for the narrative *Joseph and Aseneth*. Christoph Burchard, *Joseph und Aseneth* (PVTG 5; Leiden: Brill, 2003).

4. See the discussion by Christine M. Thomas in *The Acts of Peter, Gospel Literature, and the Ancient Novel: Rewriting the Past* (New York: Oxford University Press, 2003).

5. Bart Ehrman discusses examples of this problem in *Studies in the Textual Criticism of the New Testament* (Leiden: Brill, 2006). On the mechanics and history of Christian literature production, see Harry Y. Gamble, *Books and Readers in the Early Church: A History of Early Christian Texts* (New Haven: Yale University Press, 1995).

6. Eusebius refers once to Artapanus's work as *Judaica*, but elsewhere he calls it *On the Jews*, the title also used by Clement of Alexandria. The two titles probably refer to the same work. See John J. Collins, "Artapanus," in *OTP* 2:889; Carl R. Holladay, *Fragments from Hellenistic Jewish Authors*, vol. 1: *Historians* (SBLTT 20, SBL Pseudepigrapha Series 10; Chico, Calif.: Scholars Press, 1983), 189 and 227, n. 12; Jacob Freudenthal, *Alexander Polyhistor und die von ihm erhaltenen Reste judäischer und samaritanischer Geschichtswerke* (Breslau: H. Skutsch, 1875), especially 206.

7. Freudenthal, *Alexander Polyhistor*, 143-53; see the summary of scholarly positions from Freudenthal until the early 1990s in Gregory E. Sterling, *Historiography and Self-Definition: Josephos, Luke-Acts and Apologetic Historiography* (Leiden: Brill, 1992), 179, n. 218.

8. Howard Jacobson, "Artapanus Judaeus," *JJS* 57 (2006): 210-21. The term "Jewishness" is taken from Shaye J. D. Cohen's discussion, in which the term signifies all the features of a person's life and worldview that constituted her/his self-identification as "Jewish" (*The Beginnings of Jewishness: Boundaries, Varieties, Uncertainties* [Berkeley: University of California Press, 1999], 1-10). As Cohen also discusses, the overarching features that constitute "Jewishness" are related to the identity formulation of ethnic groups. The content of "Jewishness," then, can be understood in a general way according to Jonathan M. Hall's definition of ethnic groups (*Hellenicity: Between Ethnicity and Culture* [Chicago: University of Chicago Press, 2002], 9-10). Although the concept of "religion" is arguably more than a "sur-

Although the issue here is not whether Artapanus was Jewish as opposed to Christian (rather, it is whether he was Jewish as opposed to non-Jewish Greek), the debate entails similar problems to those scholars face when studying other noncanonical literature that is preserved by Christian writers. The challenge rests upon presumed constructions of identity and upon discerning which construction best corresponds to the content of the text. The greatest conundrum regarding Artapanus's work is his declaration that Moses assigned an Egyptian god for each nome and even chose the animals that would be associated with these gods (27.4). The man who would later inscribe the covenantal agreement between God and the Hebrews is credited with acting in opposition to a fundamental tenet of that very agreement: according to Artapanus, Moses promoted polytheistic religious practices. For this reason, it is tempting to conclude, as Howard Jacobson does, that "No Jew would have used the tale of Moses as institutor of Egyptian animal worship."[9] In disagreement with this position, I will argue in support of the Jewishness of Artapanus, but I will also propose a subtle paradigm shift concerning how to describe formulations of Jewish identity in antiquity. The very obstacle that Artapanus constructs, and which raises questions for scholars about his identity, contributes to a Jewish critique of the religious and political systems that Artapanus and his peers encountered.

I. Detecting Jewish Authorship

Artapanus's work is preserved in fragmentary form because only parts of the text are quoted in the works of two Christian writers, Clement of Alexandria and Eusebius of Caesarea. A small fragment of Artapanus's work is preserved in Clement's pedagogical work *Stromata*, which was composed in the latter half of the second century C.E. The longest fragments are preserved in Eusebius's *Praeparatio Evangelica*, which he wrote in the early fourth century, shortly after becoming bishop of Caesarea. Eusebius explicitly cites that his source for Artapanus's work is an ethnographical composition entitled *On the Jews* and written by the Greek historian Alexander Polyhistor (dated to the mid-first century B.C.E.).[10] Since the fragment from Clement is be-

---

face pointer" for Jewish identity in antiquity, much of the way Hall defines ethnicity is helpful when dealing with evidence for Jewish life in Ptolemaic Egypt.

9. "Artapanus Judaeus," 219-20.

10. On the writings of Alexander Polyhistor, see Freudenthal, *Alexander Polyhistor*, and Felix Jacoby, *Die Fragmente der griechischen Historiker*, vol. 3A (Leiden: Brill, 1954).

lieved to be taken from Polyhistor as well,[11] and the association of Moses and the Egyptian animal cults is preserved only in the Eusebius quotations, I will focus on Eusebius's preservation of Artapanus's work.

Eusebius quotes from Polyhistor extensively in chapter nine, where he presents his case that the "Greeks" knew a significant amount about Jewish history.[12] Previous to this chapter, Eusebius presents a Hebrew narrative of descent that outlines the superiority of the ancient Hebrews over the Greeks but at the same time distinguishes them from contemporary Jews of Eusebius's day (chaps. 7–8), setting up his argument for why Christianity embraced the Hebrew traditions.[13] In chapter nine, Eusebius launches into his second string of attacks against the "Greeks," arguing that they were well-informed about the Hebrew traditions (which the "Greeks" called Jewish traditions), and then proceeds to present the case that the "Greeks" were "thieves and plagiarizers" of traditions more ancient than their own (chaps. 10–13.13).[14] The rhetorical purpose of chapter nine, then, is to emphasize the Greekness of Eusebius's sources and not the Jewish works that may underlie them.[15] When Eusebius quotes from Polyhistor, he is more interested in the Greekness of Polyhistor than the precise background of Polyhistor's sources. As Sabrina Inowlocki has demonstrated, Eusebius appears to closely copy Polyhistor's text, so much so that he "takes pains to cite the editorial notes which Polyhistor inserted between the different excerpts of the Jewish authors."[16] Our knowledge about Polyhistor is limited, but he is credited with twenty-five writings that focus on geography and culture, specifically eth-

---

11. According to Sterling (*Historiography and Self-Definition*, 147), Clement presents excerpts from Eupolemus, Artapanus, and Ezekiel the Tragedian in a sequential order that is similar to that of Eusebius, who explicitly cites Polyhistor as the source for these literary texts (cf. Clement, *Strom.* 1.23.153-55, and Eusebius, *Praep. Evang.* 9.26-28).

12. Aaron P. Johnson, *Ethnicity and Argument in Eusebius'* Praeparatio Evangelica (New York: Oxford University Press, 2006), 128-52.

13. Johnson, *Ethnicity and Argument*, 94-125; Sabrina Inowlocki, *Eusebius and the Jewish Authors: His Citation Technique in an Apologetic Context* (AGJU 64; Leiden: Brill, 2006), 105-38.

14. Johnson, *Ethnicity and Argument*, 128-52. On Eusebius's rhetorical strategy in his construction of social groups (e.g., "Jews," "Hebrews," "Greeks," and "barbarians"), see ibid., 25-54.

15. This explains, for example, why Clement does not mention Polyhistor in using his material but Eusebius does. Inowlocki, *Eusebius and the Jewish Authors*, 275.

16. Inowlocki, *Eusebius and the Jewish Authors*, 276. On the reliability of Eusebius's quotations from Polyhistor, see Freudenthal, *Alexander Polyhistor*, 3-16; and Sterling, *Historiography and Self-Definition*, 142. On Eusebius's rhetorical strategy in his citation technique in general, see Inowlocki, *Eusebius and the Jewish Authors*.

nography. He appears to have been a collector and compiler of writings, and for this reason, most scholars believe that Polyhistor copied faithfully from Artapanus's work.[17] Yet we cannot discern from our evidence what Polyhistor's perception of Artapanus's identity was; he records both Greek (i.e., non-Jewish Greek)[18] and Jewish writings (e.g., from Demetrius the Chronographer and Ezekiel the Tragedian) in his compilation *On the Jews*. Neither Eusebius nor Polyhistor, then, either negates or confirms the Jewishness of Artapanus.

Because the sources of Artapanus's work do not provide explicit clues about its background, it is the content of the text itself that provides the basis for our analysis. Artapanus's level of knowledge of the Genesis and Exodus narratives and his portrayal of the superiority of the Hebrew ancestors over Egyptian leaders are the predominant reasons why most scholars think that he was Jewish.[19] Howard Jacobson challenges these assumptions based on the argument that non-Jewish Greek writers knew Septuagint texts and that they sometimes portrayed the superiority of other non-Greeks in their writings.[20] I will evaluate these two points separately.

With regard to non-Jewish writings that demonstrate familiarity with the Septuagint, Louis H. Feldman presents the evidence in two categories: (1) literature that paraphrases verses from Genesis 1, and (2) literature that was likely written using the Septuagint as a source.[21] One of the examples from the book of Genesis comes from the work, *De Universi Natura*, where Ocellus discusses the purpose of sexual intercourse:

---

17. J. Strugnell, "General Introduction, With a Note on Alexander Polyhistor," in *OTP* 2:778; Sterling, *Historiography and Self-Definition*, 145.

18. For example, passages from Timochares and the "Syrian measurer." Inowlocki, *Eusebius and the Jewish Authors*, 275, n. 285.

19. Carl H. Holladay, *"Theios Aner" in Hellenistic Judaism: A Critique of the Use of This Category in New Testament Christology* (SBLDS 40; Missoula, Mont.: Scholars Press, 1977), 216-32; Collins, *OTP* 2:890-95; idem, *Between Athens and Jerusalem: Jewish Identity in the Hellenistic Diaspora*, 2d ed. (Grand Rapids: Eerdmans, 2000), 37-46; Sterling, *Historiography and Self-Definition*, 167-86; John M. G. Barclay, *Jews in the Mediterranean Diaspora: From Alexander to Trajan (323 BCE–117 CE)* (Edinburgh: T. & T. Clark, 1996), 127-32; Erich S. Gruen, *Heritage and Hellenism: The Reinvention of Jewish Tradition* (Berkeley: University of California Press, 1998), 155-60.

20. Jacobson, "Artapanus Judaeus," 217-19.

21. Louis H. Feldman, *Jew and Gentile in the Ancient World: Attitudes and Interactions from Alexander to Justinian* (Princeton: Princeton University Press, 1993), 311-14. Feldman builds upon the work of Menahem Stern, *Greek and Latin Authors on Jews and Judaism*, 3 vols. (Jerusalem: Israel Academy of Sciences and Humanities, 1974-84).

Constructing Jewish Identity in Ptolemaic Egypt

People have to think over these matters beforehand and thus not come to sexual intercourse like irrational animals, but to consider as necessary and good that which good men think necessary and good, namely, *that households not only will abound in men and the greater part of the earth will be filled* (man is indeed the gentlest and best of all creatures) but, which is the most important thing, that they will also have an abundance of good men. (§46)

Greek text of the italicized portion above:

τὸ μὴ μόνον πολυανδρεῖσθαι τοὺς οἴκους καὶ τὸν πλείονα τῆς γῆς τόπον <u>πληροῦσθαι</u> (ἡμερώτατον γὰρ πάντων καὶ βέλτιστον ζῷον ὁ ἄνθρωπος), ἀλλὰ καί τὸ μέγιστον εὐανδρεῖσθαι.[22]

In Richard Harder's reconstruction of Ocellus's original text, he primarily uses four fifteenth-century manuscripts that best preserve the work.[23] Only one of the manuscripts, M, exhibits the word πληροῦσθαι, which Harder and others argue is an allusion to Gen. 1:28 (ὁ θεὸς λέγων Αὐξάνεσθε καὶ πληθύνεσθε καὶ <u>πληρώσατε</u> τὴν γῆν καὶ κατακυριεύσατε αὐτῆς).[24] The verb πληροῦσθαι is necessary neither in the logic of this sentence nor in the overall argument of Ocellus, and without πληροῦσθαι, the contrast of πολυανδρεῖσθαι and εὐανδρεῖσθαι makes sense in his discussion. Ocellus argues that the social location of sexual intercourse should be within marriage for the purpose of procreation, but he outlines the ways that men can ensure good progeny (so in a sense, εὐανδρία) who contribute appropriately to the household, the city, and the world.[25] The ending of section 46, then, could have read: "that not only households and the greater part of the earth abound in men, but, which is the most important thing, that they also have an abundance of good men." Harder argues that such a reading would be

---

22. Translation is taken from Stern, *Greek and Latin Authors*, 1:133; and the Greek text is from the commentary by Richard Harder, *Ocellus Lucanus: Text und Kommentar* (Berlin: Weidmannsche Buchhandlung, 1926), 22.

23. Harder (*Ocellus Lucanus*, iii-x) provides the following categorization: manuscript A (Parisinus graecus 1928), M (Marcianus 263), B (Parisinus graecus 2018), and R (Florentinus Riccardianus 70).

24. Discussed by Harder (*Ocellus Lucanus*, 128-32), and supported by Feldman (*Jew and Gentile in the Ancient World*, 312) and Stern (*Greek and Latin Authors*, 1:131-32).

25. He discusses the kind of women men should marry, the diet for both men and women, and the form of instruction for boys and girls (§§43-57).

nonsensical and would create an asymmetrical syntax whereby πολυανδρεῖσθαι has two subjects and εὐανδρεῖσθαι has one.[26] Immediately preceding this verse, however, Ocellus mentions the superior role of humankind (ἄνθρωπος) on the earth (γῆ) and the importance of humankind's everlasting presence on the earth (§§38-40). Likewise, the parenthetical comment "man is indeed the gentlest and best of all creatures" (§46) also alludes to this previous point. Section 46 lies within Ocellus's extension of his argument about humanity's purpose by discussing the motivations by which men should perpetuate their species. Harder's choice appears to be influenced, at least in part, by his position that the Hellenistic philosophical circles were more sophisticated and intellectually open than their politically and economically minded contemporaries, and so he supports the likelihood that some of these philosophers studied Jewish legal material (the LXX) as they studied other "foreign" legal tracts and traditions.[27] As a general theory, I agree that scholarship needs to be open to the idea that such kinds of transactions occurred (e.g., such as with the case of Pseudo-Longinus, discussed below), but I do not consider this particular case to be a convincing example.[28] It is equally possible that at some point during the sixteen centuries after this work was written πληροῦσθαι was added. That is, a Christian scribe, sensing an allusion to Genesis (πολυανδρεῖσθαι . . . τὸν πλείονα τῆς γῆς τόπον) may have interpolated πληροῦσθαι in order to align Ocellus's discussion more closely with Genesis 1.[29] This is not to say that a minority attestation in a manuscript tradition always dictates that the particular textual witness does not preserve the original composition; in this case, however, Harder's argument does not convincingly demonstrate that πληροῦσθαι is authentic.

26. Harder, *Ocellus Lucanus*, 128-29.
27. Ibid., 129-32.
28. Harder also mentions that manuscript M seems to preserve the correct attestation (or closer to correct) in three other places against manuscripts ABR (in §10, since M reads ἐπειδεῖ καὶ against ABR ἐπειδὴ καί, so Harder produced ἐπιδεῖται in his reconstruction; in §21, M reads καὶ ἡ ὕλη instead of λευκὸν; and in §45, M reads πολιτικῆς, against ABR πολίτης [however, in manuscript M there is apparently a citation that R reads πολιτικῆς]) (*Ocellus Lucanus*, iv). Harder admits, however, that these attestations cannot alone prove that πληροῦσθαι is authentic (p. 128). See also Willy Theiler's reservations on the choice of depending on πληροῦσθαι in the reconstructed text (review of Richard Harder, *Ocellus Lucanus: Text und Kommentar, Gnomon* 2 [1926]: 589-90).
29. Ocellus's image of the abundance of humankind on the earth and his association of procreation with divine intention and the good (§§43-47) also may have triggered the scribe's connection with the first creation narrative in Genesis.

Constructing Jewish Identity in Ptolemaic Egypt

Another set of LXX Genesis references are supposedly made by Pseudo-Ecphantus, but the argument for these literary allusions is based on conceptual connections and not literal or contextual correspondences. The first example is an alleged allusion to Gen. 2:7 in Pseudo-Ecphantus 4.6.22; in Genesis, God fashions the human being by breathing into him the breath of life (ἐνεφύσησεν εἰς τὸ πρόσωπον αὐτοῦ πνοὴν ζωῆς), and in Pseudo-Ecphantus humanity was given "some sort of divine inspiration, which attached him to the eternal living being, displaying to his better part the holy aspect of the Creator" (θεομοιρής τις ἐμπνοίησις ἀιδίῳ ζῴῳ συνᾶψεν αὐτὸ τῷ κρείσσονι μέρει δεικνῦσα τὰν ἱερὰν τῷ γεννάτορος πότοψιν).[30] What complicates matters is that Pseudo-Ecphantus shares more in common conceptually here with Philo's writings (e.g., *Opif.* 135; *Leg.* 1.38; and *Det.* 86), and, given the lack of a verbal connection with the Genesis verse, the question remains whether Pseudo-Ecphantus took from Genesis directly or rather borrowed ideas from other Jewish thinkers.[31] The second supposed reference is to Gen. 1:27, in Pseudo-Ecphantus 4.7.64; in the former, God created humanity in the image of God (κατ' εἰκόνα θεοῦ ἐποίησεν αὐτόν), while in the latter, the king "was made by the best craftsman, who wrought him using himself as a model" (ὑπὸ τεχνίτα δ' εἰργασμένος λῴστω, ὅς ἐτεχνίτευσεν αὐτόν ἀρχετύπῳ χρώμενος ἑαυτῷ).[32] Again, the conceptual, but not literal, correspondence weakens the direct link to Genesis 1, and even the conceptual parallel is not exact, since Pseudo-Ecphantus discusses only how kings are made according to a divine model, not all of humanity.[33] Finally, neither example clearly alludes to the narrative context of the Genesis creation accounts (such as mentioning other elements of their respective plotlines), which would better indicate that these Septuagint passages were sources for Pseudo-Ecphantus.

The strongest argument for a non-Jewish Greek writer's direct familiarity with the Septuagint is Pseudo-Longinus's reference. In chapter nine of his work *On the Sublime*, Pseudo-Longinus discusses the "successful and un-

---

30. Translation and Greek text of Pseudo-Ecphantus from Stern, *Greek and Latin Authors*, 3:36.

31. Holger Thesleff argues for a Stoic influence here (*An Introduction to the Pythagorean Writings of the Hellenistic Period* [Acta Academiae Aboensis, Ser. A, 24.3; Åbo: Akademi, 1961], 68-70), and Walter Burkert proposes the LXX influence ("Zur geistesgeschichtlichen Einordnung einiger Pseudopythagorica," in *Pseudepigrapha I* [Entretiens sur l'antiquité classique, vol. 18; Vandoeuvres-Genève: Fondation Hardt, 1971], 49-51).

32. Stern, *Greek and Latin Authors*, 3:36-37.

33. See discussions by Stern, *Greek and Latin Authors*, 3:37; Thesleff, *Introduction to the Pythagorean Writings*, 69-70; and Burkert, "Zur geistesgeschichtlichen Einordnung," 52-53.

successful ways of representing supernatural beings and of exciting awe."³⁴ One of the effective examples is a clear reference to Genesis 1:

> A similar effect was achieved by the lawgiver of the Jews — no mean genius, for he both understood and gave expression to the power of the divinity as it deserved — when he wrote at the beginning of his laws, I quote his words: "God said" — what? — "Let there be light. And there was. Let there be earth. And there was." (9.9)

> ταύτῃ καὶ ὁ τῶν Ἰουδαίων θεσμοθέτης, οὐχ ὁ τυχὼν ἀνήρ, ἐπειδὴ τὴν τοῦ θείου δύναμιν κατὰ τὴν ἀξίαν ἐχώρησε κἀξέφηνεν, εὐθὺς ἐν τῇ εἰσβολῇ γράψας τῶν νόμων "εἶπεν ὁ θεός" φησί, — τί; "γενέσθω φῶς καὶ ἐγένετο· γενέσθω γῆ, καὶ ἐγένετο."³⁵

Not only does Pseudo-Longinus refer to the pentateuchal tradition (with an allusion to Moses), but also the first part of his quotation corresponds very closely to Gen. 1:3.³⁶ Even though the second part of the quotation never appears in Genesis 1, it conveys the sense of supernatural power that Pseudo-Longinus intends in a manner consonant with the book of Genesis. Pseudo-Longinus often adjusts his presentation of other sources in order to make his points,³⁷ so his paraphrase does not seem out of place here. This example seems to be well represented in the manuscript evidence,³⁸ and since it is clear that this writer knew Genesis 1, scholars have debated whether Pseudo-Longinus was Jewish.³⁹ Those who have argued *for* Pseudo-Longinus's Jewish-

---

34. D. A. Russell, ed., *Longinus: On the Sublime* (Oxford: Clarendon Press, 1964), xv, referring to lines 4-11.

35. Translation and Greek text from Russell, *Longinus,* 93 and 11-12, respectively.

36. LXX Gen. 1:3: καὶ εἶπεν ὁ θεὸς γενηθήτω φῶς. καὶ ἐγένετο φῶς.

37. For example, in the same chapter, (1) in line 4, he briefly alludes to but does not literally quote from a story about Alexander the Great and Parmenio that both Arrian and Plutarch narrate (in *Anabasis* 2.25.2 and *Alexander* 29.8-9, respectively); and (2) in line 6, he conflates several lines from the *Iliad* to illustrate Homer's presentation of the "Battle of the Gods" (21.388, 5.750, and 20.61-65), and then in line 8 he conflates a different set of lines from the *Iliad* to demonstrate ways in which Poseidon's power is expressed (13.18, 20.60, 13.19, and 13.27-29). See Russell, *Longinus,* 10-11.

38. Russell bases his text on the tenth-century manuscript Parisinus 2036 (P), from which eight of the ten other extant manuscripts descend (xlix-l). He does not mention any variant readings of 9.9 from the manuscript tradition.

39. See Russell, *Longinus,* xxix-xxx, 93-94, and the review in Stern, *Greek and Latin Authors,* 1:361-63.

ness base it on the implausibility that a non-Jewish writer would know the Septuagint, and those who have argued *against* his Jewishness base their position on the unlikelihood that a Jewish writer would refer to himself as "Greek" ("Ελλην). The "Greek" self-reference, however, is used to unite the writer and the named recipient of this treatise, Terentianus (e.g., "we Greeks," in 12.4), so it is difficult to separate the Greek reference from the intended effects of the work. Given the flexibility of the term "hellene" in the ancient world,[40] such an identifier does not necessarily mean "non-Jew." Furthermore, since some Jews, like Philo of Alexandria, participated in Hellenistic educational systems, cross-cultural transactions between educated Jews and non-Jewish Greeks are not out of the question.[41] The difference between this passage in Pseudo-Longinus and Harder's Ocellus text is that the manuscript evidence better supports the authenticity of the use of LXX Genesis in the former than in the latter.

Although Pseudo-Longinus provides the best textual link to the Septuagint (linguistically and contextually), his brief example from Genesis 1 is overshadowed by the numerous literary examples from non-Jewish Greek literature that make up most of his work (chaps. 9–43). Other non-Jewish writers wrote about Jewish traditions,[42] but in most of these cases it is difficult to ascertain whether their sources were particular Septuagint texts or other traditions that may have circulated about Jewish history. Even if some did have pentateuchal texts at their disposal, we are mostly left with few literal references to the Septuagint or with even more fragmentary evidence than we have for Artapanus. The number of cases in which non-Jewish writers provide literal and contextual links to particular Septuagint texts is small and therefore not sufficient to support Jacobson's claim that Artapanus was not necessarily Jewish.

40. For examples, see the essays in *Ancient Perceptions of Greek Ethnicity*, ed. Irad Malkin (Cambridge, Mass.: Harvard University Press, 2001), especially the article by Dorothy J. Thompson, "Hellenistic Hellenes: The Case of Ptolemaic Egypt," 301-22; see also Hall, *Hellenicity*.

41. On the likelihood of Jewish participation in Greek educational circles, see Feldman, *Jew and Gentile in the Ancient World*, 57-63; Erich S. Gruen, *Diaspora: Jews amidst Greeks and Romans* (Cambridge, Mass.: Harvard University Press, 2002), 104-32.

42. Feldman lists the following writers: Apollonius Molon, Teucer of Cyzicus, Apion of Alexandria, Herennius Philo of Byblos, Pompeius Trogus, Tacitus, Celsus, and Numenius of Apamea (*Jew and Gentile in the Ancient World*, 312-13). The last two demonstrate the most convincing examples of Septuagint usage. In his composition *The True Doctrine*, Celsus makes significant references to the Septuagint (primarily to the book of Genesis), and Porphyry quotes Numenius where he paraphrases Gen. 1:2 (Stern, *Greek and Latin Authors*, 2:224-305 and 215, respectively).

In comparison with these examples, Artapanus fragment 3 relies extensively upon the book of Exodus in two ways. First, his history of Moses is constructed within the narrative time frame of Exodus 1–16. Artapanus shares the following specific events with the Exodus account: (1) the rise of a Pharaoh who mistreated the Israelites (Artap.: Ἰουδαῖοι) and commissioned building construction in at least two Lower Egyptian cities, one of which was Heliopolis (Exod. 1:8-11; Artap. 27.1-2); (2) the adoption and naming of Moses by Pharaoh's daughter (Exod. 2:5-10; Artap. 27.3); (3) Moses' slaying of an Egyptian and his subsequent flight from Egypt, residence with Raguel, and marriage to Raguel's daughter (Exod. 2:11-12, 15-21; Artap. 27.17-19); (4) God's speaking from the unnatural fire and commanding Moses to confront Pharaoh and lead the people back to their ancestral land (Exod. 3:1–4:17; 6:1-8; Artap. 27.21); (5) Moses' first approaching Aaron before confronting Pharaoh (Exod. 4:27-31; Artap. 27.22); (6) Moses' initial court encounter with Pharaoh/the king and his demands for the release of the Israelites/Jews (Exod. 5:1-3; Artap. 27.22); (7) magical acts performed with a rod (turning the rod into a serpent and affecting the Nile so that it was incapable of sustaining life and of producing drinkable water), and the comparable magical acts performed by Pharaoh's/the king's professionals, which cause Pharaoh/the king to ignore Moses' demands (Exod. 7:8-23; Artap. 27.27-31); (8) six more plagues: winged creatures that attack solely Egyptians and not the Israelites/Jews (Exod. 8:20-24; possibly referred to in Artap. 27.31); body sores that affected even medico-magical professionals (Exod. 9:8-12; Artap. 27.31 [although in Artapanus, the sores are caused by the winged creatures]); frogs (Exod. 7:25–8:15; Artap. 27.32); locusts (Exod. 10:1-20; Artap. 27.32); gnats (Exod. 8:16-19; Artap. 27.32); and hail (Exod. 9:13-35; Artap. 27.33); (9) Pharaoh's/the king's release of the Israelites/Jews, whom Egyptians furnish with clothing and precious items (Exod. 12:31-36; Artap. 27.34); (10) the people's departure and approach to the Red Sea (Exod. 12:37-39; 13:17-18; Artap. 27.34); (11) the people's crossing of the Red Sea after Moses is instructed by God to use his rod to divide it, and Pharaoh's troops being defeated by fire and the flooding waters (Exod. 14:15-18, 21-29; Artap. 27.36-37); and (12) God's provision of manna in the wilderness (Exod. 16; Artap. 27.37).[43] Even though Artapanus adds a great deal to the

---

43. See also Sterling, *Historiography and Self-Definition*, 173-75. Eusebius's presentation of Artapanus includes the death of the Egyptian ruler, Chenephres (Artap. 27.20), and, in the next verse, Moses' encounters with God through the divine fire (27.21). This sequence of events corresponds with the report of the Egyptian king's death in Exod. 2:23 and the narration of Moses and the burning bush in the following verses (Exod. 3:1-10). The short por-

period between Moses' birth and God's appointment of him, this fragment stays faithful to the overall plot of Exodus.[44]

Second, fragment 3 provides a few linguistic connections with the Septuagint text. Both texts use ῥάβδος for the rod of magical performance (Exod. 4:2-4; 7:9-10, 17-19; 8:5-6, 16-17 [belonging to Moses and Aaron]; Artap. 27.27-29 [belonging only to Moses]); ἕλκος and ἐξελκόω for the plague of body sores (the nominal use in Exod. 9:8-12 and the verbal cognate in Artap. 27.31); βάτραχος, ἀκρίς, and σκνίψ for the plagues of pestilent creatures (Exod. 8:1-19; 10:3-20; Artap. 27.32); χάλαζα for the plague of hail (Exod. 9:13-35; Artap. 27.33); χράω for the furnishing of materials by the Egyptians (Exod. 12:36; Artap. 27.34); and ἐρυθρὴ θάλασσα for the "Red Sea" (Exod. 13:18; 15:22; Artap. 27.34).[45] In Artapanus 27.28, Moses strikes (πατάσσω) the Nile with his rod (ῥάβδος), and the stagnant water begins to smell (ἐπόζω). Although in Exodus the actor is Aaron, the description of his actions and the effects on the Nile correspond in content and words to LXX Exod. 7:18, 20-21.[46] Likewise, in Artapanus 27.30, the Egyptian priests use incantations (ἐπαοιδοί) and make (ποιέω) a serpent (δράκων), and in Exodus, Pharaoh's enchanters (ἐπαοιδοί) help to make serpents (ποιέω δράκων) (7:10-12).[47] Compared to the examples above of how non-Jewish writers may have used pentateuchal traditions, Artapanus's considerable use of the Book of Exodus stands out. It supports the argument that he was Jewish, but it is not the only indicator.

Jacobson also argues that Artapanus's glorification of Moses, Abraham, and Joseph does not confirm that he was Jewish. Hecataeus of Abdera,

---

tion provided by Clement of Alexandria, however, portrays Chenephres as the Pharaoh whom Moses confronts when demanding the release of the people. For a comparison, see Holladay, *Fragments from Hellenistic Jewish Authors*, 1:218-19.

44. Aaron's role, however, is significantly reduced in Artapanus's version. For example, whereas in Exodus Aaron uses his rod to enact certain plagues (stagnation of the Nile and production of the frogs and gnats; 7:19-20; 8:5-6, 16-17), Artapanus gives credit to Moses and *his* rod for these acts (27.28-29, 32).

45. Collins, "Artapanus," 894.

46. Sterling, *Historiography and Self-Definition*, 174-75, n. 197.

47. According to Sterling (ibid., 174, n. 196), Artapanus also agrees with the Septuagint in six out of twenty personal names, although "it should be noted that the basic distinction is that in Artapanus the names assume a fully declinable form instead of the indeclinable transliterations of the LXX." In terms of place names, Artapanus agrees four times (out of eleven) with the Septuagint, but two times Artapanus uses anachronisms ("Syria" for "land of Canaan" and "Arabia" for "land of Midian"), and five times Artapanus uses names that are not attested in the Septuagint.

for example, "elevated Egyptians over the Greeks," so it is conceivable that a non-Jewish Greek "elevated Jews over Greeks and Egyptians."[48] Such an argument, however, diminishes the rhetorical design of the texts that these writers produced. Certainly in Hecataeus's ethnographic work on the Egyptians he places a higher priority on indigenous Egyptian sources than on Greek sources, and he portrays Egypt as the origin of civilization.[49] Yet Hecateaus came to Egypt at the beginning of Ptolemaic rule (Diodorus Siculus 1.46.8), and he most likely composed his historical work *Aegyptica* under the patronage of Ptolemy Soter.[50] His historiography helped to produce a new "Greek" identity in Egypt whereby perceptions of successful pharaonic rule in the past served as the model for Ptolemaic kingship in the present,[51] but by no means does his work promote Egyptian rule during his lifetime. Hecataeus's attention to Egyptian traditions corresponds well with other near contemporaries (e.g., Callimachus, Theocritus, and Apollonius of Rhodes), who formulated a new identity for Ptolemaic Greeks that separated them from classical traditions and rooted their history in the Egyptian pharaonic past.[52] Such a literary attempt corresponded to early Ptolemaic diplomatic ventures with the Egyptian priesthood and Ptolemaic

---

48. "Artapanus Judaeus," 218.

49. Sterling, *Historiography and Self-Definition*, 64-72; Bezalel Bar-Kochva, *Pseudo-Hecataeus "On the Jews": Legitimizing the Jewish Diaspora* (Berkeley: University of California Press, 1996), 13-14, 192-98.

50. Oswyn Murray, "Hecataeus of Abdera and Pharaonic Kingship," *JEA* 56 (1970): 141-71, here 166; Sterling, *Historiography and Self-Definition*, 74; Bar-Kochva, *Pseudo-Hecataeus "On the Jews,"* 7-8.

51. Susan A. Stephens, *Seeing Double: Intercultural Poetics in Ptolemaic Alexandria* (Berkeley: University of California Press, 2003), 32-36. On Hecataeus's use of Egyptian sources, see Stanley M. Burstein, "Hecataeus of Abdera's History of Egypt," in *Life in a Multi-Cultural Society: Egypt from Cambyses to Constantine and Beyond*, ed. Janet H. Johnson (SAOC 51; Chicago: University of Chicago Press, 1992), 45-49. Some scholars suggest that Hecataeus intended to motivate other Greeks in Egypt to respect Egyptian traditions so as to prevent conflict (Bar-Kochva, *Pseudo-Hecataeus "On the Jews,"* 16-17) or to motivate the Egyptian power base (i.e., the priests) to provide their support of Ptolemaic rule (Sterling, *Historiography and Self-Definition*, 74-75). Certainly Hecataeus's work could have aimed at these effects. Based on recent scholarly discussions about the various forms of cultural transactions that took place in Ptolemaic Egypt, it is important to add that his approach is best understood as a "convergence" of Egyptian and Greek ideas that produced a new way for Greeks in Egypt to think about themselves and their history (John Dillery, "Hecataeus of Abdera: Hyperboreans, Egypt, and the *Interpretatio Graeca*," *Historia* 47 [1998]: 255-75, esp. 255-60).

52. D. Seldon, "Alibis," *Cl. Ant.* 17 (1998): 299-412.

Constructing Jewish Identity in Ptolemaic Egypt

constructions of a distinct royal identity in Egypt,[53] and these transactions produced more cultural expressions of lasting value (as best exemplified in the Sarapis cultic traditions).[54] So, although Hecataeus elevates Egyptian traditions, he does so with implications for his and other Greeks' identity in Egypt. It is within this kind of rhetorical context that Artapanus is best understood.

Artapanus's work was composed during the Ptolemaic period in Egypt, no earlier than the mid-third century B.C.E. (given its extensive reliance on LXX Genesis and Exodus) and no later than the mid-first century B.C.E. (before the compilation by Polyhistor).[55] In this environment, Jews along with non-Jewish Greeks reconstructed their respective group identities, and many chose to root their histories in the land and traditions of Egypt. This process did not lead to an embrace of all aspects of Egyptian indigenous life, but it produced perspectives distinct from those in the homelands from which these groups came or with which they had initially iden-

---

53. For a helpful summary of this phenomenon, see Ludwig Koenen, "The Ptolemaic King as a Religious Figure," in *Images and Ideologies: Self-Definition in the Hellenistic World*, ed. Anthony G. Bulloch et al. (Berkeley: University of California Press, 1993), 25-115.

54. As another example of how a Greek wrote favorably of a non-Greek culture, Jacobson refers to Herodotus's positive portrayal of Egyptians in Book 2 of his *Histories* ("Artapanus Judaeus," 217-18). The object of Herodotus's discussion, however, is to articulate how to "be Greek" in the world. As James Redfield argues, with Herodotus's discussions of Egyptian, Scythian, Persian, and other cultures in the ancient Mediterranean world, he "calls upon the Greeks to be critical assimilators, to experience cultural change not as a mere diffusion but as a thoughtful choice between options" ("Herodotus the Tourist," *CP* 80 (1985): 97-118, here 117). Herodotus's discussion about Egypt aims ultimately to construct "Greek" identity and history in relation to other cultural groups (and their histories) in the Mediterranean world. For a discussion about Herodotus's use of Egyptian history in rewriting Greek tradition, see Ian S. Moyer, "Herodotus and an Egyptian Mirage: The Genealogies of the Theban Priests," *JHS* 122 (2002): 70-90.

55. See Sterling (*Historiography and Self-Definition*, 168-69, n. 175) for a summary of past scholarly positions (from 2000 and before) on more specific dates for Artapanus's work within this time range. Holger M. Zellentin ("The End of Jewish Egypt: Artapanus and the Second Exodus," in *Antiquity in Antiquity: Jewish and Christian Pasts in the Greco-Roman World*, ed. Gregg Gardner and Kevin L. Osterloh [Tübingen: Mohr-Siebeck, 2008]) argues that the work was written during the latter half of the second reign of Philometor VIII (145-116 B.C.E.), specifically as a reaction to the decree of amnesty issued by Ptolemy and Cleopatra II in 118 B.C.E. There is a general consensus in scholarship on the topic of provenance; Artapanus's particular interests in Egyptian traditions and history still make Egypt the most convincing location for the production of this work. See Collins, *Between Athens and Jerusalem*, 39; Sterling, *Historiography and Self-Definition*, 169; Holladay, *Fragments from Hellenistic Jewish Authors*, 190; and Zellentin, "The End of Jewish Egypt."

tified themselves.[56] Fragment 3 of Artapanus is an illustrative result of such a process.

II. Artapanus, the Apis Cult, and Memphis

In addition to the controversial line about Moses establishing Egyptian ritual practices throughout the land (27.4), Artapanus describes a few other Egyptian practices that are related to Moses. The soldiers of Moses, possibly with Moses' assistance, consecrate the ibis in the Hermopolite region and name the city in honor of Moses (27.9);[57] Hermopolis, or "city of Hermes," alludes to the association of Moses with Hermes three lines prior (27.6). When his adoptive mother, Merris, dies, Moses buries her and renames the place "Meroë," whose inhabitants end up honoring Merris as much as Isis (27.15-16). Finally, during the period of the plagues, the Egyptians reinterpret Moses' actions in ways that fit their ritual sensitivities; Moses' rod becomes associated with Isis (27.32).

The formation of the Apis cult, however, stands in stark contrast to the religious practices that Moses establishes and inspires. Whereas Moses wanted to assign oxen for agricultural production, Chenephres originates the worship of the Apis bull in Memphis and commands that the very animals that Moses assigned to the nomes for worship (27.4) are to be brought to Memphis and buried there (27.12). If there is a question as to Chenephres' motives, Artapanus confirms the confrontational nature of this decision: Chenephres wished to conceal Moses' inventions (κατακρύπτειν θέλοντα τὰ τοῦ Μωΰσου ἐπινοήματα) (27.12). According to Artapanus, the Apis cult and the ritual traditions of the necropolis of Memphis were created in opposition to Moses, who was popular with the Egyptians (27:6), and to all other social infrastructures of Egypt. In the context of Ptolemaic Egypt, this condemnation of dominant Memphite religious practice would not have been missed by Artapanus's audience.

---

56. The latter is what Hall refers to as fictive histories of descent that nonetheless carry significant weight in group self-definition (*Hellenicity,* 9-19).

57. τοὺς οὖν περὶ τὸν Μώϋσον διὰ τὸ μέγεθος τῆς στρατιᾶς πόλιν ἐν τούτῳ κτίσαι τῷ τόπῳ καὶ τὴν ἴβιν ἐν αὐτῇ καθιερῶσαι... (27.9). The subject can include Moses ("Moses and those around him" [i.e., the soldiers]), as similar constructions of οἱ περί τινά in other historiographical works include τινά as a subject of the action (e.g., Xenophon, *Hellenica* 5.4.2 and *Anabasis* 2.4.2; Acts 13:13). The sentence can also be read, however, to indicate that only the soldiers performed the actions in this line ("those who accompanied Moses..."; cf., e.g., Xenophon, *Anabasis* 1.5.8).

Constructing Jewish Identity in Ptolemaic Egypt

By the Ptolemaic period, Memphis consisted of several non-Egyptian peoples along with Egyptian inhabitants. Ionians, Carians, Phoenicians, and Idumeans all had their own temples in Memphis,[58] and they functioned in a full-fledged metropolitan environment. Although all of these communities were Greek-speaking to some degree,[59] they were not equal in the political context of Ptolemaic Egypt, where Macedonian descent initially carried significant weight.[60] In terms of religious practice, none of these communities was a key player in the balance of political and economic power over the city and its assets.[61] The Egyptian high priesthood of the temple of Ptah and the Ptolemaic court developed a long-term working relationship that would ensure Ptolemaic financial control over and Egyptian priestly administration of Egyptian cultic life in Memphis.[62]

---

58. The Ionian temple, the Hellenion, the temple of Carian Zeus, the Phoenician temple to Astarte, and the Apollonieion for Idumeans. See Dorothy J. Thompson, *Memphis under the Ptolemies* (Princeton: Princeton University Press, 1988), 82-105.

59. There is indication of bilingual usage among Carians and Phoenicians in the Memphite region, at least during the late Persian and early Ptolemaic periods. See Thompson, *Memphis under the Ptolemies*, 88-95. For evidence of bilingual non-Egyptians in the Persian period, see Philip Kaplan, "Cross-Cultural Contacts among Mercenary Communities in Saite and Persian Egypt," *Mediterranean Historical Review* 18 (2003): 1-31, esp. 18-19.

60. For example, in Alexandria and Ptolemais, those of Macedonian descent were chosen for priestly leadership (both male and female) in the dynastic cult. See Jan Quaegebeur, "Cleopatra VII and the Cults of the Ptolemaic Queens," in *Cleopatra's Egypt: Age of the Ptolemies,* ed. Robert S. Bianchi, Richard A. Fazzini, and Jan Quaegebeur (Brooklyn, N.Y.: Brooklyn Museum, 1988), 41-42; W. Clarysse and G. Van der Veken, *The Eponymous Priests of Ptolemaic Egypt (P.L. Bat. 24): Chronological Lists of the Priests in Alexandria and Ptolemais with a Study of the Demotic Transcriptions of Their Names* (Papyrologica Lugduno-Batava 24; Leiden: Brill, 1983).

61. The respective religious leaders of these groups also were mindful of each temple's affairs. See especially PSI V.531, a letter in which the priests of Astarte of the Phoenician-Egyptians (φοινικαιγύπτιοι) in Memphis request oils from Zenon, "as is granted to the temples in Memphis of the Carians and the Hellenomemphites [i.e., Ionian-Egyptians] (τὰ ἱερὰ τῶν Καρῶν καὶ Ἑλληνομεμφιτῶν τὰ ἐν Μέμφει)." The request concludes with the observation, "The temple of Astarte is similar to those of the Carians and Hellenomemphites. As is done to them, let it be done to us." Translation by Thompson, *Memphis under the Ptolemies,* 90.

62. Thompson provides a thorough description for Memphis (*Memphis under the Ptolemies,* 106-54). Especially in the first half of Ptolemaic rule, the Ptolemaic-Egyptian priesthood relationship was sustained throughout Egypt. For a summary of this relationship, see Ludwig Koenen, "Die Adaptation ägyptischer Königsideologie am Ptolemäerhof," in *Egypt and the Hellenistic World,* ed. Edmond Van't Dack, P. Van Dessel, and W. Van Gucht (Studia Hellistica 27; Leuven: Lovanii, 1983), 143-90, and idem, "The Ptolemaic King as a Re-

Patricia D. Ahearne-Kroll

Most significant for this discussion is the Ptolemaic patronage of the Apis cult and of Egyptian religious practices associated with the necropolis of Memphis. The live Apis bull was kept in the Temple of Ptah in the valley of Memphis, but when the bull died it was mummified and it received an elaborate funeral procession to the Sarapieion in the necropolis, where it was buried and worshiped as Osiris-Apis.[63] The ritual practices surrounding the death of an Apis bull lasted seventy days, and for much of this time cultic functionaries in the Temple of Ptah carried out the process of mummification and preparation of the bull for the afterlife. In correspondence with the activity within the temple, Memphites and visitors participated outside the temple space in mourning the death of Apis,[64] and on day sixty-nine the people could partake in a public ceremony whereby Apis was transported in a procession to the Lake of Kings (i.e., Lake Abusir), located near the necropolis, and then returned to the temple.[65] The procession would act out the re-

---

ligious Figure"; Ragnhild Bjerre Finnestad, "Temples of the Ptolemaic and Roman Periods: Ancient Traditions in New Contexts," in *Temples of Ancient Egypt*, ed. Byron E. Shafer (Ithaca, N.Y.: Cornell University Press, 1997), 185-237.

63. The description of the Apis mortuary ritual is primarily taken from *P.Vindob.* 3837 and the commentary by R. I. Vos (*The Apis Embalming Ritual: P. Vindob. 3873*, [OLA 50; Leuven: Peeters and Departement Oriëntalistiek, 1993]). See also Thompson, *Memphis under the Ptolemies*, 198-207. According to Vos, the recto of the papyrus is written in Hieratic and Demotic and appears to be an official manual; the verso is mostly written in Demotic and provides "complementary notes" to the guidelines on the recto (*The Apis Embalming Ritual*, 3-7, 41-42). Based on the correspondence between the script in this document and other Egyptian writings, Vos dates this papyrus to the late Ptolemaic period (roughly, the second half of the second century B.C.E.; *The Apis Embalming Ritual* 7). The archeological evidence for the Memphite necropolis (especially the discovered vaults and hieroglyphic stelae for deceased Apis bulls) confirms that a significant burial procedure took place for Apis bulls at least from the rule of Psammetichus I (seventh century B.C.E.) to the late Ptolemaic period (30 B.C.E.) (Jean-Philippe Lauer, *Saqqara, the Royal Cemetery of Memphis: Excavations and Discoveries since 1850* [New York: Charles Scribner's Sons, 1976], 25). See also Auguste Mariette, *Le Sérapéum de Memphis* (Paris, 1857) and *Le Sérapéum de Memphis: Publié d'après le manuscrit de l'auteur par G. Maspero* (Paris, 1882); Jean Vercoutter, *Textes biographiques du Serapeum de Memphis: Contribution à l'étude des steles votives du Serapeum*, BEHE IV (Paris, 1962); and Michel Malinine, Georges Posener, and Jean Vercoutter, *Catalogue des steles du Sérapéum de Memphis* (Paris: Impr. Nationale, 1968).

64. According to Vos, adherents would perform public gestures of lament (e.g., wearing "mourning-garments" and making vocal expressions of mourning) and would restrict their diet during the seventy-day period (*The Apis Embalming Ritual*, 31).

65. *P.Vindob.* 3837 in particular notes that *wꜥb* priests draw out the coffin from the Embalming House "while all people raise a great lamentation" (Recto IV, line 15; translation by Vos, *The Apis Embalming Ritual*, 52).

juvenation of Apis; the deceased bull would be accompanied by Egyptian gods (some of whom were played by real people, such as twin sisters who represented Isis and Nephthys);[66] and priests would recite narratives that recounted the journeys of Osiris and Reʿ in primeval times.[67] The end of this ritual would mark the rebirth of Apis, and on the seventieth day he would be taken to the necropolis, where adherents would have gathered, some of them since the beginning of the mourning period.[68] Not all these worshipers, however, were Egyptian; Hellenomemphites especially participated in the cultic traditions involving Osiris-Apis.[69] As part of the Sarapieion complex, a semicircle of Greek statues stood at the eastern end of the dromos, and along the dromos lay stone decorations of Dionysian imagery.[70] During the

---

66. According to P. Vindob. 3837, Isis and Nephthys carry two natron jars and 12 linen cloths, so the manual presumes that people acted out the roles of these goddesses (Recto IV, line 16). When the Apis bull of the cow Ta-Renenutet II died (164 B.C.E.), the twins Thaues and Taous performed this role during the seventy-day ritual ceremony for the deceased bull. For a discussion of the papyrological evidence about them see Thompson, *Memphis under the Ptolemies*, 233-45. The evidence for her discussion can be found in *UPZ* I.17-54. *P. Vindob.* 3837 also lists the following gods that accompany Apis in the procession: Wepwawet of Upper Egypt, Wepwawet of Lower Egypt, Horus, Thoth, and an object associated with Ptah (Recto IV, line 17). It is not clear, however, whether these gods were represented by people or objects. The Wepwawet gods may have been performed by priests who wore masks, but Vos leans toward the idea that the priests carried standards bearing the images of these gods and of Horus and Thoth (*The Apis Embalming Ritual*, 40 and 165).

67. At the shore of the Lake of Kings, the Apis bull was placed on a sand bank (with head facing south), and the wʿb priests boarded a boat (the "Bark of Papyrus") across the lake and read aloud nine books. According to Vos (*The Apis Embalming Ritual*, 161-62, 166-67), it appears that the priests ritually enacted the process by which the deceased Apis bull was perceived to fight off cosmic enemies (primarily understood in terms of Seth and Apopis) and rise to eternal life (primarily in the forms of the resurrected Osiris and Reʿ).

68. *P. Vindob.* does not provide a description of the ceremony after day 69, but inscriptional evidence from the Sarapieion confirms that the Apis bull was taken on day 70 for final burial procedures (Vercoutter, *Textes biographiques du Serapeum*, 125-26; Vos, *The Apis Embalming Ritual*, 41). Thompson notes that there was increased police protection of the necropolis, and she estimates that thousands likely attended this ceremony (*Memphis under the Ptolemies*, 202).

69. Thompson, *Memphis under the Ptolemies*, 202-3. An early example of Hellenomemphite participation comes from the Greek papyrus in which Artemisia the daughter of Amasis appeals to "Oserapis" and the gods "who sit with him" in the necropolis to curse her husband, who did not provide for a proper burial of their deceased daughter (*UPZ* I.1; late fourth century B.C.E.).

70. Eleven statues were located in this space; the subject of one has been identified (Pindar, whose name was on the base of the statue when discovered), and three others have been argued to represent Plato, Pythagoras, and Homer. The stone designs included three

Patricia D. Ahearne-Kroll

Ptolemaic period, Osiris-Apis as Sarapis represented the complex product of integrated chthonic traditions, visually expressed in multiple ways.[71] Two smaller shrines located along the dromos reflected this phenomenon: one was Egyptian in architectural design and contained an Apis bull statue, and the other was Corinthian and contained an inscription referring to it as a λυχνάπτιον.[72]

In several ways the Ptolemies communicated their close connections with Egyptian religious life in Memphis. Some funded building projects in the necropolis that served the Egyptian cults. For example, Ptolemy II Philadelphos likely supported the work of a master builder on an Apis vault in the necropolis as well as on the construction of two temple sites between 253 and 248 B.C.E.[73] More construction was financed during the reign of Ptolemy V Epiphanes, including the Anoubieion gateway, where an inscription of Ptolemy V offering incense to Anubis was found.[74] At least half of the Ptolemies (but maybe more) — from Ptolemy I Soter to Kleopatra VII — provided funds to support the Apis cult.[75] Kings Philometor, Euergetes II, and Soter II were associated with Apis in their Egyptian royal titles,[76] which

---

statues depicting a young Dionysus. See Jean-Philippe Lauer and Charles Picard, *Les statues ptolémaïques du Sarapiéion de Memphis* (Paris: Presses universitaires de France, 1955), 108-18 and 173-245. Thompson also mentions that Greek graffiti were discovered along the dromos near the burial chambers but were not recorded (*Memphis under the Ptolemies*, 27-28).

71. For a discussion about the relationship between the Sarapis tradition and the Osiris-Apis cultic traditions, see Philippe Borgeaud and Youri Volokhine, "La formation de la légende de Sarapis: Une approche transculturelle," *Archiv für Religionsgeschichte* 2 (2000): 37-76.

72. Lauer and Picard, *Les statues ptolémaïques*, 176-80. According to LSJ, λυχνάπτιον is a hapax legomenon that most likely means "a meeting place for λυχνάπται" (lamp-lighters), which LSJ also cites as a gloss for δαδοῦχοι ("torch bearers," often associated with the Eleusinian mysteries) (1067). The λυχνάπτιον was apparently some kind of organizational center for those who oversaw the lamps used in cultic practices in the necropolis (Lauer and Picard, *Les statues ptolémaïques*, 178-80; Thompson, *Memphis under the Ptolemies*, 28).

73. Louvre stele 82, in Heinrich Brugsch, "Der Apis-Kreis aus den Zeiten der Ptolemäer nach den hieroglyphischen und demotischen Weihinschriften des Serapeums von Memphis," *ZÄS* 22 (1884): 114. Many of the details in this paragraph are taken from Thompson, *Memphis under the Ptolemies*, 116-19.

74. H. S. Smith and D. G. Jeffreys, "The North Saqqara Temple-Town Survey: Preliminary Report for 1976/77," *JEA* 64 (1978): 19-20.

75. For specific examples, see Thompson, *Memphis under the Ptolemies*, 114-25 and 284-96.

76. Philometor was titled "twin of the living Apis upon their birth brick," likely because he was born the same year as the Apis bull of the cow Ta-Renenutet II, 186 B.C.E.; Euergetes II was "distinguished through the start of his reign coinciding with that of the liv-

united the importance of the Temple of Ptah and the Ptolemies, at least in the eyes of the Egyptian priesthood. At the Temple of Ptah, Ptolemy IV Philopator supplied an architectural embellishment of its eastern gate,[77] and in it Ptolemy V Epiphanes participated in a coronation ceremony that was facilitated by the high priest of Ptah.[78] Supposedly, after Ptolemy V, similar coronation ceremonies took place in Memphis for the remainder of the Ptolemaic period.[79] Whereas the dynastic cult in Alexandria was led by priests of Macedonian descent (and then later, of other Greek ethnicities), the dynastic cult in Memphis was administered by members of well-known Egyptian priestly families.[80] The Temple of Ptah and the necropolis constituted a formidable part of the economic industry of Memphis,[81] and, given the annual support of the *syntaxis* that funded Egyptian cultic practices,[82] the Ptolemies

---

ing Apis"; Soter II was "shining out in Egypt at the same times as the living Apis" or "distinguished in his birth together with that of the living Apis," according to Thompson, *Memphis under the Ptolemies*, 121-23.

77. W. M. Flinders Petrie, *Memphis I* (London: School of Archaeology in Egypt, University College, 1909), 14.

78. As described in the Rosetta Stone. Greek text: André Bernand, *La Prose sur pierre dans l'Egypte hellénistique et romaine*, vol. 1 (Paris: Centre national de la recherche scientifique, 1992), 44-56; hieroglyphic text: Stephen Quirke and Carol Andrews, *The Rosetta Stone: Facsimile Drawing with an Introduction and Translations* (New York: Abrams, 1989); Demotic text: R. S. Simpson, *Demotic Grammar in the Ptolemaic Sacerdotal Decrees* (Oxford: Griffith Institute, Ashmolean Museum, 1996), 258-71.

79. Willy Clarysse, "The Ptolemies Visiting the Egyptian Chora," in *Politics, Administration and Society in the Hellenistic and Roman World*, ed. Leon Mooren (Leuven: Peeters, 2000), 35, cited in Thompson, *Memphis under the Ptolemies*, 139.

80. Thompson, *Memphis under the Ptolemies*, 127-35, especially with regard to the cult of Arsinoe II. According to Jan Quaegebeur ("The Egyptian Clergy and the Cult of the Ptolemaic Dynasty," *Ancient Society* 20 [1989]: 93-113), an Egyptian version of the dynastic cult developed early on during the Ptolemaic empire, and, after Ptolemy II Philadelphos instituted the Arsinoe cult, forms of the dynastic cult were incorporated into temple activity all across Egypt. Quaegebeur cites the Mendes Stele, CGC 22181, in Herman De Meulenaere and Pierre MacKay, *Mendes II* (Warminster, England: Aris & Phillips, 1976), 173-77, 205-6.

81. Thompson presents an extensive description in *Memphis under the Ptolemies*, 3-81.

82. The *syntaxis* was a grant supplied by the Ptolemies to Egyptian temples, which was based on the revenue from land that had been owned by the temples but was taken under Ptolemaic control. This grant appears to have funded much of the temple activity (Thompson, *Memphis under the Ptolemies*, 77-78). The *apomoira* tax, which was a tax on income produced from vineyards and orchards, was assigned to the dynastic cult (Greek and Egyptian forms) during the Ptolemaic period (Koenen, "The Ptolemaic King as a Religious Figure," 66-69); this is yet another indicator of the pronounced economic and political relationship between the Ptolemies and the Egyptian priests.

instituted administrators (primarily, *epistatai*) who would oversee the distribution and use of this grant. In Memphis, as was the case in other Egyptian temples, these positions were assigned to Egyptian cultic leaders.[83]

The close ties between the Ptolemies and the Egyptian priesthood in Memphis are evident: financial contributions to Egyptian ritual practices and building projects as well as leadership assignments in the city's main industry gave Egyptian cultic personnel more access to economic influence and political power than other groups in Memphis and the surrounding region could achieve. Certainly, the Ptolemies supported the religious practices of other groups in Egypt, but the forms of communication and patronage differed for these groups. One example from Memphis illustrates this point. From an Idumean temple, the Apollonieion, we have an inscription of an honorific decree given by the temple's leaders to a *strategos* named Dorion.[84] The inscription records how Dorion provided payment for temple restoration projects and, in return, a ritual ceremony was held in his honor. The son of an Egyptian priestess (Heranch, serving Horus of Athribis), Dorion was a priest of Horus, Onnophris, and Osiris, and he served as a military commander and royal scribe.[85] In the decree, Dorion is also referred to as one of the priests of the Idumean mercenary unit that was associated with this temple, but the autobiographical record of his career (written in hieroglyphs) does not include this position; rather, this title appears to have been honorary, and Thompson suggests that such appointments "[might have played] a valuable part in protecting the corporate interests of minority ethnic groups."[86] Non-Ptolemaic and non-Egyptian Memphites had less access to funds and royal support than the Egyptian cultic sites received.

Jewish communities in the *chōra* sought out patronage relationships similar to the example of the Idumeans; the dedicatory inscriptions from the *chōra* that honor the Ptolemies for the construction of Jewish prayer houses (*proseuchai*) are cases in point.[87] There seems to have been a Jewish commu-

---

83. Koenen, "The Ptolemaic King as a Religious Figure," 69; Thompson, *Memphis under the Ptolemies*, 109-14.

84. *OGIS* 737. See Thompson's discussion in *Memphis under the Ptolemies*, 101-3.

85. This record comes from two hieroglyphic stone records found in the necropolis at Memphis, in Pascal Vernus, *Athribis, textes et documents relatifs à la géographie, aux cultes, et à l'histoire d'une ville du delta égyptien à l'époque pharaonique* (Cairo: Institut français d'archéologie orientale, 1978), 214-18, nos. 177-78, cited by Thompson, *Memphis under the Ptolemies*, 102-3.

86. *Memphis under the Ptolemies*, 103.

87. In *CPJ*, vol. 3, Appendix I ("The Jewish Inscriptions of Egypt," ed. David M.

nity living in Memphis,[88] and at the very least there were significant communities living near Memphis (in the Delta region and in the Fayûm) whose lives would have been affected by Egyptian religious practice in the Memphite area.[89] During the Ptolemaic period, there were thirteen Apis bulls; on average each bull lived for about twenty-two years.[90] The Jews who lived in or near Memphis likely witnessed or at least were highly aware of the extensive ritual that surrounded the death of the Apis bull, and they would have noticed the discrepancy between the support that the Egyptian cultic leadership received and Ptolemaic support for their own religious practices.

When we combine the fact that Artapanus presents the Memphite religious practices as inauthentic Egyptian traditions within the context of Memphite religious practice during Ptolemaic rule, Artapanus's condemnation of the Apis and necropolite cults is quite clear. Juxtaposed to this critique, the latter half of fragment 3 several times depicts the superiority of the Israelite God. God's might is demonstrated when the king falls over speechless and a priest dies from the power of the divine name (Artap. 27.25 and

---

Lewis), inscriptional dedications of *proseuchai* are identified with the following locations: (1) in Lower Egypt: Schedia (1440), Xenephyris (1441), Nitriai (1442), Athribis (1443-44); (2) in the Fayûm: Krokodilopolis (1532); and (3) one of unknown Egyptian provenance that was found at Cairo (1449). The inscriptions from Schedia and Krokodilopolis date to the reign of Ptolemy III (246-221 B.C.E.), those from Xenephyris and Nitriai to the second reign of Ptolemy VIII (145-116 B.C.E.). Athribis dates to either the second or first century B.C.E. (dedicated to "King Ptolemy and Queen Kleopatra"), and the inscription of unknown provenance could date to the reign of either Ptolemy III or Ptolemy VIII (it mentions only "King Ptolemy Euergetes"). See also William Horbury and David Noy, *Jewish Inscriptions of Graeco-Roman Egypt* (Cambridge: Cambridge University Press, 1992).

88. Thompson, *Memphis under the Ptolemies*, 17. Thompson argues that the Berlin stele 2118 (third century B.C.E.), which mentions a Jewish quarter and was posted and written in Memphis (Saqqara), likely refers to a Jewish district in Memphis (17, n. 39, and 91-93). On the Berlin stele 2118, see L. Stern, "Die biligue Stele des Châhap," ZÄS 22 (1884): 101-9.

89. Such as Leontopolis in the southern Delta; and in the Fayûm region, Hephaistias, Herakleopolis, Krokodilopolis, Philadelphia, Psenyris, Samareia, and Trikomia. See *CPJ*, vol. 1, and Appendix 1 in vol. 3; Horbury and Noy, *Jewish Inscriptions*. For the Herakleopolite Jewish papyri, see *Urkunden des Politeuma der Juden von Heracleopolis (144/3-133/2 v. Chr.) (P.Polit.Iud.): Papyri aus den Sammlungen von Heidelberg, Köln, München und Wien*, ed. James M. S. Cowey and Klaus Maresch (Papyrologica Coloniensia, 29; Wiesbaden: Westdeutscher Verlag, 2001), and Robert Kugler's analysis of Artapanus based on what these documents suggest about Jewish life in the Egyptian *chora*, "Hearing the Story of Moses in Ptolemaic Egypt: Artapanus Accommodates the Tradition," in *The Wisdom of Egypt: Jewish, Early Christian, and Gnostic Essays in Honour of Gerard P. Luttikhuizen*, ed. Anthony Hilhors and George H. van Kooten (Leiden: Brill, 2005), 67-80.

90. Thompson, *Memphis under the Ptolemies*, 198, 284-96.

26). God's sovereignty is also implied by the guidance of the divine voice (27.21 and 36) and by the plague of hail and earthquakes that destroy "most of the temples" (27.33).[91] Significantly, it is shortly after Artapanus's condemnation of Memphite religious practices that he aligns his narrative of Moses quite closely with the Exodus account, and the cosmic power of the Israelite God and the story of deliverance are left intact in his story. This synthesis of the divine salvation of the Israelites and the criticism of dominant religious practices in Egypt makes most sense as a Jewish tradition from Egypt.[92]

Artapanus's claim that Moses created Egyptian cultic practices has been a stumbling block for scholars in constructing his identity, but the rhetorical use of this claim in fragment 3 discloses monotheistic ideals. The context of Jewish life in antiquity is often depicted too simplistically as polytheistic without much attention given to the different religious traditions within that polytheistic world or to the particular social power that individual traditions exercised in different geographical regions. The subtle paradigm shift that I have proposed with Artapanus is to read fragment 3 in light of the influential polytheistic traditions that Jews encountered in Egypt. I agree with John Collins's assessment that Artapanus's work is a "competitive historiography," but not simply with regard to Manetho-like accusations. Artapanus is particularly antagonistic toward Ptolemaic-Egyptian religious relations in Memphis. He does not mark average Egyptians for his attacks, and so it is unclear whether he opposed them. This leaves open the question of whether Jews in Egypt, like Artapanus, considered *all* Egyptians as "other" (in the binary-oppositional sense) or focused more specifically on dominant social forces in the construction of their distinct identity.

---

91. See also the summary by Kugler, "Hearing the Story of Moses in Ptolemaic Egypt," 77.

92. The publication by Holger M. Zellentin ("The End of Jewish Egypt") came out too late for me to fully engage with in this essay; the social context I propose for the composition of fragment 3 does not conflict with his thesis, and I find aspects of his hypothesis about the compositional time frame of Artapanus's work compelling.

Dispelling an Illusion of Otherness?
Juridical Practice in the Heracleopolis Papyri

Robert A. Kugler

Introducing the first volume of *Corpus Papyrorum Judaicarum* (*CPJ* I), Victor Tcherikover confidently asserted that the Judeans of Ptolemaic Egypt were permitted to form within the cities and villages where they dwelt *politeumata*, ethnic groups living in Egypt that possessed certain privileges, including "the right 'to live according to their ancestral laws.'" For Tcherikover, "'the ancestral laws,' as concerning Jews, could have only one meaning: Jewish autonomous organization based on the laws of Moses. Thus the Torah was the fundamental law of all Jewish communities in Egypt."[1] According to Tcherikover, this ensured that Jews experienced a comfortable life in Ptolemaic Egypt, but one marked by its Otherness vis-à-vis the dominant culture of the land. However, later in the same synthetic introduction to *CPJ* I, Tcherikover wrote that in the mixed legal context of Hellenistic Egypt there were "two contradictory tendencies in Egyptian Jewry: the desire to follow old national and religious traditions, and the desire to participate vigorously in all aspects of Hellenistic life," and that "individual Jews, when faced with the innumerable petty problems of everyday life," preferred the latter over the former.[2] At least in terms of legal practice, Judean Otherness was not so certain.

Tcherikover's admission regarding the wanness of Egyptian Judeans'

---

1. V. Tcherikover and A. Fuks, eds., *Corpus Papyrorum Judaicarum*, vol. 1 (Cambridge, Mass.: Harvard University Press, 1957), 7.

2. Ibid., 36.

Robert A. Kugler

Otherness when it came to keeping their distinctive laws foreshadowed a trend in more recent research to elide the Judeans of Egypt with the Greco-Egyptian culture of the Ptolemies, to dispel what some might consider to be an illusion of Otherness conjured by Tcherikover and scholars of an earlier generation. This trend, however, depended for the most part on analysis of the literary texts from the Judeans of Hellenistic Egypt, not the documentary texts that preoccupied Tcherikover.[3] Now a recently published cache of documentary papyri from Heracleopolis has been taken to further undermine the notion of Judean exceptionalism in Hellenistic Egypt.[4] Sylvie Honigman has observed that, although the papyri prove beyond doubt that Judeans in Ptolemaic Egypt had the right to form *politeumata* and to govern themselves by their ancestral traditions, at least the Judeans of the Heracleopolite nome played mostly by the general Ptolemaic (Greco-Egyptian) procedural and substantive laws. Indeed, in a review of the *editio princeps* of the papyri, Honigman recalls Tcherikover to remark that he "depicted the *politeuma* as a pattern of autonomy that the Jews would have looked for. He conceived of the willingness of the Jews to enjoy a legal pattern enabling them to abide by

---

3. See especially Erich Gruen, *Heritage and Hellenism: The Reinvention of Jewish Tradition* (Berkeley: University of California Press, 1998); idem, *Diaspora: Jews Amidst Greeks and Romans* (Cambridge, Mass.: Harvard University Press, 2002); John M. G. Barclay, *Jews in the Mediterranean Diaspora: From Alexander to Trajan (323 BCE–117 BCE)* (Edinburgh: T&T Clark, 1996); idem, "Jewish Identity Strategies under the Hegemony of Hellenism," in *Ethos und Identität: Einheit und Vielfalt des Judentums in hellenistisch-römischer Zeit*, ed. M. Konradt and U. Steinert (Munich: Ferdinand Schöningh), 13-25; Sylvie Honigman, *The Septuagint and Homeric Scholarship in Alexandria: A Study in the Narrative of the "Letter of Aristeas"* (London: Routledge, 2003). Resisting the trend is John J. Collins, *Between Athens and Jerusalem: Jewish Identity in the Hellenistic Diaspora*, 2d ed. (Grand Rapids: Eerdmans, 2000); idem, "Hellenistic Judaism in Recent Scholarship," in his *Jewish Cult and Hellenistic Culture: Essays in the Jewish Encounter with Hellenism and Roman Rule* (Leiden: Brill), 1-20. Barclay underscores Collins's resistance when he accuses him of remaining loyal to a "dissonance model" for understanding the relationship between Judaism and Hellenism against the weight of what Barclay thinks are significant "new" theoretical insights that argue for a contrary view (John M. G. Barclay, "Review of J. J. Collins, *Between Athens and Jerusalem: Jewish Identity in the Hellenistic Diaspora*, 2d ed.," *JJS* 52 [2001]: 363-68). As this essay indicates, at least from the perspective of the documentary evidence, Collins seems to have the better angle of vision on the matter, and in general I would argue that he also wins the day on the basis of the literary texts. In any case, his resistance is firmly rooted in his habit of privileging texts over theory, a virtue those of us who have been mentored by him can only hope to emulate as effectively as he evinces it.

4. James M. S. Cowey and K. Maresch, *Urkunden des Politeuma der Juden von Herakleopolis (144/3-133/2 v. Chr.) (P.Polit.Iud.)*: Heidelberg, Köln, München und Wien (Papyrologia Colonensia XXIX; Wiesbaden: Westdeutscher Verlag, 2001).

their own laws as a highly self-conscious and self-reflective process." By contrast, she says of the papyri, "It seems to me that the new documents from Heracleopolis prove just the opposite."⁵

This essay honoring John J. Collins casts a critical eye on this reading of the Heracleopolis *politeuma* papyri to suggest that greater nuance is necessary in characterizing the legal reasoning of these Judeans. My initial analyses of the juridical reasoning in the papyri summarized here indicate that, while the Judeans of Heracleopolis drew heavily on the hybrid Greco-Egyptian common law of the Ptolemaic kingdom, they also relied on the juridical norms of their Judean ancestry to achieve their litigation goals, and in at least one instance the Judean normative system determined a litigator's goal.⁶ While much more remains to be done to confirm my initial assessment, at least on the basis of the evidence summarized here from the perspective of juristic papyrology we should not be so quick to use the Heracleopolis papyri to further dispel an illusion of Otherness. They may turn out to suggest just the opposite.

I. *P.Polit.Iud.* 4 and 7: The Cases of Philotas and Dorotheos

Recovered from mummy cartonnage discovered at the site of ancient Heracleopolis on the edge of the Fayûm region of Egypt, the Heracleopolis papyri date from 144/3 to 133/2 B.C.E. and provide a glimpse of life for Judeans living under Ptolemaic rule, as well as proof that Judeans formed *politeumata*, self-governing communities of people sharing a common ethnos.⁷ The cache includes citizen petitions to the archons of the Judean

---

5. S. Honigman, "The Jewish Politeuma at Heracleopolis (Revision of Cowey and Maresch, *Urkunden*)," *SCI* 21 (2002): 251-66 (264).

6. My full study of *P.Polit.Iud.* 7 will appear as R. Kugler, "Dorotheos Petitions for the Return of Philippa (*P.Polit.Iud.* 7): A Case Study in the Judeans and Their Law in Ptolemaic Egypt," in *Proceedings of the XXVth International Congress of Papyrology, August 2007* (Ann Arbor: University of Michigan Press, forthcoming); a study of *P.Polit.Iud.* 4 (along with 3 and 5, also concerned with marriage and dowry agreements) is in progress.

7. Until the papyri were published in 2001 by Cowey and Maresch, doubt remained as to whether the Judeans of Ptolemaic Egypt had the right to form *politeumata*. Indeed, the uses of the term *politeuma* in association with Judeans known prior to publication of the papyri were ambiguous in their meaning (*Letter of Aristeas* 310; *CIG* 5361-62 [two inscriptions of the first century B.C.E. from Berenice in Cyrenaica]; for discussion of the texts, see G. Lüdertz, "What Is the Politeuma?" in *Studies in Early Jewish Epigraphy*, ed. J. W. van Henten and P. W. van der Horst [Leiden: Brill, 1997], 183-225, esp. 204-21). The papyri settle

politeuma (*P.Polit.Iud.* 1-16) and correspondence between the archons and other officials in the nome (17-20). The petitions that are sufficient in scope to permit analysis address disputes regarding personal honor (1-2), marriage arrangements and dowries (3-5), the law of persons (6-7), and business transactions (8-12). The letters between officials address a release of prisoners and the fallout from a disturbance in Peempasbytis, and record summonses to appear before judges.

The significance of the petitions for understanding the way these people used the *politeuma* privilege of relying on Judean normative systems to regulate their affairs is disputed. The editors of the papyri argued mildly that specific phrases (e.g., ἀποστασίου [[τὸ]] βυβλίον in *P.Polit.Iud.* 4.23-24; see below) and more general practices (e.g., the purported cession of a daughter to a relative to pay off a debt in *P.Polit.Iud.* 7) attested in the papyri indicate the authors' dependence on distinctively Judean normative systems.[8] Sylvie Honigman has replied that most such aspects of the papyri are just as easily understood within the context of non-Judean, typically Ptolemaic practices and that "Ethnic particularism among these Jews does not seem to go beyond religious belief..., cultic praxis and marriage customs."[9] The following overview of my analyses of *P.Polit.Iud.* 4 and 7 indicate that, while

---

this issue once and for all. The phrase "the *politeuma* of the *Ioudaioi*" in *P.Polit.Iud.* 8.5; 20.8-9 leaves no doubt as to the ethnicity of the *politeuma* members. The petitions also provide significant new evidence reinforcing the view that military settlers who shared the same ethnicity formed the core of Ptolemaic-era *politeumata* (see S. Honigman, "Politeumata and Ethnicity in Ptolemaic and Roman Egypt," *Ancient Society* 33 [2003]: 61-102 [64-67]). See especially *P.Polit.Iud.* 1, which concerns a dispute in the wharf area of Heracleopolis, the location of the fortress where soldiers were garrisoned; see also James M. S. Cowey, Klaus Maresch, and Christopher Barnes, *Das Archiv des Phrurarchen Dioskurides (154-145 v.Chr.?)* (*P.Phrur.Diosk.*): *Papyri aus den Sammlungen von Heidelberg, Köln, München und Wien* (Papyrologica Coloniensia XXX; Paderborn: Schöningh, 2003), an archive that shows that the powers exercised by the garrison commander (*Phrourarch*) at Heracleopolis correspond well with the leaders of the politeuma. An added bonus is *P.Phrur.Diosk.* 1, which addresses a neighborhood brawl involving a *Ioudaios*.

8. Cowey and Maresch, *Urkunden*, 23-29.

9. Honigman, "The Jewish Politeuma at Heracleopolis," 264; for a reply to Honigman, see James M. S. Cowey and Klaus Maresch, "'A Recurrent Inclination to Isolate the Case of the Jews from Their Ptolemaic Environment'? Eine Antwort auf Sylvie Honigman," *SCI* 22 (2003): 307-10. In her review Honigman argued that the practices of the Judeans in Heracleopolis evidenced in the papyri were not distinctively Judean, but rather were consonant with general Greek customs. Cowey and Maresch replied, saying in so many words that they in any case do not consider themselves authorities when it comes to the ways of Judean law and await the insights of others.

Dispelling an Illusion of Otherness?

Honigman is correct to argue that the Judeans of Heracleopolis drew heavily on the hybrid Greco-Egyptian common law of the Ptolemaic kingdom, at least these instances argue in favor of greater caution and further research before passing judgment on the ethnic particularism of the Heracleopolite Judeans.

> *P.Polit.Iud.* 4 (P.Heid. Inv. G 4931), January 12, 134 B.C.E.
> An die Archonten wegen Auflösung einer Verlobung
>
> 19th of Choiak, in the 36th year. Concerning marriage. We consent to make a ruling. To the archons, from Philotas, son of Philotas of the *politeuma*. In the present year I courted/engaged Nikaia, daughter of Lysimachos. Her father, just named, promised to give her to me, along with the dowry determined for her, with which I was pleased. Thus not only did we make determinations/oaths in common, but also according to the law an oath became *binding* and under these circumstances we went our separate ways. After a short time, without cause Lysimachos joined Nikaia to another man before receiving from me the customary writ of separation. Therefore I ask you, if it seems just, to consent to write to the Jews in the village that they decree to Lysimachos to come to you, so that, if it is as I write, it will be decided concerning him according to the law, to compel [him] to . . . me. . . .

According to *P.Polit.Iud.* 4, Philotas of the *politeuma* courted Nikaia, daughter of Lysimachos, and Lysimachos promised to give Nikaia to Philotas as a wife, along with a negotiated dowry. In recalling this, Philotas remarks that he and Lysimachos made a pact sealed by an oath and by common agreements. Lysimachos, however, joined Nikaia to another man before Philotas completed the marriage by bringing Nikaia under his roof. Philotas argues that Lysimachos is in violation of contract because he had not issued the ἀποστασίου [[τὸ]] βυβλίον, the "customary" writ of separation necessary to terminate a marriage agreement (cf. LXX Deut. 24:1). The remedy Philotas sought is not entirely clear because the petition is broken at the end; he may have hoped to acquire the dowry he had lost, he may have still wanted to marry Nikaia, or he may have been seeking to achieve both results.

Indicating the hybridity of Ptolemaic legal reasoning and practice in the *chora*, the petition echoes a cornucopia of customary norms for marriage agreements with roots in Egyptian, Greek, and Judean practices.[10]

---

10. It is important to stress that, while I address these as though they are distinctly

Philotas indicates that he courted Nikaia (ἐμνηστευσάμην Νείκα[ι]αν); this is hardly the arranged marriage of Greek and Judean practice, but it is typical of the freer romance culture of ancient Egypt.[11] However, Philotas indicates that he did conform to Greek (and Judean) norms, arranging with Nikaia's father for their marriage.[12] That Lysimachos swore an oath to honor his unwritten agreement to give Nikaia to Philotas is typical of Greek and Egyptian contractual practices (ὀμ[ό]σαντος δώσειν).[13] The negotiated

---

identifiable as Greek and/or Egyptian and/or Judean in origin, they were surely simply "Ptolemaic" in the practice of Philotas, Nikaia, and Lysimachos.

11. Philotas courts Nikaia (μνηστεύω, middle + acc., "to woo, seek in marriage," or "woo and win, espouse"; cf. LSJ μνηστεία II 2; Preisigke s.v.). Michael Satlow has argued that the LXX's use of μνηστεύω to translate ארש, "to betroth," is explicable by analogy with the way Elias Bickerman explained the use of φερνή in place of *mohar* ("Two Legal Interpretations of the Septuagint," *Revue internationale des droits de l'antiquité* 3 [1956]: 81-104): the Greek translator did not understand the concept of betrothal as "inchoate marriage," and replaced it with a related term and practice from Greek culture, the agreement to marry, the promise of a daughter to a suitor (*Jewish Marriage in Antiquity* [Princeton: Princeton University, 2001], 69-73). Satlow's point calls for some nuance, and when taken as such helps to explain what Philotas declares here. In LXX Deut. 20:7; 22:23, 25, 27, 28, the verb is in the passive voice and does mean "promised." But in LXX Hos. 2:21, 22, the prophet uses μνηστεύω in the middle voice with a direct object, the woman, to signal his effort to woo her; he "courts" his intended directly because she is without a paternal sponsor. Indeed, this active pursuit of a woman's hand by the groom, without the direction and/or assistance of her father, departs from normative Judean and Greek practice of Persian- and Ptolemaic-era Egypt (Greek marriages: *P.Eleph.* I 1 [Greek, 312 B.C.E.]; *P.Tebt.* I 104 [Greek, 92 B.C.E.]; Judean marriages: *TAD* B2.6; B3.3; B3.8 [Aramaic, fifth century B.C.E.]; *P.Yadin* 18 [Greek, 128 C.E., Palestine]; cf. R. Katzoff, "Hellenistic Marriage Contracts," in *Legal Documents of the Hellenistic World: Papers from a Seminar Arranged by the Institute of Classical Studies, the Institute of Jewish Studies and the Warburg Institute, University of London, February to May 1986*, ed. M. J. Geller and H. Maehler [London: University of London, 1995], 41, for the continuity between Judean and Greek contracts over time and among disparate loci). It conforms well, however, with practices among native Egyptians. From the 26th Dynasty (e.g., *P.Berl.Dem.* 13614, 536 B.C.E.), marriage deeds began with the formula, "The man has said to the woman, 'I have taken you as a wife,'" or in the alternative, the woman says she has undertaken "to take a husband." Note also the second-century B.C.E. Demotic oracle question of Stotoetis son of Imouthes to the crocodile god Soknebtynis whether he should marry a certain Tanous daughter of Taapis; see *Women and Society in Greek and Roman Egypt: A Sourcebook*, ed. Jane Rowlandson et al. (Cambridge: Cambridge University Press, 1998), 318. This independence of the couple remained the norm among Egyptians into the period of our petition.

12. See especially the well-known instance of *P.Eleph.* 1.

13. That Philotas does not cite a written document but rather recalls oral exchanges indicates that this was an "unwritten marriage contract" (on the full status of which see H. J. Wolff, *Written and Unwritten Marriages in Hellenistic and Postclassical Roman Law*

dowry (τὴν σταθεῖσαν ἐπ' α[ὐ]τῆι φερνήν) reflects an Egyptian and Greek practice.[14] In assenting to the agreement with the expression "with which I was satisfied" (ἐφ' ἧι κἀμοῦ εὐδοκοῦντος), Philotas uses an Egyptian (Demotic) contractual formula.[15] The remark that Lysimachos had given Nikaia

---

[Haverford, Pa.: American Philological Association, 1939]; see the updated comments of Uri Yiftach-Firanko, *Marriage and Marital Arrangements: A History of the Greek Marriage Document in Egypt, 4th Century BCE–4th Century CE* [Munich: Beck, 2003], 81-104). This may explain the unusual claim that Lysimachos swore (ὀμ[ό]σαντος) to give his daughter to Philotas. Even when we have much later, clear evidence for the details of marital agreements among Judean grooms and fathers-in-law in the Mishnah (see esp. *Qiddušin*), fathers are not found to be swearing by oath to deliver their daughters into a marital relationship. Yet the petitioner in *P.Polit.Iud.* 3.6 uses the same verb, ὄμνυμι, to describe how his prospective father-in-law guaranteed a vineyard as part of a dowry. That binding oaths were a means of ensuring adherence to unwritten agreements may be supported indirectly by a Demotic text from 20 June 223 (*P.Berl.Dem.* 13587 lines 13-14), wherein the writer offers to swear an oath by Osiris before "the first prophet" that he did not receive a contractually agreed amount of money (for which apparently no written contract was in existence).

14. The lack of any mention of a *mohar*, the "bride price" customary in Judean marriages, reflects a change from the Aramaic papyri of fifth-century B.C.E. Elephantine that included the *mohar* and a dowry (not named as such, but rather described with the phrase, "N. brought in to me/to my house X, Y, and Z"; e.g., *TAD* B3.8.5). Moreover, the petitioner adds the peculiar participial adjective σταθεῖσαν, "established" or "determined." There is no negotiation of the dowry amount in the Elephantine papyri from the fifth century B.C.E., but by the time we come to the marriage agreements from the Judean Desert dated to the early second century C.E. (*P.Yadin* 18, 37) there is no doubt that dowries are reckoned according to the needs of the bride for maintenance in the marriage and/or survival in the event of a divorce (see *P.Yadin* 18 line 7, προσφέρω; *P.Yadin* 37 = *P.Hever* 65 line 8, τιμογραφία, τιμογραφεῖν [DJD XXVII, 224-37; see esp. 234 on the noun and verbs]), and the language of the divorce agreement from 13 B.C.E. in *BGU* 1102 = *CPJ* II 144 line 19 suggests much the same. Before that time, Egyptian marriage agreements — deeds of property in reality — were mostly about the negotiation of amounts to be exchanged between the suitor and the bride's father for the bride's maintenance in marriage or divorce (and on occasion for the husband too; see P. W. Pestman, *Marriage and Matrimonial Property in Ancient Egypt: A Contribution to Establishing the Legal Position of the Woman* [Papyrologica Lugduno-Batava 9; Leiden: Brill, 1961], passim). Similarly, the Greek contract, *P.Tebt.* I 104 lines 12-13 (92 B.C.E.), refers to a dowry as διωμολογημένην, "negotiated" or "agreed upon." Thus Nikaia's dowry seems to have been determined more along the lines of Egyptian and Greek juridical practices than according to traditional Judean custom. That said, it seems likely that this had become the Judean custom by Philotas and Nikaia's day.

15. This statement of satisfaction echoes the formulaic response in the Aramaic papyri from Elephantine to the receipt of a *mohar* or a dowry (*TAD* B2.6.5, 15; B3.8.5; 6.1.5), but also the purchase price for a house (*TAD* B3.4.6), a general payment (*TAD* B3.2.4), or an oath (*TAD* B2.8.5). However, this clause is not unique to the Aramaic Judean documents from Elephantine; it first appears in Demotic among the papyri found at Elephantine in

to another man without cause or reason (ἄνευ λόγου) implies that a suit for divorce by man *or woman* was permissible so long as it was justified, a practice that was normative among Greeks into the second century B.C.E.[16]

For all of this reliance on general Ptolemaic practice, at two points Philotas fortifies his legal standing by invoking norms drawn from the Torah. As noted above, Philotas unequivocally invokes Deut. 24:1 in arguing that he had not issued the writ of separation necessary to release Nikaia for betrothal to another man. More subtly, he invokes LXX Num. 30:3, 14 to strengthen his assertion that the agreement he made with Lysimachos could not be broken. He remarks, οὐ μόνο[ν] ὁρισμῶν γεγομένων κα[τ]ὰ κοινὸν ἀλλὰ καὶ τῆς κατὰ τὸν νόμον ἀπωμρ[σία]ς γενθείσης εἰς δ[εσμὸν], "Not only did we make determinations in common, but also according to the law an oath became *binding*."[17] The word ὁρισμός is used in other published papyri only to refer to property boundaries, typically in documenting the *parachoresis* of land.[18] One depends on LXX Num. 30:3 to find in Hellenistic literature a use of ὁρισμός that refers to an oath or determination.[19] But-

---

P.Moscow 135 line 1 (349 B.C.E.), a transfer of stipends, and it continues in use in Demotic in marriage contracts from the late third and early second centuries B.C.E. onward (e.g., *P. Hausw.* 6 [229 B.C.E.]; *P.Mich.* A I [199 B.C.E.]; *P.Berl.Dem.* 10229 [78 B.C.E.]). This clause is, in any event, a hybrid formula.

16. ἄνευ λόγου suggests that a wife can request a divorce with adequate explanation. Egyptian and Judean marriage contracts from the fifth century B.C.E. onward permit divorce without cause stated by both parties, and Greek contracts make divorce the outcome of various acts damaging the relationship (*P.Eleph.* 1; *P.Giss.* 2; *P.Gen.* 21; *P.Tebt.* 104), but by the second century B.C.E. contracts permit simple declaration of divorce by both parties. This comment suggests adherence to a somewhat antiquated Greek norm.

17. For the readings ἀπωμρ[σία]ς (= ἀπομοσία) and εἰς δ[εσμὸν] see my full study of *P.Polit.Iud.* 4 (see n. 6 above).

18. The other seventeen times it appears in papyri recorded in the *Duke Databank of Documentary Papyri*, ὁρισμός refers to the boundaries of houses and fields, mostly in deeds of sale or other legal texts relating to real property (*PSI* 796 [222-23 C.E.]; *P.Giss.* I 48 [203-4 C.E.]; *P.Alex.Giss.* 4 [113-20 C.E.]; *P.Petaus* 13 [184-85 C.E.]; *P.Thmouis* 1 [180-92 C.E.]; *P.Amh.* II 97 [181-82 C.E.]; *P.Cair.Masp.* III 67353 V [569 C.E.]; *W.Chr.* 363 = *BGU* II 599 [II/III C.E.]; *P.Oxy.* XXXVIII 2847 [272-73 C.E.]; *P.Bub.* I17 [after 224 C.E.]; *P.Fay.* 23A [II C.E.]; *P.Strasb.* I 31 [II CE.]; *BGU* IV 1091 [212-13 C.E.]).

19. ἄνθρωπος ἄνθρωπος ὃς ἂν εὔξηται εὐχὴν κυρίῳ ἢ ὀμόσῃ ὅρκον ἢ ὁρίσηται ὁρισμῷ περὶ τῆς ψυχῆς αὐτοῦ οὐ βεβηλώσει τὸ ῥῆμα αὐτοῦ πάντα ὅσα ἐὰν ἐξέλθῃ ἐκ τοῦ στόματος αὐτοῦ ποιήσει, "Person by person — if he vows a vow to the Lord or swears an oath or determines for himself with determination against his soul, he shall not profane his word; everything that proceeds out of his mouth he shall do" (30:3; NETS; for this meaning of ὁρισμός, see LSJ s.v. A v, which cites Num. 30:3). Cowey and Maresch, *Urkunden*, 65, acknowledge the occurrence of ὁρισμός in Num. 30:3, but miss its exclusive use otherwise in

tressing the link between Philotas's argument and Numbers 30 is his use of ἀπωμο[σία]ς, which derives from the verb ὄμνυμι, "to swear," also used in Num. 30:3 (with ὅρκος, "oath," as its direct object). And if the reconstruction εἰς δ[εσμὸν] (a supralinear insertion) is correct, Philotas may have added further rhetoric from Numbers 30 by echoing the highly restrictive language of v. 14 that decrees, "Every oath and every vow of binding [δεσμός] to afflict the soul, her husband shall establish for her."

P.Polit.Iud. 7 (*P.Köln* Inv. 21038), June/July 134 B.C.E.
Eingabe, das Dienstverhältnis eines Mädchens
betreffend, und Urteil der Archonten

To the archons from Dorotheos of the Politeuma. In the 32nd year, when my wife's brother Seuthes stayed with me (παρ' ἐμοὶ) while he was sick and things were going badly for him, I doctored him for a sufficient time, expending much from my own means. Next, upon learning that his daughter had been thrown into debtors' prison I sent for her, and while the two of them were living with me (παρ' ἐμοὶ) Seuthes also gave Philippa into my charge {as a member of the household?} so that she might be with me (παρ' ἐμοὶ), [first] on account of what I had expended for the two of them, and second, on account of his confidence in my wife. But Iona, his wife, took Philippa and made her at home with her sister in Paanamei. I ask, if it seems right, that you summon her to compel her to afford me justice. Live well.

P.Polit.Iud. 7 also evinces this strategic use of Judean norms to achieve a litigator's goals. In a forthcoming study I argue that Dorotheos requests that the archons require Iona, mother of Philippa, to return her young daughter to him not as a household servant, as was warily suggested by the editors, but as an orphan to her guardian.[20] Dorotheos was the young girl's

---

papyri to describe real property boundaries, and add, oddly, that while promises were perhaps meant here, the word was to be taken in the text as "gewiß nicht Gelübde im Sinn von LXX Nu. 30,3" (ibid.).

20. See n. 6 above. On the general topic of guardianship in Greco-Roman Egypt, see R. Taubenschlag, *The Law of Greco-Roman Egypt in the Light of the Papyri, 332 B.C.–640 A.D.*, 2nd ed. (Milan: Cisalpino-Goliardico, 1972), 157-70; L. Mitteis and U. Wilcken, *Grundzüge und Chrestomathie der Papyruskunde*, 2 vols. (Leipzig: Teubner, 1912), 1:374-83; 2:248-56; E. Seidl, *Ptolemaische Rechtsgeschichte* (Glückstadt: Augustin, 1962), 109. To understand guardianship we depend on texts from the Hellenistic and Roman periods. On continuity in *Privatrecht* during the Greco-Roman period, see H. J. Wolff, *Das Recht der griechischen*

uncle. In 136 B.C.E. he had taken her and her father, Seuthes, under his care when Seuthes was ill and Philippa had been delivered into debtor's prison. Dorotheos reports that Seuthes had turned Philippa over to his care on account of Dorotheos's generosity and Seuthes' trust in his sister, Dorotheos's wife. Presumably Seuthes died not long after that, and Dorotheos continued to house the orphan Philippa for the next four years. Iona, Philippa's mother, removed her from Dorotheos's home in 132 B.C.E. to place her with her sister in Paanamei, and Dorotheos apparently appealed for Philippa's return to him.

Dorotheos bases his claim that Philippa should be returned to him on a combination of the Greek customary law pertaining to the guardianship of an orphan (a minor predeceased by her father) and a Torah stipulation, the duty of an individual to care for destitute kinfolk (LXX Lev. 25:35-38). Greek law recognized guardians as fiduciaries for orphans until they reached the age of majority, and thus required proof of their reliability.[21] Greek law also

---

Papyri Ägytens und der Ptolemaeer und des Prinzipats. Vol. 1: *Bedingungen und Triebkräfte der Rechtsentwicklung* (Munich: Beck, 2002), 35-43; H.-A. Rupprecht, "Greek Law in Foreign Surroundings: Continuity and Development," in *The Cambridge Companion to Ancient Greek Law*, ed. M. Gagarin and D. Cohen (Cambridge: Cambridge University Press, 2005), 328-42, esp. 329, 338. On Judean practice of the law of orphans in the Roman period in Judea, see especially N. Lewis, *The Documents from the Bar Kochba Period in the Cave of Letters: Greek Papyri* (Jerusalem: Israel Exploration Society, 1989), 47-64, 116-17; Ann Ellis Hanson, "The Widow Babatha and the Poor Orphan Boy," in *Law in the Documents of the Judaean Desert*, ed. R. Katzoff and D. Schaps (SJSJ 96; Leiden: Brill, 2005), 85-103; for the view that the archive reflects foremost Roman law, not Greek, see in the same volume, T. Chiusi, "Babatha vs. the Guardians of Her Son: A Struggle for Guardianship — Legal and Practical Aspects of P.Yadin 12-15, 27," 105-32; and see also H. Cotton, "The Guardianship of Jesus Son of Babatha: Roman and Local Law in the Province of Arabia," *JRS* 83 (1993): 94-108. Against this view (and in support of the notion that one can look to the Babatha archive for insight into practices across time and the Mediterranean world), N. Lewis observes that, even at the level of scribal practice, evidence of influence from Ptolemaic Egypt is present in the Babatha archive: the abbreviated form of the *Doppelurkunden* in the archive (the inner text is only an allusive summary of the outer text and depends on a public registry of the full document) is a holdover into the Roman period from Ptolemaic Egypt (Lewis, *Documents*, 9).

21. Taubenschlag, *The Law of Greco-Roman Egypt*, 162, nn. 28-30; see, among others, *BGU* IV 1070 (218 C.E.); *P.Harris* I 68 (225 C.E.); *P.Tebt.* II 326 (266-267 C.E.); *SB* V 7558 (173 C.E.) exhorting the appointment of guardians who are ἐπιτήδεος and ἀξιόχρεως, "suitable" and "reputable." For instances of poor guardians and the consequences they could incur for their bad performance, see *P.Lond.* VII 2017 (242-241 B.C.E.); *P.Dryton* 33 (136 B.C.E.); *P.Bingen* 74 (second century C.E.); *P.Oxy.* VII 898 (123 C.E.); XVII 2133 (308 C.E.); *PSI* IV 281 (second century C.E.); see also H. F. Jolowicz, "The Wicked Guardian," *JRS* 37 (1947): 82-90.

established that fathers could name guardians for their children, and in the absence of clear evidence for such an appointment before a father's death, the task often fell to local officials.[22] Dorotheos relies on these common law principles. He argues in the petition that he was at least informally appointed by Seuthes precisely because he was reliable, and, in any case, his behavior toward Seuthes and Philippa independently proved his reliability and gave the archons sufficient cause to formally appoint him and thus to require Philippa's return to him. What captures our attention in particular is the way he documents his reliability: he hints that it is proved by his adherence to the law requiring care for destitute kin in Lev. 25:35-38. His reliance on Lev. 25:35-38 is suggested by two elements in the petition. The first παρ' ἐμοί with reference to Seuthes alone might evoke Lev. 25:35a (ἐὰν δὲ πένηται ὁ ἀδελφός σου καὶ ἀδυνατήσῃ ταῖς χερσὶν παρὰ σοί ἀντιλήμψῃ), but its repetition to reference Seuthes and Philippa together, and then to establish where Seuthes sought to locate Philippa for her future good, seem too intentional to ignore.[23] Bolstering this intuition that Dorotheos seeks to invoke Lev. 25:35-38 on his own behalf is his repeated emphasis that to care for Seuthes and Philippa he expended freely from his wealth without return: he reports that he helped Seuthes (cf. ἀντιλήμψῃ αὐτοῦ in Lev. 25:35c) by safeguarding his well-being for a considerable time (προ{σ}εστάτησα αὐτοῦ ἐφ' ἱκανὸν χρόνον; cf. Lev. 25:35b; 36c) and spending much on Seuthes' care from his own resources (ἐκ τοῦ ἰδίου πλείονα δαπανῶν; cf. Lev. 25:36a; 37);[24] he rescued Philippa from debtor's prison so father and daughter could live with him (ἀμφοτέρων διαιτωμένων), and Seuthes gave his daughter into

---

22. For a father's designation, see SB VI 9065 (first century B.C.E.); BGU IV 1113 (14 C.E.); SB V 7558 (173 C.E.). Appointment could also be made for unborn children through the instrument of a marriage contract (e.g., P.Oxy. II 265 [first century C.E.]). Officials make the designation in BGU VIII 1813 (62-61 B.C.E.). P.Oxy. III 496 (127 C.E.) also permits a mother to make an appointment if the father's will is unknown. For instances of the mother seeking help in making an appointment, see SB XVI 12720 (142 B.C.E.); SB V 7568 (36 C.E.). Jolowicz, "The Wicked Guardian," 82-90, describes a number of papyri where guardians are not juridically established, but instead took on the role without specific appointment (e.g., P.Lond. III 1164 (g) + (i) [212 C.E.]; P.Oxy. XIV 1638 [282 C.E.]).

23. It is also worth observing that the use of παρὰ + dative was the preposition's least frequent use in Hellenistic Greek, making its threefold appearance here and in Lev. 25:35a all the more notable. For example, παρὰ occurs with the dative case 167 times in the LXX, while it appears with the genitive 421 times, and with the accusative 243 times.

24. Although it may make too much of the language in both texts, it is hard to ignore the assonance between the prohibition against earning πλεονασμόν from the needy in Lev. 25:37b and Dorotheos's expenditure of his own πλείονα in line 7.

Dorotheos's care because of what he had expended for them (ἀμφοτέρους δεδαπανήκειν).²⁵ Dorotheos's unusual integrity according to the Torah's standard of care for the destitute could not be questioned.²⁶

The difficulty with this reading of Dorotheos's petition, however, is that an appeal to regain the responsibilities of guardianship once removed is unheard of. The task was onerous, brought no rewards, and could land persons in court for failing in their obligations, and we even have evidence of guardians seeking release from their appointments.²⁷ So why would Dorotheos make such an extraordinary request? Here I think we encounter an instance of Judean juridical norms not merely working as useful tools in achieving litigation goals, but actually shaping the goal itself in a way that is distinctively Judean: it is only understandable that Dorotheos would have sought out the burden of guardianship because the Torah required it of him as a Judean (LXX Exod. 22:21-24; Deut. 10:18; 14:29; 24:17, 19, 21; 26:12-13; 27:19).

II. Conclusions

The two petitions surveyed here reveal Judeans who participated fully in the general Ptolemaic legal system that was a hybrid of Greek and Egyptian norms, yet who also were aware enough of their unique ancestral traditions to call upon them to achieve their litigative goals, and perhaps even to determine those goals. On this reading it seems hard to deny that Philotas's and Dorotheos's use of the Torah was in some measure a "self-conscious and

---

25. For the loss of the *epsilon* augment and the unusual ending on δεδαπανήκειν (both typical of papyri), see E. Mayser, *Grammatik der griechischen Papyri aus de Ptolemäerzeit* (Berlin: Walter de Gruyter, 1938), I.2, 80-81, 98, cited in Cowey and Maresch, *Urkunden*, 89.

26. Dorotheos may even have been invoking what we know was stipulated among the rabbis by the early first century C.E., that one who boards an orphan for a lengthy period becomes a guardian by default (*m. Giṭ.* 5.4). See LXX Prov. 23:10; Philo, *Quod deterius potiori insidiari soleat* 145; *De somniis* 1.107; and P.Yadin 12-15, 27 for further evidence that Judeans had integrated into the simple mandate to care for the orphan Greek customs of guardianship.

27. For an example of someone seeking relief from the burden, see *SB* V 7558 (173 C.E.), where "Iulius Lucullus, the honorable *epistrategos*, from Gaius Apollinarius Niger, Antinoite, of the Osirantinoan tribe and of the Hermaian deme," asks to be relieved from the "guardianship of Valeria Tertia, alias Thaisarion" to which he was appointed by the will of the veteran Marcus Anthestius Gemellus.

self-reflective process." At least in this narrow sense it seems that the Heracleopolis papyri show not only that Judeans were very much like their neighbors but also that they had a consciousness of the ways in which they were *not* like their neighbors. The Otherness some impute to Judeans of Hellenistic Egypt may not be such an illusion after all.

Clearly, though, two cases do not constitute anything more than suggestive anecdotal evidence that in terms of juridical reasoning and practice some Judeans in Egypt under the Ptolemies were distinctive. Much more remains to be done to confirm and flesh out that possibility. First, it is necessary to analyze the legal reasoning of the remaining Heracleopolis petitions and of other Judean-related legal documentary papyri revealed since the completion of *CPJ*. Inasmuch as the evidence gathered in *CPJ* has escaped careful study from the perspective of juristic papyrology, it also requires fresh analysis. Second, to further validate such analysis it must be paired with comparative evidence for the legal ethos of other ethnicities within their *politeumata*. Do they similarly deploy their unique legal norms instrumentally and/or to establish litigative goals?[28] Third, the case needs to be made that juridical distinctiveness is meaningful evidence of a group's larger self-understanding. Although it might be tempting to allow theoretical perspectives and comparative models from the sociology and philosophy of law to do our heavy lifting in this regard, it is also, fourth, necessary to amass evidence of unique Judean self-consciousness from other areas of life in the ancient world, many of which can also be traced in the documentary papyri. The project that lies ahead is large and challenging.

The project I just described is confined largely to the documentary papyri and will lead to a portrait of non-élite Judeans far removed from the literary texts that have usually been our source for imagining Judean self-awareness in Hellenistic Egypt. That said, the outcome of this project is not irrelevant to the study of the literary texts. For all of our fascination with determining the precise mind of the authors of literary texts — and our inclination to extrapolate from those postulated imaginations general portraits of Judean identity — the Judeans who received those texts were likely the sort of people we encounter in the documentary texts. Just so, having been transformed by receiving those literary texts and by their changing circumstances, these non-élite Judeans and their descendants were also the likely

---

28. While the paucity of evidence for the legal systems of other ethnicities as compared to Judeans poses difficulties for this aspect of the enterprise, it requires doing all the same.

targets of still later writing élites. To fully understand the literary texts and their authors, then, requires equal appreciation of the documentary texts and their Judean figures. Whatever Otherness there was among Hellenistic Judeans we can know legitimately only if we pay attention to both kinds of evidence.

Index of Authors

Aaron, D. H., 51
Abegg, Martin, 362, 375
Abrams, Judith Z., 281
Abusch, Ra'anan, 370
Ackerman, Susan, 90
Adams, E., 245
Adams, Samuel L., 187, 191-93
Aharoni, Yohanan, 385
Ahearne-Kroll, Patricia, 413
Aitken, J. K., 403
Albertz, Rainer, 96, 117
Alexander, Philip S., 63, 371
Allison, Dale C., 369
Allport, Gordon, 263
Alter, R., 235
Amir, Yehoshua, 303
Anderson, A. R., 241
Anderson, Frank, 110
Andrews, Carol, 453
Apple, A. L., 230
Arazy, A., 391
Argall, Randal A., 164, 253
Ashton, John, 253, 396
Assis, Elie, 21, 151
Atkinson, Kenneth, 275
Attias, J.-C., 403
Avalos, Hector, 281

Avigad, N., 81

Bakhos, Carol, 28
Bahrani, Zanib, 33
Barclay, J. M. G., 407, 415, 420-21, 458
Bardtke, H., 351
Bar-Kochva, Bezalel, 404-8, 410, 418-22, 425, 446
Barkun, M., 228, 230
Barnes, Christopher, 460
Barr, James, 392
Bauckham, R. J., 235
Beal, Timothy K., 106, 283
Beard, Mary, 400
Beardslee, William A., 260-61
Beaulieu, Paul-Alain, 42, 44, 46
Becker, Jürgen, 342
Bedford, Peter Ross, 117
Beentjes, Pancratius C., 174
Begg, Christopher, 311
Ben Zvi, Ehud, 117
Benbessa, E., 403
Bene, Brigit, 139-40
Bengtsson, Håkan, 350-51, 353, 356-67
Berg, Shane, 334-36, 338, 340
Berlin, Adele, 382-83
Berman, Joshua, 77

471

Index of Authors

Bernand, André, 453
Bernays, J., 405
Bernheimer, Richard, 133
Bernstein, Moshe, 53, 54, 381, 383, 385-87
Berquist, Jon, 68-69, 79
Berrin, Shani, 344
Berry, W., 245
Berthelot, Katell, 56, 402
Bickerman, E. J., 45, 177, 394, 423, 462
Birnbaum, E., 393
Bishop, Doyle W., 122
Blenkinsopp, Joseph, 39
Bilde, P., 395
Blidstein, Gerald, 330
Boccaccini, Gabriele, 165
Bollansée, J., 418-19
Bond, Helen K., 329
Bonnington, Mark, 303
Bonwetsch, G. Nathanael, 304, 324
Bordo, Susan, 67, 70
Bourdieu, Pierre, 67, 70
Borgeaud, Philippe, 452
Bowley, James M., 304
Bowman, John, 185
Boyer, P., 229, 244
Box, G. H., 174, 304-6, 320, 324
Braun, Roddy L., 43
Breech, Earl, 295
Briant, Pierre, 46
Bright, John, 99
Bringmann, Klaus, 424-25
Brooke, G. J., 53, 54, 338, 344, 347
Brown, Peter, 79
Brown, Ruppert, 122, 129
Brownlee, William, 342, 356, 358, 360-61, 366
Brugsch, Heinrich, 452
Bruneau, Philippe, 183
Buber, M., 238
Bull, Robert J., 181
Bultmann, Rudolf, 249
Burchard, Christoph, 435
Burke, David, 146, 148-49, 151-55
Burke, Kenneth, 36
Burkert, Walter, 441
Burkes, Shannon, 156, 159, 194, 293, 299

Burney, C. F., 91
Burns, Rita J., 88-89
Burnstein, Stanley M., 446
Bush, Frederic, 111
Butler, Judith, 34
Bynum, Caroline, 67

Calduch-Benages, Núria, 162
Callaway, Philip R., 358
Camp, Claudia V., 173, 189, 195
Campbell, Edward, 105, 109-11
Caquot, A., 53
Carney, James, 133, 137-38
Carson, Rachel, 283
Chadwick, Henry, 325
Chang, C. S., 176
Chapman, Cynthia, 33, 68
Charles, R. H., 66
Charlesworth, James H., 374
Chazon, Esther, 179, 370-71, 382
Cheng, Weikun, 71
Chiusi, T., 466
Cifarelli, Megan, 68
Clark-Soles, Jaime, 216
Clarysse, W., 449, 453
Clemencea, 237
Clifford, Richard J., 192, 280
Coggins, Richard J., 174, 176-78, 285
Cohen, J. J., 241, 283
Cohen, Shaye, 17, 391, 435
Cohn, Robert L., 49, 402-3
Coleman, K. M., 430
Collins, Adela Yarbro, 257, 283, 296
Collins, John J., 3, 4, 17, 47, 48, 159, 163-70, 173, 178, 181, 185-86, 199-200, 204, 214, 222, 231, 238, 251-52, 260-62, 280, 287, 289, 293, 295, 299, 305, 323-24, 328, 333-35, 337, 339, 342, 348-49, 368-69, 403, 415, 435, 445, 447, 458
Cook, D., 229
Cook, Joan E., 291
Corley, Jeremy, 183
Corsten, Thomas, 428
Cotton, H., 466
Cowey, James M. S., 458-60, 464
Crenshaw, James L., 153, 161, 163, 191, 193

Index of Authors

Cross, Frank Moore, 88, 96, 176, 362
Crossan, John D, 248-49
Crown, Alan D., 176, 183
Crüsemann, Frank, 346

Daise, Michael, 181
Daley, B. E., 241
Davies, Philip R., 353
Davila, James R., 379, 434
Davis, Lennerd J., 281-82
Dawson, L. L., 228
Day, John, 31
de Jonge, Marinus, 434
Delcor, Mathias, 350
Derrida, Jacques, 34
Deutsch, H., 231
De Vaux, Roland, 352, 364
Dey, J., 236
Dexinger, Ferdinand, 176, 386
Diamond, J., 245
Dick, Philip K., 234
Dicou, Bert, 21
Di Lella, Alexander A., 161-62, 167, 170, 173, 178, 183-84, 186
Dillery, John, 446
DiTommaso, Lorenzo, 222, 224-25, 229, 231, 236, 239, 289
Doniger, Wendy, 68
Doob, Penelope B. R., 133
Doran, Robert, 4, 167, 176, 178
Dorman, Joanna, 281
Doudna, Greg, 351
Douglas, Mary, 70
Douglas, Michael C., 340-42, 346
Drawnel, Henryk, 180
Dumont, S. Bakchine, 51
Duncan, Julie A., 91
Durham, M., 237
Dyer, K. D., 245

Eck, W., 400
Edwards, Mark, 401
Ehrman, Bart, 435
Eilberg-Schwartz, Howard, 68
Eiseley, Loren, 237
Eisland, Nancy L., 281

Eliade, Mircea, 139
Elliger, Karl, 350, 352, 363
Eshel, E., 60, 63, 65
Eshel, Hanan, 384
Exum, J. Cheryl, 86-37, 99

Falk, Daniel, 371, 377
Feldman, Louis H., 52, 58, 181, 404-6, 419, 438-39, 443
Ferch, Arthur J., 280
Festinger, L., 227
Fewell, Danna, 105
Fiedler, Fred E., 122, 282
Fiedler, Leslie A., 282
Fiensy, David A., 196
Finnestad, Ragnhild Bjerre, 450
Firth, Raymond, 70
Flinders Petrie, W. M., 453
Flint, Peter W., 374
Fossum, J., 177
Foucault, Michel, 67, 71
Fowler, Robert, 259
Fox, Michael V., 150
Fraser, P. M., 411
Freedman, David Noel, 88, 111
Frerichs, Ernest S., 262
Freudenthal, Jacob, 435-37
Frey, Jörg, 177, 186
Fried, Lisbeth, 44-45
Fuks, Alexander, 427
Fukuoka, Masanobu, 283
Funk, Robert, 248-49
Funkenstein, A., 225

Gabba, E., 405-6, 419
Galpaz-Feller, Pnina, 82
Gamble, Harry Y., 435
Garland, Robert, 286
Gatens, Moira, 67
Geach, P., 231
Geffcken, Johannes, 11
Geller, Stephen A., 146, 149-50
Gilmore, David D., 282-83, 286
Ginzberg, L., 50
Goering, Gregory, 187

473

Index of Authors

Goff, Matthew J., 196-97, 199, 202, 252, 335-37, 386
Goldenberg, D. M., 50, 52
Goldenberg, Robert, 17, 28, 188
Goldingay, John E., 170
Goldstein, Jonathan, 177-78, 424
Goldstein, Morris, 325
Golka, Friedemann W., 193
Goodblatt, D., 391, 393-94, 396
Goodman, Martin, 24, 392-93, 395, 397-98, 401
Goodwin, Frederick K., 141
Gorman, P., 420-21
Gould, S. J., 226
Gow, A. C., 241
Gray, J., 239
Greenberg, Moshe, 19, 383-84
Greenfield, Jonas C., 180
Grabbe, Lester, 45, 69, 314
Gropp, Douglas M., 179
Grosz, Elizabeth, 67
Gruen, Erich S., 413, 415, 417, 424-25, 431, 438, 443, 458
Guizot, François, 237
Gunkel, Hermann, 283, 288
Gunn, David, 105
Gutman, Y., 414-15

Haberman, Avraham M., 362
Habicht, Christian, 426
Hahne, H. A., 245
Hakuin, 229
Halbertal, Moshe, 303
Hall, Jonathan M., 435, 443, 448
Hall, J. R., 239
Hall, Robert G., 322, 324
Hallpike, C. R., 71
Halperin, David, 317
Hanson, Ann Ellis, 466
Hanson, P. D., 117, 223
Harder, Richard, 439-40
Harink, D., 234
Harkins, Angela, 341, 346
Harnack, Adolf von, 249, 400
Harrelson, Walter, 149, 280
Harrington, Daniel J., 190, 204, 211, 251

Hartman, Louis F., 67, 170
Harvey, Graham, 183, 391, 394-95
Hatch, Edwin, 275
Hayes, Christine, 17
Hays, Christopher B., 133, 142
Helfgott, Benjamin, 24
Helm, Robert, 314
Hengel, Martin, 12, 415, 423
Henze, Matthias, 133, 139, 142
Himmelfarb, Martha, 168, 171, 315, 324
Hinkle, Steve, 129
Hirshman, Marc, 24, 26
Hjelm, Ingrid, 174, 176-77, 180-81, 186
Hobsbawm, E. J., 239
Hodges, Frederick M., 430
Hoftijzer, Jean, 110
Holden, Lynn, 281
Holladay, Carl H., 438
Holladay, Carl R., 413-14, 435, 445
Holloway, Steven W., 33
Hölscher, G., 63
Honigman, Sylvie, 458-60
Horbury, William, 455
Horn, D. G., 226
Horsley, Richard, 255
Horst, Pieter W. van der, 317
Howard, Albert, 67
Hughes, Julie, 382
Humbert, Paul, 109-10
Humphrey, Edith McEwan, 294-95
Humphreys, W. Lee, 167, 171

Inowlocki, Sabrina, 434, 437-38
Isaac, E., 51
Isager, Jacob, 286

Jackson, Kent P., 102
Jacob, F., 223
Jacobsen, Thorkild, 140, 142
Jacobson, Howard, 420, 435, 438
Jacoby, Felix, 436
Jaeger, Werner, 405, 407
James, William, 141
Jameson, Fredric, 36
Jamison, Kay Redfield, 141
Janowitz, Naomi, 303

Index of Authors

Japhet, Sara, 117, 120
Jassen, Alex, 344-45
Jastrow, Morris, 60, 77
Jeffreys, D. G., 452
Jeremias, Gert, 342, 353, 355-56, 361-63, 365
Johnson, Aaron P., 437
Johnson-Debaufre, Melanie, 248
Jokiranta, Jutta, 344
Jolowicz, H. F., 466-67
Jonas, Hans, 235
Jones, Christopher P., 428
Jones, P., 32
Joüon, Paul, 104
Julian, James W., 122
Jull, A., 351
Juster, J., 391, 396

Kaminsky, Joel, 4, 17, 150-51, 188
Kaplan, Philip, 449
Katzoff, R., 462
Kehoe, Alice Beck, 139
Kermode, F., 234-35
Kessler, John, 117, 119, 121, 124, 128
Kiberd, Declan, 132
King, Philip J., 84
Kippenberg, Hans G., 181
Kittel, Bonnie, 382
Klaassen, W., 241
Klein, Ralph W., 92
Klihn, A. Frederik J., 284
Knibb, Michael A., 280, 285, 289, 385
Knoppers, Gary, 69, 80
Koch, Klaus, 191, 223
Koenen, Ludwig, 447, 449, 454
Kolarcik, Michael, 206, 210-11
Kraemer, Ross, 396
Kraft, R. A., 234, 434
Kratz, Reinhard, 48
Kristeva, Julia, 298
Kronholm, Tryggve, 107
Krüger, Thomas, 194
Kugel, James L., 175, 178, 180-81, 194, 304, 378
Kugler, Robert A., 386, 455-56, 459
Kuhn, Heinz-Wolfgang, 342

Kulik, Alexander, 305-6, 8, 310, 313, 316, 320, 324, 326
Kurzman, D., 392

Landsman, J. I., 304-6, 320, 324
Lange, Armin, 335, 347
Lauer, Jean-Philippe, 450, 452
Lawrence, D. H., 227
Lebram, J. C. H., 169
Lee, M. F., 244
Lee, Thomas R., 183
Leopold, Aldo, 283
Leprohon, R. J., 32
Levi, Jaakov, 110
Levinas, Emmanuel, 35
Levine, Etan, 106
Levinson, Jon D., 216
Lewis, Bernard, 263
Lewis, David M., 455
Lewis, N., 466
Lewy, Y., 66, 406
Lichtenberger, Hermann, 337
Lieb, M., 229
Lieberman, S., 228
Liesen, Jan, 164
Lieu, Judith M., 396-97
Lim, Timothy, 103, 114, 351, 354
Linafelt, Tod, 106
Lipschits, Oded, 68-69
Lock, Margaret, 69-70, 72, 78
Lombroso, Cesare, 226
Lorrentzen, L. A., 244
Lovelock, J., 243
Luckenbill, D. D., 42
Lüdertz, G., 459
Lunt, Horace G., 305

Ma, John, 429
MacDowell, Douglas, 427
Mack, Burton L., 164, 183
MacKay, Pierre, 453
Madden, F. W., 394
Magen, Itzak, 177, 186
Mageo, J., 71
Magness, Jodi, 352
Malinine, Michel, 450

475

Index of Authors

Marböck, Johannes, 164, 187
Marcus, R., 175
Maresch, K., 458-60, 464
Margalit, Avishai, 303
Mariette, Auguste, 450
Martyn, J. L., 224, 234
Martínez, Florentíno Garcia, 179, 262
Marx, Tzvi C., 281
Masanobu Fukuoka, 283
Mayr-Harting, H., 232
Mayser, E., 468
McCarter, P. Kyle, 92
McGhee, G. S., 227
McGinn, B., 229, 233, 238-39, 241
Mélèze-Modrzejewski, J., 404-5
Mendels, Doron, 145, 181, 183, 186
Meshorer, Y., 393
Messner, B. A., 230
Meulenaere, Herman, 453
Meyers, Carol, 88-89, 95, 97, 118-20, 124, 128
Meyers, Eric M., 118-20, 124, 128
Millar, Fergus, 423, 429
Miller, Barbara D., 70
Milne, Pamela J., 167
Mitchell, David T., 281
Mittag, Peter Franz, 424
Mitteis, L., 465
Mobley, Gregory, 68, 133, 139, 142
Momigliano, Arnoldo, 285, 406, 424
Moore, Carey A., 145, 147, 149, 152
Mor, Menachem, 176-77
Morgan, M. Gwyn, 425
Moyer, Ian S., 447
Moyers, B., 243
Mueller, James R., 329
Mulder, Otto, 174-75, 177-78, 184, 186-87
Müller, H.-P., 339
Muir, John, 246
Mukenge, André Kabasele, 145, 147-48, 155-56
Murphy, Catherine M., 199
Murphy-O'Connor, Jerome, 342
Murray, O., 411, 446
Musurillo, H. A., 398
Myers, Jacob M., 291

Neusner, Jacob, 262
Newsom, Carol A., 370, 374-75, 379
Nicholson, Ernest, 96
Nickelsburg, George W. E., 154, 157, 163, 169, 190, 198, 252, 263-68, 270, 274-75, 277-78, 315
Niditch, Susan, 4, 68, 83-84, 167
Nielsen, Kirsten, 105
Niewiadomski, J., 241
Nitzan, Bialik, 357, 362, 370
Noonan, H., 231
North, J., 400
Noth, Martin, 73
Novak, David, 24
Noy, D., 396, 455

Obeyeskere, Gananath, 70, 72, 79, 82, 141, 147
O'Connor, Flannery, 249
O'Connor, M., 377
Oeming, Manfred, 69
Oesterley, W. O. E., 174
O'Keeffe, J. G., 133
Olivelle, Patrick, 72
Olyan, Saul, 68, 77, 182, 281
O'Regan, C., 223
Orlov, A. A., 234, 305, 312, 316
Ōshio Heihachirō, 246
Osten-Sacken, P. von der, 223
Otzen, Benedikt, 181

Paget, J. Carleton, 397
Palmisano, M. C., 187
Pardee, Dennis, 377
Parente, F., 411
Parker, Simon, 102
Parsons, Mikeal, 281
Pastor, Jack, 201
Pennington, A., 305
Perdue, Leo G., 162, 164
Pestman, P. W., 463
Petersen, David L., 119-21, 123-25, 127-28
Philips, Anthony, 180
Philonenko, Marc, 305
Philonenko-Sayar, Belkis, 304
Picard, Charles, 452

476

Index of Authors

Pippin, Tina, 249, 258, 298
Pleins, J. David, 193
Poethig, Eunice, 87
Poirier, John C., 319
Pollan, Michael, 283
Popović, Mladen, 262
Porton, Gary, 24
Posener, Georges, 450
Postgate, J. N., 32
Pound, Ezra, 232
Price, Simon, 400-401
Puech, Émile, 181, 341
Pummer, Reinhard, 176, 180-81, 183
Purvis, James D., 174, 177

Qimron, E., 371, 386
Quaegebeur, Jan, 449, 453
Quast, Udo, 104
Quirke, Stephen, 453

Rajak, Tessa, 401
Raphael, Rebecca, 281
Rappaport, U., 225, 395
Ravid, B. C. I., 392
Redfield, James, 447
Redpath, Henry A., 275
Reicke, Bo, 351
Reymond, Eric D., 378
Riches, John, 249
Rietz, H. W. L., 374
Rinehart, J. F., 227
Ritschl, Albrecht, 249
Roberts, J. J. M., 355
Rovit, E., 235
Rubenstein, Arie, 305
Rubinkiewicz, Ryszard, 305-6, 319, 323-24, 326
Rudolph, Wilhelm, 104
Rupprecht, H.-A., 466
Russell, D. A., 442

Sabatier, Pierre, 132
Saldarini, Anthony J., 145, 147-48, 152
Sanders, James A., 273-74, 374
Sanders, E. P., 11
Sanders, J. T., 243

Sandoval, Timothy J., 192
Sasson, Jack M., 105, 114
Satlow, M. L., 405-7, 462
Schäfer, Peter, 315, 325
Schall, J. V., 235
Scheper-Hughes, Nancy, 69-70, 72, 78
Scherer, G., 243
Schiffman, Larry, 22
Schipper, Jeremy, 281
Schmidt, F., 63
Scholem, Gersham, 316
Schuller, Eileen, 179, 381, 383-87
Schürer, Emil, 186, 415, 421
Schwartz, Daniel R., 329, 427
Schwartz, R. M., 403
Schwartz, Seth, 177, 183, 186, 201
Schweitzer, Albert, 249
Scott, J. M., 63
Scott, Jr., N. A., 235
Segal, Alan F., 168, 216
Seidel, L., 232, 465
Seldon, D., 446
Sen, Amartya, 232
Seow, Leong, 69, 80-81
Sharef, Z., 392
Sharp, Carolyn, 41
Shea, John, 301
Sheppard, Gerald T., 152-53, 155, 163
Sherif, Muzafer, 122
Sherwood, Y., 236
Silberstein, Laurence J., 403
Simon, M., 400
Simon, Uriel, 378
Simpson, R. S., 453
Skehan, Patrick W., 161-62, 173, 178, 184, 186, 374
Smith, H. S., 452
Smith, J. Z., 202, 252
Smith, Mark, 31
Smith, Morton, 44
Snyder, Sharon L., 281
Soggin, J. A., 51, 91
Sokolowski, F., 428
Soltysik, A. M., 230
Sparks, H. F. D., 305
Spector, S., 237

477

Index of Authors

Speiser, E. A., 51
Spina, Frank Anthony, 4, 18, 403
Stager, Lawrence E., 84
Steck, Odil Hannes, 145, 147, 153, 155, 157
Stegemann, Hartmut, 353, 356, 363
Stenhouse, P., 185
Stephens, Susan A., 446
Sterling, Gregory E., 435, 437-38, 444-47
Stern, L., 455
Stern, Menahem, 394, 404-5, 408-10, 422, 438-39, 441-43
Stern, Sacha, 27, 396
Stewart, Bruce, 134
Stone, Michael E., 154, 163, 223, 225, 275, 279, 284-95, 298
Strickland, D., 241
Strugnell, John, 11, 190, 438
Stuckenbruck, Loren T., 313
Sumner, William G., 122
Szuchewycz, B. G., 373

Tajfel, Henri, 129-30
Talmon, Shemaryahu, 364
Tantlevskij, Igor R., 351, 361, 366
Tanzer, Sarah, 254
Taubenschlag, R., 465-66
Taylor, Charles, 205
Tcherikover, Victor, 189, 423-25, 457
Theiler, Willy, 440
Thesleff, Holger, 441
Thiering, Barbara, 355
Thiessen, Matthew, 386
Thomas, Christine M., 435
Thomas, Dylan, 301
Thomas, L., 238
Thompson, Alden L., 280, 284
Thompson, Dorothy J., 443, 449, 450-55
Thomson, Rosemarie Garland, 281
Thordson, M., 179
Thordson, T., 179
Tigchelaar, Eibert J. C., 154, 182, 196
Tolbert, Mary Ann, 257
Tomson, P. J., 391, 393
Tov, Emmanuel, 146
Towner, Sibley, 47
Trafton, J. L., 53

Trenchard, Warren C., 173
Trehuedic, K., 53
Tromp, Johannes, 303
Tronier, Henrik, 256
Tropper, Josef, 111
Turner, Victor, 71-73, 129
Tuveson, E. L., 241

Udoh, Fabian E., 321
Urbach, Ephraim, 330
Ullendorff, Edward, 101-2

Van De Water, Rick, 353, 362-65
Van der Meer, F., 232
Van der Woude, 363-64, 366
Van der Veken, 449
Van Ruiten, J. T. A. G. M., 63
Vanderhooft, David, 42
VanderKam, James, 62-64, 66, 175, 177, 181, 198, 225, 347
Vawter, Bruce, 193
Vercoutter, Jean, 450
Vermes, Geza, 350, 357, 361
Vernus, Pascal, 454
Vezin, G., 232
Violet, Bruno, 284-85
Volf, Miroslav, 35, 242
Volokhine, Youri, 452
Von Rad, Gerhard, 117, 161, 339
Vos, R. I., 450-51

Wall, D., 244
Walter, N., 413-15
Waltke, Bruce K., 377
Watts, James, 69
Wehrli, F., 406
Weiss, Johannes, 249
Weitzman, Steven, 316
Welch, Robert, 134
Wenham, G. J., 51
Werman, C., 63
Westermann, Claus, 51
White, Lynn, Jr., 245
Whitney, K. William, 279, 288
Whybray, R. N., 193
Wilcken, U., 465

Wilder, A., 235-36
Wilkinson, John, 281
Williamson, H. G. M., 45
Willis, John T., 92
Wills, Lawrence M., 4, 166, 175, 262, 276-77
Wilson, Robert R., 83
Winston, David, 57, 205
Winter, Irene, 68
Wise, Michael O., 342
Wojcik, D., 232
Wold, Benjamin G., 196
Wolff, H. J., 462, 465
Woude, Adam Simon van der, 363

Wright III, Benjamin G., 163, 165, 182, 187, 189-90, 195-97
Wright, Jacob, 68

Yiftach-Firanko, Uri, 463
Yoder, Christine, 81
Young, Frances, 401

Zakovitch, Yair, 104-5
Zeigler, Joseph, 138
Zeitler, S., 391
Zellentin, Holger M., 447, 456
Zimmer, H., 226
Zimmerli, Walther, 117, 385
Zsengallér, József, 178, 186

Index of Scripture and Other Ancient Texts

HEBREW BIBLE/OLD TESTAMENT

Genesis

1–3	337
1–2	337
1	207, 291, 337, 438, 440-43
1:2	443
1:3	442
1:27	210, 441
1:28	439
2–3	337
2:24	106
2:7	441
3:1-24	210
6:4	152
9–10	65
9	6, 50-51, 57-59, 63
9:1	52-53, 59
9:2	245
9:6b	30
9:18	56
9:18-19	54
9:18-27	402
9:21-27	50, 52, 58-59, 62, 65
9:22	55-56
9:24-25	52
9:25	60-61
9:25-27	56, 59, 62
9:26	51
9:26-27	54
9:27ab	52-54
10	50, 58, 62-63
11	128
11:28	304
12	306, 327
12:1	306, 310
12:3	150
12:6-8	175
12:7	53
13:15-17	53
14:22	316
15	310-11, 314, 316, 327
15:1	311
15:5	319
15:7	53, 310
15:7-21	310
15:9	311
15:9-11	314
15:10	314
15:11	315
15:12-21	311
15:13-14	327
15:17	316
15:18-21	53
16:7-14	312
17:4-6	319
17:14	429
17:17	92
17:20	28
18:11	92
22:11-18	312
22:13-14	312
22:17	319
23:6	65, 416
25:2	150
25:6	61
25:12-16	150
25:15	150
25:20	92
25:26	92
25:27	27
27	21
27:40	416
28:4	53
33	21

33:18-30	175	10:3-20	445	7:27	431
34	175, 178, 180-82	10:20	37	10	78
34:7	180, 182	10:27	38	10:8	78
34:30	181	11:10	38	11	431
35:4	175	12:15	431	12:8	80
35:12	53	12:19	431	15:24	358
36	150	12:31-36	444	15:26	358
37:27	59	12:36	445	17:10	431
39:12	137	12:37-39	444	18:3	65
49:5-7	181	12:48-49	19	18:19	358
49:9-10	293	13:10	90	19:8	431
		13:17-18	444	21:1-5	76
Exodus		13:18	445	21:1-6	76
1–16	444	14:4	38	21:5	76
1:8-11	444	14:8	38	21:10	76
2:5-10	444	14:15-18	444	22:3	431
2:11-12	444	14:17-18	38	23:29	431
2:15-21	444	14:19-20	312	24:22	20
2:23	444	14:21-29	444	25:35-38 (LXX)	466-67
3:1–4:17	444	15	37	25:35a (LXX)	467
3:1-10	444	15:1	88	25:35b (LXX)	467
4:2-4	445	15:1-18	87-88	25:35c (LXX)	467
4:21	37	15:20	89	25:36a (LXX)	467
4:27-31	444	15:20-21	85, 87-88	25:36c (LXX)	467
5–15	31	15:21	88	25:37 (LXX)	467
5:1-3	444	15:22	445	25:37b (LXX)	467
5:2	38	16	444	25:44-46	20
6:1-8	444	19:3	155	27:2	73
7:8-23	444	19:5-6	151		
7:9-10	445	19:18	316	Numbers	
7:10-12	445	20:2	327	3–4	97
7:17-19	445	22:21-24 (LXX)	468	6	67, 69, 71-79, 83-85
7:18	445	23:20-21	313		
7:19-20	445	23:23-33	49	6:5	74
7:20-21	445	23:28-30	56	6:6-7	77
7:25–8:15	444	24:10	313	6:9	74
8:1-19	445	28	314	6:11	78
8:5-6	445	31:14	431	6:12-13	75
8:16-17	445	34:24	90	6:16	78
8:16-19	444	34:28	312	6:20	78
8:20-24	444			9:13	431
9:8-12	444-45	Leviticus		11:1-3	182
9:12	37	1:9	76	12	85
9:13-35	444-45	7:20	431	13:32-33	152
10:1	37	7:21	431	15:30	431
10:1-20	444	7:25	431	17	314

19	76	24:1 (LXX)	461, 464	5:2	74, 76
19:13	431	24:17 (LXX)	468	9:27	90-91
19:20	431	24:19 (LXX)	468	11:29-40	75
21:1-3	75	24:21 (LXX)	468	11:34	89
25	184	26:12-13 (LXX)	468	11:40	90
25:12	184	27	175	13	78
30	465	27:19 (LXX)	468	13:5	74
30:2	75	28	362	13:7	78
30:3-15	75	28:36	124	13:14	78
30:3 (LXX)	464-65	28:64	124	16:17	74
30:14 (LXX)	464	29:22-23	178	19:23	180
31:19	76	29:25 (LXX)	21	19:24	180
33:51-53	49	30:12-13	152	20:6	180
		30:19	231	20:10	180
Deuteronomy		32	42	21:15-25	90, 93
1:28	152	32:8-9 (LXX)	21	21:19	90
2	21	32:9	27		
2:4-6	150	32:15	178	**Ruth**	
4	146	32:20	178	1	103, 112
4:6	147	32:21	178-79	1:1-2	113
4:6-8	158	32:22	178	1:3	113
4:19	153	32:39	302	1:4	113
4:19 (LXX)	21	32:42	74	1:5	113
4:38	152	33:2	25	1:6	113
7:2	49	33:24	376	1:7	113
7:14	376	33:29	157	1:8	110, 113
7:20-22	57	33:29 (LXX)	158	1:9	110, 112
10:14-15	151			1:9-10	103, 114
10:18 (LXX)	468	**Joshua**		1:11	110, 112-13
12:31	56	2	18	1:12	106
13:2	124	6:21	49	1:13	110
14:1	30	7	18	1:14	106, 113
14:29 (LXX)	468	8	175	1:14	113-14
16:13	90	8:26	49	1:16	20, 128
20	49	9	50	1:16-17	103, 115
20:7 (LXX)	462	10:28	49	1:19	110-13
20:16-18	24	24	306	1:22	111, 113
20:17	49	24:2	306	2	103
22:21	180	24:2-3	304	2:1	113
22:23 (LXX)	462	24:32	175	2:2	113, 115
22:25 (LXX)	462	24:33	185	2:4	113
22:27 (LXX)	462			2:5	106, 113
22:28 (LXX)	462	**Judges**		2:6	106, 113
23	21	1:5-7	33	2:7	108, 113, 115
23:4	105	5:1	87	2:8	104-7, 110, 112-13
23:4-9	402	5:1-31	87-88	2:9	107-10, 113

Index of Scripture and Other Ancient Texts

2:10	113-15	2:11	91	**1 Chronicles**	
2:11	113-14	2:19	90	6:3	85
2:13	113, 115	2:21	92	15:16-22	96
2:14	104	5:3-5	307	15:24	96
2:15	113	10:1	92	16:7	95
2:18	113	10:17-27	92	17:4	43
2:19	113, 115	14:24-46	75	17:7	43
2:20	113	18:6-7	89	20:6-8	152
2:21	103-6, 110, 112-15	18:10-11	137	29:25	379
2:22	104-7, 113	31:4	137		
2:23	104, 107, 113			**2 Chronicles**	
3:1	113-14	**2 Samuel**		6	151
3:2	104, 107	1:6	137	6:18-21	151
3:4	110	1:6-10	137	20:7	52-53
3:5	115	1:20	89	32:20-21	32
3:6	113	1:24	94	33:11	33
3:9	113, 115	3:18	43	34:4	374
3:10	106-7, 113	7:5	43	35:15	95
3:11	113	7:8	43	35:25	95, 97
3:12	113	13:12	180	36:7	33
3:15	115	21:18-22	152	36:13	42
3:16	113	22	382	36:18	33
3:17	103, 113-15			36:23a	45
3:18	110, 113	**1 Kings**		46:13	43
4	103, 112	5	187		
4:1	113	8	151	**Ezra**	
4:2	113	8:27-30	151	1:2	45
4:3	113	11:13	43	2:41	95
4:5	20, 113	11:32	43	2:70	95
4:8	113	11:34	43	6:21	19
4:9	112-13	11:36	43	9:6	374
4:10	20, 113	11:38	43	10:1-2	402
4:11	110-13	14:8	43		
4:12	106	16:24	176	**Nehemiah**	
4:14	113			3:14-15	371
4:15	113	**2 Kings**		9:5	371-73, 376-77, 380
4:16	107, 113	4:8-37	83		
4:17	113	17	176, 183	10:29	19
		19:34	43	10:29-31	402
1 Samuel		19:37	32	11:22	95
1:1—2:10	90-91, 93	21:10-15	321	13:1-3	402
1:3	90	23:8	96	13:7	80
1:11	74, 76	23:8-9	96	13:23-30	402
1:28	91	24:13	33	13:28	80, 177
2:1-10	91	25:5-7	33		
2:5	92	25:13-17	33		

Index of Scripture and Other Ancient Texts

Esther		68:29	89	14:20	193
3:1	25, 375	73–83	95	14:35	192
9:27	19, 128	74:12-14	31	15:16	193
		74:13-14	288	15:17	137
Job		79:1	384	17:1	137, 193
1:19	104	83:7	151	17:5	193
3:13-19	215	88:10-12	215	17:7	192
7:12	288	89:3	43	18:4	148
21:13	362	89:10-11	31, 288	18:23	193
26:12-13	288	89:20	43	19:4	193
28	146, 148-50, 152, 253	89:20-21	32	19:12	192
		89:23	32	22:4	191-92
28:1	148	89:30	172	22:7	193
28:6	148	92:12	187	22:23	193
28:12	148	104:16	187	23:10 (LXX)	468
28:13	150	106:39	321	24:3-4	191
28:15-19	149	108:5	375	25:1	192
28:20	148	108:10-11	151	25:2	258
28:23	148, 150	110:1	32	28–29	192
28:23-27	153	115:3-8	307	28:10	192
28:24	153	119:14	375	28:12	193
28:26-27	153	119:53	383	28:25-26	192
28:27	153	135:4	27, 155	30:4	152
29	208	137:7	151	30:18-19	150
38:35	153-54	145:11-12	379	31	81
40–41	288	147:4-5	153		
				Ecclesiastes	
Psalms		Proverbs		2:18-21	149, 194
2	34	1:20-33	160, 170	4:1-3	194
2:3	26	3:13-14	193	4:13	149
2:7	32	3:18	156	5:7	194, 375
9:17	23	6:10-11	193	5:8	194
18	382	8	213, 253	9	194
21:7	372	8:1–9:6	160	9:14-17	149
31:9	362	8:4	160	9:16	194
31:16	362	8:15-18	149	10:19	194
33:6-12	151	8:18	192	11:9	207
37:32-33	365	8:21a (LXX)	253		
37:35	187	8:22-31	153, 253, 256	Isaiah	
50	95	8:26	319	6:3	372
57:6	372	8:30-31	160	6:9-10	119
57:12	372	8:35	160	8:6	119
60:9-10	151	8:35-36	156	8:12	119
68:11-12	88	12:24	192	10	39
68:12	97	13:21-22	192	10:5	40
68:24-25	88-89	14:14	375	10:5-14	39

Index of Scripture and Other Ancient Texts

10:5-19	39	51:9	288	20:7-18	82
10:7	40	51:9-10	31	21:8	231
10:15	40	51:9-11	98	22:26-28	385
10:15-19	39	51:11	98	22:28	124
10:16	40	52:7	98	24	118
13–23	231	52:8	98	24:7	128
14:1	19, 128	53	208	25	41
14:12-14	277	53:3	128	25:9	43
19	21	53:6	128	27–29	41
22:25	384	54:1	92	27	158
27:1	31	55:5	158	27:5-7	149
34–35	98	56	19	27:5-7 (LXX)	41-42
34	21, 151	56:6	19	27:7	43
35:1-2	98	56:6-8	158	29:7	157
35:10	98	56:7	20	29:23	180
37	39	60:4-16	158	30:1–31:40	99-100
37:21-29	39	65	22	30:23–31:4	99-100
37:24-25	39	65:13-15	21	31:1	128
37:26	39	66	20	31:3	128
37:35	43	66:1	151	31:4	100
37:38	32	66:18-21	158	31:10-14	93
40–66	154, 158-59	66:20	22	31:12	93
40–55	98	66:22	20	31:13	93, 99-100
40:9	97-98	66:23	20	31:15	94, 99
40:9-10	97	66:24	20	31:21	100
40:25-26	153			31:29-30	82
40:26	153	**Jeremiah**		31:31-34	129
42:6	156	2:13	148	33:21	43
42:10-12	98	2:20-24	321	33:22	43
42:13	98	4:11	119	33:26	43
42:15-16	98	7:4	41	37–38	41
43:5-9	158	8:7	124	39:10	117
43:9	25	8:13	124	40:10	117
44	307	9:17	95	46–51	231
44:1	155	9:17-18	84	49:7	150
44:9-20	307	9:17-21	94	49:7-22	151
44:23	98	9:19	94	50:2-3	31
44:24–45:13	43-44	10:1-16	307	50:5	128
45:1	44	10:6-7	153	50–51	41
45:5	302	10:12	153	50:31-32	41
45:18	153	10:12-16	153	51:7	41
46:1	31	10:16	153, 155	51:34-39	41
48:12-13	153	13:23	231	51:44	31
49:6	156	15	82	51:59-64	41
49:18	158	15:16-18	82		
49:22-23	158	16:13	385		

485

Index of Scripture and Other Ancient Texts

Lamentations	
4	383
4:1-5	383
4:21-22	151
5:2	117
5:10	383

Ezekiel	
1	317
1:26	313, 317, 376
8	321
10	317
11:15	117
11:15-21	118
11:20	128
16:13	383
17:2-27	258
17:11-21	43
18:2-4	82
18:14-20	50
21	384
21:21	383
21:23-27	383
21:24-26	385
21:26	10
21:28-29	383
22:3-4	321
27:24	383
28:1-10	277
32:2-8	34
33:15	147
33:23-29	118
33:24	117
34:23-24	43
35	21, 151
36:17	358
36:28	128
37:23	128
37:24-25	43
40–48	19
40:1	96
40:44-46	95, 97
44:6-16	96
44:11	96
44:13	96
44:15-16	96
47:22-23	19

Daniel	
1–6	46-47, 166
1–4	46-47
1	312
1:2	33
1:4	171
1:8-16	166
1:17	166, 171
1:20	171
2–6	166
2	48, 167
2:10	166
2:14	166, 171
2:18-19	166
2:20-23	254
2:23	171
2:27-28	166
2:30	167, 171
2:31-45	285
2:35	48
2:38	149
2:47	167
3	167
3:17-18	167, 170
3:28	47
4	133-34, 136-37, 139, 142
4:8-9	166
4:9	171
4:12	141, 149
4:14a (OG)	138
4:18	135, 167, 171
4:19 (OG)	138
4:28 (OG)	138
4:29 (OG)	139
4:30	133
4:30 (OG)	139
4:34b (OG)	139
4:37	47
5	167
5:11	167, 171
5:11-12	171
5:14	167, 171
6	167
6:3	171
6:26	47
7–12	166
7	37, 166, 285, 316
7:2-8	169
7:8b	37
7:9	313
7:9-12	169
7:10	171
7:12	170
7:15	169
7:16	168, 171
7:19-27	169
7:20b	37
7:23-27	168
7:25	170
7:25a	37
7:26-27	169
7:28	169
8:10-11	169, 277
8:11-13	169
8:12	170
8:14	169-70
8:15-16	171
8:15-17	168
8:17	169, 387
8:18	169
8:19-26	168
8:23-25	169
8:25	169
8:25b	37
8:26	170
8:27	169, 171
9	170
9:2	171
9:4-19	145, 147
9:17	169
9:22	168, 171
9:23	171
9:24-26	171
9:24-27	170
9:26-27	169
9:27	169
10:1	171
10:2-3	168
10:8	169

486

10:9	169	**Amos**		**Haggai**	
10:10	169	1:3–2:3	231	1:2	119
10:10-14	168	4:13	153	1:12	119
10:11	171	5:8	153	1:14	119
10:12	171	5:26	153	2:2	119
10:13	224	5:27	153	2:4-5a	120
10:15	169	9:5-6	153	2:5	121
10:16	169			2:6b-8	121
10:16-17	169	**Obadiah**		2:14	119-20
10:18-19	169	8–9	150	2:21b-22	120
10:18–12:4	168				
10:19	171	**Micah**		**Zechariah**	
10:20	224	3:12	384	1–8	117
10:21	171	6:4	85	1:2	123
11	37			1:3	123
11:1-45	170	**Habakkuk**		1:4	123
11:20	379	1:2-4	354	1:5	123
11:28-30	424	1:4	350, 354	1:6	123
11:30	170	1:12-17	354	1:18-21	126
11:30-31	169	1:13	350, 354	2:6	124
11:32	170	2:1	354, 358	2:6-7	125
11:33	254	2:2-4	355	2:9a	127
11:33-35	169-70	2:2-20	354	2:10-11a	128
11:34	19	2:5	356	3	315
11:35	170, 387	2:5-6	356	3:7	118
11:36	37, 377	2:5-8	356	3:8-10	46
12:1	169, 171	2:5-17	354	3:9	118
12:1-3	169, 216	2:7-8a	360	4:6-7	46
12:2	216	2:7-8	358-59	5:5-11	127
12:2-3	170, 254	2:8	359	6:8	126
12:3	170, 214	2:8b	361	6:15	125
12:4	169-70, 387	2:9	356	7:5	124
12:7	170	2:9-11	356, 363	7:14	118
12:8	169, 171	2:12	355-56	7:14a	124
12:9	169-70	2:12-13	355	8:6-8a	125
12:9-13	168	2:13-14	355	8:8	128
12:10	169-70	2:15	356, 364	8:10	118
12:11-12	170, 236	2:15-17	356	8:11	119
12:13	170	2:16	364	8:13	124
		2:17	365	8:14	123
Hosea		2:18-20	355	8:16-17	124
2:12	180	3:3	25	13:4	79
2:21 (LXX)	462	3:6	26	14	20
2:22 (LXX)	462			14:12	20
5:3	321	**Zephaniah**		14:16-21	20
		2	231	14:18-19	20

487

Index of Scripture and Other Ancient Texts

Malachi	
1:2-5	151

NEW TESTAMENT

Matthew	
7:17-18	228
12:30	228
21	27
25:1-13	26
25:31-46	217

Mark	
1:27	257
4	257
4:10-11	257
4:22	257
4:23	258
6:2	256
12:18-27	216
13	249, 258, 259
15:27-32	210

Luke	
6:17-49	198
6:43	228
12:13-21	198
22:3	325

John	
1:14	155
5:18	325
6:40	216
7:12	325
7:20	325
8:41	325
8:48	325
9:2	386
10:33	325
13:2	325
13:27	325
14:6	19

Acts	
3:13	448

4:12	19
6:1	397
16:19-23	398

Romans	
6:3-9	216
8:19-22	244

1 Corinthians	
1:18-25	256
7:29-31	256
8:2-4	256
11:26	256
15:51-56	256
16:22	256

2 Corinthians	
5:1-10	217
5:10	217
6:14-15	272-73
11:22	397

Galatians	
4	27
6:15-16	399

Philippians	
1:23-24	217
3:5	397

Colossians	
1:18	216

1 Thessalonians	
1:9-10	256
4:13-18	256

2 Peter	
3:5-10	244

Revelation	
2:8-9	398
2:16	239
4:8	316
4:11	316
5:9-10	316
5:13	316

7:12	316
12:7-9	277
12:7-12	224
15:3-4	316
16:7	239
18:1–19:10	232
19:1b-2	233
19:2	239
19:10	313
20–21	239
22:8-9	313

APOCRYPHA

Baruch	
1	253
1:1-14	145
1:11	157
1:12	157
1:13	146
1:15–3:8	145, 147
1:19-20	146
2:14	158
2:17	148
2:21	158
2:23	158
2:24	158
3:4	148
3:9	146, 148
3:9–4:4	145-47, 157
3:9-14	147-48
3:10-13	146, 148
3:11	148
3:12	148, 154
3:13	148
3:14	146-48
3:15	147-48, 152
3:15–4:1	147
3:16-17	149
3:16-19	149, 152, 157
3:16-31	149
3:20-21	150
3:20-23	150
3:23	150, 154
3:24-25	151

3:26	152	9:2	181	7:37	426	
3:27	151	10:5	312	9:5	38	
3:29	152	11:7	149	9:12	38	
3:29-31	152	12:19	312	9:17	38	
3:31	152			9:18	38	
3:32	152, 154	1 Maccabees		10:29-30	224	
3:32-35	153	1:17	425	11:24	426, 429	
3:32-37	153	1:20	425	11:31	426	
3:32a	153	1:29	425	12:37	426	
3:32b	153	1:29-35	424	14:30	176	
3:33	153	1:41	425	15:1	176	
3:34	153-54	1:61	430	15:29	426	
3:34-35	153	2:23-26	185			
3:35	154	5:65	186	4 Maccabees		
3:35-36	156	5:65-68	186	18:12	185	
3:36	154-55	5:66	186			
3:36 (LXX)	154	5:66-68	186	Psalm 151		
3:37	155	6:12-13	38	4	153	
3:37 (LXX)	154	13:12-24	361			
3:38 (LXX)	155	14:33	186	Sirach		
4:1	146, 155			1:9-10	173	
4:1a	155	2 Maccabees		2:1-5	161	
4:1b	155-56	4:15	426	2:10	161	
4:2	156	4:34	184	3:21-24	165	
4:2-4	147, 156	5-7	432	4:11-19	162, 170	
4:2b	156	5:1-16	425	4:27	182	
4:3	156	5:11	425	5:4	162	
4:4	157	5:15	426	6:20-22	162	
4:5–5:9	145, 158	5:22	431	6:23-31	162	
4:9	158	5:22-23	176	9:11-12	162	
4:9-29	158	5:24-26	425	10:19-22	187	
4:12-13	146	6:1	425	10:30	194	
4:14	158	6:1-2	177	11	253	
4:24	158	6:2	177	11:26-28	162	
4:25	158	6:6	426	13:23	189	
4:36-37	158	6:7	429	13:24	195	
5:5-6	158	6:9	430	14:16	195	
		6:10	430	14:17	362	
Epistle of Jeremiah		6:11	430	15:10	173	
3	308	6:18-31	312	15:18	153	
		6:21	431	15:6	182	
1 Esdras		7	216	16:9	178	
4:50	186	7:2	426	16:12-14	162	
		7:8	426	16:26-30	162	
Judith		7:24	426	16:27	162	
5:16	176, 181	7:27	426	17:3	187	

489

Index of Scripture and Other Ancient Texts

17:8	187	44–50	175	1:16–2:1a	205, 212
17:11	147	45	182	1:16–2:24	205, 211
20:9-11	165	45:5	147	2	205, 209, 214-15
21:10	162	45:9	182	2:1-5	206, 207
23:18-21	162	45:15	171	2:1a	205, 207
24	147, 155, 157, 164, 253	45:23	182, 184	2:1a-20	213
		45:24	184	2:1b-20	212
24:6	187	46:6	178	2:2	207
24:8	155	47:17	182	2:2-5	213
24:8-12	163	47:23	183	2:5	207
24:13	187	48:10	184	2:6	207
24:23	155, 158, 163	48:15	183	2:6-9	207
24:25-27	155	49:4b-5	156	2:7-9	207
24:28	155	49:5	178-79, 182	2:10-11	208
24:28-29	165	49:16	185	2:12	209, 215
24:30-34	164	50	174-75, 178, 182	2:12-20	208
27:2	194	50:1	182	2:13	209
31:8-9	195	50:1-24	174-75, 179	2:16	209
33:1	161	50:8	187	2:17-20	209-10
33:5	182	50:12	187	2:18	210
33:12	188	50:13	183	2:20	209-10
33:16-19	164	50:20	183	2:21	205
34:1-8	165	50:24	184-85	2:21-24	210, 212
36	163, 187	50:25	178, 182	2:22	210, 212
36:3	182	50:25-26	8, 173-75, 178-79, 184-87	2:23	210
36:11	184			2:24	213
37:25	182	50:26	176, 178, 182, 186, 386	3–5	214
38	253			3	212
38:1-3	251	50:27-29	164, 174	3:1	212
38:24-27	257	51	174	3:1-9	212
39:1-5	164			3:1-12	212
39:4	187	**Tobit**		3:1–4:20	211
39:6	164	12:16-22	313	3:7	214
39:7	253	14:6	20	3:13-19	212
39:8	13			4	212
39:12	164	**Wisdom**		4:1-6	212
39:12-35	173	1–6	8, 204-5, 210-11, 214-17	4:6	212
39:23	178			4:7-20	213
39:26-27	162	1:1	211, 213	4:16	213
39:32	164	1:1-15	211, 213	5:1-23	211
40:29	195	1:1–6:21	210	5:4-13	212
42:14	173	1:6-7	211, 214	5:4-14	215
42:15	164	1:12	212	5:6	213
42:15–43:33	162, 173, 378	1:13	210, 212	5:7-8	213
42:16	173	1:15	211-12	5:13	213
42:17	378	1:16	213	5:15	213

Index of Scripture and Other Ancient Texts

5:15-23	213	8	306	18:8-11	318
5:17-20	215	8:1	310	18:14	318
5:21-23	215	8:3-4	310	19	318
6	211-12	8:6	310	19:1–29:13	306
6:1	213	9–32	305	19:3	317, 319
6:1-21	211, 213	9–14	305, 310	19:8	319
6:4	215	9	310	19:9	319
6:9-11	213	9:1-5	310	20:1	319
6:12-16	213	9:3	310	20:1-3	319
6:12-21	213	9:5	311	20:3	319
6:18c	215	9:6	311	20:5	319
6:21	211, 213-14	9:7	311	20:7	320
7–9	210	10–11	310	21	320
9	253	10	312	22:4	320, 328
10–19	210	10:3	313	22:5	320
10	211	10:8-13	313	23	320
11–19	215	10:9	316, 318	23:10	320
11:15–12:27	211	10:10	318	23:12	320
12:6	57	11:2	313	23:13	320
12:11	57	12	310, 312, 314	23:14	321
13–15	211, 212, 307	12:1-2	312	24:1-4	321
13:10	308	12:6	312	24:6-9	321
14:21	308	12:8	314	25	329
		12:9	314	25:1	321
		12:10	314	25:1-6	321
PSEUDEPIGRAPHA		13–14	310	25:4	321
		13	314	26	321-22
Apocalypse of Abraham		13:1	314	26:1	322
1–8	305	13:4-5	314	26:2-3	322
1–2	306	13:7-8	315	26:3	318
1	306	13:14	315	26:4	322
3–4	306	14:4	315	26:5	322
3:2-4a	308	14:5-7	315	27–28	322
3:8	308	15–18	305, 310	27:3	322
4	324	15	316	27:7	323
4:3	308	15:2	314	28:1–29:3	323
5	306	15:4–17:3	316	28:5	323
5:7	307	16:3	316, 318	29:1-2	323
5:14	307	17	315	29:4-6	323
5:17	307	17:1	316, 318	29:4-13	323
6–7	306	17:4-21	316	29:4a	323
6:3	308	17:8-14	317	29:5	325
6:11-17	309	17:17	317	29:6	325
7	309, 311	17:20	317, 378	29:8-13	324
7:11	309	18	317	29:9-10	324
7:12	310	18:1-2	318	29:9b	324

Index of Scripture and Other Ancient Texts

29:10	326	8:1-10	313	85–90	265, 270
29:14	328	8:15	313	86–88	265
29:14–31:12	306			88:1-3	266
29:15	328	**2 Baruch**		89:9-12	265
29:17	328	4:3-4	311	89:59-64	265
29:18	327	26:1-35	285	89:61-64	266
30:1-8	285	29:4	288	89:65-67	266
30:2-8	328	48:30-41	285	89:70-72	266
31:1	326	70:2-3	285	89:76-77	266
31:2-3	326			90:2-19	266
31:4	326, 328	**3 Baruch**	312	90:6-7	266
31:5	326			90:8	266
31:9-12	327	**1 Enoch**		90:17-19	266
		1–36	314	90:20	266
Apocalypse of Zephaniah		2–5	154	90:20-21	266
6:11-15	313	2:1	154	90:21-27	266
		5:6	253	90:30-38	266
Artapanus		6–16	263, 270, 314	91:6-7	285
27.1-2	444	6–11	152, 263, 266	91:11	267
27.3	444	9:6	253	91:14	268
27.4	436, 448	10:1-3	265-66	92–105	254, 266
27.6	448	10:17-19	265	92:1	253
27.9	448	10:17-20	266	93:4	267
27.12	448	10:21	265	93:10	253
27.15-16	448	11–16	253	94:7	267
27.17-19	444	12–16	254, 263-64	94:8	198
27.20	444	14	316-17	95:6	267
27.21	444, 456	15:8–16:1	264	96:5	267
27.22	444	17–36	312	97:6	268
27.25	455	37–71	268, 312	97:8	267
27.26	456	37:1	253	98:4	267-68
27.27-29	445	39:1	269	98:15	267, 271
27.27-31	444-45	39:10-14	316	99:2	267
27.28	445	42	172	99:3	268
27.28-29	445	42:1-2	172	99:4-9	285
27.30	445	43–44	153	99:7	308
27.31	444	50:2-4	269	99:14	268
27.32	444-45, 448	54:1-6	269	100:1-3	285
27.33	444-45, 456	56:1-4	269	100:6	268
27.34	444-45	60:7-10	288	100:10	268
27.36	456	65:6-7	269	102:3	268
27.36-37	444	67:5-7	269	103:5	267
27.37	444	69:4-5	269	103:11	267
		69:6-12	269	103:11-13	267
Ascension of Isaiah		80:2-4	285	103:14-15	267
7:18-23	313	81:1–82:4	253	103:15	267

Index of Scripture and Other Ancient Texts

104:1-3	268	6:56	292	*Joseph and Aseneth*	
104:2	198	6:56-57	290	7:1	312
104:7-8	268	7:28-29	293	8:5-7	312
104:10	267	7:48	284	15:11-12	313
104:12	267	7:96-97	292		
105:1-2	268	7:125	295	*Jubilees*	287
		8:53-54	293	3:10	234
2 Enoch		10:11	295	3:31	234
1:4-8	313	10:16	295	4:5	234
22	312	10:20	295	7–10	62, 65
39	316	10:25-26	295	7	64
		10:27	295	7:7-12	62
3 Enoch		10:27a-30	296	7:12	53
1:7	313	10:30	296	7:13-14	63
		10:50	295	7:17	63
4 Ezra		10:38-40	295	8–9	63
3:1-3	296	10:56-57	296	9:1	64
3:14	311	11:1	289	9:14-15	64
3:21-22	284	11:1-3	288	10:28-34	62
3:34-36	28	11:2	289	10:28-46	65
4:11b-12	284	11:4	289	10:29-34	64-65
4:23-25	284	11:10	289	11–12	307
4:27b	284	11:12	289	12:2-5	308
4:30	57	11:13	290	12:12-14	310
4:30a	284	11:28-32	289	12:16-21	309
5:1-13	285	11:31-35	290	20	307
5:8	285-87	11:37	293	22	307
5:9-10	172	11:38	293	22:18	308
5:9b-10	285, 287	11:39	293	23:11-25	285
5:20b-2	296	11:45	290	23:13	361
5:37	279	12:1-3	293	23:25	285, 287
5:51-55	284	12:3a	290	30:17	181
6	290	12:11	293		
6:13	295	13:1-2	294	*Liber antiquitatum biblicarum*	
6:21	285-87	13:3	294	2:9	308
6:35-37	296	13:4	294	6	310
6:38-54	287	13:5	294	18:5	319
6:39	291	13:9	294	23:6	311
6:40	291	13:9-10	290		
6:41	291	13:10-11	294	*Letter of Aristeas*	
6:44	291	14:1-6	296	2	411
6:45	291	14:13-14	297	31	410
6:49	287	14:25	296	128-71	411
6:52b	287	14:39-40	296	131	411
6:54	292	14:50	297	134-38	307
6:55-59	289				

Index of Scripture and Other Ancient Texts

135	308	8	275	DEAD SEA SCROLLS	
147	411	8:8-10	275		
161	411	8:9-10	725	CD (Damascus	
184-296	411	8:12	275-76	Document)	
189	411	8:22	276	1.10-17	342
200-201	412	9:4	277	4	358
208	411	10	275	4.3-4	358
209	411	11:2	158	4.5	358
211	411	12–16	275	4.7	358
222	411	12:1-4	276	4.11-12	358
235	412	13–15	276	4.14	358
236	411	16	277	4.14-19	358
237	411	17	31, 275	4.16–5.11	275
244	411	17:4-7	276	6.7	342
256	412	17:11-14	276	12.2	358
292	411	18:10-12	154	20.1	342
295-96	412			20.14	342
310	459	*Sibylline Oracles*		20.28	342
		2:55	285	20.33	342
Ladder of Jacob		2:154-73	285		
2:6-22	316	2:155	287	1QIsa^b	
		3:11-14	308	22.17	362
Odes of Solomon		3:29-53	307		
26:8	378	3:57-59	308	1QpMic	
26:10-11	378	3:110-28	65-66	8–10:6	342
		3:586-90	308		
Psalms of Solomon		3:796-807	285	1QpHab	
1	275	5:74	285	1.2-4	354
1:7	276	5:82-83	308	1.4	354
2	275			1.12-17	354
2:3	275	*Testaments of the*		1.13	342, 350, 354
2:3-5	276	*Twelve Patriarchs*		2–6	271
2:11-13	275-76	*Testament of Judah*		2.1	354
2:22-31	276	21:7–22:1	285	2.1-2	271
2:25	37			2.1-3	343
2:25-29	277	*Testament of Levi*		2.2	342
2:29	37	2–5	312	2.2-4	354
2:29-30	37	4:1	285	2.2-20	354
3	275	6:8	181	2.6-10	343
3:3-12	275-76	6:11	179	2.8	342
4	275, 277	7	180, 182	2.12	355
4:2-8	276	7:2	180	2.12-14	355
4:3-12	276	7:2-3	179	2.13-14	355
4:5	276	8:4-5	312	2.18-20	355
4:5-12	275			4.8-12	350
4:20	276	*Testament of Naphtali*		5.10-11	271
		3:2–4:1	154		

7.1-5	271, 343	11.12-16	364	10:17-19	340
7.4	342	11.15	366	11:13-14	379
7.4-5	366	11.17–12.1	365	11:18	197
8–9	365	11.17–12.10	365	11:20-21	338
8	360	12	365	11:20-37	272
8.1-3	271	12.2	271, 350	12–13	273-74
8.3	342, 356	12.5	362, 366	12:5-6	272
8.8	271, 350, 354	12.6-7	365	12:5–13:4	271
8.8–12.10	354	12.8	271, 350	12:8-22	272
8.8-13	356, 359, 365	12.8-10	365	12:10	272
8.9-10	357	12.10	354	12:13	272
8.12-13	357			12:18-22	272
8.16	350, 363	1QapGen^{ar}		12:21-24	272
8.16–9.2	358	16–17	65	12:27	272
8.16–9.12	358			12:27-28	343
9	361	1QS		12:27-29	340
9.1	362	3–4	272	13:11-12	340
9.1-2	362, 366	3:13	336	14:34-35	216
9.2	360, 362, 366	3:13-17	337	15:26-27	340
9.2-4	359	3:13–4:26	272, 273	15:27	343
9.2-7	359	3:17–4:16	337	16:6	340
9.7-12	359	3:19	336	18:4	338
9.8	361	3:23–4:26	224	18:12	338
9.9	271, 350	4:2-14	336	19:3	338
9.9-10	342	4:10	358	19:3-14	272
9.9-11	366	4:12	360	19:11	358
9.9-12	361	5–11	348	20:7	341
9.10	362, 366	5:8	201	20:24	338
9.11	362	8:11-12	345	20:25	338
9.12–10.5	366	8:12	342	20:26	338
9.16	350, 363			21:6	338
9.16-17	363	1QM		21:14	338
9.17	359	1.1-2	402	21:18	338
10.2	363	13.5	358	22:8	338
10.3-5	366			22:11	338
10.5	363	1QH^a		23:9	338
10.9	271	1:1	341	25:34	341
11.2-3	364	3–9	335		
11.3	365	5:21	341	1Q34bis	
11.4	271, 350	7:21	341	3 2:1-4	154
11.4-8	364	8–27	335		
11.5	342, 364-65	9:7-20	336-37	4QpIsa^c	
11.6	365	9:21-24	234	30 3	350
11.7	364	9:27-31	378-79		
11.8-11	364	10–17	335	4Q169	
11.12	350, 364	10:13-15	340	3 + 4 i 6-8	271

495

3 + 4 i 7	271	4Q286		1 i 32-33	369		
3 + 4 ii 2	271	7 ii 4	358	1 i 33	375		
3 + 4 ii 4	271			1 i 44	375		
3 + 4 ii 8	271	4Q291					
3 + 4 iii 3	271	1 5-6	370, 376	4Q404			
3 + 4 iii 6-7	271			5, 2	375		
		4Q317					
4Q171 (pPs^a)		1+1a ii 28	375	4Q405			
1:26-27	271			19ABCD, 7	369		
2:12-18	271	4Q371	179, 182	20-22 ii 8	375		
3–10 iv 7	365	1 10	179, 386	20-22 ii 8-9	375		
3–10 iv 8-10	365			20-22 ii 13	369		
3–10 iv 9	365	4Q372					
3:15	342	1 4-9	384	4Q406			
3:19	342	1 9	383, 385	1, 2	375, 379		
4:5-10	271	1 9-11a	385				
4:18	342	1 10	385	4Q415			
4:27	342	1 10-11	386	6 2	190		
		1 11	179				
4Q173 (pPs^b)		1 11-12	179	4Q416			
2 2	342	1 11-14	386	1 1-9	154		
		1 14	385	2 ii 4-6	196		
4Q174		1 14-15	386	2 ii 9-15	190		
1:12	342, 345	1 19-20	386	2 ii 17	196		
				2 ii 18-20	198		
4Q179		4Q378		2 ii 20	190		
1 ii 9-13	383	6 ii 5	374	2 ii 20-21	197		
				2 iii 3	196		
4Q216		4Q381		2 iii 7-8	199		
5, 13	374	24 4-12	382	2 iii 8	191		
		69 2	358	2 iii 9	197		
4Q252				2 iii 11-12	196, 199		
1&3 II	52	4Q385a		2 iii 12-13	198		
1&3 II, 5-8	52	6, 3	375	2 iii 15-16	197		
1&3 II, 7	54			iii 2	190		
1&3 II, 8	52	4Q393		iii 8	190		
		3, 6	374-75, 377	iii 12	190		
4Q254				iii 19	190		
1	52	4Q400					
		2, 3	378-79	4Q417			
4Q274				1 i	338		
1 i 7	358	4Q402		1 i 6-13	336-37		
		4 14-15	379	1 i 7-8	199		
4Q277				1 i 13-18	197		
1 ii 5	358	4Q403		1 i 16-18	337-38		
1 ii 6	358	1 i 10-39	369	2 i 10	202		
		1 i 28	370-71, 380				

2 i 10-11	199	11Q19		Jewish Antiquities	
2 i 12	197, 202	10.11	374	1.120	58
2 i 17-19	195	45.10	358	1.120-47	58
2 i 19-20	200	48.16-17	358	1.121-22	58
				1.134	58
4Q418		Mas 1 k		1.138	59
9 7	197	II 4-7	379	1.138-42	58-59
103 ii 3	202			1.155-57	309
126 ii 7	197			1.341	181
126 ii 7-8	197	HELLENISTIC JEWISH		9.288-90	176
177 5	190	AUTHORS		9.290-91	176
				10.21-23	40
4Q501		Ezekiel the		11.173	395
6	383	Tragedian	317	11.302	176
				11.306-12	177
4Q511		Josephus		11.329-39	46
2 ii 8	358	Against Apion		11.340-41	176
43, 7	358	1.162	418, 421	12.43	175
		1.164	419	12.142	425
4Q512		1.165	421	12.157	175
1-6	358	1.165 (quoting		12.239-54	424
9	358	Hermippus)	419	12.257	176
		1.175	418	12.353	186
4Q521	216	1.176-83 (quoting		13.254-58	186
11Q5 (Ps^a)		Clearchus of Soli,		13.275-81	186
18:1	273	On Sleep)	407	15.371	422
18:1-2	273	1.179 (quoting		17.6.3	329
18:1-14	274	Clearchus of Soli,		18.55-59	329
18:2	273	On Sleep)	407-8		
18:3	273	1.180 (quoting		Jewish War	
18:4	274	Clearchus of Soli,		1.3	395
18:4-8	274	On Sleep)	407	1.31-35	424
18:5	274	1.181 (quoting		1.62-65	186
18:7	274	Clearchus of Soli,		1.282	393
18:7-8	153	On Sleep)	407	1.648	329
18:11	273	2.137-42	431	2.8.3	213
18:12	273	2.143	432	2.169-74	329
18:15	274	2.146	408		
18:17b-20	273	2.165	419	Philo	
18:18	273-74	2.168-69	418	De Abrahamo	
22:12	374	2.170	408	68-80	309
		2.252	308		
11Q14		2.257	418	De aeternitate mundi	
2	179	2.281	418	13-19	416
21	179			112	151

497

Index of Scripture and Other Ancient Texts

De cherubim
52 — 151

De decalogo
52-81 — 307
66 — 308

Legatio ad Gaium
200-201 — 393
299-305 — 329

Legum allegoriae
1.12-13 — 308
1.38 — 441
1.105-8 — 416
2.10-14 — 320
2.15 — 417
4 — 393

De migratione Abrahami
20 — 394

De mutatione nominum
152 — 416

De opificio mundi
21 — 151
135 — 441
165 — 320

De plantatione
134 — 393

Quaestiones et solutiones in Genesin
1.45-48 — 320
2.6 — 417
2.65 — 54
2.70 — 54-55
2.75-76 — 54
2.77 — 54-55

Quis rerum divinarum heres sit
11 — 320
207-14 — 416

Quod deterius potiori insidari soleat
86 — 441
145 — 468

Quod omnis probus liber sit
53-57 — 416
72-75 — 422

De sobrietate
30-69 — 54
31 — 55
44 — 55
48 — 55
51-68 — 56

De somniis
1.107 — 468
2.244 — 416

De specialibus legibus
1.1.2 — 430

De vita Mosis
1.23 — 417
2 — 416

RABBINIC LITERATURE

Mishnah
'Abodah Zarah
3:3-4 — 330

'Abot
1:2 — 175
3:14 — 30

Gittin
1:5 — 176
5:4 — 468

Hagigah
3:4 — 312

Tosefta
Hagigah
3:30-32 — 312

Sanhedrin
13:2 — 23

Babylonian Talmud
'Abodah Zarah
2b-3a — 25
36a — 312

Berakot
57b — 28

Hagigah
15a — 312
25a — 312

Sanhedrin
17b — 312
70a — 50, 61
91a — 61
96b — 25

Sotah
35b — 25

Targums
Targum Ruth
2:21-22 — 106

Midrash
Genesis Rabbah
26:3 — 62
36:2 — 60
36:7 — 50, 60
38:13 — 309
38:19 — 304
44:7 — 62
44:12 — 319
56:10 — 60
61:7 — 60, 62
84:17 — 59-61

Lamentations Rabbah
1:3 — 323

Midrash ha-Gadol — 304

Midrash Proverbs
19:1 — 24

Midrash Tanhuma, Beshalah
25 — 323

Ruth Rabbah
5:11   105

Sifre Deuteronomy
32:1   154
238   25
312   27

Tanna debe Eliyahu
2:25   304

GREEK AND ROMAN LITERATURE

Andokides
I.83   427

Apollodorus
iii 13   226

Aristotle
Politics
1322b   430
1328b   430

Arrian
Anabasis
7.2-3   408
2.25.2   442

Celsus
On the True Doctrine   443

Cicero
De Divinatione
1.132   431

De Natura Deorum
1.56   431
2.71   431

Demosthenes
De Corona
92   428

Diodorus Siculus
1.46.8   446

Diogenes Laertius
1.1   408
1.9   408
2.125-44   412
5.1   419
8.3   420
8.7   419
8.32   420
8.36   419
8.41 (quoting Hermippus)   419
9.1   419

Epictetus
2.8.13-14   308

Galen
De usu partium corporis humani
11.13   430

Heraclitus
B frg. 2   447

Herodotus
Historiae
2   447
4.95   420

Hesiod
Works and Days
106-201   285
130   287
181   287

Homer
Iliad
5.750   442
13.18   442
13.19   442
13.27-29   442
20.60   442
20.61-65   442
21.388   442

Horace
Satirae
1.8.1-3   308

Iamblichus
Vita Pythagorae
14-15   420
146   420

Juvenal
Satirae
13   308
14   308

Livy
37.11 15   427
39.15.2-3   431
39.16.6-9   431

Lucian
Philopseudes
20   308

Ocellus
De Universi Natura
10   440
21   440
38-40   440
43-47   440
43-57   439
45   440
46   439-40

Ovid
Metamorphoses
15.234-36   228

Plato
Laws
10.909-910d   430

Republica
5.473D   416

Pliny
Epistles
10.96   398

Index of Scripture and Other Ancient Texts

Plutarch
Alexander
29.8.9	442
65	408
69	408

De Iside et Osiride
71	308

Polybius
2.47.3	427
2.70.1	427
4.25.7	427
21.6	427
21.45.7	427
30.25.1–30.31.3	432

Porphyry
De abstinentia
2.26 (quoting Theophrastus, Peri Eusebeias)	404-5

Vita Pythagorae
6	420
11	421
11-12	420
14-15	420

Pseudo-Ecphantus
4.6.22	441
4.7.64	441

Pseudo-Heraclitus
Epistula
4	308

Pseudo-Longinus
On the Sublime
9–43	443
9.9	442
12.4	443

Statius
Achilleis
I 269	226

Strabo
Geographica
7.3.5	420
15.1.59	410
15.1.61-68	408
16.1.31	422
16.1.68	406
16.1.70	406
16.2.39	406
16.4.5	430

Suetonius
Nero
16	398

Tacitus
Annals
15.44.2-8	398
15.44.3	398

Thucydides
8.76.6	427

Xenophon
Anabasis
1.5.8	448
2.4.2	448

Hellenica
5.4.2	448

EARLY CHRISTIAN LITERATURE

Apocalypse of Peter
25	239

1 Clement
29.1-2	399

Clement of Alexandria
Paidagogus
1.7	400

Stromata
1.5	400
1.15.70.2	406
1.15.71.4	408
1.15.72.4 (quoting Aristobulus)	413
1.15.72.5 (quoting Megasthenes, Indica)	409-10
1.22.150.1 (quoting Aristobulus)	414
1.22.150.2 (quoting Aristobulus)	415
1.22.150.3 (quoting Aristobulus)	414
1.23.153-55	437
5.14.97.7 (quoting Aristobulus)	414
5.14.99.3 (quoting Aristobulus)	414
5.14.101.4b (quoting Aristobulus)	414

Eusebius of Caesarea
Chronicon
151 (quoting Aristobulus)	414

Praeparatio evangelica
7–8	437
7.13.7 (quoting Aristobulus)	414
7.32.16 (quoting Aristobulus)	414
9 (quoting Artapanus)	437
9.6.6 (quoting Aristobulus)	413
9.6.8 (quoting Aristobulus)	414
9.6.9 (quoting Numenius)	422
9.7.1 (quoting Numenius)	422
9.22.1-11	181
9.26-28	437
10–13.13	437

Index of Scripture and Other Ancient Texts

13.11.3 (quoting Aristobulus)	413	
13.12.1 (quoting Aristobulus)	414-15, 421	
13.12.4 (quoting Aristobulus)	414	
13.12.6-7 (quoting Aristobulus)	414	
13.12.8 (quoting Aristobulus)	415	

Julian
Contra Galilaeos
253A   398

Justin
Dialogue with Trypho   399

First Apology
53   397

Melito
Peri Pascha
505-8   397
693-95   397

Origen
Contra Celsum
1.15.334   421-22
1.28   325
1.32   325
1.69   325
5.59 (quoting Celsus)   398

De Principiis
3.8   400

Tertullian
Apology
16   401
21.2   399

INSCRIPTIONS AND PAPYRI

P.Alex.Giss.
4   464

P.Amh.
II 97   464

P.Berl.Dem.
10229   464
13587, 13-14   463
13614   462

P.Bingen
74   466

P.Bub.
I 17   464

P.Cair.Masp.
III 67353 V   464

P.Dryton
33   466

P.Eleph.
1   462, 464
I 1   462

P.Fay.
23A   464

P.Gen.
21   464

P.Giss.
I 48   464
2   464

P.Harris
I 68   466

P. Hausw.
6   464

P.Heid.
Inv. G 4931   461

P.Hever
65, line 8   463

P.Köln
Inv. 21038   465

P.Lond.
III 1164   467
VII 2017   466

P.Mich.
A I   464

P.Moscow
135, line 1   464

P.Oxy.
II 265   467
III 496   467
VII 898   466
XIV 1638   467
XVII 2133   466
XXXVIII 2847   464

P.Petaus
13   464

P.Phrur.Diosk.
1   460

P.Polit.Iud.
1–16   460
1–2   460
1   460
3–5   460
3.6   463
4   459-60, 464
4.23-24   460
6–7   460
7   459-61, 465
8–12   460
8.5   460
17–20   460
20.8-9   460

Index of Scripture and Other Ancient Texts

P.Strasb.		IV 1091	464	3.2.4	463
I 31	464	IV 1113	467	B3.4.6	463
		VIII 1813	467	B3.8	462
P.Tebt.				B3.8.5	463
104	462, 464	CIG		6.1.5	463
104, 12-13	463	5361-62	459		
II 326	466			UPZ	
		CPJ		I. 1	451
P.Thmouis		II 144 line 19	463	I. 17-54	451
1	464	3, App. 1	454		
P.Vindob.		OGIS		OTHER	
3837	450-51	737	454		
3837, R. IV, 15	450			Annals of Sennacherib	
3837, R. IV, 16	451	PSI		1.1-4	42
3837, R. IV, 17	451	796	464	1.10-15	42
		IV 281	466		
P.Yadin		V 531	449	Berlin Stele	
12-15	468			2118 17, n. 39	455
18	462-63	SB		2118 17, n. 91-93	455
18, line 7	463	V 7558	466-68		
27	446	V 7568	467	Louvre Stele	
37	463	VI 9065	467	82	452
		XVI 12720	467		
W.Chr.				Mendes Stele	
363	464	TAD		CGC 22181	453
		B2.6	462		
BGU		6.5	463	Mesha Stele	
1102	463	B2.6.15	463	l.2	108
II 599	464	B2.8.5	463	l.3	108
IV 1070	466	B3.3	462	l.5	108

www.ingramcontent.com/pod-product-compliance
Lightning Source LLC
Chambersburg PA
CBHW021112300426
44113CB00006B/125